Tactics for Criminal Patrol

*"Every vehicle stop
is a story waiting
to be told."*

—Sgt. Wayne Corcoran
Phoenix (AZ) Police Dept.

(overleaf)

Bullets fly during a traffic stop of an alleged drug trafficker in Honolulu. He attacks unexpectedly with an assault rifle with a 60-round magazine. 40 rounds are fired as Officer Stanley Cook fights back with his S&W 9mm pistol. Cook survives, despite being shot 7 times. The assailant dies after being hit 9 times.

Tactics for Criminal Patrol

Vehicle Stops, Drug Discovery & Officer Survival

CHARLES REMSBERG
author of STREET SURVIVAL
and THE TACTICAL EDGE

photography and design
DENNIS ANDERSON

 Calibre Press • Northbrook, Illinois

Published by:
CALIBRE PRESS, INC.
666 Dundee Road, Suite 1607
Northbrook, IL 60062-2760

800-323-0037 • (847) 498-5680
Intercontinental: 800-2323-0037
FAX: (847) 498-6869
E-mail: staff@calibrepress.com

Library of Congress Catalog Card Number: 95-067002
ISBN 0-935878-12-2

Printed in the United States of America

for **Larkin Smith**

Chief, Gulfport (MS)
Police Department (1977-1983)

Sheriff, Harrison County (MS)
Sheriff's Department (1983-1988)

A caring administrator,
a special human being,
and a pioneer proponent
of Criminal Patrol.

Killed in a 1989 plane crash
while serving as a member of the
U.S. House of Representatives.

CONTENTS

ACKNOWLEDGMENTS

This is the third in a distinctive series of books about how you stay alive and uninjured as a police officer while confronting potentially violent criminals and criminal situations.

The first text, *Street Survival: Tactics for Armed Encounters*, deals with how you prevent (if possible) and win (if inevitable) attacks by armed offenders. *The Tactical Edge: Surviving High-Risk Patrol* concerns how you must think and act to control successfully the most dangerous calls you are likely to encounter. Now **Tactics for Criminal Patrol** explores the strategies behind a particular style of working the streets; specifically, how you can *safely* turn one of your most common activities—vehicle stops—into on-site investigations that lead to significant felony arrests. Much of what is revealed here, as you'll see, can be applied to other of your assignments and emergency calls, as well.

Like the other volumes, **Tactics for Criminal Patrol** evolved over a number of years. It began nearly a decade ago during a delicious seafood dinner on the Gulf Coast with **Larkin Smith**, then sheriff of Harrison County, Mississippi, and **Randy Cook**, his major in charge of patrol operations. They proudly mentioned the successes of one of their deputies, **Bill Collins**, in applying many of the tactics and techniques described in these pages. They expressed the hope that through Calibre Press's Street Survival® Seminar we could share his methods with other officers throughout the United States and Canada. Initially a small block of instruction was developed for the Seminar, and that has been expanded several times as the topic has grown in popularity and urgency.

Three years ago, we decided to produce *the first comprehensive instructional treatment in print* of Criminal Patrol and its related tactics of officer survival. During many months of intensive research, writing, and photography, scores of officers, trainers, and other authorities contributed their first-hand experiences and unique insights to this project.

Some of those who helped have asked to remain anonymous. These include a number of convicted drug offenders, who shared the tactics and motivations of their trade from prison. I would like to thank the Illinois Department of Corrections for allowing access to their facilities, particularly Director **Howard A. Peters III** and **Robert J. Jones** of the Planning and Research Unit.

Also, in respect for privacy, I have granted anonymity to officers and agencies described in many of the case histories I have used to underscore tactical concepts. To all these unnamed individuals—as well as any whose valuable assistance has inadvertently been

1

unacknowledged in these pages—I extend my profound gratitude.

Special thanks goes to eight reviewers who read and critiqued this book in full before its final editing. These individuals were selected because of their experience and expertise with the tactics of Criminal Patrol and/or its legal parameters. Some were also interviewed at length during the research phase of this project. The reviewers are:

Master Sergeant **Bill R. Collins** of the Tupelo (MS) Police Department and formerly of the Harrison County (MS) Sheriff's Department;

Daniel Heinz, instructor/coordinator at the North Carolina Justice Academy;

James P. Manak, publisher of the *Law Enforcement Legal Defense Manual* and the *Law Enforcement Legal Review;*

Trooper **Robert V. Stevens,** K-9 handler, and Trooper **Dick Unger,** members of the Traffic Drug Interdiction Team, Ohio State Highway Patrol;

Sergeant **Robert H. Stasch** of the Chicago Police Department;

Sergeant **Patrick Mahaney,** legal counsel and administrative officer for the Alabama Department of Public Safety, Narcotic Division;

Julia W. Stoner, assistant county attorney for Blackhawk County (IA) and formerly deputy county attorney for Yavapai County (AZ).

In addition, Instructor **Robert Willis** of the Street Survival® Seminar and Sergeant **Michael Irwin** of the Illinois State Police offered valuable assistance with the chapter on defensive tactics. **Charles Kirchner** of Canine Consultants, Inc., and retired senior trainer for the Metropolitan (DC) Police K-9 Unit, reviewed and provided helpful comment on the chapter about searching vehicles with dogs. **Emily L. Battin,** an independent trucking consultant and a compliance counselor with the Illinois Commerce Commission, and **Dave Bagby,** professional truck driver, provided guidance on regulations and practices of commercial carriers. Insights regarding mobile clan labs from Chief Agent **John Duncan** of the Oklahoma Bureau of Narcotics and Dangerous Drugs Control are also appreciated.

Besides the attorneys who reviewed the manuscript, I drew on the knowledge of other legal authorities, including: **Wayne W. Schmidt,** executive director of Americans for Effective Law Enforcement, Inc.; **Margaret Nave,** deputy prosecuting attorney for King County (WA), and Prosecutor **Joe Weeg** of Polk County (IA). I would like also to thank the reference librarians, in particular **Marcia Lehr,** at the Northwestern University Law School for assistance in tracking court cases and verifying citations on many occasions.

Senior Instructor **David Grossi** of the Street Survival® Seminar supplied many valuable leads mined from among attendees at our programs. His intelligence gathering helped me keep in touch with issues of greatest concern to field officers and stay focused on practical, realistic information that is of the most help to them.

Russell Arend, director of the Institute of Police Technology and Management, merits commendation for offering outstanding courses on Criminal Patrol techniques at IPTM's training facility in Jacksonville (FL). In particular, I would like to thank four of his instructors for sharing their materials unselfishly: Training Specialist **Harry Walters**, Florida Marine Patrol (Reserve); **Bruce Parent**, state law enforcement officer and drug recognition technician, Florida Department of Transportation; Investigator **Don Klein** of the Anaheim (CA) Police Department, and Patrol Officer and FTO **Greg DiFranza**, Jacksonville Sheriff's Office.

A note of appreciation is also due the organizers and instructors of other training programs that were attended for background information, including those presented by the Missouri Sheriffs' Training Institute; the Narcotic Enforcement Officers Association; the Institute for Law and Justice; the American Society of Law Enforcement Trainers; the California Narcotic Canine Association, and Operation Desert Snow. Likewise the Drugs and Crime Data Center and Clearinghouse in Washington (DC) proved to be an important resource for statistics on drug-use patterns and other trafficking information.

Early in our research, the Iowa Department of Public Safety permitted ride-alongs with one of its Criminal Patrol Enforcement Teams. Especially helpful in demonstrating successful tactics of interviewing and contraband detection were Special Agent **Scott Leighter** with the Iowa Division of Narcotics Enforcement and Trooper **Wayne Neville** with the Iowa State Patrol and their colleague, Officer **Ron F. Glover**, K-9 handler for the Davenport (IA) Police Department.

Officers and trainers from a variety of agencies submitted to extensive and in some cases repeated interviews about their practices and experiences on Criminal Patrol and/or related activities. They include: Corporal **John Scarberough**, Arkansas State Police; K-9 Trooper **Orlando J. Saavedra**, Florida Highway Patrol; Corporal **Wally Cowart**, Baton Rouge (LA) Police Department; Trooper **Rich Jimerson** and Trooper **Kyle Moomau**, Kansas Highway Patrol; Senior Special Agent **Jim Crotty**, U.S. Customs Service, Federal Law Enforcement Training Center; Officer **Sandy Pritchett**, Arizona Department of Public Safety (retired); **Stephen Mackenzie**, K-9 specialist, Schoharie County (NY) Sheriff's Department; Detective **Patrick Gannon**, Lansing (IL) Police Department, stationed with the Drug Enforcement Administration, Chicago; Captain **Tony Miller**, West Memphis (AR) Police Department; Patrolman **Daniel Dyer**, Wyoming Highway Patrol; Trooper **Jim Jenkner**, Illinois State Police; Special Agent **Paul W. Roemer**, Federal Bureau of Investigation (retired); Supervisory Customs Inspector **Dennis Doherty**, U.S. Customs Service; **Chet Jernigan**, training manager, North Carolina Justice Academy; Special Agent **Mark Thomas**, Drug Enforcement Administration; **Charles (Twig) Rollins Jr.**, special deputy, Anson County (NC) Sheriff's Department and director of Anson County Emergency Services; State Traffic Officer **Dick Himbarger**, California Highway Patrol; Trooper **John LeBlanc**, Louisiana State Police; **Jim Foster**, formerly a sergeant and trainer with the New York State Police; Officer **R. J. (Bob) Wortham**, Little Rock (AR) Police Department.

Also interviewed at length were Training Instructor **Edward F. Davis** and Forensic Psychologist **Anthony Pinizzotto** of the Federal

Bureau of Investigation, who spearheaded a study of police murders and helped identify the "fatal tendencies" commonly shared by victim officers.

Other important sources who cooperated fully by supplying lesson plans, private and official documents, personal experiences, and officer survival tactics include: Sergeant **Wayne Corcoran,** Phoenix (AZ) Police Department; Detective **Walt Markee,** Oregon State Police; Sergeant **Steve Rapich,** Utah Highway Patrol; Chief **Jack D. Compton,** Alice (TX) Police Department; Chief **Don Clark,** Wildwood (FL) Police Department; Sergeant **Jeff Greene,** Ohio Highway Patrol; Sergeant **John Danko,** Shaker Heights (OH) Police Department; Assistant Chief **F. E. Piersol** and Police Officer III **Michael Parlor,** Los Angeles Police Department; Personal Protec-tion Trainer **Scott Weaver** of Silent Resolve, Inc.; Officer **Michael Kabasinski,** Millcreek Township (PA) Police Department; Sergeant **Mike Dohanic,** State Police of Crawford and Erie Counties (PA); **Kevin M. Maurer,** law enforcement training specialist, Wake Technical Community College (NC); **Frank G. Packwood,** special agent in charge, Shasta-Trinity National Forests (CA); Lieutenant **Gary Klugiewicz,** Milwaukee County (WI) Sheriff's Department; Special Agent **Paul Hagerty,** Bureau of Alcohol, Tobacco, and Firearms; Sergeant **Rob Bishop,** Traffic Enforcement/Drug Inter-diction Division, Butts County (GA) Sheriff's Department; Lieutenant **John Morrison,** San Diego Police Department (retired); Staff Sergeant **Ross MacInnes,** Calgary (Alberta) Police Department Organized Crime Division.

My gratitude as well goes to these additional sources, who furnished a varied array of other materials and answered diverse important questions: Agent **Billy Artiaga,** Ortero County (NM) Narcotics Enforcement Unit; Deputy First Class **Shawn Callaghan,** Orange County (FL) Sheriff's Office; Sergeant **Robert Dunn,** Illinois State Police; Chief **Scott E. Penny,** Fairmont (IL) Police Department; Detective **Murrell Dillard,** Lake County (FL) Sheriff's Office; Patrolman **Gene Baker,** Jacksonville (FL) Sheriff's Office; Special Agent **Jay Rominger,** Federal Bureau of Investigation; Officer **Jeff Metts,** formerly with the Stuart (FL) Police Department; Agent **Robert Cole,** Agent **Chris Parkerson** and Agent **Steve McDonald,** U.S. Border Patrol; Officer **Greg Kilpatrick,** California State Police; K-9 Officer **Blake Hunt,** Irondequoit (NY) Police Department; State Traffic Officers **Eric Marmont** (retired) and **Richard Moss,** California Highway Patrol; Constable **Mark C. Maeers,** Ontario (Canada) Provincial Police; Officer **James Smith,** Milwaukee (WI) Police Department; Constable **Mark Johnstone,** Vancouver (British Columbia) Police Department; Deputy **Sarah Hardaway,** Sevier County (TN) Sheriff's Department (Reserve); Officer **Carl Diblasi,** Coconut Creek (FL) Public Safety Department; Deputy **Robert G. Igo,** Tillamook County (OR) Sheriff's Office; **Leopold T. Altman III,** President, Law Enforcement Training Society, John Jay College of Criminal Justice; Trooper **Curt Fiechtner,** South Dakota Highway Patrol; Patrolman **Gerald Machurick,** Ft. Lauderdale (FL) Police Department; Detective **Tracy Sparshott,** Montgomery County (MD) Police Department; Detective **Rena Epting,** Special Investigations Unit, Albany (NY) Police Department; Supervisory

Special Agent **Steve Merrill,** U. S. Immigration and Naturalization Service; Trooper **Mark Belew,** Virginia State Police; Sergeant **Dave Wheeler,** Los Angeles Police Department (retired); Corporal **Michael Dolan,** Dearborn (MI) Police Department; Sergeant **Brian Stover,** Los Angeles Sheriff's Department; Detective **Keith Werner,** Wauwatosa (WI) Police Department; Constable **F. Scott Stewart,** New Westminster (British Columbia) Police Service; Trooper **Chris Dew,** North Carolina Highway Patrol; Instructor **Carlos F. Ortiz,** supervisor, Advanced Drug Enforcement Training, Georgia Public Safety Training Center; **Margarita Patmore,** Translation & Editorial Services, Lincolnshire (IL); Safety and Security Manager **Andy Anderson,** Avis Rent A Car System, Inc.; Trooper **Grant Willis,** Louisiana State Police; Sheriff **Don Blankenship,** Phelps County (MO) Sheriff's Department; **Javier A. Ortiz,** formerly a reserve deputy with the Fulton County (GA) Sheriff's Department.

Throughout this project I have been ably assisted by Calibre Press's director of research, **Scott Buhrmaster.** With his creative and dogged determination, he opened many doors and performed many near miracles in corralling people, photographs, and materials that contributed immeasurably to the success of this effort. My deepest appreciation for his ability and willingness to go the extra mile many times over. I want to thank other members of the Calibre Press staff, too, for their enthusiasm and assistance and the Reference staff of the Northbrook (IL) Public Library for many research favors.

It is difficult to express in words the gratitude I owe to my partner, **Dennis Anderson,** cofounder of Calibre Press. During this project, as through nearly twenty years of collaboration, he has served as an invaluable sounding board, wellspring of creativity, lifter of spirits, and sharer of many burdens and challenges. His heart, soul, and talents touch each of these pages.

I would like to thank my family, immediate and extended, for their interest, motivation, and encouragement. And finally, my wife **Colleen** deserves special mention. She lived this long project with me day upon day, patiently enduring many lost nights and weekends and never wavered in her loving support. She is truly the wind beneath my wings.

Charles Remsberg
Northbrook, Illinois

A Note About Legal Content

The success of certain Criminal Patrol techniques depends on a clear working knowledge of search-and-seizure law and case law. On the street, when you are confronting a potential criminal encounter, you want as few uncertainties as possible to distract you from making the bust and staying alive. Consequently, this book has made legal considerations an integral part of discussions about patrol tactics and officer survival.

Traffic stops which lead to the discovery of narcotics trafficking and the arrests of dealers and couriers are a relatively new and volatile area of the law. Legal principles dealt with herein derive mainly from the federal constitution as interpreted by the federal courts, particularly the United States Supreme Court. Some state constitutions, state laws, state courts, and department policies impose more stringent guidelines, plus there is not always consistency even among the federal jurisdictions.

If you are uncertain how the foundation doctrines of Criminal Patrol are interpreted in your jurisdiction, your local prosecutors or legal advisors may be helpful. Unfortunately, depending on your jurisdiction, you may encounter prosecutors who are overworked, relatively inexperienced, and unfamiliar with important subtleties of search-and-seizure law. The case law cited in the Chapter Notes beginning on page 483 may be useful to them in better understanding the problems you face and in supporting the procedures you need to use. In some cases, you will find experienced, well-trained, and highly motivated police trainers and field officers to be reliable sources of legal guidance, as well.

Remember that new cases reinforcing or contradicting existing case law arise constantly. Become a regular reader of case-law newsletters, such as *Narcotics Law Bulletin, Search and Seizure Bulletin* and *Law Enforcement Legal Review*, to keep abreast of important developments.

INTRODUCTION: MAKE-A-DIFFERENCE PATROL

Traffic that flows along the streets and highways of your beat is like a moving city. And like any city, it has its criminal element.

Some of the vehicles around you are going to or from crimes. Some are involved in criminal activities even as they move. They may be stolen...they may be carrying evidence from a murder or a burglary...they may conceal abducted or abused children or rape victims or fugitives on the run...they may be transporting black-market guns, smuggled drugs, dirty money, poached plants and animals, untaxed goods, illegal aliens, or other contraband. And this is true whether you patrol in Philadelphia, Pennsylvania (population 1,600,000) or Philadelphia, Mississippi (population 6,800).

As you think about the crime-related possibilities streaming by, you probably feel both frustrated and challenged. Frustrated because you can't know *all* the dark secrets of the cars, trucks, vans, campers, and motor homes you see...challenged because you'd like to discover more about them than you currently are able to.

The techniques you'll learn and reinforce in this book can help you meet the challenge and reduce the frustration. They can help you become part of an elite group of patrol officers: top-notch criminal investigators whose crime scenes are common vehicle stops. And these techniques can help you stay alive and uninjured in the process.

Take this quick test. And to measure accurately how you presently perform, answer *honestly*.

While you're on patrol, a car drives by with a piece of newspaper flapping out from behind its front bumper. Acting typically, you:

❏ A. Don't notice it.
❏ B. Think the driver's a jag for not
  stopping and removing it.
❏ C. Are curious about why it's there.
❏ D. Are suspicious.

If your answer is D, explain why.

When a state trooper in central Illinois was tested by this incident in real life, his reaction was a blend of C and D. He swung in behind the car, a nine-year-old white Cadillac Seville with Texas tags, and followed it for about a mile. When he saw the driver improperly change lanes and repeatedly swerve onto the shoulder, he flipped on

7

his overheads and pulled the car over.

The driver was a nervous, sixty-two-year-old Hispanic, traveling alone. He said he was headed to Chicago to visit friends, but the trooper could see no luggage in the car. As conversation developed, the driver couldn't recall his friends' names, addresses, or phone numbers.

The flapping paper, the trooper now observed, was a page from a San Antonio newspaper that seemed to be coming from inside the car's bumper assembly. He also noticed that as he approached the front of the car, the driver became even more nervous and turned away, as if not wanting to witness what was about to become the unraveling of his life.

Before that stop was over, the curious and suspicious trooper, with the help of backup officers, a K-9, and some nearby service station attendants, had discovered fifteen packages of marijuana wrapped in duct tape and newspaper behind the front bumper and another sixteen lodged behind the rear one—sixty-two pounds in all, with an estimated street value at that place and time of $187,000. The flapping newspaper apparently had protruded all the way from Texas, unnoticed by the driver—*and* by other police officers he'd undoubtedly passed by en route.

Everybody knows that cops see things that civilians miss. And then there are certain cops who see things even other cops miss. They look at the same person, the same vehicle, or the same scene...or they hear the same voice or same story...or they inhale the same air, but they *comprehend* it differently. They notice details that conform and those that conflict, those that are present when they shouldn't be and those that are inexplicably absent. To these special officers, individual elements add up to a vastly different whole. And because of that, they consistently make the most of their enforcement contacts and produce the kinds of arrests that elude most of their fellow officers.

This happens, at times, even in circumstances that seem blatantly unambiguous. Hours apart, two troopers in Utah stopped the same vehicle for speeding. The first ticketed the sixteen-year-old driver for the moving violation and for having no registration certificate and sent him on his way. The second became almost immediately curious about more than those infractions. Approaching the car, he noticed that there was no rear license plate—just a dealer's advertising placard. When the driver couldn't produce proof of registration, the officer asked where he was coming from. He'd been vacationing in Las Vegas, the driver said—but the trooper could see no luggage. The picture on the driver's license only slightly resembled the driver, so the officer asked him to step out. When he did, the trooper could see that he was covered from his shirt collar to his shoelaces with dried blood. A quick frisk turned up a second license. And a check of that through NCIC revealed that the driver was wanted for stabbing his grandmother to death. The car was stolen, too.

A stop that the first officer had dismissed with what now seemed an embarrassing and pathetic pair of cites became for the second a major homicide arrest. The same evidence was available to both; one saw it or found it, one didn't.

The success of exceptional officers is not a matter of luck or accident or some birth gift of unerring instinct. It's a matter of *training* and *motivation.* These officers have conditioned themselves to be super observers and to work in a systematic way that is most likely to produce remarkable results. They approach patrol—especially traffic enforcement—as more than just riding around between hot calls and occasionally hanging tickets on errant motorists. To them, watching traffic and conducting vehicle stops is a unique opportunity to search for and unmask *felony* offenders and pull off make-a-difference busts. They fully understand and exploit the fact that *every vehicle stop carries the potential for discovering serious criminal conduct,* especially drug offenses. In making stops, they regard themselves as first-line criminal investigators...*total-commitment* law enforcement officers. And in many cases, although they work on uniformed patrol, they have become the top investigators on their departments, making more and better cases than plainclothes or undercover officers.

Their kind of patrol—characterized variously as Aggressive Criminal Patrol, Criminal Awareness Patrol, Criminal Apprehension Patrol, or Criminal Interdiction Patrol—seeks to maximize the number of citizen contacts on vehicle stops during each shift and, through specific investigative techniques, to explore the full arrest potential of each. In effect, officers using this approach try as often as possible to advance to the top of this Criminal Patrol Pyramid:

BONUS BENEFITS

ARREST

PROBABLE CAUSE

SEARCH (usually by consent)

REASONABLE SUSPICION

SUSPICION

DIALOGUE

SENSORY ASSESSMENT (especially observation)

LEGAL CONTACT

© Calibre Press, Inc.

With the foundation of a *legal contact,* they use *observation* and *dialogue* to learn more about the subject(s) they've stopped. If they become *suspicious* of wrongdoing, they mentally identify the reasons why, so they can later articulate their feelings as facts that courts will accept as reasonable. With *reasonable suspicion,* they ask *consent to search* the suspect's vehicle. Ideally, they then discover incriminating evidence that gives them *probable cause* for an *arrest,* converting the stop to a far different outcome than may originally have been anticipated. When circumstances are appropriate, they also lay the foundation for *bonus benefits* beyond the primary bust, including arrests of coconspirators and the seizure for forfeiture of crime-related assets.

This method of policing can be as demanding and dangerous as it is productive. But in the opinion of one Iowa officer, "It's the most fun you can have in law enforcement. When you score, it feels like hitting *bar-bar-bar* on a slot machine."

The work pattern of these committed officers is identifiable. It's learnable. And in **Tactics for Criminal Patrol,** you'll follow it step by step. You'll see in action exactly how small, seemingly inconsequential details can add up to significant revelations of criminal activity, *if* you understand their meaning and importance and properly manage the suspects associated with them. You'll share little-known insider methods, gathered from throughout the U.S. and Canada, that have taken outstanding Criminal Patrol officers and their trainers years to perfect—but that you can now employ on your next shift. And in these pages you'll also be able to study never-before-published photographs showing how transporters of drugs and other contraband really work. "Once you learn how and make your first bust," says a Criminal Patrol officer, "the next time comes so easy." The principles are simple enough, when known, that just a week after a rookie was instructed in Criminal Patrol tactics at a Kansas academy, he busted 300 pounds of marijuana on one of his first traffic stops.

Core to successful Criminal Patrol is determination, particularly the commitment to look beyond simple driving violations and not be hopelessly blinded to the bigger picture of your job by a tunnel-vision Traffic Cop Mentality. With determination—plus patience, an awareness of the full range of legally acceptable tactics at your disposal, and the understanding that this is a continuous learning process—you can develop a reliable system of your own for turning "routine" traffic stops into felony arrests. Even if you don't specialize exclusively in Criminal Patrol, integrating any of these principles and tactics into your daily operations will enhance your patrol effectiveness.

The foundation you need is presented here in the context of just *one* Criminal Patrol objective: *the interception of illegal drugs in vehicles.* This is the policing activity for which this style of patrolling is best known, on which many of its techniques have been razor-honed, and to which they can be most readily applied. You'll learn how best to:

1. **Improve your observation skills;**

2. **Evaluate vehicles, drivers, and passengers for subtle clues to contraband transporting;**

3. **Confidently engage subjects in revealing conversation to identify potential suspects;**

4. **Detect lies and other evidence of deception;**

5. **Obtain voluntary consent to search vehicles and their contents in the absence of a warrant;**

6. **Quickly uncover drugs and other illegal goods in even the most clever hiding places and the largest vehicles;**

7. **Use K-9 assistance when it's available;**

8. **Expand investigations beyond roadside encounters for even more significant results;**

9. **Cement your cases legally from start to finish, so they are "bulletproof" in court and you are shielded from civil liability;**

10. **Most important, tactically control the stop and the suspect(s) throughout, so you avoid mistakes that have gotten less prepared officers injured or killed.**

Keep in mind: *The same investigative and control principles you learn and apply to drug interdiction can also help you succeed and survive in a broad range of other potentially treacherous enforcement situations, including high-risk complaint calls, field interrogations, and witness interviews.* In fact, the drug problem could end tomorrow and the principles of Criminal Patrol would still endure, so long as there is crime and mobile criminals. The tactics revealed here constitute a *way of working* that can—and should—pervade all your patrol experience, including even foot patrol.

Where the Billions for Drugs Go...

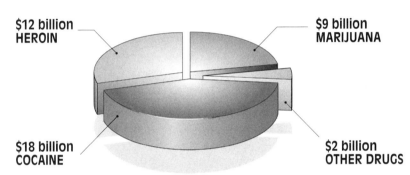

$12 billion
HEROIN

$9 billion
MARIJUANA

$18 billion
COCAINE

$2 billion
OTHER DRUGS

According to the Office of National Drug Control Policy, Americans spend more than $41 billion every year on illegal drugs. This is more than annual expenditures for all tobacco products. An interesting comparison: The entire Gulf War cost taxpayers $36 billion.

This seizure was unloaded from 3 tractor-trailers involved in a single bust in southern California. You are looking at 2.5 tons of cocaine. Drug trafficking has been called the greatest crime problem in U.S. history; with less than 5% of the world's population, this country consumes 60% of the world's illegal drugs.[1]

(background)
Lebanese police officer sorts through 8 tons of hashish confiscated in Beirut en route to Europe.

(below)
Officer stands amidst a forest of 18-ft.-high marijuana plants in northern California. Each was expected to yield at least 2 lbs. of marijuana. Estimated street value of this crop: over $170,000.

(lower right)
NYPD narcotics detectives take 4 Israelis to central booking after arrests in an international drug-smuggling operation that netted $1,000,000 weekly.

(bottom)
Vigorous outdoor eradication efforts have prompted pot growers to move indoors with high intensity lamps, fans, sprinklers, and automatic fertilizing systems. Once harvested, these drugs are most commonly moved by vehicle.

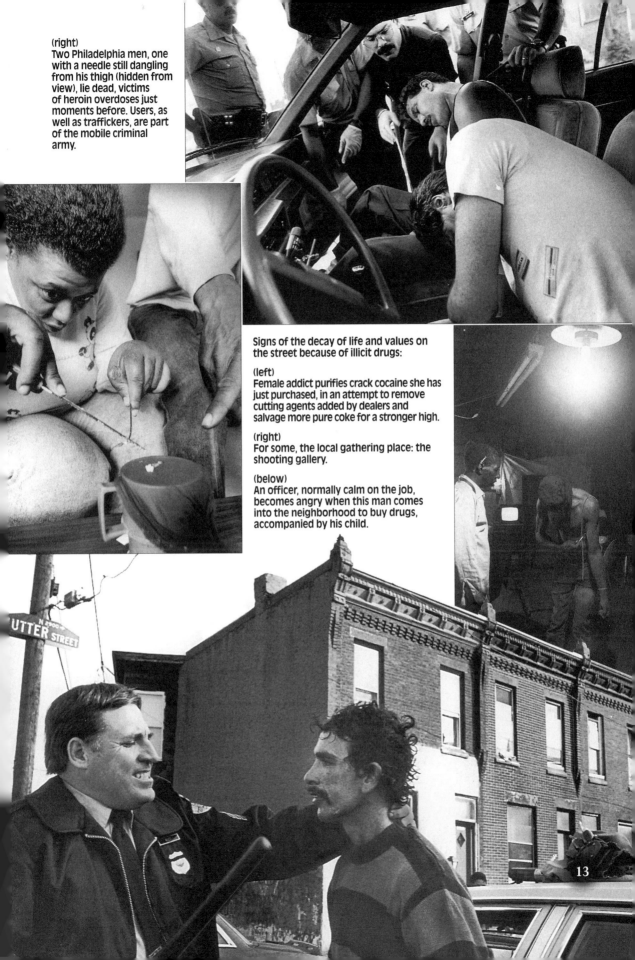

(right)
Two Philadelphia men, one with a needle still dangling from his thigh (hidden from view), lie dead, victims of heroin overdoses just moments before. Users, as well as traffickers, are part of the mobile criminal army.

Signs of the decay of life and values on the street because of illicit drugs:

(left)
Female addict purifies crack cocaine she has just purchased, in an attempt to remove cutting agents added by dealers and salvage more pure coke for a stronger high.

(right)
For some, the local gathering place: the shooting gallery.

(below)
An officer, normally calm on the job, becomes angry when this man comes into the neighborhood to buy drugs, accompanied by his child.

UTTER STREET

13

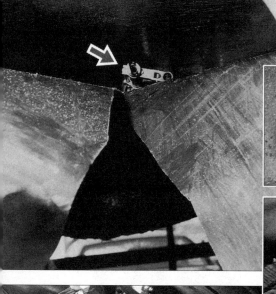

(top left)
Barrel of an AK-47 (fires 600-rounds per minute) peeks out of a section of a false roof inside a mini-van in California. Officer's search on a vehicle stop produced more weapons and considerable ammunition.

(top right/above)
Semiautomatic rifle, which looks like a machine gun, is assembled here from component parts that were discovered by a deputy, hidden in the rocker panels of a car stopped for a traffic violation.

You may stop someone who is hauling more surprises than just drugs.

(above)
You easily see the barrel and forehand grip (arrow) of a 9mm Uzi inside the trunk of a car stopped for a minor violation. Are you curious about what might be inside the other travel bags visible inside this trunk?

Despite the mounting drug tragedy, most departments, unfortunately, have not actively recruited ordinary patrol officers as soldiers in the war on drugs. Criminal Patrol is a foreign concept to many traditional administrators who, according to one New Jersey trainer, "have learned nothing in their careers about this kind of law enforcement." They regard narcotics enforcement as the mission of undercover squads, SWAT teams, and special task forces with special equipment; the budgets, training, and attention of such administrators go to support buy-bust operations, raids, stings, and occasional sweeps of streets and neighborhoods. One cynical officer observes that patrol personnel too often are dealt with on a need-to-know basis: "If you need to know, you aren't told." This separatist mystique so pervades some agencies that patrol officers aren't trained even to recognize many of the drugs and drug paraphernalia that they do happen to encounter! Indeed, one trainer contends that most patrol officers have not seen a kilo of cocaine or heroin except on TV.

This is a grave and costly misuse of human resources. The size of the drug problem is growing and now exceeds what can be handled by specialized units alone.[2] In a recent year, a single drug organization

(left)
Drug couriers may carry a variety of weapons when they travel. One offender had these pipe bombs hidden inside his attaché case.

(top left)
Common travel items for today's mobile offender: black canvas tote bag, Cobray M11/Nine with silencer, extra magazines, survival knife, lots of ammo, and a ski mask.

(top right)
.44 Magnum Desert Eagle semiautomatic "hand cannon." Probably the most powerful handgun available, this weapon is said to be capable of killing anything.

(above)
.45 Colt semiautomatic conversion with Mauser stock for a steady aim and a high-capacity drum magazine for extended fire.

operating in New York reportedly made an annual profit three times the size of DEA's entire worldwide budget.[3] Against this kind of enemy, law enforcement can no longer afford ineffective, underutilized officers.

Potentially, *uniformed patrol officers constitute the most vital resource available against narcotics traffickers.* One North Carolina trainer calls them "the front-line, last-defense, street-level, street-fighting people who can make a difference." Even in some major metropolitan areas, several hours are available during an officer's typical shift for discretionary use—time that he or she could use for working traffic in an investigative frame of mind. Thus deployed, patrol officers would significantly augment the 4% of sworn law enforcement personnel in this country who are assigned full time to special anti-drug units.[4]

Not only would this dramatically increase arrests for narcotics offenses, but with officers applying Criminal Patrol techniques the detection and solution of *other* crimes, including the confiscation of illegal weapons, would measurably improve, as well. When certain officers began patrolling with these techniques in Indianapolis, for example, they proved to be *ten times* more productive in seizing guns than "regular" patrol officers.[5] Moreover, studies have shown that Criminal Patrol techniques also produce a substantial *deterrent* effect on the

15

crime rates for robbery, burglary, and various other offenses.[6]

Where Criminal Patrol tactics have been encouraged, the results usually have far *surpassed* those of specialized narcotics units. One federal study concludes that on a per-dollar-spent basis, interdiction techniques yield nearly twice as much confiscated cocaine and more than twice as much marijuana as conventional drug-investigation measures.[7]

A trained and observant uniformed officer on Criminal Patrol in the Midwest, for example, discovered seventy-two kilos of cocaine in the roof of a station wagon he'd originally stopped for a traffic violation. He recovered more in that one bust than his agency's detectives had gotten in *three years* with elaborate and costly buy-bust operations.

When a Louisiana agency formally adopted a Criminal Patrol philosophy, an evaluation of the first forty-five days showed that 345 criminal arrests had been made by twenty-one uniformed officers—far beyond expectations and a marked contrast to the relatively low ratio of criminal arrests customarily resulting from traffic contacts; in the first twenty months, Criminal Patrol produced 2,465 arrests for this agency, including 575 narcotics offenders, 310 other criminals, 1,035 aliens, and 235 fugitives, including one on the FBI's "Ten Most Wanted" list. (As proof of Criminal Patrol's across-the-board effectiveness, note that only about 23% of the arrests were narcotics-related.) Officers recovered more than $700,000 in stolen vehicles and other goods, discovered more than $3,000,000 in crime-connected U.S. currency, and confiscated more than $21,000,000 worth of narcotics, drug paraphernalia, and deadly weapons. With time and experience, the agency's stats have gotten even better.[8] Arrests aside, one sheriff's department in Mississippi calculates that for every dollar it spends in salary and equipment for Criminal Patrol, seventy-five dollars worth of drugs and assets are seized.

"All things considered," says a law enforcement consultant who specializes in drug enforcement strategy, "interdiction efforts [by patrol officers] offer the most effective and efficient return on manpower and resources of any narcotics enforcement programs."[9]

Some county and municipal departments dismiss a major role for patrol in drug interdiction as a concept that's relevant only for state police or highway patrol agencies or only in certain drug-intensive Southwestern or Southern states like Florida, where the DEA once estimated that an average of seven kilos of cocaine are flowing through certain counties every hour. This narrow attitude usually goes hand in hand with the belief that sizable quantities of drugs are being transported only along certain "cocaine corridors" of the Interstate highway system. Incredibly, administrators in some suburbs, small towns, and rural areas removed from the Interstate network have declared flat out: "We don't have drugs moving through our jurisdiction!"

Many patrol officers who should know better buy into this ostrich thinking, too, and it becomes the mind-set behind their failure to perceive evidence that virtually screams out to the contrary.

Undeniably, Interstates are bloodlines for drug distribution; some authorities have estimated that *one out of every 100 vehicles* whizzing along them is carrying narcotics contraband.[10] State police and highway patrol officers on Interstate beats certainly have played a leadership role in Criminal Patrol, with the help of federal funding, training, and support assistance through the Operation Pipeline interdiction program. Many of the techniques you'll learn here troopers developed through hundreds of thousands of vehicle stops, roadside interviews, and exhaustive search

State Cuts Road Patrols

Short-Staffed Troopers
Face Overtime Limits,
Ignore Some Highways

By Tom Brune and Rebecca Carr
Staff Writers

...ictions have reduced patrols on
...iminated them alto-
...ute areas.

(top left)
To avoid state interdiction nets, many cross-country couriers have moved off the Interstates onto secondary roads like this one, where you may patrol.

(above)
Budget cutbacks for state agencies mean greater opportunities for traffickers to escape detection and greater opportunities for local law enforcement to make arrests.

es. Their spectacular successes undoubtedly will continue to amaze and inspire other officers.

But the transporting of contraband never has been a problem limited *only* to the Interstates. It is even less so now, in part because of the lightning-strike impact that committed troopers have had.

Even when Interstates are utilized by traffickers between cities, the vehicles involved must at some point drive onto local streets and make delivery. As drugs are cut and distributed, they are moved along different streets and alleys to lesser dealers, who may drive them to other neighborhoods or outbound to satellite markets. Outlying customers drive to suppliers and drive home with personal-use quantities or more. At other times, the end users may drive drugs along with them on vacation or to school or to parties or to concerts or to places of work. "There are so many drugs in transit, constantly moving back and forth out there in every direction," says one officer, "that you can almost hold a snorting straw up to the wind and get high."

Day in and day out, cops everywhere are dealing with cars, some of which incontestably are carrying contraband. Yet, inconceivably, in one recent twelve-month period, a startling 14% of the nation's police departments made *no* arrests for marijuana; 30% had no cocaine busts; 62% registered no arrests for amphetamines, and 83% lacked arrests for heroin. Sheriff's departments did somewhat better but usually only by thin margins.[11] Little wonder that only an estimated 5% of narcotics are intercepted before they reach an end user.[12]

When county and municipal officers do use Criminal Patrol techniques, they score, in *all kinds* of jurisdictions. For example:

In one of Chicago's wealthiest suburbs, an officer working graveyard clocked an old Buick speeding 24 mph over the limit and weaving in its lane. Through the officer's investigative skills, what looked like a probable DUI turned into one of the largest drug seizures in that county's history. Multiple kilos of coke with an estimated street value of $1,300,000 were found in secret compartments in the rear armrests, along with an automatic money counter and nearly $38,000 cash, some of it counterfeit.

In a small town in central Florida (population 3,400), a municipal officer stopped an old van for speeding and in casual conversation with the nervous driver and passenger quickly elicited conflicting stories about where they were headed. While he worked, a backup officer with a K-9 circled the vehicle. The dog alerted and before long, from a compart

17

ment cut into the van wall and carpeted over, the officers recovered a plastic bag filled with a pungent mixture of mustard and spices—and twelve kilos of cocaine. In just three years of Criminal Patrol, this twelve-officer department, incidentally, has seized 170 pounds of cocaine and nearly $600,000 in cash.

In rural upstate New York, sheriff's deputies found three-and-a-half pounds of pot in a van they'd stopped, along with $7,000 cash...and that was only the beginning. Confronted with their discovery, the driver confessed that he and a partner, who had met through their sons' Boy Scout troop, were cultivating marijuana in a string of indoor "grow factories," part of a mounting trend among drug traffickers to move operations to secluded suburban locations. Armed with search warrants, deputies seized nearly 800 luxuriant plants, each capable of yielding about $3,800 worth of weed, in elaborately outfitted rooms and basements of three houses scattered in three tiny hamlets—the most sophisticated indoor greenhouse operation some veteran narcotics investigators had ever seen.

A corporal in Louisiana stopped an empty automobile-transport trailer in his city of 220,000 because the license plate was obscured. The more the stop progressed, the more nervous the violator became, sweating profusely and apparently unable to tell a coherent version of where he'd been and where he was going. Although he claimed to have been transporting cars, the corporal noticed that all the truck's chains looked rusted and unused. Presently, the officer's attention focused on a sheet metal plate he found bolted to one of the truck's vertical support bars. After a dog alerted to it, the plate was popped. Inside was 160 pounds of marijuana.

Soon after, the same officer stopped a car carrying four women, one of them seventy years old. The nervous driver told him where they were headed, but he noticed that the destination she named was different from a city that was highlighted on a map lying open on the front seat. This time, on a consent search, the corporal discovered fifty pounds of pot sealed in wax in a hidden compartment behind the back seat.

Near a hamlet in Georgia one night, county police stopped two vehicles for weaving: a Ford pickup, driven by an older man, that was tailgating a Chevy Lumina, driven by his son. The father seemed exceptionally nervous and certain aspects of his body language suggested that he was being deceptive, officers thought, so they asked the pair to sign Spanish-language consent-to-search forms. Moments later, the officers discovered the cause of the nervousness. When they removed a plastic bed liner from the back of the pickup, they found thirty-seven bricks of cocaine stacked along the walls. They found another thirteen kilos in a phony gas tank. In all, it was the biggest bust ever made on a Georgia highway, worth possibly $20,000,000.

Says one Eastern sheriff: "If anyone thinks drugs today are limited to the inner city, they'd better wake up and smell the coffee." A DEA intelligence report states that "Major trafficking groups are extending successfully their operations from large cities to street corners and dwellings in virtually every state." Even in some national parks, which much of the general public considers to be away-from-it-all retreats, law enforcement rangers estimate that after dark one out of two cars on the roads contain marijuana, methamphetamine, crack cocaine, or other dope.[13] States a high-ranking federal official: "Most of the USA is now a high-intensity drug-trafficking area."

"It's Everywhere..."

"Some people believe all the dope in the world is in Miami or Houston or Los Angeles or New York," says a U.S. attorney. "Actually, it's everywhere." Wisconsin, for example, is considered a typical middle-America state, with extensive rural areas dotted with constellations of small towns. Yet according to the Wisconsin State Patrol:[14]

• Of its 4,900,000 residents, almost half a million have used drugs.

• 25% of regular cocaine users admit to criminal activities to support their habits.

• Drugs and alcohol are factors in over half of the state's homicides, 40% of suicides, 33% of sexual crimes and child abuse cases.

• 47% of 12th graders have tried an illicit drug.

• 51% of high school seniors are "chemically at risk."

• 65% of the state's adult prison population has drug treatment needs—a 65% increase since 1984.

Nationally, according to the latest federal reports available:[15]

• 11,700,000 people in the U.S. admit to using drugs at least monthly.

• 5.1% of eighth graders smoke pot at least monthly, and among 8th, 10th, and 12th graders use is increasing. Overall, marijuana use is "virtually exploding" in almost every area of the country.

• Heroin use, now considered fashionable and chic in certain social circles, is on the upswing, with younger users becoming involved.

• Cocaine-related ER visits grew more than 18% and marijuana/hashish-related visits by 22% in a recent 12-month period; heroin-related emergencies increased 44% in six-months (see graph below).

• Drug users 35 years old and older now constitute 28% of illicit users, compared to 10% in 1979.

Considering statistics like these, what do you think are the chances that you have stopped someone transporting drugs in personal use or resale quantities and not realized it?

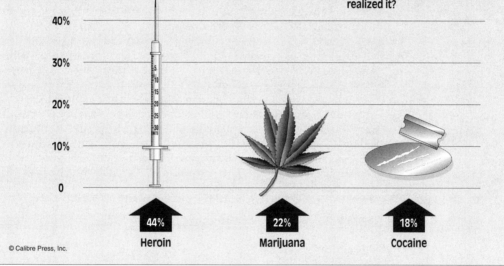

| 44% | 22% | 18% |
| Heroin | Marijuana | Cocaine |

© Calibre Press, Inc.

Besides the public service and career value of nailing contraband and its associated suspects, officers who can pull off major busts or even a steady series of minor ones on their beats can reap impressive professional benefits for themselves and fellow officers. State and federal asset-forfeiture laws allow money, vehicles, and other property related to illegal activities to be seized and liquidated. In most cases, significant portions of the proceeds revert to the department responsible for the seizure, to be used for training and equipment that will enhance officers' safety and drug-fighting performance. From Maine to California, law enforcement agencies have used forfeited assets originally seized on vehicle stops to fund better retirement perks, new personnel, new semiautomatic weapons, new firearm stress ranges, new surveillance and nighttime reconnaissance gear, new patrol cars, new computer-aided dispatch systems, new body armor, new automated mug-shot filing systems, new jails, new body-bug transmitters for undercover operations, new helicopters, new laser-disc projection systems for shoot/don't shoot simulations, new gym equipment, new high-tech radar gear, new in-car video systems, and a wide variety of other "wish list" benefits. Without uniformed officers on Criminal Patrol, such improvements would not be possible in many instances in these tight-budget times.

If the stakes are high in contraband detection, it's axiomatic that the risks are high, too. Nearly one-third of the officers killed in narcotics enforcement situations are *not* killed conducting raids, serving warrants, or making undercover buys. They're killed performing what's classified as "other enforcement," which includes contraband vehicle stops.[16] Ironically, one of the great risks of Criminal Patrol is the rush you get when you succeed at it. Seeking that reward, you can become so focused on the *investigative* aspects of this policing style that you forget or ignore *survival* concerns. Thus, the underpinning theme of **Tactics for Criminal Patrol** is officer survival, just as it was in *Street Survival* and *The Tactical Edge*.

The truth is that in many situations on Criminal Patrol, you're up against a stacked deck. Compared to many of the drug haulers who cross your path, you and your fellow officers are understaffed, underfinanced, and at a firearms disadvantage. Many more transporters on streets and highways are armed than those who pass through security-conscious airports, so the potential for an armed encounter with the travelers you meet is much greater. Moreover, couriers with large loads are likely to be more afraid of the people who hired them than they are of you. They operate today with what an Arkansas officer calls "a rougher edge than they've ever had before." Often they harbor a two-part plan: Their first effort is to con you into accepting them as just one more traffic violator; failing that, they may intend to hurt or kill you to get away. Your coming out unscathed depends on your alertness, knowledge, resourcefulness, and tactical skills in detecting Plan A...and outwitting Plan B.

Drug-Related Officer Slayings...

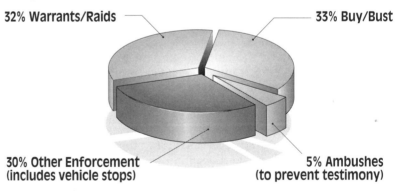

32% Warrants/Raids

33% Buy/Bust

30% Other Enforcement
(includes vehicle stops)

5% Ambushes
(to prevent testimony)

The critical core of peak performance on Criminal Patrol, as with any police activity, must always be the protection of yourself and fellow officers. In the end, that's the most essential element of excellence.

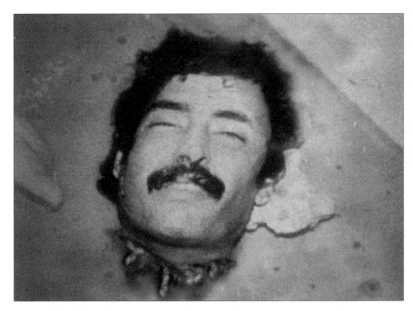

This is a drug courier who failed to deliver his load. Actually, this is one of the larger pieces of him found in Tennessee after his job performance was critiqued—with a chain saw. Remember him.

Do you think the threat of this might provide strong motivation for a courier to take you on, if he thinks you're standing between him and his delivery?

As a sobering reminder of risks, consider the fate of Sergeant Ronald Slockett. At the wheel of his patrol car, alone, at 4 o'clock one morning, Sergeant Slockett was heading toward the station to end his shift in Sugar Land, Texas (population 25,000). With one minute left to go, he spotted a white Toyota with three occupants driving erratically on an old highway that runs through town. He decided to make one last traffic stop for the night.

Initially, he tried to pull the car over opposite an all-night grocery store. The driver paused there, then slowly rolled forward for another three-tenths of a mile—until he was in a spot that was dark all around. *Sergeant Slockett failed to read this as a danger cue.* He apparently was anticipating just another drunk driver. But as he began his approach on foot after finally getting the car stopped, *this* driver started crawling out through the front window. Sergeant Slockett put his hand on his gun, shined his flashlight on the driver, and yelled: "Stop! Don't move!"

(above)
Sgt. Ronald Slockett

(left)
Dark stains beside his patrol car are where the thin blue line ran blood red one night in Sugar Land (TX).

21

He may not have seen the front passenger bolt out of the car. With a .357 Magnum in one hand and a 9mm Beretta in the other, the passenger opened fire from the shadows. Three rounds struck Ron Slockett in the chest. He was dead when he hit the pavement.

What he was *really* stopping that night were three Colombian coke dealers, products of a country and a culture in which hundreds of police officers each year are killed as just part of the game. They had cash from drug trades in their car, and in their trunk was a hostage—a rival dealer who'd welshed on a debt. It's now believed they were taking him on a last ride to a killing ground when Sergeant Slockett unwittingly became their victim.

As you read the pages ahead, you will have flashbacks to motorists you have pulled over and to some you didn't pull over. If you're out there making traffic stops, it's very likely that you already have narrowly escaped deadly confrontations. It's virtually guaranteed that you have unknowingly missed significant loads of drugs or other contraband. But many more are in transit.

From the moment drugs penetrate our borders or leave the burgeoning number of domestic fields, laboratories, and greenhouses that produce them until the moment they are finally squeezed into a vein, sniffed up a nostril, dissolved on a tongue, gulped down a throat, or sucked into lungs, they generally are destined to ride in many vehicles, along many routes. Transportation by motor vehicle, especially automobiles, is the most common method of narcotics distribution.[17] Some trips cover hundreds of miles, some only a few blocks.

People who have contraband in their vehicles almost always are frightened and desperate, with good cause. Great sums of money, reputations, their very lives may hang in the balance once you flip on your overheads and initiate a stop. At that moment, they want nothing more in life than to get rid of you and be back on their way. With a strong enough motivation and an opportunity when you are vulnerable, they may get rid of you any way they can. *Any* way.

The next vehicle you see may be carrying Mr. Wrong and his secret cargo. He knows who *you* are the instant he lays eyes on you. Through what you see, say, hear, smell, feel, sense, and do, can you find out about *him*—and control him—fast enough to win your brief encounter?

I

TACTICS OF ENCOUNTER

5%ER MIND-SET

A good cop stays a rookie at heart, excited by every shift.
—David Hunter, *The Night Is Mine*

Of the uniformed officers who slide into patrol cars at the end of roll call, there are RODs and there are 5%ers—and a shifting sea of blue and brown in between that could drift either way. RODs don't succeed on aggressive Criminal Patrol. ROD means: Retired On Duty.

For these officers, says a Southern trainer, "their climate-controlled cruiser is a fortress. They roll up the windows and set the temperature at sixty-eight to seventy-four degrees, they adjust the seat just right, they have a soft cushion for their broad ass, they tune in their favorite radio station at a volume that's one decibel below where they can hear their call number. They don't leave this comfortable 'home' unless they absolutely have to. Each day to them is just another day toward pulling the pin. They spend their shift going to coffee, coming from coffee, going to bullshit with someone, leaving someone they've just bullshitted with—and occasionally handling a call. When they do stop traffic violators, they're just 'mail carriers'—they deliver the ticket. They don't look for anything more, they don't think about anything more. Their philosophy is: 'Little cases, little problems...big cases, big problems.' They build a career on sliding by."

And in today's violent world, their lackadaisical attitude not only is a waste to the taxpayers but because of the tactical indifference that's usually part of it, it's *dangerous* to the RODs themselves, to you, and to other officers, as well.

You either already are or want to be a 5%er—one of the *exceptional* minority committed to outstanding performance on patrol.

Along with the relative handful of other elite officers on any agency, you are *aggressive* about enforcing the law, not in the sense of a John Wayne hot dog or a thug who tramples people's rights, but in the way you seek out chances for *pro-active* police work, rather than mark time with *reactive* coasting. While you respect legal restraints, you're more interested in making the most of what you *can* do legally than in feeling paralyzed by what you can't do. You know search-and-seizure laws inside-out because they are your tools—and you know how to use them. You enthusiastically embrace the core concept of Criminal Patrol: *that vehicle stops are golden opportunities for unique field investigations which, with the right volume of contacts, the right knowledge and creativity, and the right approach, can lead to major felony arrests.* Your body hums when you're on the street. You want to see just how sharply you can hone the fundamental patrol skills of *observation, conversation,* and *tactical thinking.* To sharpen your alertness to detail and your readiness for trouble, you practice *mental conditioning exercises* like those described in *The Tactical Edge,* such as Crisis Rehearsal, Positive Self-Talk, and the Survival Resource.

Suspicion! You never leave home without it. You're motivated by a passion for the job, pride in its purpose, and competitiveness with fellow officers, with the bad guys, and with yourself for results. You are self-confident without being arrogant. *You expect to succeed.*

You share the focused drive of two highway patrol officers who have built enviable reputations for Criminal Patrol in Ohio. One morning these two, Robert Stevens and Jim Slagle, were scheduled for court. When they arrived, the prosecutor said it would be about ninety minutes before they'd be called. Rather than loll around the courthouse, they decided to drive their units out to the nearest major roadway and watch traffic.

Moments after setting up, Stevens clocked a white Ford van with Florida plates exceeding the speed limit, and Slagle stopped it down the road. The two males inside said they were en route from Florida to Michigan to look for an apartment. Scanning the van's interior, Slagle noticed a want-ad publication from a city in Ohio, which didn't seem to jibe.

Chatting with the driver, Slagle without warning asked: "Do you have a toothbrush with you?" Until then, the driver had appeared extremely calm. Now he suddenly started stuttering and shaking, apparently unnerved by the unexpected query. With Stevens as backup, Slagle got the driver's consent to search the van and uncovered $18,000 cash, quantities of Valium and cocaine, electronic surveillance equipment, and telephone repairmen's climbing shoes (when the suspects wanted to place a phone call, they just scaled a pole and tapped into a line!).

Later, the driver admitted they were drug runners. He gave up a ministorage spot in Ohio containing ten pounds of pot, a kilo of coke, and a MAC-10. He also cooperated in busting his supplier in Florida, and that individual set up *his* supplier in Mexico, resulting eventually in multiple arrests and the federal seizure of an aircraft and 800 kilos of cocaine. All

Another drug detection victory involving Tpr. Stevens.

This time the vehicle was a rental truck with a "cover" load to fool unsuspecting officers. It didn't work.

Drug packages discovered hidden inside a sofa from the truck.

this because two officers had the 5%er penchant to "kill time" productively.

This avid orientation is not rookie fever. It grows from a special professional spark that you can ignite—and sustain—at any point in your career, including at a very common but critical turning point.

A trainer who is a former federal agent explains: "After a few years in law enforcement, you come to a crossroads. By now you've been beaten on by your department, by the public, by civilian friends, by family members who don't understand. You've lost your initial hope that you can make the world a happier place. You feel that what you do doesn't matter.

"You can continue with disillusionment and cynicism and spiral on down—into alcoholism, divorce, drug abuse, excessive complaints, burnout. You might even lose the edge to the point that you get killed. Or you can turn *up*, where you start doing the *best job you can do.* Not because your administration wants it or the public wants it—but because *you* want it, for the pride you can take in your work."

Taking traffic stops seriously—consciously working to go "beyond the ticket" successfully and safely—is one way of helping yourself in making this important transition. It can literally save your life, on and off the job.

Trooper with the 5%er Mind-Set: Robert Stevens.

An older officer in Iowa who was feeling "terminally burnt out" happened to see photographs of a vehicle-stop drug bust made by a young colleague. "I decided I was going to try it," the officer recalls. "In the fourth car I stopped, I found eighty pounds of marijuana. Now I'm hooked! When you stop a guy for not wearing a seat belt and you turn it into a $200,000 contraband seizure, there's just no other feeling like it."

Those who are good at it agree: *The 5%er Mind-Set is the most essential factor behind successful Criminal Patrol.* A root component is the willingness to work hard. Criminal Patrol in large part is a numbers game; you have to stop a lot of vehicles to get the law of averages working in your favor. You have to be able to tell quickly whether the driver you've stopped *this time* is a likely contraband offender. If so, you have to know how to get him or her to cooperate with your desire to search the vehicle. Then, given that opportunity, you have to be able to find whatever the suspect may be hiding. All this requires high energy, fast thinking, psychological agility, and persistence. Your *attitude* determines whether you'll learn what you need to know to do the job...apply what you've learned...stick with it through discouragement, setbacks, and moments of impatience...maintain the mental and physical stamina required...and operate with the right tactical balance of courage and caution to overcome what at times will be life-threatening risks.

27

A deputy in Florida discovered a memorable coincidence you can use to remind yourself that on the street *attitude is everything.* Starting with A, he numbered in sequence each letter of the alphabet and then designated those numbers to be percentage points. The word *attitude* adds up like this:

A	1
T	20
T	20
I	9
T	20
U	21
D	4
E	5
	100%

On Criminal Patrol and any other assignment, you should periodically conduct a personal "attitude check," in the interest both of success and survival. You need to be sure every moment you're on patrol that your mind-set—*your most powerful weapon*—is working 100% to *your* advantage, not to your adversary's.

Fatal Tendencies

Just how critical attitude is to your survival is revealed in an in-depth study of more than fifty randomly selected officer murders, 22% of which occurred during vehicle stops or pursuits.[1] Agents conducting the study exhaustively videotaped the incarcerated killers describing their fatal encounters and also probed the personalities and professional performances of the slain officers by interviewing their administrators, supervisors, and peers. Analyzing this data, the investigators then were able to identify certain behavioral characteristics that tended to be shared by many or all of the victims.

Without exception, these characteristics were rooted in attitude, and often they played decisive roles in the officers' deaths. Undoubtedly these same "fatal tendencies" are at play in other confrontations where officers are injured or killed. They need to be carefully studied and contemplated so you can *avoid* them in your own patrol practices.

According to the investigators, the murdered officers tended to:

1. Operate with an unbalanced public relations/service orientation. They were hard-working, friendly, easy-going, well-liked by their community and fellow officers—all highly desirable traits. But—on the street they were so focused on the *service* side of policing that they seemed to see themselves more as public relations figures than as law enforcers. In their desire to help, they forgot the potential danger they faced as officers and the survival tactics needed to cope with it.

2. Use less force than peers. Officers who got killed tended to use *less* force than their fellow officers say they would have used in similar circumstances. Interestingly, they also used less force than their *killers* say *they* would have used had they been the officers involved in their encounters.

3. Use force later than peers. The victim officers also tended to use force as a last resort—typically later in a confrontation than their fellow officers say they would have in comparable situations. This apparently stemmed from a reluctance to hurt anyone. Unfortunately,

(above)
CHP officers maintain control during arrest of 4 felony suspects on a high-risk stop. Inside the vehicle officers later found a scanner, 2 revolvers, a rifle, and a machine gun.

Do you tailor your tactics to the potential risk you're facing?

The fantasy of having control of an uncontrolled suspect has resulted in many officer deaths. A sergeant and officer stand distracted, leaving this drug suspect with multiple opportunities for attack.

29

(upper left)
Suspect in the shooting death of a New Jersey state trooper. Killer was alleged to be a member of a heavily armed drug-dealing gang from New York.

(upper right)
New Mexico cop killer stands remorseless after the jury announces his death sentence. Many suspects have no moral hesitation in taking advantage of officers' fatal tendencies.

(below)
In the battle to control the streets, the risks of tactical errors can be extreme.

(above)
Grisly scene of a DEA agent found slain on-duty in New York City.

by delaying the application of appropriate force to resistant suspects, they extended the time they themselves were vulnerable to assault.

4. Shortcut rules and procedures. The slain officers tended not to closely follow their departmental rules and procedures. Instead, they took shortcuts, either for convenience to themselves or "courtesy" to the offender. These included violating procedures for vehicle stops, arrests, prisoner handling, and the wearing of body armor.

5. Act without waiting for backup. Often backup was available, but the victims tended to go ahead on their own in high-risk situations. The training instructor who headed this study estimates that 75% of the officers killed made *procedural errors* that impacted on their deaths. *Failure to wait for backup is the single greatest tactical mistake* emerging not only from this study, he says, but from the national Officer Killed Summaries tallied year after year by the FBI.

6. Rely heavily on "reading" people. The victim officers generally took great pride in their abilities to "read" people and situations. They depended more on their gut than on observable, articulable facts. If they felt "good vibes" early on, they were inclined to let their guard down, rather than use caution and *continuously* evaluate people and circumstances throughout the contact.

7. Relax when "good" is perceived. The murdered officers characteristically looked for good in other people—and tended to drop their guard when they perceived evidence of it. A smile, a kind word, cooperation—any of these from a suspect often was enough to convince them that this person would cause no trouble. Tragically, this attitude in many of the cases set the officers up for their fatal assaults.

Remembering the potential grim consequences of these traits is especially important on Criminal Patrol because often you will find it necessary to fake a relaxed attitude in order to properly probe and evaluate the subjects you're up against. As you'll see, projecting an easy-going friendliness and helpfulness can be an important strategy in building quick rapport, with an eye toward detecting deception and the concealment of evidence. You, too, will need to rely heavily on your ability to "read" people and circumstances as part of your investigation. And up to a point, you may sometimes be more effective working alone, without backup present. What's crucial is to be able

The Darrell Lunsford Stop

The rubbing of Darrell Lunsford's name you see above was made at the National Law Enforcement Memorial wall in Washington, D.C. A small-town traffic stop made his one of the first officer murders ever photographed by in-car video as it happened.

With a history of successful drug stops behind him that fateful night, Constable Lunsford pulled over an old GM sedan with Maine license plates and three Hispanic occupants. His instinct for building suspicion was right on target, but his behavior, unfortunately, was a sad medley of tactical errors and fatal tendencies.

Lunsford was known to detest backup, so one deputy who approached the scene and could have offered help deliberately passed on by. The driver met Lunsford half way. Favoring the camera, Lunsford stood with him in the "sandwich meat" position between the cars, fully illuminated by his own headlights. At one point, while talking to the passengers, he put his upper body fully into the suspect vehicle, even though it was still occupied. One of the passengers disobeyed his command to stay in the vehicle, but Lunsford did not escalate his force to control the situation.

With two young suspects out and unrestrained against a middle-aged officer who was all alone, the countdown to a killing began....

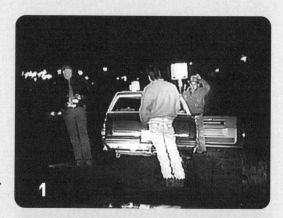

(1) Essentially abandoning his effort to get the persistent passenger back in the vehicle, Lunsford now misses an important danger cue. The passenger removes his cowboy hat—indication in that part of the country that a fight is coming. (2) Lunsford begins to search the trunk, later found to contain about 40 lbs. of marijuana. He turns his back on the driver, whose hands are hidden in his pockets, and allows himself to be bracketed by the two suspects. (3) He permits the suspects to get close enough to each other to converse. Speaking Spanish, the passenger tells the driver: "I'll take his feet, you get the top."

4

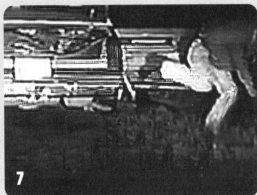

7

5

8

6

9

(4) Suspect's attack catches Lunsford by surprise. He continues to clutch his flashlight and suspect's ID, not freeing his hands to fight back. (5-6) Second assailant joins in. Lunsford is big and hard to control, but as he fails to fight back effective he is moved to the side of the road, where a leg grab finally topples him. The third occupant now gets out.

(7) Lunsford is kicked in the head 3 times and disarmed. (8) With Lunsford's own .357 Magnum, suspect shoots the fallen constable once through the base of the skull. 14 seconds have elapsed since the assault began. (9) Suspect slams trunk lid shut and gets the dope back on the road. Lunsford is found later, dead in the ditch—emphatic rebuttal to the myth that marijuana transporters aren't dangerous.

to distinguish between a calculated plan that you follow as part of an investigative strategy and bad habits that you slip into through carelessness, complacency, and poor judgment. At some moments on Criminal Patrol the two may *look* and *sound* about the same. The difference is that when you're behaving a certain way by *tactical choice*, you stay fully alert to your environment and to the subject(s) you are dealing with and you are fortified by a readiness to respond *instantly* to defeat any threat that may arise.

Your Goal

To meet the practical challenges of Criminal Patrol, you need to detect and interpret certain telltale cues to deceit and contraband concealment, much like a mantracker reads "sign" in pursuing his prey.

These cues or "indicators" not only can alert you to the possible presence of criminal activity but they also can warn you at the earliest possible moment that you may be dealing with a high-risk situation. That's especially important because certain techniques for advancing the *investigative* aspects of your Criminal Patrol stops may require you to temporarily compromise ideal survival tactics, and if you can't quickly read danger cues you risk compromising yourself into fatal vulnerability.

Some red-alert indicators associated with the vehicle or its occupant(s) will be evident to you *before* you make a stop or approach; indeed, they may be what prompts you to single out potentially suspicious vehicles from the stream that flows across your field of vision in the first place. But most cues can be detected or developed only after you establish contact with the vehicle and whoever is inside.

In practice, you look for and test for these incriminating tip-offs much as an overworked medic conducts triage among the wounded on a battlefield. Unable to treat all the injured because of limitations of time and resources, he assesses wounds and vital signs and selects out those he feels are *most likely* to respond to his expert attention; the rest, in effect, he abandons.

For legal and practical reasons, you must be selective, too. You need to determine which of the vehicles you stop are likeliest to be worthwhile searching. Even if you had the time and zeal to search every vehicle you pulled over, you'd still want to make choices. For while you are snooping through cars or trucks that are not carrying contraband, dirty drivers may be whizzing by unstopped and undetected.

Being selective, you'll probably develop enough suspicion to search only a small minority of the vehicles you stop, perhaps as few as 1%. Not that you'll ever be infallible. There is no foolproof diagnostic formula; predicting who's carrying drugs or other illegal goods is much more an art than an exact science. But with training and practice you can, like the battlefield medic, learn to read the "symptoms" that are most promising of positive results. The vehicles and occupants exhibiting those characteristics are the ones you want to zero in on for extended attention. With them, you move as high as you can up the Criminal Patrol Pyramid, while the others, after appropriate initial exploration, you send quickly on their way with a ticket or warning.

Your vigilance for giveaway indicators must be *habitual*, at work

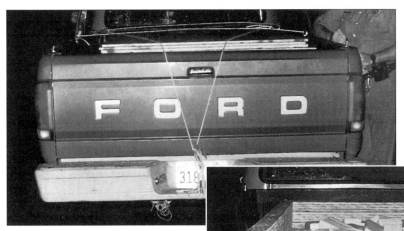

Pickup pulled over at night in Texas with a burned-out taillight. The visible load is 22 sheets of 4-ft. x 8-ft. plywood panels. What's wrong with this picture?

Tpr. Mark Parks did see something wrong when he approached. Despite being loaded with wood, the pickup's bed wasn't riding low as if under heavy weight. Center of plywood was cut out, concealing 248 kilos of Colombian cocaine.

during *all* your contacts. Cues may crop up at unlikely moments, apart from traffic stops. As examples: In New Mexico, an officer approached a car in a traffic jam at an accident scene, intending just to ask the driver to stop honking his horn. Because she was alert to the visual cues of Criminal Patrol, the officer ended up instead arresting the driver for transporting drugs, drug money, and a firearm.... Another officer investigating a collision in the Southeast learned from one driver that the three occupants of the other car had offered him

35

$2,500 cash not to report the crash to the police. Building on that remark, the officer eventually discovered in the suspect vehicle handwritten notes in a "narcotics-related code," plus $50,000 in currency hidden in the trunk and $3,000 cash and $90,000 worth of jewelry concealed on the suspects themselves—all potentially forfeitable.... In California, one officer seized 801 kilos of marijuana from an unoccupied vehicle that first attracted his attention because it was parked on a median strip with a flat tire; another stopped to check on a pickup truck that had caught fire—and ended up discovering 202 pounds of marijuana hidden under the hood, while in Illinois an officer checking on a junker van that had konked out and been left beside a roadway spotted thirteen garbage bags inside that eventually turned out to hold 650 pounds of heroin and cocaine (as the Buck Savage character used to say in the old police-training films: "Bad guys' cars break down too").... Two Texas troopers recovered over 1,800 pounds of narcotics during two abandoned-vehicle calls; one involved a van that had been in an accident and the other a Chevrolet Suburban that had gotten stuck in a field.... A Mississippi deputy was waiting in the drive-through line at a hamburger joint anticipating lunch when he noticed two Hispanics approach a white Lincoln Continental at a motel next door. The way they looked around before getting into the car piqued his curiosity. Within fifteen minutes, the deputy had discovered that structual cavities in both sides of the Lincoln were filled with packages of dope.... In Chicago, patrol officers inspecting a college student's car that was double-parked in a residential neighborhood with flasher lights blinking at 4 o'clock in the morning discovered a personal arsenal inside: a Chinese assault rifle with attached bayonet, a .25-cal. Beretta semiauto, a machete and two other large knives, an expandable police baton, lead-filled gloves, body armor, a two-way radio, and 300 rounds of ammunition....

In short, *you may encounter contraband circumstances at any time, day or night, on any citizen contact.* The key is awareness and a pro-active approach to your job. Avoid assumptions.

- **If you assume you can never find contraband, you'll never look;**
- **If you assume you'll only find small quantities, you'll never press hard enough to find big loads;**
- **If you assume you'll only find big loads, you'll quickly get discouraged.**

An obvious clue that eventually led to a sizable seizure by an alert deputy.

"It's a lot like fishing," says an Ohio officer. "You go to the stream with positive expectations. You catch a lot of little fish for every big one you catch, and some days you don't catch anything. But the law of averages says if you fish enough, you'll hit something eventually. What keeps you coming back is knowing that there *are* big ones out there and they *can* be caught. But you'll *never* catch anything if you don't put your line in the water."

A Diamond Day

"Some days are diamonds, some days are stone," says the country song. For Traffic Officer Ryan Briceland of the California Highway Patrol, a memorable diamond day began when he stopped a passenger car for an obstructed driver's view and no license plate.

Conversing with the lone male driver, Briceland detected what he considered "obvious signs" of narcotics trafficking: a peculiar nervousness and apparent confusion by the driver in presenting a straight story about where he was coming from, where he was headed, and why.

After obtaining the driver's verbal consent to search the vehicle, Briceland started by walking his drug-trained K-9 partner, Greif, around the vehicle. The dog immediately alerted at the right rear. Briceland then noticed that screws in the rear quarter panel molding looked new and scratched as if recently replaced.

When he removed the quarter-panel vent plate he saw what looked like numerous drug packages. A thorough search of the car uncovered thirty-four bricks of marijuana—eighty-seven pounds—inside the quarter panel, the right front door panel, and a spare-tire well in the trunk that had been sealed with Bondo, painted over, and hidden with carpeting.

Approximately five minutes after making this stop, Briceland noticed a similar type of vehicle with a single occupant pass his location. The driver looked straight ahead without making eye contact as he passed—cause for suspicion to Briceland.

The officer radioed another CHP location about this vehicle and down the road it was stopped by another officer. Another K-9 alerted on this car, and this time a search discovered twenty-eight other packages—sixty-nine pounds—of marijuana hidden in quarter panels.

When you have a choice, you're most likely to reel in good catches where there's good traffic volume and especially where you think drugs are most likely to be flowing on your beat. Work a street or road that feeds a known drug area, for example; "The only way traffickers are going to get in there," says a Midwestern trooper, "is by car—they can't be beamed in." At night, you might patrol around all-night fast-food places, gas stations, or convenience stores where couriers might pull in on quick stops. Suburban malls or shopping center parking lots are often where mid-level drug deals go down. In rural areas, watch highway rest stops, as well as roadways, and watch pay phones at truck stops for truck drivers who stand out as not looking like the typical unshaven, unbathed, disheveled rig jockey. (Because they may be driving trucks infrequently and only to carry dope, couriers often fail to blend in with legitimate truckers, and while they often carry cellular phones they are reluctant to use them because conversations can be monitored. If you have a CB, you can easily eavesdrop on other conversations at truck stops. Personal drug deals among truckers are often blatantly discussed amidst other CB chatter.)

Fishing for "trouble" productively takes planning: You plan where you're going to work...you may set a mental goal of how many vehicles you'd like to stop on your shift...you decide how tactically you're going to make contact with the driver and how you're going to position yourself to get a look inside the vehicle...you know certain key words, phrases, or questions you're going to use to try to catch people in lies...you have a strategy in mind for getting inside the vehicles you decide you want to search and the search pattern you're going to use...you anticipate the role that a K-9 may play...you understand how you need to document and handle any physical evidence that you uncover...and you think out how you're going to employ backup and control suspects for safety. *You plan your work and work your plan*—always maintaining flexibility to improvise and adapt to overcome barriers you may confront.

Expect the unexpected.

That's the primal law both of Criminal Patrol and of officer survival.

An Emergency Services officer from New York City, for example, thought he was just stopping to help a stranded motorist when he pulled up behind a Nissan Maxima with tinted windows parked on the shoulder of a nearly deserted expressway about 2 o'clock one morning. The car was a model known to be favored by a local Jamaican crack-dealing gang called the Forties Posse, and in the front seat were two young black men. The officer, mentally focused on being a Good Samaritan, walked straight toward the driver's door.

When he was less than five feet away, the driver suddenly spun out of the car with a gun in hand and opened fire. The officer, a seven-year veteran, took three hits to the chest and wildly fired back six ineffective rounds as the Nissan sped off.

The attack caught the officer completely by surprise. With a better reading of danger cues he might have anticipated trouble in time to prevent it.

At least in one regard he *had* expected the unexpected. When he left for work that shift, he put on soft body armor. The vest stopped the driver's rounds and kept the officer alive.

Expect the unexpected. One night in southern California an officer was murdered in the line of duty. When his body was discovered, officers noted that he had not been wearing his body armor that shift. An inspection of his patrol car later revealed why the vest had not been on to protect him.

Cartels: Hidden Puppeteers Who Pull the Strings

Law enforcement sources estimate that the Colombian Cali Cartel, the world's main cocaine supplier and "the most powerful drug-trafficking organization in history," is responsible for the shipment of 70 to 90% of all cocaine entering the U.S., the world's most ravenous drug market. The leaders of this group and other major controllers of drug supplies to this country may seem far removed from the streets you patrol. But their impact is never really far away.

The Cali Cartel smuggles cocaine into the U.S. via courier, private aircraft, cargo vessels, and land conveyances. It tracks shipments closely by assigning a subject in a key distribution area to act as overseer. This subject is often well-established and has a legitimate business cover to conceal illegal activities. Cocaine shipments often are routed via transshipment countries (Venezuela, Brazil, Panama, Costa Rica, El Salvador), and a Cartel representative in the transshipment country further monitors the shipment. When it finally arrives here, another subject is dispatched from Colombia to coordinate delivery with the local overseer.

Most of the cocaine shipped into the U.S. by the Cartel is transshipped and staged in Mexico, Puerto Rico, and the Virgin Islands. In Mexico, private aircraft fly to airstrips in Agua Prieta, Guadalajara, Mazatlán, Veracruz, and Nogales, where cocaine is offloaded and warehoused. It may then be shipped out of there by vehicle, aircraft, boat, or foot traffic. Southern California, Arizona, south Florida, and Texas are preferred staging and distribution areas used by the Cartel within the U.S. Cocaine may also be carried from Mexico to Oregon by boat for distribution east, or brought in from Canada. Key "gateway" and distribution sites include Houston, Los Angeles, Chicago-Gary, Miami, Washington-Baltimore, the Gulf Coast, the Southwest Border, and New York.

The Cartel operates numerous independent "cells" within large metropolitan areas, staffed by controllers who receive their orders directly from the Cartel in Colombia. One cell may be unaware of the existence of another cell operating in the same area. Each is equipped with the latest technology: computers, fax machines, pagers, cellular phones, et cetera. (Cellular phones are often scrapped after limited use to deter law enforcement interception.) An estimated 4,000 Colombians living in Los Angeles alone make their living working for the cocaine Cartel (which is now aggressively expanding into heroin distribution because of the surging popularity of that drug).

To launder some drug proceeds, Colombian traffickers employ teams of people, generally called "smurfs," to convert substantial sums of drug dollars into money orders, usually in denominations between $500 and $1,000. Going bank to bank, some smurfs are able to purchase with cash up to $100,000 in money orders during a single day. The money orders are then coded with various symbols used as accounting tools by the Cartel (the U.S. Postal Service has catalogued over 800 such markings) and smuggled out of the U.S. to Colombia. They are eventually returned here for collection through the foreign and domestic banking system in transactions originating in Colombia, Panama, Ecuador, and other countries, giving the appearance that they represent payment for legitimate goods and services. Drug money is also often laundered through foreign currency exchanges. One in Canada accepted more than $200,000,000 a year in illicit funds. Canadian authorities estimate that 40% of exchanges are involved with suspicious transactions.

Besides Colombian organizations, other top-echelon suppliers compete for power and profit in the drug trade. Among them: Nigerian groups, which are estimated to smuggle 35% to 40% of all heroin arriving in the U.S....ultra-secretive Asian Triads, still operating traditional heroin pipelines from the Golden Triangle (Burma, Thailand, and Laos)...growing Russian criminal mafias smuggling heroin from Afghanistan... cutthroat Mexican cartels, warring with one another, both to help Colombians penetrate our porous border and to disperse their own flood of brown heroin and marijuana...and myriad domestic street gangs which, through ruthless drug retailing, are fast replacing the Mafia as our most murderous and visible practitioners of organized crime.

The glue that holds any drug superstructure together is green and red: money and blood. At every level—including the point at which you intercept the drug flow—violence is always waiting.[2]

Agents of DEA, U.S. Coast Guard Intelligence, and U.S. Customs jointly contributed to this investigation which resulted in seizure of approximately 9,000 lbs. of cocaine found aboard this fishing vessel off the coast of Long Island (NY).

Seized in another incident, a cocaine package wrapped with translucent tape and Colombian newspaper pages.

The Hunted

Whether illegal substances are produced here (America is currently the most popular country for marijuana production) or flow in through our sieve-like borders and coastlines, sooner or later the problem of narcotics contraband gets down to a couple of people in a couple of vehicles: you...and someone transporting drugs. An important part of your 5%er preparation is to understand the mindset, motivation, and methods of the *other* person behind the wheel. The success of any good hunter, after all, is enhanced by knowing the habits of his prey.

Plaster bust of Jesus Malverde, patron saint of drug traffickers, sits in a shrine in Culiacán, Mexico. In the Mexican countryside, drug desperados often are viewed as heroes.

Loads intended for resale may range from a kilo or less tossed into a gym bag or tucked under the dashboard on up to a semitrailer or tanker truckful headed to a warehouse or other central collection point to be split into smaller shipments for distribution. One major marijuana trafficker is said to disperse more than two tons of his product a month. He uses a network of drivers who haul pot over established routes from El Paso to North Carolina, where it's shipped out to other locations. Another organization ships bales of marijuana from New Mexico to storage facilities in Pennsylvania, where it's repackaged in babyfood cans and sent on to New York City. Out of Los Angeles, Bloods and Crips street gangs oversee the transportation and selling of crack cocaine in a myriad hinterland markets, including hamlets in Idaho and South Dakota, just as Jamaican Posse gangs do in the East and Midwest.

Overall, drug movement within the U.S. is highly diverse and often haphazard. But to cite just one well-defined pattern, cocaine and heroin coming from Mexico under the auspices of the most powerful and structured Colombian criminal organizations generally go first to staging points like Los Angeles, Houston, and Phoenix (some authorities estimate that 70% of imported drugs now come in through the Southwest[3]). From these warehousing locations, drugs are moved out by vehicle to dozens of regional hubs, which can be as large as Denver or Omaha or as small as Cedar Rapids, Iowa, and Rockford, Illinois. And from there illegal loads reach into the American heartland and sometimes backtrack the route they have traveled. One $8,000,000-a-month ring run in Rockford by a former migrant worker and lathe operator, for example, shipped drugs in cargo vans to lesser dealers in Utah, Illinois, Michigan, Iowa, Wisconsin, Missouri, Oklahoma, Arizona, and California. Operating at various levels in the drug trade are crews that build hidden compartments in vehicles, experiment with packaging methods in hopes of eluding detection by drug-trained K-9s, hire drivers (from a cross-section of ethnic groups), enforce discipline, launder money, set up safe houses, pay off corrupt officials, and so on. Besides their involvement in smuggling, some of these may also operate legitimate businesses.

The transporter you encounter behind the wheel may be at virtually any level on the distribution food chain. He or she may be a "mule" hired by an individual trafficker or an organization to move goods from Point A to Point B, which may be across the border, across the country, or across town. Or he may be an entrepreneur who's bankrolling the load himself, with his own money as well as his free dom at risk (like the cash-squeezed Illinois nightclub owner who arranged to pick up a kilo of cocaine in Florida on consignment, sell it to a contact he'd made up north, and use his share of the proceeds to transfuse his ailing club). He may be a small or large street dealer with drugs for his customers, or he may be an end user.

With any category suspect, you may find drugs, drug ingredients, drug paraphernalia, or drug money. With some, you may also find black-market guns intended for sale to street criminals, run as a profitable sideline. Jamaican Posse gangs, for example, move sizable firearms ship

A Mule on the Move

Antonio is one rags-to-riches example of how an ambitious immigrant became a criminal kingpin—and then a federal prisoner—by transporting drugs. He talks about his career moves from a penitentiary in Arkansas:

He first came to the U.S. dirt-poor from Mexico and worked at legal jobs in Illinois until he saved enough money to buy a red El Camino truck. Then he drove back down to his hometown of San Martín Peras, Mexico, where an acquaintance sold him thirty-one pounds of marijuana for $1,200. He packed the drugs into a bolted compartment in the back of the truck and headed for the border.

"At Del Rio, I got in line," Antonio recalls. "I started praying. My leg was shaking. When I got to the checkpoint, the officer just waved me through. I couldn't believe it." He peddled the drugs back in

Illinois for $12,000 and soon he was headed south of the border again for another load.

As his business thrived, he recruited others to help. He and his mules would drive vans to rendezvous points just across the border in Mexico, where drugs were delivered into staging areas in the blistering Sonora desert by private airplanes.

After months of participating in deliveries himself, he developed so many contacts that he became a broker, taking orders from dealers in dozens of towns in the Midwest. Like scores of other high-level traffickers, he could contact a Colombian connection and, once a deal was struck, the drugs he'd ordered would arrive at his base of operations in Illinois via automobile from just about anywhere in the country. There they'd be broken down into small-

er loads and shipped back out again to dealers lower on the dope ladder.

In his neighborhood of poor Hispanic immigrants, he became a Godfather. Many paid homage to him. His money financed new bars and restaurants, and satellite dishes sprouted in modest back yards. He donated generously to his church, sponsored block parties for Mexican festival days, was president of a soccer league. He bought new homes for his employees, several airplanes, and dozens of automobiles.

Then after five flourishing years in the drug trade, an extensive federal investigation brought him down.

Today Antonio is serving a forty-five-year sentence. But some of his former compatriots have taken up the slack and continue to run drugs, much as he did before.[4]

What's the Load?

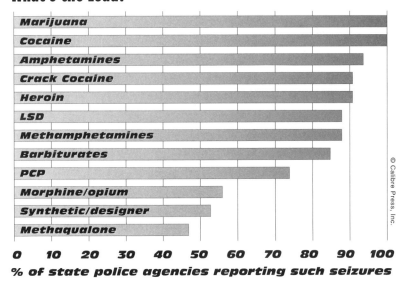

What are you most likely to find in a vehicle which is used to transport narcotics? Here is what state police agencies found as a result of their drug-interdiction efforts in one 12-month period.[5]

© Calibre Press, Inc.

41

ments from state to state, sometimes hiding both guns and dope in the door panels of stolen luxury cars. Customs agents say that gun smuggling of assault weapons from South America and Mexico has increased significantly since Congress passed federal anticrime legislation.

Mules commonly draw fees ranging from flat rates of $1,000 to $5,000 or piece rates of $500 per kilo or more plus expenses per trip, depending on distance and the volume they're hauling. Some are recruited to what one DEA agent calls "the ant army" of drug movers by strangers who strike up conversation—at a bar, say—and end up offering quick bucks for a quick trip and zippered lips. One transport recruit was nursing a beer in a barrio bar in Chicago one night when a friendly fellow illegal from Mexico whom he'd never seen before offered him $500 to move a car from one neighborhood of the city to another.

He was to park the car on the street, leave the ignition key in the ashtray, lock the door, and walk away. He was not given a trunk key or told the purpose of the twenty-minute drive. "I had no job," the man explains in Spanish. "I had a wife and hungry kids in Mexico. I needed the money." No questions asked, he agreed. He claims he did not know there were five kilos of coke hidden in the trunk. He found out soon enough. Federal agents were lying in wait at the delivery point, and he is now doing forty years in a maximum-security prison.

Although mega-size loads of both drugs and money can be—and are—found in any type of motor vehicle, the consistently biggest cargoes are moved by truck. These drivers, who tend to be closely controlled by drug cartels, may be paid a small percentage of the value of what they're carrying, but they are always owed money as one means of keeping them obligated to the distribution boss and ready for the next run. A trucker may travel empty hundreds of miles from his home base to a rendezvous point where he picks up his drug load, possibly a cover load, and an assigned destination. From there, he may caravan cross-country with other dirty haulers to a major delivery or redistribution center. Because of some colossal busts in the past, bosses now try to limit loads to no more than 500 kilos per truck, but greedy couriers may actually be hauling more than that because of accumulating shipments from several bosses on a single run.

Most couriers at any level, with any vehicle and with any size load, are known personally to those who engage them, or they're a friend of a friend. It's a matter of trust...and it's a hook. If a mule who's personally connected fails to deliver because he rips off the load or gives it up to the police, he can more easily be held accountable by those higher in the narcotics network; if he himself can't be found, a family member he cares about certainly can. "We'll kill the family," says a distributor. "That's our insurance." Despite the lore that drug trafficking organizations expect to lose a certain percentage of loads "as just a part of doing business," few criminal groups in reality—especially groups like ruthless and predatory street gangs and subsidiaries of the 300-odd Colombian cartels estimated to be operating in this country—accept courier missteps and the loss of profits casually. Drivers who lose a load may be "offed" in prison, if not on the street, and their bosses are expected to pay back to the organization the street value of the loss.

Many mules are employed in legal jobs full-time and make contraband runs for side money, sometimes only once a month or less. They may leave with a load on Friday and return Sunday night, driving straight through. One network of drivers for a Mexican organization,

From Here to You...

One popular entry point for drugs and dispatch point for mules to the rest of the U. S. is Starr County, Texas, a rambling chunk of border brushland along the Rio Grande. Officially, Starr is the poorest county in the Lone Star state. Unemployment in some of its dozen scattered towns is 50%. The average reported income per capita is about $3,600 a year. Many neighborhoods have no running water or sewers, only privies that overflow on rainy days. Yet authorities estimate that 75% of the county's 40,000 residents are involved somehow in trafficking illegal drugs, and an estimated $200,000,000 in drug profits is on deposit in banks throughout the county. Here's how this one "source area" for drugs that may end up on your beat looked to one reporter:

It is shortly after dusk when the first of the "choo-choos" roll into town. Their drivers hidden behind blacked-out windows, the customized pickups parade

through Rio Grande City [the dusty county seat of 9,900] with arrogant abandon.

First they glide by the U.S. Border Patrol station to see how many agents are on duty. Then it's on to the Pizza Hut a block away to show off their $25,000 special-order rigs.

Behind the wheels are drug dealers, some of them millionaires, cruising their turf on a warm spring evening, playing out a nightly ritual. They dress in designer shirts and pants. They drape themselves in gold chains and religious medallions. Their feet are wrapped in eel, ostrich, or sharkskin cowboy boots. Their jackets are leather. They like black, flat-brimmed Stetsons. "We have more unemployed truck drivers living in $300,000 houses, driving $25,000 trucks, and wearing $750 boots than any other place in the world," says a supervisor of the Border Patrol's night shift.

He says the dealers often carry fully automatic weapons and are

"particularly fond" of AK-47s capable of firing 600 rounds a minute. "They wouldn't hesitate for a second to blow your head off if you got in their way. They're mean, they're organized, and they're very deadly.

"There used to be an unwritten peace agreement between the Border Patrol and the drug dealers. Most of them never carried weapons, and when they did, it was to protect themselves from other dealers." Now agents [in the area] average at least one armed encounter a week.

In one raid, authorities found a stockpile of military assault rifles, police scanners, two-way radios, and infrared night goggles. They also located notebooks that detailed the movement of Border Patrolmen in the region, including the agents' lunch break schedule.

"We're facing an epidemic," says a thirty-year veteran lawman, "a very dangerous epidemic...."[6]

The fruits of planning and commitment: the seizure of 14,676 lbs. of cocaine that will never reach the streets of any American communities. This investigation also involved the arrest of Cali cartel drug kingpins from Colombia, as well as their highest ranking managers in the U.S. 14 law enforcement agencies from the greater Miami area worked in cooperation with each other to effect this mission.

hauling cocaine, heroin, and marijuana hidden in the headliners and behind the dashboards of vehicles, customarily drove directly from south Texas to Chicago, Florida, or California, distances of up to 1,900 miles each way, stopping only for gasoline. When a transport *team* is used, members often don't know each other. Increasingly these days they are a male and a female, paired to blend into traffic as an unexceptional married couple. Having two or more on a transport helps with the driving and increases security; as strangers, it's believed they'll tend to watch each other and be less likely to conspire on a rip-off.

"You're scared the whole time you're in the car," says a frequent mule. "Maybe you don't know *exactly* what you're hauling or *exactly* where it is, but you know you're not being paid for a vacation trip. You have the feeling that sooner or later there'll be trouble. You tell yourself you'll just do it for one more trip, then it's one more trip after that, and one more trip after that....The money gets you."

Just how many drug couriers are in transit on any given day or night is anybody's guess. Smuggling contraband into the U.S. is said to be the largest business on earth, and the steady flood of drugs to the streets testifies that the ant army is overwhelmingly successful on its mission. And with the diminished federal interest in border interdiction of late, more drugs than ever are moving on our streets and highways.[7]

As part of your motivation to succeed on *your* mission to intercept contraband, imagine a load of drugs headed toward this country.

Without detection:

- The load gets past DEA, U.S. Customs, U.S. Border Patrol, and enters the U.S.;
- It continues to evade detection and gets four to five states away from you;
- It gets past officers in states around you and enters your state;
- It gets past your state troopers and into your county or town;
- It gets past other officers in your community and into your neighborhood and your children's school. Your kids' friends and aquaintances are touched by it;
- **It gets into your home.**

"I *personalize* Criminal Patrol as protecting *my* family," says the trainer who constructed this hypothesis.[8] "A mule who tries to go right by me may be carrying drugs that somewhere down the line are headed toward my house, and I'm going to do my damnedest to stop him."

Your hunt for transporters protects your *blue* family, too. Most of the crime and violence you and your fellow officers must deal with today is drug-driven; its perpetrators are intoxicated by drugs (in some cities, 70% of males arrested for felonies test positive for illegal drug use), desperate for drugs, greedy for drug profits, fearful of drug penalties. Drugs or drug use play a role in almost half of all murders and other violent crimes in the U.S.,[9] and in the chemical warfare of the streets, *cops* end up as some of the victims. "When I seize a load," says an Illinois trooper, "I think, If this had gotten through, somehow, somewhere it might have resulted in an officer getting hurt or killed."

"Whether it's a roach in the ashtray or a truckload, it's all part of the problem," says a New Jersey trainer. And as a 5%er on Criminal Patrol, *you* are a vital part of the solution.

LOOKING FOR MR. WRONG

Q. What does a drug courier look like?
A. Just like anyone else.

That's what a course plan for drug interdiction prepared by the Wisconsin State Patrol says, trying to persuade officers to stretch beyond a style of "mule hunting" that has been popular since the cross-country transporting of drugs and illicit money in vehicles was first acknowledged as a major law enforcement challenge back in the early 1980s.

Back then, officers assigned to intercept contraband were trained through DEA's Operation Pipeline interdiction program to recognize a "profile" of the drivers and vehicles considered most likely to be involved in drug shipments. These characteristics were derived largely from the subjective impressions and arrest experiences of DEA agents, especially those who'd worked drug interdiction at airports. The identified characteristics were then reinforced and modified as they bore fruit in the field. Although officers on patrol generally offered the excuse of a traffic violation for stopping a profile driver or vehicle, in fact many motorists (especially Colombians, Cubans, Mexicans, Puerto Ricans, Haitians, Jamaicans, and African-Americans) were pulled over primarily—sometimes even solely— because they exhibited some or all of the profile earmarks.

Today, officers rarely utter the "P word" except among themselves. For good reason, profiling has sparked controversy, lawsuits, and condemnation and is now officially prohibited by most agencies. Yet in practice the old "traditional profile pattern" continues frequently to be used. Monitoring traffic, its adherents watch for:

- male Hispanics, blacks, or "any swarthy, dark-haired outlander," sometimes accompanied by a white female or white male...
- roughly twenty to forty-five years old...
- possibly displaying an overindulgence in gold jewelry or other flamboyant style of dress...
- often "unshaven and unkempt in appearance"...
- traveling on an Interstate highway...
- driving a rental car with a Florida license plate, or a heavy, roomy "road car," often an older, two-door General Motors model, possibly with heavily tinted windows but definitely with a commodious trunk, big natural "dead-space" cavities inside doors and quarter panels, powerful engine, and large-capacity gas tank...
- hauling dope north or east and cash south and west...
- frequently traveling at night, when cops are scarcer in many jurisdictions (virtually nonexistent in some), when darkness can camouflage personal features, and when vehicle searches are harder to conduct thoroughly and safely.

There's no doubt that targeting vehicles and occupants who match

Who's Carrying Drugs?

Using traditional profile characteristics, which of these would you suspect is carrying drugs?

(Answer: ALL these were arrested with drug loads. Avoid prejudgments. Read on!)

46

the profile has yielded countless caches of hidden drugs and cash and has resulted in numerous spectacular arrests. Traditional profile characteristics still *do* correlate closely with a sizable portion of drug couriers. In fact, a Rutgers University study found that 80% of arrests on an Eastern turnpike involved "late-model cars with out-of-state plates driven by black males," even though less than 5% of the traffic on that highway fit that description.[1] Confidential teletypes from the El Paso Intelligence Center (EPIC), the restricted federal clearinghouse for drug-interdiction data, confirm that, nationwide, blacks and Hispanics are still heavily represented among the arrested runners of most major drugs; a lot of couriers still drive big GM boats, some twenty years old or more; drugs are still moved via long road trips (over half the cocaine in L.A. is believed to go by vehicle to New York); "dirty" truckers, especially, still like to drive at night when many weigh stations are closed, and the Interstates are still our great national sewer system.

But—the profile as a reliable absolute has been discredited. The full picture of who's out there with contraband today has grown much more complex than the profile suggests...if, indeed, it ever was quite that simple. "It's a game," explains one officer. "The dopers have a strategy and we have a strategy. When ours gets better than theirs, they change."

"Profiling" Today

To counter successful profiling, traffickers who hire mules have become shrewder and more eclectic. For "talent," they now recruit:

- *All* races, *all* ethnic groups, and *all* nationalities; the drug trade today offers equal opportunity employment. (One Midwestern Criminal Patrol team claims that about 80% of the drug couriers it finds now, including independent operators, are white);

- Clean-cut, all-American college students, attorneys, businessmen, even shady cops who "badge" their way out of any trouble;

- People who would never move a package normally but who've been laid off and need money;

- Grandma and grandpa who've been suckered into driving drug-loaded Winnebagos on "free trips" or hired outright as mules to supplement Social Security (the elderly, who tend to be virtually "invisible" to officers when they travel, are said to be among the fastest-growing segments of transporters, the oldest on record believed to be an eighty-seven-year-old man caught with five kilos of coke);

- The disabled (including deaf people, who traffickers think will be treated leniently by police and whose difficulty in communicating is considered insurance against incriminating slips of the tongue);

- Juveniles ("When we had a lot of dope, the man gave us guns. I carried a .38," says a seventeen-year-old from Milwaukee who, along with others as young as thirteen, regularly delivered drugs in cars with hidden compartments);

- Women with children who rent themselves and their kids out to accompany men they don't know so a dope run will look like a "family outing" and be ignored by officers who are locked into traditional profiling. (Often there's a ten- to fifteen-year age difference between the male and the female, and the kids tend to be young, under six years. Women, in fact, have become like gold on contraband transports because many officers are inclined to be less suspicious of females, despite the fact, as one deputy says, "Women are just as dirty as men...and just as mean." Jamaican Posses often use white female drivers, but almost always there will also be a Jamaican in the car "because they don't trust Anglos completely."[2] Boasts a drug trafficker: "I like to put a nice-lookin' lady wit' a couple kids in a decent car and have her dress nice. When a cop pull the bitch over, he want her phone number. He not gonna go no fu'ther, he not gonna look in the car, 'cause his mind on somethin' else. Next thing you know, she gone, without even a ticket.").

Routes. Mules and drug entrepreneurs driving cross-country often avoid the more knowledgeably patrolled Interstates altogether these days. Or they may jump off the Interstate onto secondary roads to detour past sections where busts have recently occurred. In municipal areas where local drug-running or personal use is concerned, virtually any street is potentially part of a transport route. Dope and money travel in all directions now, depending on where the contraband enters the country and is staged, where delivery points are, where currency is collected and laundered, and so on. "There's no rhyme or reason any more to travel patterns," says a California investigator.

Transport vehicles. Intercity and intracity couriers drive every conceivable carrier, from Volkswagen Bugs to forty-foot-long refrigerated semitrailers to James Bond specials (a Jamaican Posse drug car—a Mercedes—seized in New York City was equipped with a tear-gas

ejector, siren, bulletproof glass, armor plating, high-speed racing tires, and a police-conversion, high-performance engine). Some transporters use limousines with deeply tinted windows. Some hire wreckers to carry dope or to tow cars or trucks loaded with it, figuring cops are around tow trucks so much they won't notice one—even if it incongruously bears out-of-state tags. In Ohio, cartons of drugs and TEC-9 submachine guns were smuggled in a horse trailer. Sheriff's deputies in Texas found a cement hopper hauling 3,720 pounds of marijuana in its inside chambers. In Maryland, a man with a suspended New York driver's license was nabbed with multiple kilos of cocaine hidden in a tractor. In Georgia, a courier hired a taxi cab to drive him on an Interstate from one city to another

Wrecker stopped en route from Houston to Chicago. For this kind of vehicle to travel out-of-state is suspicious. Drugs were discovered under the hood and in the spare tire.

to deliver a suitcase filled with nearly $1,000,000 in cash, and in some urban areas cab drivers not only transport drugs but deal directly from their vehicles. One of the largest cocaine shipments ever intercepted in the Chicago area—500 kilos—was confiscated from a van with "Happiness Flowers" painted on the side, masquerading as a florist's truck. Traffickers now favor small cars as often as big ones, willing to sacrifice hiding space to blend better with traffic. All cars, after all, have at least some natural cavities; all a shipper has to do is devise a way to get drugs into them and back out again, or they just put them in a suitcase, box, or bag in the passenger compartment or trunk, figuring they won't get stopped and searched. Smaller quantities of drugs are easier to hide, and if the courier is busted, less is lost. (Fewer drugs per load, of course, means that more vehicles are needed, increasing the odds that the cars and trucks you stop have some contraband connection. But beware: *A person with a small load is not necessarily any less dangerous.* Inner-city drug runners working for street gangs now often use bicycles for local deliveries. In Michigan, an officer stopping a cyclist to check for drugs at 1 o'clock in the morning was fatally wounded when the suspect whipped a gun from his pants and started shooting.)

Time of travel. "Dope is in transit *all* the time," a Midwestern trooper flatly declares. Rather than nighttime being the most productive, some jurisdictions report the greatest success during daylight hours, especially midmorning and early afternoon.

Monday	Tuesday	Wednesday	Thursday	Friday	Saturday	Sunday
2%	21%	14%	5%	9%	47%	2%

Transporting heroin, for example, is an every-day-of-the-week enterprise on I-95, from Florida to Maine. Percentages show seizures by days of the week, with Saturday the busiest arrest day, according to the DEA. What is the level of drug activity on primary and secondary routes in your patrol area?

In short, the mix of people and vehicles carrying contraband today, whether in resale or personal-use quantities, is a true cross section of what you see on the streets and highways. "It would be nice if only Eskimos smuggled drugs on dog sleds," says a captain in Georgia. "But unfortunately, everybody is in the business."

© Calibre Press, Inc.

Consequently, basing decisions about who warrants your investigative attention only on profile characteristics creates three serious problems:

1. You will miss a lot of good busts because you are too narrowly defining who could be a suspect;

2. Sooner or later—probably sooner—you will run afoul of courts that reject that style of selective enforcement as discriminatory.

3. Most important, you'll make yourself vulnerable to violence from *non*profile-type transporters because you'll tend to dismiss them as potential threats.

That's not to say that many drivers and vehicles carrying contraband don't often share certain "diagnostic" characteristics. Many do, and these suspicious distinctions should be in your mind as you survey traffic and make stops, and they should tickle your curiosity to investigate further. In that sense, the search begins when you see the vehicle.

However, as you'll see in later chapters, the key indicators that enable you to truly "profile" someone as a likely contraband courier are generally more subtle than the broad brush strokes of the traditional pattern. And the most pivotal of these normally can't be discovered until after you make the stop and establish contact with the vehicle and its occupant(s). In other words, most of your contacts with couriers will—and should—start out as "routine" traffic stops, with no immediate clues that they're anything more. Discovering that there is more is where your investigative skills come into play. **Stay open-minded. Don't fall into the trap of prejudging.**

- Don't initiate stops only in circumstances where suspicious indicators are immediately visible;
- Don't fail to explore who and what you've stopped even though you may not detect any potential contraband indicators before you confer with the driver;
- *Never* assume that because a vehicle or driver does not readily fit a suspicious "profile" that it's a "clean" situation and that you're safe to let your guard down.

Beating the Profile

The downfall of many contraband haulers has been that they stand out...they look to cops like what they are. A how-to book about being a successful smuggler offers pointers to contraband couriers on avoiding the "profile" look when traveling roads paved with bad intentions:

- The most important thing you can prepare in this business is your mind. You are the aggressor. You pick the time and the place. The opposition is too small to be everywhere all the time....

- Learn the art of toning down [your] lifestyle. One problem the average smuggler has is that he lives his lifestyle: long hair, gold jewelry, fast cars, lots of girls. This creates problems....

- Dress is very important. Always wear good clothes, a dark suit or sport coat, and quality wingtip shoes. Buy a Rolex watch or a counterfeit Rolex watch. Be a business executive, not a devious planner. You are in the game for money, just like Exxon....

- Keep your hair short and your appearance neat and clean. One of the worst things you can do is look sloppy. Many smugglers are originally targeted by law officers because of appearance and flamboyant attire....

- Rent or lease a simple standard vehicle. Never use a good expensive car for work. They tend to stand out, and in your business you must blend in....

- Have business cards printed showing that you are a lawyer. You'll whistle [by]....

- There is an expression that holds true for the drug business: "big balls, big bucks." Most dopers are not real fearful people. Most get caught because of their own belief that they are invincible. Prisons are overflowing with dopers with egos too big for their own good....[3]

Many drug traffickers have seen the wisdom of advice like this, making them harder to spot. But with the right Criminal Patrol tactics, you can still unmask them.

Curiosity Ticklers

Even though you're not profiling in the traditional sense, you want habitually to perform a "visual pat-down" of the exterior and what you can see of the drivers and passengers in the vehicles around you as you watch traffic. Although couriers today blend in better than ever, some will rouse your suspicion on sight, if you understand what to look for.

When you first notice any vehicle and then throughout your contact, you want to note things that *don't quite fit* with what you know to be normal appearances and behavior. *Train yourself to regard out-of-the-ordinary as potentially criminal.* When such aberrations blip onto your mental radar screen, ask yourself: "What's wrong with this picture?"—and then set about getting answers.

Some things you see at the pre-stop stage may prove significant in the context of Criminal Patrol, even though in and of themselves they are noncriminal in nature and do not legally justify your conducting a stop. What makes them tickle your curiosity is your unique experience and perspective as a Criminal Patrol officer. Your 5%er mind can draw inferences from these otherwise benign observations, because you can relate them to common drug courier behavior and practices.

Following are visual cues that frequently correlate to contraband hauling. Most are relevant to municipal streets and freeways as well as rural highways. "Cops 'see' these kinds of things every day," says an Ohio officer, "but they don't 'observe' them because their minds are on other matters or because they don't appreciate their potential significance." Individually, these potential indicators may not mean much; *clusters* of them are more likely to be significant. But when you see any of them, either satisfy yourself that they have a legitimate explanation as you progress with your contact or use them as a first step toward building suspicion on the Criminal Patrol Pyramid. Do not, however, concentrate solely on vehicles that display these characteristics. Not all drivers with contraband will exhibit them.

Sometimes you may think the driver's alone, but a buddy is really sacked out in the back seat, out of sight. If you see someone sitting up in the back seat, he or she may have just awakened, and that is worth noting.

Team-Driving Cues. A sleeping passenger or the visibility of pillows and bedding may suggest a team that's splitting the driving to keep moving on long runs. Mules often drive straight through to cut delivery time and expenses and also because they're afraid to leave the car unattended. Although many hauling cross-country still drive alone, a two-person team is used at least half the time, according to experienced interdiction officers. Rarely on long transports do you find more than three occupants in the vehicle, unless some are children.

Rental Vehicles. These offer traffickers reliability and a certain "distancing" from contraband. Generally late models and well-maintained, rentals are unlikely to break down and thereby cause delays or lead to unwanted contacts with officers who might pull over to help or with mechanics who might stumble onto hidden stashes while making repairs. A car, van, or truck that's rented by one party with cash or a phony credit card, then left at a designated spot where someone else picks it up and drives it on a delivery is often harder for you to trace back to the group that's responsible for the shipment than a privately registered vehicle. And if you discover drugs in a rental vehicle, the distributor doesn't also then lose a personal auto through seizure and forfeiture. Plus the driver can say he just rented the car—he didn't know anything illegal was in it.

Rental cars are getting harder for you to spot before you make a stop; rental firms in many parts of the country are getting rid of visible identifiers because these have made it too easy for street criminals to target tourists and business travelers. But some companies and some states at this writing still do mark rental cars in distinctive ways. Of course, most rental *trucks* are readily identifiable because they generally are painted with blatant advertising.

If a rental car comes with identification and advertising stickers on trunk lids, bumpers, and side windows, couriers may peel these off in hopes of being less conspicuous to cops who key on rentals as a part of traditional profiling. Usually, though, dirt and road dust will cling to the adhesive residue, so you can see that something has been removed. The average legitimate renter has no reason to remove these stickers, so that's a what's-wrong-with-this-picture indicator.

Coded license plates may help you identify rentals from some states. Examples:

- Illinois—names of major rental agencies are abbreviated at the beginning of the plate number: HRZ (Hertz)....NCR (National Car Rental)....BCR (Budget)...AVR (Avis), and so on;
- Virginia—first alpha character is R, then two other letters plus three numbers.

Some old reliables are gone or going. Florida rentals, for example, all used to start with Y or Z or bear the word RENTAL; New York used to start with Z and the District of Columbia with R, and Maryland started with D over R, then had five numbers. All these are now being phased out.

In an effort to avoid getting cars with revealing tags in states that still have them, sophisticated criminals may surreptitiously inspect a rental car lot before going to the counter, then ask for any out-of-state car they've seen there that they think does *not* have a coded plate. Or they may simply switch plates before the trip begins. In some places, authentic-looking replicas of private-registration tags from major states—even diplomatic corps plates—can be bought over-the-counter in souvenir shops.

Temporary Registration. Despite the appeals of rentals, Criminal Patrol specialists estimate that from 50% to 80% of contraband haulers currently use privately owned vehicles. For one thing, it's usually more convenient to build secret compartments in these. Various trafficking groups, including street gangs, favor *newly* registered cars because they're usually harder to trace through NCIC. Sometimes a car is bought new under a phony name just before a run, then once the contraband is delivered and extracted the vehicle is given to the mule as payment. On I-95 along the East Coast, nearly 40% of all the crack seizures made during one six-month period involved vehicles with temporary registrations. Design and placement of temporary registration placards or stickers vary, but in most states they are required to display the vehicle's VIN number. Later when you approach the car, check that all seventeen digits of the VIN appear on the permit and that it matches the vehicle's other visible VIN numbers. Blank temporary stickers are commonly stolen and fenced within the criminal community and may be filled out incorrectly before they're applied to the vehicle. Also be sure the sticker is current; these usually are good for only ten to twenty days, and often on a drug vehicle the registration will be expired. If you can see an expired date from your patrol car, that, of course, is legal grounds for a stop.

Would a temporary registration placard impress you as a potential contraband cue?

"Protective Coloration." Because they know officers tend to notice out-of-state cars when they're watching traffic (especially those from notorious drug-source areas like Florida, Texas, California, Arizona, New Mexico, Kentucky, and New York), some transporters carry separate license plates for each state they enter, and switch near the state line. If you see a driver crouched down at the front or rear of his vehicle at a highway rest area or beside the road, don't automatically assume he's just checking his oil or changing a tire. Look closely. *Is he really changing plates?* Sometimes shiny bolts will give away that the plate has been removed, causing the bolts to be handled or wiped clean.

Two-Plate States

A missing front license plate may be more than just a registration violation. This sometimes is a clue that plates have been carelessly switched by a contraband courier. As you visually pat down the vehicle, check plates front and rear. These jurisdictions require two plates:[4]

Alaska	Iowa	New Hampshire	Texas
California	Maine	New Jersey	Utah
Colorado	Maryland	New York	Vermont
Connecticut	Minnesota	North Dakota	Virginia
District of Columbia	Missouri	Ohio	Washington
Hawaii	Montana	Oregon	Wisconsin
Idaho	Nebraska	Rhode Island	Wyoming
Illinois	Nevada	South Dakota	

You may pick up on switched plates by first noticing something else about the car that doesn't fit with your locale. If tinted windows are illegal in your state, an "in-state" car that has them might really be from a Southern or Southwestern state, bearing bogus plates as it passes through. Also an *old* car with shiny *new* plates is incongruous in most jurisdictions. Such a vehicle stopped in Texas for a possible registration violation yielded more than 100 pounds of marijuana in its trunk.

Watch also for evidence that someone has tried to obliterate obvious links to a common drug-source area. Couriers from Florida may pop off dealer logos that say Miami, or Dade, or Broward counties, leaving the drilled holes in the body visible. Or they may install a license plate holder that obscures the county name at the bottom of the tag, or cover it over with a bumper sticker.

Drug couriers have been caught on-camera changing license plates just short of the state line. A definite warning sign for the observant officer.

(left)
To conceal the stamped plate designation DADE (Dade County, FL), the courier driving this vehicle stuck a piece of bumper sticker over the letters.

(right)
Now DADE is visible as curious deputy pulls away the camouflage. His observation was rewarded when he found drugs hidden inside the vehicle.

Don't be fooled into disregarding vehicles with "good guy" decals, bumper stickers, or other "reassuring" messages. Some couriers write "Just Married" on their cars; religious and antidrug slogans are often displayed, and police decals, like PBA or FOP stickers, are available at black-market prices in the drug community in hopes they'll lull you into fast—and false—assumptions. *Trust no one;* accept nothing at face value. One municipal officer in Mississippi says that over half the dope cars he catches bear some kind of police association sticker. Some California street gangs have transported cocaine in vans and buses with church names painted on them; the vehicles are loaded with kids from housing projects, and the drivers are black females who, if stopped, say they're headed for church camp. One trucker hauling marijuana up from Mexico in a semitrailer made more than twenty trips to multiple delivery sites without being checked out even at the border, where federal agents have wide legal latitude to conduct inspections. He didn't even try to disguise his load—just stacked bags of pot in the unlocked trailer, with no other freight. He painted a "Just Say No!" slogan on the back door and figured that would deflect suspicion. It did—until finally a Border Patrol agent with a K-9 decided not to believe everything he saw.

As another means of protective coloration, male couriers sometimes try to camouflage themselves by wearing neckties on cross-country runs. They intend to look like business travelers, forgetting that on long car trips most legitimate businessmen won't put on a tie until they get to their destination.

Stay alert even when approaching what looks like a "safe" motorist assist. Some couriers and gang members carry guns attached to the battery or hidden elsewhere among engine components. They may be stopped with the hood up, appearing innocently to be fixing things. But they may actually be arming themselves, fixing to fix you.

Lifestyle Statements. On the flip side of protective coloration, vehicles that sport roach clips with feathers hanging from the rearview mirror or decals of marijuana leaves or names of certain rock groups associated with heavy drug use are virtually screaming for your attention. Although it's by no means legal justification for a stop in and of

(left)
Load after load of marijuana was transported inside this semitrailer, and the driver didn't even bother disguising it with legitimate freight. He figured the antidrug signage in plain view would work and it did!

(upper right)
"Good guy" symbols may serve as protective coloration to distract you. Among criminals, police decals are sold for premium prices.

(above left/above)
Grateful Dead stickers can be prime drug cues.

(left)
Religious stickers and artifacts in plain view may be calculated to lull you.

55

itself, experienced Criminal Patrol officers insist that a driver whose vehicle flaunts a decal from the Grateful Dead is virtually "100% guaranteed" to have at least personal-use quantity of an illegal substance on his person or in his car. One seventeen-officer Criminal Patrol unit in Maryland reports that all the LSD it has seized has come from followers of this rock group.[5] Nationally, roughly 500 Dead followers are serving federal terms for LSD violations, with up to 2,000 more in state prisons. Fans of any rock group are probably more likely than symphony aficionados, say, to be drug users. If a rock concert is scheduled in your area, a good place for you to be making Criminal Patrol stops would be along thoroughfares leading to and from the event.

What first sparked a highway patrolman's curiosity about a car he saw pulling out of a 7-Eleven parking lot in South Dakota was a pair of handcuffs dangling from the rearview mirror, a walk-on-the-wild-side symbol you don't see in the average automobile. He stopped the vehicle and issued a warning for obstructed vision. During an eventual search of the trunk he found a pistol, large amounts of money, a bank bag full of pennies, a crowbar, a tire iron, and five screwdrivers. From the floor of the passenger compartment, he recovered a map with circles and Xs over several towns, one of which had recently been the site of a burglary. End results: burglary convictions for both occupants.

Glitzy Trucks. Although commercial rigs of all kinds have been caught with dope, some experienced officers regard fancy semitrailers with expensive, garish accessories to be especially suspect. These "tricked out" rigs (especially Peterbilt models, which offer the most customizing opportunities in the industry) twinkle with lights all over them (even blue lights, which are illegal in some states), glint with lots of stainless steel, feature costly chrome lug nuts, may have nicknames painted on, display "designer" mud flaps, and so on. Among some courier groups, flash is part of the competitive macho image, and some believe that cops are less likely to stop a truck that looks ultra clean and expensive. Ordinary truckers humping to make ends meet rarely have the surplus cash—or taste—for luxuries.

Also be alert for units that have side doors on the trailer. These are often favored by drug couriers because they allow easier unloading of contraband that is placed near the front of the trailer and camouflaged by legitimate cargo behind.

Improper Signage. Watch for truck drivers who get plain sloppy in conforming to U.S. Department of Transportation regulations, including rules for the signage trucks must display. Officers spotting such violations, which are legal grounds for making a stop, have produced a number of significant drug busts, especially where propane tankers from Mexico are involved. One sharp-eyed Texas officer saw a sparkling new white propane tanker with the words PROPANO painted in big red letters on its side. He knew that DOT regulations require that contents be identified in English, not Spanish, in this country. Also he noticed there were no hazardous-materials placards on the truck—another DOT violation. He pulled the truck over...and during the stop discovered that the tanker was loaded to the brim with more than a ton of marijuana.

Discovering one indicator often leads to more. This tanker, originally stopped for improper signage, was freshly painted. When the belly-side was tapped, it produced a dull thud, not a resonant ring. On the scales, the tanker weighed significantly more than it should with a proper propane load. Inside was 6,240 lbs. of marijuana.

Also visually check for annual fuel-stamp decals on big rigs, which you should see on the left side of the cab. Each state has its own distinctive style and color. Absence of a fuel stamp is cause for a stop.

Air Shocks. On passenger cars, can you see a valve at the rear (usually near the license plate) and lines running from it underneath, indicating that the vehicle is fitted with air shock absorbers? Or, if the shocks are new enough and you're back far enough, can you see shiny nuts on the mounting brackets underneath, indicating their fresh installation? Usually people add heavy-duty air shocks to level out their vehicle when they pull a heavy load. So it's normal to also have a trailer hitch on the rear bumper. If you see air shocks but no hitch, that's different from what's normal; they may be there to level out a heavy load of contraband concealed within the vehicle. A profitable shipment of marijuana can weigh 100 to 500 pounds and without air shocks would cause a car without factory load-levelers to ride abnormally low or tilt to the side—which, of course, can be other visual cues.

(lower left)
Spotting an air-filler valve may be your first cue that a car is outfitted with heavy-duty air shock absorbers. Often valves are mounted low on the rear frame or even penetrating the license plate.

Abnormal Windows. Tinted windows make you wonder what they're hiding, of course. But also watch for windows being down, either on hot summer days when most cars have them up with the air conditioning on or in winter when they should be up for warmth. They may be down to keep drug odors from building up inside, especially if marijuana is being hauled or smoked. One Northern officer stopped a car for driving 3 mph over the limit in subzero weather with all four windows down. The family inside

Hose lines that dangle underneath the bumper indicate a fast "home-brew" installation. Air shocks without a trailer hitch are especially suspicious.

was trying to keep warm with a kerosene heater. The windows were open to keep the fumes from overcoming them. Their car heater couldn't work because cocaine was stuffed in the air vents; marijuana was packed wall-to-wall under the hood.

Misaligned trim: a curiosity tickler that led to the discovery of 100 kilos of cocaine in a false bed.

Modification Flaws. More and more traffickers these days disassemble parts of a vehicle to create or install hiding places for contraband—but most aren't very good at it yet; they aren't always able to get things fitted together again quite right. Example: When gas tanks are removed and altered to conceal drugs, the tailpipe assembly often ends up hanging lower than normal, not up close to the undercarriage. In one case after false compartments were built into the bed of a pickup truck, the horizontal paint stripes along the side no longer lined up like they should with those across the door. In New Jersey, an alert trooper noticed that the molding on the side of a Ranchero seemed too high to protect it from the doors of other vehicles opening against it. That led to the discovery that the molding actually had been moved to cover up the seams of a special panel that had been cut into the body. Inside this hiding place the trooper found $1,500,000 cash, in denominations of $20 or less.

With pickup trucks , compare the bed level to the rear tires. The bottom of a legitimate pickup bed should be about even with the tops of the tires or a couple of inches higher, as you look into the wheel wells. If the bed extends below that, it may be overloaded with weight—or extra inches have been created by a compartment built underneath it.

Courier pickup with an obvious plain view modification. Note the bottom of the bed extends below the top of the tire.

Abnormal Tires. To reduce the risk of flats during long, tortuous driving, a full set of new tires may be bought just before a run to make the car "road worthy." Couriers often are lazy and may not take time to wipe the color coating off white sidewalls, making their newness easy to spot. New tires should especially pique your curiosity when you see them on an older car; they may be worth more than the jalopy itself.

Also be alert for spare tires in odd places, like strapped to the roof or riding in the back seat. They may have been moved out of the trunk to make more room for contraband. Or they may be extra spares, as more insurance against breakdown delays. With trucks, if you see more than two spare tires on racks under the trailer, that's an unusually high number. Maybe they're packed with dope.

To compensate for a heavy load elsewhere in the vehicle and to try to keep the car level, radial tires may be pumped up and the suspension may seem stiff. Going over bumps, the bounce won't seem right.

Multiple Deodorants. Ornamental deodorizers hanging from the rearview mirror, particularly in multiples, may be an effort to mask the smell of drugs on board. In the minds of many interdiction experts, clusters of fresheners are "almost a 100% indicator." Air fresheners hanging in a rental car are particularly suspect. Other deodorizing agents may be visible or sniffable to you later when you're able to approach the car close up.

Dirt. Are the taillights clean, but the rest of the car is dirty? Maybe they got clean by being removed, handled, and wiped off during the hiding of contraband. If tires are clean but the rest of the car is dirty, maybe they're fresh ones, bought and installed already loaded with drugs. A clean license plate on a dirty car may have been installed after a run began, or it may have been wiped off in the process of stashing contraband behind the bumper. Likewise a rear license tag with insect splatter may signal a plate switch. So could a supposedly in-state vehicle that's noticeably dirtier overall than the

Multiple air fresheners, and vehicles that are dirtier than others you see, may be contraband cues.

rest you see on the road. It may have come through heavy weather somewhere else. Cross-country couriers often start their trips deliberately in bad weather, figuring fewer inspection points will be open then and fewer cops will bother to stop minor traffic violators. By the time they get where you are, the weather has changed but evidence of the earlier, distant storm remains. "I watch the Texas weather reports very carefully," says an officer in Iowa. "I figure when it's raining down there, there's going to be more dope coming through." Sometimes different layers of dirt—country clay, road salt, urban grime—give away that a "local" car has been in different locales.

Unnatural Driving. Be alert for signs of self-conscious or nervous driving behavior, especially once the driver and any passenger(s) know you're near and possibly watching them. If you're behind the vehicle, the driver may anxiously and repeatedly look in the rearview mirror, even reposition it to see you better; the passenger may turn around and look to confirm that you're there (a small act, incidentally, that is regarded by some interdiction experts as "a 99% sign of some kind of criminal activity"). The driver may be so intent on watching you that he drifts between lanes or drives in the emergency lane, then overcorrects when he realizes it. He may sit up unusually stiff, grip the steering wheel tightly with both hands, and become meticulous in following traffic laws. Upon seeing you, he may slow down or change to a slower-speed lane, even though traffic does not warrant it. Some will stroke their hair or reposition their right arm to the top of the seat—nervous mannerisms.

If you are beside the vehicle at a light or moving in traffic, say, the occupants may avoid looking at you, staring resolutely straight ahead like statues, avoiding conversation among themselves, and averting all eye contact. The passenger may even begin staring out of his or her side window, directly away from you. One officer calls this behavior the "No-Look Rule," and he tests for it by deliberately pulling alongside without turning on his overheads to see if the occupant(s) will glance his way, as people normally do. He may tap his horn or roll

No-Look Showdown

What can an indicator as simple as the No-Look Rule sometimes lead to? Ask James Stevens and Ray Stachnik, veteran officers with the San Diego Police Department.

Patrolling a city street one hot August night, they noticed a blue Ford Ranger with a white camper shell approaching in the opposing lane of traffic. As the Ford went by, Stevens and Stachnik glanced at the driver—who immediately broke eye contact with them and deliberately stared straight ahead.

Experienced with hard-core criminals, the officers recognized the No-Look cue—plus they noticed that the driver was "buffed," exceptionally muscled as if from years of lifting weights in prison.

The truck offered the necessary PC for a stop: a broken taillight. But when the officers whipped in behind it and turned on their overheads, the driver accelerated. Through the rear window of the cab, Stevens, driving, could see the suspect driver move his right arm down to his lap, then hand something to his male passenger. Stachnik thought it could be a gun. Within seconds, he knew it was.

The passenger leaned out of the cab window and began spraying the squad car with rounds from a MAC-11 machine pistol. As bullets peppered their vehicle, the officers slumped down in their seats to make themselves smaller targets.

Stevens swerved from side to side to hamper the gunman's accuracy. He maintained the pursuit as Stachnik grabbed their dash-mounted 12-ga. and prepared for urban warfare.

Over the next ten minutes, some forty rounds were exchanged, Stachnik firing the 870, Stevens his 9mm, and the two offenders passing their MAC back and forth between them. "There's no doubt they were trying to kill us," Stachnik later told investigators. "I could literally see rounds passing by us, illuminated by the headlights. I could see bullets to the right of our vehicle, close to where I was. The driver was fishtailing just to give the passenger clearer shots at us."

The pursuit ended in a thunderous crash as the suspects tried to negotiate a right turn. Their vehicle center-punched a parked car and knocked it several feet in the air.

The gunfight continued. "I knew we were dead if we didn't return fire," Stevens said. The officers shot their guns empty, reloaded, and came back up fighting, their muzzle flashes lighting up the scene.

When incoming rounds finally stopped, the officers ceased fire. The passenger suspect was sprawled face-down on the pavement. The driver was hanging head down out of his door opening, his foot caught in the steering wheel.

Both appeared dead. But when a helicopter, a K-9 unit, and other backup arrived, approaching officers discovered that the two were just faking death.

Aware now that a twitch would result in immediate protective gunfire, the suspects submitted to handcuffing without resistance. Both had spent most of their adult lives in prison and were currently wanted for parole violations. The driver was on San Diego's Ten Most Wanted list.

Although sixty rounds had been fired, a hand wound to the suspect driver was the most serious injury inflicted. Ironically, what saved the ex-cons was the low penetration power of the police ammunition. None of the thirty-five rounds fired by Stevens and Stachnik was capable of penetrating the thin side panels of the truck bed or the thin metal of the cab.

The suspects were prosecuted federally under the Armed Career Criminal Act. Each was sentenced to thirty-five years to life.

Officers Stevens and Stachnik received the Medal of Valor, their department's highest award for bravery.[6]

down the window and shout, "Hey! Hey! Over here!" trying to attract the driver's attention. If you try this and then go on around the car, watch in your mirror. A driver who's hiding something will often pull off or turn at the next opportunity. You can then come back to pick up on him again. Another option is to drop your speed as you're alongside the No-Look car. He'll drop his, too, and you may be able to stop him for going under the limit.

The more determined an occupant is not to look, the more determined you should be to look further. A No-Look almost always leads to something—a suspended license or more. An officer in South Dakota used the No-Look Rule to catch a motel robber. When the robbery was broadcast, the officer, who was several miles away from the site, parked his unit facing against traffic and watched cars going by from the direction of the motel. The first eight or ten drivers acknowledged his presence by looking over at him. Then a man drove by who conspicuously ignored him. The officer calculated that if the robber had driven in his direction from the motel at the speed limit, he would have been passing by at about that same time. Alerted, other officers down the road stopped the driver and, after discovering an eight-inch knife with brass-knuckled handle and a sawed-off shotgun in the vehicle, arrested him.

Erratic driving that you may first think is caused by intoxication may really reflect fatigue and stress. A motorist who was stopped one afternoon in New Jersey because he kept swerving onto the shoulder was found to be falling asleep at the wheel even in broad daylight because he'd been driving nonstop since the previous day. Eventually the officer got his consent to search and discovered forty-one pounds of cocaine in a hidden compartment in the trunk. Some haulers can go forty-eight hours or more at a stretch, if they take stimulants to keep them up. Beard stubble, red eyes, or a generally disheveled look may tip you off to them. Another cue to long, nonstop driving can be headlights on after daybreak, because the suspect has forgotten to turn them off after driving all night.

Erratic driving may also result from drug intoxication. A Tennessee study found that eighty-eight out of 150 motorists stopped for reckless driving tested positive for cocaine, marijuana, or both—even though most were able to pass conventional sobriety tests. Drivers on cocaine typically took turns too fast or weaved through traffic, while those on marijuana drove inattentively and displayed poor reflexive actions.[7]

Watch for drivers who, even on high-speed roadways, make a point of driving 5 to 10 mph less than the speed limit when you're around. A Wyoming highway patrolman likes to consciously patrol at 10 mph under the limit and watch for cars that seem reluctant to pass him. He has found that drivers hauling contraband are more likely to violate even *minimum* speed limits than to pass him, not only making themselves obvious but giving him legal grounds for a stop. Using this technique one day, he noticed a Mercury Marquis from Arizona come up behind, hesitate a long while, then almost creep around him. The male driver appeared to be in his late thirties, with unkempt hair and a ragged cap. His age seemed unusual, the officer thought, because that model car generally appeals to older people. When a radio check of the license plate surfaced some apparent inconsistencies about the registration, he pulled the car over. Minutes later, he was putting handcuffs on the driver after discovering in a consent search of the trunk twelve cylindrical packages wrapped in duct tape—250 pounds of marijuana, headed for Rhode Island.

Upon seeing you, some drivers may pull to the side and wait until you pass, or they'll turn at the next intersection or pull off abruptly at the next possible exit from a throughway. An Indiana officer with a long record of successful contraband stops says that when he sees drivers acting in unusual ways, he always asks himself: "When most do not, why do a few?"

"Repeat" Vehicles. Often from knowing your beat well, you'll know which cars "belong" there and which are "strangers." If you watch closely, you may become aware of a strange vehicle that makes repeated trips back and forth through your area, possibly at fairly regular intervals. This could be a mule or dope dealer traversing your territory on a delivery route. In urban areas, watch cars that pull up in front of bars, schools, parks, convenience stores. If someone gets in, the car drives around the block, and then returns quickly to discharge the passenger, that can be an indicator of a drug transaction. More dope, guns, or other contraband may be in the car if you're able to stop it.

Fortunately for police, drug runners tend to be creatures of habit. If you stop a vehicle and fail to find dope one time, chances are the driver will be back through your beat again, offering you fresh opportunities. Be observant; develop your memory.

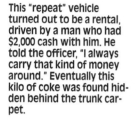

This "repeat" vehicle turned out to be a rental, driven by a man who had $2,000 cash with him. He told the officer, "I always carry that kind of money around." Eventually this kilo of coke was found hidden behind the trunk carpet.

Remember: The presence of these or other curiosity ticklers does *not* automatically mean you've spotted a car or truck involved with criminal activity, just as the absence of them does not guarantee that something illegal is not afoot. If present, you should regard these primarily as consciousness raisers at this point. Staying alert for what a Milwaukee patrolman calls "Stop-Me Cars" and using their suspicious qualities to motivate you to find out more can help keep you in Condition Yellow, the mind-set of heightened awareness necessary for safe and effective patrol.

Making a habit of scrutinizing traffic strengthens your powers of observation, just like working a muscle makes it stronger. "The first two months I tried Criminal Patrol," says a Southern deputy, "I made only one arrest. Then I started to look closer." In one seven-month period, he bagged forty-two felons and seized $171,200 in cash, 261 pounds of pot, seventy-eight pounds of coke, half an ounce of methamphetamine, twenty-two units of a controlled prescription drug, an ounce of hashish, more than a dozen handguns, a couple of boot knives, and twenty-one vehicles employed in criminal enterprises, including a $50,000 BMW. Total street value of these confiscations and forfeitures estimated by his department: over $7,000,000.

Different pre-stop cues may become important in the future, while current ones could become less significant with time. Develop sources who can keep you abreast of the latest trends. Besides intelligence officers in your own department, cultivate friends in DEA, ATF, state police narcotics interdiction teams, and other outside groups who tend to have a broader picture of what's happening than you can obtain just locally and who will trust you with sensitive data.

A Tripper's Hot Tips

Drug-oriented magazines regularly offer their readers "alerts" on how to avoid detection when transporting contraband. This excerpt from "High Times" is typical—and a good reminder to you of some things to watch for:

Transport is laughably easy—if you know what not to do.

Never transport anything, not even head stash, in a vehicle with Florida tags, particularly Florida rental tags. That's a sure way to attract attention. One luckless duo was arrested with beau coup reefer shortly after New Year's Day. The reason? Florida tags, with the typical tinted windows found in many Florida vehicles. After the vehicle was stopped, the trooper spotted two packs of untaxed cigarettes on the dash...probable cause.

If you're carrying, don't hurry. The vast majority of busts start with a speeding violation. Get yourself a radar detector.

Obey all traffic rules, right down to keeping your license plate clean and signaling when you change lanes. Make sure your lights work!

Avoid the Delaware Memorial Bridge in the southern terminus of the [New Jersey] Turnpike. Delaware is cool, but once you cross that bridge you're right where the cops concentrate the heat.

Make sure your car or truck's exterior has been washed. The Man looks for a vehicle that has obviously been on the road nonstop.

Be cool when you pass through toll booths. The toll-takers, I've noticed, have started eyeballing drivers for signs of intoxication.

If you're unlucky enough to be stopped, DON'T waive your freedom from unreasonable search and seizure. Most busts occur when the bustee signs a consent-to-search form. If you don't give verbal or written consent to search, your chances might be a little better.

I've traveled [with drugs] literally hundreds of times, with absolutely no problems. If you use your head, you can do the same. Use your head—or lose it.

Justification to Stop

Under the blitz of complaints, lawsuits, and other legal actions raining down on law enforcement these days, some officers have become so obsessed with what they *can't* or *shouldn't* do legally that they timidly back off even from situations in which they are fully justified in taking assertive action.

Obviously, it's essential to know your legal limitations. If you callously trample across the bounds of what's permissible, you'll destroy good cases, discredit your professional reputation, expose yourself and your department to lawsuits, and possibly provoke otherwise unnecessary, stringent restrictions on yourself and other officers in the future.

But to be successful on Criminal Patrol, your *primary* focus has to be on what you *can* do legally and getting that to work for you, sometimes even pushing to the edge of established legal limits, *when appropriate.* One officer likens it to a football game: "You don't always run the ball straight down the middle of the field. Sometimes to do the job you take an end run that brings you right to the boundary line. So long as you don't go over that line, the play's still legal."

Later we'll explore legal principles and precedents you can use to detain travelers for further investigation and to search their vehicles without a warrant, areas that are at the heart of Criminal Patrol but that are frequently misunderstood. Here we'll concentrate on what you need legally to stop a vehicle, another important area that sometimes is also clouded by myths and misinterpretations.

The questions posed below are ones that officers and agencies new to Criminal Patrol techniques often ask. Even if you're a seasoned veteran, they're worth your quick review to be sure your practices are up to date.

1. Can I use common, visible indicators of possible drug trafficking (like those described earlier in this chapter) as my legal grounds for stopping a vehicle? Maybe—but don't count on it. Much more often than not, the answer will be *no*. Under the Fourth Amendment, which governs search and seizure, you can legally stop a vehicle when you have either reasonable suspicion or probable cause.

Reasonable Suspicion requires that you be aware of specific, articulable facts, together with rational inferences drawn from those facts, that lead you plausibly to conclude, given the totality of the circumstances, that some crime has occurred or is occurring or is about to occur, involving the vehicle you wish to stop and/or its occupant(s). Mere curiosity or an "unparticularized" hunch ("I just had a bad feeling"), even though you may be acting completely in good faith, is not enough; your suspicion must be anchored to details you can explain. Where you have reasonable suspicion of wrongdoing, you can conduct a brief investigative stop to seek additional information to confirm or dispel your concern. Any facts suggesting criminal activities that you obtain after the stop commences cannot be used to justify the stop itself, although such facts can be used to justify continuing your detention from that point on. Moreover, reasonable suspicion to stop a vehicle does not automatically give you the right to search it for evidence or even necessarily to frisk its occupants.[8]

Probable Cause for stopping a vehicle involves a higher degree of likelihood that wrongdoing is afoot. PC requires articulable facts (evidence) that would induce a reasonably intelligent, cautious, prudent, and trained officer to believe than an individual in the vehicle is subject to arrest or citation for a crime or infraction. Stated another way, reasonable suspicion means a subject *could* be involved in criminal activity; probable cause means he or she most likely or probably *is* involved. Considerably *less* evidence is required for PC than for a conviction.[9] To some extent, probable cause, like reasonable suspicion, is in the eye of the beholder. An officer of greater training and experience may look at the same set of facts as a less-experienced officer, come to a different conclusion, and be able to justify it, because he can perceive and explain nuances that may appear wholly innocent to the lesser-trained eye.

Neither of these slippery concepts can be readily reduced to a neat set of rules or hard certainties, especially in a dynamic undertaking like Criminal Patrol, where circumstances—and your ability to explain them—can be everything. But this much is clear:

"Curiosity ticklers" often associated with contraband hauling, like those cited previously, normally *do not* by themselves add up to probable cause justifying your stopping a vehicle. (An exception, of course, would be those indicators that are actual law violations, like improper truck signage and driving below minimum speed limits.)

On occasion, however, *multiple cues* that are not themselves illegal may cumulatively be considered to constitute reasonable suspicion, giving you the right to stop, even in the absence of any specific violation.

One case where such common indicators were considered sufficient involved a DEA agent in an unmarked car, patrolling a coastal area of North Carolina that was under surveillance for drug trafficking. He noticed a pickup truck with a camper shell, its windows covered with a quilted material instead of curtains. The truck was riding low in the rear and appeared to be heavily loaded. As the agent observed it over a distance of about twenty miles, it seemed to be traveling together with a passenger car. Knowing that vehicles with such characteristics are often involved in contraband runs, the agent decided to make an investigative stop with the help of a marked unit. After initial evasive action and a brief chase, both vehicles got stopped. A short time later, the agent smelled marijuana when he pressed his nose against the window of the camper. Making entry with the officer, he discovered bales of pot inside. Given the agent's experience, the court found that his reading of potential contraband characteristics provided grounds for reasonable suspicion to justify the stop. In other cases, courts have ruled that seeing something like a broken left vent window can be legal grounds for an investigative stop, considering that 80% to 90% of stolen cars have broken side windows. Some courts have also accepted tips from reliable informants as reasonable cause to stop a vehicle, absent any other violation. These tips can even be anonymous, if the information has a "special ring to it" that suggests that the tipster has actual familiarity with the subject of the tip and the information seems sufficiently supported by independent police observation.[10]

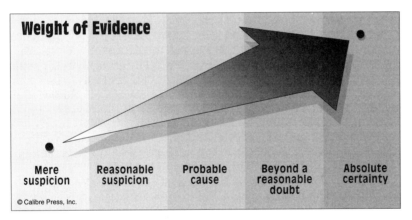

Weight of Evidence

| Mere suspicion | Reasonable suspicion | Probable cause | Beyond a reasonable doubt | Absolute certainty |

© Calibre Press, Inc.

More typical, however, are the outcomes of two drug busts involving vehicle stops by Border Patrol agents in Arizona.

In one, an agent watching heavy morning traffic on a state highway saw a Mexican male driving a typical "profile" road car, a large Pontiac with a big trunk; it appeared to be "loaded down in the rear." The agent followed it for four or five miles and noticed fresh hand prints on the dusty trunk. A radio check showed the car was registered to an old mining town in Arizona "known to have a high concentration of drug and alien smuggling." The agent concluded that he had a drug shipment in transit and stopped the car. Sure enough, he noticed two large bags in the back seat as he approached, and when the driver agreed to open them, they yielded 104 pounds of marijuana. Despite this evidence, a federal appellate court reversed the driver's conviction of possession with intent to distribute. If the agent's observations and conclusions were accepted as justification for making the stop, the court said, they "would also justify the [stopping] of every Mexican male driving to work in an old Pontiac on the state highway if the car was dusty, contained packages," and was registered in a drug-intense locale. More is needed than such observations alone "to create a founded suspicion of criminal conduct."[11]

In the second case, another Border Patrol agent was helping direct traffic around an accident site when one of the passing motorists caught his eye. The driver appeared to be young enough that he ought to be in school instead of out on the highway. He was driving an old car with a large trunk, and he seemed to be traveling in tandem with another car. As he passed the accident, he failed to meet the agent's gaze (an apparent example of the No-Look Rule) and sped off faster than other cars going by. Based on these potential indicators, the agent gave chase and pulled the kid over. As soon as the agent approached the car, he detected a strong odor of marijuana, and eventually found over 100 pounds of it stashed in the trunk. This time in reversing the initial conviction, the appellate court ruled that there was "nothing suspicious" about the juvenile's failing to look the agent in the eye, that his driving was "not so unusual," that there was "no proof" he was "part of a rolling drug caravan," and that his car "merely" had a large trunk and was "not specially outfitted for drug trafficking." In short, the agent's subjective inferences were "insufficient" to support his stopping the vehicle in the absence of other evidence.[12]

Unfortunately, no "bright line" has been established by court rulings between what is sufficient and what is insufficient to support stopping a vehicle on reasonable suspicion alone. If you try this tack, your success will depend on the number and nature of cues you can detect, your ability to articulate why they seemed suspicious to you, your track record of previous successful interdiction arrests and seizures, and the court's inclination to understand and acknowledge the ways of the street.

The more characteristics you can cite that are potential contraband cues, the better your chances of making the stop stick. Check the vehicle carefully, so you can describe all the specific facts and circumstances justifying the stop in your written report. If you have a "gut feeling" something is wrong, analyze that sensation. What is your subconscious picking up on that your conscious mind is missing? With discipline and practice, you'll better be able to articulate exactly what suspicious elements you observed.

Never use red-flag buzzwords like "profile" and "profiling" to explain in your report or testimony why you became suspicious or stopped a given driver. Avoid these terms on the radio, too; tapes may be subpoenaed. Such terminology will diminish your chances dramatically in any case, particularly one where you based the stop on reasonable suspicion alone. Courts generally have held that to stop vehicles and/or occupants because they "fit" some version of a drug-related profile is unacceptable, considering that many elements of the traditional profile also "describe a very large category of presumably innocent travelers."[13]

Likewise, *don't cite race or ethnicity* as a major factor in your decision to make a stop. A New Jersey detective driving an unmarked car saw a passenger vehicle pull up in front of a housing project known to be a drug-trafficking site. A black passenger got out and entered the project while the white driver parked a street away. When the driver saw the detective's car, he shielded his face with a magazine and slouched down. When the passenger returned and they drove off, the detective stopped them. Approaching the car, he saw cocaine inside and later found other drugs and paraphernalia—not surprising to anyone who understands the street. In court, the detective testified that in his experience it was "typical for a white drug user to employ a minority" to make a buy for him. Because the activities of the two suspects "fit the usual pattern in every way," race was a "primary factor" in arousing his suspicion. Even though his suspicion proved dead right, the court suppressed the seized contraband. "No rational inference can be drawn" about criminal activities from a person's race, the court ruled; thus the officer had "no valid legal basis" for stopping the vehicle.[14] Similarly, a sheriff's department in Colorado that stopped travelers on the basis of profile characteristics, including race, was held to violate the constitution. The court found that officers involved were not entitled to qualified immunity because they should have known their actions were illegal. This opened the officers to both compensatory and punitive damages.[15]

If you persist in stopping vehicles on the basis only of broad, ambiguous, noncriminal characteristics, like race or type of car, you could find your career as well as your cases profoundly damaged. In one Colorado jurisdiction, an officer became so notorious for profiling and stopping cars only because they had out-of-state plates or were driven by blacks or Hispanics that the local DA flatly refused to prosecute his arrests. In one instance, the officer saw three young black men whom he'd nailed with twenty pounds of coke in their car walk without trial "because it was so clear that [he] did not have a lawful reason to stop them."[16]

Ironically, courts have *accepted* the use of drug-courier profiles in airports, bus depots, and train stations.[17] Plainclothes officers regularly approach travelers they feel fit a profile—paying cash (especially small-denomination bills) for tickets, traveling under false names, going to or from source cities for narcotics, making quick turnarounds on long trips, appearing unusually nervous, checking no luggage, et cetera—and, as a first step in checking them out, ask permission to talk to them for a moment. Despite controversy about the reliability of such profiling, courts have sanctioned it because the subject is legally free to *ignore* the request and keep walking; if he or she *agrees* to be questioned, it becomes a consensual encounter, one the suspect voluntarily participates in. Such encounters in public places are not considered Fourth Amendment seizures, so long as the subject is not involuntarily detained. Vehicle stops, on the other hand, are not consensual events. They're forced detentions in which you intrude on a subject's right to travel freely. Consequently, the basis for your interrupting his trip and ordering him to stop must be stronger.

With moving vehicles, your legally safest strategy is generally to forget trying to justify pullovers on reasonable suspicion and to base your stop decisions instead on clear-cut probable cause.

With luck, you might get PC by actually seeing a crime in progress. A North Carolina deputy one night spotted an elderly driver lighting and puffing on a crack pipe, which gave PC for stopping the car; soon after, the deputy discovered forty-three grams of coke inside. Other officers from Alabama to Oregon have initiated stops—and been sustained in court—after observing handrolled cigarettes being held by or passed among occupants. One Border Patrol agent's stop was sustained on grounds that he *smelled* a crime in progress—the odor of marijuana blowing back from a pickup truck he was following along a gravel road in Texas; as it turned out, more than 200 pounds of dope was hidden in a compartment of the vehicle. Sometimes binoculars can help you establish PC. A Missouri officer patrolling past a nightclub noticed three men smoking in a car parked outside. He turned off his lights and surveilled them from a distance with field glasses, confirming what he'd suspected: The cigarette they were sharing was a joint, leading to their arrest and the eventual forfeiture of the car.

On-view crime is great, if you have it. But *usually* you'll establish PC in the most common and dependable way for Criminal Patrol: Whether you're initially suspicious about the vehicle you've spotted or not, you'll use a *traffic infraction* or *equipment violation* as your legal basis for pulling it over. This will be your humble but vital justification for making contact to see what more might be developed. [18]

Sometimes your mere presence can provoke a stoppable violation. One officer, knowing that some of the most popular dope markets in his city are in dead-end streets and cul-de-sacs, just parks there and watches. Often drivers will get close before seeing his squad, then stop suddenly (improper stopping in a roadway) or hastily back up (improper backing in a roadway). "There's two offenses," he says, "before I even pursue the car!"

2. Is it legal to be curious about a car or driver first, then find a traffic infraction to justify pulling him over so I can make contact and check him out? According to the U. S. Supreme Court, yes. In a 1996 decision,[19] the Court sanctioned your becoming suspicious about a vehicle first (perhaps because of curiosity ticklers) and then finding another unrelated but legal reason to stop it. If your actions are objectively valid—in other words, if you have probable cause to believe that a traffic infraction or other violation has actually taken place—your true motivation for wanting to effect a stop doesn't matter.

The overwhelming majority of state courts follow this thinking, too. In Los Angeles, two marked units spotted a truck that they knew had been fingered by a narcotics agent for suspected drug activity. They tailed it until they saw it make an illegal U-turn and later an unsafe lane change, then stopped it. A few minutes later, during a consent search, the uniformed officers found a quantity of cocaine and a firearm. The truck's two occupants ended up going to prison. Their lawyer claimed that the stop was illegal because it was pretextual, but in line with the Supreme Court's thinking, a state appeals court declared: "The issue is whether a reasonable officer 'could have'...stopped a vehicle for the observed traffic violation," not whether the officer had a "subjective desire to search for drugs." As another state court put it: "Motorists have no legitimate expectation of not being stopped when they violate laws."[20]

Before the Supreme Court ruling, there was considerable controversy about "pretextual" stops. Some courts allowed a stop only when "a reasonable officer *would* have made [it] even if he had lacked the additional motivation of investigating another offense."[21] If you wouldn't ordinarily have stopped the car in question but did so because of your suspicions, in these jurisdictions you were guilty of conducting a pretextual stop—one where the traffic infraction is just an excuse for checking into an unrelated, usually more serious offense for which you lack reasonable suspicion or PC. This was termed the "usual police practices" or "objective reasonableness" approach to the pretextual issue, as contrasted with the more liberal "authorization" or "could test" to the pretextual stop issue.[22]

Even today state jurisdictions technically could be more restrictive, although few if any still are. Be certain. You need to know the guidelines that prevail in your jurisdiction. But even a police-practices restriction does *not* necessarily keep you from stopping cars after you become curious about them, as you'll see next. Understand, though, that the right to stop does not automatically give you the right to search in *any* jurisdiction.

3. How can I protect myself against accusations of profiling or arbitrary stops? By following the normal Criminal Patrol work pattern. Remember, you need a *lot* of contacts to find the relatively few felony offenders you're most interested in. To get the volume you want, you're going to have to intensively enforce the traffic laws.

Air hoses rubbing against metal (arrow) can provide cause to stop a large commercial truck. But if you stop trucks for such violations only when you suspect drug hauling, you may be accused of improper selective enforcement.

Sure, you'll catch some contraband haulers on relatively major common violations. Tired from long miles of nonstop driving, under pressure to deliver fast, a lot more confident of not getting caught after they've been on other successful runs, they frequently do speed or drive erratically. But there'll be times you'll want to stop people who scrupulously avoid these ordinary blunders. You may then need to call upon more *trivial* violations or public safety considerations, like having a taillight out or a cracked windshield, changing lanes without signaling, impeding traffic, following too closely, failing to dim lights, speeding 3 to 5 mph over the limit, wearing no seatbelt, allowing air hoses on trucks to rub against metal or liquid to drip onto the roadway from under the back doors of semi-trailers, and so on. This level of enforcement requires an intimate and resourceful working knowledge of the motor vehicle codes, as well as knowing the outer limits of what prosecutors and courts in your jurisdiction will stand for. But you don't want to wait until you're following someone you think might be a contraband transporter before enforcing these laws.

You should maintain a "rolling resume," an anecdotal and statistical written log, not only of your training in Criminal Patrol but also of your enforcement activities and any contraband busts that result. Jot down a brief description of each vehicle and occupant you stop on each shift, including race, sex, age; why you made the stop (the specific violation); the location and the outcome, even if it is just a verbal or written warning.

This should show fair and consistent enforcement of a wide variety of minor (as well as major) infractions on a regular basis, even if you just write warnings for them. These violations are your bread and butter on Criminal Patrol. They allow you to contact a wide range of motorists, which is what you need, not only for your record but because you understand that the least likely parties often turn out to be the very ones you're looking for.

If you're accused of profiling or arbitrary stops, you can bring your daily logbook to court and document that pulling over motorists for "stickler" reasons is part of your customary pattern—not a glaring exception conveniently dusted off in the defendant's case. This makes it difficult if not impossible for the defendant to claim that the stop was unfairly targeted against just him or her as part of inappropriate selective law enforcement. (Moreover, include in your log all the times you make contact with the motoring public to *assist* them for their convenience and safety, such as changing tires, giving directions, et cetera. This will help build your credibility in court as a "good guy" who makes frequent contacts as a normal part of your daily activities.)

Certainly you're not obligated to *ignore* potential suspect indicators that you observe on patrol. One officer accused of profiling by a defense attorney answered this way: "Counselor, when you sit down to dinner and you have steak, green beans, and mashed potatoes on your plate, don't you take a bite of the one you like best first? That's not profiling, that's *assessing,* and police officers do this all day long."

When you do stop someone you're already suspicious about or become suspicious of, don't get so focused on finding out more about him or her that you forget to issue a warning or ticket for the offense you witnessed. You need that written record to confirm that you didn't pull him over "just" to check him out. In a case that was decided against the prosecution, a Utah trooper stopped a driver for drifting within his lane on an Interstate. The trooper found forty-three pounds of marijuana behind a partition in the vehicle. In court, he testified that he initiated the stop because he believed the driver had been drinking. But in reversing a favorable lower-court decision, an appeals court pointed out that the trooper made no effort to check whether the driver was impaired, casting doubt on his story. The stop was declared invalid and the drug evidence suppressed.[23]

Be truthful. An officer in Georgia stopped a male Hispanic driving a rental car and, during a consent search, found cocaine in the bottom of a cooler. The officer claimed he stopped the suspect for driving without headlights in misty weather and for weaving "all over the travel lane." In court, however, a videotape from the officer's in-car camera showed that the offender's lights were on and that his driving was not erratic. In fact, like the Utah trooper, the officer made no inquiry during the stop about the violator's ability to drive. The court ruled that the officer's reason for the stop was "impeached by the tape" and suppressed the evidence.[24]

Trivial Pursuit?

Common infractions can sometimes lead to uncommon busts. Consider the following cases as proof that thorough enforcement of motor vehicle laws—which some might consider a trivial pursuit—is a key to successful Criminal Patrol, because increasing the number of laws you actively enforce increases your chances of contacting criminal activity. In short, any motor vehicle contact may result in a seizure.

Two officers in Texas were driving behind a car that switched lanes after its turn signal blinked only once. Texas law requires a minimum of 100 feet between signaling and changing lanes—plus the car cut quickly in front of three tractor-trailers. The officers pulled it over.

The driver acted nervous, his hands were shaking, and he would not look the officers in the eye. Conflicts quickly surfaced between information the driver gave and answers to the officers' questions from his female passenger.

During a consent search, one officer noticed a new bolt and scratches on the strapping holding the gas tank. Sure enough, the tank had been moved to get access to a hollow compartment above it. Concealed inside, the officers found the payoff for their trouble: a kilo of cocaine.[25]

One morning an Illinois trooper and his supervisor were reviewing patrol assignments at a rest area. They saw a man asleep in a BMW parked nearby with Florida plates and what appeared to be a shattered rear window.

When the man drove out of the rest area soon after, the trooper stopped him for failing to signal a right turn before entering the highway and for driving with an obscured window.

While advising the subject of these violations, the trooper noticed a hunting knife next to the driver's seat, which he retrieved for his own safety.

A computer check revealed that the driver was not the owner of the car and that he had a previous record of weapons and drug violations. A K-9 was recruited, and during a consent search officers recovered several containers of cocaine in the vehicle. More coke was found on the driver himself.[26]

Early one evening a Wyoming highway patrolman saw a Volvo with California dealer plates whiz by him. In Wyoming, a dealer transporting a vehicle through from out of state must stop at the border and register it, receiving a sticker for the rear window. Because it was too dark to see if the sticker was affixed, the officer pulled the car over to investigate.

With "a strange feeling," he approached from the passenger side. While examining the driver's license and registration, he noticed that the subject seemed nervous and swallowed a lot. The driver was not the registered owner, but he said he was driving the car to Ohio as a favor for a friend who'd been called back there suddenly from California to visit a sick relative.

The patrolman asked permission to look in the trunk. After hesitating a moment, the driver said OK. Bad answer—for him. Inside, the officer found half a dozen nylon duffel bags. Inside them, hidden under layers of towels, were seventy-five pounds of marijuana.[27]

In Missouri, a highway patrol officer stopped a motorist for driving at 30 to 40 mph on a rural road, causing a traffic backup.

The driver produced a temporary, handwritten, photoless, out-of-state driver's license and a handwritten registration application, each document in a different name. Asked for more ID, the driver acted nervous and tried to hide the contents of his wallet as he retrieved a Social Security card. The officer asked to see the wallet and found three more out-of-state licenses in three different names, each bearing a photo of the suspect.

During a consent search of the car, the officer found burglary tools, instructions for cracking safes and making false IDs, and a loaded gun.

The driver was arrested. Fingerprints revealed his true identity—and the fact that he was wanted on two federal warrants. Although he argued that the officer had stopped him on a mere pretext, his conviction for being a felon in possession of a firearm was upheld.[28]

---

4. Can I set up a roadblock checkpoint and force people to stop? Yes... but with some big "ifs." Roadblocks can be highly effective. At one in Utah, for instance, officers discovered and seized over half a million dollars in drug money from two vehicles traveling in different directions within the first hour of operation. But here, in something of a hair-splitting exercise, courts have said that intent is important.

If the primary purpose of the roadblock is to check drivers' licenses and registrations and detect drunk-driving violations, that's considered valid under constitutional guidelines. It's okay if such a roadblock also produces a "collateral benefit" of discovering and deterring drug trafficking.

However, if the principal purpose is to catch drug haulers, that's not acceptable, because then the roadblock becomes a subterfuge for detecting crimes other than licensing and sobriety offenses.

Moreover, you must stop vehicles at a checkpoint according to some established numerical formula: every car or every fifth car or every tenth car, et cetera, under a plan that places explicit, neutral limitations on officers' actions. *Random, arbitrary stops are forbidden at checkpoints just as they are on patrol,* again in an effort to discourage discretionary and discriminatory profiling. If a motorist evades a clearly marked checkpoint, it is "a proper police response" for you to pursue and stop him or her. But this, too, must be done in a "nonarbitrary, uniform" fashion, "with officer discretion kept to a minimum."[29]

Under no circumstances does stopping someone at a checkpoint permit you to search the vehicle, unless you have consent or probable cause to do so. However you're free to examine the exterior of the vehicle for contraband cues as part of your checkpoint duties. Peering under one car, a New Mexico officer noticed what appeared to be a new clamp on a gas line. This small clue led eventually to the discovery of thirty-nine pounds of marijuana hidden in the gas tank.

Some departments have been successful with drug seizures by only pretending to be working a checkpoint. Officers set up signs, warning: "Narcotics Inspection Ahead" or "Drug Dog at Work," then watch to see which vehicles whip U-turns or quickly pull off the roadway. A U-turn, especially across a highway median, may be illegal and justify an immediate stop. Otherwise, these cars are kept under rolling surveillance, until a legal reason can be found to stop them for a closer look.

Signs announcing roadblocks that don't really exist are a legal means of identifying suspected haulers of contraband in some jurisdictions. Just watch for motorists who make abrupt U-turns, then stop them for legitimate traffic violations to make contact.

When the sign ruse was tried in Kansas, one car with out-of-state plates abruptly left the highway at a rarely used exit, drove several miles down a gravel road, and finally pulled into a service station in a sparsely populated hamlet. A trooper who'd been following it pulled up behind and engaged the driver and passenger in conversation. Both seemed unusually nervous and gave conflicting stories about the purpose of their trip. They said the only reason they left the highway was to get gas—yet less than five miles earlier they'd passed an exit clearly marked as leading to gas stations and now their tank topped off after only four dollars' worth. Before this "consensual" encounter ended, the trooper got their permission to search the car with a drug dog, and the dog alerted to a trunk full of marijuana.

In court, the offenders argued that the checkpoint that caused them to leave the highway and resulted in their contact with the trooper was unconstitutional. But the court said no—because no checkpoint was ever actually set up. Just a "warning" sign had been posted.[30]

Again, check with your local legal authorities. Narcotics-sign ruses have been rejected by courts in some jurisdictions.

Of course, when it comes to over-the-road commercial vehicles like semitrailers, there's no problem forcing them to stop at checkpoints like weigh stations, for example, even in the absence of any individualized suspicion. One state supreme court has ruled, typically, that "commercial drivers of motor vehicles have low expectations of privacy" and that fixed checkpoints like weigh stations "constitute reasonable seizures" for them.[31]

5. Can I approach people who are already stopped and try to develop suspicion about them? Yes. You can walk up to anyone in a public place and attempt to engage them in conversation. You do not need even reasonable suspicion of wrongdoing to do so—provided that they are free to leave at all times, their exit is not blocked, and they are not ordered or coerced in any way to stay and respond to you.[32]

On any shift, in addition to your enforcement-related contacts, you have opportunities for contacts that are *voluntary,* both for you and the subjects. When you pull up to get coffee at a stop-and-rob or a filling station, greet the people around you in a friendly way and watch their reactions. Someone in the crowd may look down, not reply, refuse to establish eye contact with you, or otherwise appear nervous or uncomfortable. A guy pumping gas may reflexively jerk the nozzle out of the tank and spill fuel all over. The unaware officer would think, Dumb ass!, and go on to coffee. With the 5%er mind-set, you want to zero in on that subject for more "friendly" banter, to see if you can find out *why* he had such an overreaction. Likewise, if you stop to check on someone with a disabled vehicle in your "community caretaker" capacity and they seem anxious for you to leave, that's unusual. Most people in that predicament welcome help and will ask for more favors.

Some uniformed officers regularly take advantage of voluntary contacts at highway rest stops, "working" people who are just sitting in their stopped vehicles or are out on foot, like plainclothes officers work airports and depots. They watch for travelers who exhibit characteristics they consider suspicious and then try to develop enough indicators through casual, consensual conversation to warrant asking them for permission to search their vehicle. This tends to be an especially good place to contact elderly travelers (the "blue hairs"). Often just asking about their vehicle ("I've been thinking about a motor home like that myself. Do you like it?") is enough for you to read their willingness to talk versus a terse brush-off that may suggest they have something they don't want you to find out.

Of course, if during the conversation you develop articulable facts for suspicion, you may then have grounds for escalating the contact from voluntary to an official, compelled investigative detention.

Tactical Reminders

Counting officers' murders and accidental deaths from traffic together, more than one out of eight police fatalities occur during vehicle stops. So whether you've picked up on early indicators of suspicion or not, remember: *Conducting a vehicle stop is one of your highest-risk activities,* not only because of an offender who may be armed and assaultive but because of the environment in which you're working.

Here are some reminders of tactical elements of caution and control that are important while you are initiating the stop. Unfortunately, they often get forgotten or ignored in the potentially mind-numbing repetition of conducting multiple pullovers day in and day out. Consciously integrating good procedures on every stop can keep your "routine" from becoming a deadly routine.

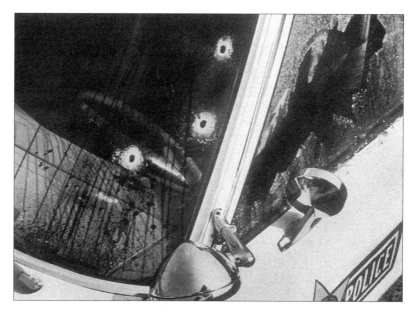

Your survival can be threatened at any stage of a vehicle stop—even before you exit your patrol car. From the moment you try to initiate the stop, stay alert for danger cues.

1. If at all possible, make your radio check before you effect the stop. If you can get feedback that the car's hinky, you'll have a valuable survival edge at the outset. Among other things, you may prevent this nasty surprise: Some offenders plan to wait until your car stops and you pick up your mike, then they'll jump out and start shooting when your mind and hands are occupied. So it is important—some say mandatory—to call in the license plate, the vehicle's description, the number and description of occupants, and the location before you kick on your overheads. If you wait to call in until there's a crisis, you may not be able to deliver that information so clearly or completely under a stress overload.

If for some unavoidable reason it isn't possible for you to check in before the stop, you or your partner should at least try to record the plate and descriptions, while maintaining visual contact with the vehicle and occupants.

Beyond survival considerations, calling in preliminary data before the stop helps shorten your detention of the violator. A favorite defense ploy is to claim that a stop took too long. To keep the detention short and still test for suspicious circumstances, you want to utilize as much of your time as possible in actual contact with the driver and passenger(s).

2. Be cautious about what you say on the radio. Ideally, don't tip suspicions you may have going in; the suspect or confederates in another vehicle may be listening on a scanner. However, if you feel you are going to need backup or K-9 down-range, call for these *early*. They can be en route before the vehicle is actually stopped, cutting down on the time you need to detain it—and getting you help faster. To defeat eavesdroppers, you may want to use prearranged code words when communicating about your stop.

3. Keep your overheads and highbeams off until you close distance and move up close behind the violator. You want to leave enough space so if he spikes his brakes or turns suddenly you can react safely.

A Little Luck...and Good Tactics

Like every officer, Trooper Bob Duncan of the Florida Highway Patrol has heard the reminders about waiting for backup and about calling officers from another agency if help from yours isn't immediately available. Shortly after midnight one morning, he proved the wisdom of this advice after clocking a late-model car at 10 mph over the limit.

The area was dark and four males were in the vehicle, so Duncan called backup from the nearest municipal department and waited for it to arrive. With the local officer tactically positioned, Duncan spoke to the driver about the violation, issued a warning, and then obtained consent to search. In the first place he looked—the trunk—he found a box for a new Uzi. The occupants denied knowing where the gun was, but Duncan figured they were lying.

Now he called more backup. After it arrived to help watch the suspects, he searched the rest of the car. In the driver-door pouch, he discovered a loaded 9mm pistol, found another in the passenger-door pocket, and recovered the missing Uzi under the seat, with an instruction book and a kilo of coke next to it.

Later Duncan listened to a discussion the suspects had among themselves, recorded by a tape recorder hidden in the water fountain of the holding cell where they were brought. They revealed that they initially planned to kill him as soon as he approached the driver's window. When he didn't approach and then the first backup car arrived, they dropped the plan. They figuring they couldn't take out both officers with the 9mm pistols.

Originally they'd intended to use the Uzi to handle any cops who stopped them. But they couldn't get the rounds loaded into the magazine correctly. Either they couldn't read or couldn't understand the directions.

At the same time, you don't want to be so far back that you can't confirm his license plate and he has a tempting head start that prompts him to flee. Your first tactical goal on any stop is to get the vehicle halted without the subject rabbiting. Pursuits are highly dangerous for you, him, and third parties and the best time to stop them is before they begin. A Canadian constable who makes a high number of stops but experiences a low number of pursuits explains: "If the first thing he sees is a mirror full of cop, he'll know that you have his plate and that he'll have trouble losing you. If your highbeams and overheads do not impress him after about forty seconds, light him up with your take-down lights so he thinks you're in his back seat and give him a good, strong blast of the 'yelp' siren for two or three seconds. If he does run, you don't have to play catch up; you can back off to a comfortable pursuit distance, broadcast the plate, and have at it."

4. Continuously monitor actions of the car's occupant(s) from the moment you decide to make the stop. Watch for guiltily nervous or fearful behavior—"reacting signs"—once they notice you. *Don't neglect to watch passengers.* In a contraband situation, they may display much more agitated movement than passengers in cars where just a traffic infraction is involved (as implied by the photograph on the cover of this book, for example). It's important that you develop a sense for how people *normally* react upon seeing your patrol car, so you have a basis for comparison.

Note: If the car you're stopping has a sunroof, consider that a potential danger cue. Jamaican Posse gangs, which now control 70% to 80% of the drug trade in some cities, favor foreign or rental vehicles with sunroofs for transporting drugs because they can reach through the open top without hindrance to shoot back at you.

5. Always think weapons. Does anyone in the car try to change places or make rapid or furtive movements—especially under the seat, to the glove box, inside a center armrest, behind visors—as if hiding contraband or reaching for a weapon? These not only can be warning signs but may also provide you legal grounds to extend detention of a suspect after you get the car stopped.

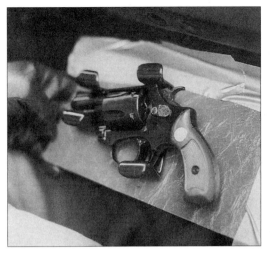

(above)
Crude but fast, this mail-order gun holder can be attached under the dash with duct tape. Furtive movements may be early clues of such devices.

(right)
Stashing guns under seats is so popular that even commercially produced lockboxes are available to let travelers quickly arm themselves.

The study of incarcerated cop killers mentioned in Chapter 1 reveals that their favorite places to carry weapons when they traveled by car was on their person; next preferred was directly under the driver's seat. (They didn't say that they liked to keep their wallet or driver's license under the seat, so if you see someone you're about to stop frantically reaching there, it's not likely he or she is reaching for ID!)

Don't limit your thinking to the obvious. Some drug runners in New York City have modified cars by installing a button under the carpeting between the driver's door and seat. When this is pushed, inside door panels on both the driver's and passenger's sides fold down to access hidden guns.

Consider the list of some additional places currently popular for hiding weapons (especially small-caliber handguns) in the passenger compartments of cars, as compiled by street-gang investigators on the West Coast and in the Midwest:

- Under a headrest, with the headrest down to conceal the weapon;
- Up inside springs under a seat, usually toward the front;
- Under a floor mat, where a section of floorboard has been cut out and a metal box installed to hold the weapon;
- Behind a removable stereo unit;
- Behind or inside speaker grilles in doors;
- Behind a glove box or inside the panel above it;
- Inside or behind armrests;
- Inside compartments above or below rear armrests;
- Inside door panels;
- Behind or inside the dashboard;
- Up inside the headliner;
- Inside tip-out ashtrays, including those in the rear seat;

- Inside upholstery;
- Inside the rear window deck;
- In a sun visor, hollowed out to conceal the weapon.[33]

Furtive movements to such places not only warrant extra caution, including an *immediate* call for backup, but may also give you grounds for frisking occupants and for conducting a limited, protective search inside the vehicle, as explained in later chapters.

Deadly example of "Expect the unexpected." Back seat of this vehicle seized in Louisiana was removed, and 2 occupants knelt in back with long guns aimed through portholes in the rear trunk wall. When they released a wire (arrow), trunk lid would fly up and they could fire on pursuing or approaching officers.

6. Watch for contraband or weapons that may be dropped or thrown out of windows once your presence is known. Using these as grounds for custodial arrests can give you the right to search inside the vehicle. Even if what's tossed can't be fully recovered, what you estimate that you've seen may be important. During a high-speed chase of two suspected drug couriers, a Missouri detective saw the passenger open eight to ten plastic bags and dump white powder from them onto the road. Later, after a stop and arrests were effected, only about sixty grams of the powder (coke, of course) could be recovered. But drawing on what the detective estimated he saw, a judge sentenced the offenders on the basis of possessing with intent to distribute 2.5 kilos.[34]

7. Control the environment for your stop, to the extent possible. Once he sees your lights, the driver may slow down but continue traveling, then after a delay pull over with a sharp veer and a hard stop. This can indicate an impaired driver, but it may also suggest a stall while occupants get a story together, hide incriminating evidence (some may try to eat small quantities of drugs), retrieve guns from hiding places, or select a spot where they want the stop to take place. By stopping abruptly, they may try to catch you off guard, then jump out and rush you. Use your P.A. system to direct the driver to move if he stops where you don't want him to. If you're in an urban area, avoid letting him park near an alley or other potential avenue of escape or pull over in front of a tavern, gang hangout, or other spot where you'll have an instant—and possibly hostile—crowd to watch and deal with. Also avoid buildings with reflective windows that may expose all your movements to people inside the car. Unless you feel you can use darkness to help conceal your moves outside your unit, try for a well-lit area, keeping in mind that the extra illumination will help you if you progress to searching the vehicle.

On highways, try to pick a straight stretch of level road, away from hills and curves where traffic hazards are greater. Where there's a median strip, try to stop near a cut-through so that backup coming from the opposite direction can reach you quickly. Avoid spots where a guardrail, deep ditch, or other obstacle cramps your mobility and may prevent a passenger-side approach. Ideally you want close availability of cover—for you, not for the occupant(s)—in case a gunfight erupts. Put the suspect at the disadvantage. In rural areas, try to make your stop near a plowed field or other open area. If he tries to flee on foot, he can be easily spotted for a considerable distance in daylight, and he'll leave tracks in the turned earth that can be readily followed. Most fields have access roads that can be driven at least by police four-wheel-drive vehicles, making a search faster and simpler. In rain, you may be able to get him stopped under an overpass, so you'll have shelter while you talk to him and later search the vehicle. Be certain, however, that your radio transmits and receives reliably in this location; sometimes overpasses block out radio signals and your screams for help would go unheard.

8. Maintain distance for added protection as your car and the violator's come to a stop. Whereas earlier you may have moved up close to discourage flight or to test for the No-Look reaction, you now want to build a reactionary gap. Some officers park so close they can't even see the subject's rear license plate when they're behind the wheel. You're safer from firearms assault or the offender suddenly throwing his car into reverse if you stay back at least far enough that you can see his rear wheels touching the ground. By buying yourself distance, you also buy greater opportunity to throw your car in reverse and back up if someone comes out shooting before you can step out. On the other hand, you don't want to be so far back that you can't quickly reach your patrol car as a cover option should a threat suddenly develop during your foot approach to the vehicle or driver.

Whatever vehicle you're stopping and whatever your stop positioning, try to give yourself maximum flexibility. Here being so close to the suspect vehicle and having limited cover may work to the officers' disadvantage if shooting erupts. Any stop can become a high-risk stop at any moment. Be positioned so you can escalate to high-risk stop tactics if necessary.

9. Remember that you can reposition your patrol car. Officers typically freeze their car in the original stop position, which is often dependent on where the violator stops, rather than back up or reangle to create better distance or cover to their advantage.

10. Watch for brake lights staying on or backup lights coming on as warnings that the stopped vehicle may be preparing to flee or to reverse ram as a means of activating your air bag and delaying your exit. In fact, interstate car-heist rings in New York and New Jersey have instructed their juvenile thieves to back into squads on vehicle stops and suddenly step on brakes during pursuits to force collisions and detonate the bags—a serious threat to officer safety.

11. Anticipate survival concerns. If you've seen furtive movement or are otherwise concerned, consider increasing your parking distance 20-25 feet to allow time for better scrutiny and, if terrain permits, off-set your car to the *right*. If you line yourself up between the suspect's driver and passenger seats as you sit behind your steering wheel, you're harder to hit with gunfire from either side of that car, unless an assailant exits or shoots through his rear windshield.

Normally, you'll probably off-set your unit about one-quarter to one-half its width to the left to create a safety lane. Positioned properly, your left headlight can shine into the suspect's side mirror (day or night) and your right headlight will illuminate his vehicle's interior.

Setting this up so your unit is not jutting unduly into the traffic lane requires your getting the violator to pull to the far right.

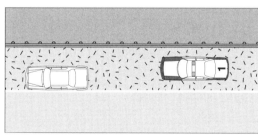

An alternative: off-set to the right. Here the offender will have a hard time targeting you in a gunfight. However, terrain may prevent this option.

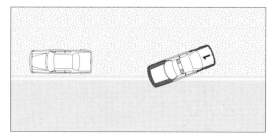

Another possibility is to angle your unit at about 45 degrees from the rear of the suspect vehicle, with your driver side turned away. You'll gain added protection from your vehicle, including the engine block. But this tactic may make it harder for you to back up quickly, and you lose effective use of highbeams at night.

79

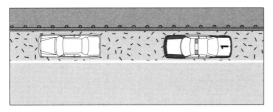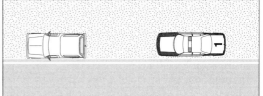

(above)
In some circumstances, parking directly behind with no off-set may be desirable. On a narrow shoulder with heavy, high-speed traffic on your left and barrier on your right, this may be most practical.

(above right)
Or if you are riding with a partner, an in-line position behind a van or camper will allow him or her to monitor the passenger side more readily.

12. Remember the special challenges of large commercial vehicles. Getting semitrailers and the like stopped is different from pulling over cars. Because of their size and weight, you have to anticipate that trucks will require more time and distance to get stopped. Also you need to direct them to a wider, flatter, more solid shoulder or emergency lane for pulling the vehicle out of the traffic flow. Then there's the problem of getting the truck back into traffic without creating more of a hazard than the original violation presented.

The noise and bulk sometimes makes it difficult for the truck driver to notice that you are trying to initiate a stop. To get his attention, you may need to straddle the center stripe when safe to do so, with your overheads on until he starts to slow and pull to the side.

In directing the truck to a stop, you need to anticipate where you will ultimately position your vehicle. If you feel you're tactically safest to park ahead, you'll want at least forty-five feet between you and the truck. Parking behind, you'll need to be at least twenty feet back to maximize your visibility. Also assess the stop location for permitting you to off-set or angle your patrol car for better visibility and cover and for allowing backup to deploy for greatest advantage.

With semitrailers, once the truck stops, you may decide to park your patrol car ahead of the cab and signal the driver to meet you at that position.

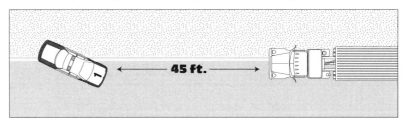

Some officers feel more secure parking behind the truck and deploying on foot from there. Relative merits of these positions are discussed in Chapter 3.

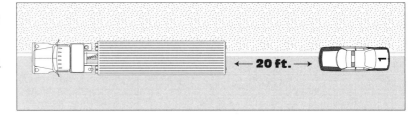

13. Stay alert for escort vehicles. From the beginning, note what other traffic is around. When you spot a car you want and perhaps you're waiting to get into traffic to pursue it, don't let other cars just go by in a blur. Contraband couriers commonly travel in teams, in two or three separate cars or sometimes a car and a truck, especially if "mother" loads are involved. If the load car breaks down, they can transfer the goods to another vehicle. Also an extra car can be used to draw an officer's attention away from the load carrier. Watch especially for the next vehicle with plates from the same state and county as the car you're after, or with similar occupants, or even drivers passing signals back and forth.

Sometimes a trail car will quickly pull over nearby or at least slow down and the occupants scrutinize you as they go past if you're out with a load car. Soon after, you may notice that the car has come back on the other side of the road or street and perhaps even parked there. Watch also for any vehicle that speeds up when you start to stop someone else. In New Jersey, two black subjects in a car with North Carolina plates zipped past two troopers parked on a highway median. Although the subjects were speeding over the limit, they grinned and waved as they passed. They were headed home from New York City after buying five pounds of cocaine, which was hidden under their bumper. They expected a chase car that normally traveled with them—driven by a white deputy sheriff—to whip around them and recklessly weave in and out of traffic as a decoy to bait the officers into pursuing it instead of the load car. But unknown to the first subjects, he'd gotten detained at a construction blockade and wasn't within sight—until too late. By then, the troopers had stopped the load car and were on their way to finding the secret goods.

Although some transport teams travel in tandem, another strategy is for the escort vehicle to follow about ten to fifteen minutes behind the load car. The thinking is that it will take about that long for an officer to develop suspicion, get a consent form signed, and be underway with a search. If the load car gets in that kind of trouble, the escort vehicle will arrive at about the time the officer is most vulnerable, while searching. If it's not that kind of stop, the load car will probably be back in traffic by then and the escort won't have to reveal itself.

Escort Assault

About 7:30 one November morning, Border Patrol Agent Jorge Gonzalez was working alone in sparsely populated canyon country of Arizona, along a well-known drug-trafficking route. He saw a Ford Ranger emerge from a remote canyon, and began to follow it. As he got closer, he was able to see bundles of marijuana in the truck bed.

Gonzalez had made lots of marijuana busts and anticipated nothing exceptional. But when he activated his emergency lights, the vehicle refused to yield. As he followed behind in his Blazer at about 35 mph, he noticed an International Scout approaching from his rear. The pursued driver began signaling to the driver of the Scout. Gonzalez realized they were working together, and the Scout was preparing to ram him.

He radioed dispatch that he was in danger. Backup was dispatched, but the nearest unit was at least forty minutes away.

Gonzalez tried to pass the load vehicle to avoid being rammed, but the Ranger blocked his attempt. He then went to the right side of the road and stopped on the shoulder. The truck stopped, too, blocking his path. The Scout was roaring up from the rear, a collision imminent.

To avoid a direct hit from behind, Gonzalez maneuvered his Blazer so the Scout struck it just behind the driver door. The Scout skidded sideways, spun around so it was headed forward again, and rammed the patrol vehicle a second time, with Gonzalez still inside.

Fearing for his life, he drew his sidearm and pointed it at the Scout driver, who was preparing to ram a third time. The driver exited his vehicle and tried to flee on foot, but was subdued and arrested by Gonzalez. Later the Ranger, which took off during the struggle, was found abandoned. The pot Gonzalez had seen had been removed, but more than a pound was found under the truck seat.

The courier was tracked down and arrested. Both drivers were subsequently convicted of assault on a federal officer, possession of marijuana with intent to distribute, and conspiracy. The courier drew eight years, the rammer seven.

For you to take on a possible transport team *alone* is highly risky. In some cases if a bait car fails to lure you away from a load car you've stopped, there may be a *third* car or van—a weapons vehicle. This "tail-gunner" can deliver a drive-by ambush or deliberately run into you.

Fortunately, attacks on officers from escorts so far have been rare. But any time you perceive what might be tandem travelers before you start to make a stop, you're safest to follow the tactics of an off-duty Tennessee officer who spotted three vehicles that seemed to be together on an Interstate. He followed from an unobtrusive distance and even watched the occupants stop and talk together briefly while he was awaiting backup. When a comfortable level of manpower was present, officers stopped two of the vehicles: a Mercedes clocked at 7 mph over the limit and a truck that was weaving because the driver was intoxicated. Before the dual stop was completed, a drug-sniffing K-9 was summoned and nearly 4,500 pounds of marijuana was discovered and seized from both vehicles. Watchful deployment and the avoidance of rushing prevented any violence.

Team Attack Tactics

Vehicles traveling together can pose special danger for you if criminal activity is involved. The threat is graphically conveyed in these excerpts from a law enforcement intelligence bulletin issued regarding a "training seminar" held in Idaho for members of a right-wing extremist group known for maintaining connections with ex-convict gang members and other highly mobile criminals—types you may well encounter on Criminal Patrol:

The seminar was given by a white male...wearing a ski mask to hide his face. [He] was believed to be a law enforcement officer, either past or present. Following is a brief overview of methods covered:

• KILLING POLICE OFFICERS ON ROUTINE CAR STOPS. The group was told to always travel in groups of at least two vehicles. The first car would contain the [criminal] team. The backup car would be a family-style car (station wagon, etc.) driven by a man and a woman. If you are stopped, you have three to five minutes to make up your mind whether to kill the officer(s) before backup arrives. The primary responsibility of killing the officer(s) is with the second car. This can be done in two ways:

1. The [criminal] backup car turns off its headlights and coasts [up] behind the patrol car. Backup personnel exit the car quietly, walk to the passenger side of the patrol car, and shoot the officer(s) once in the torso and once in the head.

2. The driver of the first car starts arguing with the cop and distracts his attention from the backup car. Backup personnel run to the cop yelling: "Can we help you, officer?" as if to assist the cop. At point-blank range the officer is shot in the torso and head....

• Radio scanners should be installed in vehicles....

• All members should learn how to start making their own bombs and have them available....

• All members should keep "heavy weapons" but use them only for major assaults...At night [cops] will be fumbling around trying to reload while you'll be killing them. Small .22 caliber weapons are now available with [extra] round capacity. Extra barrels are available and should be obtained. If the weapon is fired in a criminal activity, the barrel should be changed immediately....

• All members [criminals] should wear body armor....The cops are trained to shoot at body mass and will do so automatically in a gun battle....

As your vehicle and the suspect's come to a stop, you can never be sure how the driver's perspective of this moment compares to yours.

As you exit your vehicle, you must be ready to play it as it lays.

There is a lot to do now in a short amount of time: *Your first priority—always—is your survival.* So we'll first explore survival tactics for controlling the driver and vehicle once the stop is made, then we'll detail your investigative strategy for finding out the truth about the subject(s) you are about to meet.

Going in, you may know only that the car you've stopped has a burned-out taillight. But don't be quick to formulate an opinion that you are in a low-risk situation. The suspect may not even be aware of the violation you've stopped him for. But...he may know that he is transporting illegal drugs or guns...or is high on dope...or is on parole...or is wanted on an outstanding warrant...or is fleeing the scene of a crime. And he may *assume* that you know this, too, and that's why you're stopping him.

With these thoughts running through his mind, he just may be gearing up to launch the attack of his life.

POSITION
OF ADVANTAGE

3

As soon as his vehicle comes to a stop and before you can exit your patrol car, the violator scrambles out and rushes back toward you, possibly with his driver's license in hand. Even if both hands are in plain view and you can see he's not brandishing a weapon, *what's wrong with this picture?* A couple of things:

1) This can be a strong contraband cue. If he's hauling illicit goods with a distinctive odor, like marijuana, or if other incriminating evidence is readily detectable inside the car, he wants to keep you *away* from the vehicle. By preempting your approach, he's creating distance to his advantage. Moreover, he may figure that by showing how "accommodating" he is by saving you the "inconvenience" of coming up to his car, he can lull you into keeping the detention brief and perfunctory, out of appreciation. Anytime someone exits immediately and heads back to intercept you, chances are that something is wrong about his vehicle or about him.

2) More important, by unexpectedly initiating action rather than waiting for your instructions, he is seizing psychological and tactical control of the stop. And that is your job.

Whether you avoid attack and find what you're after on a Criminal Patrol stop is often a matter of who best controls the element of surprise. If you can anticipate the suspect's thinking and thwart his surprises with unexpected measures of your own, that's ideal. If you can't, you want at least to minimize the damage he can inflict and quickly neutralize his threat. And that means from the outset *taking charge.*

When you've stopped a suspect with criminal secrets, jockeying for control can become a deadly contest. He or she will be pitting deception and possibly unexpected violence against your investigative skills and tactical talents. Whatever wrongdoing you may suspect or evidence you may develop, if you can't maintain control of yourself, the suspect(s), and the stopped vehicle, you could still end up losing.

"Too many cops today seem afraid to assert control, reluctant to tell anyone what to do," observes a Wisconsin officer. "People are allowed to move as they want, to stand where they want, and then officers try to adapt to what the suspect does." Instead, *you* need to orchestrate the event. A vehicle stop or any other citizen contact should be like directing a movie, and a movie has only one director; you call the shots, things get done your way. When you let the suspect run the show, you invite assault. He may just be waiting for that "window of opportunity" when he can use deadly surprise. But if you close the window by the way you manage the scene, he may still *want* to attack but he won't get the chance.

From the beginning of the stop through the end, you want to engineer for yourself a Position of Advantage. That is, you situate yourself and the suspect where you have a tactical superiority that will discourage assault and give you the edge for defeating any threatening action that's attempted. In general terms, you choose positions relative to the vehicle, the driver, any passengers, and passing traffic that let you:

- **Use distance and barriers to separate yourself from potentially dangerous people and locations;**
- **Visually monitor possible threat sources;**
- **Protect and conceal your personal movements at the scene;**
- **Physically dominate any contact that turns sour.**

These principles apply on any vehicle stop you make, whether you suspect the driver at the start or not. The better your position accommodates these priorities, the more to your advantage it is.

On *each* stop, before you leave your patrol car, have firmly in mind how you intend to deploy this time. Base your decision on answers to this five-point checklist for tactical planning, remembering that each stop is unique:

1. What is the situation? Evaluate: early danger/courier indicators... type of vehicle stopped...number of occupants...NCIC results... immediate environment...lighting conditions...backup availability... other factors that may influence your tactical choices.

2. What are my best tactics initially? Given the situation as it appears now, decide how you should position yourself to: establish first contact with the driver...get a look inside the vehicle...talk to other occupants...be protected from traffic and possible escort vehicles...run additional radio checks...issue a citation or warning... obtain permission to search, if you decide to do so. Re-evaluate your plans: once you meet with the driver...at the point you ask consent... and at any other time new information is available that potentially changes the situation.

3. What am I going to do if...? The nature of any contact can change in a heartbeat; you can discover at any moment that someone is ready to kill you. Be prepared to shift quickly to new tactics, such as high-risk vehicle-stop procedures, based on the suspect's actions or statements or your sense of the situation. Consider how you'll handle variables that might occur, like: the suspect coming out shooting...or throwing his vehicle into reverse...or physically assaulting you...or fleeing...or other occupants exiting the vehicle on their own. If you plan in advance and mentally rehearse how to resolve such problems, you can usually cope with them successfully; if you don't plan, you're relying on spur-of-the-moment luck for your survival. For the best problem-solving mind-set, don't think "if" something goes wrong... think "when." Expect not only the unexpected but the worst. Ask yourself: If it happens right now, am I ready? And remember: In any interaction, the party with the *most options* usually wins.

4. What are my goals? Before the stop is concluded, you want to: evaluate the driver and any passengers for deception, impairment, other evidence of wrongdoing...look into the vehicle for plain-view evidence...inspect the vehicle for equipment and maintenance violations...run radio checks...warn or cite the driver...get consent to search if you develop sufficient suspicion...search thoroughly...arrest if you discover contraband...pursue any other objectives unique to this stop, such as persuading the suspect to cooperate in a controlled delivery of his contraband or seizing property for possible legal forfeiture. But remember: *All* these goals are *always* secondary to your safety. That must be the most important aspect of any Criminal Patrol stop. *No amount of contraband and no arrest is worth your life.*

5. What equipment or assistance do I need to accomplish these goals? The tools for investigation and control most often left behind and then regretted are your flashlight and your baton. If you've detected early indicators of a possible contraband situation, consider getting K-9 started toward the scene, if it's available. Also get backup en route— an absolute if more than one occupant is visible. Know how far away your nearest backup is, even if he or she is from a different jurisdiction. Once most officers become involved with the driver, they tend to forget about other occupants within about thirty seconds. This is where problems often start. At any point the situation appears threatening, seek cover and don't proceed further until help arrives.

A sixth question on this checklist should be carefully considered after you complete each stop: *What could I have done better?* Candidly critiquing yourself—and the stops you see other officers make—is an important element of improvement. Tapes from in-car video cameras make excellent teaching tools and will almost invariably reveal mistakes you didn't know you were making at the time, as well as contraband cues that you may have failed to pick up on.

In contrast to 5%er planning, the "average" officer on a traffic stop falls into the "victim rut" of rigid, "routine" approach and violator contact. He forgets—or feels immune from—the grim fact that over half of officers killed on vehicle stops die during approach and initial contact with the violator.[1] The truth is that what you may perceive as a low-risk traffic stop is always an *unknown*-risk stop going in; you don't yet know the full story of that encounter. Once you decide to initiate a stop, you should be asking yourself throughout: Are things still the same as I thought they were when this started?

One drug courier says he has been stopped occasionally for traffic violations on his dope runs, but never busted for the loads he carries. He has observed three alarming patterns common to the officers who've pulled him over:

- They never treat him as if he were armed, although he always is;
- They exhibit no real curiosity about what might be in his car;
- They seem to have a low level of awareness about ways in which they make themselves vulnerable.

He says none of the officers got hurt because he chose not to hurt them.

With these respective mind-sets, who do you think really controlled those stops? And who had the greater capacity for surprise?

To maintain the Position of Advantage over an offender who is determined to attack, given the chance, you will likely need to think

85

beyond traditional vehicle-stop tactics, just as you have to think "beyond the ticket" in order to find contraband. You need to be *unpredictable*. And that may mean frequently avoiding the standard driver-side approach for contacting the violator.

How and where you initially make contact with the violator has a lot to do with avoiding the consequences of taking a "position of disadvantage" and getting assaulted or disarmed.

Driver-Side Risks

As it's usually done, walking up on the driver side undoubtedly holds more potential bad surprises for you than for the suspect. It's the most predictable and easily detectable approach you can make, the ultimate example of your trying to adapt to the suspect rather than directing his position, and it's as potentially dangerous as it is common.

First, even with a safety lane, you risk direct exposure to traffic, statistically your greatest threat on vehicle stops.[2] Like a long and tragic roster of officers before him, a federal agent in Arizona was quizzing a suspicious motorist at what seemed like a safely designed checkpoint when he suddenly realized that a car coming from behind and apparently piloted by a drunk driver was headed right for him. Just before impact, the agent leaped as high as he could, trying to dive onto the hood of the car he was standing beside. The hurtling mass of metal still caught his right leg, broke it multiple times against the window frame, and spun him like a dervish for about twenty feet down the concrete. Remarkably, he managed to remain conscious and even to direct fellow officers in stabilizing him medically.

He considers himself fortunate, given that hundreds of officers have been killed or permanently crippled in similar accidents. It's easy to forget the extraordinary hazard of traffic by thinking that your emergency lights alone make you safe. They don't. Drunks, in fact, may see your lights and aim right toward them. Other motorists may pass by at frightening speeds. Many drivers operate in Condition White—with the radio on, their heads in the clouds, and their minds on everything but their driving skills.

Moreover, a committed suspect is probably anticipating that you'll make your contact with him on the driver side; that's how he has

seen virtually every cop on TV and on the street do it. By watching his face in his rearview mirror, you may be able to read signs of fear, panic, or over-interest that would alert you to danger. But this is chancy at best and may be impossible at night. If he does launch an attack or suddenly exit the vehicle after you've passed his rear bumper, you may be forced to retreat into open territory and perhaps into traffic.

Considering that over 200,000,000 firearms are in circulation in this country,[3] it stands to reason that many occupants of vehicles you stop are armed, particularly those engaged in illegal activities. In fact, says a city officer from North Carolina, "I'm at the point where I assume almost everyone I contact is armed." Just because you haven't seen any furtive movements before starting your approach does not mean that the driver or other occupant hasn't already accessed a weapon and now has it ready and waiting for you. He doesn't have to see the color of your eyes to hurt you; he just has to know where you are or accurately anticipate where you're going to be.

No Guns? No Way!

A team of officers in New York City watched two twenty-two-year-old males enter a known drug house, emerge a few minutes later with a shopping bag, and drive off in a Pontiac Grand Prix. The officers pulled them over and quickly discovered five kilos of coke in the bag, but no weapons.

"Unarmed?" exclaimed their cap-tain, back at the precinct station. "Carrying $100,000 worth of cocaine with no weapons to protect it? No way!"

The second time around, the officers searched in less-than-obvious places—and found two electronically operated hatches built into the car above the back-seat armrests. Inside were $18,500 cash, a 9mm machine pistol, a .357 Magnum, and enough ammunition to assure that the suspects were "ready for anything" if they decided to shoot it out with rival dealers or the police.

Drugs and guns are a common combination you need to consider as you plan your tactics for making contact.

When a suspect and a gun are inside a vehicle and you are outside, the element of surprise can work strongly in his favor. Not only does the vehicle's interior afford numerous hiding places for weapons, but also its structure often blocks your view of what's in his hand, in his lap, under his thigh, or tucked behind his hip until you are well into his immediate kill zone. Even if you pause at the back window to scan the interior, you may not see as much as you need to. His right hand, the one likeliest to produce a weapon, is the one farther from you as you approach the driver's door, and if it comes up and toward you with a gun, the threat may be difficult to recognize and probably difficult to control. The hand may even be empty the first couple of times you see it, tempting you to become lax.

Some courier hideouts require only the subtlest movements to retrieve or activate weapons. Consider the possibilities seen here:

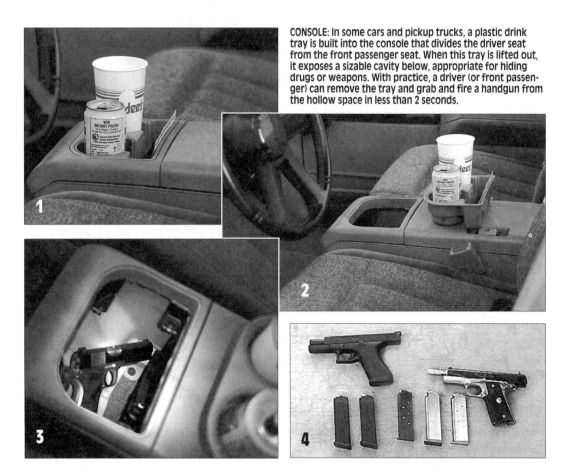

CONSOLE: In some cars and pickup trucks, a plastic drink tray is built into the console that divides the driver seat from the front passenger seat. When this tray is lifted out, it exposes a sizable cavity below, appropriate for hiding drugs or weapons. With practice, a driver (or front passenger) can remove the tray and grab and fire a handgun from the hollow space in less than 2 seconds.

STEERING WHEEL: At least one company commercially manufactures a kit that permits a driver to replace the factory-made horn cover on some car models with a hollowed-out version where a semiauto and an extra magazine can be secreted. The fake cover, identical in appearance to the legitimate one, can be pulled off with one hand and the gun grabbed with the other in lightning speed. Similarly, some couriers are removing air bags and placing guns in those compartments.

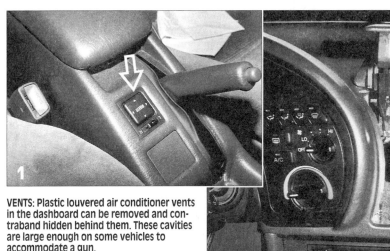

VENTS: Plastic louvered air conditioner vents in the dashboard can be removed and contraband hidden behind them. These cavities are large enough on some vehicles to accommodate a gun.

The offender in this car prepared himself to greet officers on driver-side approaches. When the mirror button is pushed, a vent grille pops open, revealing a hidden compartment where a gun is concealed.

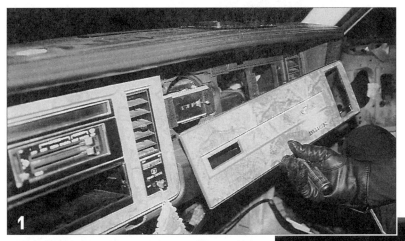

DASHBOARD: Traffickers will take out a portion of the front dash and apply Velcro strips to the back, allowing quick removal of the panel and access to hidden guns or drugs.

GLOVEBOX: Still one of the most popular and accessible hiding places for guns and edged weapons.

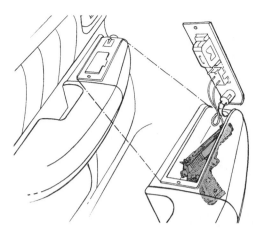

ARMREST: In some models, the metal plate that holds the window- and door-lock controls on top of the arm-rest can be removed to access a hollow core big enough to hold a short-bar-reled revolver or semiauto. If the plate is laid back in place but not screwed down, it can easily be knocked aside for a fast draw.

SPEAKERS: A drug transport group in Michigan carried 9mm Berettas and SIG SAUERs inside speaker wells in the driver doors of its vehicles. They were wired so the driver just hit a switch, the speaker cover flipped down, and a gun was then available in a holster mounted at the back of the speaker.

This maneuver could not be seen by an approaching officer.

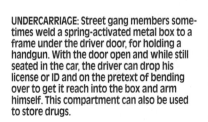

UNDERCARRIAGE: Some dope runners in urban areas have installed a spring-loaded, 4-ft. steel bar under the driver door on their vehicles. When an officer stands directly opposite the door, the driver can pull a metal pin out of the floorboard to release the steel bar. It then flies out and hits the officer, potentially breaking his or her ankle(s) or leg(s).

UNDERCARRIAGE: Street gang members some-times weld a spring-activated metal box to a frame under the driver door, for holding a handgun. With the door open and while still seated in the car, the driver can drop his license or ID and on the pretext of bending over to get it reach into the box and arm himself. This compartment can also be used to store drugs.

Voluntary Victims

Despite extensive reinforcement by academies, in-service training, and independent instructors to use good survival tactics in approaching vehicles, probably the positioning most often used for driver-side contacts is the worst: where an officer stands directly outside the driver's window to examine documents and engage in dialogue.

The enormous risk of this mindless deployment was illustrated by two tragic incidents just a month apart.

First in Texas, an eighteen-year veteran trooper stopped a car one evening for operating with only one head-light. Unknown to the trooper, the eighteen-year-old driver was a crack dealer on probation who had

just stolen a 9mm pistol from his mother's house. The trooper called in the stop, but then proceeded with his approach before getting the NCIC response, which would have warned him that the car was hot. He moved past the center doorpost and stopped directly opposite the driver, making himself a straight-on target.

Apparently at the last second he saw the suspect holding the stolen pistol by his chest. A hollow-point round tore through the trooper's hand as he raised it in futile defense, and struck his trachea, severing it. He died three days later.

Just 24 days after that during the morning rush hour in Atlanta, two officers stopped a traffic violator whose car had heavily tinted

windows and a Florida tag. One officer took a "cover" position at the rear of the suspect vehicle, but he couldn't see inside because of the dark glass. His partner walked up first on the passenger side, then, frustrated by the smoked windows, circled around the front of the car and stopped at the driver's open window. Behind the wheel was a fifteen-year-old criminal who had once threatened to kill a cop. Before the officer could speak, the juvenile fired a .38 and hit him in the temple. The cover officer fired five blind shots through the back window and killed the driver. But by then his partner was already dead.

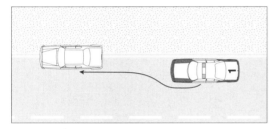

Failing to stand slightly to the rear of the center doorpost leaves you vulnerable to being knocked off-balance—or shot—in a surprise attack.

Trying to reduce the dual risks of traffic and surprise attack, officers and trainers have sought to improve on the standard approach for driver-side contact. One suggestion: At night as you walk from your car, turn on your flashlight, hold it in your nongun hand at the side of your leg with the beam shining behind you, and quickly shake it back and forth, aiming it toward traffic approaching from your rear. This movement serves as a sign to passing cars that you're out of your vehicle. When you get near the violator's car, you can aim the light into the driver's window.

Also officers have worked to improve on the standard positioning for contact at the driver side. This is where you stand just to the rear of the left center doorpost with your body bladed parallel to the car. This positioning has traditionally been favored because to target you, the driver will probably have to reach his gun hand up and out, giving you some time to react, either with disarming or distracting moves or by dropping down to create more lag time for him and more response time for you. Also from this location you can glance into the vehicle and follow his hand to the glove box if he has to reach there for documents, using your flashlight to illuminate his movement if it's dark.

One modification some officers like is to initially establish contact with the driver at this doorpost location. Then after an assessment there, when you're comfortable with the circumstances and can see that there's nothing threatening in his hands or inside the glove box,

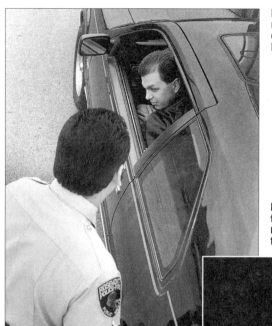

Behind the doorpost parallel to the car, you're in the spot most awkward for the driver to attack during a driver-side contact. Avoid the temptation to move up directly opposite his window.

Motorists are being checked at a roadblock in an attempt to find 3 maximum-security prison escapees. Considering the risks of a driver-side approach, what's wrong with this positioning?

One risk of driver-side positioning is the tendency to creep out into the roadway as the stop progresses. This not only makes you an easier target for the occupants, but also exposes you more to traffic hazards coming from the rear.

There are tradeoffs to almost every tactic. This positioning affords a better view of the driver's hands and oncoming traffic, but you present a far more direct target to the driver, as well.

move to the front of his door by the windshield post. Turn to face him and traffic, and continue dialogue from that vantage point. In this position you can keep a visual on activity in the front seat, plus you can better see what's coming toward you on the street or road. If you decide to direct the driver to get out, you can use his door as a barrier once it's opened, and you're positioned to follow him from behind to wherever you want him to go. The significant downside risk of wind-shield-post positioning, of course, is that you could be in a kill zone for him or a front passenger while they're seated in the vehicle if, during a moment when you're distracted, they do manage to access a hidden gun. In the dark, especially, you may miss such aggressive movement. And if you shortcut this tactic by going straight to the windshield post without pausing to assess things at the doorpost, you increase your vulnerability even more.

An option which can work at night, if traffic and street lighting are at a minimum, is practiced by a veteran suburban sergeant and FTO in Ohio. He lines up the center of his unit with the left taillight of the suspect vehicle, parks about ten to fifteen feet back, and immediately turns off his headlights upon stopping. He keeps his light bar on and aims his spotlight at the driver's side mirror, angled in slightly toward the driver. He exits without slamming his door and does not use his flashlight, to promote undetected movement. Quietly approaching the violator vehicle, he stays outside the spotlight beam (alert for traffic risks, of course); with the headlights off, he's not silhouetted. Blinded by the light in the mirror, the driver can't track his approach, but the officer can see better because his night vision is not affected by his headlight beams bouncing off the bumper and trunk of the violator car, as they do on a conventional stop. "On numerous occasions," he says, "I've gotten right up by the suspect's door and watched him for awhile trying to find me in his mirrors, without me being noticed. When I finally activate my flashlight and speak, people are startled."

Even when you take a proper position on the driver side, the violator may suprise you with a gun. Skill at disarming is crucial in how you respond to an imminent threat. Pictured here are two of the many response options worth practicing and having confidence in:

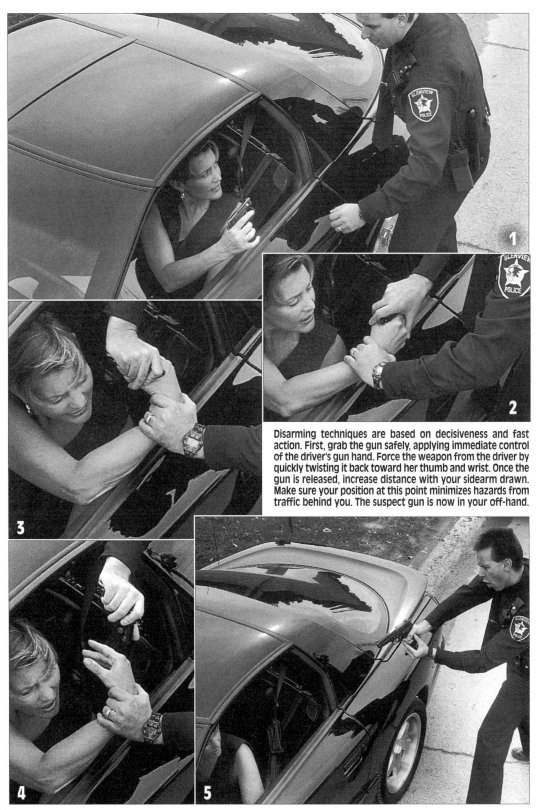

Disarming techniques are based on decisiveness and fast action. First, grab the gun safely, applying immediate control of the driver's gun hand. Force the weapon from the driver by quickly twisting it back toward her thumb and wrist. Once the gun is released, increase distance with your sidearm drawn. Make sure your position at this point minimizes hazards from traffic behind you. The suspect gun is now in your off-hand.

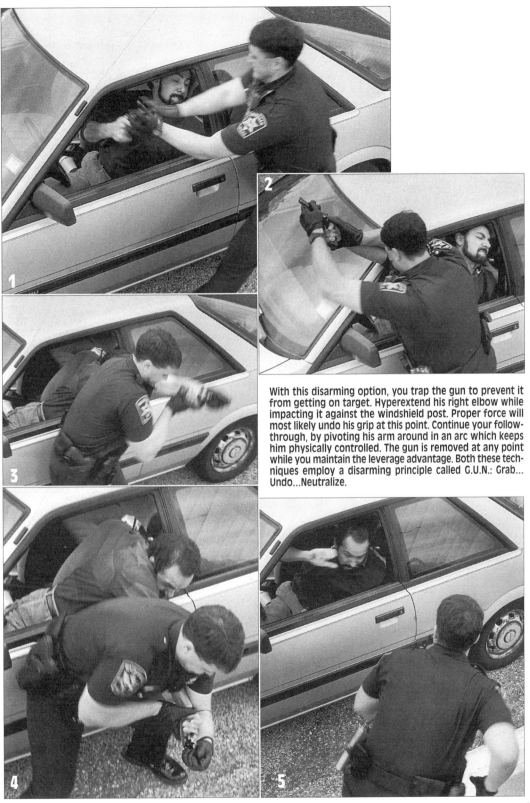

With this disarming option, you trap the gun to prevent it from getting on target. Hyperextend his right elbow while impacting it against the windshield post. Proper force will most likely undo his grip at this point. Continue your follow-through, by pivoting his arm around in an arc which keeps him physically controlled. The gun is removed at any point while you maintain the leverage advantage. Both these techniques employ a disarming principle called G.U.N.: Grab... Undo...Neutralize.

Some officers try to reduce their lag time by having a surprise weapon of their own at the ready. A Midwestern trooper, for instance, carries a .38 snub-nose in his right-rear pocket as a backup gun. As he approaches a vehicle, he tucks his right index finger down into the pocket across the trigger guard and tugs the butt out enough with his thumb that the hammer is clear. The rest of his hand conceals the weapon. When he stops just short of the driver's door to initiate dialogue, he appears from the subject's perspective merely to have his hand resting casually on his hip, maybe to support a sore lower back—

less high profile than keeping his hand on his regulation sidearm.

In Pennsylvania a sergeant rigged up a beeper shell as a camouflaged holster. Besides hiding a five-shot derringer inside, he installed electronic components that enable him to surreptitiously cause the unit to sound off loudly like a real pager. If he starts to get nervous about a contact, he discreetly activates the sound, then grips the "pager" as if turning it off. With a fast twist, it's off his belt, his hand is on a lever trigger that protrudes from the case, and he can shoot before the suspect realizes what has happened.

"Pager" used by the Pennsylvania sergeant.

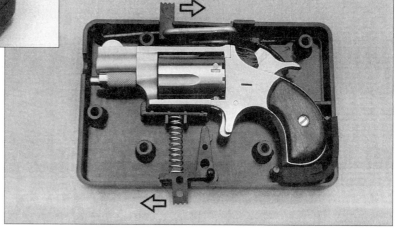

Some officers who work with K-9 use the dog for a psychological edge by having it "speak" when they begin a driver-side approach. This reinforces the K-9's presence and may intimidate suspects.

Or, if you have a human partner, you may have your fellow officer covering the passenger side of the vehicle while you move up on the driver side. Often the second officer stands by the right-rear fender of the suspect car where it's difficult for anyone inside to attack. But there his view of the occupants—and thus his ability to warn you of hazards—is extremely limited. He'll see better if he moves forward and flanks out to the right, hopefully to cover. There he can get a good look into the front seat, at the occupants' hands and laps, while still not advancing past the doorpost, and the two of you have a good triangulation of fire if trouble develops. (Of course, if there are back-seat passengers, he won't want to move in front of them unless he can be protected by cover.)

There's no doubt that a left-side approach is generally the most efficient method of contacting the driver, and sometimes it's necessary. If you need to escort an impaired or confused driver to protect him from wandering into traffic or if you must physically extract a subject, you'll normally need to be at his door to do it. Also on some one-way thoroughfares, the passenger side may expose you to traffic, or occasionally there may be special environmental or situational hazards that make the driver side more protected.

But generally speaking, it's one of the most dangerous places to be on a vehicle stop, especially at night, when you're working alone, when there is more than one person in the suspect car, or when you have early indications that you may be about to make contact with Mr. Wrong. With rare exception, other deployment will more reliably establish you in a Position of Advantage.

Passenger-Side Edge

A Maryland officer came to appreciate one viable alternative to a driver-side approach after he stopped a car carrying four males one night. He sensed that he might be walking up to a carload of trouble, so instead of heading directly for the driver door as he usually did, he opted for the approach on their passenger side. It was the best tactical choice of his career.

As he quietly moved up on their right, he could see that the suspects were all looking to their *left*, expecting him to come up that way. The left-rear passenger was leaning way back in his seat. The one on the right-rear was perched forward. He was wearing surgical gloves—and gripping a .45.

These guys were on their way to a drug transaction—and, they admitted later, they were planning to kill the officer for interfering...until his use of surprise proved better than theirs.

Your approaching on the right is so rarely anticipated that it usually catches occupants completely off-guard. It allows you to concentrate better without the distraction and danger of traffic, affords you a superior visual inside the car, and usually gives you extra time before your location is detected to size up what you're dealing with. It also provides you the mass of the vehicle as something of a cover barrier against ambushes from tail cars. In fact, one Connecticut academy trainer states emphatically: "Officers should prefer a right-side approach unless there is some specific and important reason to do otherwise."[4]

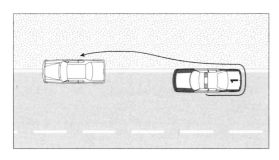

Passenger-side approach usually gives you the advantage of surprise because the violator assumes you will approach on the driver side.

The passenger-side approach works best at night, when your lights bouncing off rearview mirrors will severely limit the occupants' ability to see back. Even in daylight, though, lights on mirrors can have a distinct effect. But in daylight, you'll probably be more dependent on moving discreetly and capitalizing on the nervous distraction that motorists generally experience in the early stages of a stop.

If you're alone, probably your safest and most reliable option is to circle around the rear of your car and begin moving forward from there. That gives you more distance, cover, and concealment than you'll have cutting between the cars and reduces the risk of being crushed if the violator suddenly backs up or your unit gets rammed from the rear. Also you won't be silhouetted at night by your headlights.

Note: Some violators may reposition mirrors to try to track your movements. At night, some may step on brake lights in an effort to illuminate you. Brake lights being on may also mean that the driver has now shifted gears, creating potential for him to back up suddenly or speed away as you get closer.

When you reach the rear of the suspect vehicle's passenger side, pause a moment. This gives you a chance in darkness to "readjust" your night vision and to scope out the interior from a new angle. If you see the driver appearing to be reaching for a license or registration, wait until he has completed his movement before continuing to close the gap between you.

At the right rear you can also check the trunk lid as precaution against a hidden suspect waiting in the trunk to ambush you. Running your fingers across the crack will tell you if the lid's ajar but won't give away your position by rocking the car like pushing down or lifting up on the lid may. If the lid feels ajar, then instantly push down hard. Don't pull up; the last thing you want is to raise the lid when someone is hiding under it, quite likely armed. Back off immediately to cover, get your gun out, get backup, and convert to a high-risk stop. If the lid's okay, some officers like to press their open hand *gently* against the surface before moving on. This leaves your print on the car for identification if things go sour later and the driver flees.

If any passengers are in the back seat, don't advance past the rear-door crack, even if they appear asleep. (This applies on a driver-side approach, as well.) The driver can pass his license back to you via the passengers. If the back seat is clear, move up to a point just behind the front door. Here, with your flashlight, you can see into the glove box if the driver opens it to find his registration or insurance card, and you'll get a good view of the area around his feet, something that's tough to see fully from the left side. When the driver leans across the front seat to open the passenger door or roll down the window to hand you his papers, you may be able to visually pat down at least part of his waistband. In this "yoga-stretch," he's at a decided physical disadvantage. Also the driver will probably have already rolled down the window on his side, anticipating your approach there. When he now opens the passenger door or lowers that window, it creates a draft through the car that will help you smell marijuana or other aromatic indicators that might be inside.

While the driver and passengers generally see less of you as you're walking up on a right-side approach, you tend to see more of them. In what proved to be a startling experiment, a tactics trainer with the Los Angeles Police Department instructed 100 patrol and motor offi

(far left)
When the driver stretches to hand you his license on the passenger side, you may be able to visually pat down his waistband. Your hand kept close to your sidearm will be blocked from his view.

(left)
When a passenger is present, he or she can hand you papers. Stay where occupants have to move awkwardly to reach you.

With 2-door cars especially, you can converse with the driver from the passenger side, while still maintaining limited cover and a higher degree of concealment.

cers to make a conventional driver-side approach during a vehicle-stop exercise. Unknown to them, a role-player was lying face up on the back seat with a gun in his hand. This man was big—6'4", 235 pounds. Yet 96% of the officers approaching on the driver side never noticed this suspect as they walked by. They apparently were so habitually focused on reaching a position by the driver door where they could establish contact and on looking for the driver's hands that they did not even glance into the back seat. By contrast, fifty other officers were told to make a passenger-side approach. They were given no hint about the hidden suspect. Yet all of these officers detected the gunman lying in wait before passing beyond the rear passenger compartment! Even if they concentrated on the driver and watched for his hands on the steering wheel, their line of vision was more likely to cross the supine suspect from the passenger-side angle.

If someone inside the vehicle does draw a gun and tries to fire on you, a passenger-side position should help protect you, assuming you're not standing full-view in the front passenger window. First, the assailant will have to turn around to locate you and swing his arm over the seatback to get on target, signaling his intent. About 90% of the population is right-handed, and it will be awkward for a right-handed assailant to shoot quickly at a rear angle toward the right side of the vehicle. Attackers are far less accurate in hitting targets from this position, generally pulling the shot high and to the left or striking the center doorpost. If you've stayed close to the side of the car, you can immediately drop down out of sight below window level the moment you perceive a threat and can move anywhere around the vehicle. You're likely to have more options here under fire than on the driver side. Even if you're hit, you won't have to fear falling back into traffic as you would on the left side. Although not a guarantee, the body of the car also may provide you some cover against subsequent rounds.

In a two-officer unit, your passenger partner is the logical one to approach, since he's already on that side. As he advances, he leaves his door open. As the driver officer, you come around the rear of the patrol car and take position behind his door where you can be clear of traffic, watch the occupants ahead, and provide extra security. By staying back, you keep your field of vision wide enough to see the big picture. Also you are near the best radio at the scene (portable mikes are not always reliable) and probably your heaviest firepower, the shotgun or patrol rifle. If better cover is nearby that allows you to safely monitor your partner and the suspect vehicle, use that.

One option for 2-officer deployment. Officer who stays behind can flank out to cover, if available, for maximum surprise and protection. At night especially offender may be fooled about officers' locations.

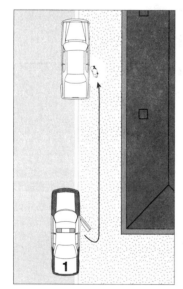 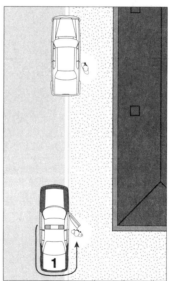 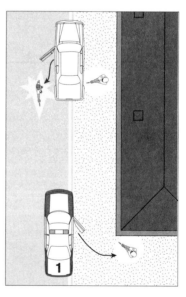

Approaching on the passenger side will often better position you for spotting contraband, as well as danger signs. Occupants expecting the usual driver-side contact will often toss drugs or other evidence out of passenger windows, or passengers may hold or try to conceal illicit goods inside the car, thinking they'll be farther away from inquisitive police eyes than the driver. As a Massachusetts trooper was stopping a car for speeding, for example, he noticed the passenger twist forward as if he were stuffing something on the right side of his seat. The trooper made a right-side approach and knocked on the passenger's window. Startled, the suspect quickly opened the door. The trooper spotted a small leather object lying on the floor. Thinking it a holster, he grabbed it and slammed the door shut. "Put your hands on the dash

100

where I can see 'em!" he commanded the occupants. He then realized that the item he'd snatched was not a holster but a small pouch, partially opened. Inside he could see and smell marijuana. Before that stop was over, the officer had found pot, other drugs, and assorted drug paraphernalia several places in the car and had recovered from the trunk a duffel bag crammed with $168,000 in drug money.

Once the driver perceives that you're on the passenger side, watch his first response. Often suspects will glance at the spot where they've placed contraband to double check that it's hidden from view when they realize that you can now look inside from a different angle than they anticipated. Ask the driver to turn his dome light on. This will better illuminate him, other occupant(s), possible weapons, and any contraband in plain view, as well as test his cooperation.

A Haunting Question of Tactics

Michael Hartmann, a trooper with a Criminal Patrol team in southern Illinois, usually makes a passenger-side approach. He doesn't know why he didn't when he stopped a pickup driver one dreary morning in January. The question still haunts him.

Hartmann had pulled the Chevy truck over after spotting it tailgating a semitrailer at 10 mph under the limit. Early indicators abounded. The pickup's Virginia plates checked out to a Dodge. The driver, a long-haired, bushy-bearded biker type, wouldn't immediately submit to the trooper's red lights. He crept along at 20 mph and eventually exited the highway to a secondary road before finally pulling abruptly to a stop on the shoulder. He and his female passenger seemed unusually nervous... "jumping around, acting fishy."

For reasons he still "can't figure out," Hartmann changed his usual practice and went up on the driver side. "I got to the tailgate," he recalls, "and I saw the driver's door crack open about half an inch like he was going to come out and meet me. I didn't say anything because he closed it right away. When I was right next to the back tire, he opened the door again. He brought his right hand around. His feet never left the controls. I remember thinking that with that salt-and-pepper beard he looked just like a raccoon. Then I looked down and saw the gun."

He felt a round slam into him "like somebody jabbed me in the ribs. I thought, 'Aw, shit, I'm hit.' I turned and automatically ran between the vehicles to take cover by the passenger side. Somewhere in there I drew my gun and spun around and fired." His first round missed, but he forced himself to slow down and aim. "The second shot hit him right square in the back of the head. His hair puffed up and he slumped forward."

At first, Hartmann thought his vest had stopped the suspect's bullet, but the slug had glanced off the edge. Through the gap between panels, it had torn into the right side of his chest and bored down to his abdomen, partially collapsing his right lung. Bleeding, fighting for breath, Hartmann called for help.

The next minutes were a blur of action. The truck, apparently kicked out of gear during the shoot-out, rolled into the ditch and nearly crashed into a telephone pole.... The female passenger jumped out with a baby bundled in her arms and hysterically started to flee. "I would have shot her," Hartmann says. "I wouldn't have had any trouble with that." But she stopped and sat down when he yelled at her.... He discovered that his backup gun was missing from his ankle holster. Evidently it had bounced out when he was running for his life. Fearing the consequences of a loose gun at the scene, he scrambled around

searching until he found it.... Backup arrived and paramedics started treating Hartmann.... Meanwhile, the head-shot suspect revived and tried to spin the truck out of the ditch. Officers drew down on him. He began haltingly to step out of the cab, then retreated back inside. Twenty seconds later, he put the gun to his head and pulled the trigger. His head lurched back and shattered the back window. Then he pitched forward, dead at last.

The suspect was an ex-con crack-cocaine addict who pulled armed robberies and burglaries to support his habit. He and his girlfriend had been criss-crossing the country from Virginia to California and back to Illinois on a violent crime spree. In the process, the girlfriend had borne the baby and the suspect had murdered three people, including his own brother and sister-in-law. He'd promised his friends, "If the cops ever stop me, we're going to hold court right there." Later the girlfriend testified that the attacker had smoked crack the morning of the shoot-out.

Hartmann has recovered from his wound. In the months since then, he has played that fateful day over and over in his mind. About the only unanswered question that still nags him is why he broke from his usual pattern and approached a suspicious vehicle on the driver side.[5]

Despite its strengths, the passenger-side approach is not a cure-all. Do not attempt to push it beyond its intended purpose. Recognize and accept that *it is not a substitute for high-risk stop tactics when threats to your safety are known or when you know you are dealing with criminal suspects* before you start an approach.

A corporal for a municipal department in Michigan saw a van with South Carolina plates blow a red light. He pulled it over. Approaching the rear doors, he peeked into one of the bubble windows—and puckered so hard he nearly sucked his uniform off.

The driver's right arm was reached behind his seat, holding a handgun. The passenger was squatting behind the other seat with a shotgun across his lap. Both were concentrating with deadly intensity on the driver's window.

The corporal hurried back to his patrol car and called for backup, which was far away. He was advised to wait. But then an off-duty officer from a nearby city pulled up and offered help. Contrary to procedures for high-risk stops, the two decided to approach the van, rather than command the occupants out one at a time with their hands up and order them back to a position where they could be controlled, cuffed, and searched, while the officers remained behind cover.

Instead, the officers chose to sneak up on the passenger side. Fortunately, the suspects were still riveted on the driver's window. The corporal yanked open the passenger door, reached around the seat, and jerked the shotgun man out from behind it "before he had a chance to even think about using the gun." When the door flew open, the driver was so startled he dropped his weapon. Other guns and a horde of ammunition were stashed in the van, the officers discovered, and the two suspects were wanted in the South for armed robbery.

Later the corporal boasted that his passenger-side approach "saved" him and his fellow officer. In a sense, yes. But more accurately, they were saved by incredible good fortune. Their macho impulse to rush up to the action and immediately do something brought them within a hair's breadth of disaster. What turned out to be a dramatic arrest of dangerous criminals could just as easily have been an officer bloodbath.

Investigative Positioning

The U.S. Supreme Court has noted "the inordinate risk confronting an officer as he approaches a person seated in an automobile" and has ruled that you can *routinely* order the driver *out* of his vehicle and direct him to a nearby location on any lawful stop.[6] A reasonable, generalized concern for your safety is all you need. That can come from the fact that traffic poses a hazard if you approach or that any seated driver is, in fact, half concealed and therefore a potential danger. You do not have to articulate a suspicion that criminal activity is afoot, nor do you need specific grounds for fearing that the driver is a threat.

In seeking the best Position of Advantage, you can make full use of this ruling by directing the driver to meet you at the curb or roadside for your initial contact—away from traffic, away from weapons that may be hidden in the car, away from other occupants who could be coconspirators in illegal activity, away from surprises he may have planned. The new location becomes your base of operations for assessing the driver, for launching a controlled approach to the car later to visually pat down its interior, and for questioning and evaluating passengers. Here, isolated from the comfort of a familiar, sheltered setting inside the vehicle and the psychological support of traveling companions, a subject is likely to be under less pressure to save face in front of friends or relatives and may ultimately be more truth ful. In any case, you are directing him out of an environment he controls—his vehicle—and forcing him to adapt to an environment you control—the street.

Properly executed, this deployment not only reasonably accommodates the principles of good positioning—use of distance and barriers, visual monitoring, protected movement, and physical domination—but also can aid your development of suspicion about contraband, as you employ the special interviewing and observational techniques we'll describe in subsequent chapters. Generally, this tactic provides you better protection than a driver-side approach and it incorporates many of the advantages of going up on the passenger side, plus some others as well.

This "investigative positioning" is particularly appropriate anytime you are dealing with vehicles that are difficult to see into, such as vans and panel trucks, cars with tinted windows, or semitrailers or other carriers with raised cabs...vehicles with additional occupants besides the driver...or "Stop Me" vehicles that radiate early-warning cues or possible contraband characteristics. However, it does require that you know how to control an ambulatory subject and defend yourself against physical assault, the same as with any field-interview contact.

Think of the movement necessary to reach the investigative position you have in mind as consisting of three blended tactical phases:

1. Mutual exit. If the driver exits his vehicle impromptu and heads back toward your unit, instruct him to pass quickly in front of your patrol car and meet you at the side. *Don't instruct him to get back into his vehicle.* That only re-introduces him to a largely concealed environment where weapons may be hidden and where he may be able to confer with visible or hidden companions to formulate a plan.

Ideally, you'll be on your feet out of your unit *before* the violator exits, giving yourself the best chance for drawing and shooting easily if you have to. If he's out first, he can run back to you in about a second and a half, possibly trapping you behind the steering wheel. If he does beat you out, put your squad in reverse and back up. Direct him through your open window or PA to the roadside and wait for compliance before taking your foot off the brake and shifting to "Park."

If you are out first, stand behind your door as something of a barrier. Opening the door only to the first notch lets you slide up right behind it but keeps you close to your car and lessens the chance of your stepping into traffic. Command the driver, by PA if necessary, to

As you exit, pause momentarily and observe the driver's demeanor. Your open door gives you limited cover before you circle behind your patrol car, as he crosses between cars to meet you.

That momentary pause before you move does not mean multiple officers clustering behind your door for a sustained period of time. This civilian vehicle contains 5 Skinheads and numerous guns.

get out and come back toward you. Order him to exit as quickly as it's safe to do so. As part of your strategy, you usually won't want him to have time to collect all his identification papers or, of course, to arm himself. If it's night or he has tinted windows, tell him to turn on his dome light before he exits, to better illuminate the interior. If you've off-set to the left, the safety lane should protect him as he walks.

As he exits, watch for items that may fall fom his lap or that he may try to drop under the car. These may be drugs, drug paraphernalia, or other evidence. If he's wearing a beeper or a fanny pack, tell him to keep his hands away from it. Versions of both these items that conceal guns inside are widely available commercially. One beeper "holster," for instance, allows an assailant with a quick flick of his wrist to fire a .22-cal. mini-revolver from inside the case by moving just two levers, one to cock the hammer and one to push the trigger. Other versions shoot 9mm or .357 rounds at the push of a button, as if the suspect were moving to retrieve a phone number. If the

A real beeper that has been converted to shoot at the push of a button.

beeper is really a beeper, the subject may be reaching for it to turn it off. This could be a contraband cue; legitimate motorists generally don't turn off their beepers during a traffic stop.

If the driver emerges with a briefcase, purse, or day-planner in hand, command him or her immediately to put it back in the car or set it down on the pavement and move forward. If he wants it with him, you *don't* want it with him. Briefcases are often used to carry money for drug deals, but can also be used as blunt instruments; plus some are designed so a MAC-11 with sound suppressor and full-auto capability can be mounted inside and fired through a hole in the end just by tripping a lever on the bottom. On some drug runs, briefcases have also been used to carry pipe bombs, as well as loose handguns. Innocent-looking purses have been designed with built-in shotguns hidden inside, and street gangs often conceal semiautos inside personal-organizer cases.

104

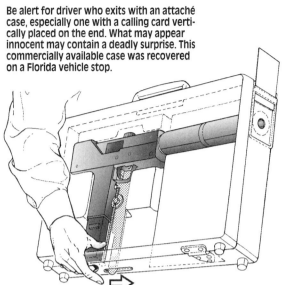

Be alert for driver who exits with an attaché case, especially one with a calling card vertically placed on the end. What may appear innocent may contain a deadly surprise. This commercially available case was recovered on a Florida vehicle stop.

Trigger is activated by moving the index finger forward. Vertical rod then presses against the trigger of the MAC-11 inside. On full-auto this can be a devastating weapon. A MAC-11 fires 1,200 rpm.

Here's a good "what–if" moment. When the driver exits and starts back, you tell him to take his hands out of his pockets. He responds with disregard and taunting. What do you do?

(right)
Act immediately. Move from your door to better cover, draw your gun, and call backup. Trying to argue him into compliance without adequate protection leaves you vulnerable to his sudden moves.

Keep occupants other than the driver in the car for now. If you try to deal with two or three people out at once, then you'll have four to six arms and legs to overcome if a fight develops; that's like wrestling an octopus. Keep it one-on-one. If passengers get out, order them back in. Draw your gun to reinforce your commands if you feel threatened and if verbal commands alone don't win compliance.

2. Mutual movement. As the driver heads back, be sure his hands are visible, check his clothing for bulges, and watch for other indicators of concealed weapons as he walks. Getting out of a car, a subject with a gun in his waistband (where 90% of concealed weapons are carried[7]) may automatically reach to that spot and readjust the weapon from outside his outer clothing. You may notice that his shirttail is out, or he may have discordant clothes because an inappropriate sweater or jacket is worn to conceal a firearm. When he walks, the leg on the gun side often takes a slightly shorter stride and that arm a shorter swing because it tends to stay close to the body, instinctively guarding the weapon. He may pull up his pants because the weight of a gun is pulling them down. Or he may bump his foot against the opposite ankle, tapping an ankle holster or knife sheath. When you start talking to the violator, he may touch his weapon from time to time with his elbow, forearm, or hand (a "security feel") or glance at where it's hidden ("security peek") to be sure it's still concealed. He'll also most likely turn the side that the gun's on away from you, just as you do when you take an interview position. Be alert, too, for indications that the subject is wearing soft body armor.

Wait until the driver reaches his rear bumper, then suddenly direct him to the sidewalk or roadside. This unexpected instruction may momentarily divert his thinking and disrupt any plan he may be formulating, as well as helping you continue to judge his level of cooperation as an important barometer in your early threat assessment.

As the driver walks quickly between the cars toward the curb or shoulder, close your door, move around the rear of your patrol car and come up to meet him. This gives you distance and employs your unit as a barrier and limited cover while you're moving and evaluating him. En route you can also monitor his vehicle and any visible passengers without losing your visual on him.

Note: Before leaving your unit, hide your PA mike under the seat. One North Carolina deputy got into a vicious fight with a motorist he'd pulled over. A passing civilian ran to the patrol car to call for assistance—but in his ignorance of the equipment, he grabbed the PA instead of the radio mike. His frantic cries for help boomed out all around the car, but never reached the dispatcher. Leaving only one mike visible eliminates confusion if someone else needs to use it to save you.

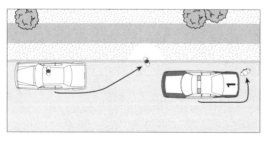

As you come around to the rear, pause. You have distance, limited cover, a good view of the driver and his vehicle—all to your advantage.

106

Deputy in Colorado meets resistance, but in this position he has the advantages of distance and some cover. Does the 22-year-old suspect have a clear target if he decides suddenly to take this officer on?

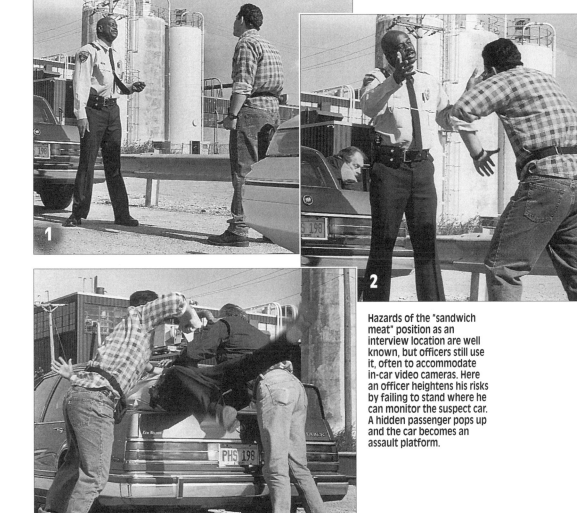

Hazards of the "sandwich meat" position as an interview location are well known, but officers still use it, often to accommodate in-car video cameras. Here an officer heightens his risks by failing to stand where he can monitor the suspect car. A hidden passenger pops up and the car becomes an assault platform.

107

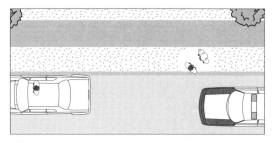

Maintain your Position of Advantage when you reach the interview site at roadside. Stand where you have a visual on the driver and his vehicle, as well as any occupants inside. Keep your hands in a ready position, and maintain proper separation, while you further assess the suspect, with your gun side away.

3. Taking position. Contact should occur near the right-front fender of your patrol car. In an urban setting, you and the suspect can stand on the sidewalk out of the street. Along a highway, if your car is off-set left, use the space directly behind his right-rear fender, exercising caution not to stand between the vehicles in the "sandwich meat" zone, where a drunk driver or tail car could crush you. If you want a little extra protection initially, open your passenger door and stand a couple of feet back from it while directing him to stand about eight to ten feet forward from it. Instruct him to stay there and remove his license. Once his hand is in the clear and you can see he's not holding a weapon, close the door and motion him forward. In any tactical encounter, you want as much as possible for the suspect to come to you, not the other way around. *Don't stay behind the door when he's close;* he can easily use it as a weapon against you. At night with your high-beams on, you and he are now behind a curtain of light from the perspective of any other occupants.

You can buy some additional reaction time by having the driver lean forward and place both hands palms-down on your hood, if you feel uneasy while talking to him. If he decides to assault, he then has to move around the fender to make contact. However, this position does create potential liability for you if your unit is rammed and he is hurt.

Some officers like to position the driver in front of their unit, while they stand at the side and instruct him to hand documents across the hood and fender. This does impose a barrier, but may create liability for you because he is between the vehicles. Some courts have held that if a motorist is injured or killed because you have directed him to stand between cars, you are responsible. You place a driver in custody when you order him to stop, therefore you owe him a "duty of care" to minimize the hazards he's exposed to.[8] You can gain some protection for the driver in this position if you turn your wheels all the way to the left before exiting your vehicle. Then if your car is struck from the rear, it will be pushed out to the left rather than straight forward. Even if the suspect isn't crushed, though, he may still be knocked down by the impact.

Some officers mistakenly believe they and the violator must stand between the cars to accommodate their in-car video cameras; in a sense, they feel they must sacrifice safety for "performance." Eventually you may gain more flexibility, because higher-tech cameras will routinely come equipped with sensors that cause the lens to follow wherever you move. But even without that feature, you can adjust for greater safety. You can widen the angle of your camera lens by positioning your car farther back from the suspect vehicle initially, perhaps ten to fifteen feet more. Before you exit, rotate the camera on its side-to-side axis so it's aimed slightly off center toward the right. Now you can conduct your dialogue where it's safer and still stay "in frame." If that's not feasible, go with just the audio portion of the recording, which usually will adequately convey the circumstances. Better to sacrifice the picture than yourself. If you move your car too far back to accommodate the video, you're just lengthening the distance you may have to run to reach the cover it provides in case you're threatened.

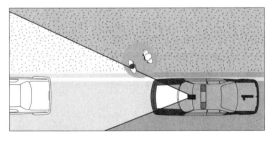 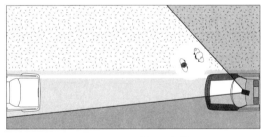

Stand so the driver is between you and his vehicle. Remain aware of what any occupants are doing. If a front passenger leans forward, he may be trying to use the right-side mirror to watch you. In some drug-smuggling operations, it's the right-front passenger who's armed. When so, an attack is most likely to occur after you reach your final position at the curb or roadside. You want anyone contemplating assault from inside the vehicle to have to shoot through the driver to hit you. It's not a guarantee, but it is a calculated edge.

As you take your stance, give the suspect some simple directives: "I need you to stand right over here, please"…"Could you move a little to your left?"…"Please just keep your back to your car and face me while I ask you a few questions," and so on. Again you're testing him. One Southern officer, when he senses that he's dealing with a punk, deliberately drops the subject's license, then tells him: "Pick that up!" to establish who's who. That's unnecessarily offensive and potentially provoca

(above left)
Typical in-car camera angle may not tape you and the driver if you are positioned with the driver safely.

(above right)
Aiming the camera slightly off-center and increasing your parking distance allows for a safe interview, as well as a desirable video recording.

tive, but by setting a few *reasonable* parameters that you expect the driver to observe, you're stringing invisible "trip wires." If he fails to respond or violates an order, it should trip a signal to you. Is it because he doesn't understand... because he's insubordinate...or because he's setting up an attack? Any time you get resistance, expand your reactionary gap (if traffic noise permits, it normally should be at least one of his leg lengths between you), seek cover, escalate your verbal commands, and be prepared to move up the force continuum until you get compliance.

Remember: You must stay in control of the stop.

Tell the driver to extinguish any smoking materials and don't let him light up again during the stop. A cigarette flicked at you can be a pre-attack distractor, plus smoke may help mask incriminating odors that you'd otherwise pick up from his presence.

Some officers who ride with K-9s like to open the dog's door at this point, but have him remain in the car. A subject who reacts uneasily about this is reassured: "The dog won't come out unless you try to hurt me or I signal him."

When you're working with a partner, he or she can flank out to the right of the suspect vehicle to monitor passengers while you deal with the driver, you can take positions similar to what you might on a domestic beef, where you can see each other (at least in peripheral vision) while keeping your primary concentration on your respective areas of responsibility.

Deployment option when working with a partner. You deal with the driver, while partner monitors passenger(s) and suspect vehicle.

With good planning and a favorable environment, you may also have been able to select a spot for the stop where you're close to cover. Trees and rocks are some of the best friends you can have in a shitstorm!

3

Passenger's hands are visible from your partner's vantage point.

You and your partner assume the "W" position just as you do when positioning complainants on a domestic. This prevents eye contact between driver and passenger, but gives you a potential triangulation of fire for both suspects.

4

Furtive movements by suspect now or earlier, bulges in his clothing, or other reasonable, articulable grounds for suspecting he's armed will allow you to pat him down for weapons at the beginning of your contact.[9] For the pat-down, have him face his vehicle while you frisk his pockets, waistband, collar, and up and down each leg from behind, crimping his clothing, pulling it tight, and squeezing his boots with your off-hand. (Be sure in your report later that you state you thought he was moving to conceal or retrieve a *weapon*, not contraband; contraband can't legally put you in fear of your safety. As we'll discuss in more detail later, furtive movements or discovery of weapons can also give you the right to make a limited search of the suspect's vehicle. A vehicle search is additionally justified if you find contraband that you immediately recognize as such during the pat-down and this leads to a custodial arrest.)

During your contact, try to keep your hands empty to the extent possible. Tuck your flashlight under your armpit on your nongun side, for example, and scan his license quickly, trying to memorize a couple of important items before tucking it into your belt while you talk to him. Under high stress, muscles constrict, and if you're attacked when something's in your hand, chances are you will hang onto it harder than ever. You want your hands free to defend yourself fully.

Occasionally officers who conduct stops at highway rest areas con front subjects who immediately say, "I have to go to the bathroom." This can be a ruse to get away from you so they can flush drugs or other evidence down the toilet. One trooper finds he can often foil this by asking, "Do you know why you have to go so bad?" "Yeah," the driver usually responds, "because I've been driving a long time." "No," says the trooper, looking him solemnly in the eye, "it's because you're about to tell me the truth about what's going on." Pause. "Now, if you still want to go, go ahead." Usually the subject stays, and dialogue begins.

Amidst the basics—obtaining his license, explaining why he was stopped—you can begin the kind of seemingly casual, friendly inquiry that tends to flush out deception and contraband cues, as described fully in Chapter 5. There's survival thinking behind telling him why you stopped him (the traffic violation, not any other suspicions) as soon as you have his license: Hearing this may convince him that you're not aware of any criminal activities and thereby increase your safety. This also gives you a chance to read his level of nervousness. Especially if you say you're going to issue just a warning, most legitimate people will calm down. If the violator's nervousness persists, wonder why.

Near the beginning, ask: "Are you traveling with any other vehicles?" and "How many people are in your car?" He may tell you about an escort car or about a hidden passenger.

During the contact, you'll have opportunity to look for potential indicators like tattoos that may suggest street- or biker-gang affiliation or past prison terms. This inmate displays multiple tattoos which show his association with the Spanish Cobra street gang of the "Folk Nation."

You can also check the driver for revealing tattoos and scars. One unique disfigurement displayed occasionally by drug runners is a "crack smile." This is a wicked, permanent scar, inflicted with a straight-edge razor or knife from the ear to the corner of the mouth, sometimes on both sides of the face and deep enough to damage nerves and cause facial paralysis. Somewhat resembling the Joker's rictus grin, this "life mark" is administered by drug dealers to low-level cocaine and heroin couriers and users—most often black males in their late teens or twenties—as punishment for nondelivery, theft of drugs or cash, or other business transgressions.

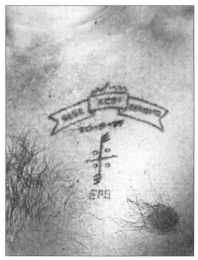

Drivers or passengers without shirts can be walking billboards of danger cues. This subject, arrested in a small town in Illinois, makes revealing statements with his "skin art." On his back (right) are symbols of the cultish Santeria religion, embraced by some drug traffickers: the Virgin, flanked by heads of Indians, above 3 men in a boat, one of them black. On his chest (far right) is another cue: the design with the intersecting lines and 4 circles symbolizes a sub-cult within Santeria called Palo Mayombe. Its hardcore criminal members are involved in drug trafficking and murder.

Controlled Approach

If the violator responded quickly to your original command to exit his vehicle, he'll probably have only his driver's license with him, so you'll now have a built-in excuse to approach his car at your discretion to get his registration and insurance card or rental agreement. (If he has everything all ready for you, be suspicious; it probably means he has been stopped before and knows the drill.)

Going to the car under controlled circumstances gives you a chance to scope out the interior and conduct the kind of potentially revealing "sensory pat-down" described in the next chapter. When you feel comfortable starting an approach, *take the driver with you* so you don't have to turn your back on him. Ask where the documents are before you start toward the car so you'll know where he should be reaching once you get there. And if you have grounds for a pat-down, conduct it before starting your approach. One Southern officer stopped a driver he thought might be a drug runner and determined at roadside that he had altered ID—clear cause for suspicion and concern. But without patting him down, the officer suggested they go to the car and get the registration. En route, the offender suddenly pulled a gun from his waistband and spun around. The officer was carrying his flashlight in his gun hand—and was shot. (Fortunately the wound was not fatal, and he made the most of a desperate situation by breaking the suspect's neck with his light!)

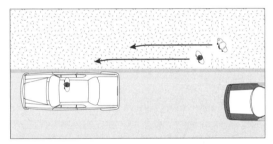
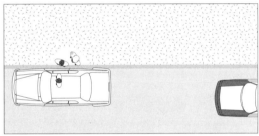

Keep the subject between you and his vehicle as you move toward it. If you haven't had legal grounds to pat him down, you may now be able to touch him lightly in a few places (like the small of his back) to feel for weapons and bulky contraband, under the guise of "guiding" him.

113

At the car, adapt your positioning to the circumstances.

1. If there are no passengers and the needed documents are somewhere other than the glove box, let the driver open the front passenger door and reach in to get them. Initially, you stand behind him. But as he's reaching, put your hand on your holstered gun for readiness and move silently around to stand *in front* of the open door. He won't be able to see this shift (role play it; you'll see) and if he comes out intending to attack you where he thinks you are (still behind his back), you won't be where he's expecting. (This same tactic will also work if you opt to have him reach into the car at the driver door, as seen below.)

2. If the documents are not in the glove box but there is a front-seat passenger, you may still want the driver to reach in from the left side of the car. Here, however, moving around surreptitiously to stand in front of the door while he's occupied may put you in the passenger's line of fire. In this situation, you're probably safer to stay behind the driver and keep him between you and the passenger as a barrier. Before the driver ducks into the car, get the passenger's hands where you can see them.

3. If the documents are in the glove box, which overwhelmingly will be the case, you are now inviting movement toward a potential high-risk location. Approach from the passenger side, but before the box is opened, position yourself where you can exert immediate phys

(left/above)
Before the driver reaches into the car, be sure you can see the passenger's hands. Don't let the driver block your view. You cannot react to hazards you cannot see.

(bottom left/below)
A safer approach is to control where the driver stands before accessing the glove box. Now you can see the passenger, the glove box as it is opened, and can react immediately to hidden surprises.

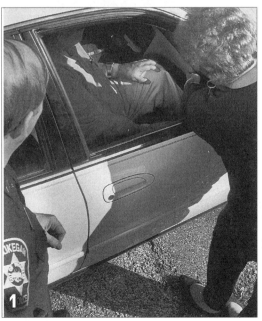

ical dominance, if necessary. One option, even if there's a passenger sitting in the front seat, is for the driver to open the vehicle door, *slowly* open the glove box, and retrieve what you need. (In some states, the driver opening the door must be *voluntary* to be legal; if you instruct him to do it, that constitutes a seizure.) With the door open, the passenger's right side is exposed to your scrutiny. Make sure his hands are where you can see them, and stand about a foot behind the driver where you can visually follow his hands. Shine your flashlight to illuminate hands and the box interior, *even in daytime.* By bobbing around a bit behind the driver, you should be able to see inside the box. This is an opportunity not only to be warned of weapons but to see contraband that may be in plain view inside.

A second option is to keep the door closed, have the passenger lower the window, then tell the driver to reach through it with his left hand to open the glove box. The closed door provides more of a barrier between you and the passenger, and it will slow him down if he becomes aggressive. Even if he gets a gun, he'll probably bring it up to window level to shoot.

Either way, it's important to use the *driver* to open the glove compartment. If you let the passenger do it, you'll be focused on his movements, and the driver may seize upon your distraction to assault you. By using the driver, you keep him occupied and you have both of them at a disadvantageous angle for targeting you. With any false move from either, shove the driver hard from behind. His body unexpectedly slamming into the passenger in the open doorway or against the car door will cause momentary disruption or immobilization, buying you time to back up, get behind the right-rear corner of the vehicle or to other cover, draw your sidearm, and assert control.

4. If there are any back-seat passengers, do *not* approach the vehicle. Trying to deploy safely against that many people when the driver is reaching into the car is too precarious. Instead, when you first instruct him to exit the vehicle, tell him to bring all the documents you're going to want with him. This means you may have to sacrifice a close-up look into the car, but you'll still have ample opportunity to develop suspicion through dialogue. If he ignores your instructions and leaves papers behind, that's a trip-wire signal. *Don't be lured up to the car.* Get backup there to help get the passengers out and positioned where they can be watched while an approach is made. Any inconvenience they may complain about is the driver's doing.

Assuming you've approached with the driver, return to your investigative positions once you've looked inside and he has retrieved the needed document(s). If you've seen incriminating evidence, you may now have grounds to arrest him and search him and the vehicle interior. Otherwise, instruct him to stay at the interview site while you run radio or computer checks. With a portable, you may be able to stand at the rear of your unit to lengthen the distance from him and stay on your feet. If you must get inside your vehicle, be sure, if you are in an urban setting, that your right-side mirror is angled to pick up any pedestrian traffic approaching from the right rear. Keep close watch on the violator and any other occupants of his car. This potentially is a very vulnerable time for you.

Passenger Positioning

In 1997, the U. S. Supreme Court ruled that the philosophy that permits you to order a driver out of his vehicle at will also permits you to order *passengers* out.[11] In the past, some courts have been more restrictive, requiring *reasonable grounds* for commanding a passenger out, because passengers are not automatically considered to be under detention to the extent that a driver is on a vehicle stop.

Even if your agency were to require reasonable grounds before you maneuver passengers, one acceptable reason certainly should be any articulable concern for your own safety. For example, a woman in Idaho touched off a pursuit when she failed to yield after committing several traffic violations. During the chase, officers saw her male passenger lean over in his seat as if retrieving a weapon. When the car finally stopped, officers ordered the occupants to get out and put their hands on the hood. The passenger refused, instead keeping his hand over a bulging pocket in his coat. Officers physically sought to control him, he fought, and after he was successfully arrested a search of the car revealed two loaded guns, drugs, and a drug ledger. The passenger's attorney protested that the officers had acted improperly. But they were found to have had a reasonable fear for their safety.[12]

Another good reason for ordering a passenger out is when suspicions about a driver's story make you feel that it is necessary to interview a passenger with privacy.

In one such case, a California municipal officer stopped a sedan with three occupants and no license plate about 3 o'clock one morning. When the driver was unable to produce even a license, the officer told him to step from the car and, after some questioning, turned him over to a backup officer on the sidewalk. He then decided to quiz the two passengers separately, one of whom was sitting in the right-rear seat, the other in front. To avoid having to put his back to the rear passenger, he ordered him out first. When this man exited, the officer saw him drop two baggies of crack cocaine. The suspect was immediately arrested and searched, and more cocaine was discovered on him. In court, the defendant's lawyer claimed that the officer exceeded his authority in commanding the passenger out. However, an appellate court ruled that the officer had a legitimate need to interview the passengers "in an effort to establish the identity of the driver." His decision to separate them was "a legitimate concern…for his own protection," the court declared.[13]

Even if you decide not to order passengers out, you should still consider talking to them, asking them for ID, and posing questions. Even if there are multiple passengers, you generally won't need to talk to more than one to develop suspicious inconsistencies with the driver's story.

In any case, ask or instruct *no more than one passenger to exit the vehicle at a time.* The driver should be physically *separated* from you and that subject, both to discourage a gang-up attack and for interview privacy.

Your options for controlling the scene now include:

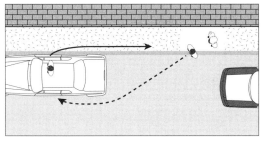

1. If you have no backup, one possibility is to let the driver go back to his car and sit inside while you call the passenger out to the investigative position. Although this prevents two people from being out and ambulatory at once, it has the strong *disadvantage* of returning the driver to a location where weapons may be hidden. Legally, you have the right to search the car's interior *before* allowing the driver to re-enter, if you have reason to believe he may have access to a weapon there (see Chapter 6). But practically speaking, the logistics of doing that by yourself with two or more subjects to manage simultaneously are likely to be more than you can safely attempt. Probably your best defense if you have the driver return to the car is to position yourself so the passenger stands as a psychological barrier between you and the driver seated inside.

2. Better, if you have a cage, is to place the driver in the back seat of your unit, after patting him down, then call the passenger out. This can be done for safety purposes without the driver being under arrest. In fact, with the right phraseology and tone of voice, it can be accomplished as a "voluntary" move on his part. Rather than directly "ordering" him into your car, say: "Sir, would you please have a seat in the back of my car while I talk to your passenger?" It's not put as a pleading question, but as a firm directive disguised as a request. Technically, he can refuse, so his compliance is consensual. Likewise, you can get his permission for a pat-down in a similar off-handed manner. (Unless you have reason to believe he is armed or dangerous, some states do not permit you automatically to pat down a subject you're placing in your patrol car,[14] except when he is under arrest. However, *you don't want anyone getting into your unit without being patted down.* If he refuses to comply with your request, that's a significant warning sign.) With the driver in your unit, you want your investigative positioning with the passenger to be far enough back beside your patrol car that you can maintain a *three-way* visual: on the *passenger* you're interviewing...the *driver* in your back seat...and the *suspect vehicle.*

3. An alternative is to direct the driver to stand at the center-front of his vehicle, while you call the passenger back to the usual investigative position at the rear. As he's walking back, you can stand behind the open passenger door of your unit while you appraise your new interviewee, then move up to meet him once you feel comfortable. Although this puts two subjects outside the car at once, an undesirable circumstance, you do have distance 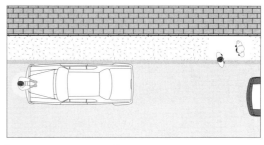 from the driver working to your advantage, and you can position the passenger between you and the driver. If the driver takes off running, you still have his ID, the car, and passenger(s), plus reason then to believe something is amiss. And if the driver moves toward you, you've got time to react. If there's a child along who's old enough to open car doors and no one else is left in the car to tend her, have the driver carry her to the front of the car so you don't have to worry about her getting out into traffic.

Note: Be aware that some criminals now affix handguns to the underside of the black vinyl "bras" that cover the fronts of some sports cars. Velcro that is glued to the gun's barrel and grips and to the bra holds the gun where it can be easily grabbed. In these circumstances, you'll want to keep subjects away from the front of a vehicle.

Also don't position *yourself* in front of a suspect vehicle so long as anyone else is inside it. Inspecting a courier car that had been confiscated along with four kilos of coke in a suburban town in upstate New York, a police mechanic discovered a small toggle switch under the dash. He flipped it. The engine started, and the car kicked into forward gear, lurched ahead, and smashed into his workbench. The device apparently had been rigged to cream an officer who passed or stood in front of the car during a vehicle stop or checkpoint inspection.

During interviewing, you may develop grounds for an arrest or become nervous about your safety. If both the driver and a passenger are outside at that point, one option is to direct the one you're interviewing at the inves-

The suspects are "propped" against the car only for the purpose of being watched. This is not a proper search position. Handcuffing should occur only when backup is present.

tigative position to face away from you, and brace his or her hands on the trunk of the suspect vehicle at the right rear. While you stand or crouch behind your open passenger door, most likely with your gun out, command the other to stand on the passenger side of the suspect vehicle and place his or her hands on the roof where you can see them. This puts both suspects in roughly the same cone of fire from your perspective. If additional passengers are inside the car, order them to keep their hands visible. Stabilize the scene until backup arrives.

Assuming the stop progresses peacefully, stay aware of your Position of Advantage when writing the citation or warning. Some officers continue to use barriers and distance, standing at the right rear of their vehicle or behind their open passenger door (or better cover, if available) for writing. You can more easily maintain your mobility and a visual on the suspect(s) there than from inside your car, where the tendency is to look down while writing in your lap.

On the other hand, inside your unit you have protection from the elements, access to communications, a means of escape, and possible concealment at night if your high-beams and spotlight are blinding the suspect(s). Writing in the front *passenger* seat of your patrol car can be confusing to the suspect and may force him into time-consuming, awkward movements to attack you. It also gives you opportunity for a fast exit to open ground and cover, without being encumbered by the steering wheel or directly exposed to traffic. Periodically look up from your paperwork directly at the driver and occupants, such as after making each entry on the ticket, to confirm that all is well.

Distance and alertness are essential if you write the citation inside your vehicle while the driver is positioned outside of his car. Consciously keeping your cite book up will keep your eyes up—and the violator in your peripheral view.

If you sit in the driver seat, write high on the steering wheel, as close to eye level as possible. Then you'll always maintain some peripheral vision of the suspects and their car. One officer noticed in his peripheral vision while writing that a female passenger was turning around and apparently pinching an infant in a rear car seat. She hoped the baby's piercing screams would hurry the officer into concluding the stop. Because he caught her, he extended the contact—and discovered a sizable quantity of drugs hidden in the vehicle. When people think you're not looking may be when they do things you're most interested in seeing.

120

After you're done writing, consider your reapproach to the driver, whether he's inside or outside his vehicle, as a fresh contact, requiring your maximum alertness for new threats as well as for contraband indicators not visible before. Do not assume that a heretofore cooperative violator will remain cooperative during your reapproach. For some subjects, a seemingly "routine" traffic citation can mean a significant change in their lives which they may wish to fight or even kill over. Consider reapproaching the car on the right-hand side and have the driver sign the cite through the passenger window. If you do approach on the driver side, don't give him your ticket book for signing. Turn the book around for him and brace it for him with your off hand, keeping your gun hand free. Give him your pen to use; one he pulls from his pocket may in fact be a disguised weapon. If he tries to use your pen against you, you can shove your ticket book in his face.

At no time during the stop, start to finish, turn your back on a driver or passenger. In moving from place to place, either walk backwards or sideways looking back to keep all subjects in view. This lesson was learned the hard way by a K-9 officer in Mississippi who stopped a car with no license plate early one winter morning. Approaching the vehicle, he noticed two VCRs on the back seat. The driver said he had no license, but knew the number. Suddenly two passengers started to exit the vehicle. The officer ordered them to stay in the car and started back toward his patrol car and his K-9 partner. As he later regretted, he turned his back to do so. Before he reached his vehicle, he was jumped from behind by one of the passengers, clutching a butcher knife. As the officer struggled with this attacker, another occupant rushed up and shot him twice in the abdomen with a .25-cal. handgun. Fortunately, his vest stopped the rounds.

Large-Truck Considerations

Tactical problems with making contact can be even more complex when you're dealing with a semitrailer, tanker truck, or other large commercial carrier. Indeed, the logistics of contacting truck drivers can be as intimidating as trying to decipher the paperwork they'll give you, and the sense that it's a no-win proposition is one reason more patrol officers (even highway patrol officers) don't even consider nailing trucks except for the most blatant, absolutely must-stop violations.

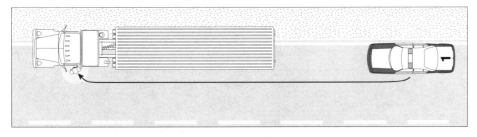

Approaching for contact on the driver side is even more dangerous with trucks than with cars. The long trailer extends your exposure to traffic and heightens your risk of becoming "road pizza." The side of the trailer can create almost the suction of a wind tunnel when vehicles whiz by at high speed, especially other 18 wheelers. You're in a danger zone all the way, but especially each time you're opposite wheels, gas tanks, or other low obstructions that would prevent you from darting or rolling under the trailer for cover or escape if the driver pops out shooting.

Poor positioning on the driver side or failing to monitor the driver in the mirror during a passenger-side approach can make you vulnerable if he exploits a truck's height and bulk to his advantage.

Coming up on the driver side, you may be able to watch the trucker's head and shoulders reflected in the side mirror as you advance, but there's little hope of seeing his lower body or inside his cab while you are standing on the ground with his door closed. Climbing up, you're vulnerable to him opening the door suddenly and smashing you, plus the narrow toeholds may be slippery, especially in inclement weather.

Among the relatively few officers who contact trucks a lot, most favor alternatives to a driver-side approach. No option is perfect; all have risks and trade-offs. But if nothing more, perhaps you can use these as springboards to something better.

Option 1. Ironically, your position of greatest advantage with a large truck is one you would scrupulously avoid with a smaller vehicle. That is, after the truck has come to a halt, quickly swing your patrol car around it and park about forty-five feet ahead of the truck, with the front of your car pointed toward the right at about a 45° angle. As you exit your driver door, you have the body of your unit to use as a protective barrier. You can see up into the cab and possibly even into the sleeper berth, depending on light conditions, and, starting from a standing stop, the truck cannot cross the reactionary gap fast enough to harm you before you can retreat.

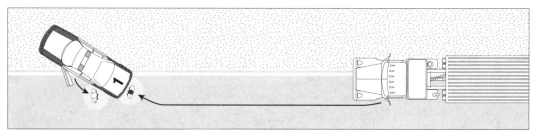

Signal the driver to come down and walk toward you. This gives you a chance to assess him while still behind your patrol car. Protected from traffic, you can conduct dialogue and hand documents back and forth across the corner of your trunk. As you finish with a document, lay it on the trunk lid and let him occupy his hands to keep it from blowing away.

Normally, a trucker will bring all the paper-work you need with him, including his log-book and manifest (if he doesn't, that may be cause for suspicion). If he does need to retrieve anything, you can remain behind your car for cover and maintain a visual on him while he returns to the cab. From your position, you are also able to monitor any passenger(s) visible in the cab. If the driver becomes hostile, you have some protection from your patrol car, as well as distance, working to your advantage.

Option 2. Park behind the truck as you would with other vehicles—but at least twenty feet back, so that you increase your visibility on the rig. Now call the driver back. If he can't hear your PA because of engine noise or the racket of his refrigerator unit, you may be able to contact him by CB or attract his attention with hand signals; indeed, experienced truckers may get out on their own, because they know officers don't like to approach along the driver side.

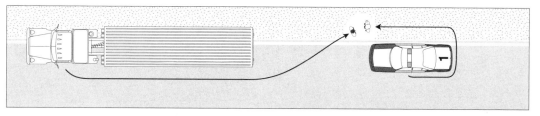

You want the driver to meet you with his papers near the right front of your patrol car. Stand so he's between you and the truck and where you can watch down the passenger side of the trailer. You'll be able to see under the trailer enough to spot legs walking down the driver side.

Some officers incorrectly interpret Option 2 as a technique which permits contact near the rear of the trailer rather than near your patrol car. A position near the trailer makes you highly vulnerable to surprises from a hidden passenger, who can sneak up undetected.

This option offers excellent distancing from possible concealed occupants while you assess the driver and the circumstances at your initial meeting place. However, if he needs to fetch anything from the cab, complications arise. Because of the configuration of semitrailers, it will be difficult to maintain a good visual on him without accompanying him forward. And then you may be vulnerable to passengers you haven't seen or to the driver himself when he climbs up to the cab and thereby gains the advantage of being able to make concealed movements in a high-ground position.

Option 3. A passenger-side approach. Instruct the driver by hand or speaker to come back to your unit, parked behind the truck. But just as he opens his door and loses sight of you in his mirror, dart between your car and the rear of his trailer. As he walks back, you start walking forward on the passenger side. You can glance under the truck to monitor his legs, but chances are he won't think to look under for you because he expects you to be waiting for him at the back.

126

Watch the passenger-side mirror and window for any sign of other occupants. At the cab, watch up as you quickly swing out to a position forward from the front right fender. This position gives you a head-and-shoulders view of anyone sitting in the cab and may even expose some of the sleeping compartment. At night, use your flashlight to illuminate the interior and blind anyone you see. You're in the kill zone of the cab, a definite risk, but you are protected from the more common hazard of traffic.

(above left/above)
As you begin your approach in Option 3, you can track the driver's movement by watching under the trailer. He's not likely to watch you because he assumes you're waiting at the rear.

If the driver remains in the cab during your approach, you can watch him in the side mirror as you advance. Remember, though, that he can watch you, too.

Option 4. Don't call the driver back but make an approach on the passenger side to the forward observation point where you can look through the windshield into the cab. If there's a passenger visible, motion the driver to your position and have him stand as something of a barrier for you, where you can monitor the passenger.

If the driver's alone, cross in front of the cab (about fifteen to twenty feet out from the bumper) to the rear of his door. He can't get the truck moving quickly enough to run you down, so that's not a problem. Keep your left hand on the door as you pass across it. This blocks any

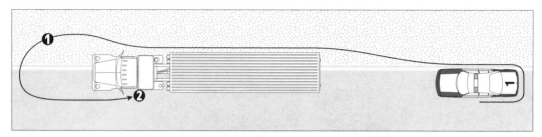

(above)
Driver can be signaled out to meet you at Position 1, if there's a passenger.

If the driver's alone, you can move to Position 2, protecting yourself from his door as you pass it. Your suddenly opening the door may expose weapons or contraband and give you better observation during contact.

attempt by the driver to open it suddenly. As soon as you reach the rear of his door, standing where it's awkward for him to reach you, pop the lower latch and swing the door open.

You can articulate this legally as being necessary for your safety because of the poor observation of dangers in the cab you would otherwise have from ground level. Unexpectedly opening the door may reveal weapons or contraband on the floor, in the door pocket, taped to the steering column, or in his lap, or it may disclose incriminating odors before the driver can react to your surprising move.

Get his hands on the steering wheel where you can see them. At this point, one Florida officer likes to ask a quick series of questions for his safety before asking for the driver's license and registration:

"Do you have any weapons in the cab?"
(Some officers experienced with truckers claim the majority do carry firearms, usually in the sleeper or under their seat.)

"Do you have anything that's going to hurt me in any way?"

"Got any wild women in there?"
(indicating the sleeping berth)

"Anyone else?"

"Got any coolers or containers?"

"Any alcoholic beverages?"
(forbidden in the cabs of commercial vehicles)

The driver customarily answers each of these readily, usually regarding them as routine or even stupid. Then, without pausing, the officer quickly pops the last in the series:

"Any drugs?"

If the driver hesitates before answering this one, you have a guilty indicator right off the bat.

Assuming he answers "No" at this point, you can have the driver gather his papers, step out of the vehicle, and move to an interview location. Although Option 4 can be surprising and revealing, it means extensive movement for you through the kill zone—plus a prepared driver is in a superior position to launch a physical or firearms attack once you pop the door open.

Moreover, some instructors add to the risks of this option by advocating that once the driver door is open and you "feel comfortable" with the subject, you should climb up to his level! They say to brace your back against the open door with your feet on the top step and conduct your interview there. The door will hold you surprisingly securely and you will have a good visual on the driver, the cab, and usually some of the sleeping berth (even if the curtain is closed, you'll likely be able to see or hear movement behind it). *But* a violent driver can easily attack you in this position. You may *think* you can grab the hard rail and roll away from him, but in reality he will probably land the first blow.

Even without this dangerous element, Option 4 (like Option 3) places the point of contact a long way from your shotgun and other safety features of your patrol car. If you have to return to use the radio, you have the awkward problem of bringing the driver with you or the risk of leaving him alone, unobserved, where he may arm himself or destroy evidence in your absence. These options are safest to attempt *only when you have backup*, which you should try to get whenever you decide to stop a large truck. The sheer bulk and design of big rigs requires at least two officers (preferably more) for adequate security. Then there can be someone always watching the suspect(s)—and discouraging trouble.

As you try to tailor your approach tactics to the circumstances of your stop, it may take conscious effort to break old habits. Psychologists say it takes about twenty-eight days of conscious action to establish a new habit. Be patient. Stick with it. There may be much that is new to you about the tactics of Criminal Patrol, including techniques appropriate to the next phase of your stop. But the enhancement of your survival and your professional success will make a persistent effort to change worthwhile.

A violent driver can easily launch a vicious attack against you in this position with a thrust of his left leg. The theory that you can grab the hand rail and roll out of the way to dodge trouble simply doesn't work well when role-played realistically.

Do you always role-play tactics like this to see if they're valid?

This officer, who had never practiced the tactic above before deciding to use it, just assumed it would work. You be the judge.

II
TACTICS OF INVESTIGATION

SENSORY PAT-DOWN

The red Chevy pickup was racing like the searing wind across the high plains of western Kansas when it hit Trooper Richard Jimerson's radar at 81 mph, an easy catch. At roadside, the twenty-four-year-old, white driver was polite and clean-cut—neat blue jeans, buttoned-up shirt, no different to look at than a hundred guys with a heavy foot you might stop on any street or highway. But in the fading dusk, Jimerson's Geiger-counter senses were soon buzzing.

The young man's hand trembled when he handed over his license. He avoided eye contact. On the gale scooping through the truck bed, Jimerson could smell the strong aroma of ether, yet there were no containers of chemicals visible to account for it. As they talked, the trooper's eyes kept moving. Something about the pickup didn't look right; the bed seemed to sit too high, and an unusual quarter-inch crack ran along its length. The driver said a friend in Colorado had loaned him the vehicle. He'd just lost his job in a tile factory up in Canada and was driving from Denver to St. Louis "on vacation." For a long trip, he was traveling light, Jimerson noticed. Only a single small duffel bag rode in the cab beside him. A road atlas was also open on the seat, although the route from Denver to St. Louis is a straight-shot no-brainer on I-70.

Bit by bit, little things like these started to add up. And what they totaled to by the time the stop was over was huge.

The driver agreed to follow Jimerson to a nearby sheriff's station for a voluntary search of the vehicle, no questions asked. The odor seemed to be coming from inside the floor of the bed. Touching, tapping, and inspecting it closely, Jimerson finally confirmed what he had come to suspect: The bottom had been built up with a thick false compartment.

Tpr. Richard Jimerson.

From inside, with the help of deputies, he pulled out more than 293 pounds of cocaine. Authorities believe the load was actually headed from California to Chicago, and estimated its value, even before being "stepped on," at over $13,000,000—the largest coke bust to that date in the history of the state. The closed-mouthed courier, a Polish national, said only that he had been paid $1,000 to leave the truck in the parking lot at the St. Louis international airport....

With your stop legally made and your tactics for maintaining a Position of Advantage in place, you now enter an *investigative* phase as you work to ascend the Criminal Patrol Pyramid. This is the pivotal period when you must quickly decide whether the subject you've stopped is "just" a traffic violator who should be warned or ticketed and sent on his way—or a felony suspect who warrants the full Criminal Patrol treatment. And as Trooper Jimerson so spectacularly proved that evening in Kansas, this make-or-break stage done right is an adventure of the senses.

Usually you have only a few minutes before the motorist's detention becomes "unreasonable," so you need to use your time wisely. The visual assessment you began when the vehicle was still mobile expands now into a multisensory "pat-down" from a different perspective. You'll probably never want to *taste* anything on Criminal Patrol (except the sweet taste of success!); certainly touching your tongue with samples of unknown substances to see if they "taste like" drugs is about as smart as sticking your toe in a piranha pool to see if the fish are biting. But besides that, you do need to see, hear, smell, and feel things the average officer won't take the time and effort to explore, lacks the knowledge to properly interpret, or doesn't even detect, if you are to base your actions regarding the motorist on articulable facts and not on some seat-of-the-pants hunch.

Whether you've already briefly met the driver at an interview location or are approaching directly, your first close-up contact with the vehicle you've stopped offers precious opportunities for intercepting revealing sensory signals that the violator may not even know are being transmitted. On occasion your case will be made at the window of the car by what you observe, what you hear, and what you smell; at the very least, you may accumulate indicators that can advance your suspicion to a new level. "When I'm on foot at the car," says a Midwestern officer, "my eyes, my ears, my nose are on red alert. I watch the people in my peripheral vision, but I look around while I talk to them. My eyes sweep the outside, dart around the interior. I'm conscious of what I'm smelling. I listen to the details of what they're telling me, not tuning them out. I let my senses shake down the entire scene, trying to get impressions of the whole picture."

Some impressions will come to you from the vehicle's exterior, potential contraband cues that are open to scrutiny for the first time now that you're closer. Dealer logos, parking decals, inspection seals, bumper stickers, and similar "location-specific" displays may reveal where the car has been. Are any of these from high-intensity drug trafficking areas, like Florida, Los Angeles, New York City, Houston, the Southwest, Chicago, San Diego, or the Baltimore-Washington metropolitan area? Are they from smaller distribution or use areas near or even within your community? Are there inconsistencies that make you wonder about the history of the car, like a license plate from one state but a dealer decal from another? Such details may soon be useful in developing conversation with the driver or in checking his story. At a minimum, such things can be small mosaics in the portrait of the car and occupant(s) you're trying to piece together.

Be alert also for modification flaws or other puzzling abnormalities you may have missed before but now are in position to detect, like Trooper Jimerson discovering the mysterious crack and the unusual height of the pickup bed. Make sure you continue to ask yourself

"What's wrong with this picture?" and "What doesn't fit with what's 'normal'?" Remember that *small* details, individually or as part of a collective buildup of characteristics, can have big significance. A Border Patrol agent approaching a truck at a license checkpoint in New Mexico saw what appeared at a distance to be a common spare gas tank. But then close up he noticed there were no feeder lines running to it, a rather critical omission. He figured right: It was a phony—filled with cocaine.

Usually you won't have the legal right to physically penetrate significantly into the vehicle during this investigative phase. Some courts permit a *minimal* intrusion into a vehicle without considering it an

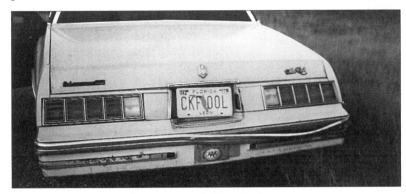

Disrepair? Or evidence of tampering? Plain-view abnormalities like this sagging bumper strip can give you something to talk about with the driver. In this case, a stash of Ecstasy tablets was hidden in the bumper.

Checking the underside of this van as part of his plain-view examination, a Canadian officer found an extra gas tank. Later he discovered that it held a drug cargo, accessed though a hole in the floor.

unconstitutional violation of privacy. A state court in Rhode Island approved when an officer seized a gun he saw on the floorboard after sticking his head through an open window to watch a driver rummaging in the glove box for documents.[1] An officer who leaned into a van to question passengers of an unlicensed driver and then saw marijuana was supported by a federal court,[2] and under certain circumstances intrusion to inspect a VIN plate may be okay.[3] But usually, you'll be on safer legal ground if you keep your head, hands, and other parts of your body outside the vehicle for your sensory pat-down. But what your *senses* detect about potential contraband indicators inside can help focus your dialogue with parties in the vehicle...build grounds for extending their detention and for asking consent to search...direct your searching to the most productive places...and keep you motivated if the search gets tedious or frustrating. Under certain circumstances, your sensory assessment may even yield PC that will allow you to shortcut the normal progression of the stop and actually begin an interior search immediately, without having to obtain either a warrant or the suspect's consent.

Guidelines in this chapter will help you understand the rules of play and how to score against cunning and dangerous adversaries.

Sensory Pat-Down

Just how far your sensory pat-down takes you may depend on your ability to:

• Perceive
• Recognize
• Remember
• Describe.

Perceive even subtle sensory signals from the vehicle and occupants that may be easily missed.

Recognize those that suggest the possible or probable presence of contraband.

Remember these signals when talking with occupants, deciding appropriate action, writing your report, and giving testimony.

Describe (articulate) the indicators you detected in context with the habits and practices of drug traffickers so a judge or jury will understand.

© Calibre Press, Inc.

Reading "Ambiguous" Cues

On Criminal Patrol, as on the street generally, things are not always what they seem. There rarely is black and white; virtually *everything* is subject to interpretation. Like the curiosity ticklers you may have seen before the stop, certain ambiguous sensory cues you're now in position to detect may, by themselves, mean only that more investigation is needed. Certainly they don't normally constitute probable cause to search or arrest, even when you detect them in clusters. Yet often they do prove to be early, fertile seeds that blossom eventually into reasonable suspicion.

Once you perceive these cues and recognize their potential, you'll be highly motivated to investigate further. The brain finds ambiguity annoying and seeks resolution about what it perceives. And resolution is one of the important roles to be played by what you *hear*, what the violator soon tells you during dialogue.

In the perception stage of observation, you're expected to follow only a few simple rules. So long as you do not enter a vehicle, you're entitled to make a visual inspection of its interior (as well as the exterior, including its underside). Just looking at what is in open view in a car you've stopped does not constitute searching,[4] therefore is not subject to the Fourth Amendment's many constraints. (You can also peer into parked vehicles you encounter, just as any inquisitive passerby can, without violating an occupant's expectation of privacy.[5]) As long as you had a lawful basis for making the stop and you maintain a vantage point where you have a legal right to be, you can:

- Shift your position, bend down, or lie down to get a better view;
- Use your flashlight to illuminate any areas that would be visible to your naked eye under better lighting conditions;[6]
- Look in any windows, including those of camper shells;
- Ask if you can see inside suspicious containers you may spot in the interior (if the subject indicates a willingness to let you look, he's consenting to a voluntary search of that item[7]);
- Take advantage of "free glances" into spots that would normally be off-limits, such as a wallet, purse, briefcase, glove compartment, or possibly even luggage while a suspect has it open to retrieve his or her license, registration, or insurance card.

Keying on your *first* potential indicator is always hardest. Once you have something to build on, you usually can quickly develop other evidence, provided that you are in fact dealing with a contraband offender.

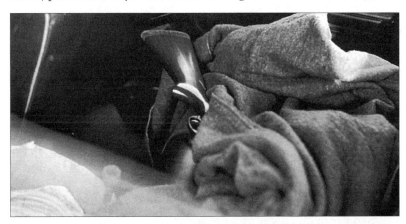

Being alert for sensory cues is important on every stop. This Remington shotgun was in plain view of the officer who walked up to make contact with the driver. But it could have been missed if the officer had been preoccupied or unobservant.

(far left)
Some officers like to subtly check the state tax stamps on visible cigarette packs to see if they jibe with the violator's story of where he has been.

(left)
Another plain-view opportunity in a back seat. Regional souvenirs, such as oranges, may be a sign of travel in a source area. Inside this travel bag was 33 lbs. of coke.

137

This lawn-care rig is pulled over for having a faulty "slow moving vehicle" placard. Approaching, the officer notices that 2 large, stacked containers don't fit together snugly. He also notices a "plain smell" cue: the odor of marijuana. Guess what kept the trash cans from stacking properly?

If you have not already detected a cue that has aroused your curiosity or suspicion by the time you approach the vehicle, one or more from the following common cues may offer you a start. If you've already perceived something, these may help you add to your mental roster of suspicion. Some of these you may already have perceived on past stops without realizing their possible significance.

"Masking" odors. Suspiciously strong smells may be evident even as you approach the vehicle. One possibility is that these are intended to mask the odor of drugs to protect against narcotics-detection dogs. Most such efforts don't work very well, but often the smell of the masking agent itself becomes so powerful in close confines that you can easily pick up on it without a dog when you're standing nearby. Cocaine traffickers, for instance, may wrap each kilo in plastic, then slathered it with a thick coat of grease and pungent spices before loading it into a vehicle's natural cavities. A drug runner stopped on a rural road in upstate New York en route to Toronto with a load of marijuana had packed it amidst a trunkful of smelly fish. In some cases, drug runners concentrate masking odors most heavily on the driver side, anticipating your approach—and their greatest need for protection

138

from you—there. Strong masking scents may also cling to the clothes of occupants when you move them away from the vehicle for dialogue.

In addition to air fresheners, which you may see hanging inside in multiples even before you make the stop, all of the following are commonly used for masking, either placed independently in the vehicle or packed with the goods:

- Fabric softener (probably the No. 1 mask for marijuana);
- Baby or talcum powder ("Another ultrastrong cue," says one Criminal Patrol specialist. "If you smell it, hang in. Dope is in that car somewhere!");
- Fresh coffee or coffee grounds (packages of pot are commonly wrapped with tape first, then a layer of coffee is added, then more tape wrapped around);
- Detergent;
- Chili powder;
- Cut citrus fruits;

- Heavy perfume (especially suspicious if no women are in the vehicle);
- Cologne, after-shave, or deodorizer spray (used to saturate clothing packed with drugs in luggage);
- Spoiled produce (especially common with refrigerated trucks, to serve as a cover load as well as a masking scent);
- Cedar shavings;
- Grease;
- Mothballs;
- Mustard;
- Carpet freshener;
- Heavy incense.

Officers in Missouri smelled ammonia, sometimes used as a masking agent, coming from the back of a Hertz rental truck. Consent to search was denied, but the driver agreed to drive to the department for further inspection. 797 lbs. of cocaine were inside these freezers and 3 cardboard boxes. Also found were a bottle of K-9 repellant, air fresheners, and a bottle of ammonia.

Body-work odors. You may detect other odors that relate to materials used in body work and other vehicle modifications. In the drug-trafficking world, these may signal that the vehicle has recently undergone installation of hidden compartments or other alterations to accommodate contraband. Be sensitive to the smells of:

- Bondo, the plastic body-filler compound;
- Automotive paint;
- Glue and tar (used to hold down carpeting and rubber stripping);
- Putty sealant;
- Undercoating.

"Lived-in" look. Travel habits of cross-country mules often create a distinct ambiance inside their cars; the vehicles look like they've been "lived in" under combat conditions. As the trip progresses, evidence builds up of the long hours of straight-through driv-ing and of the couriers' reluctance to leave their vehicles unattended.

"Lived-in" look.

Male occupants may have a day or two's growth of beard and a disheveled look, indicating they have not spent time in a sleeping room. You may see beverage cans and fast-food wrappers on the seats or floor, suggesting meals grabbed on the run from drive-up windows...wrappers from several different restaurants, indicating a long trip with a series of no-stop meals...an ice cooler for sand-wiches...coffee cups and pack-ages of NoDoz or other anti-drowsiness compounds...toilet paper or a "piss jug" to eliminate the need to stop in public places...scattered papers, dirty clothes (including soiled diapers lying open)...trash, which may reflect messy lives—or a calcu-lated effort to discourage a search. One ring of Haitian smugglers that used couriers in Datsuns deliberately infested the cars with hordes of cockroaches and palmetto bugs, on the accurate theory that most cops wouldn't take on a search to find the drug packages concealed under the seats. What finally stopped them were Criminal Patrol officers who carried cans of Raid and sprayed hell out of the interiors before entering.

Sometimes to fight fatigue or as partial compensation, couriers who are also users are given cocaine to take while they drive. Take note of any uneaten fast food, like a cold burger that looks like it has been unwrapped once but not consumed. This is where dopers sometimes hide their personal stashes. You may also see lots of dis-carded Kleenex, indicating frequent nose-blowing; if speckled with blood, that's a strong cocaine cue.

There may be a makeshift bed with a pillow and blanket on the back seat to accommodate rotation driving (if more than one person is in the car) or a quick nap at roadside (if the driver's alone).

Note: Remember that bedding can easily conceal weapons. A sleeping bag can hide even a long gun.

Is someone sacked out so soundly that he or she appears not to awaken during your contact? Even if it's a child, this person may be playing 'possum, protectively lying over the very spot where con-traband is hidden.

Nonmatching colors. Trim, carpeting, upholstery, and other inte-rior colors are usually coordinated when a vehicle comes from the factory. Something that stands out as not blending in well may indi-cate replacement material necessitated by modifications for a hid-den compartment.

Luggage. Sometimes brand new luggage is an indicator. It may have been bought just for the trip, to carry cash or bulky drugs like marijuana...or to serve as window-dressing for occupants pretending to be tourists. Or is the only luggage you see a small ditty bag, capable of holding just a few clothes and personal items for a fast turn-around? If so, remember it later if the driver tells you he's on an extended vacation or business trip, which would normally require more luggage. Careless or complacent couriers not expecting to be stopped often put the dope in small bags. Because of media attention to ultrasophisticated smuggling schemes (like cocaine mixed with fiberglass and molded into bathtubs and dog houses), you may forget that a great deal of trafficking is still very crude; one municipal officer who stopped a luxury car in Little Rock and got curious about an unzippered bag sitting in plain view on the seat eventually found over $100,000 cash, a quantity of cocaine, and a gun inside it. If you see a bag that's empty, maybe it's a money satchel, yet to be filled with payment for a load.

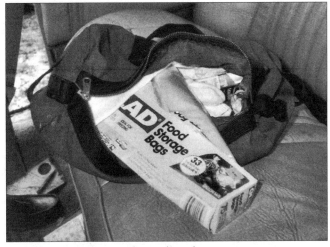

Dialogue with the occupant(s) will help you evaluate "ambiguous" items you may see in plain view. The Hispanic driver of this vehicle told the officer a "weak" story, plus his point of origin was from a source city. A quantity of marijuana was eventually found.

On the other hand, what seems like too much luggage for the number of occupants you see may, in fact, be luggage filled with contraband...or it may prompt you to wonder what's in the trunk that necessitates carrying so much baggage in the passenger compartment. A combination of luggage and young children in the back seat is something unusual that also raises questions about the trunk. Traveling parents normally want to give squirmy, restless kids as much room as possible.

Maps. Is a road map open for reference? Most travelers covering any distance across unfamiliar territory these days stick with the Interstate system, and most legitimate people who use secondary roads are short-trippers who know their way around that area. So if you've stopped someone on a non-Interstate highway who needs a map to find his way, that's unusual...and potentially indicates a courier hitting backroads in hopes of avoiding state-police interdiction teams. (Cross-country trucks caught on circuitous routes off the Interstate should be immediately suspected.) In fact, some maps have been confiscated with warnings to couriers to specifically avoid sharply patrolled communities. These cautions may include this symbol: $\oslash$, which is the international symbol for *no*, advising a detour. One map confiscated in Utah had "Watch out" scribbled near one city—the one where the stop was made, appropriately enough. Forty-eight pounds of coke were recovered from the driver, who evidently wasn't much at following directions.

If you see an open map with a string of cities marked, that could indicate a distribution route a courier is servicing. One map that was part of a cocaine bust in Nebraska showed cities circled all across the Northwest, from Seattle to Omaha. That run was being covered by a young unmarried couple in a Toyota pickup who had ties to a Crips set in Los Angeles.

A Mississippi deputy stopped a 58-year-old retired telephone company employee, driving a VW Jetta from Miami to Oklahoma. All his luggage, including a big garment bag and several suitcases, was inexplicably crammed into the tiny back seat. After the deputy got consent to search, he found out why. The only thing in the trunk was a single overnight bag—filled with $150,000 in 50- and 100-dollar bills. The boss who'd hired the courier had just told him to stay out of the trunk. The man figured something was fishy, but unquestioningly jammed his luggage up front and started driving.

Keep maps and their markings in mind later—along with any out-of-town newspapers or regional souvenirs you may see, like bags of Florida oranges or boxes of Southwestern cactus candy. If you've seen a map from some state the suspects don't mention or it's folded open to a route that's different from what they claim, *why?*

Checklists. Watch for lists of instructions on car maintenance and driving: "Keep gas half full...✓ turn signals...✓ headlights..." and the like. Prepared reminders may be given to couriers to help avoid breakdowns and police contact.

Manufacturing materials. Some innocuous items found in the ordinary household when found together in a vehicle become more suspicious, because they can be used in drug production (including the converting of cocaine base to cocaine powder, an aspect of the drug trade that's starting to move to this country). These commonplace items include: Rubbermaid trash cans, a quantity of cheesecloth or coffee filters, microwave ovens, heat lamps, large drums that don't appear to fit the vehicle. The drums may be unmarked or carry labels of acetone, ethyl acetate, ethyl ether, hexane, methyl ethyl ketone, hydrochloric acid, sulfuric acid, and corrosive liquid N.O.S. *Note:* If you find evi dence of such chemicals, get help immediately. Some are extremely dangerous and require handling by haz-mat specialists.

Packaging materials. Do you see rolls of ultrasticky tape or boxes of strong deodorizing fabric softeners, like Downy or Bounce? These are very strong clues of possible transporting. Traffickers favor them to wrap around bales of marijuana or package kilos and odd sizes of cocaine and other drugs. The dryer sheets help mask odors and the tape—most commonly duct tape, masking tape, white filament tape, or brown polypropylene carton-sealing tape—is waterproof, opaque, and tough to tear open. Also watch for quantities of one-pound and gallon-size food storage bags, which may be visible on seats or floors, in map pockets, or behind visors. These are often used to package pot.

One Missouri crank dealer, gunned down execution-style with his girlfriend, was reputed to smuggle methamphetamine by feeding it in plastic packets to snakes, which he then carried with him in his vehicle. When he arrived at his destination, he slit their stomachs and retrieved his shipment.

Often personal drug kits (especially for heroin users) and sometimes guns are concealed inside the purple Crown Royal whiskey bags with the gold draw strings at the top. An officer noticing a driver trying to hastily conceal one of these on a stop in Minnesota led first to a physical attack on the officer—then, after the offender was subdued with a flashlight, to the discovery of $80,000 in drug money in the trunk. Other personal-use quantities are commonly carried in 35mm plastic film canisters, which you may see on a dashboard, seat, or console without any camera being visible.

(below)
Wrapping material and duct tape are commonly used for drug packaging and may be observed on your approach to the violator's vehicle. Note the road atlas, another possible plain view cue.

(left)
Gallon jugs or thermos bottles may not look like drug packaging, but smugglers sometimes pour cocaine into water because it will so finely suspend that it's virtually invisible. 6 gallons of water can hide 8 kilos of coke. At the end of the transport, the liquid is evaporated and the drug recovered and repackaged.

143

Monitoring/communication devices. Cellular phones and radar detectors are commonplace these days in private vehicles and are no longer the potential courier cues they once were. But a police scanner in a car is still out of the ordinary—and cause to wonder why the driver is so concerned about monitoring law enforcement activity. You may be able to hear a scanner, even if you can't see it. If you see a

CB radio, give it the once-over, too. Is it set to some channel other than the ones used by most people in your area? That may be for communication with an escort vehicle. Rather than CBs, some couriers may use marine two-way radios. With truckers, watch for SkyTel pagers, capable of paging anywhere via satellite; the average legitimate trucker doesn't use one because he can't afford it. Binoculars are rare in legit cars but may be visible in courier vehicles. Not only can a passenger use them to watch for cops on the road, but when the vehicle reaches the delivery site it's common for the runners to drive around scrutinizing the area for officers before making the drop-off.

A deputy became suspicious of a vehicle he'd stopped for a traffic violation after he saw this assortment of police gear and communications equipment inside. Guns were later found hidden behind vents in the body.

"Good guy" symbols. Like the "straight-arrow" bumper stickers and decals you may have noticed on the exterior, certain items you spot inside the vehicle can also be calculated "protective coloration."

These may include: police caps and antidrug materials, religious literature, crosses hanging from the mirror, statuettes stuck to the dashboard, and what one Midwestern trooper calls "the Number 1 indicator:" a Bible in prominent view on the seat or dash.

Bibles and other books can be jerry-rigged or purchased with the center of the pages cut out. One such Bible was recovered by a small-town officer in Illinois who stopped a driver for weaving. As they stood outside the car, the observant officer noticed that the driver, who appeared to be high on pot, kept looking back in at a Bible on his front seat. At one point, the suspect asked permission to re-enter the car. At that moment, the officer experienced a flashback to an old movie he'd seen where an evil preacher carried a derringer inside a book. The officer grabbed the Bible—and beat the suspect to a small handgun hidden inside.

Be aware also of lone male drivers with women's and children's clothing visible, possibly intended to create a "family" look. "If you find a lone male driver with a lot of baby gear, ask a *lot* of questions—where the baby is, what sex it is, how big it is, the color of its eyes—and see if you get answers that seem hesitant or deceitful," one deputy advises.

Tobacco. Young people who smoke cigarettes are many times more likely than others to use drugs, so their cars are probably more worthy of suspicion about hidden illegal substances. According to one study, smokers between the ages of twelve and seventeen are twenty-three times more likely to use marijuana and twelve times more likely to use heroin than those who have never smoked.[8]

(left)
Commercially available smoking pipe that looks like a cigarette but is really a "1-hitter," with space enough to pack a small amount of marijuana. Would you recognize this common drug paraphernalia if you saw it inside a car?

(below)
Dope smokers, especially of college age, sometimes flaunt Phillies' red-and-white logo on T-shirts and baseball caps because this cheap cigar is often adapted to drug use.

(left)
Phillies Blunts and other brands are often hollowed out and filled with pot, creating a super joint called a "blunt," which may contain as much marijuana as 6 standard joints. Be alert for cigars which look crumpled, have cracked leaf wrapping, or green plant material exposed at the ends.

Cash cues. Are there receipts for cash purchases lying around or clipped to the visor? Drug runners generally don't use credit cards, either to avoid a "paper trail" or because they don't qualify for credit. But they keep receipts so they can get reimbursed when the run's done.

You may also see rolls of quarters on the floor or seats (possibly for pay phones, especially in urban areas) or other money indicators, like cashier's checks, money orders, or Western Union receipts (possibly representing payment for drugs or for smuggling them). Also change purses are frequently used to carry small amounts of marijuana.

Lying on a seat or console, you may notice what at first seem to be just loose scrap papers or a memo pad or notebook with names, locations, and cryptic numbers. This may be a drug dealer's "pay-and-owe" register, on which he records orders, deliveries, debts, and so on.

Cache cues. Some visual cues are "two-fers": they not only suggest that contraband may be in the vehicle but hint at where it's hidden.

Do you see a screwdriver perhaps lying on the floor like it rolled out from under a seat? It may have been used to remove door panels, armrests, vent plates, or rocker-panel kick strips. Window crank handles that are missing or lying around may have been taken off so doors could be loaded with contraband. Likewise, if the driver opens the door to talk to you or hand you his license, consider that the window might not roll down because it's blocked by hidden dope. Or the driver's window may roll down half way but other windows don't go down at all. On a rental car this would be extremely suspicious.

Note: Just because a window does roll down doesn't prove that the door is *not* loaded.

Socket wrenches may suggest specially constructed secret compartments, which commonly are in the rear or underneath the vehicle. A tire jack or toolbox in the passenger compartment, like a spare tire riding there, may mean the trunk is filled. Is the rear seatback ajar or excessively bowed? A favorite spot for hidden compartments is in the seatback or between the seat and trunk. If the back isn't replaced just right after being loaded, it will ride slightly forward, not locked in place, and a full load may push the seat out unnaturally. If no rear seatbelts are visible, the seat likely has been removed at some point. Also check for corners of newspapers or plastic bags that may be sticking out from armrests because hidden compartments in those areas are not sealed tightly.

As you scope out the driver's area, check the ignition. Is there only an ignition key visible? Most people keep a bunch of keys on their vehicle ring...certainly a companion trunk key and usually at least a house key, too. But on drug transports when the goods are in the trunk, that key may be mailed ahead to the destination to discourage the driver from tampering with the load; the ignition key may have been left for him in the ashtray, without a ring, when he picked the car up. A *rental* vehicle with the trunk key missing is extremely suspicious.

Note: In some cases, the "missing" key is just a ruse to deter you from searching the trunk. It may actually be taped behind the ashtray or hidden elsewhere in the vehicle.

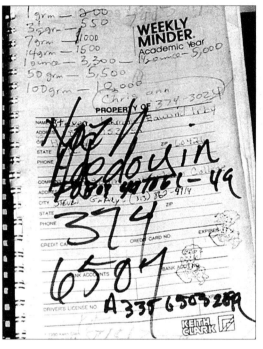

(above)
Datebook found in a courier car implicates the driver with multiple drug transactions, dates, key contacts, drug prices, and several related phone numbers.

(right)
Pay-and-owe ledger confiscated from a drug distributor reveals the crude but effective accounting practices of the drug trade.

146

"Free" zones. Your legal right to glance into private areas that the subject voluntarily opens to you can reveal a lot. If he says he's unemployed but you spot a jackroll as thick as a salami when he empties his pockets to find his license, you're going to want more answers. Pot smokers may carry folded rolling papers between documents in their billfolds. In New Jersey, a flustered speeder claimed she and her eight-year-old son were on their way from Miami Beach to Boston when stopped. Fumbling for her license, she spilled the contents of her wallet. The watchful trooper noticed several business cards for lawyers flutter to the ground. That became the first cue that ultimately led to his discovering eight pounds of cocaine packed among clothes in the back seat. In Florida, a driver parked in a handicap spot to use the restroom at a highway rest stop. When he returned, deputies were waiting for him. As he looked for his license, they noticed a snapshot in his wallet showing him wearing four gold rope-chain necklaces, gold bracelets on both wrists, huge gold rings on each finger—the classic "Mr. T Starter Kit" dope-dealer regalia. He was carrying five kilos of coke in a hidden compartment and granted consent to search because he erroneously thought no cops were sharp enough to find it.

Customized release buttons inside a glove box. All 3 buttons are labeled "trunk." One of the buttons is the trunk release, the others activate hidden compartments in the trunk used to hide drugs and cash.

When the glove box is open, do you see extra trunk-release-type buttons? These may be tied into the vehicle's electrical system to activate hidden compartments. If you see that a glove box is empty except for the registration or insurance card, that's highly unusual in private vehicles regularly in use for legitimate purposes. In Arizona, that subtle, ambiguous first cue started a sharp-eyed Customs inspector on an investigative track that led ultimately to the discovery of

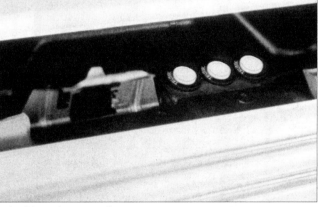

285 pounds of cocaine in the false bed of a pickup truck.

A speeder stopped in California told an officer that his registration was in his trunk. When the violator opened the lid, the officer noticed a large nylon bag and got verbal permission to open it. Inside was a lot of radio equipment that the driver said belonged to his father. The officer ran a check on the radios and discovered one had

147

been stolen. He also found that the driver had a long criminal record, ranging from possession of a controlled substance with intent to distribute to the manufacturing of dangerous weapons. After arresting the driver, the officer thoroughly searched the car and recovered 900 grams of marijuana and fourteen grams of methamphetamine.

Drivers of most commercial trucks are required to carry fire extinguishers, which must be available to law enforcement inspection on demand. Often they are carried in a storage compartment that is accessed from outside the cab. When the driver opens it at your request to confirm that the extinguisher's there, you can also scope out whatever else might be visible.

Caution: During this high-risk period of initial contact, don't allow yourself to become so tunneled in on possible contraband cues that you ignore danger cues. One Louisiana officer who did so failed to see the butt of a gun plainly sticking out from under the center armrest, inches from a driver's fingers, while he was at the driver's window. Only later when he was searching the vehicle did he notice it. "I was just lucky he didn't want to take me on," said the shaken officer, "because hidden in his door was $30,000."

You want to maintain the perceptual acuity of a suburban officer in Minnesota who approached a traffic violator slumped behind the wheel with his hands between his legs. Instead of dismissing this as fatigue or dejection, the officer looked closer. Between the man's fingers, he could faintly make out the dark bluing of a gun barrel, a .380 semiautomatic. At almost that instant of recognition, the offender grabbed the gun and jammed it out the window toward the officer. But the split-second advance warning the officer had gained from his visual alertness allowed him to grab the gun and rip it from the suspect's hand before a single shot could be fired.

It's Not Always Drugs

The pot of gold at the end of your investigative rainbow is not always filled just with drugs. Ambiguous cues properly developed can lead to other crimes, too. That's why, when you approach any vehicle on Criminal Patrol, a fully open mind rather than a pre-set expectation is your most important investigative tool. Don't get locked into looking just for drug cues.

A traffic officer and his drug-dog partner, for example, stopped a red Camaro after it tried to evade a checkpoint in California. As the officer talked with the male driver and female passenger, he noticed that the car's interior was littered with what looked like collectible coins wrapped individually in plastic jackets.

The dog alerted at the passenger's door, giving the officer PC to search. He did find an ounce of crystal meth inside an eyeglass case in the woman's purse. Of more interest, though, were over a dozen credit-cards in the purse, all bearing different names, and several hundred dollars worth of credit card receipts with what looked like forged signatures, indicating a recent spending spree.

In the back seat, the officer opened two pillowcases and discovered gold coins, rolls of old silver dollars, negotiable stocks and bonds worth thousands of dollars, travelers checks in another person's name, and $68,000 in cash.

The goods, as it turned out, had come from the desert home of a couple who were on a vacation cruise. Telephones had been ripped out to defeat the alarm system, every room had been methodically ransacked for valuables, a Jaguar had been stolen from the garage, and the concrete floor had been torn up to remove a 400-pound safe.

In all, over $400,000 in cash and property had been taken by the driver and his girlfriend passenger. The driver's criminal history was three pages long. His former occupation was listed as: Security Alarm Installer.

148

Plain View/Plain Smell PC

During your sensory pat-down, you'll occasionally hit on something about which there is little or no ambiguity. If you know what you've discovered, your "plain view" or "plain smell" of this incriminating evidence can give you probable cause to enter the vehicle and search. Most likely you'll end up making an arrest, too, without the effort of having to carefully build reasonable suspicion and psychologically manipulate the driver to cooperate.

In order to cut directly to the bottom line in this way, you not only must be lawfully present in the place from which you see or sniff the relevant evidence, but what you observe or detect cannot commonly be found with innocent persons; it must have an *immediately apparent association with criminal activity*, without further examination.[9] (An additional aspect of plain-view evidence—*inadvertent discovery*—which once was essential no longer applies federally but may still be a requirement of some state courts.[10])

The Supreme Court has ruled that "immediately apparent" does not mean absolute certainty. Rather, you need reason to believe that the plain-view item more likely than not has a criminal association.[11] What qualifies as being "immediately apparent" to you will depend not only on the item or odor, but on your training and experience (as well as on the latitude allowed by courts in your jurisdiction). Not all officers are equal in their ability to recognize crime-associated evidence, and because of this disparity many stops that could become felony busts are lost.

Hopefully, seeing a weapon or some weapon indicator (like loose bullets, a magazine, or a gun rug) is understood by all officers as PC for entering a vehicle. Even if the weapon is legal to transport in your jurisdiction, you can truthfully claim that its presence makes you fear for your safety. You're entitled to confiscate it, at least for the duration of the stop, and then legally search at least those places in the passenger compartment where a weapon might be hidden, including a locked glove compartment. You can seize any contraband you encounter in the process. What you seize may then serve as probable cause for you to search more of the car.[12] Finding drugs up front, for example, could entitle you to search the whole car (depending on your state laws), including the trunk and closed containers. (Details of this and other types of warrantless searches are explained more fully in Chapter 6.)

The frequent relationship between weapons and drugs can make any weapon a productive contraband cue, apart from its own importance, provided you remember to seize this legal opportunity and look *beyond* the weapon itself. A traffic officer in California, for example, who stopped two males in an old Camaro that had burned rubber peeling away from a stoplight, noticed several .38-Special rounds lying in the center console as he peered in through the driver window. He searched, using this as his PC, but found no gun. Behind the front passenger seat, however, he discovered a gallon plastic jug filled about one-third full with white powder that proved to be methamphetamine, worth over $40,000. A Missouri officer who saw .22-cal. rounds on a console during a traffic stop searched the passenger compartment for weapons and found marijuana on the floor. With this as PC, he arrested the two occupants and then searched the trunk, where he uncovered more dope, pharmaceuticals, burglary tools, and two handguns.

(top left)
Some drug paraphernalia will be obvious to you, like this cutting mirror in plain view.

(top right/above)
Are you curious or suspicious about what you see protruding from this ashtray? The ornate handle (arrow) affixes to a roach clip. The tube is an improvised crack pipe.

(left)
LSD blotter paper of perforated squares, shown actual size. Each square, laid on the tongue or swallowed, is one dose. Printed design may help your nearest DEA field office trace the drugs to the source of origin.

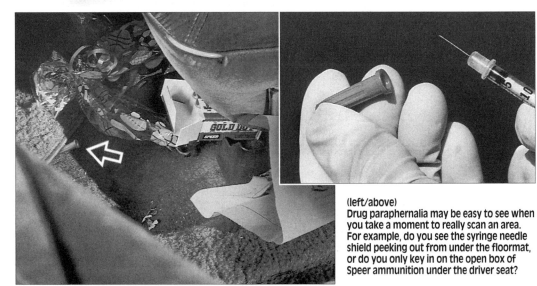

(left/above)
Drug paraphernalia may be easy to see when you take a moment to really scan an area. For example, do you see the syringe needle shield peeking out from under the floormat, or do you only key in on the open box of Speer ammunition under the driver seat?

(left)
Watch for items that easily lend themselves to preparing and using drugs. All of this evidence was plainly visible inside just one car: measuring spoons, a gas torch, a bottle of inositol (used as a bulk enhancer), cotton balls in a bag (used to absorb heroin), and a bottle of alcohol (used as a fuel source in cooking).

(below)
What looks like trash—a broken car radio antenna—you may actually recognize as an improvised crack pipe, if you understand the drug world.

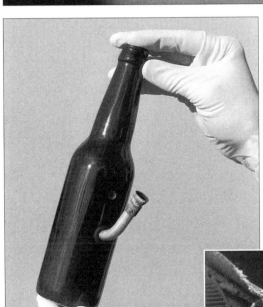

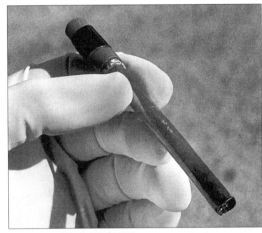

(above)
Commercially available bong may easily be mistaken for an empty beer bottle, unless you see it from the right angle and know the deceptive capabilities of pot smokers. Be curious about what you see.

(above/left)
Smoking devices can be fashioned out of many common objects. A dent and a few punched holes can turn a beverage can into a homemade crack pipe.

151

An officer who stopped a red Lincoln Continental with tinted windows for blowing a stop sign in Pennsylvania spotted the butt of an Uzi sticking up from the back seat when he shined his flashlight through the glass. Searching on this PC, he found eighty-four vials of crack cocaine. Glimpsing a .380 semiauto when the driver of a rented Buick opened the glove box, a New York officer launched a search that turned up $2,000 cash and forty-one grams of heroin elsewhere in the car, and another officer in that state parlayed an illegal can of Mace he saw in a glove box into a major cocaine arrest.

When the plain-view PC is drugs or drug paraphernalia rather than weapons, things gets more problematical. Then what you immediately recognize as having criminal connotations will depend on how knowledgeable you are about the habits and artifacts of the drug world. The more you know, the more items you can use as grounds for entering, seizing, and searching. Some officers with limited narcotics exposure might not recognize even crack rocks, sinsemilla buds, or LSD blotters. On the other hand, with training and experience at Criminal Patrol, you might see as incriminating some subtle things that others would dismiss as trash. You may also be able to identify improvised pipes made from plastic bottles, toilet paper rollers, aluminum foil, small pieces of tubing with Brillo pads for filters, and so on. Similarly, you may know that a bottle cap that's burned on the bottom with possibly a tiny tuft of cotton stuck to it is very likely a cooking vessel for heroin, with the cotton used to soak up residue, and that a radio antenna with one end burned is probably a "straight shooter," used to smoke crack.

In a landmark case from Texas, an officer at a driver's license checkpoint shined his flashlight into a car's interior and saw the driver draw his hand out of his right pants pocket. Caught between the two middle fingers was a deflated, opaque, green party balloon, knotted about one-half inch from the tip, which fell onto the seat. The driver then opened the glove box to get his license. The officer shifted position so he could look in and observed "several small plastic vials, quantities of loose white powder, and an open bag of party balloons." The officer seized the first balloon, which contained a "powdery substance," and searched the car. The U. S. Supreme Court ruled that his *experience* in knowing that such balloons are often used to deal drugs "made it immediately apparent to him that the balloon contained evidence of a crime." Consequently his plain-view seizure and subsequent search were lawful.[13]

Given that you can substantiate your familiarity and that courts in your area are mainstream in their thinking, you should be able to use as plain-view probable cause for getting into and searching at least some portions of a vehicle not only drugs themselves and residue like roaches in ashtrays and seeds on seats and floorboards, but also among other things:

- Tiny glassine or plastic envelopes or bags
  (used in packaging crack rocks, heroin, marijuana,
  PCP, and other drugs; the suspect may claim they're
  for "coin collecting");

- Paper or tinfoil "snow seals" or "bindles"
  (folded drug packets);

- Vanilla-extract bottles or other brown-glass containers
  (used to package and sell PCP to protect it from sunlight);

- Digital, hand-held, triple-beam scales;

- Grinding mills
  (for processing cocaine);

- Small glass or plastic vials
  (used for carrying crack; the suspect may claim they're
  "perfume samplers");

- Containers of the vitamin B powder inositol,
  the baby laxative mannitol, or lactose
  (cutting agents for cocaine and drugs of similar appearance);

- Rolled-up currency, glass tubes, pieces of plastic straws cut to
  three or four inches long, possibly balled up in the ashtray and
  with residue visible
  (coke snorters);

- Small mirrors, possibly with razor cuts and white residue;

- Roach clips;

- Syringes;

- Smoking pipes.

Toke a Toad?

Could you articulate a bucket full of toads seen in a vehicle as PC?

Certain green, squat, lumpy toads with big, bulging eyes (scientific name: Bufo alvarius) secrete a venom from a gland on their backs. Drying this ooze produces an illegal smokable, hallucinogenic drug called bufotenine.

Officers in California arrested one couple, a former teacher and Explorer Scout leader and his wife, for processing bufotenine from four toads they captured in Arizona. Literature seized in their home indicated a cult of underground enthusiasts for the drug, which produces a high said to eclipse even the psyche-delic properties of LSD. Some users just lick toads for their dose. The male suspect said he got so revved from the drug he could "hear electrons jumping orbitals in my molecules."

Scientific journals trace the use of bufotenine to ancient times. In the 1950s, the Pentagon and the CIA supported research on it as part of their efforts to develop brainwashing agents, but its use has been outlawed in the U.S. since the 1960s.[14]

If judges in your jurisdictions consider some of these "associated" items too ambiguous *individually* to constitute sufficient PC for you to search the entire car, they may accept them in *combination* as evidence of narcotics trade, particularly if you are in an area with a high incidence of drug trafficking.[15] Also an attempt to *conceal* one or more of these questionable items can be grounds for concluding that criminal activity is afoot.[16] Courts will generally weigh the "*totality* of the circumstances" you perceived, in judging your actions. So when justifying any seizure-and-search decision, cite *everything* you can that factors into your assessment. In a gray situation, more observation or dialogue with the driver may strengthen your position. For example, spotting rolling papers in a car most likely *won't* give you probable cause to seize and search, because too many people theoretically still use these to roll their own tobacco cigarettes (although an estimated 90% of the popular Zig-Zag brand are used by pot smokers). But if you ask the driver what brand of cigarettes he smokes and he pulls out a pack of Marlboros, *then* the rolling papers are open to a more specific, and less innocent, interpretation. (Some jurisdictions, of course, do not outlaw drug paraphernalia. There these items would not constitute probable cause.)

So far as "plain smell" is concerned,[17] if you credibly recognize a "sufficiently distinctive" odor of drugs coming from a vehicle you've stopped, that can constitute probable cause to search areas where you reasonably suspect drugs could be hidden, including closed containers that may hold the contraband.

Note: This refers to the smell of illegal drugs, *not* of ambiguous masking odors nor unidentifiable scents. Drug odor permits only a search, usually not an arrest without additional evidence, and of course you must be lawfully positioned when you detect the scent. This could include pressing your nose against a rolled-up window from outside or sniffing along the cracks of the trunk lid. Even whiffing the smell of burnt marijuana on the clothes, identification papers, or breath of an occupant as you talk to him or her outside a vehicle can give you grounds for searching inside for unburned goods. A search in Minnesota that grew from an officer smelling dope on the body and breath of a man he'd stopped for speeding uncovered eighty pounds of marijuana, cocaine, and pills and $25,000 cash hidden under a false bottom of sheet metal in his trunk.

When you detect an identifiable drug odor, one option is to "ask for the sale," as one trooper terms it. That means ask the subject, for example, "Where's the weed?" When you make clear to him that you know you're smelling marijuana, he may offer you a shortcut by revealing where the drug is located. Asked that question in California, for example, a speeding-and-weaving suspect casually pulled a small baggie from the groin area of his pants—and that, in turn, led to the discovery of two large suitcases in his trunk, filled with nearly fifty-seven pounds of marijuana.

While pot will most often be the drug you smell, either burned or raw, you may also encounter the odors of chemicals associated with drugs or drug processing. Ether, for example, is often used to process or freebase cocaine and in the manufacturing of methamphetamine and PCP. If you haven't yet encountered some of the rarer odors on patrol, narcotics detectives may have samples they can acquaint you with. The more actual contact you can document, the tougher it will be for a suspect's lawyer to challenge your plain-smell conclusions. Also in keeping your sense of smell sharp on patrol, remember: If you smoke or chew tobacco or wear heavy cologne, that may diminish your scenting sensitivity.

During your contact, stay alert for special circumstances that will allow you to expand your plain view/plain smell opportunities. On one stop, a blankly staring driver who was so unsteady he could barely walk told an officer during a curbside interview that the officer could go into his car and get the registration. It was an offer the officer couldn't refuse. Now lawfully able to "invade" the vehicle by invitation, he opened the door—and immediately smelled ether. This resulted in a drug arrest, after the officer's sensitive nose led him to a box of Sherman cigarettes which, he knew, are often dipped in ether-exuding PCP.

Officer stopped to talk with driver of this vehicle, after spotting him urinating alongside the road. Driver, whose 2 sons were in the car, was so nervous he held onto the vehicle for support. He claimed they were bound for a 3-day trip to Disneyland, but had no luggage. Officers detected a strong plain-smell odor of fabric softener—and then found 160 lbs. of marijuana in the vehicle.

In some states, courts have also held that if a driver refuses or is unable to produce an insurance card or registration, you can search for them where you reasonably think they might be kept in the vehicle, seizing any evidence you come across as you do so.[18] This is considered acceptable for your safety, rather than let the driver reach into places where weapons may be hidden.

Even though what your senses detect may give you the legal right to enter and search a vehicle, most officers who work Criminal Patrol usually like to also get a driver's voluntary consent to search. They follow the thinking of an officer who stopped a Ford Taurus headed from Houston to Ohio while running radar at a suburban location late one morning in Arkansas. As soon as he reached the driver's window, the officer detected a "very strong" odor of marijuana coming from inside. The same sweet scent came from the nervous driver when the officer got him away from the car. Although the officer now had PC for a search, he proceeded as usual, not revealing his sensory discovery: He wrote out a warning ticket, then asked consent to search, which the driver granted. In a false compartment behind the back seat, he found twenty-one bundles of the infamous "green, leafy substance," and in a briefcase found more. "Having both probable cause and consent is a legal safety net for your case," the officer explains. "It's like a cautious surgeon who puts on two pairs of latex gloves before treating some bloody mope in the emergency room. If one fails, the other may still do the trick."

Violence-Prone Abusers

On some stops, the first indication that something is wrong will come more from what you can see or smell about the driver or other occupants than from what your senses tell you about the vehicle. If a subject is under the influence of drugs, you need to recognize and deal with that as quickly as possible; any cargo he or she may be transporting that could chemically intoxicate others becomes, for the moment, a secondary concern.

The threat to you from unrecognized or uncontrolled chemical abusers is written in blood in the modern history of police assaults. In California, an officer who was hesitant in forcefully managing a PCP freak he encountered on patrol was shot to death when the suspect ripped the victim's shotgun—rack and all—out of his unit and blasted him. Other officers have been attacked bare-handed and badly injured by assailants fueled by "cocaine psychosis," a derangement marked by extreme violence toward self and others. The infamous "'roid rage," which can be triggered by even small irritations in heavy users of anabolic steroids, can flash in a twinkling into a firestorm of violence. In Wisconsin two suspected steroid users took on two deputies, a male and a female. Before their savage attack was finally stopped at gunpoint by responding officers, the male deputy had suffered a concussion, a broken leg, badly torn muscles, and such severe bruising that surgery had to be performed to relieve blood clots. The female deputy also suffered a concussion from repeated head slams, several of her teeth were knocked out, and she was rendered unconscious with a knee drop. She was left with permanent facial-nerve damage and partial loss of vision. Plastic surgeons who tried to repair her said she was smashed and ripped like someone beaten with a baseball bat.

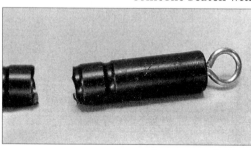

An altered state can lead to sudden and shocking strength. This "unbreakable" police mini-baton was snapped in half by a violent arrestee whom an officer was trying to control.

Abusers do not always have large amounts of contraband in their vehicle, but *violence is not necessary proportionate to quantity.* Casual users with small amounts of dope may have a lot to lose—family, job, reputation—if detected and arrested, and consequently they may take desperate action. Sophisticated training is available on drug recognition, including how to thoroughly examine and test a subject in the controlled environment of a booking location. But you need to be able *at the scene* to identify swiftly and with reasonable accuracy behavior and appearance cues associated with drug influence, especially when it poses potential danger to you.

The following reference charts are provided to help you better understand the appearance and behavioral cues exhibited by drug users that you may come in contact with on patrol:

Cocaine, Crack, Amphetamines, Methamphetamine and Other Nervous System Stimulants

Often taken by truckers to fight long-haul fatigue and frequently abused by other motorists, stimulants create exhilaration, super energy, hyperactivity, increased alertness, and a feeling of powerfulness. They can also induce irritability, anxiety, apprehension, and high paranoia, especially around law enforcement personnel, as do most drugs.

Many officers miss these symptoms, concluding too quickly that they are dealing strictly with alcohol impairment. Often alcohol and other drugs are involved and may intensify the symptoms. As with other suspects, never let a stimulant user out of your sight or turn your back on him or her. These people may be extremely paranoid. Suddenly reaching for or touching them may prompt a violent reaction. In one case, a methcathinone ("cat" or "goob") abuser killed himself when he thought he was about to be arrested.

The line between suicide and homicide (against you) is always razor-thin.

Probably more officers than you imagine will be needed to effectively immobilize these subjects. The chances of the subject trying to escape or becoming violent are very high.

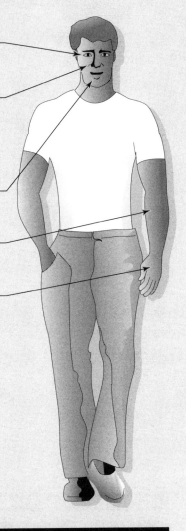

BEHAVIOR AND APPEARANCE CUES

EYES
Red, watery, or bloodshot...pupils noticeably dilated, usually more than halfway across the iris or even off the pupilometer scorecard...no nystagmus.

NOSE
If drug is snorted, very sensitive...red, runny, possibly bleeding, swollen, or scabby...frequent sniffing, like with bad cold... may be crystalline powders on nose hairs, which you may be able to see by having the subject lean his head backward while you shine your flashlight up his nose...with extensive snorting, nose hairs may be destroyed.

MOUTH
Dry, with dry spittle or slimy white coating on tongue or lips... may lick lips continually and possibly grind teeth...may be dark brown deposits on tongue and teeth or white powder residue on mustache.

VEINS
Distended, indicating elevated heart rate and higher blood pressure... may be needle marks or scar tissue if drug is injected, with possible swelling, bruising, and infection (especially in meth users).

HANDS
Trembling, wringing, excessive scratching...tips of fingers and nails may be eroded (with chronic cocaine freebasing)...nail of little finger may be exceptionally long (to serve as coke "spoon").

PERSPIRATION
Profuse, especially on forehead, neck, palms...may contribute to bad body odor, including strong chemical smell given off as drugs secrete through pores.

RESPIRATION
Rapid...may take about twenty-five breaths a minute, compared to about fifteen for the average unimpaired person.

MANNER
Hyperactive walking and talking...movements jerky, fast, uncoordinated, with exaggerated reflexes...may be startled by ambient (background) noises...rapid, rambling, "wired," motor-mouth speech...may be very nervous, fidgety, squirmy, restless...possible body tremors or uncontrollable shaking...may be either overly agreeable or disagreeable, obnoxious, and cocky...may display obvious fear or discomfort...may light cigarettes to hide odors, then put them out nervously.

MENTAL TRAITS AND SPECIAL DANGERS

Often inability to concentrate or keep up with questioning...may lack immediate recall on simple questions...slow thought processes and decision-making... not "with it"...may experience great suspiciousness, delusions, and hallucinations...during withdrawal, may be irritable and argumentative...may be excitable, unstable, hostile...may feel false sense of power, super strength, abundant self-confidence, omnipotent invincibility...can easily be triggered into state of overreaction and panic, in which he or she will be very quick, very strong, and wholly committed to self-defense in every way conceivable. "Even with low blood levels of cocaine," says a Florida medical examiner, "cases of people who go absolutely berserk are now as common as dirt."

PCP, LSD, MDMA, and Other Hallucinogens

Some of these drugs are currently making a strong comeback among adolescents.[19] The massive impact they have on the brain makes them danger-ous for the same reason they are favored by their users: They divorce an indi-vidual from reality, through visual, auditory, and other illusions and delusions. Each time they are taken, the specific behavioral effect is unpredictable, but the potential threat they represent to you is constant.

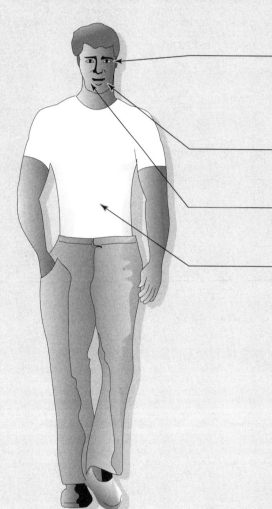

BEHAVIOR AND APPEARANCE CUES

EYES
Tearing...may show evidence of blurred vision...usually won't establish eye contact...with PCP, both horizontal and vertical nystagmus...blank stare...pupils near normal...with LSD, may stare at something intently... pupils noticeably dilated...no nystagmus.

MOUTH
Grimacing...possible clenching or grinding of teeth... may drool...with PCP, breath may have an ether smell.

FACE
Flushed, sweating because of rise in body temperature... may feel warm to the touch.

GENERAL APPEARANCE
With PCP, agitated, excited, combative...muscular rigidity... with LSD, dazed, disoriented, possibly nauseated.

MANNER
Confused, disoriented...if driving, may sit forward and hug steering wheel in seeming super concentration... may have difficulty standing, with legs far apart and braced...may slowly bob and weave...poor coordination... speech often slurred...muscle rigidity may cause spastic jerking of arms...with PCP, may be uncommunicative, responding to simple questions or commands by nodding or giving incomplete, repetitive answers...may be nude because of high body temperature...with LSD, may talk about bizarre things, like the sides of your squad car moving in and out as if it is breathing... may reveal an illogical mix-up of senses, like referring to "the color of the wind"...may experience body tremors...poor perception of time and distance.

MENTAL TRAITS AND SPECIAL DANGERS

Emotional instability...concentration generally difficult, but may focus intently on very minute things...memory impaired...following directions difficult...may misperceive surroundings and self, not knowing where he or she is or why...poor perception of distance and time...exaggerated emotional reactions to what is seen, heard, or imagined... may perceive you as part of persecuting plot...extremely defensive about personal space...mood can swing unpredictably and fast between tranquility and paranoid, "fired up" violence...minor, ordinary occurrences may pro-voke extreme overreactions for no apparent reason... frightening hallucinations may cause you to be perceived as a life-threatening apparition, giving rise to a "fight-for-life" attack, or (especially with LSD) subject may vividly imagine his own body is being dismembered or destroyed.

Marijuana

For most people, smoking pot, possibly the most abused drug other than alcohol (some say cocaine is the most popular) and generally a depressant, has a calming effect. But some people react just the opposite. Also, along with stimulants to the central nervous system, marijuana is probably the drug most likely to be used in transit by persons with drugs. Thus your detection of its symptoms can be an important factor in your sensory evaluation.

BEHAVIOR AND APPEARANCE CUES

EYES
Bloodshot, with pronounced veins in eyeballs...glassy... pupils usually normal but may be slightly dilated... lids drooping, possibly tremulous...no nystagmus... pupils slow to react to changes of light.

MOUTH
Dry...may be spitting or plucking of cigarette debris from tongue...tongue may have greenish cast...possible hacking cough and mouth breathing.

HANDS
May be burn marks on thumb and forefinger.

MANNER
May experience mild body tremors...slow, slurred speech... often drowsy appearance and giddiness...poor muscle coordination... slow gait...poor balance...impaired depth perception may cause subject to step unusually high.

MENTAL TRAITS AND SPECIAL DANGERS

Short attention span, with difficulty concentrating... impaired perceptions of time and distance...disorientation and mild confusion...slow reaction time...relaxed inhibitions. Often used with cocaine, crack, PCP, and other drugs with erratic results...abuser may be volatile and aggressive. Heavy doses may produce psychosis and paranoia, causing your presence and actions to seem unduly threatening to the suspect. Most marijuana now on the street has a significantly higher level of THC, the active ingredient, than in the past, intensifying reactions.

Says the executive director of a Miami-based drug information center: "We are seeing [marijuana users] more and more in the criminal justice system and [marijuana more often] reported as resulting in violence."[20]

Anabolic Steroids

An estimated 1,000,000 to 3,000,000 Americans, many of them adolescent athletes, abuse these body-building "chemical time-savers," which, in fact, destroy both body and mind in time. About two-thirds of abusers began using 'roids at or before the age of sixteen, getting them from coaches, medical personnel, mail order, or the black market.[21] Ironically, these are still not viewed by many people as drugs of abuse, although they are commonly taken in quantities 100 times the "recommended" dose. Some authorities warn that they are more dangerous than most "recreational" drugs. People who use them are also more likely to use other drugs, like marijuana and cocaine. Certainly steroids are dangerous to you. Abusers may feel more aggressive and are two to three times more likely to have committed recent violence than non-users.[22]

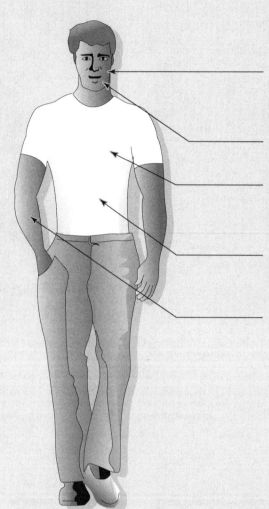

BEHAVIOR AND APPEARANCE CUES

FACE
May be badly broken out with acne or skin rash... possible jaundice, due to liver damage...facial hair on females...males may have heavier than normal body hair, but thinning hair on temples and forehead.

VOICE
Nonreversible deepness in females.

BREASTS
Males may develop what they call "bitch tits," breasts that actually protrude...female breast development diminishes as musculature increases.

GENERAL APPEARANCE
Very muscular...may look bloated, like the Michelin Man, because of fluid retention...possible "pumpkin head."

ARMS
Needle marks may be present, as steroids can be injected as well as taken orally.

MENTAL TRAITS AND SPECIAL DANGERS

Mood may swing abruptly and unpredictably from euphoria or giddiness to depression and aggressiveness...can suddenly become extremely violent over small things. The strongest steroids are injectibles, so users may carry needles with them, like heroin abusers. Guard against getting stuck when searching their clothing, luggage, seat cushions, or other potential hiding places in vehicles.

Officer Ken Wrede, 26, lies dead under a sheet after a PCP suspect reached inside his patrol car and ripped his Remington 870 shotgun and mount right off the dash, charged the shotgun, still in its mount (right), and killed Wrede.

Michael Jackson, 29, a daily PCP user and now a convicted cop-killer.

(above/right)
Unpredictability of drug abusers can quickly turn "routine" tasks into violent encounters. Rather than offer a potential weapon, most officers prefer using their index finger to conduct nystagmus tests. Officer (right) nearly lost an eye when a suspect used her writing instrument in a way she'll never forget.

Anyone in an altered state, including drunks and characteristically passive heroin addicts, should be considered unpredictable and therefore potentially dangerous, just like a person who's emotionally disturbed from mental illness. The delusions of hallucinogen abusers are strongly held and completely believed—and they will react to *their* view of reality, not yours. In particular PCP, a powerful analgesic, may imbue the user with a sense of superhuman strength and virtual immunity to pain. Trying to use single-officer control techniques that depend on pain compliance may only get you hurt or killed. Until you have sufficient backup—perhaps five to eight officers—remain as reassuring, calming, and non-threatening as possible. If you are attacked, an immediate high-level force response will probably be necessary, such as shots that impact the spinal cord.

Unfortunately, many officers, once they perceive a mental and physical impairment, let their alertness for danger subside. It should *increase.* Although symptoms of a generally "nonviolent" drug like marijuana may predominate, you can never be sure what combination of other drugs may also have been taken; in some drug-treatment programs, up to 40% of abusers report that they prefer marijuana laced with LSD.[23] Moreover, you cannot predict what effect the stress of a potential search and arrest may produce.

Officer frisks a man suspected of being on heroin, while another heroin abuser watches. Although heroin users are generally considered passive, would you feel comfortable trying to manage these 2 unstable suspects alone?

The driver of this car was stopped for weaving in Arizona. The officer recognized signs of amphetamine use (sweating, slurred speech) and handcuffed the driver, who managed to escape on foot but was quickly captured. In this trunk was a cargo of methamphetamine.

162

"Assume": It Makes an "Ass" of "U" and "Me"

About 10 o'clock one morning, a deputy sheriff in Mississippi stopped a rental car from Alabama carrying two males, for weaving. Both appeared to have been snorting cocaine and the driver seemed severely impaired, drooling from his mouth as he talked. The deputy, who had a rookie with him, put the passenger in the back of his squad car, then started to pat down the driver. He didn't handcuff him first because he "assumed he was too impaired to be dangerous." Big mistake. The deputy reports:

As I touched him he said, "Man, I gotta tell ya som'thin'. I got a gun."

I said, "Don't move!"

I started patting for it, then all hell broke loose.

With his left hand, he pulled a piece of aluminum foil—his coke—out of his left-front pocket and started to eat it. With his right hand, he grabbed a five-shot .22-cal. revolver out of his right-rear pocket. I grabbed him in a bear hug, and we went to the ground.

His hand was so big it encompassed his entire gun. I grabbed his hand with both my hands, trying to get it. I kept telling him I was going to shoot him if he didn't let go of it.

Then out of the corner of my eye, I saw my gun, lying on the side of the road! The rookie was just standing there in a daze. I yelled at him, "Pull your gun out!" but he just stood there, looking at me. He was so scared he didn't know what to do.

Finally I smashed the driver in the face with my fist. Coke, blood, and spit spewed out of his mouth. I hit him a couple more times and eventually was able to get control of the gun.

Back at the station, I took some Popsicle sticks from a rape kit and scraped fluid from his face and neck so I could test it and charge him with possession of cocaine.

The whole thing was a tactical embarrassment. I sharpened up after that and was glad to be alive to do it.

Unless you're in imminent danger, take your time in dealing with anyone who seems drug-impaired. Trying to rush is likely only to aggravate these people. Talk slowly so the subject can comprehend you. As with an EDP, you may get farther by *requesting* what you want done rather than ordering or threatening. The subject may already be afraid. More fear may just trigger him to explode. Acts that tend to stimulate the senses—loud or aggressive questioning, a body search for weapons, lights flashed in the eyes of a PCP abuser especially, or an attempt to handcuff the suspect—may set off violent reactions. Any abuser can change behavior *instantly*, going from calm to incredibly violent without warning. Your goal, even after backup arrives and certainly before, is to get or keep the subject calmed down. Having only one person speak to him usually helps in that regard because it reduces the amount of stimulation and confusion. If he's delusional, don't argue with him. No amount of logic or proof from you will shake his fantasy; arguing will just keep him agitated. More effective may be to reassure him that he's just having a bad trip...that you're there to help him...that everything's going to be all right. As with EDPs, stay alert for signs that the abuser is hearing voices. You may hear him "answer" someone who isn't there...or cock his head as if he's listening to sounds you can't hear...or perhaps even say that someone gives him instructions. If he's hearing voices that give commands, he's potentially very dangerous, because you have no way of knowing what "orders" he is "receiving."

Be prepared to significantly escalate your level of force, even as you're talking and attempting to calm him.

Assuming a conservative initial approach on your part, just where your contact leads—and with what level of violence—will depend on the drugged suspect's behavior. For the majority of drivers and passengers you stop who are not on drugs, you move now toward the heart of your investigative stop: the probing through dialogue for more contraband cues, including evidence of deception, and then the decision about whether they have dirty little secrets—or dirty big secrets—to hide.

163

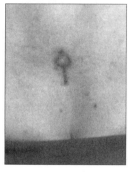

Thomas Hoyeson (top right) did something one night that had never happened before in Milford, CT. He killed a cop. When Officer Daniel Scott Wasson (inset) made a stop for an expired registration, he was unaware that Hoyeson was under the influence of cocaine. In the re-creation of the shooting (above) you see where Hoyeson was standing when he fired the fatal shot with a .44 Magnum.

Hoyeson, whose brother had also killed an officer, made a daily practice of taping a handcuff key to the small of his back. Note the impression of the key on his skin, even after removal.

(above)
At one point in his career, West Haven (CT) Chief John Mariano (now retired) made a decision not to shoot a gunman who was firing at him. That gunman was Hoyeson, who 11 years later killed Officer Wasson.

(left)
At Wasson's funeral, fiancée Melissa Piscitelli, also a Milford officer, salutes farewell next to "General," Daniel's K-9.

164

DETECTING DECEPTION

"Before I knew what I was doing," says a Mississippi officer after more than seven years on Criminal Patrol, "I stopped two guys in a pickup truck that was loaded with shoeboxes. They claimed they were going to New Orleans from Miami to deliver shoes. Looking back, I'm sure those boxes were loaded with coke. *I knew* they weren't right, but I didn't know what I could do...."

When a detective interrogates a suspect, he's often able to carefully construct an environment that actively promotes his success and safety. The questioning may take place in a stark, isolated room with no distractions. It may continue for hours without interruption. At least one other officer is usually available for the old "bad cop/good cop" routine. The suspect's criminal past and violent inclinations are probably well known. He has been thoroughly searched, he may be restrained. And in the end, he may be hooked up to a polygraph for a couple of hours to see if he's telling the truth before he's cut loose.

On the street when you're trying to learn the truth about a vehicle stop, these are luxuries you can only dream of. Rain, snow, howling wind, blistering heat, hostile crowds, roaring traffic, pressure from other calls, computers that are down, dispatchers who are busy, bored, or bitchy—these may be your environment. The suspect knows exactly who you are, but at the outset you probably know nothing about him, maybe not even a gut feel that he's wrong. He may be secretly armed, plotting attack with help from coconspirators only a shout or a signal away. Initially you are likely to be alone. You are under legal obligation to keep your contact brief. The person you want to know about the worst may be able to lie the best, yet the only lie detector you have at the scene is yourself. And like the Mississippi officer quoted above, there undoubtedly are times when you feel that's just not enough.

Yet despite these hefty handicaps, you can successfully and safely ferret out wrongdoers—by adapting to the turmoil of the street some of the same principles and tactics the skilled interviewer brings to his controlled interrogation room...and that the Mississippi officer and many others on Criminal Patrol have now mastered through trial, error, and long study.

The minutes you spend with the driver and other occupant(s) after your initial contact are most likely to be the turning point of your stop. What you see and hear during this contact will ultimately determine whether you're suspicious enough to ask permission to search...or should just give the violator a ticket and a quick good-bye.

As you conduct your evaluation, you and guilty subjects will be working to con each other. They'll be trying to convince you that they are unexceptional, legitimate motorists. "Lie, Lie, Lie," advises a hand-printed manual for drug dealers confiscated from a suspect in Denver—and they will. They can conceal (withhold) information from you, which is their preferred MO, and/or they can actively falsify what they do offer, which is harder for them to pull off because they must invent the "facts." Usually they do a little or a lot of each. As you silently analyze their stories, their verbal mannerisms, and their body language for deception cues, you'll be trying to convince them that suspicion is far from your mind. To expose their deception swiftly, you need to create a nonthreatening atmosphere that encourages even reluctant people to reveal information, without realizing that because of your special insights it may work against them. The longer you can delay their tumbling to the fact that you are actually appraising them, their vehicle, and their reason for being in transit, the more likely they are to unwittingly provide you with incriminating evidence and the less likely they are to feel so jeopardized that they decide to clam up, flee, or attack.

In drawing them out, you're conducting a "concealed interrogation"; in effect, a polygraph exam without a polygraph. In some ways, you can be even more effective than the machine. A polygraph measures only blood pressure, pulse rate, perspiration, and breathing; but with the right style, questions, and alertness to auditory and visual feedback, you can explore far more. Plus, what you detect can be used not only to build your case at the stop site but to strengthen it in court.

Every vehicle stop is a story waiting to be told. The characters and setting you can see. The plot—bland or bold—is hidden in the documents, the conversation, and the involuntary disclosures you now are able to address.

Getting the *true* story depends, first of all, on wanting to. Most liars, says one expert, "escape detection because the targets of their deceits don't care enough to work at catching them."[1] The 5%er essence of Criminal Patrol, of course, is *caring.* And by applying the strategies described here, you'll be amazed at how easy catching people in lies can be.

Fighting the Clock

It's surprising how fast people reveal that they have something to hide. Watching time-coded videotapes of stops where contraband is eventually found, you'll notice that often within about *two minutes* of the officer making contact with the driver, strong verbal or behavioral deception cues that are readily identifiable begin to emerge.

That's good, because from the moment the violator's vehicle comes to a halt, you're operating against a legal stopwatch.

The U. S. Supreme Court has never stated exactly how long you're entitled to detain a traffic violator against his or her will. But generally courts have held that an involuntary detention can last only as long as it takes you to expeditiously accomplish certain "reasonably necessary duties."[2] These primarily include:

- Instructing the violator to move the vehicle, if necessary for safety;
- Obtaining his or her license, vehicle registration, insurance infor

mation, and other pertinent documentation;

- Explaining the violation;
- Listening to any explanation the driver may offer;
- Running warrants, registration, and license checks;
- Checking for prior recent moving violations;
- Examining the vehicle for unsafe conditions;
- Writing out a citation or warning;
- Explaining follow-up actions that are necessary by the driver;
- Answering any questions he or she may have.

Extending the detention beyond that, "routinely and without any cause whatsoever," violates legal guidelines. So does directly "interrogating" the driver about narcotics trafficking or other possible offenses or seeking permission to search his or her vehicle during this *enforcement* portion of the stop, if you do so "on a mere hunch."[3] (When and how you *can* pursue these important concerns is explained in Chapter 6.)

In effect, what this means is that, initially at least, you must subtly integrate your probing for incriminating information into an efficient performance of more obvious tasks.

So long as you do not create "undue" delays, nothing forbids you from engaging the driver and passenger(s) in what appears to be casual conversation while you are carrying out your laundry list of "necessary duties." If this dialogue or your observation of the vehicle or occupant(s) raises reasonable suspicions in your mind regarding possible criminal activities, you can then prolong the detention temporarily while you investigate and resolve these suspicions.[4] Likewise, concern for officer safety can justify extending the contact, as in a case in California where a driver was delayed longer than normal after officers recognized his name as having been associated with past confrontations with police.[5]

Once you manage to unearth reasonable suspicions that require exploration, you are operating in a less restrictive time frame. If trying to clarify the circumstances gets complicated, extending the detention to forty-five minutes or even more might be considered reasonable.[6] But usually, you'll want to make a decision about asking permission to search in no more than five to twenty minutes maximum, so that you minimize your "intrusion" into the suspect's right of free movement until you have grounds for a custodial arrest.

Courts will consider whether you were actively involved in an investigative process during the time you kept the driver; that is, were you diligently directing your efforts toward completing the stop and "quickly confirming or dispelling" any suspicions.[7] So keep the conversation and your activities moving briskly. This keeps you legal...helps keep the suspect from perceiving that he's being detained...and gives him less time to think about and construct effective deception.

Instant Rapport

Because you must work fast, the personality you project must be calculated to get the violator quickly to let his or her guard down. Most people are naturally inclined to be reticent when they're trying to conceal wrongdoing, and magazines like *High Times* and other "trade journals" for the drug crowd repeatedly caution transporters to stay as mute as possible when stopped by the police. You want to get people *cooperating* with you and *talking*. You do it by establishing rapport, the feeling of acceptance and trust. Then they'll often talk themselves right into incrimination or what one observer calls a "jailhouse built out of bullshit."

A simple formula explains the influence you can bring to any interaction with a suspect: Stimulus...Object...Behavior. You are the Stimulus when you talk to the suspect, who is the Object, and his or her Behavior, either cooperative or uncooperative, is a reaction to the stimulation you present; in short, *your approach affects the suspect's response.* This is easy to remember because the acronym is S.O.B. But if you act like an s.o.b., as too many officers do on vehicle stops, you'll never establish the instant rapport you need for a good concealed interrogation.

In recruit school, you probably were trained to keep your contact with traffic violators to a minimum. In so many words, this may have been framed as "Just deliver the mail"—issue your citation, get the driver back on his way, and you get back on patrol. This does accommodate the legal strictures on detention time and, theoretically at least, promotes officer survival by lessening your exposure to the violator and to traffic, hostile crowds, and other environmental hazards. In the field, though, this minimum contact often becomes either indifferent contact, which reveals virtually nothing about the circumstances beyond the traffic violation, or rude, curt, and intimidating contact, a power-trip approach that fosters resentment, hostility, and resistance from the Object.

On Criminal Patrol, *this demeanor is a guaranteed recipe for failure.* People loosen up and talk most easily to those they consider friendly, understanding, trustworthy, helpful, and nonthreatening. Think of Columbo on TV: affable, laid back, not too sharp, just a chatty, nosy but "undiscerning" cop seeming to have no interest or talent for detecting anything serious. If what one officer calls "this dumb country-fuck routine" is a bit much for you or your beat, "Think how your dentist treats you when you walk into his office," suggests a North Carolina trainer. "That's the approach: professional friendliness." You want the violator to think you could almost be buddies.

By deliberately projecting that personality, apparently just trying to make small talk while you're hanging a ticket, you disarm guilty parties psychologically and encourage overconfidence on their part. This, in fact, suckers them right into the conversational traps you're setting up. In short, you can convict them with your "stupidity."

Remember, though: *this good ol' boy role is strictly an act.* In truth, you know what you are doing. Behind the guise, you stay watchful at all times. You don't want the people you're questioning to be the last people you see on this earth. Don't *ever* become so caught up in playing the part that you become careless about your safety. And don't do anything *tactical* that lets people you've stopped think you are easy prey. If they are involved in criminal activity, they'll likely be watching for such "windows of opportunity" and weighing the odds of taking you on. You can smile and still be on guard, and if you need to be assertive, do so without hesitation.

A deputy who stopped what seemed like a down-and-out couple and their two boys sympathetically encouraged them to tell him all about their welfare woes. But he stayed acutely aware that the woman seemed unusually tense in clutching her purse. Fearing a weapon was inside, he asked if he could look in it. She unzippered it and started to thrust her hand in. *Gun!* he thought. He slapped the purse from her grasp. As it hit the ground, a fried-chicken bag tumbled out—not with the weapon he expected but with what proved to be $15,000 cash the "welfare" couple earned from a drug transaction. In this case, his ability to conduct concealed interrogation without forgetting officer survival exposed a phony cover story. But if the woman had been drawing a gun, his alertness could have saved his life.

Sometimes the genial approach itself can enhance your safety. One Arizona trooper with an enviable record of drug busts claims that her friendly demeanor and "next-door-neighbor" appearance—short, chunky, fortyish—consistently fool contraband carriers into assuming she's no threat. One day she stopped two males and searched their Toyota 4-Runner, which had expired registration tabs. She found eight kilos of coke in a suitcase, and from behind a seat she retrieved a .45-cal. pistol and eleven cartridges. The offenders were street-gang members; one had ninety-nine misdemeanor warrants outstanding from all over the country. The passenger later testified that when they were first stopped, he planned to shoot the officer but then decided against it because she seemed so harmless. "If I'd known I was going to jail, I would definitely have shot her!" he declared. By the time they discovered how sharp she really was, she had outmaneuvered them.

Keep rapport working for you, not the suspect(s). If you're a female officer, a male offender may try to develop his own rapport with you, as a means of taking advantage. Female couriers may do the same if you're male, through tears, flirting, or other manipulative behavior—or by playing on a feminist bond if you are female. One drug hauler tells of being stopped with a load one time when he had a For Sale sign on his car window. He managed to get the officer so interested in buying the car that the cop let him go without a ticket in exchange for a (phony) phone number where he could reach the "owner" to close the deal. *Always stay conscious of who's controlling the interaction.*

Be careful not to weaken rapport by taking personally any negative Stimulus you may get from the suspect. Some officers, for instance, go ballistic if they're lied to, as if it's a personal affront. You don't belong

169

Gender can be a dangerous element where rapport-building is concerned. For example, who do you think is in control here?

on Criminal Patrol with that attitude. A crook's job is to break the law and lie to the police. Your job is to catch him at it. You *want* him to lie, especially by falsifying, because you probably can detect it.

With the right approach, you usually can get a guilty party to lie within about three to four questions. Finding out the truth may not be possible until after you've searched the vehicle, but that's fine. Your goal at this stage is to build reasonable suspicion, not elicit a formal confession. And detecting a lie is generally the Number One flag to you that something is wrong.

Deception in Documentation

Among the first things you examine closely on most stops are documents associated with the driver and vehicle, such as license, registration, perhaps a rental agreement, and, with commercial carriers, shipping papers and logbook. These are often fruitful starting places in detecting deception. The credentials—or lack of them—may themselves be questionable, thus justifying delay for more investigation, or they may provide information you can capitalize on in developing revealing dialogue with the people you're detaining.

Just how you analyze documentation to pinpoint suspicious aspects depends on whether you've stopped a vehicle that's private... rental...or commercial.

1. Private. With a private vehicle, the most important immediate question is: *Who is the registered owner?* Private cars on contraband runs often are alleged to be "borrowed" and to belong to a relative or a friend of the driver or passenger or to someone who just hired the driver to take the vehicle to a destination and drop it off; in short, it belongs to someone who isn't present...it's a so-called "third-party vehicle."

Identification of the owner may be very confusing. In some states, cars bought at auction or from small used-car lots may carry a non-specific "open" title from the time of sale until the buyer gets around to registering it. Drug-running street gangs acquiring such cars sometimes keep these titles open indefinitely to deliberately obscure ownership.

Other times, registration information may be virtually nonexistent. A driver stopped for speeding in Utah handed a trooper a bill of sale for the car as his "registration." The bill was handwritten on the back of an envelope and didn't have a notary seal, nor could the driver produce a signed title. During a consent search, the trooper discovered that the violator was illegally transporting guns.

Any time you stop a vehicle where the owner isn't in it, ask for a phone number where he or she can be contacted. When pressed, the occupants may not even be able to tell you the name of the owner without looking at the registration themselves, or they may only know a first name ("Vince, from down the block"). You need to confirm that the owner has not been harmed and that the vehicle is not stolen. Thus you have valid grounds to detain until you can verify that the driver is legally in possession. If you can identify the owner, try to get a criminal history check on that individual as well as the driver and any passenger(s) through your communications center. Any drug-related charges or other shady background that show up will give you more cause to be suspicious.

Is there a geographic cohesion to the vehicle and occupants? The first clue that led to 150 pounds of pot hidden in the trunk of a Crown Victoria in Missouri came when a deputy noticed that the car bore Missouri plates and had the caps of Missouri sports teams in its rear window, but the driver carried an Arizona driver's license. With most legitimate travelers in private vehicles, the registration, driver's license, current residency, various inspection stickers, dealer's logo, and other decals displayed on the car will all be from the same state. With contraband traffickers in third-party cars, not only are documentation sites frequently scattered, but the occupants often live in different parts of the country from each other, too. Although they'll generally claim to be "friends," sometimes of long standing, they may not even know each other's last names.

Minor Violator...Major Fugitive

Two things about the blue Olds Cutlass caught the eye of Officer Michael Kabisinski when the car zipped past him as he patrolled his township beat adjacent to Erie, Pennsylvania:

1. The vehicle lacked a state inspection sticker that should have been affixed to the lower left corner of the windshield;

2. Although the car bore a Pennsylvania license plate, an automobile dealership sticker on the trunk was from Indiana. Not illegal, but unusual.

Noticing Kabisinski behind him, the driver tried to elude him by ducking through a series of side streets. After about five minutes of cat-and-mouse, Kabisinski got him stopped.

Approaching for license and registration, Kabisinski saw a highway map on the dashboard in front of the one visible passenger, and numerous fast-food wrappers and bags on the floor.

The nervous driver claimed he had left his wallet with license and registration in his hotel room. He said the car belonged to his mother, "Jan Cunningham." But when Kabisinski asked him to spell her last name, he stumbled to a stop about two-thirds of the way through. "At that point," says Kabisinski, "my belief that something was way wrong really escalated."

Waiting back at his unit for backup, Kabisinski learned from dispatch that the Olds' license plate really belonged to a Chevy from Pittsburgh. When backup arrived and the two occupants were ordered out, the officers discovered that the passenger, who was dressed as a male, was really a female. An extended verbal exchange with the driver eventually revealed their true names. An NCIC check disclosed that they were wanted in Indianapolis for nearly twenty armed robberies, including the stickup of a shoe store where a clerk had been killed.

Later the driver said that if Kabisinski had returned to the vehicle to question him further, the officer would have been shot. "He could have shot me," Kabisinski acknowledges, "because during a search of the vehicle we discovered a Glock 9mm under the driver seat with eight rounds in it. When I asked him why he decided not to shoot me, he said that when he saw the backup officer arrive he got nervous and put the gun back under the seat."

Courier cars that are owned by the driver crop up more often now than in the past because drug bosses trying to avoid the third-party stigma may give the vehicle to the transporter as full or partial payment for the run. How long has the car been registered in the driver's name? If only a few days and he or she is already on a long trip, that could be an indicator.

In most states, the registration papers will indicate whether the car has been paid for in full or still carries a lien. An expensive, new car that's completely paid for could be a drug vehicle that was bought with cash. Keeping in mind the dealer logo you've seen on the trunk or license frame, ask where the car was purchased. If there's a conflict, something's probably wrong. Also check the odometer. High mileage on a new vehicle is another potential courier clue.

Sometimes guilty drivers try verbally to "distance" themselves from the car. Then if you find contraband, they feel more confident in claiming they didn't know it was there. A blatant example occurred in Connecticut when a subject said he didn't own the Ford Taurus he was driving and didn't know who did. When an officer asked him why he had the car's keys, he threw the keys into the car's open window and said: "I don't have any keys." A brown bag later recovered from the car contained both cocaine and heroin. In California, a young driver claimed not to know where the vehicle's registration was and insisted the car wasn't his; he "just picked it up a day ago to drive up north" for some guy. The officer suspected he was hauling drugs, but didn't immediately challenge the story. A few minutes later while inspecting the exterior, the officer pointed to the mag wheels. "Damn, those are nice tires! Where'd you get those?" he asked, playing the good ol' boy. "I'd sure like to get a set like that! Did you buy 'em around here?" "Yeah," the driver said proudly, "and they were on sale!" "Really! Think it might still be going on? How long ago did you put 'em on the car?" "Right after I got 'em—about a month ago." Oops! The officer's mental polygraph needle just took a jump. And when he searched later, he found the drug load he suspected.

A driver's license may yield deception cues, too. If it's from your state, you probably know how to detect a counterfeit. But if it's unfamiliar, check a pocket identification manual showing licenses from every state that you can carry in your patrol car for indications of tampering unique to the driver's jurisdiction.[8] (Asian gangs, among others, are reportedly responsible for mass producing false driver's licenses, enabling members to stay in this country illegally, travel state-to-state, and go underground after being involved in crimes.)

A new license may motivate you to question the violator more closely about his past whereabouts. Common practice among L.A. street-gang "pioneers" heading for new drug-peddling frontiers, for example, is to go first to Texas or Oklahoma, get new licenses there (often with phony addresses), and then go on to their "homesteading" destination, having eliminated obvious evidence of their L.A. roots.

Also note the first three numerals of the Social Security number that appears on most licenses. These are code for the state where the subject was living when the card was issued or (if issued before

Detecting a Doctored Driver's License

When checking a driver's license for validity, check it both front and back.

Use the helpful hints below, as reprinted from a National Park Service law enforcement bulletin.

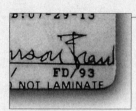

LAMINATION: Check lamination closely. Laminations/protective coatings applied by the issuing agencies usually are tightly sealed to prevent alterations or fraud. Laminations added by others to mask an altered or forged license may show separation or peeling. Some states may prohibit lamination.

COLORS: There are usually two or more colors on driver's licenses from most states. Colors may be on picture background and/or in format.

CLARITY: When checking clarity, check following on both front and rear formats:

> Sharpness of lines and print: Issued licenses are printed by typewriter or by computer. Lines in format are sharp and distinct. Ditto printing. In license you're examining, does the thickness in the same line vary?

> Smudges/Mistakes/Erasures/"Cut and Paste": Presence of same indicates altered or fake ID. Check for tape-overs, cutting/piercing, areas added or deleted. Hold license up to light to aid in detection.

> Uneven lines or print: Indicators of false, forged, or altered ID. Check all lines and printing closely. Are lines off-center, lines or spacing uneven, unusual forms of printing present?

> Other: Staple holes in license usually indicate a valid license with prior traffic offenses (many jurisdictions staple a driver's license to issued violation notices until fines are paid). Large hole (from a punch) may indicate expired/out-of-date license. Staple holes in photo of licensee may indicate an "attitude" problem on a previous stop.

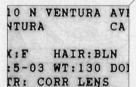

PHYSICAL DESCRIPTION: Compare with picture and person.

PICTURE COLOR: Is the background of photo consistent with the color of issuing state? NOTE: Some states may have an alternate color for minors, others may have profile picture.

PICTURE EDGE: Has picture been added? There should be no raised edges on photo. Issued licenses imprint photo directly on license.

OVERLAP OF SIGNATURES/SEALS/REFLECTORIZED PRINTING: Majority of all issued licenses have overlapping of one or more of these elements on both format and picture. Overlap onto picture is usually a state seal, commissioner's signature, issuing station number, driver's signature, or reflectorized printing in the issued lamination process. Only a few states do not have some form of overlap on their pictures. If one of these ends abruptly at a picture's edge and a portion is cut off or blocked at the edge, it indicates a forged license. If hologram is present, check 3-D picture closely. A fake will not appear as 3-D.[9]

1973) at least the state where he or she first registered with Social Security. (The other card numbers have no special meaning.) In our highly mobile society, it's not unusual for a driver to live in an area far afield from where he first registered with Social Security. But by decoding these numbers via the chart printed below, you'll have a bit of intelligence with which you can test a driver's reaction to an unexpected question. If his license shows a current address in Vermont, say, but his Social Security number starts with 403-, ask him casually: "What was it like living in Kentucky?" If he denies he ever did, something's wrong.

Social Security Codes by State

S.S. #	ISSUING STATE	S.S. #	ISSUING STATE	S.S. #	ISSUING STATE
001-003	New Hampshire	416-424	Alabama	575-576	Hawaii
004-007	Maine	425-428	Mississippi	577-579	District of Columbia
008-009	Vermont	429-432	Arkansas	580*	Virgin Islands
010-034	Massachusetts	433-439	Louisiana	580-584	Puerto Rico
035-039	Rhode Island	440-448	Oklahoma	585	New Mexico
040-049	Connecticut	449-467	Texas	586*	Guam, American
050-134	New York	468-477	Minnesota		Samoa, Philippines,
135-158	New Jersey	478-485	Iowa		Northern Mariana
159-211	Pennsylvania	486-500	Missouri		Islands
212-220	Maryland	501-502	North Dakota	587-588	Mississippi
221-222	Delaware	503-504	South Dakota	589-595	Florida
223-231	Virginia	505-508	Nebraska	596-599	Puerto Rico
232	North Carolina	509-515	Kansas	600-601	Arizona
232-236	West Virginia	516-517	Montana	602-626	California
237-246	North Carolina	518-519	Idaho	627-645	Texas
247-251	South Carolina	520	Wyoming	646-647	Utah
252-260	Georgia	521-524	Colorado	648-649	New Mexico
261-267	Florida	525	New Mexico	650-699	Not assigned or issued
268-302	Ohio	526-527	Arizona	700-728**	Railroad Retirement
303-317	Indiana	528-529	Utah	729-799	Not assigned or issued
318-361	Illinois	530	Nevada		
362-386	Michigan	531-539	Washington	* Some numbers from this area also assigned to SE Asian refugees from 1975-1979.
387-399	Wisconsin	540-544	Oregon	
400-407	Kentucky	545-573	California	
408-415	Tennessee	574*	Alaska	** Not been issued since the 1960s.[10]

2. Rental. With a rental car, get your hands on the contract as soon as possible to forestall the suspect trying to "speed read" it to learn the information you'll be asking about. (He's required to hand the contract over to you on request.) First determine whether the rental agreement is in the driver's name. If not, is the lessee present? If not, how is that person connected to the people in the car? Is the driver's name even on the contract as an alternate authorized operator? If the lessee is not in the car and the driver's name is not on the contract, you are entitled to detain the vehicle and contact the rental agency for instructions. (In some jurisdictions, you may also be entitled to search the car, on grounds that the driver is not authorized to possess it and thus does not have a reasonable expectation of privacy in it.[11])

Considering that for a drug transport a third party usually contracts for the vehicle and then gives it to the mule without the knowledge of the rental agency, the driver may not even know the actual lessee's name, or where or when the vehicle was rented, if he hasn't studied the rental agreement. Test him. If the contract says the lessee is Tom Jones, ask the driver, as if you are reading from it, "So, Bobby Smith rented this for you?" If he says, "Yeah," then ask who Bobby is, to see how far he'll go and what you'll learn from his fairy tale.

Was the rental charged on a credit card? That's how almost all legitimate people rent cars these days, and what most mainstream rental agencies require. But drug traffickers sometimes find secondary firms that will accept cash. Indeed, a cash rental was one of the first cues an officer in Arkansas picked up on after stopping a motor home for a traffic violation. This small beginning eventually led to the discovery of $4,000,000 worth of cocaine bricks hidden under a drawer inside. Any rental vehicle without credit-card documentation on the rental papers calls for special scrutiny.

If it was rented by credit card, does the card belong to a third party not present in the vehicle? Be sure your radio request for a criminal-background check includes the name of the person renting and paying for the car, whether or not he or she is along. Also, is the card number imprinted (as it should be) or hand-printed. The latter may suggest a phony card number listed as a cover by a rental company employee who is providing the car surreptitiously. (Some rental firms have such poor inventory control that they don't realize quickly when a vehicle is missing.) If the driver claims to be the renter of the vehicle, ask him or her to produce the credit card whose number appears on the contract.

Does the license plate check out to the car? Rental agencies often switch plates among their vehicles, so this is not necessarily an indicator. But it will take time to investigate, creating more opportunity for you to converse with the occupant(s).

Do you see any plug-in electronics—radar detector, CB, scanner, mobile phone—that could be more indication of an unusual need to travel fast and stay in touch on a long haul? Note how long the car has been out and how many miles have been driven. Does the total jibe with where the driver says he has been? If a lot of mileage has been clocked in just a few days, that could suggest day-and-night driving.

With rentals, always assess the financial feasibility of the trip. If a *passenger car* was rented from the same city where the driver or lessee resides, this is unusual for legitimate purposes; why didn't the driver just use his own car? Likewise, if the rental is one-way, requiring a drop-off fee and perhaps an airline ticket back home, does the stated purpose of the trip seem to justify that level of expense? On a stop in Nebraska, two men said they'd rented a U-Haul truck to transport $10,000 worth of new furniture they'd just bought in Omaha back home to Texas. That didn't seem to make sense, decided the trooper who'd stopped them, considering that identical goods were surely available hundreds of miles closer. He discovered the real reason for the trip hidden behind the seat in the cab: $120,000 cash and two kilos of cocaine. On a windy, rainy day in Arizona, another officer observed a U-Haul swerving about the highway. While preparing a warning for poor lane usage, she casually asked the male driver and female passenger where they were

Building Suspicion with a Rental Contract

Checkpoints on a vehicle rental contract to help you develop reasonable suspicion for wanting to detain the driver for more investigation and/or search the vehicle:

In addition, ask the subject questions about his current employment situation to detect deception: What is your employer's name? What are your duties? Is this trip job-related? What is your company's business address and phone number? Ask yourself if the type or absence of employment justifies the expense of a rental car.

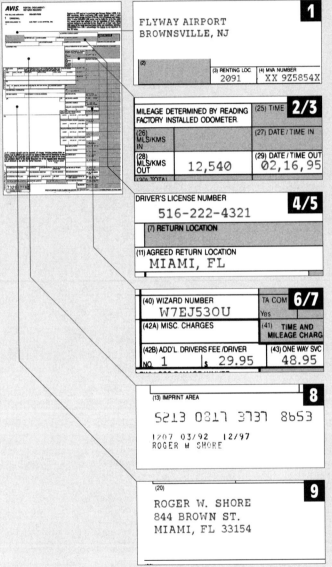

1. **RENTAL LOCATION.** Has the car been rented from a known source area for narcotics distribution?

2. **DATE AND TIME OUT.** Be suspicious of short turn-arounds. It's common for drug traffickers to rent a car in upstate New York, for example, drive to New York City, and return in the same day.

3. **TOTAL MILES DRIVEN.** The starting odometer reading is filled in here by the rental company computer before the car leaves. Calculate the miles driven up to the point of your stop. If the driver claims he went to visit relatives in a city 200 miles away, but your mileage calculation reflects 1,500 miles driven since checkout, you have something to talk about.

4. **DRIVER'S LICENSE INFORMATION.** Use this information for NCIC and criminal-history checks. Run a suspension/revocation check if driver is not able to produce a license.

5. **WHERE CAR IS TO BE RETURNED.** Is the car being returned somewhere other than where it was rented? Is the drop-off point a demand city? Is it the driver's home? If not, how will he get home? If so, how did he get to the city where he picked up the car? Do the time, effort, and cost involved seem justified?

6. **DROP-OFF CHARGE.** A substantial drop-off charge may amount to more than it would cost to fly from the city of origin. Why is the extra expense of driving worth it to the driver?

7. **ADDITIONAL DRIVER.** If the driver is not the renter, he must be named. If the driver's name is not on the rental agreement, you may detain the vehicle until the rental agency is notified.

8. **CREDIT CARD IMPRINT.** If the renter is in the vehicle, ask to see the credit card used for renting the vehicle and match it with the imprint. A driver with a phony ID or who's "borrowing" the renter's ID probably will not have the credit card.

9. **RENTER'S NAME, ADDRESS, PHONE NUMBER.** Is the driver the renter? Ask him his full name, address, phone number, and d.o.b. and check all that against the rental information and driver's license. If he's evasive, you may have indications of a criminal impersonation or contraband transport. If the driver is not the renter, be sure you also check the renter's name via NCIC.

176

An Arizona officer pulled over this rented U-Haul truck for weaving. The driver and passenger said they were "thinking" of moving to Chicago. The officer played along with their story. When asked what they had in the back to "move," the passenger responded "clothes" and granted the officer a look. She discovered a small bag and a considerable amount of chemical material, which the driver claimed was racing-car fuel. Actually cooler was filled with liquid PCP, "enough to blow up the town nearby."

going. Chicago, they said—because they were "thinking" of moving there. The officer had never heard of anyone renting a cargo truck to travel to a place they were just thinking of moving to. Actually, as a search later disclosed, the couple were hauling raw materials to manufacture PCP and had enough chemicals in the cargo area "to blow up the town" they were stopped in.

3. Commercial. Semitrailers, tankers, and other commercial carriers are frequently inspected by commercial enforcement personnel at weigh stations and other checkpoints for size, weight, and equipment violations, but rarely are they scrutinized for illegal activities not connected to trucking. As an aggressive officer on Criminal Patrol, that's a pattern you want to break, for eighteen-wheelers by and large haul the biggest single loads of drugs, stolen goods, and other contraband. In addition to stopping trucks in transit, be alert for situations that allow you to make contact at truck stops and other places frequented by truckers, which are often rife with drug dealing, prostitution, and other criminal activities.

Basically, there are three methods of moving drugs and other illegal items by commercial carrier:

1. The contraband is secreted in among legitimate cargo as a valuable "add on" to the run;

2. There is a "cover" load of produce, fuel, or consumer goods whose sole purpose is to camouflage contraband;

3. The traffickers are so confident that the truck won't be stopped and checked that the cargo area has nothing in it but contraband and maybe a few empty pallets.

In some cases, the driver is an unwitting accomplice; he thinks he's

177

Maintaining a good reactionary gap while questioning truckers is ideal. But traffic noise, wind, and the need to build rapport may make it impractical. When you violate survival principles, do so by conscious decision and with heightened alertness, not through carelessness.

Commercial drivers typically have lots of paperwork. This can yield invaluable contraband cues if you know how to evaluate it and take time to do so.

on a legitimate run and does not realize that an unscrupulous employer or crooked personnel who've had contact with the truck have given him a "polluted" load. Honest drivers can make dishonest loads tough for you to detect. But such circumstances are relatively rare, and for most others a combination of "reading" the driver and reading between the lines of his documentation will yield the kind of cues you're looking for. An FBI intelligence report on the tactics of tractor-trailer drug haulers states:

> "[T]wo male drivers is the most preferred scenario used by traffickers. This is a telling point, as most legitimate trucking companies cannot afford the luxury of a second driver. The second driver allows the truck to be driven straight through, nonstop, from coast to coast. Often the drivers are Latin, either Colombians, Cubans, Puerto Ricans, or Mexicans, because of a basic lack of trust of non-Latins [with this size load] within the trafficking organization....If the drivers of illicit cargo are Colombian, Cuban, or Puerto Rican, the truck will in most instances be carrying cocaine. The Mexican drivers are most likely to transport marijuana and in some cases various forms of heroin. The driver or codriver will in most cases have a criminal record, although the charges may not necessarily be in drug trafficking. *Most drivers should be regarded as carrying weapons and be considered armed and dangerous.*"[12]

From the blizzard of paperwork that typically accompanies over-the-road rigs, four documents are of prime interest to you in develop ing sufficient suspicion to want to search a truck's cab and cargo area. If there's something illegal in the load, flaws in the documentation are almost a certainty.

Driver's License. First, does the driver have a valid *commercial* license? Incredibly, one of the biggest loads of drug money yet intercepted—over $4,000,000 in cash, found in a truck that was stopped one Thanksgiving Day in Colorado—was entrusted to two teenagers too young even to qualify for commercial licensing. An early clue to the contraband was the fact that the driver was only nineteen and could show only a learner's permit.

Check with the issuing state via communications to see if the driver's license has been revoked or suspended. Also be alert for evidence of multiple licenses from different states, bearing different names and Social Security numbers, even different ID photos. Since 1987 it has been illegal for a truck driver to have more than one license if his vehicle weighs over 26,000 pounds or transports hazardous materials requiring placarding, but shady drivers sometimes still do. Ask the driver the last time he got a ticket of any kind, including for weight violations. Run a license check for him in any state he admits to having been ticketed in. Also run the state next to the state where he lives; you'll be surprised how many suspensions you come up with.

Big-rig drivers should carry just one Commercial Driver's License (abbreviated CDL in some states). Check states surrounding driver's home base to surface "hidden" suspensions, violations, and possibly other licenses.

As with noncommercial drivers, request a criminal history as part of your radio check, if possible. Most truckers involved in drug transport have been arrested for at least petty crimes—and many for serious felonies—most of their lives. Check out any passenger's identification, too. Although they're not supposed to, truckers frequently pick up hitchhikers, who'll turn out to be fugitives or missing persons. Moving-van drivers frequently pick up off-the-street passengers called "lumpers" to help them unload at their destination. Not uncommonly these characters have unsavory backgrounds. You'll find a lot of wanted people around trucks. Even if they're not wanted, any unauthorized passenger in a long-distance commercial truck is a violation of federal rules and regulations for motor carriers.[13]

Registration. Experience shows that independent owner-operators, driving expensive, fancy, late-model rigs (above the industry average), have a much higher likelihood of being drug couriers than do employee-drivers for large established trucking firms. The operator may be driving for his own one- to two-truck company, or he may have leased his truck to a major shipper. The most common states of registration for "dirty" rigs currently tend to be: Florida, Texas, New Jersey, New York, California, and Illinois.[14]

As with private and rental vehicles, if the registered owner of a commercial carrier is not present, he or she should be checked for a criminal history, as well as the driver and passenger(s). Check registration papers for both the tractor and trailer, and be certain that the

Interpreting Truck Driver's Logbook Entries

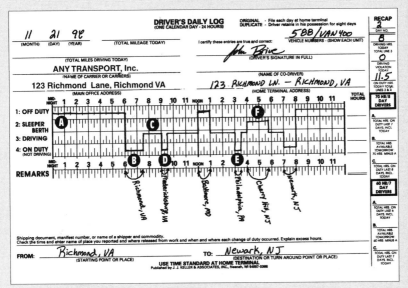

Logbook gives you a valuable tool for checking a driver's story. In this case, entries jibe with his version of how and when he spent his time:

A. Midnight - 6 AM: Off duty.

B. 6 AM - 7:30 AM: Reported for work, helped load truck, checked with dispatch, performed pretrip vehicle inspection, completed other in-office duties.

C. 7:30 AM - 9:00 AM: Driving.

D. 9 AM - 9:30 AM: Minor accident in Fredericksburg, VA. Details handled with local police.

E. 3 PM - 3:30 PM: Delivery made in Philadelphia.

F. 4 PM - 5:45 PM: Stopped in Cherry Hill, NJ. Entered sleeper berth for rest break.

DRIVER'S VEHICLE INSPECTION REPORT

AS REQUIRED BY THE D.O.T. FEDERAL MOTOR CARRIER SAFETY REGULATIONS, I SUBMIT THE FOLLOWING:

DATE: 11/21/9C   TRACTOR/TRUCK NO.: #588   TRAILER(S) NO.(S): VAN 400

☐ I detect no defect or deficiency in this motor vehicle as would be likely to affect the safety of its operation or result in its mechanical breakdown.

☒ I detect the following defects or deficiencies in this motor vehicle as would be likely to affect the safety of its operation or result in its mechanical breakdown.

Indicate whether defects are on TRACTOR/TRUCK or TRAILER - Use sufficient detail to locate for mechanic.

Fuel tank strap cracked

DRIVER'S SIGNATURE: John Brive
☒ Above defects corrected   ☐ Above defects need not be corrected for safe operation of vehicle
MECHANIC'S SIGNATURE: Bob Smith
DRIVER'S SIGNATURE: John Brive
© Copyright 1983 & Published by J. J. KELLER & ASSOCIATES, INC.

FRONT SIDE

Distances and times should correspond. If not, this may be an indication of falsified entries.

Be wary of prolonged "down time." Drivers make money driving; down time represents financial loss. If a driver has logged an abnormal amount of down time (i.e. three days with no movement), question the reason. Be alert for signs of nervousness and lack of solid explanation.

Be wary of noticeably indirect routes: If a driver's goal is to make a delivery from Albuquerque, NM, to Amarillo, TX (a straight shot east on I-40) and he's included a brief stop in El Paso (a border town approximately 200 miles in the wrong direction), question why.

Be wary of cross-outs, erasures, white-outs, and multiple corrections: Legitimate truckers should have minimal mistakes in their logbooks.

Be wary of illogical trips: A driver hauling oranges should not have Nashville, TN, listed as his starting point and Miami, FL, as his final destination; an orange-producing state wouldn't logically be receiving such a shipment.

Be sure logbook entries are up to date: Drivers are required by law to keep them current. A violation is grounds for detention and further investigation.

BACK SIDE

Missing information, indicating that a daily inspection has not been conducted, may suggest equipment negligence, sometimes associated with contraband runs.

papers you're handed actually correspond to the tractor and trailer you're checking.

At the other end of the spectrum, older rigs *below* the industry standard also seem inordinately involved in drug running. Like the drivers of many "third-party" automobiles, these operators may have no knowledge of who the owner is, which should be a cue to you.

Logbook. With smugglers, the journal of charts that a driver is required by law to sketch in to show where and how he spends his time is likely to be screwed up. If you analyze his entries for the last week, you may see that they are not up to date...or that gaps are unaccounted for...or that he has driven out of his way rather than taking the most direct route toward his destination...or that he has spent several days in one location. Contraband truck drivers often rent motel rooms for three days or more, waiting while smaller loads in smaller trucks come from storage areas to be combined into a "mother" load. But such static time is highly unusual with legitimate operations where rig and driver must keep moving to make money. The log of one driver stopped in Illinois showed that the truck had sat empty for four straight days in Los Angeles (a source city), then had left for the East Coast (a heavy demand area) with only empty pallets in the trailer. Suspicion confirmed: Officers searching the truck found ninety-five kilos of coke under the pallets.

Confirm that logbook pages have not been ripped out. Take the book and examine it, don't just let him show it to you. This allows you to ask questions without him being able to glance at it for the answers. Be sure to ask about the driver's point of origin and where he has been and has stopped. Don't rely just on what you see in the book. Stopped in the Midwest for following too close, one trucker who was hauling a secret load of drugs told the officer he was carrying vegetables from Idaho. The logbook said he was coming from Arizona—the first cue that he was hinky. Also ask to see his fuel receipts so you can confirm the stops and routing he claims. If you have a road atlas in your unit, you can check the total mileage between two points entered in the logbook, then calculate an average 50 mph speed while the vehicle supposedly was in motion. Does the actual mileage and time required approximate what's in the logbook? If not, this should be a subject of inquiry.

Be alert for any evidence that the driver has more than one logbook. Some keep two: one for the police if stopped, one for the trafficking organization.

Shipping orders, manifest, invoice, bill of lading, or whatever he calls the documentation that specifies the shipper, destination, weight, and nature of the cargo he's carrying. You may be entitled to see some or all of this paperwork, depending on your state law. These papers are often the most fertile field for unearthing discrepancies, inconsistencies, and mysteries that can become the seeds of suspicion. Some smugglers won't have shipping papers or other evidence of a valid, dated purchase order stating quantity and often price for the commodity supposedly being transported. This is highly irregular among legitimate truckers.

Where a manifest does exist, does the driver look like he's trying to read it hurriedly before handing it over to you? Ask what he's hauling and compare the manifest with what he says. If there's something on the bill that he doesn't mention or a quantity is different, that's not

Shipping orders. Where data is missing, you have grounds for asking questions.

normal. Legitimate drivers know what they're carrying; an illegitimate one with a cover load may not.

Look for type-overs, white-outs, erasures, or other signs that the papers have been altered. Are names typed in where signatures are called for? Is the destination address a P.O. box or incomplete? Are there spelling errors? Is the manifest dated, with the freight specified? Legitimate papers are not casual; they're filled out to the max, with dates, destinations, times, refrigeration temperature, possibly even prices—lots of detail.

Does the load make sense economically...can he make any money hauling it the way he's hauling it? You might strongly suspect a cover load, for example, if:

- The truck is transporting merchandise or produce from a distant area to a destination where the same kind of goods are plentifully available (a load of potatoes going from Long Island to Idaho, or asphalt coming from Arizona to Chicago);

- The merchandise on board is so cheap or in such poor condition that it could be thrown away without major economic loss;

- The cargo area is only partially full.

Under such circumstances, how is the company justifying the high cost of fuel, manpower, and equipment for the run, unless something else more in demand or more profitable is also on board? That's the question U.S. Customs asked recently in issuing an intelligence bulletin that advised officers to watch for a pair of suspected couriers who regularly ferry loads of squash up from Mexico, a source country, into Texas. They incur the expenses of truck rentals and various fees and drive their loads all the way across three more states to Los Angeles, despite the relatively low value of squash and its ready availability much closer to the destination. Similarly, a trooper newly assigned to a Criminal Patrol team in New Jersey, thought that a

A trucker traveling cross-country with an empty trailer is immediately suspicious. A truck needs to be loaded to economically justify the trip. If it's not, explore why.

trucker hauling used cars from Houston to the East Coast didn't make economic sense—until he found $4,200,000 worth of cocaine hidden on the truck.

If the trailer is alleged to be "empty" on a long run, that's equally suspicious from a cost-effectiveness standpoint. *No* commercial truck going cross-country should be unloaded. Legitimate drivers can't afford to run that way.

With some trucks, you'll notice a certain "triangle" pattern repeating itself in the logbook or other documents. The driver lives in Houston, say, picks up a load in Los Angeles (source city) and drops it in New York City (demand city) before returning home. If the outbound and/or return leg of a triangle like that shows him hauling empty, that is a superstrong cue.

If you have access to scales, check for weight discrepancies. Authorities first alerted to the truck carrying the $4,000,000 in Colorado, which was alleged to be empty, when its weight registered more than it should. On the other hand, a tanker purportedly hauling fuel but actually carrying marijuana will generally weigh lighter than it should. The driver, if he's transporting contraband, may not even know the empty and loaded weights for his rig or be able to present a bona fide scale ticket.

With refrigerated units, is the temperature being maintained at the level specified on the shipping orders? A big load of marijuana hidden inside, for example, will generate heat that may fight with the cooler, melt ice faster, and produce an unexpected rise in temperature. Is the refrigeration unit even on? If the shipment is produce or other perishable goods, which it most commonly is on contraband runs, it will rot if not cooled, but if the true load is drugs the courier probably won't care. Indeed, produce that's just marginally fresh is often sought out as a cover load because it's cheap. Some traffickers believe officers will be intimidated about detaining or carefully investigating a perishable load for fear of liability for damage. Also operators who haul produce are exempt from many of the permits required for rigs that haul heavy equipment or hazardous materials.

A lightweight cover load is also often preferred. This allows two to three individuals working in a "safe" location to unload it by hand to reach the drugs without having to back into a commercial off-loading site.

In some cases, truckers keep hauling the same cover load back and forth cross-country on drug and money runs. A North Carolina K-9 trooper suspected this might be the case after he stopped a semitrailer for tailgating and discovered that the bill of lading, showing a load of furniture, was dated more than six months earlier. When he brought his dog to the vehicle, it immediately alerted. A search subsequently disclosed the aging furniture close to the tailgate, hiding boxes that were piled up at the nose of the trailer. These contained more than 1,400 pounds of cocaine, said to be worth over $86,000,000 street value.

With cover runs, the "customer" listed on the manifest usually will either be phony, or will be a legitimate company or individual who hasn't really ordered a shipment. If the driver's nervousness and other indicators seem strong, consider calling the would-be recipient. If the consignee can't be located or nothing is known about the load at its presumed destination, you'll definitely want to search. Ditto, obviously, if there is no customer or no shipper listed on the papers. As always, small details can become big clues. On one manifest for a load of asphalt shingles, no street address was given for the consignee, and the nervous trucker couldn't adequately explain how he intended to make delivery. Concealed among the shingles were hundreds of pounds of coke.

Besides closely inspecting the four primary pieces of documentation, verify that any driver of a long-distance, big rig you stop is also carrying a medical card, current fuel stamps, permits for each state he is traveling in, and insurance papers on his tractor and trailer. Although legitimate truckers will usually have this information in order (often in a well-organized, three-ring binder), contraband haulers often are provided their documentation by "facilitators" working for a drug cartel. If the facilitator is sloppy and unknowledgeable about what is required, the driver may end up with inadequate documents.

Concealed Interrogation

Putting together the true story of a contraband stop is like assembling a jigsaw puzzle. You do it one piece at a time. And to get the pieces of suspicion you need, you may have to ask a lot of questions as you go about examining documents and performing other tasks of the stop. To the object of your inquiries, these should appear unobtrusive, random, and pointless..."just conversation." In fact, they are "conversation with a purpose." For many officers, this is the fun part of the stop, and in most cases it will prove to be the most important factor in your conclusions about the vehicle and its occupant(s).

Except for commercial drivers, who are subject to closer scrutiny because of their closely regulated occupations, a driver or passenger is not required to answer questions that don't pertain to the official business of the stop. If he or she has been coached about the techniques of Criminal Patrol, they may not answer. If they ask why you're asking questions, you can say: "I'm just curious. I know you're not up to anything bad. I didn't think you'd have anything to hide." Most people will respond because they won't perceive your "idle" inquiries as part of an investigation. In event you get stonewalled, try to get a narcotics-sniffing K-9 to the scene ASAP. Legally, the dog can walk around the exterior of the vehicle and sniff the "public" air outside it, without any suspicion or justification required. If the dog then alerts to contraband odors coming from the car, you have probable cause to at least detain the vehicle and obtain a search warrant. (See Chapter 11 for details.)

Depending on the violator's level of reticence and your own personal style, you may pose hidden-agenda questions directly ("Where are you headed today?" or "Nice tan! Been down to Florida?") or more gradually weave them into your official dialogue about the violation. For instance, you could start the ball rolling with something as simple as a rapport-building remark about the weather ("Boy, it sure is hot, isn't it?") as you examine the driver's papers. That can lead to: "Is it gonna be any cooler where you're headed?" And that, of course, can lead to where he is headed, without him feeling that he's getting the third degree. Whatever your style, you do not need to give a Miranda warning prior to this type of questioning.[15]

You want the driver isolated where the other occupants can't hear, and you want to quickly establish this core information:

- **Whose vehicle he's driving** (Is he vague or completely stumped? Is it a third-party situation?)
- **Where he's coming from** (This usually should be one of your first questions after getting his license and registration. You want to know where he started the trip, plus where he's coming from *today*. Are these origins a known source area, demand area, or distribution area for narcotics?);
- **Where he's going** (Where he's coming from and going to may suggest whether you'll most likely be looking for drug money or undelivered narcotics.);
- **Why he's traveling** (Don't suggest an answer, like: "Are you on vacation, or is this a business trip?" Let him come up with the information on his own.);
- **What he does for a living** (Does his stated occupation seem consistent with the nature and expense of the trip? Does he have documentation that fits?);
- **How long he plans to stay** (Is this consistent with his vocation, reason for the trip, and gear visible in the vehicle?).

These fundamentals should be sought from everyone you stop. The answers will help you decide if you need to get "nosier." Asked of a guilty subject, such questions tend to elicit noticeable nervous behavior, compared to simple questions like: "What is your name?", "How tall are you?", and "Where do you live?" The more you can get the subject to elaborate, by posing questions that require *narrative* rather than straight yes-or-no answers, the more you'll have to check up on and evaluate. Keep the subject off-balance. You want him *not knowing* what kind of question is coming next.

Listen analytically. Remember: A good listener isn't someone who has nothing to say. A good listener is someone who is *after something.* So listen with a purpose (the same as you converse with a purpose), don't supply possible answers when he pauses, and be attuned not only to what is said but *how* it is said.

As you listen and observe, consciously ask yourself three key questions. These will give you a framework for identifying things about the vehicle and its occupant(s) that "just don't fit." They are a far more accurate means of "profiling" a probable contraband courier than trying to pick him out of a stream of traffic on the basis of his race or nationality.

Does the driver (or passengers) fit the vehicle? For example, if, during your "casual" conversation, he says he's unemployed or works some minimum-wage job or you see that the heels on his shoes are ready to fall off, yet he's driving a $49-a-day rental car, where's he getting the money to pay for it? On the other hand, is he driving a cheap rental car, but wearing expensive jewelry? Is he a young kid driving an LTD sedan, typically an older person's car (but popular with drug haulers for its large body with many hiding places)? Is he behind the wheel of an elegant Lincoln Town Car, but has callused hands and dirty fingernails (like you'd usually find on the driver of a junker)?

In Maryland, the driver of a welding truck was stopped for speeding. He said he was on his way to a job in Delaware. He was dressed in a velour running suit and brand-new tennis shoes, his nails were manicured and polished, his hair was blow-dried, and his beard neatly trimmed. Suspicious officers uncovered 167 pounds of marijuana in his truck. Two black teenagers riding in a limosine told New Jersey troopers they were headed home to Baltimore after attending a Broadway play in New York City. A subsequent consent search revealed two pounds of crack in a caramel corn box.

With over-the-road trucks, how knowledgeable does the driver seem to be about his industry and his equipment? A dope hauler, even if properly licensed, may be relatively inexperienced with the truck he's jockeying; in fact, his maneuvering of the vehicle may be what prompt

Drug ring in suburban Chicago over a period of 4 years sold 275 kilos of coke, worth millions. One of the couriers for this group was a high school punk who made deliveries in a Corvette with vanity plates. Before he finally was busted, he was no doubt stopped for speeding and other traffic infractions by officers who never registered that an average teenager just doesn't fit with a luxury sports car. Tactics to ponder here: handcuffing in front, the officer's hands in his pockets, and almost no "reactionary gap" from arrestee.

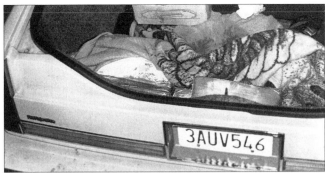

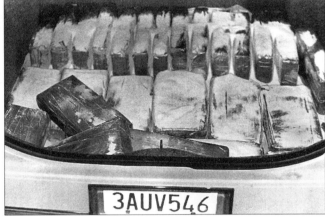

Size up the driver. With a trucker, are his clothes and grooming like other highway jockeys you see? Is he familiar with how equipment on his rig works?

Officer who pulled this vehicle over in Wyoming thought the young, disheveled driver didn't fit with a clean, new, conservative, family-type car. Soon, underneath the pile of blankets (above), the officer discovered 155 lbs. of marijuana, wrapped in duct tape and covered with laundry detergent to mask its odor.

ed you to stop him. See if he has confident, credible answers when you ask him about the prescribed temperature for his refrigerated trailer, the gross weight of his rig, the number of pallets his truck will carry (a normal forty-eight-foot trailer has room for twenty-four pallets on the floor, with possibly a second layer on top), the *previous* load he hauled, the explanation for his routing, and so on. Certain tanks and valves on the rig are capable of being bled during a safety inspection. See if he can demonstrate this for you, or does he not even know where to start? A dirty trucker may have been hired less for his driving skills than for his availability and loyalty to the trafficking organization.

Does the driver (and car) fit his story? "The truth," says one experienced investigator, "generally sounds like the truth and a lie sounds like bullshit." Example: When a couple in a Texas rental car were stopped for speeding in Mississippi, some 400 miles from home, the female passenger insisted that she didn't know where they were going ("I'm just riding with him," she said, pointing to the driver) and claimed the purpose of their trip was to "just ride around looking," something they did "sometimes twice a month." Obviously that wasn't plausible, but apparently it was the best she could come up with on short notice to cover the fact that in two small Gucci bags in the back seat were fifteen kilos of coke they were carrying on a regular run between Miami and Houston.

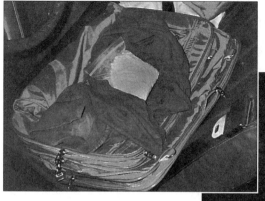

Discovery of these Ecstasy tablets began with the most basic deception cue: The driver gave a false identity. That justified investigative detention and resulted in an incriminating consent search.

Examples abound that you're not always up against rocket scientists when it comes to launching a credible story into orbit:

An Arkansas trooper who's adept at playing dumb-like-a-fox stopped a station wagon one night for speeding. The driver said he was taking the wagon from California to New York for a friend he'd just met on vacation. Yet he couldn't remember the "friend's" name and couldn't say for sure just where he was supposed to deliver the car. While they were talking, the trooper noticed that all the visible luggage looked brand new, and most of the clothing he could see still had price tags on it. That didn't fit with the typical vacation wardrobe but it could jibe with items bought as "window dressing" for a drug run, he figured. After getting the driver's consent to search, he found a secret compartment under the carpet in the rear of the wagon. Packed inside were seventy-six bundles of cocaine, with an estimated street value of $21,000,000.

In Wyoming, an officer pulled over a driver on a two-lane road for failing to dim his high beams. Extremely apologetic, the man said he and his passenger were headed back to Denver after a shopping spree—but no packages were visible in their two-door Lincoln. They really were hauling marijuana in a duffel bag on the back seat. Another supposed shopper was stopped for speeding in Ohio. He said he was headed back to Detroit after buying Christmas presents in New York City. It was January at the time. Nearly thirty-nine kilos of coke were found under a false floor in his trunk.

A Chicago officer who stopped a traffic violator noticed a suspicious number of water-filled jugs in the back seat. The driver insisted he needed them because his car overheated. But the car was nearly new. Actually, the water held cocaine in suspension as a means of concealed transportation.

Two men pulled over for seat-belt violations in Iowa turned out to have $225,000 worth of cocaine hidden in a rear panel of their Thunderbird. The first clue was when the driver said they were traveling from Utah to Buffalo—but couldn't say why. The passenger didn't know either; he "just came along for the ride." Despite the cross-country trek, the two had brought along no extra clothing.

A traffic violator in Oregon told an officer that the Dodge he was driving had been loaned to him by his uncle to head north from California to look for work. He couldn't remember his uncle's name, but said it was on the registration. The officer, who was holding the registration, glanced down at it and asked, "Is your uncle's name Rosas Ramirez?" That happened to be a name the officer had fabricated at that moment. Yeah, the driver agreed, that's it. Moments later, his hidden load of marijuana and methamphetamine was uncovered.

An Indiana officer stopped a driver in an old car with Florida tags who said he was en route to Chicago to sell his vehicle at auction. The officer asked if he expected to make a profit, and the guy said, yeah, about $200. How was he planning to get back South? "Fly," the driver said. To drive 1,300 miles to make a couple hundred bucks and then spend probably more than that to get home didn't make any sense at all—and that conclusion led the officer ultimately to a jackpot of hidden drugs.

In Mississippi, a deputy stopped a sixty-eight-year-old man for speeding. His Olds Toronado had Texas plates, but he said he lived in New Orleans and was returning home after driving to Miami (860 miles one way) to see a doctor. He showed the deputy a nasty cyst on his hand. "How'd the examination go?" the deputy asked, dripping concern.

"Well, the doctor wasn't in," the old man said.

"You didn't have an appointment?"

"No."

"Who does the car belong to?"

"My son."

"Where's he?"

"In prison."

"For what?"

"He got caught with some drugs."

Now father and son are reunited for an extended visit, for under the back seat the deputy found a kilo of cocaine. The son, ironically, had been busted in the same car with a load of marijuana.

Whatever the suspect's story, the more you dig for *details* the more likely you are to expose deception and develop grounds for suspicion. If you ask enough questions, eventually you will hit one the subject didn't think you would ask, no matter how prepared he is. If your subjects say they're on vacation, it's only natural for a friendly "good ol' boy" to ask where they're planning to stay, what sights they're going to see, and so on, as well as where they stopped, what they did, and where they spent the night yesterday. Do they seem to know what they're talking about and does what they say make sense? "One thing smugglers definitely don't want to talk about is where they're going," says an Illinois trooper, "so that's something we definitely should talk to the public about." Drug runners will usually say, with little elaboration, that they're headed toward some major city, generally to visit a friend or a relative, with a quick turn-around. Ask: the friend's name, where he works, his street address and telephone number. Usually they won't be able to give you a name (or at least a last name) or other pertinent information because they haven't thought their story through to that level of specificity.

Often they'll offer a sympathy story associated with poor health or death—like the Hispanic van driver who told the city corporal who stopped him in Louisiana that he was rushing his sick mother to the hospital for stomach cramps. The woman was moaning as if in agony. Not easily convinced, the corporal asked who the van was registered to. The driver said he didn't know. Actually, the corporal discovered, it was registered to the driver himself; his drug supplier had put the vehicle in his name so he'd have no registration problem if stopped, but then forgot to tell him. With the help of a K-9, the corporal eventually found 100 kilos of coke in a false floor.

In an urban setting the driver may say he's headed to work. Ask where that is, then tell him: "Oh, my cousin works there. You must know the foreman, Bill Smith" (using a name you invent). If he says he does know this imaginary person, something's haywire.

Once the violator tells you where he lives or some spot he's recently visited, pretend that you're familiar with that territory, too. Test if he's telling the truth by making up some "local landmark" that you "remember" ("Do they still have that famous pie house on the square downtown?"). A person who has lied will often go along with your invention, faking that he knows what you're talking about, while a legitimate party from that area won't know what you're referring to. Or you can tell him: "I'm thinking of going on vacation around there. What are some of the things we should see while we're there?" Legitimate people can tell you. (Between stops and off-duty, you and a partner can role-play concealed interrogation. Practicing ways to dig details out of the "bad guy's" story will teach you to improvise faster and smoother.)

When you've established where the driver says he's coming from and headed to, you then can determine whether he's on the normal route between those points. If he's "off course," why? Sometimes you may be able to spot newspapers, souvenirs, or other items that will contradict the alleged route or denial of having been in a source city. One driver insisted to a Southern deputy that he was not coming from Miami—yet visible in the car, the deputy could see a poster of Miami at night; fifteen kilos of coke were also in the vehicle. If the suspect is smoking, perhaps you can see the tax stamp on his cigarette pack. Is it consistent with the state(s) he says he's been through? Are any visible maps folded open to locations off the supposed itinerary? How familiar does he seem to be with the details of daily living in the places he claims are his origin and destination? Street-gang members who've come into your area from out of town to set up satellite drug distribution will often try to convince you they're locals. They may be able to offer an address you recognize, but ask them the zip code and area code for your community. They usually won't know these, but they may try to bluff by reciting ones for L.A., Chicago, or wherever they really hail from.

Asked about occupation, mules most often will say they are unemployed or part-time workers. Or they'll allege a livelihood that allows freedom of movement and flexible hours, such as seasonal worker, student, or self-employed. Do they look the part? A female drug runner in a prim business suit looked like the sales rep she claimed to be, but when an officer asked her for a business card she couldn't produce one. One Eastern officer stopped two couriers who told him they were migrant farm laborers. He was certain they were lying because "they had nice new Levis on, nice shoes, rings. Their hands were softer than my wife's!" If the business the subject claims to be involved in deals with a product, ask specific questions about its use to see if he appears knowledgeable. Does he have any samples or is he able to speak confidently about the nature of his company, how many workers it employs, how long it's been in business? Alleged students should be able to tell you their major, the names of professors, their source of income while attending school.

If the driver says he's going cross-country to seek employment—another common story among couriers—that in itself is suspicious; most people don't look for jobs that way. Does the amount and type of clothing and professional equipment he has with him seem to fit this stated purpose? A New Jersey officer stopped a courier from Ohio who said he was going to New York for a week to audition for a band. He had no clothes and no musical instruments with him. Another violator told a deputy he was driving his Ram Charger from Texas to Virginia on a job quest, but the only "luggage" visible was a rectangular blue box (see below), not the sort of container that clothes and personal effects are usually packed in for an extended trip. That was what the deputy searched first when he got consent; inside: twenty pounds of marijuana.

The "blue box" stop.

Ideally you want to reconstruct the subject's story beginning with his activities even a few days before he left on his trip. Once you understand it in chronological order, get him to repeat the order of events backwards. This may be difficult even for a truthful person—nearly impossible for a liar, because he usually makes up and rehearses things as they move forward.

Are there conflicts among the occupants? In Louisiana, a rental truck with a driver and a passenger failed to stop at a highway weighing station. When a trooper caught up with it, he isolated the driver and asked what they were carrying. Answer: "Furniture." But when the trooper got the passenger alone and asked the same question, he said: "Antique pottery." In the rear of the truck, the officer noticed sheets of Bounce on the floor and lots of mothballs scattered around a load of cardboard cartons. As it turned out, the first three rows of these boxes were filled with pottery, most of it broken. But the rest of the cartons contained 1,600 pounds of pot.

It's crucial to get occupants of a vehicle *separated* and kept apart during the contact—to check their stories for consistency. Ask each

An officer scored a victory because he took the time to explore conflicting stories between 2 occupants. 5 kilos of coke were hidden inside an armrest compartment.

Rewards for having curiosity: 2 sisters were pulled over for following too closely. Both were nervous, their stories conflicted about their travel plans, and they were unable to agree as to who owned the pickup. 264 lbs. of marijuana were hidden in the truck.

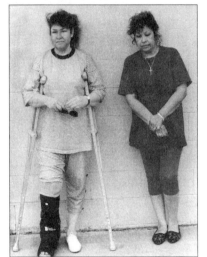

the same questions independently, including: "Who's that in the car with you?" and "How long have you known her?" File away everything each tells you to be double-checked against answers from the other. With people who really know each other and are traveling for legitimate purposes, their independent responses should jibe. But with drug traffickers and other contraband couriers, this technique will run the best of them smack into a wall. You will *always* be able to surface conflicts with them. Some may be glaring inconsistencies, like the driver of a semitrailer with a contraband load who claimed he and his partner were headed to Chicago to line up a contract with a major dairy-food company; his passenger, an amputee, said they were going to pick up a prosthetic arm.

Even if the suspects have rehearsed and agree upon a general, superficial story, they can't possibly rehearse and remember every little specific that you might ask about, like names, hair color, height, weight—anything likely to be unexpected. They tend to invent details to seem more credible, and inevitably end up crossing each other up. Like two

192

Colombians in their twenties who were stopped in an Eastern state. The driver spun an elaborate story: He said they were coming from a remote airstrip in the mountains of Pennsylvania...that a friend had taken him out there, dropped him off and asked him to drive a car that was parked there back to the Bronx as a favor...that he couldn't get it started...and that the fellow who became his passenger had walked out of the woods at that moment carrying a tool box, started the car, and asked for a ride in exchange for his help. The passenger's story was shorter: They were driving back to New York after vacationing in the Midwest. The officer who searched found no toolbox, but he did find a socket and wrench—and $350,000 cash in a hidden compartment in the trunk.

Sometimes a little mind-screwing is productive. Say you're a patrol officer in Milwaukee and you stop a rental car with two occupants for running a red light. As you develop dialogue with the driver at an isolated interview location, ask him when they left on their trip and where they left from. If he says they left from Omaha at 10 o'clock last night, then ask the passenger: "What time this *morning* did you leave *Minneapolis* to start your trip?" If they're hinky, the passenger may try to jump on what he thinks is the story his buddy has given you. Then you've got a suspicious conflict—and a reason to detain them longer and ask more. You may also be able to develop differences by asking the passenger(s) and the driver, separately, about their destination and route of travel: what towns they've been through...where they've stopped...how often they've gotten gas...who they've visited, et cetera.

When you talk to occupants who claim they live together or are married—a common story with male-female trafficking teams—work questions into your independent conversations with them about things they both should know and be consistent on: their anniversary date, how many kids they have, where they lived before their current residence, what their house looks like. One couple en route from Texas to Chicago with two youngsters couldn't "remember" how long they'd been married when they were stopped in downstate Illinois. He said they were going to a wedding, she said to a funeral; neither could name who was being married or buried. The woman and kids, it developed, were hired camouflage for the mule, who was delivering twenty-three kilos of coke, hidden under his back seat. Don't assume that the occupants will agree even on their marital status. A woman stopped for speeding in Delaware nervously stammered that she was traveling from Miami to Long Island for a vacation with her husband, the passenger. He said she wasn't his wife and that he was headed to New York on business. The true purpose of the trip was to peddle the cocaine hidden under a false floor in their trunk.

A base to touch in testing the driver's story: Is the passenger in the vehicle of his or her own free will? "I always ask," says a Florida trooper. "You'd be surprised how many people say they aren't, especially kids."

Even if the driver's alone, you can often surface inconsistencies by repeating certain questions at two or three different points in the conversation. "Ask him a wad of questions real quick," advises one officer, "then after a bit, come back and ask the same questions again."

Example: He says that's his wife in the car with him; later, you ask casually, "You said that's your cousin in the car with you, right?" If he had to make up answers to the first barrage on the spot, he'll be sure to have forgotten, under stress, some of what he told you; lies are difficult to remember. Two small-town officers in Tennessee stopped a car because its license plate was displayed in the back window instead of being properly affixed. The driver first said he was moving a woman's possessions from that town to Memphis. But when he was asked again later, he said he was moving a different person from Nashville to Memphis, which was opposite to his direction of travel. Searched, the car yielded the usual array of fenceable burglary booty, including an arsenal of stolen guns.

Be alert for even small discrepancies. As he approached a traffic violator driving an old Oldsmobile, one Criminal Patrol officer noticed handprints in the dust on the trunk lid, as if it had been opened and shut. Then he observed that the driver's hands were grimy. The officer asked if there had been tire trouble; the suspect insisted there hadn't. That doubtful response led to a search of the trunk where the officer found $25,000 in small bills in plastic bags under the spare tire, plus a money-transfer receipt for another $5,000. Not through with inconsistencies, the driver then gave three different versions of where the money was from. Eventually, he admitted that the cash was from a drug transaction, after the officer found a page in the car that had been torn off of a desk calendar. When the courier was leaving on the transport, his boss told him: If you get stopped, tell the cops "the money belongs to someone else." He didn't think he could remember that, so he jotted it down on the calendar page and took the note along for rehearsal.

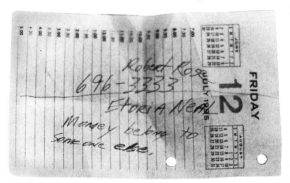

No matter how ludicrous or patently false some or all of a suspect's story may seem, your best strategy is to appear to believe him and stay calm and friendly, at least early in the stop. Like Columbo, prompt him to supply more and more detail so you can fully "understand" what he's trying to explain, and let his confidence build that he is successfully "selling" it to you. In reality, if you can get him to offer something ridiculous, it will sound good for your side in court.

Your goal, after all, is not to be confrontational and prove to him that he's a liar at this point, but only to identify grounds for suspicion. By continuing to ask questions and getting specious answers, you strengthen your case as you move your stop on to the next stage. If the suspect does not sense that you are "catching" his lies or even scrutinizing very closely what he is saying, he will feel less need to try to cover his tracks, anticipate questions, prepare excuses, and in other ways be cautious about what he reveals. Later, if he refuses to grant you permission to search, you will have compiled more grounds for pursuing a search warrant.

Deception Cues

Even when a violator tells you a story that seems plausible, you may be able to detect evidence that it's shaky, if you understand the relationship between speech patterns and deceit. One compelling study of police interview subjects in Maryland found that certain phrases and styles of responding to questions are as much as nine times more likely to be used by persons who are being deceptive as by those giving honest answers.[16] In other words, liars tend to talk a certain way, and they'll frequently identify their lies for you, provided you know how to interpret what you're hearing.

When a subject uses the verbal deception cues explained here, he or she probably merits further investigation. This is true, of course, in more than just contraband situations; these cues and the stress "leaks" described later are relevant anytime you are trying to elicit information from a potential suspect or witness on a call or during a field interview.

Bear in mind, however, that *no single verbal or nonverbal behavior automatically means a subject is lying.* These are *tentative* indicators for suspicion, not absolute proof of prevarication. Nor are these indicators or signs of exceptional stress legal grounds for searching a vehicle.[17] Nonetheless, the deception cues that follow will more often than not mean that the suspect is trying to evade answering your question(s)...manipulate you out of negative impressions...put you on the defensive...or is being untruthful in a specific response or in his general story:

Hesitancy. The suspect pauses, even if briefly, before answering a simple question that would ordinarily prompt an immediate response, like, "Where are you headed today?" Unless your query legitimately requires reflection or a search of memory, hesitancy usually means that he's deciding whether to lie and, if so, what lie to invent and how big a lie to make it. A deceitful subject knowing he has something major to hide may, in fact, be so disorganized that he will delay even in giving his own home or business address.

Hesitating before answering "yes" or "no" to a question is an especially accurate deception cue, particularly if yes-no answers earlier in the conversation have been "on time." A truthful person does not generally have to ponder over an answer. The truth tends to come very quickly, because the subject has only one answer that doesn't have to be thought out. It will be substantially the same, regardless of how often you repeat the question.

A version of hesitancy is *minimal response,* in which the subject gives puny, monosyllabic answers when what you're obviously looking for is fleshed-out information. Example:

"Where are you from?"
"Texas."
"What part of Texas?"
"South."
"Where?"
"Down around the border."

Three questions and you still don't have a town mentioned. Any time you must repeat a question more than twice before a person finally answers it, deception is a high probability. *Don't accept evasion.*

Notice also if a suspect's lips keep moving after he has stopped talking. This is often an indication that "there's more to tell."

Stalling. The subject skirts or delays a direct answer in order to buy time to edit or concoct his response. Typically, he repeats the question you just asked...clears his throat or coughs...makes noises like "Aahhh," "Eerrr," "Uummm," "Uuhhh"...comments that your question is "hard," "tough," or "good"...asks you to repeat or clarify it...

states he wouldn't "dignify" it with an answer...says he has already answered that question...or replies with a question of his own, such as: "Why are you accusing me?"..."Do you really think I could do something like that?"..."Are you talking to me?" (when he's the only one being questioned)..."Why would I do something like that?"... "How would I know?" and so on.

Usually the best antidote to this type of stalling is: Don't say anything, just look blank. Eventually the subject will answer; most people can't bear the pressure of long silences in conversation. If you do speak, simply repeat your question while looking at his eyes. If he's not looking at you, chances are he's busy fabricating. Or if you ask a question and he responds with "Huh?", give him a "Huh?" right back. He will then usually answer your question. Example:

"How long have you been on the road?"
"Huh?"
"Huh?"
"Since yesterday morning."

A variation of stalling is "the rambling dissertation." Here the violator volunteers extraneous information not relevant to what you asked him. You ask where he's coming from and he starts telling you about all the car trouble he's had, how much bad weather he's been through, what grief his wife gives him, how tough it is to make a living these days, or a host of other smoke-screen topics in hopes you'll forget what you asked, while he's making up an answer in case you persist.

A close twin is the nonanswer. The suspect wants you to think he has answered your question because of an inference that could be drawn from his response. Example: You ask if he has been to Los Angeles, and he says, "I wouldn't be caught dead in Los Angeles!" Even though he wants you to accept this as a "No" answer, it really is no answer to the question you asked. Critically examine the suspect's exact words and keep probing until you get the information you want. If he doesn't say "no" to a question that an innocent person would answer with an emphatic "no," then the answer is probably "yes."

Religious affirmations. When you get a sudden "religious conversion" during dialogue, you've likely hit a hot spot. The subject starts talking about his religious devotion, his being recently "born again," the impossibility of his doing bad things because of his faith, or swearing religious oaths. He may raise his hand to the "swearing" or "oath" position or even start to pray. Statements to which he adds religious tag lines are especially suspect: "Honest to God"..."As God is my witness"..."I swear to God (or on the Bible)"..."If there is a Creator in Heaven," et cetera.

Bargaining. The suspect "lobbies" for a better standing in your eyes by trying to build rapport or play on your emotions. He may talk about an illness or some personal problem...testify to his good character ("I'm not the kind of person to do anything like that," "I've never done anything in my life I'm ashamed of," or "I don't do drugs")...mention past or current good deeds...flirt...give up a companion...or tell you he knows another cop, a celebrity, or an acquaintance of yours. Ignore bargaining unless you can turn it to your advantage.

Changing answers. In response to a key answer that a suspect gives you, ask: "Are you sure?" Act as if what he has said doesn't make sense or is factually wrong. If he changes his answer, hedges it slightly, or hesitates before answering again, be suspicious.

Politeness. "When in possession of drugs, be polite to police officers," advises a magazine popular with substance abusers. "They consider attitude to be very important, and that [is] no time to make a bad impression." When the suspect is overly deferential or courteous, it's virtually a given that you're being conned. He may constantly repeat "Sir," "Ma'am," or "Officer" when addressing you...will willingly accept the traffic violation ("I know you're just doing your job") and may be overly apologetic about it ("I'm really sorry, Officer. I promise I won't do it again")...and will strain at every opportunity to demonstrate his composure and his "niceness," including frequent forced laughter and the use of "empathy" statements, like "I understand what you're saying." When he wants to speak, he may ask permission ("Uh, could I say something?") and may even raise his hand, as if in class. Some subjects may be almost comical in showing cooperation. A former drug courier now in prison agrees politeness is often the key to being cut loose without suspicion. "Don't cuss. Show the officer he's got the authority, and give him good conversation," he advises.

In contrast, most legitimate people you stop tend to be annoyed, embarrassed, angry, resigned, impatient, or at best distantly formal. If they feel they've been unjustly stopped, they'll be emphatic and possibly emotional in their denials of wrongdoing ("I did *not* run that stop sign!"). Overpoliteness is so closely linked to deception that some officers insist that a suspect who's smart-ass with you probably doesn't have anything to hide. But don't take that for granted, either.

Also, don't let your guard down from a survival standpoint because of politeness and cooperation. The more unnaturally cooperative a suspect becomes, the most observant and cautious you should be. He could be setting you up for assault.

Fake Smiles. Dishonest emotions often go with dishonest people. Most genuine smiles last about five seconds; longer than that, they're usually contrived to deceive. A true smile crinkles the skin below the eyes slightly and causes tiny wrinkles to appear around the eyes; these can't be conjured during a phony smile.

Watch also for sudden changes in facial expression: The suspect answers a series of questions with a straight face, then when you ask a hot one, he smiles briefly when he answers.

A subject's mouth can offer cues to deception and stress, beyond what she says. Watch for smiles that are inappropriately timed and last too long and for body language that seems to "hide" what's being said.

Diversion. The subject tries to get you off the track that your interest and questions are on, often by asking you questions. He may question your understanding of his position, ask about your experience and training, compliment your uniform, ask what kind of gun you carry—anything to change the subject. If you tell him your sidearm is a "Jekler and Manlich 690 that fires .95-cal. bullets and never needs reloading," he'll just nod and say, "Yeah, cool, I read about it" because he isn't really listening. He just wants to take control of the conversation by shifting the attention off himself. Remember: Who asks the questions is who's in control. You need to keep that ball always in your court.

"Flag" expressions. These are hedgers, qualifiers, or validations that a suspect may add to the beginning or end of a sentence, trying to influence your judgment. Examples that should raise a red flag of attention when you hear them: "Really"…"To tell you the truth"…"To the best of my knowledge (recollection, remembrance)"…"Let me see now"…"I wouldn't lie to you"…"To be honest"…"Talking openly"…"To be perfectly frank"…"On my mother's grave"…"May God strike me dead"…"Believe me"…"You're just saying that because I'm (black, a woman, from a foreign country, old, young, or whatever)"…"Why would I want to…." A favorite is: "…and that's about it," which means that's about it but not all of it; what's the rest of the story? One way to find out is with "mirroring." You repeat or summarize everything the suspect has said up to the point of that flag expression, then pause and just look at him quizzically. Nothing makes most people more uncomfortable than silence. He's likely to fill the vacuum by supplying more information.

Repetition. The suspect keeps repeating his story or some aspect of it, putting a lot of emphasis on it. Apparently he thinks if you hear his lie enough, you'll believe it. More truthful information may have to be dug out of him.

Another form of repetition is uttering a string of "No's" to a hot question: "No, no, no, no, no." This is sometimes called the "Hummingbird No." Similar is the "Five-Second No": "Nnnnnnooooooooo."

Faulty speech. For the first time in the conversation, the suspect starts slurring words, stammering, stuttering, mixing up sentences, abruptly stopping sentences then restarting in the middle, or leaving off the ends of sentences. Some experts claim such flaws in speech indicate deception at least 90% of the time.[18]

A common speech pattern with liars is to mumble or to speak so softly that they can't be heard clearly (perhaps so that later if something they said turns out to be incriminating they can claim they were misunderstood). The end of a key sentence may just trail away, or the answer "no" may be given breathlessly.

Also, lying suspects are more likely to make incriminating slips of the tongue, saying, for example, "I'm doing everything I can to convince you I'm guilty" (instead of innocent) or, "All I've got is a kilo of tobacco I've been smokin'." One trainer calls these "fraudulent slips."

Listen for changes in the rate, pitch, and volume of the subject's voice. If all change at the same time, some authorities claim there is a 95% probability of a lie at that point.[19]

Convenient incomprehension. A subject readily communicates with you until you ask a troublesome question, then suddenly he can't understand what you're saying. For example, a county sergeant stopped a father and son driving two vehicles in tandem in Georgia. Initially, the sergeant asked routine questions and delivered compliments about one of the vehicles, a longbed pickup; the two responded appropriately. Then he asked, "How come you're not riding in one vehicle?" Suddenly: *"No habla."* The two were transporting an estimated $20,000,000 in cocaine hidden in the truck.

Hurry. Great interest in getting the transaction completed is often a cue to evasion or deception. The suspect urges you to "just write me a ticket and let me get going," and he may want to know, "How long will this take?" He may claim that you are making him miss a plane, be late for an appointment, or are "costing me money" with delays, but he really wants to get away from you as fast as possible to reduce the risk of detection. The legitimate driver, by contrast, will often contest your accusation of a traffic violation or try to talk you into issuing just a warning and will not show an interest in leaving until the matter is cleared up; he'll keep talking so long as he thinks he stands a chance of swaying you.

Let the hurried subject know that you are in no hurry, that you have all the time in the world to fill out the boxes on your citation, and that you want to make sure you get everything right. This may provoke a deeper stress reaction and reveal more deception cues.

Memory lapses. Forgetfulness or ignorance about routine or important things that most people automatically know (like their zip code) is highly suspect. Legitimate memory loss usually involves insignificant matters or things that happened some time ago. "Clean" people rarely forget or have to hesitate in telling you their birth dates, the number of children they have, where they're coming from, where they spent the previous night, and other facts that are recent or significant in their lives. They also know how to spell both their first and last names (people using aliases sometimes can't even get the first name right). Verbal deception cues involving memory lapses include: "I don't think so"…"I can't recall"…"I was too drunk (or stoned) to remember"…"Not that I can think of"…"I can't say"…"I couldn't tell you." Rather than automatically accept such responses, keep trying to pin him down.

Sometimes a lying subject will have a mental block that will keep him from answering at all. He may be so distraught that he becomes completely disorganized in his attempt to evade detection of deception and thus is unable to speak. Example: On one stop, the driver said he and the passenger were *brothers* and that they were planning to visit relatives. The officer asked, *"Your* relatives or *his?"* No answer.

Unusual smoothness. In contrast to the subject who can't remember what he should, this subject remembers things in unusual detail, and his answers may seem too pat. He's so much smoother than the average motorist who is somewhat rattled at being stopped that you suspect his story has been well-rehearsed. Indeed, some couriers are given audiocassettes with details of their cover story that they are instructed to listen to en route, to reinforce where they're coming from, where they're going, why, where they work, and so on.

One way to trip a too-smooth subject is to get him to repeat everything over and over again. Ask him to respell his entire name and to repeat his street address, Social Security number, date of birth, height and weight, and other driver's license information several times. Unless he has his lies etched in his brain, it will be hard for him to remember what falsehoods he has told you. If you deliberately make errors in repeating back to him some of the basics he has told you—like his home or business address—a liar is less likely than a truthful person to correct you. He may be so mentally occupied with bigger deceits that he'll completely miss your "mistake."

Another ploy is to call his bluff by telling him you will now act on his information. Tell him: "Let's go call that home telephone number you just gave me" or "Let's put all your information into my computer and see what comes out." This tactic may prompt a more truthful response, but shouldn't be used until you feel you've gotten all the untruths you're going to out of him.

Caution: If the suspect thinks you are about to discover him, this is a likely time for him to attack.

Besides these verbal cues, be attentive for certain physical indicators involving the suspect's eyes, as he speaks. Involuntary or unconscious eye movement is often the hardest part of the face for a deceitful subject to mask while he talks, so "lying eyes" often become a window to his lying mouth.

When a subject is being deceptive, his eye-blink rate often increases significantly, from one blink every few seconds to one to two blinks per second.[20] Some researchers contend also that a "third white area" will appear under the iris, in addition to the white of the eyeball normally visible on each side.[21]

When you ask questions that require more than a yes-or-no answer, deception may be indicated by how his eyes shift. First you need to watch his eye movements when you ask questions that you believe will be answered truthfully. Perhaps state your inquiries in a slightly unusual way, so he'll have to think for a moment ("What is your legal given name?"..."Why is your name John?"..."What's your current home address, with the zip code first?") According to one theory, as he genuinely recalls or reflects on the answers, his eyes will tend to shift consistently either to the left or right. Try to ask at least three "neutral" questions that will allow you to establish his normal eye movements. Then when you ask a question that causes him to "construct" an answer, his eyes will shift in the *opposite* direction. In a law enforcement context, construction is most likely to involve deception—either inventing or editing information. Watch for the change in direction. Some instructors claim that most people look to their left when truthfully replying and to their right when constructing an answer.[22] But you need to know what their normal action is before the shift is useful in building suspicion. Also understand that some subjects tend to analyze each question and this may cause "construction" movements that don't necessarily mean deception.

With yes-or-no questions, you want to watch what his eyes do when the subject says "No." Be suspicious of deception if he says:

"No," then closes his eyes or looks away;

"No" with an "empty or vanished look";

"No" while suddenly locking your eyes in a "hypnotic" gaze;[23]

"No" after looking around with a vacant stare;

"No" while folding his arms across his chest and looking to the side, at the ground, or up to the sky (as if looking for divine guidance).[24]

Is he lying when he looks to the upper right?

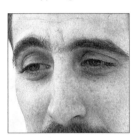

Is he lying when he looks to the lower right?

Is he lying when he looks to the upper left?

Is he lying when he looks to the lower left?

Some behaviorists believe that most people tend to look to their left when answering questions truthfully and to their right when "constructing" answers. But be careful about putting too much faith in such theories. What a subject says and how he says it are usually more reliable cues to deception than body language.

The nature of other eye contact can sometimes also stir suspicion. During dialogue with you, contraband couriers will often display excessive eye contact with other occupants of the vehicle—a kind of "Oh, shit!" look, signifying that "trouble's coming." But they may be very reluctant to establish direct eye contact with you, or they'll break off eye contact suddenly and look down when being evasive or deceptive.

Understand, though, that eye contact is by no means a universally reliable indicator because of marked cultural differences. Depending on where they were reared, some Hispanics will not look directly at you, out of respect for your position and authority. Also as a general rule, men in our society tend to establish less eye contact during conversation than women, and people as a whole tend to look at eyes more while listening than speaking. In addition, some liars may concentrate very hard on maintaining an unwavering gaze in hopes of making their falsehoods seem convincing.

In trying to watch and interpret eye movements, don't succumb to tunnel vision that interfers with your observations of other body language—or with your perception of threats.

Remember: A single indicator is *never* conclusive proof of deception; it may be just an idiosyncrasy of the suspect's speech or behavior. But clusters or "constellations" of at least three or four deceptive acts warrant your strong suspicion of evasion and deception.

Think of deception detection as a point system. Each verbal or physical indicator, along with each discrepancy, inconsistency, contradiction, and implausibility you detect in the suspect's story and documentation, is a point against him. The more points he racks up, the more suspicious of his "lie-ability" and the more determined to search his vehicle you should be.

Stress "Leaks"

Some trainers claim that a suspect's "body language"—his physical posture, movement, and manner—is a virtual picture window to deceit. Unfortunately, it's not that simple. One respected researcher estimates that about half the information in police training materials about nonverbal clues to deceit is wrong.[25] Other experts, comparing the "signs" that are often *cited* as evidence of lying to the behavior that actually *accompanies* lies, found that most of the presumed correlation does not exist.

Moreover, most people who think they can "read" a suspect's

demeanor to detect deception really can't when tested under controlled conditions. One such test measured the abilities of "professional lie catchers"— police officers, judges, trial attorneys, forensic psychiatrists, and polygraphers for the CIA, FBI, and National Security Agency. Astonishingly, only one small subgroup—Secret Service agents — did any better than chance at detecting liars from behavioral clues![26] In fact, after reviewing nearly fifty studies of people (including police officers) as lie detectors, one prominent team of psychologists concludes that

Even with his 21-year-old daughter, granddaughter, and dog along for protective coloration, the driver of this car could not mask his nervousness enough to evade detection. In the trunk: 70 lbs. of marijuana.

when it comes to body language, as with deception cues generally, "There are no foolproof signs of lying."[27]

What are often labeled as physical indicators of deceit are really indicators only of *stress*. Along with verbal cues and the responses to your concealed interrogation, they definitely can be helpful to you in deciding which vehicles seem most worthy of searching. But it's important that you know what you can reasonably extrapolate from them and what you can't.

A pathological liar usually won't display much in the way of stress symptoms, because conscience, anxiety, and fear do not impact on his or her emotional system in customary ways. However, when a more normal person feels under pressure mentally, emotionally, or physically, his or her body automatically kicks into a state of arousal internally, gearing up for action. Depending on the intensity of the stress and the subject's ability to suppress it, some clues of this physiological agitation may "leak" out in the form of involuntary or unconscious movement or mannerisms as his body releases energy in an attempt to dispel its anxiety.

With most people in a traffic-enforcement situation, these leaks emerge as mild to moderate nervousness; their stress level tends to be highest at the beginning of the stop and decreases with the passage of time. With some, however, you will see significant stress reactions beyond what is customary, and the longer you are in contact with them the higher their stress level becomes. Moreover, the *passenger* may display these stress signals equally with the driver—unusual on normal traffic stops.

When a suspect repeatedly engages in these nonverbal activities in conjunction with suspicious verbal responses, that significantly strengthens the possibility that he or she is being deceitful.[28] Even then, discrepancies and implausibilities in stories and documents are always the most reliable indicators for building suspicion.

With the limitations understood, then, watch for the following exceptional stress leaks and factor them into your "point system" as you evaluate the suspect. The more important it is for the subject to lie, the more likely he is to betray these stress symptoms. They'll be easiest to see if you have him out of his car, at an interview location where you can view his full body as you talk.

Restlessness. An exceptionally stressed subject will often be inordinately fidgety, shifting position frequently...possibly jumping from foot to foot...pacing...crossing and uncrossing his or her arms in stiff, fast movements. The typical motorist may seem a bit rigid at the beginning of the stop but then will become more "fluid" in his motions as he comes to accept being pulled over and knows he has nothing major to hide. The exceptionally stressed responder stays rigid, worsening if anything, as your contact continues.

Watch also for suspects who try to move away from you. They're attempting to increase their comfort zone in order to defuse anxiety.

"Fatigue." What look like signs of fatigue may actually be efforts by the subject's body to release stress. Frequent yawning and sighing are especially likely to be stress relievers in these circumstances. Listen for a big sigh after you tell him the stop is for a traffic violation (and not for the crime he knows he's guilty of).

Dry mouth. Does the suspect swallow repeatedly...make clicking noises with his tongue when he talks...lick his lips...show white discharge at the corners of his mouth? All these can be signs of stress-induced dryness in mouth and throat. Occasionally, just the opposite occurs: The suspect has a surplus of saliva, causing him to spit or swallow excessively.

"Leaky" neck. Although many officers watch a suspect's face expecting to find clues to deception and stress, the neck is often more revealing. You may be able to see pronounced activity in the carotid arteries as blood pressure and pulse rate rise under stress...the larynx may bob up and down... the skin will flush. Women tend to move their hands to their throat in highly stressful situations; men often rub the backs of their necks.

Sweating. Often suspects with contraband will perspire profusely when you're talking to them, sweat pouring down their faces unrelated to weather conditions. This may be aggravated by discomfort from drug loads packed under their clothing. Stress sweating will be more noticeable on the brow, but also watch for suspects wiping hands on clothing to remove excess perspiration.

Anxious hands. When the violator wants to hand you a document, don't take it immediately. Let him hold it out for a bit and see if his hand shakes from stress. As he responds to your inquiries, what are his hands telling you? Is he wringing or squeezing them, scratching excessively, or playing with his fingernails or jewelry, as people in trouble are inclined to do?

Does he try to put both hands in his pockets, even though it's not a cold day? Especially coming right after he has handed you his license or other papers, this can be a very defensive gesture, like he's trying to "keep within himself." Does he tap his own chest (perhaps subconsciously fingering the culprit for you) or point away from himself (possibly an attempt at misdirecting your attention)? Do his hands approach or cover his mouth (potentially a subconscious reaction to thinking, "I shouldn't be saying this"), or cover his eyes ("I don't like what I'm seeing"), or rub his nose ("What I'm telling you stinks"), or hold his forehead with a hand for an extended period of time ("The truth is going to hurt!")? Does he perform "grooming" gestures or cosmetic adjustments, such as repeatedly combing or smoothing his hair, readjusting his jewelry or clothing, cleaning or adjusting his glasses, dusting his clothes, picking or chewing his fingernails, or continually picking lint, threads, or hairs from his clothes? Or, revealing even higher stress, does he try to pick lint off of *you?*

You are watching hands for safety as well as surveillance. It's as true on Criminal Patrol as anywhere else on the street: *Hands kill!*

Inactivity. Sometimes inactivity is suspicious. A Midwestern trooper who stopped an eighteen-wheeler for weaving over the center line had the driver beside him in the front seat of his patrol car when he issued the citation, handed the trucker back his license, and told him he was free to go. The nervous violator just sat there, immobile and silent. The trooper figured something was amiss. A consent search showed what. Beneath a pile of stacked pallets of produce in the semi-trailer, he discovered a blue cloth bag and two boxes, containing ninety-five bricks of cocaine.

High stress can also be revealed by facial immobility; i.e., an unusually calm, emotionless expression in response to "hot" questions, particularly if accompanied by a lot of arm and foot movement.

"Give up" signal. This is when a subject turns his palms up in kind of an uncertain or helpless gesture when he supposedly doesn't know or can't remember something you're asking about. Some experienced Criminal Patrol officers claim that if a suspect responds with an upward swing of both hands more than twice during your conversation, subconsciously he's giving up; he has expected to get caught at his wrongdoing, and now he realizes he is.

Obviously, in order to pick up on these stress semaphores you have to observe the subject you're talking to. Don't get so involved in hearing what is said that you forget that watching can yield important cues, too. If you see evidence of stress persisting, casually ask what skillful interviewers call "symptomatic questions": "Is anything wrong?"..."Do you have a nervous condition?"..."Are you feeling okay?" Perhaps point out specific stress leaks you've picked up on. If your subject fails to offer an explanation, you then have more reason to believe that it's your contact that's provoking the reaction. Suspects with something to hide very often will ignore symptomatic questions, but their displays of nervousness will usually get worse.

If you're not seeing stress reactions but your gut tells you that the person you've stopped is suspicious, ask the same questions, but add: "You seem so calm." Or try this: "Is there something you're afraid I'm going to ask you about?" This unexpected query may make him think you've picked up on something or suspect that he has something to hide and may begin to undermine his composure.

Again, this is done in a friendly way. You don't want to crank the pressure on him so much that he stresses out and won't talk to you.

Background Checks

Obviously your communications center is often a first line of attack in punching through a violator's false façade. You want to run at least a warrants check on all drivers you stop. Statistically, narcotics offenders are more likely than other criminals to jump bail, whether for drug charges or for property and violent offenses.[29] They're also more likely to fail to appear on simple citations, such as traffic or trespass violations, leading to the issuance of bench warrants.

Discovery of an outstanding warrant gives you cause for an immediate custodial arrest and search of the suspect and his vehicle.

Besides your customary traffic-stop checks through NCIC and local and state records, you may be able to access special state or federal data banks for intelligence on a subject's current suspicion of drug involvement or criminal history. For example, your dispatcher may be able to run a special Triple I (Interstate Identifying Index) check through NCIC, which will tell you every place a subject has been arrested and for what. Obtaining such background as early as possible in a stop can be invaluable for your safety, as well as for building suspicion. With the trend to "three-strikes-you're-out" laws, offenders with two past falls may be more inclined than ever to take you on, figuring they're looking at a life sentence anyway should you detect what's wrong. That apparently was the thinking of a drug dealer stopped in Maryland for having no tag light. Unknown to the officer who approached him, he had two priors and an outstanding arrest warrant. Hoping to avoid a last ride to the joint, he opened fire and struck the officer twice in the chest. The officer was saved by his vest.

If you're a federal agent or an officer whose department is involved in the national Operation Pipeline drug-interdiction program, you may also have access to the computers of EPIC (El Paso Intelligence Center), a restricted, worldwide information clearinghouse headquartered in Texas and managed by DEA. By contacting EPIC with a pre-assigned access code, a participating agency can get information for patrol officers not only from EPIC's vast in-house system, but also from the interlocking computers of TECS (Treasury Enforcement Communications System) and NADDIS (Narcotics and Dangerous Drugs Information System).[30] TECS is operated by U. S. Customs to provide lookout information on smugglers and their vehicles; NADDIS, operated by DEA, supplies data exclusively on known drug offenders. Highway seizures are reported in EPIC's databank if they exceed one pound of cocaine, ten pounds of marijuana, one ounce of crack, a gram of heroin, or $1,000 in drug-related currency. EPIC's target response time is about five minutes. Check with your administrators or call EPIC's toll-free number (800-351-6047) to see whether or how you can reach its data banks, which are considered the world's best drug-trafficking resource.

If you can't get a criminal history through dispatch, try bluffing it out of the suspect by asking in a presumptive way, "When was the last time you were arrested?" Also watch for gestures that may subconsciously signal an unusual familiarity with the criminal-justice system, such as the subject getting out of his car with his hands automatically raised or moving his hands behind his back in a cuffing position as you talk to him.

Be prepared for rare but jarring instances in which sophisticated traffickers try to surprise and intimidate you with intelligence information of their own. An Arizona officer stopped a female driver in a vehicle that turned out to be associated with a biker gang. She used a mobile phone to call a number in California, and when he presented her with the citation she told him a disturbing amount of personal information about himself and his family, including an abbreviated credit report.

Cue After Cue...

How do verbal and nonverbal responses from a subject during concealed interrogation fit together to indicate a portrait of deceit? Here are real-life examples of how cues surface and cluster—if you look closely, analytically listen, and persistently probe for detail with unexpected questions:

Deputy Bill Collins of the Harrison County Sheriff's Department in Mississippi wasted no time the night he stopped the Mercury Lynx. He developed his first cue from the last name of the driver as it appeared on his license: Tovar. "What kind of name is that?" Collins asked in his good ol' boy style. "It's not common around here. Where you from?" Venezuela, the man said, which Collins knew "is right next door" to Colombia; Colombian criminals often claim it as home.

The Mercury was a rental that the man said he was driving back to Miami after a trip to New Orleans. The rental agreement seemed in order, but Collins noticed that the longer they talked the more nervous the driver became. He was visibly shaking and sweating profusely, although the night was cool.

The driver claimed to be in the import-export shoe business. When Collins asked him the purpose of his trip, he hesitated, then blurted out a complicated story about his girlfriend working for an airline and being able to get him discount tickets. "So I thought I'd fly up to New Orleans to see the city."

"Why didn't you fly back?" If the fare was so cheap, Collins thought, most people would have gotten a round-trip ticket. "Well," the driver said, "I found a luggage rack for my all-terrain vehicle and I decided to bring it back with me." The answer made little economic sense.

As he progressed with his paper work, Collins asked what the girlfriend did at the airlines. The driver said, "Ticket sales," then embarked on another lengthy spiel about how long they'd known each other, when they'd moved in together, and what Collins regarded as "other irrelevant tangents." The deputy mentally noted the excessive answer.

The luggage rack—an early suspicious indicator.

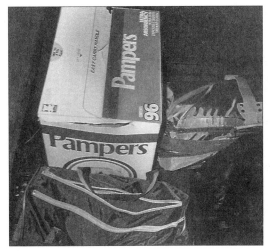

The Pampers payoff.

When Collins had first approached the car, he'd noticed through the hatchback slats a box of Pampers sitting on the floor. With the driver yakking about his girlfriend, Collins thought it a good time to ask:

"How many kids do y'all have?" "None," the driver responded.

Bingo! Collins thought. What's a guy with no kids doing with a big box of disposable diapers in a rental car? The answer came during a consent search a few minutes later, when Collins cut into the Pampers box with a pocket knife. Inside the box and hidden elsewhere in the car were stashes of cocaine, estimated to be worth more than $6,000,000.

The streets of Chicago's Northwest Side were nearly deserted at 0130 when Officer Richard Holmes and his partner saw the red Cadillac with New York plates speed through a stop sign. The officers trailed behind, but the three men inside wouldn't look back—evidence of the No-Look Rule, Holmes decided. After two blocks, he pulled them over. The driver had a thick foreign accent, but no driver's license; he couldn't explain why. Holmes noticed brand-new workmen's gloves, with price tags still attached, lying on the car seats.

"What are those for?" he asked.

Construction, the driver said; he and his companions were laborers from New York, in Chicago to work a job. Right, Holmes thought. Like there are no construction workers in Chicago, so we got to import 'em from New York.

"Where are you going in such a hurry?" he asked, still cordial.

To their motel, the driver said. But neither he nor any of the passengers could remember the name of it. When asked where it was, they hesitated then named a street that was in the opposite direction to where they were headed.

The driver voluntarily agreed to open the trunk to show proof that they were construction workers. Inside, Holmes saw pry bars, wedges, sledgehammers, and chisels of every size. These aren't instruments for construction, he thought. These are for destruction. Plus there were two walkie-talkies, a police scanner, and a police code book for radio frequencies of departments throughout the Midwest. Holmes closed the trunk and suggested the men come along to the station.

Before the night was over, Holmes had discovered the motel where the three suspects were really staying. In their room was a mother lode: oxygen tanks, an electromagnetic core drill, rotary hammers, wire cutters, and 150 burning bars which bore through safes like a needle through an orange.

This was the biggest collection of burglary tools the Chicago Police Department had seen in over thirty years. The traffic violators Holmes had stopped were all Albanian immigrants from the East Coast and were eventually linked to the biggest, most highly sophisticated burglary ring in the nation.[31]

A Minnesota officer on duty late at night in a remote area noticed two men in a van pull up to a stop sign next to where he was parked. He shined his flashlight on them and asked where they were going. "Home," they answered vaguely. Approaching the van to ask more questions, the officer noticed the two were covered with mud. He also saw a muddy pickaxe in the back seat. The men said they'd gotten muddy helping a stranded motorist, but the officer knew the site they mentioned for this assist was on a paved road.

He ran a check on one subject's ID, found an outstanding warrant, and made an arrest. Canvassing the area later, the officer and backup found tire tracks leading to an abandoned farm where someone had recently planted a crop of marijuana plants. In the men's house, officers with a search warrant discovered fertilizer, scales, grow lamps, and more marijuana plants.

In court, the men claimed the officer's initial questioning was an illegal seizure. But the court said that until the outstanding warrant was discovered, the men had been free to leave; the officer never said they had to stay and answer his inquiries. Convictions affirmed.[32]

Edwin Bradley, a patrolman with a city-county drug task force in West Memphis, Arkansas, stopped a Pontiac Grand Prix for speeding. Although the driver's ID seemed in order, Bradley noticed that he was sweating heavily and couldn't seem to stand still. The driver said he was employed by the Department of Transportation in another state.

Bradley returned to his patrol car to run a criminal-history check. He noticed the driver watching him in the rearview mirror. Waiting for the radio response, Bradley picked up his cellular phone and pretended to be making a call. He hoped the driver would think he was checking on his stated employment. Back at the violator's window, Bradley asked: "Are you *sure* you're employed with the Department of Transportation?"

Now appearing even more nervous than before, the driver said that actually he was a "subcontractor" and hadn't worked for the DOT in months. The driver refused to sign a consent-to-search form. But he did agree to open the trunk so Bradley could look inside. In addition to a small quantity of marijuana, Bradley found $149,000 cash in bundles inside a duffel bag.

The driver vehemently denied that he had any knowledge of money in the vehicle. His attorney said he knew nothing about it, either. The money was declared abandoned property—and given to the officer's task force.

The traffic violator Trooper Danny Herring stopped on an Interstate in Florida was dressed all in white. He looked like what he said he was—a nurse's aide—but that's about all of his story that rang true.

Herring was suspicious early on when he noticed a box of Bounce on the floor of the car and read it as a possible masking agent for drug odors.

When he explained to the driver that he'd stopped him for an improper lane change, the driver nervously started talking about "only going 55 mph"—both unresponsive and an indication that he was watching his speed, unusual with Interstate travelers. The car had been rented for him by his wife, the driver said. Herring asked her name. After hesitating, the driver gave the name of a woman whose last name was different from his own.

Interspersed with questions and comments about the driver's ID and the violation, Herring asked three different times how long the driver and his wife had been married. First the violator said four years, then three years, then a year and three months.

He claimed he had been on vacation in Miami and now was driving home to New Jersey. He said he'd left his wife at home and had only been in Florida three days, also unusual, Herring thought.

"Where'd you stay while you were in Miami?" the trooper asked casually. No answer.

Herring turned and looked down the road at a billboard advertising a Holiday Inn. The violator followed the trooper's gaze, then said:

"Oh, the Holiday Inn!"

"The one on 79th Street?" Herring asked.

This was an "insider" reference to a notorious drug-dealer hangout in Liberty City.

"No, no, no, no, no, no!" the driver exclaimed. The Hummingbird No. Moments later, Herring was in the car on a consent search. Results: the discovery of marijuana hidden inside all four car doors, totaling 120 pounds.

Like other aspects of your sensory investigation, roadside lie detection requires *practice.* An Iowa trooper estimates, "It takes about six months just to learn to ask the right questions." Reviewing the fundamentals of these chapters frequently and applying them daily on the street will hasten the process for you.

However quickly you eventually are able to recognize when you're dealing with a motorist who has something to hide, remember that your suspicious impression in most cases is probably comprised of multiple small components. When a bust results, you'll need to replay the stop frame by frame in your mind before you write your report. Each indicator you detected—no matter how trivial—should be itemized, so that the cumulative effect firmly supports reasonable cause for extending and expanding the stop. If you can document that a suspect has been guilty of "lying in the first degree" during your conversation, all the better. That will make it harder for him to convince a judge or jury that he was unaware that he was hauling contraband.

CONSENT TO SEARCH

Q. A mule hauling ass cross-country with $250,000 worth of cocaine stashed in his trunk tries to sneak through your beat, undetected. You nail him for an illegal turn. During your initial approach, you notice fast-food wrappers, skimpy luggage, a marked-up map, a roll of duct tape, and other indicators. In answering questions during your concealed interrogation he's nervous, evasive, contradictory. You know he's dirty, but you don't have PC to search, so you write him a warning and tell him he's free to go.

Then, just as he's about to leave, you ask if he'd let you look through his car in search of drugs. If you find any, he'll be arrested, the load will be seized, and God knows what will happen to him. He has a perfect right to say "No" and drive on. Instead, without any objection or even much hesitation, he says, "Sure, go ahead."

The scenario described above is realistic: ❏ True   ❏ False

If the transporter you've stopped is typical and you've related to him correctly, the answer is: *True.*

It happens every day. Nationwide, 92% of major narcotics seizures from automobiles in both urban and rural areas have resulted from consent searches.[1] A Midwestern trooper who statistically analyzed hundreds of investigative stops he made over a four-year period says he is denied permission to search only 4% of the time; ninety-six out of 100 drivers readily say "yes." Other experienced officers insist they never get a turndown. Some even wangle repeat permissions from suspects who've granted them consent on previous stops and have been arrested as a result!

Does that make any sense? Is it logical for someone who knows he's hauling illicit goods to voluntarily invite a suspicious officer into the vehicle to find them?

As savvy as criminals are today about their rights and considering what's at stake, you'd think that getting consent from an offender would be virtually impossible. But according to a North Carolina trainer, that's because "We all think that other people think like the police do. *The reasons for giving consent are not affected by logic.*" Explains another officer: "It's a matter of perception. The average patrol officer is thinking, 'This guy can't be dumb enough to give me consent to search his car.' Some officers are afraid to even ask for it, for fear of being rejected. But the average suspect is thinking, 'This guy is just a cop on the street. How can he find my dope?' If the suspects keep their false perception and we get over ours, we'll win."

Getting consent can be one of the easiest things you do on Criminal Patrol. But getting it in the right way can be a bit like tap dancing across a mine field. Stretching between your avid state of mind (suspicion) and your coveted state of action (searching) is the treacherous ground of the Fourth Amendment, with its formidable protection of personal privacy and restrictions against unreasonable search and seizure. Unless certain special circumstances exist, that Amendment obligates you to get a warrant to search a vehicle you've stopped, a demand for which you may have neither the time nor the probable cause. By giving you permission to search, the suspect eliminates the warrant requirement; in effect, he opens a passageway for you through the Fourth Amendment's impediments by voluntarily agreeing to surrender his right to be secure in the privacy of his vehicle.

He does not have to do this. If he's guilty of criminal activity, it is indisputably against his interest to do it. And if he is not dealt with skillfully, he won't do it (or if he does you'll have your case blown out from under you when you get to court. And if you do uncover contraband, your search may very well be challenged. One source estimates that consent searches "probably generate more litigation than any other area of Fourth Amendment law."[2])

Gaining his cooperation requires that you extend the play-dumb guise that you've used already to elicit deception cues and provoke "stress leaks." As you bring your concealed interrogation to a close and wind up the exploratory stage of your contact, you need to decide, finally, whether you want to search the suspect's vehicle. If you do, you now need to position him emotionally to grant you his permission.

With the right timing, the right atmosphere, the right word pictures, the right respect for his legal rights (and your own), you must push him to the edge of a psychological cliff, where he freely puts his fate in your hands. You want him to feel compelled to give you what you ask without feeling *coerced* to do so.

And you need to know what to do next if that doesn't work.

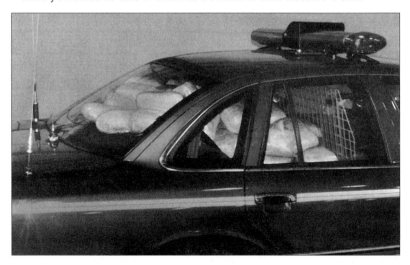

Bringing home the bacon. The impressive result of a consent search asked for, obtained, and conducted in the right way.

The Magic Moment

Some officers try to search every vehicle they stop, as a hedge against offenders who are successfully deceptive during dialogue. That's generally a waste of valuable time. The whole purpose of a sensory patdown and concealed interrogation is to select out those travelers who seem most likely to warrant closer inspection. Moreover, in many jurisdictions indiscriminate searching is simply not permitted.[3]

Although some jurisdictions are more flexible than others, legally you're on safest ground if you have articulable reasonable suspicion before seeking consent to search. That means that during your contact your curiosity, your hunches, or your mere suspicion have grown to the point that you can now identify and describe specific, relevant facts that suggest the possibility of criminal activity, like the potential indicators we've discussed. This probably will be interpreted liberally, but be able to cite at least something(s) about the vehicle and/or its occupant(s) that led you to infer that contraband might be present. If you can't, finish up your paperwork, get the driver back into traffic, and go on to your next stop. You're not going any higher on the Criminal Patrol Pyramid this time.

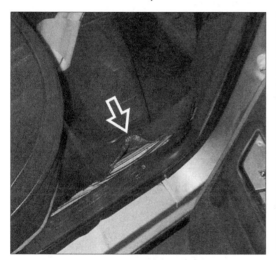 

Search cues like the disturbed carpet (above left) can lead to important discoveries like the stacks of cash (above right) from money compartment under it. But unless you've laid the proper groundwork before asking consent, your prized evidence may be thrown out of court.

For those relatively few vehicles you do want to search, your timing and manner in asking permission now become critical.

First of all, the moment you know you're going to ask for consent you should get backup on the way, along with a drug-trained K-9 if one is available. Even without a dog, you'll ideally need one or more extra officers to monitor the occupant(s) while you scrutinize the vehicle inside and out. Backup should arrive about the time you obtain consent so you minimize the wait before you start to search. That keeps your detention time reasonable and gives the suspect the least opportunity for reconsidering. If backup pulls up before you complete the consent process, have him or her deploy at a distance so as not to add intimidating overtones to your request.

For a consent search to be valid, not only must the stop itself be lawful but the suspect's permission must be considered voluntary. Specifically: *Consent must be asked for and granted when a "reasonable" person would believe he is legally free to disregard further con*

(above left/above)
When you return a suspect's documents before asking for consent to search, you may become so focused on legal procedures that you forget about physical tactics. Remember: Careless positioning can be dangerous at any moment during the stop.

(left/below)
Stay alert, balanced, and tactical. But make sure that backup does not crowd the suspect and make him feel coerced to sign consent.

tact with you and leave your presence.[4] In other words, your request must be posed when the suspect is in what could flippantly be called a "screw you" period.

Legally this period begins when you have concluded the reason for the stop (issued him a ticket or warning, for example) and have returned his license, registration, insurance card, and any other documents. In most jurisdictions, so long as you retain these items, courts will likely conclude that a reasonable person in the position of the violator would not feel free to leave. Asking for consent under those circumstances will be considered tainted by the possibility that he felt coerced to cooperate because he was still being officially detained.

You may want to mark the end of your official detention by saying casually, as a "throw-away" line: "Okay, you're free to go; have a safe trip," as you hand him the papers. Some officers feel this "purifies" your actions and lets you "stand tall" in the courtroom. But the U. S. Supreme Court says such notice is *not* required.[5] All federal jurisdictions (but not necessarily all state courts) now conform to that rule. These courts presume that a reasonable citizen knows that constitutionally he does not have to remain once the purpose for the stop is ended. If he does stay after that point, it's presumed that he's sticking around by "choice" and engaging in "consensual conversation" with you. Whatever he agrees to then, in these courts' view, is more likely to be voluntary.

Understandably, most Criminal Patrol officers do not like to draw attention to the suspect's option to ignore them in this consensual period, so they try to avoid an abrupt break when the detention technically ends and the contact de-escalates into a voluntary encounter. Heading toward the finish, they keep the conversation flowing as they're filling out the paperwork—a mix of irrelevant chatter, continued probing for deception cues, and perhaps a segue into the kind of "pin-down sequence" we'll discuss shortly. One officer tries to time it so he's able to ask a question about the weather in whatever locale the suspect says he has come from at just about the time he hands back the driver's license. "This keeps him focused on something nonthreatening at that moment," the officer explains, "and it all kind of blends together." With a "seamless" transition, the suspect is less likely to register the fact that his status has officially changed.

Psychologically, though, the chances are overwhelming that the average person won't leave at that "break" point, even if he understands intellectually that he could. After all, you're the police and you're still talking to him. As a practical matter, his freedom to disregard your questions and split simply don't occur to him.

If you lack confidence in this and try to crowd specific questions about contraband and a request for consent into your dialogue too early, you can end up with bitter legal consequences. A deputy in Utah stopped a driver whose Cadillac he'd clocked at 12 mph over the limit. The car cleared okay on a computer check and the driver showed no sign of substance abuse, but the deputy noticed that he was so nervous his hands were shaking. The deputy asked if he had any drugs, weapons, or serious money in the car. The driver denied it, but said he did have $1,600 cash in the glove compartment and $150 in his pocket. Without writing a speeding citation and while still holding the suspect's license and registration, the deputy asked for and got permission to search the car. Eighty-six kilos of cocaine were discovered hidden inside, indicating that the deputy certainly knew something about reading culprits. But in a decision that the U.S. Supreme Court refused to review, a federal appeals court ruled that the deputy had violated the suspect's Fourth Amendment rights by posing questions about contraband and consent before the driver was free to leave.[6] This underscores the rule: *Return everything to the driver first, then ask for consent to search.*

Once they're in the consensual period, most officers favor a fairly direct approach. One option is to pretend that the idea of searching has occurred to you as an afterthought. If you're at the driver's window or standing outside with him, turn as if you're going to walk away after you've returned his papers, then, still acting the good ol' boy, turn back and broach the subject cordially, lightly, almost as a joke: "Say, can I ask you a question?" Wait for him to agree, then: "You know, I sure run into a lot of strange things out here. You don't have any bazookas or drugs or atomic bombs in the car, do you?"

Technically, you've confirmed that he's agreeable to talking to you. Your tone conveys that you're posing a strictly routine, even stupid, question to which you are of course expecting a negative answer. When the driver says "No," then casually but quickly pop the $64,000 question:

"Well, you wouldn't mind if I took a look, would you?"

This phrasing, too, employs psychology in your favor. The implication is that the subject will look guilty if he *does* mind. An assumption is built into the question. It's psychologically harder to decline than a straight-forward: "Can I search your car?"

Another option is to preface the question by revealing a bit of what you've seen or heard that has made you suspicious. This applies a little more psychological pressure. If you've picked up some inconsistencies between his story and a passenger's, for example, ask him after he's technically free to leave:

"Oh, by the way, you say you're going to Detroit?"

"Yeah."

"Hmmm. Your buddy there said something else." Don't disclose *what* the passenger said, but sound puzzled. "Something's not right here. You're not hauling anything illegal in the vehicle, are you—guns, drugs, alcohol, bad money?"

"Nnnnooooooo!"

Then, casually: "You don't mind if I look, do you?"

Or, a variation (again after the contact has become consensual): "You boys seem awful nervous. You know who I am, but I don't know you fellas. Do you have any contraband in the car?" Assured there is none, press. "You *sure* there isn't anything in the car?" With more denials, then ask permission to see for yourself.

Initially, words like "look," "inspect," and "see" are okay to keep your request sounding less alarming. But at some point in repeating your request or on your written consent form, *you should make clear that you intend to search the vehicle.* As one court puts it, you should "objectively communicate" that you are "requesting permission to examine the vehicle and its contents" in a way that a "reasonable individual" would understand. One court ruled, for example, that when an officer got permission merely to "look" in a car this meant he couldn't use his hands to search under a seat.[7] Another ruled that permission to "look" precluded removing door panels to expose multiple kilos of coke hidden behind them.[8] So be specific: You want consent to *search* the vehicle.

It is also a good practice to state what you are searching for: drugs, weapons, large sums of money, or other illegal contraband. Keep your language simple. If you try to razzle-dazzle the suspect with five-dollar words when asking consent, this can come back to haunt you later if he claims in court that he didn't understand what he was agreeing to.

If a suspect asks why you want to search, you do not have to reveal the reasons behind your suspicion. Keep it general: "We get a lot of drug smuggling through here. We check a lot of cars." Put him or her back on the defensive: "Why, do you have something to hide? A person who doesn't have anything to hide wouldn't mind me looking in their car, would they?"

A guilty suspect may stall at first: "You don't really think I'm a smuggler, do you?" or "You aren't really serious about this, are you?" In fact, a guilty party may even hedge in responding to your question about whether contraband is in the car. Instead of emphatically saying "No," for instance, he or she may respond: "I don't do drugs." If he's not saying "No" to a direct question like that, he's probably saying "Yes" or at least "Maybe." Don't strongly confront him. Tell him you don't think he's guilty; you're "just trying to do my job."

So long as you have raised the possibility that something might be wrong about the occupant(s) and the vehicle, he will usually feel a strong psychological urgency to grant your request to search in order to dispel your doubts. He may even act cocky or indignant—almost challenging you to find something. "Incredible as it may seem," says an Ohio deputy, "most individuals *ask* me if I want to search their vehicle before I even get to the consent question. They know full well there's a loaded gun under the seat or dope in the glove box. But they get so fixed on proving they're innocent, they invite me in."

Some suspects are naive enough to think that as a cop you can do anything you want and will search anyway. With others, says a trooper, "It sounds corny, but I've been friendly with them for ten minutes and they don't have the guts to say 'No' to a 'friend.'" Your casual demeanor may have convinced some that you'll just glance into the car and will miss hidden contraband. Or they may feel confident that the goods are so cleverly concealed that you'd never find them, no matter how exhaustively you search. "Basically," says a New York instructor, "a courier wants to be on his way, and he feels that cooperating is the best way to get you off his back. He may even hope that answering 'Yes' will bluff you out of searching all together."

Psychological Setup

The direct-request approach offers a certain "startle" advantage, because most people don't expect to be asked to have their vehicle searched on a traffic stop. But there may be times when you prefer a bit more of a psychological positioning before posing your consent request.

One option here is a cat-and-mouse tactic honed to a near-science by an Illinois trooper. It may help you decide whether to search in a borderline case or soften up the resistance of an overly confident subject. But to pull it off while still accommodating the legal limitations requires exquisite timing and the verbal finesse of a good actor.

The trooper asks subjects six "pin-down" questions leading up the primrose path to consent. While not absolute guarantees, they tend to separate the guilty from the innocent, he believes, based on the results of hundreds of consent searches. Once he hears the answers, he says he is never surprised when he then searches and finds drugs.

He begins blending the questions into his seemingly idle chitchat as he's writing out the ticket. Like many troopers, he usually has the violator sitting beside him in the patrol car, but the technique can work anywhere. Having the suspect somewhere away from his own vehicle establishes a small but important psychological edge for you. The separation makes it easier for him to dissociate the suspect car from his "personal zone." Thus he may feel less defensive and guarded about the problems you are soon to suggest may be associated with it.

Employing the trooper's tactic, you casually ask the suspect:

1. Are there many problems with cocaine and marijuana in your city? Innocent people tend to acknowledge the obvious right away: "Yes, there are a lot of problems. Dope is everywhere." People with drug involvement often offer denial: "No, I don't really hear of any. I stay away from it."

2. What do you think police should do to people they catch smuggling drugs? The innocent generally state an emphatic, punitive answer: "Hang 'em! Lock 'em up and throw away the key!" People with guilty knowledge of drugs often are evasive ("Aw, I don't know")...or they rationalize ("Drugs are bad, but there's lots of other things going on that cops ought to pay more attention to" or "I'm not a drug dealer, but I can see how other people might do it")...or they give an "amnesty" answer that says, in effect, "Don't hurt me" ("Maybe probation or a fine. They sure don't need to go to jail.").

Watch for signs of increased nervousness at this point. And remember that culpable people may try to consciously construct "innocent" answers. That means a "guilty" response is all the more suspicious and significant; it may be the suspect's subconscious talking.

3. What's the address you're going to in (whatever city the suspect has said is his destination)? This is a "last chance" to see if he's consistent with what he has told you before or, if you haven't raised this question previously, to test his ability to supply corroborating details for his story.

Innocent answer: "I have that address right here. It is...." Suspicious answer: "I don't know. I have to make a phone call when I get close to there. I'm not sure what I did with the number."

At about this point, complete your paperwork. Give the driver back his ID and the ticket and put away your cite book and pen to indicate that your official business with him is over. Consider even telling him that he's free to go. From here on, you're in the consensual period. With innocent subjects, their stress level should begin to decrease now that they've received either a ticket or warning. A guilty party's stress level will usually sustain or increase so long as you are present and engaging him in conversation.

With a puzzled tone, now ask:

4. Would there be any reason why someone would have called the police with your car description and said you were transporting drugs in this vehicle? For the first time, you may see innocent parties start to get a little angry or offended: "Absolutely not!" Couriers tend to give an unsure "No," or they'll attempt to explain why someone may have mistakenly associated them with drug dealings in the distant past.

"This is a real watershed question," the trooper says. "About now, many people admit that they have dope in their car." If not, continue:

5. Do you have any marijuana, cocaine, weapons, large sums of money, or other illegal contraband in your car today, sir (or ma'am)? Innocent answer: "No." A guilty person will more likely hesitate... repeat the question...ask if you think he looks like a drug dealer...say he's a family man or a religious person...say he doesn't use coke because he has stomach problems...or offer some other "smoke-screen" response that doesn't really answer your query. He may pick

When you ask about contraband, a guilty subject may look back at his vehicle, toward the spot where illegal goods are hidden. If he's personally packing a weapon, he may glance at or touch the spot where the weapon is concealed.

just one thing out of the list you've rattled off and deny having that ("No, I don't have any weapons"). That should make you wonder why he didn't deny *everything* if he really has nothing.

Watch for body language. Is the suspect saying "No" but his head is affirmatively bobbing up and down? If he breaks eye contact with you, where does he look (see above)?

After pausing for a few seconds, you then ask what the trooper calls "the Ultimate Structured Question":

6. Are you *sure?* Actually this can be asked after any of the above, to build psychological pressure. "Try to get in close when you ask it," the trooper advises. "Take your sunglasses off. Play a game. Make it appear that you already know the answer or know more than the suspect is telling. Watch him. Many verbal and nonverbal signals may now be coming at you from the guilty."

Some officers like to add a couple of "bonus" questions. One of these, again, can be asked after any of the above: *What would you say if I said I didn't believe you?* If the suspect gets angry, back off: "Hey, wait a minute. I'm not saying I *don't* believe you. I just asked what you'd say if I *didn't.* That doesn't make you mad, does it? We're just talking here." Actually, innocent people do tend to get angry when their integrity is impugned. People with something to hide are more likely to try to appear unruffled and respond with remarks like, "No, I'm not mad. I understand you have a job to do," et cetera. The second optional question is: *Have you ever thought about using or transporting drugs?* Truthful answer: Yes. Most people have thought about this subject, even if in a negative way. Lying response: No. The guilty person feels that admitting to thinking about this is threateningly close to admitting doing it.

By the time the suspect answers Question 6, he is on your hook. If you want to search his vehicle, just reel him in. Your next logical move, coming quickly, is to ask for consent.

The trooper who devised this sequence claims that a surprising 5 to 10% of guilty suspects—women especially—admit to having drugs once he poses Question 5. Some talk out of remorse, some because relieving their intense deception anxiety seems at the moment more impelling than the long-term consequences, and some to persuade you they are really victims of someone else's criminal intent. One sixty-two-year-old woman driver burst out, "I have to be honest with you. I've got eighty pounds of marijuana in my trunk. My son is traveling behind me in another car. If I get stopped he's supposed to wait for me at the next filling station." Sure enough, he was; his mother had agreed to haul for him as a favor. The trooper feels, incidentally, that by naming specific drugs in the question, you are more likely to hit on the actual contents of the load and thereby heighten a suspect's stress reaction. "If you say 'marijuana' and he's got marijuana, you can see it in his eyes," the trooper says. This increases the chances for confession.

Even if the subject lies and denies having contraband, this is still good. Later, after you find it, his lying can help you in court. A good prosecutor will use this as evidence that his consent was not coerced: "If the defendant had the nerve to lie to the officer, that indicates that the officer was not intimidating him!"

When a trooper in Ohio posed Question 5 to a driver who was en route from Alabama to northern Michigan, the driver didn't answer at all. The trooper told him: "I know from your response that it's one of the things I named. Which is it?"

"Guns," the driver admitted.

"Guns! Where are they?"

"Under the front seat. The passenger's probably gonna shoot your partner."

The trooper let out a yell to his partner who was standing at the passenger's window. The partner reached in and grabbed the startled passenger and yanked him out through the window.

The troopers benefited from the element of surprise, because what the first officer had shouted to his partner was a code word they had worked out between them, meaning: "Armed!"

New York City officers display weapons they seized from a driver who was asked, "Are you carrying any weapons, drugs, or contraband?" The man answered, "Yes," and pointed to a pile of rags on the back seat. A sawed-off shotgun and a .45 semiautomatic loaded with hollow-point rounds were found under the pile.

With psychological setups you need to stay flexible enough that you can adapt your dialogue to special circumstances. A traffic officer in California one night stopped an erratic motorist he initially thought was intoxicated. After a few moments' contact he realized the man was high on pot. There must be drugs in the vehicle, the officer reasoned—but he decided the best way to get consent to search was to guide the driver's thinking away from drugs entirely.

Throughout his roadside testing, the officer deliberately accused the suspect of alcohol consumption: "Man, you have definitely been drinking. I think you're drunk!" The driver repeatedly and vehemently denied it. Finally, in exasperation, he demanded that the officer search the car to prove there was no booze inside. At first, the officer hesitated: "I can't believe you're asking me to search your car. I know I'm gonna find booze in there!" But the driver insisted. As the officer had hoped, the suspect had become so focused on the fact that he was innocent of drunkenness that he'd forgotten about his drug stash.

With the offender in the back of the patrol car, the officer searched and found hashish and marijuana in the suspect vehicle. He also discovered a briefcase full of money. The driver said it must belong to a hitchhiker he'd dropped off a few miles back.

"Well," the officer said, "I guess I'd better count this so nobody says I stole any."

"Yeah, you better," the driver sneered. "I've heard about you guys ripping people off."

"You're right," the officer agreed. "Let's see, that looks to be about $4,000, right?"

"No way, man! That's $10,000 in cash! Count it ALL!"

Gotcha!

Caution: Keep in mind during the psychological interplay that the closer your questions and comments come to sounding accusatory, the more aggressive some subjects may become. The eventual realization that they've been psychologically boxed in may push some to violence. Stay on guard for possible sudden assault or flight.

Essentials of Consent

To be court-defensible and assure your legal survival, the consent you receive must meet certain standards set by the U. S. Supreme Court[9] and generally prevailing case law:

- Consent must be granted voluntarily;
- It must be granted by a person who has real or apparent authority to do so;
- He must understand what he is agreeing to;
- Any limitation on the scope of the requested search that he imposes must be respected, until you have probable cause that permits you to go beyond his restriction(s).

Here are some fine points of these considerations that are important to keep in mind as you pursue the driver's cooperation:

Voluntariness.[10] This is likely to be the biggest single element you'll be attacked on in court. Besides the timing issue, defense attorneys may also seize upon the atmosphere that prevails when consent is granted.

Voluntariness does not mean that the suspect is under absolutely no pressure to consent or that you cannot influence him psychologically. However, *his capacity for making independent decisions must not be "critically impaired."* If you threaten to arrest him if he doesn't cooperate or other officers crowd around him, brandishing weapons and otherwise projecting direct or implied intimidation, that is evidence of coercion.

That's why backup that arrives before you get consent buttoned up should essentially just "show up and shut up": remain at a comfortable distance from you and the suspect, ideally within earshot but not intruding on "personal space." Neither you nor other officers should display a weapon or physically touch or restrain the suspect (unless a threat occurs, of course)...use strong language or a commanding tone of voice...make threats or otherwise suggest that his consent might be strong-armed...or block his path of departure.

Obtaining consent should be a one-on-one activity. Curiously, courts have said it can occur if the suspect is sitting with you in your patrol car, a setting most people would find at least somewhat intimidating. But he or she must not be "forced" to "give in" to a show of authority. If you ride with a partner or other officers are present, don't appear to "gang up" on the offender. Also the words you choose are important; your language must convey a *request*, not an order, avoiding intimidation by volume, inflection, or ambiguous meaning.[11]

In addition, the subject's age, intelligence, education, familiarity with language, criminal history, emotional stability, and sobriety may be important as the court later looks at "the totality of the circumstances" in evaluating the degree of voluntariness.

Consent cannot be retroactive; that is, you cannot search first and then get consent. Also, if your original stop was illegal, alleged consent to search that you obtained soon after will probably also be disallowed by the courts.[12]

Authority.[13] The person who has legal authority to grant consent to search a vehicle is the one in "apparent control of its operation and contents" at the time permission is given. Normally (although not always), that's the driver.

If a passenger is present, it's desirable to get his or her consent also. If the passenger has personal belongings inside the car, you'll want to search them, and his and her consent eliminates controversy about whether these are technically off limits. However, courts in most jurisdictions have held that passengers enjoy "no ownership or possessory interest" in a vehicle and thus have little or no expectation of privacy regarding it or its contents. Thus their belongings are generally subject to search so long as the driver consents. Evidence found in the vehicle can be validly admitted against both of them, even if the passenger has no knowledge of the driver's consent.

Where conflict about consent exists between a passenger and the driver, the most conservative approach is to segregate the passenger's effects and search the rest of the car and contents based on the driver's consent. If a K-9 is on hand, a sniff of the passenger's belongings as they sit outside the car in open air may produce an alert and establish probable cause to suspect them.

Where everyone in the car denies ownership of certain luggage or containers, the object(s) in question can still be searched, based on the driver's general consent to search the vehicle and its contents, including all packages contained therein.

If the owner of the vehicle is present but not driving, his authority generally supersedes the driver's. In legal theory he has the greatest expectation of privacy regarding the vehicle and thus will be surrendering the most in waiving his Fourth Amendment rights. However, the burden is on the owner to make himself known and to protest the driver's consent. If he doesn't, the driver's consent is all you need.

Always start with the driver. If he defers to the owner, confirm that the driver himself has no objection to a search. You may be able to use that to bring the owner around if he resists: "The driver says I have *his* permission. Is there something *you* have in the vehicle that's illegal?"

Where a semitrailer or other commercial truck is concerned, the driver has the power to give you consent to search the cargo, even though he doesn't own it. The owner is considered to confer that authority over it when he assigns it to the driver's care.

Note: You may not have authority to conduct a consensual search outside your jurisdiction. This issue was raised after an officer from a major city in Oklahoma followed a driver after the officer saw a package being loaded into her trunk at a convenience store by a known marijuana dealer. In a suburban parking lot, the car stopped and the officer asked for and got the driver's consent to search. As suspected, the package contained pot. But an appeals court said the officer should have called for local backup to conduct the search. The evidence was suppressed and the woman's conviction was overturned.[14]

3. Confirmation. Depending on your state law or the requirements of your local prosecutor and judges, a suspect's verbal consent alone may be sufficient, or you may also need him to sign a consent form as a written record. The prosecution carries the burden of proving that consent was voluntary,[15] and whether a signed document is considered necessary varies among jurisdictions. Successful drug busts are validated in court every day with both approaches.

Verbal consent is probably strongest when the scene and dialogue are being recorded by an in-car video camera. Then the atmosphere as well as the exact wording of your request and the suspect's response are captured. Also the suspect's nervousness, contradictions, and other indicators that built your reasonable suspicion will be evident on the tape.

In the absence of a camera, an obvious advantage of a signed form is that it's there to impeach a suspect who claims he didn't give you consent or didn't understand what he was doing. Legally, when he signs a document, it's presumed he understands it; the burden then shifts to him to prove otherwise.

When relying solely on verbal consent, some officers try to get the suspect to repeat his agreement to a search at least three times during the course of the conversation, hopefully within earshot of another officer. If you do not patrol with a video camera and it is permitted in your jurisdiction, get not only the exchange about consent but also your earlier dialogue on audio tape, with a voice-activated recorder that slips into your shirt pocket or clips onto your belt. If the suspect later alleges he didn't understand English or tries to fake a language difficulty in court, it makes a dramatic courtroom coup when the tape is played and he can be heard conversing and granting consent in fluent English, then suddenly switching to a foreign language when you confront him with contraband you've discovered in his car.

To build credence that a person who grants verbal consent knows what he's agreeing to, some officers like to summarize for the suspect what they'll be searching for (narcotics, weapons, large amounts of unexplained cash, nontaxed alcohol, and "other contraband") and where they'll be searching (the passenger compartment, under the seats, in the trunk, in suitcases and other containers, et cetera). This helps satisfy the requirement that a suspect understand that he is consenting to an actual search. Also be sure that consent is unequivocal. Some courts have held that an affirmative nodding of the head is okay, but something open to question, like a grunt or a general waving of an arm, is not acceptable.

Unless the conversation is captured on video or audio tape, a printed consent form is usually better documentation. But it's also chancier because its official aura may frighten the suspect into second thoughts. However, you can build up to his signing it in a way that lessens that risk.

Make it seem like strictly routine, bureaucratic paper waste: "I have a standard form that has to be filled out. I appreciate your cooperation." One North Carolina deputy likes to keep a sheaf of about twenty "old," signed consent forms rubber banded to his pad of unsigned new ones. This prompts the suspect to assume that numerous motorists before him have already agreed to this "ordinary" procedure. Actually, the deputy doesn't perform that many consent searches; the "old" copies are bogus ones he has had friends and family sign to convey the impression he wants.

When you present the form, remind the suspect along these lines: "You've already given me permission to search your car. This is mainly for my protection because we look through so many vehicles out here. This just says it's voluntary and I'm not threatening you, so I don't get in trouble with my supervisor. You know how that goes! I'd appreciate it if you'd read this over and if you understand it and you're willing to let me search, would you just sign it here?" You can point to the signature line as a psychological nudge in that direction. You may even want to sign the form yourself at this point as a means of leading him to do it. But allow him whatever time he wants to read the form.

You can have the suspect fill in blanks on the form, to reinforce his voluntary agreement. This is especially desirable with those who may later claim language barriers in court. Also consider having the subject initial each paragraph to signify his agreement throughout. If time is called for on the form, a time within about five or six minutes after the citation is completed will help confirm that the consent was obtained during the consensual period.

If the suspect seems hesitant and starts arguing with you, pin him back again to his verbal consent: "You said I could search the car. I'd like to search it. It won't take long." You may be able to paint word pictures that tend to minimize the importance of permission. A New Jersey trooper likes to explain that giving consent "is not an admission of any kind. If I was to find the Lindbergh baby or Elvis in the back of your car, it's by no means an admission." And he tells hesitant subjects: "I'm not going to break anything or steal anything. If I find something I think I should have, I'll give you a receipt." This omits, of course, reference to potential dire consequences, like arrest. A light-hearted reference may also get the subject to laugh, taking the edge off his anxiety.

If the suspect insistently refuses to sign, don't badger him to the point of coercion. You may still be in the game: Courts have held that if a suspect refuses to sign a consent form but "concurrently" gives you verbal permission to search, your search can still be considered voluntary.[16] Just write on the bottom of the form: "Refused to sign." In that case, be sure that the exact wording of your request and his response are preserved in your written report. Precise language will be important in court.

Consent forms should be printed in both English and Spanish. Some officers like to have Hispanic subjects sign *both* as a precaution. Verify that the subject is able to read the language of whatever form(s) you give him. Some officers in fact, like to ask the subject if he reads English while they are still writing the ticket, so that this is established even before the consensual period begins. Some like to read the form aloud to the subject, so that his reading comprehension does not become an issue. Or you may want the subject to read the form aloud to you, especially if he is a foreign-speaker, to confirm that he knows what it says; this may also help you if a defense attorney claims later that a suspect is mentally retarded. Language comprehension is critical to validity.[17]

If a subject has difficulty speaking English and you have a consent form in his language, ask him to sign it, even if you don't usually get signed consent; try not to rely only on verbal consent in that situation. Don't be deceptive about what the form really is. One Colorado officer made a practice of getting Hispanics and uneducated blacks to sign consent forms by telling them they were warning notices for traffic violations. Needless to say, he got tromped on in court.

Note: When a suspect does not read or write, he or she can verbally consent to a search and still sign a form, if he or she understands what is being signed. Courts have held that illiteracy is not the equivalent of lack knowledge or of common sense and does not bar a subject from consenting.[18]

The form should state specifically that you intend to search the vehicle whose description you've written in—"and its contents." If some general phrase about contents is not preprinted on the form, enter it in your own handwriting before the suspect signs and be sure he initials his acknowledgment of it. This will discourage doubts later about whether he understood that you intended to search containers, packages, and personal effects you find in the vehicle.

The suspect, of course, has the right to reject your request to search, just as he or she can walk away from the consensual conversation at any time. Some consent forms include a direct notice of this right, as a legal safeguard; in some states, it's required. But if your jurisdiction follows federal guidelines, the U.S. Supreme Court has said that you *do not have to give any warning of rights nor explain specifically the suspect's right to refuse your request to search.* His "knowingly" granting consent does not mean that he has been informed of his right to refuse but that he understands that a search will result from his agreement.[19] However, some courts consider whether the subject was told about the right of refusal when they weigh whether consent was truly informed and voluntary.[20] Thus many agencies include the right of refusal in their forms, even though it's not required.

In practice, when suspect rights are printed on a consent form they tend to be bypassed by anxious subjects as just so much boilerplate.

Typically, a driver from Florida was stopped in New Jersey for speeding and was asked for permission to search after he could not produce a rental agreement and appeared very nervous. The consent form clearly stated that he could legally refuse to cooperate, but he readily signed it anyway—thereby permitting a trooper to open a suitcase lying temptingly on the back seat and discover over $87,000 in cash inside, which the driver later admitted was spoils from drug trafficking.

(left/above)
Think "survival" even when the suspect is cooperating by signing your consent form. Do you make yourself vulnerable to attack by where you stand, like the officer on the left? Or, like the officer above, do you maintain a reactionary gap and make attack awkward for the suspect?

Edged weapons may be disguised to look like pens. In a split-second this "normal" ballpoint in a pocket can becomes a deadly shaft. Don't let a subject use his own "pen" to sign a consent form or a citation.

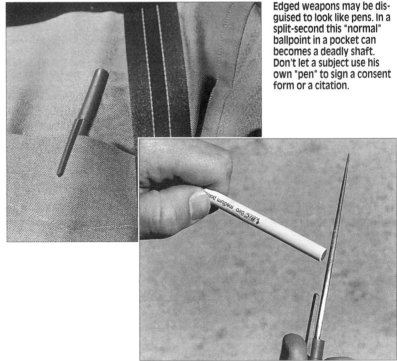

Scope.[21] If a suspect agrees to a "complete" or "general" search of his vehicle, without qualifying his permission, you are free to check it to whatever "reasonable" extent you want to. "You can take it apart and put it back as it was," in the words of one officer.

Your mention of drugs as part of what you're interested in without question confirms your right to open closed containers you encounter. The scope of a warrantless search is generally defined by its expressed object, and a search for drugs would reasonably include virtually any closed hiding place. (On the other hand, an officer in North Dakota asked permission to search the truck of a suspected DUI for "open [alcohol] containers," and the driver agreed. The officer found none of those but in a small bag under the front seat he did discover thirty-three packets of amphetamines. The court suppressed the drugs as evidence, ruling that the officer himself had specified that the search was for alcohol containers, which would have been too big to fit into the small bag.[22])

The more broadly you can describe the contraband you're looking for, the better. On a general consent search, any illicit items are fair game for seizure. An officer in Utah thought he'd find drugs after stopping two nervous individuals who had been driving through the night in a third-party vehicle. Instead, he opened a tightly wrapped package in the trunk and discovered hundreds of counterfeit Social Security and immigration cards. Other officers in Texas lifted a trunk lid and found a young rape victim, bound and blindfolded, lying inside.

If you encounter a container that's locked,[23] you are safest to ask (don't coerce) the suspect for the key or combination. Breaking into containers or compartments in such a destructive manner that you can't restore them is generally considered implicitly prohibited, unless you have the suspect's specific permission or probable cause to believe that they hold contraband. However, some courts have held that if using force to open a locked trunk, for example, would "reasonably" be interpreted as "necessary to accomplish the search," a general and unqualified consent would sanction such force. Likewise some have ruled that puncturing or otherwise accessing hidden compartments is okay, if done in a minimally intrusive manner. Again, consult your legal advisors for what's acceptable in your jurisdiction.

Whatever scope of consent you obtain applies to the use of a drug dog as well, provided that the subject does not object to the dog's being put into the vehicle.[24]

The person who grants consent is entitled to explicitly limit the physical scope of a search in any way. In other words, he has the right to give up as much or as little of his Fourth Amendment protection as he chooses. He may say, "You can't search the trunk" or "You can look in the glove box, but don't open my briefcase," for example. *Legally, you cannot go beyond any limits he imposes*, unless you develop PC or some other ground(s) for an "escalated" search. A computer check showed that the license plate of one car, stopped by Oregon officers after the driver failed to signal a turn, was connected with a semiautomatic weapons violation. The driver consented to a search, but his keys wouldn't unlock the trunk and he said he did not want that area investigated if the car would be damaged in the process. By removing the back seat, officers were able to glimpse the barrel of a gun through the trunk wall. Although they then obtained a warrant and seized the weapon, the evidence was suppressed at trial.

The court ruled that removing the seats violated the limitation the suspect had imposed.

The subject can even limit what you can look for. He may say, "You can search for a sawed-off shotgun, but you can't search for drugs." Then you would not be entitled to open containers or check places that could not conceivably contain a sawed-off shotgun. (However if you see contraband in plain view in a place that could have concealed a shotgun, then it is seizable, regardless of what he has said.)[25]

The suspect may withdraw consent at any time prior to the discovery of contraband. *If he tells you to stop searching, you must do so immediately,* unless by then you have developed probable cause to continue. Normally, his withdrawal must be specific. If he merely makes general comments to the effect of "Why are you looking in there?", you can still proceed. For example:

IF HE ASKS:	YOU (OR YOUR COVER OFFICER) ANSWER:
"Don't you need a warrant?"	"No, because you gave consent."
"Why are you doing this?"	"Because you gave consent."
"Should you be doing this?"	"That's totally up to you."
"I want you to stop."	"Ok, is it because of the drugs in there?" (If he says "Yes," some jurisdictions will consider that you now have PC to keep going or to attempt to get a search warrant.)

Sometimes even an emphatic gesture may be enough to signal withdrawal of consent. A federal court in a Western case ruled that a suspect slamming and locking a trunk signified the termination of his consent.[26] You cannot use withdrawal as grounds for arrest, nor does it constitute probable cause for searching further.[27]

If the suspect wants to limit your search at the outset, take whatever you can get him to consent to. It may lead to more. A driver of a rental truck stopped in Wyoming said an officer could search the cab but not the cargo area. Nothing physical of an incriminating nature turned up in the cab, but while searching it the officer detected an "ether-like" odor seeping through from the cargo area. Because he recognized this as a possible indicator of clandestine laboratory materials, he decided that it constituted probable cause to hold the driver and expand the search. Several hours later, a DEA haz-mat team searched the rest of the truck and discovered just the kind of contraband the officer had suspected. The court sustained this, even though the limits of the original consent had been exceeded.[28]

Salvaging Turndowns

Suppose a suspect flatly rebuffs your request to search and decides to exercise his right to leave. Then what?

Option 1: Seek a search warrant. Tell the suspect he is free to go but you intend to hold his vehicle and attempt to get a warrant. This may prompt him to give you consent. You must have *justification* (i.e., probable cause) for saying this, though. Out-and-out bluffing about seeking a warrant or the threat that you will for certain get a warrant can invalidate any consent he may then give.[29] If you have asked the right questions and made appropriate observations, you may have enough evidence to actually obtain a warrant, possibly even by phone. With a warrant, his preferences about your searching won't matter.

"DIAL-A-WARRANT"

A seldom used but very useful tool for law enforcement in some states is the telephonic search warrant, which may be available to you as an option on vehicle stops. In a manual on Criminal Patrol tactics, the Utah Highway Patrol offers this advice regarding warrants by phone:

It is imperative that the officer, the issuing court, and the county or city prosecutor have a good working understanding of this [type of] warrant before it is implemented.

The officer must be able to articulate sufficient probable cause during a telephone conversation, and have enough credibility with the court, to allow the Judge to issue the warrant on the strength of verbal communication alone.

Talk to the Judges in your area, discuss these warrants with them, and develop working relationships. If the need for a telephonic search warrant arises, the groundwork has already been established.

For the protection of the officer and the court, the entire conversation between the officer and the court must be taped. The court will probably order the tape and/or a transcription with the return of service.

Most courts have forms of telephonic search warrants on file. Go over them with your prosecutor(s) and Judge(s).

Do not be afraid of search warrants. They could be most useful [on Criminal Patrol], and, after you have worked through the process a time or two, you will find that they are not all that complicated....

[One] reason to get a search warrant, if at all practical, is because it places the burden on the defendant to challenge the search. If the search is without a warrant, the burden is always on the state to justify it. Warrantless searches are considered per se unreasonable [unless you can] bring the search within one of the exceptions.[30]

Option 2: Let him go. At the very least, if you feel the indicators are strong, you can contact the nearest DEA field office with his name, license number, and other particulars. Agents then can begin or add to the computerized intelligence trail on him in the DEA's Narcotics and Dangerous Drugs Information System (NADDIS), which may advance current investigations or help other officers in the future.

Or you can radio ahead to a jurisdiction down the road where more resources may be available. A New Mexico officer reluctantly sent one speeder on his way, after being told to shove it in regards to consent. The officer had detected a strong odor from the vehicle that he thought might be cocaine or crystal methamphetamine. A criminal-history check revealed that the driver was suspected of narcotics trafficking. Yet a judge could not be persuaded to issue a search warrant on the car. Farther down the highway, the suspect got stopped again for speeding. This time, backup was available, with a drug-trained K-9. The dog alerted strongly at the rear of the vehicle. The officers considered this probable cause to search a duffel bag visible on the floor of the hatchback trunk. Inside, they found 33,000 methaqualone tablets.[31] It took two stops to get that courier, but he did get apprehended.

Keep in mind, though, that a second stop requires a second violation or independent reasonable suspicion of illegal activity. A Nebraska trooper suspected two Hispanic males were hauling dope in a truck he'd stopped for erratically swerving onto the shoulder. He obtained permission to search, but when he couldn't get backup promptly he let them go with a warning ticket. Soon after, he learned that the passenger had a prior firearms violation. He notified another officer, who pulled the truck over again thirty miles down the road. With consent to search, that officer found two duct-taped packages of cocaine and five three-inch stacks of money in the cab and cargo compartment. The case was lost in court, however, because the second officer had not had a valid reason of his own for initiating a stop.[32]

Option 3: Turn on a little more Psychology 101. Be a salesman out there. You may still salvage consent. When a deputy in Missouri requested consent to search, the subject asked: "What would happen if I said 'No?'" "Well," the deputy replied, "I've already called the dog, so...." He shrugged and didn't finish the sentence, thereby leaving it essentially meaningless. But hearing the word "dog," the nervous driver threw up his hands and told the deputy to go ahead and look around.

If a dog is available, you can advise the suspect that you don't need his permission to have a drug-trained K-9 sniff around the exterior of the car. Telling him this legal fact may flip him, because he'll feel he stands a better chance of drugs being missed with *you* searching than with the dog involved.

If he still won't agree, try to keep the conversation going on a consensual basis until you can get a K-9 there. Or with articulable reasonable suspicion that the suspect is engaged in criminal activity, you can detain him briefly in most jurisdictions until a dog arrives, even though you do not have grounds to search inside at that point. Legal experts advise that ideally this detention be limited to thirty minutes or less. When the dog arrives, watch the suspect's reaction. Guilty parties will often become extremely nervous when they see the K-9.

Playing the K-9 card salvaged one stop in a spectacular way for two county officers in Georgia. The sloppy-looking female driver had yielded several courier cues: She was licensed in one state but lived in another, she claimed she was moving her household from one state to another but had only two wicker chairs in her minivan, and she was so nervous she was almost falling down—but she wouldn't give written consent to search. While one officer continued to talk to her, the other ran a K-9 around the van. It alerted on the passenger side. With that as PC, the handler slid the door open and began an interior search that eventually uncovered twenty-nine packages of cocaine estimated at about $13,000,000 street value.

That Takes the Cake!

Conflicting stories from occupants of a car he'd stopped led Officer Shannon Douberly of the Jacksonville (FL) Sheriff's Office to ask for consent to search. The driver thought for a moment, then replied with utter sincerity: "How about I say 'No' this time but guarantee you that you can search the next time you see me?"

Now that's a cue! Douberly decided. He called K-9 for an exterior sniff, and the dog quickly alerted on the trunk. Inside, officers found what looked like a Mother's Day cake—but:

• It was 90° out, making an even hotter trunk a strange place to transport dessert;

• It was a week after Mother's Day;

• An inscription on the cake read, "Happy Mother Day."

The K-9 officer felt the cake and realized it was really just a box covered with frosting. Under the lid were two kilos of crack.

In some cases, bluffing may work. When one Midwestern trooper gets a turn down on consent, he tries to make a search seem less threatening to the suspect. "I'm not *that* interested in personal-use quantities," he'll say. "I'm looking for the mother lode. Are you hauling a *big* load?" The suspect usually says "No" and often will then admit to having a couple of joints in the glove box or he'll let the trooper search, assuming that any small amounts found will be ignored. If the officer then discovers personal-use drugs, he promptly arrests the suspect and proceeds to search the rest of the car. "Hey," the suspect may protest, "I thought you said you weren't interested in personal use!"

To which the trooper replies: "I said, 'I'm not *that* interested,' and I'm not. Damn it, I want to find a kilo!"

Another ploy is to tell the suspect: "I'm not saying you're deliberately doing anything illegal, but did you ever think you might be transporting drugs for someone else? Who else has access to this car and knows where you're going today?" A guilty subject may seize upon this as an opportunity to distance himself from the vehicle and grant consent, especially if he's driving a rental car.

If consent is still not granted, your only remaining means of preventing a resistant driver from departing is to have legal grounds at that point that allow you to search the vehicle without his permission.

Involuntary Searches

According to most federal case law, you're entitled to launch at least a limited search of a lawfully stopped vehicle in four major circumstances, without consent and without a warrant. These are special exceptions to the usual warrant requirement. They're allowed because courts presume that a motor vehicle affords less expectation of privacy than a subject's home and because your leaving the scene of a stop to obtain a warrant or attempting to secure one even by telephone is not always feasible.[33]

Some Criminal Patrol officers prefer to use one or more of these grounds for a search whenever possible rather than relying solely on consent. Here you do not need to worry about the driver limiting the search or halting it when you get close to pay dirt.

Assuming your jurisdiction conforms to these guidelines, you can proceed over the objections of an uncooperative driver when you have one or more of the following reasons. As you'll note, these grounds for searching may overlap and blend into one another in real-life situations. Indeed, all could come into play during a single traffic stop, depending on the circumstances.

Suspicion of weapons.[34] Regardless of consent, if you reasonably suspect the presence of readily accessible deadly weapons, you can make a limited "protective search" or frisk of the vehicle's interior for your own safety. You must be able to articulate a specific basis for your suspicion and concern for safety. You can also frisk the subject himself, if you objectively consider him dangerous. In fact if you don't frisk him, courts may look askance at your frisking the car.

Even though the subject may be separated from the vehicle and under the visual or physical control of another officer or even locked in your patrol car, you can still search his vehicle. In theory, he could break away and enter it at any moment or, if not arrested, he could gain access to weapons there when he returns to the car.

If you wait until you've been refused consent before invoking your right to search for weapons, doubt may be raised in court about whether you were really concerned about your safety that late in the contact, but waiting will not necessarily sabotage your case. And of course it may very well be that during the course of writing the ticket or discussing consent you heard conversation or saw activity that led you to believe there might be weapons in the vehicle.

This type of search is sometimes called a "lunge-area" or "wingspan" search. The term refers to the radius in which the suspect might reach in going for a weapon. But it is interpreted to include areas where weapons could be placed or hidden in the entire passenger compartment. You cannot intrude into the closed trunk or into locked compartments or locked containers, though, unless you discover PC for expanding your scope. The search, after all, is to find weapons and to ensure your safety.

You can seize contraband that you encounter in plain view or while investigating spots where weapons might be hidden.[35] However, your discovery must be reasonable. For example, you should not be searching a small jewelry box (where you might find a personal-use quantity of narcotics) when you are ostensibly hunting for a knife or gun; this is sometimes referred to as the "elephant-in-a-matchbox" rule.

Even concern about a *legal* weapon can be grounds for a protective search. In a landmark case, two Michigan officers spotted a large hunting knife lying on the floorboard of a car that had swerved into a shallow ditch along a remote country road. One officer checked the passenger compartment for other weapons and in the process found a pouch of marijuana under the center armrest. The U.S. Supreme Court sustained both the search and seizure. The Court said that an offender's privacy must yield in such circumstances to the "compelling need" of police to protect themselves "in the area surrounding [a] suspect."

The same principle caused another court to uphold the actions of two California deputies who stopped a car with a burned-out headlight and were refused consent to search by the driver, an ex-convict. He was sober, properly licensed, nonresistant, and nonthreatening. A consensual pat down revealed no weapon on him. However, in dealing with him the deputies observed a four-inch knife in a sheath, lying on the open glove-box door with its handle toward the driver. This was their sole basis for believing that he could be dangerous. Although he was not under arrest at that point, they handcuffed him and ordered him to sit on a curb away from the car while one of the deputies checked it out. The deputy discovered a loaded magazine under the driver's seat and an unloaded semiautomatic hidden in a trash bag hanging from the ashtray next to the steering wheel. An appeals court upheld the search, the seizure, and the driver's conviction of being a felon in possession of a gun.[36]

Probable cause.[37] Any time you reasonably believe, based on your training and experience, that you have sufficient evidence to persuade a neutral magistrate to issue a warrant to search the vehicle, you can go ahead and search it at the scene without actually seeking the warrant. This acknowledges the "exigent" or urgent circumstances of a vehicle stop, where the driver, who is generally not under arrest, has the capability of taking off with the evidence once you're out of sight. (Exigent circumstances, incidentally, can be argued only when the vehicle you're dealing with has potential for being readily mobile; it does not apply, for example, when the "vehicle" is a stationary mobile home used primary as a residence rather than as transportation.[38])

Although searching at the site of contact is strongly preferred, PC will usually be considered to continue if you must move the vehicle to another location because of traffic impediments, weather, or unsafe conditions. However, it should be searched forthwith upon arrival at the new spot.

You have the right to search as broadly within the vehicle as a warrant would permit you to search, had it been issued. If you have PC to believe that drugs are hidden in a specific container within the vehicle, for example, you can search only that container. But if you have probable cause to believe that there is contraband *somewhere* in the vehicle, you can search *anywhere* in it that illegal goods might possibly be. That includes the trunk, other compartments, and closed and locked containers that by their shape and size might be believed to hold the object of your search. (If you were searching for a stolen lawnmower, you probably couldn't search the glove compartment, but a quest for drugs gives you maximum leeway.) Keep in mind, however, that your PC will likely get special scrutiny in court regardless of how extensively you search, if you are searching after a subject has refused you consent.

One instance where this approach was used successfully occurred in Louisiana, where an unusually nervous Florida driver was stopped for tailgating. He verbally granted consent to search after an officer learned from a records check that he had a rap sheet, including a fall for narcotics. But then when he was asked to sign a consent form, he abruptly withdrew permission. Meanwhile, a backup officer with a K-9 arrived and walked around the car. The dog failed to alert, but as the backup passed a window that was lowered about three inches, he recognized the odor of marijuana coming from inside. A search was conducted over the driver's protests and 180 pounds of pot was found in a suitcase in the trunk. The officers successfully defended their actions through appeal on the premise that marijuana smell alone justifies a warrantless search, whether the driver agrees to it or not.[39]

In another Southern case, a courier was stopped twice on separate trips by the same deputy at locations just a mile apart. The first time, he consented to a search and ended up forfeiting $70,000 of unexplained cash found in his car. The second time, he contemptuously refused to cooperate. However, the deputy had noticed two roaches in the ashtray. That was probable cause to search anyway, he decided. This time he found the suspect's trunk packed to the brim with marijuana.

Sometimes a suspect's statements during your discussion of consent may provide you PC to search, if you're listening carefully. A rental car carrying two women was stopped for speeding late at night on a highway in Missouri known as a frequent drug route. The nervous pair had driven more than 2,500 miles together from California, but the driver, a California resident, and the passenger, from North Carolina, gave conflicting stories about how they knew each other. Asked for permission to search the car for contraband, the driver first said officers could search so long as they didn't search her luggage. Then she told them, "Oh, go ahead and search the car because I'm not going to tell you where it's at." In luggage and the trunk, an officer discovered approximately 127 pounds of marijuana. The driver was sentenced to four years. On appeal, she challenged the legality of the search. What proved decisive was her saying she wouldn't reveal where "it's at." Officers could reasonably interpret "it" to mean contraband, the court ruled, because that's what they told her they were looking for. This was PC to support the search, and the evidence discovered was admissible against her.[40]

Remember, PC does not have to be a *bunch* of things; it can be just *one* thing if that thing seems incriminating enough.

An Arrest.[41] A *custodial* arrest of the driver or a passenger, of course, creates opportunity for searching, because an arrestee no longer retains a Fourth Amendment right to privacy. (An ordinary traffic stop is normally regarded as a limited seizure or investigative detention, not a custodial arrest, which generally involves transporting the subject to a police station for booking and posting bail.[42] However in some jurisdictions certain minor traffic infractions—like seatbelt violations in Iowa—can qualify for in-custody arrests.) Contempora-neous with the arrest, before the vehicle or the prisoner are moved from the scene, you may fully search the arrestee and, in most jurisdictions, the area that was within his *immediate control* prior to the arrest. That includes the passenger compartment of a vehicle he occupied. (With semitrailers, that generally means the cab, not the cargo area.)

Even a misdemeanor arrest will do. A California deputy suspected that a man he was questioning about drug sales at a truck stop was lying to him. The subject had no identification, but gave a different first name than a companion referred to him by, hesitated significantly before offering a middle name, and refused to repeat the spelling of his last name. Information he gave about having once held a Texas driver's license failed to check out by radio. After the suspect refused to grant consent to search his car, the deputy arrested him for giving false information to a police officer, a misdemeanor offense. The deputy searched the car and found crystal meth under the front seat. An appeals court upheld the arrest and ruled that it was not just a pretext for searching the vehicle.

To search "incident to an arrest," according to the federal standard and many states, you do not need any suspicion or evidence that weapons or contraband are in the car. You are not limited to checking only locations where weapons could be hidden. Nor do you have to look only for evidence related to the crime for which the suspect is arrested. You can thoroughly search the entire passenger compartment and any containers you find therein, open or closed, including luggage, clothing, boxes, bags, consoles, unlocked glove compartments, or "any other object capable of holding another object." This generally includes property that belongs to a passenger who is not suspected of criminal activity but to which the arrestee had access. (Some courts have held that you cannot search persons who are not themselves arrested, but others say the "automatic companion rule" gives you at least the right to frisk a companion of an arrestee for weapons.)

In some jurisdictions, you cannot expand your search into a closed trunk that's not readily accessible from the passenger compartment, unless you have probable cause to believe that contraband or evidence is located there. The PC you need to arrest someone does not automatically translate into PC for completely searching a vehicle with which the arrestee is associated.

However, if you discover contraband while searching the passenger compartment, that will often give you probable cause to believe that illegal goods or other evidence would be found in the trunk as well. That area then becomes open to your warrantless inspection. About midnight one night, two patrol officers in California stopped a Toyota sedan after seeing it make a left turn without signaling. Because of discrepancies about identification that arose during a records check, one of the four male occupants was arrested for giving false information. Without consent, one of the officers then searched the passenger compartment. He found a white paper napkin wedged between the back seat cushions. Inise were hard chunks that he recognized as rock cocaine. He discovered more crack next to the driver's seat, and in the glove box found live ammunition. An appeals court later agreed that this was sufficient probable cause to expand his search to the trunk, where he recovered loaded revolvers and large quantities of narcotics.[43]

Impoundment.[44] Occasionally, for reasons of public safety or to protect the interests of the owner, you may be able to impound or take custody of a vehicle you've stopped. For example, you may find that the car is stolen or has been involved in the commission of a crime, or it is not safe to drive, or no licensed driver is available or permitted to move it. Here, you may be able to legally enter the vehicle to compile an inventory of its contents, in order to protect them while in police custody...to protect yourself and others by locating potentially dangerous items...and to protect against false claims of theft or loss.

Subject to the laws of your state, this "search" often can be done without consent, a warrant, or probable cause, provided you can show that: impoundment was necessary...the inventory was conducted pursuant to standardized, preferably written, uniformly applied, department policies and procedures...and you restricted your examination to places where valuables or hazardous items might likely be concealed. This generally includes the passenger compartment, glove box, consoles, ashtrays, locked or unlocked trunk, and the contents of any closed or open containers found therein. (However, at least one state appellate court has ruled that closed containers cannot be opened and searched during a vehicle inventory.[45] Yet courts did sustain a Mississippi officer who flipped through the pages of a notebook he encountered during a vehicle inventory, where he found diagrams depicting an international drug-distribution network and the location of more than 4,000 pounds of marijuana.[46]) Normally you cannot explore inside the gas tank or other fluid reservoirs. And in some states if the owner is present, the vehicle cannot be inventoried without his or her permission. If you discover a hidden compartment or what appears to be a stash of contraband, you should stop the inventory and get a search warrant before proceeding further, because technically an impoundment inventory is not considered to be a sanctioned warrantless search; it is only an administrative procedure.

With impoundment, you can legally move the vehicle to a location where you can explore it under controlled conditions, without concern about a hostile environment or time constraints. This setting, for instance, allows careful, well-lit inspection of the undercarriage, which may be difficult on the street.

That means you *can't* use an inventory to engage in an unlimited, investigatory search for criminal evidence. A New York case in which officers tore out a back seat and thereby discovered hidden cocaine was thrown out of court as exceeding the bounds of a proper inventory, as have been cases in which officers admitted they impounded violators' cars just to have an excuse to look through them. Impoundment must be made on grounds other than the suspicion that a vehicle contains evidence of criminal activity,[47] and you should be prepared to articulate noncriminal reasons for the impoundment and inventory.

However, anything incriminating you turn up within the guidelines (like eighty-six balloons of heroin discovered in the ashtray of a pickup truck in Texas) is admissible against the owner or driver and may provide you the PC to explore parts of the car that could not reasonably be examined for inventory purposes. There are no immediate time constraints on inventories. Unlike a search incident to arrest, an inventory examination can be performed after the vehicle has been towed to another location. What's important is that an inventory must be done on *every* impounded vehicle, or evidence found when one is conducted will likely be suppressed.

One spectacular case in which an officer used impoundment to get inside a car after a suspect refused him consent occurred in Wyoming after a highway patrolman clocked a rented Lincoln Town Car carrying two females speeding at 76 mph in a 65-mph zone. The driver took suspiciously longer than usual to pull over, and the women's story seemed dubious. Supposedly they had flown to Los Angeles from Detroit to "stay with friends" and had run out of money. A "cousin" who was not in the vehicle rented the car for them so they could get back to Michigan, but they couldn't offer any plan for how they intended to get the car back to California. The officer issued a warning, returned all documents, and asked permission to search. The driver refused; she knew her rights, she declared. The officer told her that he would try to get a warrant, which might take four to five hours. She still refused.

Fortuitously, the officer got a radio message at that moment, informing him that additional information had been discovered about the driver: Her license had been suspended in Michigan. Now he wrote a ticket that required posting bond, and the women followed him to the station. There they telephoned a lawyer who promised to wire money immediately.

Waiting for it to arrive, the officer read the fine print in the rental agreement. He found that the contract was immediately voided if the driver's license was suspended or if someone other than the actual renter was behind the wheel. He called the rental company. They told him to impound the vehicle.

An inventory was promptly taken. Inside two suitcases, officers discovered 440 pounds of cocaine, valued at nearly $10,000,000. Like many before and many since, the women were arrested, and the officer reinforced his commitment not to take "No" for an answer until the last card is played.

Note: With rental cars, some courts have held that an unauthorized driver—one whose name does not appear on the rental agreement—has no privacy rights in the car. This is another opportunity for you to automatically impound and inventory the vehicle, regardless of whether the driver volunteers consent.[48] Read the contract!

If you can't get consent and you lack other grounds for searching, accept that across your career on Criminal Patrol some suspects will simply have to be released without your suspicions being satisfied.

Some officers become so addicted to finding contraband that they plunge ahead without legal foundation. It isn't worth it. One case in which you deliberately ignore constitutional limitations can be enough to destroy your credibility in court and potentially elicit other sanctions against you. Some officers carry notebooks with them that contain pertinent case law, which they review periodically to be sure they're acting properly. You never know when one of your vehicle stops may go all the way to the Supreme Court.

Even when getting consent goes smoothly, with no hint of resistance from the suspect, stay alert.

A courier was asked: "Would you ever kill a cop?"

"In a heartbeat," said the mule. "But only if he threatened my load."

"Would you let a cop search your car?"

"Sure...but only to gain the advantage."

The Mark Coates Stop

Trooper Mark Coates's name was chiseled into the National Law Enforcement Memorial wall (see rubbing above) after the night he stopped a driver from Georgia for weaving. His in-car video shows a subject who initially was soft-spoken, courteous, cooperative. He stalled and hedged a bit in answering some basic questions—like exactly where he lived—but he displayed only one major danger cue: At some point prior to Coates starting to pat him down, he casually slipped his left hand into his left pants pocket.

Coates orders the hand out, but doesn't control it, doesn't stop frisking, doesn't reposition himself.

The suspect is as fast as he is fat. In a blur, he knocks Coates off balance and to the ground and brings a gun out.

Coates tries to talk his way out of further assault. But flat on his back, no backup in sight, he needs more than words....

SINGLE-OFFICER
SELF-DEFENSE

Every time Trooper First Class Mark Coates busted a major contraband courier on the roads of South Carolina he pasted a little lightning bolt decal on the side of his patrol car, a symbol of another successful "bombing" mission in the war on drugs.

He was a member of his agency's ACE (Aggressive Criminal Enforcement) Team, and he was an ace. In little more than a year, he'd captured eight fugitives, seized a small fleet of trafficker vehicles, and recovered cocaine, marijuana, and cash worth more than $1,000,000. Twelve of the stenciled bolts (since discontinued by the agency) marched in proud formation along his left front fender. He was on his way to earning a thirteenth on a mild Friday night less than a week before Thanksgiving, when lightning of a different sort struck.

He'd pulled over an old tan Mustang with Georgia plates because the driver was weaving in traffic on a remote stretch of northbound I-95. The violator was short but huge—close to 300 pounds—with a hidden violent streak as wide as he was. As Coates talked with him at the side of the highway, the driver seemed respectful and cooperative, nothing Coates couldn't handle. Two other troopers drove by in separate units while he questioned the offender, but he didn't wave either of them over for back-up. He decided he wanted to search the Mustang, and he wrote out a warning ticket as a prelude to asking for consent. The suspect, however, had reached a decision of his own. He was carrying $1,000 cash, a supply of marijuana, and a criminal record, and he'd be damned if some cop was going to send him to jail.

During a moment when Coates was in close, standing in front of the suspect, the trooper suddenly noticed that the man had stuck his left hand into his left pants pocket. Coates told him to take it out. The suspect didn't budge. Coates repeated the command. This time the suspect hit him full force with his beefy right arm.

The startled trooper staggered off-balance and fell to the ground. His assailant yanked a .22-cal. derringer from his pocket, took it in his right hand, and pointed it directly into Coates's face. For his weight and size, he could move fast. "Just cool it! Just cool it!" the trooper urged. The offender lowered the gun slightly and blasted off a round. The slug sank into Coates's soft body armor and stopped. Fighting back from the ground, Coates kicked the suspect in the chest with both boots, drew his .357 Magnum service revolver, and emptied it at his assailant.

Five shots struck home, but the attacker's extraordinary fat just sucked them up before they could penetrate to vital organs. The suspect squeezed a fresh round from his .22. It was a one-in-a-million shot that tore through Coates's left arm, missing the bone, and bored straight through his armpit outside the edge of his vest, into his chest, and through an artery that connected to his aorta.

Normally, many officers wouldn't think of a .22 as a "killer" round but would regard a .357 as a "manstopper." Yet three days later, Mark Coates was in a flag-draped coffin on a horse-drawn caisson, headed down a muddy road to his grave.

One of the greatest hazards of Criminal Patrol, ironically, is success.

When you skillfully develop rapport and finesse cooperation from suspect after suspect, it's easy to begin anticipating compliance from every person you stop. Impelled by the "high" of achievement, you work even harder at polishing your techniques for concealed interrogation and contraband detection, while the passage of time without incident lulls you into slackening your threat awareness and slighting other training and practice. Easy-to-neglect skills like empty-hand defense especially suffer. You may start missing or dismissing danger cues, and you may embrace the persistent myth that if trouble does erupt you can always shoot your way out.

In *acting* the good ol' boy, you *become* the good ol' boy. You get seduced by your lust for the bust.

And thus a dangerous disparity seeds and grows between your verbal and observational skills related to investigation and rapport-building and your skills of personal protection.

This imbalance, while potentially fatal at any point in an investigative stop, places you particularly at risk during the dialogue and consent phases. Here you most likely are still alone, awaiting arrival of backup for the search that's to come. In building rapport, you may be physically closer to the violator than you'd really like, reducing your reactionary gap. Your focus is often fragmented between the official demands of the stop and the stimuli of your concealed interrogation. This spawns profuse temptations for distraction. As you move a subject adroitly toward the climax of obtaining consent, you may be concentrating so intently on clinching the search that survival concerns are all but forgotten. The arrival of backup, a comfort to you, may seem a critical moment for the suspect, if he reads it as evidence that this is really more than just a routine traffic stop. Indeed, if your back is to traffic coming from behind you, he may see your backup approaching before you do.

If one day or one night you encounter a suspect, as Mark Coates did, whose desperation, fear, or sheer viciousness escalates to the flash point, you may be so astonished that lag time sabotages your response...or you can't get to your gun or can't use it or it doesn't stop your attacker, and you don't know how else to defend yourself...or you understand conceptually how you need to react but you aren't adept enough to actually make the moves effectively.

That's when the vultures come home to roost in that unforgiving gap between the skills you need for winning the right to search and those you need for staying alive.

When officers are killed on Criminal Patrol vehicle stops—and on other calls—a fatal attack with a weapon often starts with a physical assault on the officer, just as it did with Mark Coates. If you don't control the attack at this first stage, you can quickly become a victim when it escalates to the next. Any resistance or move toward fighting by the suspect needs to be detected and shut down *fast*.

Anyone who attacks you indisputably has a high degree of motivation and a high desire to win. He is willing to take you on, even though you have a gun, the legal authority to kill him, and the ability to get other officers there to help you out. *He must be dealt with emphatically.*

What follows here, if absorbed, practiced, and used on patrol, can help sharpen your alertness for early danger signs and improve your immediate response tactics. If you read about danger signs here that you fail to watch for as conscientiously as you watch for investigative cues or you see depicted here physical defensive tactics that you know you could not pull off under stress, let that be a wake-up call for you.

Assaults are a reality of vehicle stops; about one in ten physical attacks on officers occurs during stops or pursuits.[1] Against this level of threat, you need every advantage you can acquire—beginning with the command presence you derive from being physically fit. Staying in shape commands respect. It reduces challenges, and if combined with a trained knowledge of defensive tactics, it can save your life if things go awry.

The measures described here are ones you can use by yourself to protect yourself as a single officer. They also can be used effectively by your backup after he or she arrives to watch the suspect(s) while you conduct the search. These techniques are applicable not only on contraband stops but on any field interview or other subject contact.

The point is not to make you shrink from conducting successful stops. You should pursue your own "lightning bolts" of achievement as aggressively as you legally can. That's the whole purpose of trying to go beyond the ticket with the 5%er mind-set.

But keep in mind that there may come a time when your investigative efforts on a stop must give way to immediate defensive action. As you negotiate your way through the thicket of risks during suspect contact and as you allocate training time off-duty, let three simple but profound truths guide you. Had the implicit messages of these been heeded, they could have saved scores of officers' lives.

1. *Always* expect the unexpected;

2. It can happen to *you*;

3. Better to have mastered a skill that isn't needed than to need a skill that isn't mastered.

Foreign-Language Trap

A fundamental part of maintaining your Position of Advantage is to understand what your suspect tells you, both verbally and with his or her body language. If the driver has a passenger present and they're conversing in a language you can't comprehend, how can you be sure they're not plotting a surprise attack against you? Likewise, if you can't interpret physical movements that are really precursors of an attack, how can you anticipate assault soon enough to avoid or counter it?

So far as spoken messages are concerned, never permit suspects to speak among themselves in any language you are not fully fluent in. Even if you think you can understand them, beware the Berlitz

Syndrome. This is a linguistic version of the John Wayne Syndrome, where overconfidence gets you in trouble. As one trainer puts it, "You may speak just enough of another language to start a fight"—or to miss a danger cue. The suspects may use a dialect or street slang that sounds like what you're familiar with but really isn't. Or they may speak faster than your mind can translate. Keeping them separated so they can't talk to each other is tactical from the standpoint of your safety, as well as your investigation.

Currently, the foreign language you're most likely to encounter among drug mules is Spanish. Considering that an estimated 35% of our population soon will speak Spanish as its first language, your learning Spanish so you can understand as well as talk it is becoming an officer-survival imperative, even apart from Criminal Patrol. At the very least, you should know and practice short, simple, self-protective commands, like: "Stop!"..."Drop it!"..."Hands up!"... "Lie down!"..."Don't move!" These may forestall an attack.

They can aid your legal survival, too. If a Spanish-speaking suspect continues to resist threateningly after you issue such orders and you end up having to shoot, it will be harder for anyone to claim that the subject did not understand what you wanted him to do if you have fluently commanded him in his own language.

These commands are among those you should be able to deliver forcefully and intelligibly, under stress:

ENGLISH	SPANISH	PRONUNCIATION
Police	¡Policía!	(poh-lee-SEE-ah)
Come here!	¡Venga aquí!	(VEHN-gah ah-KEE)
Stop!	¡Alto!	(AHL-toh)
Show me your hands!	¡Enséñeme sus manos!	(ain-SANE-yah-may soos MAN-nohs)
Drop it!	¡Suéltela!	(so-EHL-tay-lah)
Slowly!	¡Despacio!	(dehs-PAH-see-oh)
Don't move!	¡No se mueva!	(noh say moo-EH-vah)
Stand here!	¡Párese aquí!	(PAH-reh-say ah-KEE)
Hands up!	¡Manos arriba!	(MAH-nohs ah-REE-bah)
Speak English!	¡Hable inglés!	(ah-BLAY een-GLAYS)
Turn around!	¡Voltéese!	(vohl-TEH-ess-ay)
Get out!	¡Bájese!	(BAH-hay-say)
Kneel!	¡Hínquese! or ¡Arrodíllese!	(EEN-kah-say) or (ah-ro-DEE-yih-say)
Don't shoot!	¡No dispare!	(Noh dees-PAH-ray)
Lie down!	¡Acuéstese boca abajo!	(ah-QUES-tay-say boh-kah ah-BAH-ho)
Stop or I'll shoot!	¡Alto o disparo!	(AHL-toh oh dees-PAH-roh)
Quiet!	¡Silencio!	(see-LEHN-see-oh)
You're under arrest!	¡Usted está arrestado!	(oo-STEHD ess-TAH ah-reh-STAH-doh)
Give up!	¡Ríndase!	(REEN-dah-say)

© Calibre Press, Inc

An Oregon detective who trains law enforcement in "Survival Spanish" says he first asks a new class of students whether anyone knows how to say "No" in Spanish. "Of thirty-five students, normally three will raise their hands," he reports. "I then ask the remaining stu dents what they would say to a non-English speaking, Hispanic suspect if they saw him reaching for a gun. Usually there is a frightening silence.

"I point out that if the students do not even know how to say 'No' in Spanish, they are not going to be able to control this or any other type of situation [verbally]. 'No' is the same in Spanish as it is in English."[2]

If you do understand Spanish, you may want to keep that fact a secret from the vehicle's occupants unless you need to issue a survival command. That way if they are able to exchange what they probably think are covert messages in Spanish, you can eavesdrop. If you overhear remarks that seem threatening...and then instantly bark out commands in Spanish, the startling impact may shock them into submission or at least create lag time to your advantage.

Some officers feel that by speaking a little conversational Spanish to Hispanic subjects early on, you can lead them to believe that you understand more of it than you actually do and that this will discourage them from plotting among themselves for fear of being found out. If this is your approach but your grasp of Spanish is scant, be sure you revert to English quickly for the bulk of your dialogue, before the suspects realize the truth about your limitations.

The most common language trick of Hispanic mules is to speak English early in the stop and profess *"No comprendo"* only if your questioning gets too hot or you actually discover contraband. Or you may notice that their English improves significantly after you give them a ticket or warning, when they think they're about to be cut loose.

However, some will allege from the outset not to understand any English, hoping to frustrate your investigation before it begins. Or the driver will talk to you in halting English but the passenger will pretend not to speak or understand it, to stymie you in trying to develop story conflicts between them. Test their assertions, not only as a deception indicator but as a potential danger cue.

One option is to act as if you believe the suspect and start your dialogue with a few questions in Spanish. Get a rhythmic cadence going, where a fresh question comes immediately after an answer, so he doesn't have much time to think about what's being said. Ask him:

¿Cómo se llama usted? "KOH-moh say YAH-mah oo-STEHD?" ("What is your name?")...

¿Dónde vive? "DOHN-day VEE-vay?" ("Where do you live?")...

¿Es éste su carro? "ess ESS-teh soo KAHR-roh?" ("Is this your car?")...

¿Es ésta su troca? "ess ESS-ta soo TRO-ka?" ("Is this your truck?")...

¿A dónde va usted? "ah DOHN-day vah oo-STEHD?" ("Where are you going?")

In each case, the suspect will reply in Spanish. Then quickly ask your next question—***How old are you?***, for example—in *English.*

If the suspect is faking, odds are he'll slip and answer in English. Most offenders, it seems, can generally think in only one language at a time.

A variation of this trick is to quickly ask a series of questions in English, to which the suspect will answer, *"No comprendo."* For example: "Where are you going in such a hurry?"..."Where are you coming from?"..."Whose car is this?", et cetera. Then without break ing the rhythm say, "Let me see your driver's license." Often a person pretending not to understand English will reach for his or her license when he hears this command—and then you know he's faking.

An alternative is the "shoe trick," favored by an Immigration agent in Nebraska. Here you line up subjects who claim not to speak English and you tell them, in English: "I know you are all illegals. You know how I know? Because illegals always wear brown shoes." If they instinctively look down to check *their* shoes, you've got proof they understand English!

Most Hispanic suspects can speak at least broken English and often understand more English than they let on. After all, unless they're fresh arrivals from across the border they're here and functioning in this society. Even if you have to use a little broadly understood sign language—pointing to yourself, then to your eye, then to the inside of their vehicle to indicate, "I want to look in your car," for example—you can generally make yourself understood. Certainly most comprehend the "universal language of the law"—words like "jail"…"arrest"…"bond." If you perceive an attitude that could be a prelude to danger, ask sharply: "Do you want to go to jail?" Reach for your handcuffs. More than once that has provoked a response in English—and a more cooperative attitude.

As a last resort, if you have a mobile phone, call the nearest field office of the U.S. Immigration and Naturalization Service and ask for an agent. All INS agents speak Spanish and will usually be willing to translate questions and answers between you and the suspect(s) over the phone. Keep the nearest field-office phone number in your unit.

Danger "Leaks"

Just as body language and demeanor can reveal when a suspect is in a state of exceptional stress, his or her posture and behavior can also telegraph when you are in danger. Stress leaks help you defeat deception; danger leaks let you prevent attack.

Some of these indicators suggest that the subject is gearing up emotionally to take you on. Others reveal that he has already made the emotional commitment and is now positioning himself physically to assault.

Just seeing these warning signs usually will not justify a physical or deadly force response on your part. But by reading them early, you may be able to build distance…issue commands…assume a defensive stance…prepare to draw your baton, pepper-spray canister, or firearm… or take other action that will short-circuit his intentions. In short: *Alert can avert.*

These cues often come in combinations. Reading them early is especially important if, like many skilled interviewers, you try consciously to invade a subject's body space during your concealed interrogation. This can be effective because it heightens a guilty party's anxiety and susceptibility to leaking stress cues and is also believed to make lying more difficult.[3] But it obviously increases your vulnerability and your need for reliable early warning signs.

HIDDEN HANDS in a pocket should always be considered a danger cue, no elaboration necessary. If you're not already close to the suspect, *stay back, get behind cover,* and issue verbal commands from there; you don't want to knowingly get closer to what might be an armed suspect. If you're already close in, one option for forestalling an escalation of threat is to trap the suspect's hand inside his clothing by pushing his elbow down toward the pocket and securing his forearm. This will be safer for you than telling him to withdraw an uncontrolled, unseen hand. Now you can control the speed with which his hand comes out. If you perceive a threat, use a takedown.

If a suspect has *both* hands in his pockets, there's more risk in attempting an empty-hand control measure. You can't be sure which hand may be gripping a weapon, and you can concentrate on physically controlling only one at a time. If you must choose, control his right hand, since most people are right-handed. But preferably in this situation, back up, get to cover if possible, and prepare to respond to a threat.

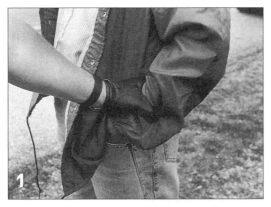

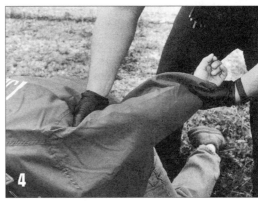

If you're close enough to a suspect who refuses to remove his hand from his pocket, trap the hand so he can't withdraw it. Secure his upper arm as you allow him to slowly remove the hand while you control it. If he continues to display resistive tension or presents any verbal or physical threat, be prepared to take him to the ground abruptly and handcuff him for your safety.

(above)
Suspect with two hands in his pockets requires a much different response than controlling a suspect with one hand hidden. If you attempt physical control with one of his hands, the other may be holding a weapon.

(right)
A far safer response is to avoid physical contact in this situation. Maintain distance and assume a ready position with your sidearm.

EMOTIONAL INDICATORS are cues, which can be verbal and/or physical and reflect an attitude of resistance. When they're evident, there's a strong probability that the suspect is motivating himself psychologically to take aggressive action. At the very least, he will be uncooperative so long as these attitude indicators persist. As some of the earliest warning signs of potential trouble, watch for:

Repetitious inquiries. This is somewhat similar to the deceptive suspect who repeats your questions in order to stall while he thinks up answers. Except here there's more defiance. If you ask where he's going, he doesn't just parrot you back ("Where am I *going?*"); there's an edge to his tone and manner, as if to say, "You want *me* to tell *you* where *I'm going?*" Or, if you ask him to do something, he asks, "Why?" He's expressing disbelief that you think you can expect answers and cooperation, plus he presenting a constant distraction.

246

Like the deceiver, he may be using this tactic to buy time—but to formulate a plan for attacking, not lying. You should be reviewing your own plans, as you warn him that you want *direct* answers *now*.

In trying to verbally persuade a difficult person to cooperate, you can follow a five-step tactical process:

1. Ask. ["Sir, will you please…"]

2. Set context [Explain the reason(s) why]

3. Present options [Explain consequences if he refuses to cooperate]

4. Confirm ["Sir, is there anything else I can say or do to get you to cooperate?"]

5. Act [Use physical control or other appropriate force measures in face of continued resistance or a threat to yourself, other officers, or bystanders].[4]

Conspicuous ignoring. Here the suspect deliberately refuses to respond to your presence or dialogue. He won't answer questions…won't follow directions…won't look at you…he may even continue talking to other occupants if you're standing by his window. He's pretending you're not there, intruding on his trip. Failure to obey commands—or even acknowledge you—is a universal indicator of trouble. His behavior is telling you, "You're not going to control me." He may be hoping to sucker you in closer—hoping, perhaps, that you'll reach in and grab his car keys or move in and grab him. If you do, *Wham!*…he attacks.

Not looking at you, not following directions, not answering questions—all signs of conspicuous ignoring, which may precede an attack.

Looking around. The suspect may be listening and talking to you, but his eyes are darting past you or to your sides or behind him—everywhere except where they should be focused; they can't stay still. Darting eyes indicate agitation and are common when a suspect feels cornered by you. Maybe he's checking to see if you have backup—or looking for backup of his own. If you've stopped him where there's a crowd, he may be looking for help or for corroboration that you're abusing him, to build up his own self-confidence. Or he may be seeking an escape route while he assesses his chances of making a run for it. And what often happens as part of an escape attempt? Assault first, then flight.

When eyes are jerking, like you might see in nystagmus testing, this can signify hallucination or mental disturbance in which the suspect thinks he is communicating with or listening to God, Satan, or other unseen beings. Depending on the messages he's "receiving," this can be a significant warning sign to create space and establish a good defensive position.

Excessive emotional attention. The suspect doesn't just grumble or make sarcastic remarks about your questions or requests, he's visibly pissed—loudly ranting and raving, accusing you of hassling him, vehemently and belligerently arguing with you or defending his innocence, cursing, maybe even issuing thinly veiled threats. Ask yourself: Why is he this upset over what at this point I am still leading him to believe is just a traffic stop? And be aware that so extremely

Excessive emotional attention and exaggerated movement can quickly escalate into an attack. This officer, by staying close, is failing to acknowledge the potential danger he's in.

overreacting emotionally may propel him into overreacting physically; there's a high correlation between emotional distress and physical conflict. Be especially cautious if he starts alleging that *you* want to use violence against *him* ("You wanna kick my ass," et cetera). He may be projecting what *he'd* really like to do to *you.*

Exaggerated movement. Here he is getting physical, although not yet aggressively so. If he's out of his vehicle and has room, he may start pacing rapidly and angrily, throwing his arms around in wild gestures, maybe kicking his vehicle as you try to talk with him. He may punch or kick his car or some other nearby object (or the air). He's physically underscoring his emotional upset. And with his body and arms moving, that ferocious energy may soon be focused in an attack. People who are physically agitated should be dealt with immediately. Start with verbal commands: "Sir, don't wave your arms around. You're making me nervous, and you don't want to make me nervous. I need you to stand still." If he doesn't, lay an option on him: "Sir, I can put you in handcuffs, then you won't wave your arms around." Be ready to escalate to physical-control measures.

Physical crowding. Consciously or unconsciously, the suspect moves in close to you. This may be an effort to intimidate you, especially if he's bigger than you are. It can also be a setup for hitting, kicking, biting, head-butting, disarming, stabbing, or otherwise assaulting you. The closer he is, the quicker and easier it is for him to launch an attack, and the harder it is for you to defend against one. Be alert for heavy, fast breathing that betrays a high level of agitation. *Create space.* Tell him: "You don't need to be this close to me. Stand still right here"—then you draw back to establish a safer reactionary gap. Remember, if the suspect initiates an attack, it will probably take you a couple of seconds to process that information and respond, especially if you haven't picked up on danger cues. Gaining distance in effect buys you more time to react.

With a suspect who continues crowding, try the "one-inch punch." As you tell him to step back, spread the fingers of your off hand and place your fingertips on his chest. If he fails to move back, abruptly

248

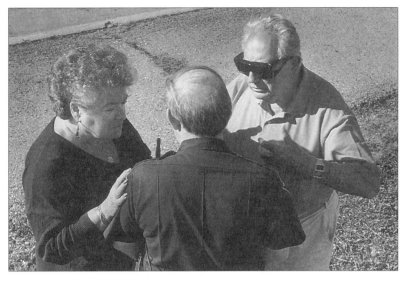

Two uncontrolled subjects out of a vehicle simultaneously is bad enough. But permitting physical crowding and even touching is asking for trouble.

slam the heel of your palm against his sternum and at the same time straighten your arm and thrust hard. Put your whole body into the move. This hurts and pushes enough to stop most people. If he grabs your arm, he'll expect that you'll try to pull away. Push *toward* him instead. His momentum and your momentum will combine to push him backwards and most likely knock him off balance. At the very least, you will "redirect" his attention and position.

Sudden cooperation. An agitated, uncooperative subject suddenly has a profound change of attitude and becomes sweetly cooperative. Maybe something you've said or done altered his thinking—or he could be tricking you into relaxing too soon.

Ceasing all movement. When an agitated subject suddenly stops cold, you may feel relieved. You shouldn't. Remember a grim rule from hostage negotiation training: When a hostage-taker who has been excited and highly mobile suddenly becomes frozen in place and ominously silent, that usually means someone's about to die. This can be the calm before the storm, a brief transition period between blowing off and taking action. It is often accompanied by the "1,000-yard stare," a radical facial change. Color drains from the suspect's face (a pale face is usually considered a more dangerous sign than a flushed one)...his mouth goes slack...his eyes look 'way through you and past you. The subject may now become violent with little or no provocation. Get ready to rock 'n' roll.

Remember, though, that these indicators are not guarantees that an attack is imminent. Don't automatically assume it is and become overtly aggressive yourself, for that could provoke an assault from a suspect who now feels he's endangered by you. Just use these caution cues as a means of subtly adjusting your levels of awareness and readiness. Be watchful for "pre-attack postures" that often suggest an assault *is* imminent.

PRE-ATTACK POSTURES occur when a suspect decides to assault and needs to rearrange himself physically to carry out his attack; it's hard to throw a punch or a martial-arts kick except from certain positions. His repositioning may take place dynamically (rapidly) or incre

249

mentally over a period of time (which you may be less likely to notice). By knowing and watching for these cues, you may be able to pick up, if only for a split second, dangerous postural changes and react to thwart their violent intent. These usually are not as direct and obvious as the suspect thrusting his hand into his pocket to grab a knife or a gun, but if you are attuned for subtle movements they are still discernible.

Certainly a physical assault in its own right is worth avoiding. But in checking it, remember that you may be warding off an even worse threat: an attack with a firearm or other deadly weapon that quickly follows or evolves out of a physical assault. Never dismiss these pre-attack cues as unimportant:

Hands that are ready for a fight can telegraph an emotional level that's ready, too. Watch out!

Boxer stance. You may first notice the suspect shifting his weight from foot to foot, somewhat like a boxer getting ready in the ring. Then he drops one foot back or steps forward to better balance himself for striking from his strong side. He may begin to bounce up and down on his toes. His fists may open and close nervously or clench tight. By bending his elbow(s), he may be getting his hand(s) up in position to slug or grab you or go for a weapon, including yours. His last move before assaulting may be to "blade" himself; that is, turn sideways to you to protect his "center line," which traverses his vital areas.

Hand set. If the suspect has martial-arts training, he may try to set his hands up into a "ready" position. Often with his fingers together in a "chopping" style, he places his hands two or three inches out from his body, one at chest level, the other down by his abdomen. If his fingers are spread rather than together, this may suggest that he's familiar with a martial arts system that features grabbing and grappling. Either way, from here he can become very aggressive very fast.

Martial artists, like this subject who's trained in grappling techniques, may give you only a split-second to perceive that their hands are moving to assault.

Some body-language experts also contend that if a suspect puts one or both hands in back of his neck, he is about to react in a physically violent way. Watch, too, for hands that go from opening and closing to closed fists. He may be about to slug you.

Shoulder shift. The suspect's body in general will tighten just before he moves, kind of a "cocking" effect to create the necessary muscle tension for his aggressive action. If he has decided to hit you, the shoulder of his striking hand may move (probably backward) and dip slightly as the trapezius muscles tighten to stabilize that shoulder for the punch. If both shoulders drop down, he may be shifting into a leg-grabbing, tackling, or wrestling position. In either case, he will not necessarily get into a boxer stance first. If heavy clothing conceals his shoulders, watch his neck for tightening muscles.

Target glance. Unless a subject is highly trained, he will instinctively look where he intends to strike, before he attacks. He may scope you out in a general way—his eyes shifting between your eyes, chest, and hands—to size you up and select what he thinks is a vulnerable spot. Then he'll maintain steady eye contact for seconds or minutes. At the last instant, immediately before he acts, he'll very likely break eye contact with you, look down or away, then quickly glance at his target point. You then may have less than a second before he strikes. If he glances at your groin, get ready for a kick...at your throat, a choke...your chin, a punch. If you catch him eyeballing your gun, tell him directly: "Don't look at my gun. Look at me!" Now he knows you won't be taken by surprise.

In fact, with any of these danger signs, clear, loud verbal commands may defuse an imminent assault. Tell the subject forcefully: "Stop and stand still!" or "Relax and look at me!" or "Open your hands and don't move!" Get prepared for a stronger response if that doesn't work.

Remember: Stay cautious with *everyone,* even those who exhibit no obvious danger cues. The totally submissive person can be the most dangerous of all, because he or she is most likely to lull you into what may be a false sense of security as a prelude to a sneak attack. Ask yourself: If you were going to attack an armed individual (officer), would you be noticeably aggressive right away—or act submissive and wait for the right opportunity?

Watching for a target glance can tell you where a suspect thinks you're most vulnerable and where he plans to strike.

Protective Stances

While you're monitoring the suspect during your concealed interrogation and request for consent, you can adjust your own stance depending on the feedback you're getting. Your level of protective preparedness rises according to the suspect's level of resistance. If you consciously stand so you're ready to deal with trouble, should it arise, you automatically cue your mind to a state of alertness that watches for trouble. Moreover, you send an important message of discouragement to the suspect. Even aggression-prone people will usually think twice before attacking an officer who appears ready and alert.

Open stance. If the suspect is calm and cooperative, the "open" stance will help you convey a nonthreatening appearance and promote rapport and communication. It may encourage him to copy your posture.

Here your feet are about shoulder-width apart, with your strong leg back slightly to increase distance between the suspect and your gun and your weight evenly distributed on both feet for balance. Your elbows are comfortably bent at about a 90° angle, with your hands roughly at waist level, above your belt. Your palms may be turned up and out, or you can stand with your fingertips together in a modified "prayer" position.

Although you appear conciliatory, your hands are deceptively close to your sidearm, your chemical-spray canister, your baton, or other gunbelt equipment if you need it.

Ready stance. If the suspect starts showing mild resistance, including verbal abuse or any of the other emotional indicators, shift into the "ready" stance.

One form of the open stance. Note the officer's bladed angle and distance from the suspect for his initial contact. If your holster is designed and positioned properly, your strong-side forearm and elbow can cover your gun for protection. From this position, you can activate a full range of defenses much quicker than standing with your hands at your sides (right). That positioning leaves you open to a sucker punch and increases reaction time to other aggressive moves.

One open stance option. Your hands look relaxed, but can move fast toward the suspect or your weapon when necessary. (Officer pictured is left-handed, accounting for his angle to the suspect.) Your partner monitors him for early warning signs, too.

If you perceive danger cues, move your hands up for possible physical-control reactions and to protect your upper body...or toward your gunbelt if you anticipate immediate weapon use.

Step farther away from him, bring your strong-side foot back more, somewhat like the boxer stance, and angle away more from the suspect. Bring your hands up to chest level, closer together with fingertips up and palms out, conveying a "calm down" gesture. You can continue talking in a nonthreatening manner, but your hands are up in "relaxed readiness," where they can quickly react to shove or strike the suspect or go for your baton, spray canister, or sidearm if necessary. Your strong-side forearm and elbow can still cover your gun.

Defensive stance. If the suspect's resistance escalates, smoothly escalate your stance into the "defensive" position. Here your strong foot is back more to brace for a blow, your elbows are in at your sides, your arms protect your chest, and your hands are up higher. Your palms are toward each other, shielding your face and ready to curl into fists if you need to make a defensive jab to keep the suspect away. Or just bring one hand up to shield your face and put the other on your gun, prepared to draw or to secure it in your holster if the suspect moves to disarm you.

253

The defensive stance is an escalation from the ready stance. The justification is due to the violator now moving into a boxer stance.

Backup Coming? Wait!

Physical assaults could often be prevented with a bit more of what seems to be a scarce commodity on patrol: patience. Consider an incident from a small town in Florida that unfortunately is not unusual:

At 0322 hours one Saturday, an officer on patrol noticed a white Chevy Camaro in front of him with a burned-out left taillight. He tried to effect a traffic stop, but the driver wouldn't pull over until he had swung into a dark and secluded alley behind a bar.

From that early warning sign, others quickly followed.

Both the driver and his passenger immediately exited the car and headed back toward the officer. When he ordered them back into the vehicle, they walked around outside, putting their hands into their pockets and not obeying.

Finally they did get in, but they ignored the officer when he ordered them to put their hands on the dash where he could see them. Instead they continued rummaging in their pockets. The officer called for backup.

Moments later, the driver and passenger exited the car again. Again they were ordered back inside and again the officer urgently radioed for backup. This time the suspects slowly sat back in the car but kept the doors open. The driver seemed to be taking items out of his pocket and placing them on the dash. The passenger was picking them up and apparently putting them into his own pocket.

The officer, unable to resist the temptation to get close to the action, walked up to the driver's door instead of waiting at a safer distance for the backup en route. He did so despite the warning signs, which he had seen and had accurately interpreted.

"The driver lunged at me, putting his shoulder into my stomach and wrapping his arms around me to tackle me," the officer later wrote. "He grabbed hold of my gun and got it halfway out of the holster. He was pulling on the gun, and I was trying to keep it from coming out.

"I struggled with him for a few seconds, then we fell to the

ground and were wrestling. He still had his hands on my gun and was trying to take it away. I punched him several times in the face to get him to let go.

"He started to calm down after I got him in a chokehold and restrained his movement. Every now and then I would loosen up on the chokehold because I did not want to hurt him, but when I did this he would become violent again, attempting to reach back toward my gun. I tightened up my hold and was able to subdue him until my sergeant arrived, at which point we were able to handcuff him."

The passenger, meanwhile, had fled. On the ground near the front-passenger side of the vehicle, the officer later recovered one small baggie of marijuana.

During the few seconds the fight lasted, the officer easily could have been killed. Had he spent those same seconds waiting for help, his brush with death probably would never have occurred.

Once resistance has reached the point where you detect pre-attack postural cues, you may not have much time to react. Some cues may be "leaked" only a fraction of a second before an actual attack. Immediately step back farther or to the side, consider drawing your baton or chemical spray or at the very least raise your hands and arms into a defensive stance if they are not there already.

If the suspect is too fast or you're too slow to avoid his first hit, even having a slight anticipation of it will help you withstand the blow psychologically. Sensing that something's coming, rather than being assaulted completely by surprise, will lessen your shock, tighten your reaction time, and allow you to come back stronger. You may even be able to move slightly to absorb some of the energy of the blow. By bringing your hand and arm into the path of the strike, you can take the hit on your forearm or shoulder rather than in a vital area.

With your partner in a gym, practice what's called "four-corners blocking." Depending on the angle of a sudden assault, learn to quickly move your hands and arms up from the various interview stances to either side of your head and down to either side of your groin to intercept first blows. Besides protecting vital areas, such blocking can buy you time to create space and launch a response.

Failure to read and react promptly to early warning signs may lead to the fight of your life—and for your life.

Defensive Countermeasures

Defensive countermeasures for a physical assault are like "immediate-action" techniques for clearing stoppages in a semiautomatic in a gunfight. You don't want to have to use them, but you're forced to. Something has gone wrong—in this case, maybe you missed an early warning indicator or were too slow reacting to one—and now the suspect is fighting you. You have to correct the problem immediately and get back in control.

Considering that you're under attack, you'd prefer to be using your baton, pepper spray, or firearm, but for one reason or another (time, distance, circumstances) you can't. So, for as short a time as possible, you fight back with your empty hands.

Rule: Avoid fighting "fair," putting up your dukes or wrestling in a conventional manner. You can lose a fair fight. You want to use tactics that will stop the assault fast, before your energy gives out and before you get injured or disarmed.

These must be surprising, highly effective, gross motor movements you can perform under stress with minimum strength and training. They must be designed to free you from the suspect's control...help you buy time and distance so you can get your baton, chemical canister, or gun out...and enable you to promptly regain the Position of Advantage.

There are many elaborate systems of defensive techniques, involving complicated wristlocks, jabs, kicks, sweeps, takedowns, and what-have-you. But for officers with limited practice time and physical skill, what's offered here is much more practical for situations where an assailant has actually grabbed you or is in close, attacking.

These few, simple, easy-to-remember countermeasures tend to work regardless of your age, gender, size, and strength relative to the suspect. They don't require "ninja-blackbelt-warrior-of-death" training, athletic ability, or exceptional agility. They won't be forgotten under stress. And they have a high probability of success, yet with relatively little risk of permanent injury to the attacker. Thus your survivability is high, your risk of legal liability low.

While you're trying to "influence" an attacker physically, be sure you inform him verbally what you want him to do. As you make physical contact, yell out *loud* an appropriate command for compliance: ***"Stop!"...* "Back!"...* "Down!"...* "Kneel!"*** Psychologically, this helps you apply the move more sharply, and makes him perceive it as being stronger. In effect, you are delivering a "multi-sensory overload"; you're touching him with the technique, your verbal stunning shocks his hearing, and the combination may even affect his vision momentarily. Yell *loud* to get past the pain barrier and grab his attention. If he doesn't hear a directive, he may just focus solely on the pain and be confused about what he has to do to get it stopped. He may react by fighting you that much harder.

Lapel push. Instead of instinctively trying to back away from a suspect who rushes you and possibly lose your balance, abruptly move in to him. This is reaction he won't be expecting. One option is to torque him off balance and out of the way with a sudden shove. Try to come at him at as near to a 45° angle as possible. Thrust both your hands at him simultaneously. One hooks into his armpit, the other lands flat where his lapel would be if he were wearing a suit. Move in and drop down slightly so you can push with the greatest leverage and thrust hard to drive him back and twist him away. As he turns, dart past him, draw your weapon, and turn and control him at a safe distance. Using leverage and drive in this way, you are fighting half of his body with all of your strength. You can move someone stronger and bigger than you are, either as they lunge toward you or to break free of a struggle.

In some cases, of course, half of a suspect's body may still be larger and stronger than all of yours. When you are clearly outmatched, modify the lapel push this way: Moving quickly to catch the suspect by surprise, grip the top of his shoulder with one hand as your forearm lays diagonally across his chest. With the other hand, grab his upper arm (or clothing) just below that shoulder and pull down violently. He may be expecting you to push him back or pull him toward you and be braced for it, but jerking down is unexpected. Your forearm across his chest will somewhat block his other arm from rising and striking you.

Caution: Your move must be dynamic and surprising. You're not going to outmuscle a superior opponent.

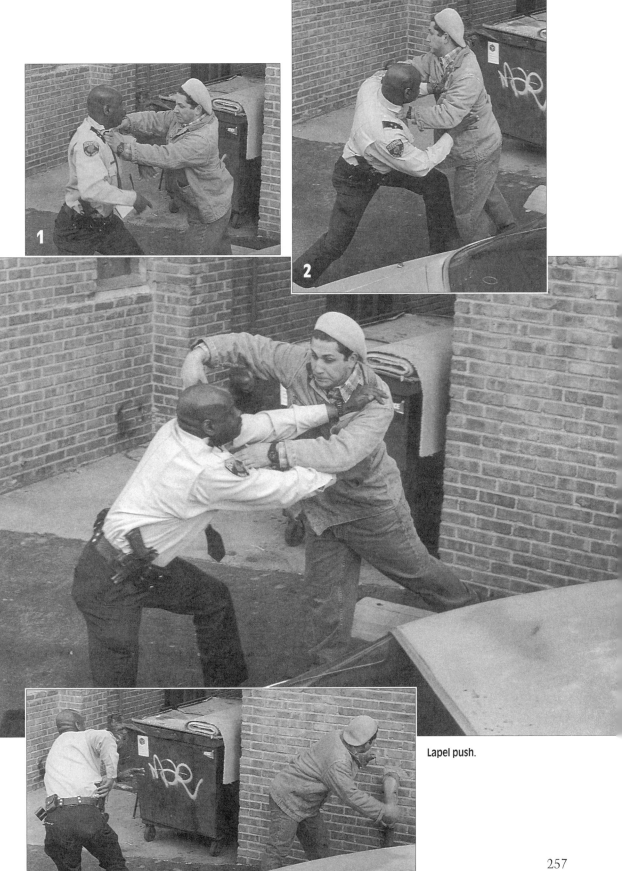

Lapel push.

257

Single-leg takedown. Here you grip the suspect's shoulder with one hand and lay that forearm across his chest. But instead of grabbing his arm with your other hand, reach down abruptly and grab behind his leg near the knee, the lower the better. Rip this leg up violently—as you push his shoulder back. He'll go airborne and to the ground.

Single-leg takedown.

Vertical stun. This is another option for surprisingly moving in to him rather than backing up. If your arms are already up in the defensive stance, you're perfectly positioned to give him a hard shove with your hands using your arm strength only, or (more reliably) to grab his shoulders or his upper clothing with both hands, yank him forward so your forearms rest almost vertically against his chest, drop down slightly for a strong push-off, then drive him backwards—hard, with your full body strength—into the nearest vertical surface. This could be your car, a tree, a utility pole, a wall—anything you can crash his full back against. The sudden backward momentum and hard impact most likely will bob his head forward, protecting it from permanent damaging impact. But the trauma diffusing across his back will momentarily stun him and knock him breathless. This should allow you to tactically retreat and arm yourself.

Shoving version of the vertical stun.

Forearm strikes. In close, your forearms can be more powerful weapons than your fists—and much less likely to break if they strike bony areas. So when you're close enough to slug an attacking suspect and lack a practical stunning surface, deliver a forearm strike instead. Bring your fists together palms down in the center of your chest to anchor your bent arms, then swing hard with your elbow so your forearm hits your desired target point. The striking surfaces should be about one to three inches forward from your elbows on the hard, bony edges of your forearms. Pivot your hips and put all your body weight behind the move for maximum impact. You can rapidly alternate blows from your strong arm and off arm, striking your assailant's chest and head until he backs off or goes down and you can get your sidearm or other weapon in your hand.

259

Forearm strike.

Knee "overload." The target here is the suspect's lower abdominal area. Your weapons are your knees. As you face your attacker, hook your hands firmly behind his neck and yank his head down and toward you, hard. As he bends forward, thrust your gun-side knee up into his solar plexus, knocking his breath out. Keep ramming him until he stops resisting, then push him to the ground for cuffing.

In extreme circumstances, you can even jackhammer his face with a knee blitz. But this can inflict serious bodily harm. Be sure you can legally justify that level of force.

Caution: A knee defense must be sudden and brief to overcome the inherent danger of standing on only one leg while you deliver the blow(s). If you are too slow or keep at it too long, the suspect may be able to grab your leg in midair and simply tip you over. To minimize this risk, you may want to strike his upper legs. Aim for the nerve groups in the thigh, anywhere between four to eight inches above the knee joint and 360° around the leg. A sharp strike here can produce pain and incapacitation similar to a groin hit. Even striking higher than that on his thigh will only slightly decrease the technique's effectiveness. Striking lower and blasting his knee joint, you may inflict permanent damage.

Also be aware that one court has described a knee strike to the abdomen as "deadly force." However, that case involved an officer who dropped from a standing position to drive his knee full force into the abdomen of a supine suspect, thereby producing an arterial tear and severe internal bleeding. With the help of another officer, the suspect was then dragged, while handcuffed, to a patrol car, where he died en route to a hospital. This subject was unarmed and resistant only to the point of being argumentative. He had not been physically aggressive.[5]

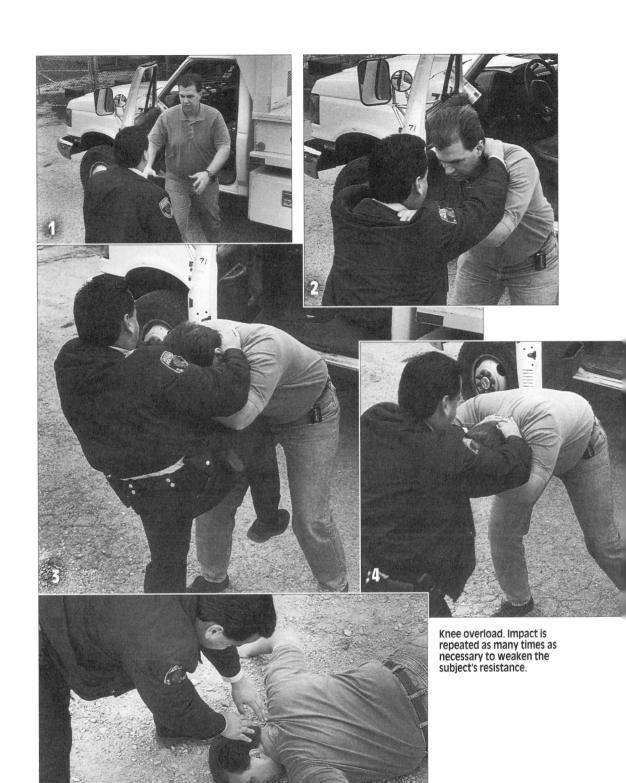

Knee overload. Impact is repeated as many times as necessary to weaken the subject's resistance.

Brachial stun. If he's grabbing or trying to choke you from the front and a high level of physical force is necessary to stop him, make a tight fist, bring your arm out about six to eight inches from the side of his neck and, keeping your arm rigid, swing so you whack his neck with the meaty muscle mass of your inside forearm. Aim for the point at the base of his neck, about half way between the side and front, where the cluster of nerves called the brachial plexus is located—not his throat, where you could fatally damage the larynx. The impact can disrupt a suspect's "mental computer" for up to seven seconds, and may also impair movement of his arm on the side where you hit him.

This blow also can work from the rear. A backup officer could come up from behind and apply it, say, if you were down, with the suspect on top of you. It can also be delivered with a backhand swing. From front or rear, the suspect can also be stunned by your striking the meaty base of your palm against the target spot on his or her neck.

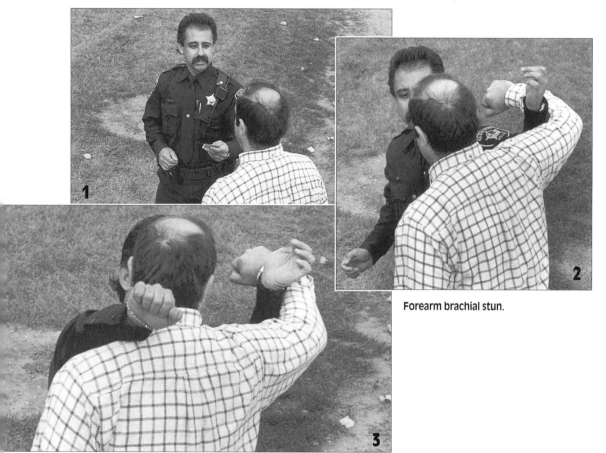

Forearm brachial stun.

Eye jabs. What some officers consider the best countermeasure is poking or gouging your attacker in the eyes, repeatedly and very hard. Even if he endures the pain and keeps attacking, he'll be hampered by not being able to see you.

Besides an old-fashioned Three Stooges jab (which sounds easy but may in fact be difficult to deliver precisely to small, instinctively protected targets), one option is "the fan." Here you simply sweep your

Backhand brachial stun.

hand laterally across the suspect's eyes so that your nails and finger-tips rake across his eyeballs. This inflicts considerable pain and is hard for him to move away from if done suddenly.

Another option for an eye jab is "the claw." Spread your fingers and stiffen your hand like talons and go for his eyes in a modified punch. This is hard to dodge, too, and may damage his face even if you don't hit bullseye on his eyes.

In contrast to some of the other countermeasures, however, eye tactics have the potential for inflicting serious permanent injury. They should be reserved for life-or-death conflicts where desperate measures are necessary for your survival.

Be effective in fighting back from the beginning. Don't start with a wimpy effort or spar around. Remember, you need to end the resistance fast, because the longer a fight lasts, the greater the chance you'll get hurt. Also, after about thirty seconds of all-out fighting, you'll suffer a significant energy loss that may result in your being defeated. So don't waste valuable time "warming up" with tentative jabs. Strike as hard as you can the first time and get it over with.

To deliver maximum power, focus all your mental and physical energy on a single point of impact. One trainer calls this "visual target designation." Once you've selected your countermeasure, imagine a red dot at the spot where you want to make impact, something like the laser beam you may use in firearms training exercises. Visualizing your total strength impacting with and driving through that spot will help channel your maximum response to that control site. Like a baseball player hitting a pitch, move in to the suspect as you deliver your action. If you're hitting, twist your hips as you do so to turbocharge your technique.

During any physical conflict, remember what a trainer from Pennsylvania calls The Laws of Creation for Defensive Tactics. These are reminders that your body is designed so that you can use the stronger parts of it to protect more vulnerable ones:

God gave you a chin to protect your throat.

God gave you shoulders to protect your jaw.

God gave you arms to protect your torso.

God gave you hands to protect your head.

God gave you hips to protect your groin.[6]

In-Car Defense

Most survival-conscious officers consider the tactically soundest deployment for conducting concealed interrogation is for you and the suspect to stand outside your vehicles at an interview location. Some officers, however, still prefer to conduct this dialogue inside their patrol cars, usually with the suspect in the front passenger seat.

They point out that: In some environments (along busy Interstates or city expressways), you're statistically at greater risk from high-speed traffic than from motorists you've stopped....On windy or inclement days, it's impractical to be outside, especially when there's lots of paperwork to review, as with truckers, and in noisy, high-traffic areas it may be difficult to hear....In the comfortable intimacy of your car, it's easier to build rapport while at the same time keeping the suspect a bit off balance, because he is removed from the reassuring familiarity of his vehicle....In your squad, you may better be able to smell evidence of drugs like marijuana on the suspect's clothes and breath.

You may argue that no one gets in your car unless he or she is handcuffed, under arrest, and behind a screen and that in-car interviewing is a classic example of sacrificing safety for efficiency and convenience.[7] But the fact is that some officers do and will continue to process traffic violators in their units, at least on some occasions. Some may even be encouraged in this procedure by their academies and agencies. Plus, if you work undercover, there may be other times when you are forced to be in cars with snitches or offenders.

Your front seat is certainly a convenient spot for processing a violator. But is comfort worth the potential risks?

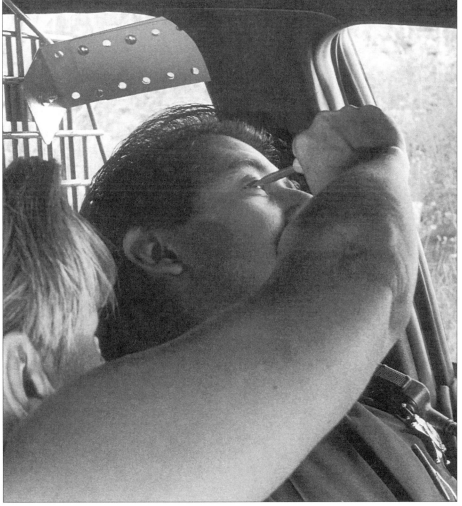

How can you make in-car positioning at least *somewhat* safer?

1. Do not permit anyone to enter your patrol car without first patting him or her down, including looking in purses and fanny packs. Technically, without reason to suspect that the subject is armed, you may have to ask permission first, to be legally correct. Just explain that you always need to do this "for my own safety and so nobody gets hurt" and ask if he objects. If he does, that's a significant danger cue in itself.

2. Instead of having the subject sit in the front seat with you, consider having him sit in the back seat, on the passenger side or in the middle straddling the floor hump. Keep the right-rear passenger door open, and you stand on the other side of it from him. You can converse and pass documents through the open door, and if he gets frisky you can slam it on him. Or you can sit on the edge of the front passenger seat with both doors open and with your feet on the ground and have him hand you documents around the doorpost. Be poised to spring up and draw your weapon if need be. This offers more comfort than standing outside and talking to him but still allows important tactical separation between you.

Anyone, no matter how harmless he or she appears, should be patted down before entering your patrol car. Appearances can be very deceiving.

Consider putting the violator in back for the interview, rather than up front. This allows you to observe him, provides a barrier to delay an attack, and permits you to keep your feet out, ready to move.

Both these positions, however, may make it difficult for you to keep a wary eye on the violator's vehicle. To solve that drawback, some officers (if they have a caged car) ask the suspect to sit in the rear passenger seat while they sit behind the steering wheel. However, this hampers rapport-building, complicates the exchange of documents, and likely weakens your observation of your primary area of responsibility, the suspect. Glancing in the rearview mirror, you probably won't be able to see below his shoulders, with your visibility even worse at night.

3. If your department policy dictates that the suspect must be interviewed in the front seat, take these precautions:

• With a split front seat, push your seat back as far as possible and bring the suspect's forward as far as possible before he gets in. If his knees are up against the dashboard, he'll be hampered in his ability to turn and assault effectively;

• If other occupants are in the violator vehicle, back up your unit once the suspect is inside. Get back about forty feet to build a bigger reactionary gap. You can always drive forward again to let him out when your work is done;

• So long as the suspect is in your car, be sure your seat belt is off. Defensively, you have some significant problems in that enclosed environment: you're sitting...your movement is restricted...if you're right-handed, your sidearm is facing the suspect...and you have a closed door on your left as a barrier to an immediate tactical retreat. Don't add further complications by being restrained by your safety harness. (When you're not involved in a contact situation, visualize and practice the movements you'd make in getting out of the car as fast as possible. Knowing how you'd effect an escape ahead of time will decrease your lag time if getting out quickly becomes necessary.);

• Tell the suspect that he must have the passenger seat belt on. Since you can't do much to gain distance in the front seat, this will at least help you gain time by slowing him down. Tell him: "I'm not planning to go any place, but you never know. I might have to suddenly take off." If he questions *your* belt being off, tell him it's department policy for any *civilian* in the car to have the rig on;

• As you sit behind the steering wheel, turn so you are angled more toward the suspect. You'll want to peripherally monitor the violator car for possible threats, but your primary area of responsibility is now to your right, not ahead. By turning, you can watch him better, plus your gun (if you're right-handed) is now wedged between you and the seat, harder for him to seize;

• If you're a large officer in a small car and can't turn much, at least plant your feet as far apart as you can. This will better brace and balance you for delivering maximum thrust and power if you have to use defensive countermeasures;

• Give the suspect documents to hold. This keeps his hands occupied and may derail his thinking. This is especially appropriate with truckers, who have multiple papers for you to examine;

• As an early warning sign, watch for a body shift by the suspect—not just his head turning, but a fuller rearrangement as he gets into a pre-attack position in the close quarters;

• If you're both in the front seat, an attacking suspect will probably go for your face or throat or for your gun, your most vulnerable areas. Your initial reaction to surprise attack will probably have to be with your "personal" (physical) weapons, specifically your forearms, knees, fists, or fingers. As with close assaults outside, use defensive countermeasures to move the suspect so you can move yourself; that is, to buy yourself time for escape, so you can get your firearm out and reestablish control. You'll have to adapt physical countermeasures that you would normally use outside to fit the interior environment. For example:

Punch. Punching an assailant with your fist is rarely a preferred choice, because the blow may break your hand or you may cut it if you hit his teeth. Indeed, gun-hand injuries are said to be the leading arrest-related injury in law enforcement.[8] But in cramped quarters this may be your immediate reaction. If you do it, one possibility is to hit with your fist vertical (like you hold a gun) and impact with the first two knuckles only, not with the whole row across your fist. This will minimize your chances of incurring a "boxer" fracture, to which your last two knuckles are most susceptible and which can affect your ability to grip your gun. Also consider striking just with the back of your fist, hurting or stunning him enough for you to break free.

Or use a palm strike. Pull your hand back as far as possible, locking the wrist, with your fingers curling slightly forward. Make impact with the very bottom of your palm, just before the wrist. A palm strike done on a slight upward angle offers a tremendous amount of leverage. Impact under the chin, for example, can produce a debilitating whiplash effect on the subject.

Another option is to deliver a "hammer-fist" blow. Instead of punching, bring your clenched fist down in a chopping fashion, as if driving a nail. Make your impact to his face, sternum, or other available target with the meaty bottom of your hand, opposite your thumb. This is a strong blow, less likely to break your hand bones, and can be executed at various angles.

Suspect's throat grab countered with stunning technique.

268

Stunning. The best object for stunning an assailant inside your unit is probably the center door post on his side of the front seat. Contact his chin with your palm (if he's facing you) or the side of his neck (if he's profile), and drive his head back against the post as hard as you can. Shoving him back by the throat will also work, but there you risk inflicting potentially lethal damage to his larynx. As an alternative surface, you may be able to stun him against your cage.

Forearm strike. Delivering a decisive blow with a conventional forearm strike may be impossible because of the limited space, your position relative to the suspect, or interference from the seat back. In that case, form a fist, stiffen your right arm, and swing your arm sharply in a backhanded manner so that your target point is impacted either by your elbow, the flat top of your forearm, or the outside bony edge. Crashing into your attacker's face can be devastating.

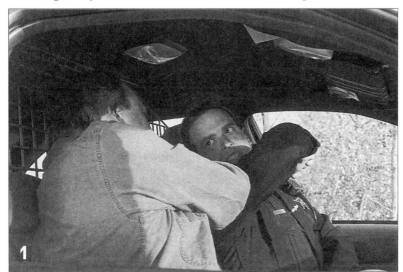

In close quarters, an elbow strike may be more practical than a forearm strike. Depending on your position and the suspect's proximity, deliver a blow that lands just to the rear of your elbow (left) or just forward from it (below). Thrust into the movement to deliver maximum power. Remember to protect your sidearm.

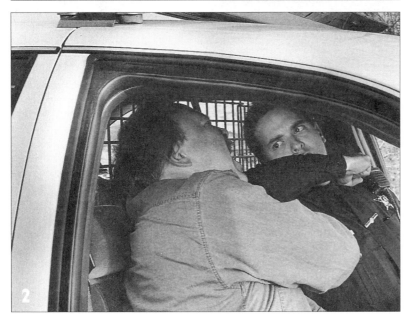

269

Knee strike. Your knee movement may be obstructed by your steering wheel, computer terminal, arm rest, or other gear. But if circumstances permit, you may be able to grab your attacker's hair or clothing or hook your hands behind his neck and pull his head down toward your knee at the same time you thrust your knee up sharply, like a spear. In effect, you are bringing the target (head) to the weapon (knee). The moment the two impact will be an experience he won't forget.

Caution: The countermeasures above are highly likely to inflict injury, potentially severe injury. To protect yourself legally, be sure you can explain why these high-force moves were "reasonable" and necessary under the circumstances.

Pressure points. Some close-quarters assailants, particularly females, attack by biting. They may be able to withstand blows or stuns, and if you try to pull away, you risk tearing your flesh and increasing the chance of contagious disease contamination. In this situation or when you're grappling in close quarters and striking is not immediately possible, try activating a pressure point instead. Probably the most effective one for these circumstances involves the mandibular angle, the hollow spot below either ear, just above where the jawbone starts to curve toward the chin. With one hand stabilizing the suspect's head, stick your other thumb against this sensitive spot and shove in hard, as if you are trying to thrust it out through the opposite eye socket. As you do so, yell loud, "*Open your mouth!*" The painful—but transitory—nerve pressure is more than most people can withstand.

A painful variation is the "cheek hook." With your left hand stabilizing the suspect's head, place your right thumb just in front of the jaw muscles below his left cheekbone. Drive your thumb in and back toward his ear. Simultaneously dig into the sensitive spot below his left ear and behind his jawbone with your fingers, creating a very painful pincer grip on his face.

An alternative is to shove your stiff index finger or first two fingers together into the bony jugular notch below the suspect's Adam's apple. Press in and down, hard. Pressure on this sensitive area tends to cause a "reversal of body movement," in which the suspect abandons his attack to reach toward the area you're counterattacking because of pain and gasping. This technique is controversial, however, because it can damage the trachea and throat, but if your safety is at stake that is strictly a secondary consideration.

G.U.N. principle. If your attacker gets your sidearm out or, despite your preliminary pat-down, unexpectedly produces a weapon of his own, consider the "G.U.N. principle": Grab...Undo...Neutralize. If he has a gun, you Grab the weapon with both your hands, trying to grip it so your fingers and/or palm(s) freeze the cylinder or slide in place to keep it from firing, and turn the barrel away from you. If he's wielding a knife, grab the hand that's holding it, not the weapon itself, so

One pressure-point option is the "nose press." Clamp across his upper face so you are pressing his nose down flat as hard as possible with your hand. Your palm blocks his vision and the pressure produces pain, inhibits breathing, causes profuse tearing, and distracts the suspect. Typically, his hands will fly up to grab your hand, but you may buy a couple of seconds to get out.

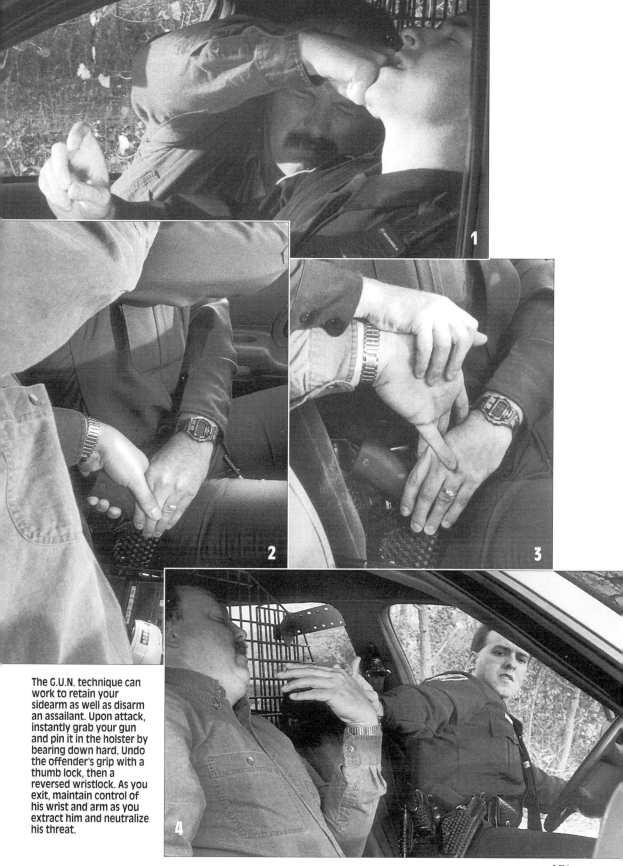

The G.U.N. technique can work to retain your sidearm as well as disarm an assailant. Upon attack, instantly grab your gun and pin it in the holster by bearing down hard. Undo the offender's grip with a thumb lock, then a reversed wristlock. As you exit, maintain control of his wrist and arm as you extract him and neutralize his threat.

you don't slice your fingers; grip with both your hands at the base of his palm so you can hold his wrist rigid, reducing his range of movement. To Undo (effect a release of the weapon), you may be able to strip or twist a gun out of the assailant's hand. If you don't have the strength or leverage for that, do what is also most likely to work against a knife: Smash his hand against the steering wheel or other hard object until he relaxes his fingers enough to release or drop it. If he's still struggling, apply defensive countermeasures until you can get out of the car and Neutralize the threat by drawing your firearm and emphatically reclaiming control. In a situation where a suspect presents a weapon threat, you want to establish the ability to protect yourself further, preferably with deadly force, as quickly as possible. Don't get into an extended wrestling match.

Note: The best time to apply the G.U.N. principle is before the weapon in the suspect's hand gets on target, especially if he's holding a firearm. If he gets the drop on you, G.U.N. can still be tried as a desperation move; using lag time to your advantage, you should be able to act before he can react, if you are fast enough and skilled enough with your move. (Theoretically, at least, if he's doing anything but actually shooting you, you have a chance of redirecting the gun off your body before he can pull the trigger.) Otherwise, your best option may be what one trainer calls "advanced BS tactics"—talk your way out. If you can't get the suspect to give up, you may at least be able to get him relaxed or distracted enough for you then to move against him with your empty hands.

A primary goal of defensive countermeasures is not only to thwart or defeat an attack quickly but to let you get out of the car as fast as possible. If the fight continues, better it be outside where your options—including deadly force—are likely to be much greater.

The most important element of in-car defense is having a plan and knowing how to use it. Study your car when you are sitting in it and nothing is happening. Practice countermeasures from behind the steering wheel and also practice getting out quickly, to rehearse and refine your techniques and build your self-confidence.

Understand, however, that because of the close quarters some movements by a suspect may be so fast and debilitating that you may not have time to respond. If he stabs your eye, for example, you will probably experience instant shock and essentially be helpless.

In-car interviewing should be recognized for what it is: comfortable but dangerous. Your best defense is to avoid it.

Tactical Ground Defense

If you're shoved, tackled, or tripped or you slip and fall during an altercation, you could end up where you'd probably least like to be: on the ground, fighting for your life. In fact, about 80% of fights that start out standing end up on the ground. In that case, your priorities are:

1. Survive, whatever it takes.

2. Get up safely.

3. If you can't get up, attack.

4. If you can't get up or attack, cover up.

Groundfighting can be a losing proposition if you don't know how to turn it to your advantage. A suspect needs 3 things to fight effectively: Air, vision, mobility. This officer is not impeding any of these—and is on his way to disaster.

He lacks a solid base to move or escape, his scissor lock is too low to be effective, and his hands and arms won't stop the attack if the suspect is stronger.

Ideally, within five to six seconds you want to be back on your feet where you can more effectively reestablish control. The longer you are down (unless you are skilled at groundfighting or able to shoot), the more vulnerable you become and the worse things are likely to be for you. Stay down for more than thirty seconds, and there's a "good chance you won't survive," according to one groundfighting expert.[9] Considering that you are likely to be injured and knocked out of breath by the fall, you may have less "quality time" even than that.

Thus you want to use it well—and you can.

Actually, the truth may not be as grim as you may think. There are effective defensive tactics you can use while you're down that will enhance your survivability significantly. These techniques will also work indoors if you go to the floor on other types of calls.

You do not necessarily sacrifice all your advantages when you hit the dirt or sidewalk. Ideally, you may still be able to use your baton against your attacker's legs or use your chemical spray or firearm to stop him. In fact, if you are down and one or more assailants are attacking you, you have strong reason to fear for your life and to legally justify the immediate use of high levels of force.

If for some reason you can't use any of your equipment, you at least are in a good position on the ground where your legs, your most powerful limbs, can become effective weapons. In fact, you can use them better on the ground because you don't have to worry about losing your balance! In order to kick or hit you, your attacker has to move

In a fight, you may hit the ground on your back. Do you keep the small of your back clear of equipment to reduce the risk of debilitating pain or spinal injury if you impact on a hard surface?

in. Once he does, you can hammer him back, possibly breaking his leg and causing him to topple to the ground while you get back on your feet. Just as you can kick and punch upright, you can kick and punch on the ground. Even in a worst-case scenario, where a bigger and stronger offender is smack on top of you, there are surprisingly effective techniques to get you free. So don't go into brain-lock and try to fight from the ground with your upper body only, as officers commonly do. You have other, more effective options. Fundamental to surviving is to believe that *you can do something,* rather than just being victimized.

STANDING ATTACKER. First, let's assume your assailant is standing. As a solid platform for either rising or fighting, you have three good ground-defense options to help you make the best of a bad situation:

On your seat. Your hands are braced back behind you to prop your head and chest up, your knees are bent, and your feet are on the ground in front of you. You can kick with one foot alone or both simultaneously from this position. Scoot around on your seat or roll back and pivot on the small of your back to turn.

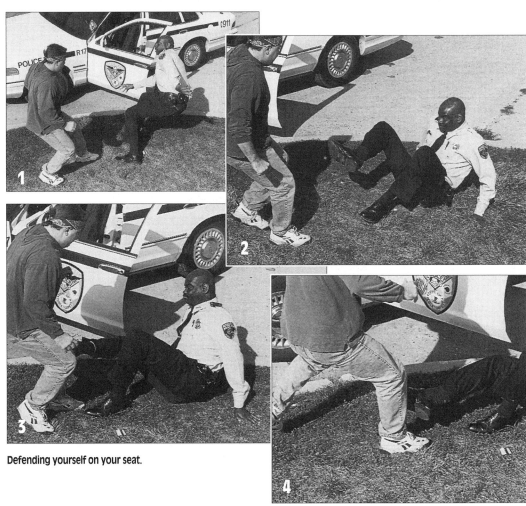

Defending yourself on your seat.

274

On your side. Here, you press both hands on the ground. Bend your lower arm so your upper body is resting almost on that forearm, and pivot on your hip to keep your attacker targeted with your feet. Because you're turning in a smaller circle, you should usually be able to move quicker than he can. If he tries to run or jump behind you faster than you can spin, you can flip from one side to the other to keep him in sight. You may find lying on your gun awkward and uncomfortable, if you still feel any pain through your adrenaline rush. But if you can fight with your gun side down, that does provide the best protection for your weapon.

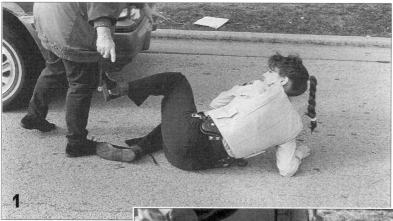

Defending on your side.

On your back. Some authorities believe this is "the most practical, economical, and versatile position."[10] Your knees are pulled in toward your chest, your ankles are crossed in front of your groin, your hands are up in the defensive position, and your chin is tucked down—something like the fetal position but on your back. This gives you ready access to equipment on your duty belt, including your gun, and good balance for using your hands and feet defensively and offensively.

If shooting is not an immediate option, you can kick out sharply with one foot while keeping the other in place to protect your groin. Or you can use all four limbs for defense or counterassault, if necessary. Faster and more powerful kicks can probably be thrown while you are on your back than from any other groundfighting position.

To change position so your feet are always pointing toward your assailant, just pivot on the small of your back, propelling yourself by one foot or the other. Or move by rocking your buttocks up and down in a rocking-chair motion. Maintaining mobility on the ground is important.

You can shoot at least one-handed from this position and if you are able to bring yourself up to a sitting position you can then get a good two-hand hold.

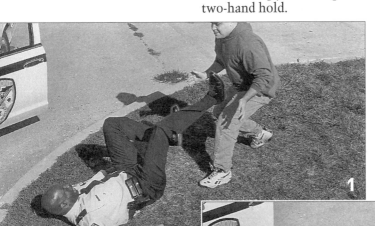

Defending on your back.

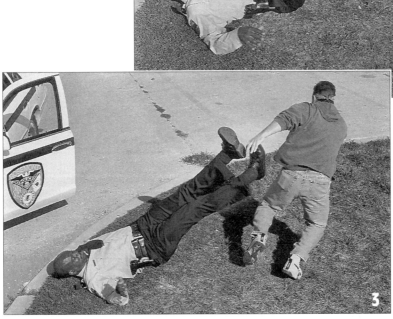

Remember, these positions all are for *desperation defense* and should not be held any longer than absolutely necessary.

When you get the opportunity to rise, one option is to sit on the ground with one leg straight out and the other tucked back under that buttock. Rock your weight onto the bent knee and stand up. This leaves both your hands free to block, strike, or draw your baton, pepper spray, or gun.

An alternative is to roll out of your down position so that one knee comes up and the ball of that foot is on the ground. The opposite knee and the palm of that hand should be touching the ground to push you up. This gives you good three-point balance. Keep your other arm extended up to grab something to pull up on, or ready to shove your assailant back or fend him off if he rushes you. Practice rising so you can learn to move fast, with economy of motion, and practice getting up from both sides.

Although getting up as soon as possible is important, getting up *safely* is essential. You want to rise when it is to your defensive advantage to do so. The suspect should be far enough away or at least temporarily incapacitated or distracted enough that you can protect yourself as you rise and regain your footing. Otherwise you may be better off defending yourself on the ground awhile longer.

In the real world of down and dirty, your form may not be perfect. But if you've practiced, you can probably get the principles of successfully repelling an attacker and getting back on your feet to work to your advantage.

Anytime your assailant is within range, attack. Take the fight to him. If you wait until he gets in closer to you, your chances of being overwhelmed multiply. Keep your techniques simple. As with countermeasures generally, the less "exotic" the technique, the more likely it will work. Fight viciously. Remember, once you're down your life very likely is on the line.

If you can't shoot and must stay down and attack with your legs and feet, aim for your attacker's knees and legs. These are the lowest possible effective targets, so you'll have the longest horizontal reach with your own legs in striking them. That means you'll be able to keep your assailant farther away. Unless he is familiar with ground-fighting techniques, he'll be surprised at your powerful counterattack and at the distance you're able to cover. When your kicks are thrusting in at this low level, it will also be harder for him to grab your legs.

Your assailant's knees are among his most vulnerable targets—weak and extremely difficult to defend. As you kick at a knee, try to turn your foot so it is horizontal (parallel to the ground) rather than vertical. This gives you a broader striking surface and lessens the chance that you'll miss the target or that your foot will slip off to the side. As you kick, push off from the floor with your hands to deliver as much explosive power as possible. As he leans down to protect his knee, he then exposes his face within your kicking range. Keep kicking until he goes down or backs off and you have a chance to get up. Constant attack is the key.

If your assailant is up by your head and you can't spin around fast enough to kick, wrap your nearest arm around his nearest leg to trap it. Then immediately shove that knee with your opposite forearm or palm to knock him off balance Or, hugging his leg, roll toward or away from him. As he falls, spin or roll away to gain distance, and get up if he is not advancing within kicking range.

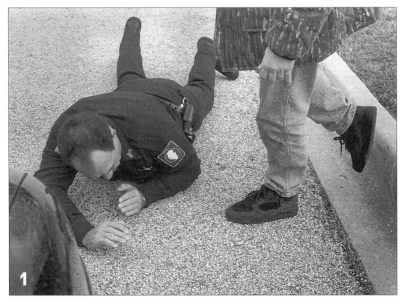

Don't just lie there and take it! If you know you are going to be kicked, move your hands to protect your head and neck from attack. Be ready to implement the "heel trap" instantly when the suspect strikes.

278

Take the kick in the shoulders and upper body. With your weight up on your toes, shift to your opposite side as you quickly trap his lower leg and heel with your arm. Brace yourself with your toes dug into the ground and roll toward his leg. As he tumbles down off balance, complete your roll, perhaps delivering a disabling elbow strike. Draw your sidearm from a safe distance. Lateral movements on your part are less likely to be anticipated than straight-line kicks and more likely to topple your attacker.

In a stomping situation, you want to try to trap his descending foot with both your hands and push or twist him off balance. Catch his foot from underneath at the highest point above you that you can. That is the least powerful and most precariously balanced position of his stomp. If you wait until his foot is lower, it will be harder to stop. If you can't catch his foot, try to redirect it away from you by shoving it laterally. Even if he still stomps, this will lessen his force. Better to take a peripheral hit than a cowboy-boot heel direct to the chest or face.

Sometimes an assailant may try to drag you along the ground. Make him pull you; don't make the job easier for him by cooperatively scooting along the ground. If he's dragging you by one leg, bend that knee. This will bring you closer to him so you can kick with the other leg. If he's dragging you by both legs, start pumping your legs furiously, "bicycle" style, trying to kick his knees. Your legs will be stronger than his hands, so it will be hard for him to continue dominating your feet. If you're being dragged on your stomach by one or both legs, roll over fast to break free.

When you are up against multiple assailants, your chances of winning from the ground diminish markedly. Although it's not easy, probably your best hope (apart from deadly force) is to try to force the offenders to work against each other. Trap one suspect's heel, for example, and topple him into the path of another attacker to disrupt their assault. If you can't get up, can't really fight back, and for some reason can't shoot, probably your best survival option then is to cover up and hope to endure the kicks and punches pelting down on you with as little damage as possible. This is the option you least want to be forced into because it requires something outside your control to distract or frighten your attackers into ending their assault. It is simply a means of trying to stay conscious and alive until circumstances change.

One option in this situation is to pull yourself into a "fetal tuck." Lie on your side with knees to chest, chin down, arms over your face, and hands trying to shield the top of your head. Scoot or roll so you can get your back against a wall, a tire, a tree, or some other object that will provide a barrier against kicks to your spine. Try to roll onto your gun side to discourage a disarming. It won't be pretty or painless, but you can withstand considerable beating in this position (your soft body armor will help absorb blows) and you may still be able to kick or elbow your way out.

If you can't protect your back, you're probably better off to stay with your back against the ground. Tuck your legs up and wrap your arms and hands around your head. Protecting your spine is essential. Even a moderate kick to your spinal column can render your arms and/or legs useless and produce long-term disability or paralysis.

Continually watch for opportunities for getting up, attacking (optimally, with deadly force), or moving to a better position that will let you more actively defend yourself or escape. Be alert also for weapons of opportunity—gravel, shards of glass, bottles, and other debris on the ground around you—that can be thrown at your attackers to distract or injure them. If you manage to deliver an effective strike to a standing attacker, be prepared for him to fall on you. Moving quickly, you may be able to dodge him. If not, one of the techniques described next can help you escape.

ATTACKER ON TOP OF YOU is probably the most terrifying of all groundfighting situations. Not only is the suspect's full weight pressing down to pin you to the ground, but you now have severely limited mobility and probably limited access to your defensive equipment. If you're on your stomach, you're extremely vulnerable to disarming. Indeed, many disarmings occur during wrestling matches on the ground.

Still, there are simple and practical techniques—based on high-school wrestling maneuvers, actually—that can work, regardless of your size, to help you escape and defend yourself.

If you are on your back with the suspect on top of you, pull your feet up as close as possible to your butt, with your soles flat on the ground to establish a platform for movement. Keeping your feet and shoulders against the ground, suddenly

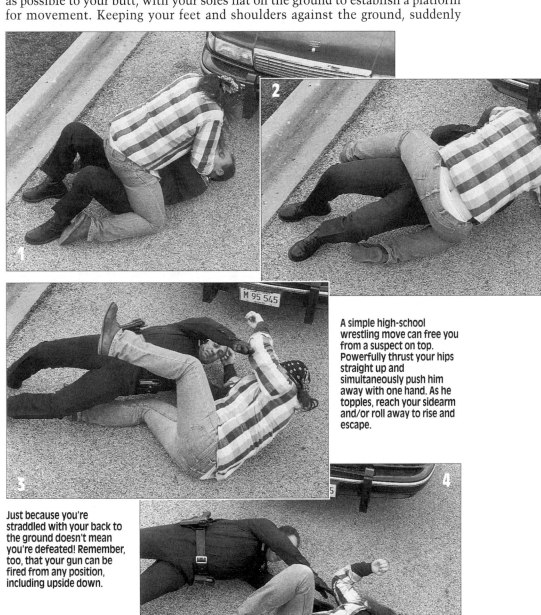

A simple high-school wrestling move can free you from a suspect on top. Powerfully thrust your hips straight up and simultaneously push him away with one hand. As he topples, reach your sidearm and/or roll away to rise and escape.

Just because you're straddled with your back to the ground doesn't mean you're defeated! Remember, too, that your gun can be fired from any position, including upside down.

281

explode your hips straight up as fast and powerfully as possible. Simultaneously push the suspect with one hand to redirect him off and away from you. (A one-handed push will deflect him one way or the other, in contrast to pushing with two hands which will only raise him up). As the suspect is thrown off you, you may then be able to reach your gun or roll onto your hands and knees and escape.

If you are on your stomach with the suspect on your back, first pull your elbows in to your sides and put your open hands on either side of your face, forming an approximate triangle. This helps protect your head and also blocks him from getting a chokehold on you or slipping under your arms and applying a dangerous full nelson. Pull your feet so they are vertical, with your toes digging into the ground to establish a base. Your weight should be on your toes, knees, and elbows to the extent possible. Suddenly and forcefully, pull your knees up and push your hips back toward your heels, as if you were going to get up on your knees. Twist your hips so one leg comes under the other while the opposite hip is thrown up. Simultaneously and quickly

You're knocked face down. What are you going to do? Before he can punch your face and head, bring in your elbows tightly to your sides and protect your face with your hands. Twist your hips with a powerful thrust.

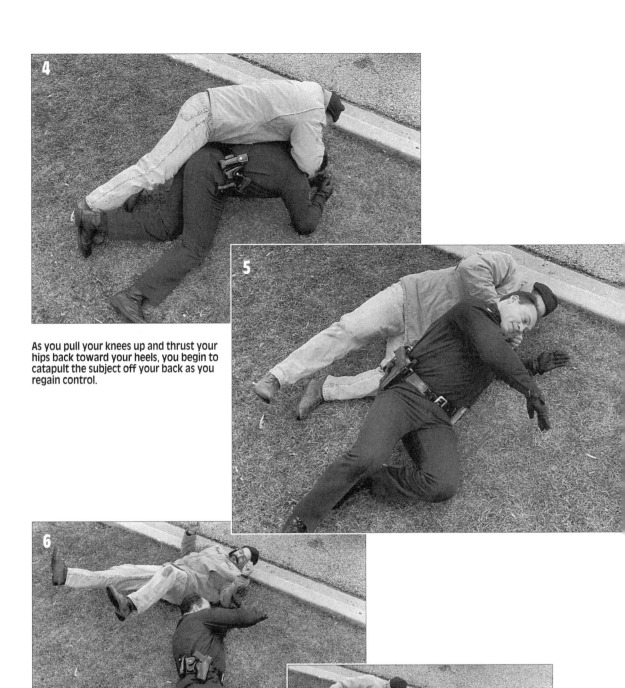

As you pull your knees up and thrust your hips back toward your heels, you begin to catapult the subject off your back as you regain control.

move the arm that's on the same side as the leg you're moving; shoot it straight out along the ground toward your head, in line with your body. As the suspect's weight shifts and he starts to slide off you, crab walk out from under him. You're using the mobility of your lower body to buy mobility for your upper body. As with other maneuvers, all this must be dynamic and explosive to be effective.

Ground-defense techniques, like other countermeasures, must be practiced to the point that they are conditioned, reflexive responses. You won't be able to think your way through them when you are under the extraordinary stress of bombardment. A good exercise to practice with a partner is to assume a position on the ground (or floor), close your eyes, and let him or her silently get into some position around you or on you. Then open your eyes and defend yourself immediately. In time, you will find yourself automatically and rapidly responding with fixed patterns to counter whatever challenges your opponent presents.

Also practice drawing and dry-firing from all positions on the ground, making certain your gun is unloaded and you are in a safe environment.

Controlled Foot Pursuit

On the January evening that Sergeant Manuel Tapia, supervisor of a metro narcotics task force, got a tip that a load of dope was going to be moved through his small Arizona border town, he did a lot of things right...and one thing grievously wrong.

Sgt. Manuel Tapia.

He recruited a deputy sheriff for backup, and in separate cars they staked out a known "trafficker street" to watch for the alleged courier, said to be driving a dark-colored Ford. When they spotted it, Tapia, in plainclothes, skillfully pulled in behind in his undercover Chevy and tailed it without alarming the lone, young driver. Anticipating a high-risk stop, he called for uniformed municipal officers and discussed strategy with them on the radio. At a traffic light, he and a city sergeant boxed the suspect in, catching him by surprise before he could peel away. Nineteen years old, the driver was nervous and shaking, but seemed cooperative. Tapia addressed him in Spanish, and he consented to open his trunk so the officers could look inside. As they moved to the trunk, the city sergeant visually checked the suspect out, but saw no evidence of a weapon.

Hands shaking, the suspect put the key in the trunk lock. Then suddenly he bolted. Apparently without a second thought, Tapia ran after him. The suspect ran down the street toward oncoming traffic, then veered away toward a grassy park, across from a motor hotel. Tapia was ten feet behind him and gaining when the courier reached in his front waistband, stopped, and turned around with a 9mm Manurhin Pistolet in his right hand.

Sergeant Tapia didn't draw his SIG SAUER P220. He couldn't. It was fifteen yards away, lying on the front seat of his vehicle. No one knows for sure why he left it there; maybe he'd taken it out and tucked it under his leg to have it "handy" while he was tailing the suspect car, and then had forgotten it in the excitement of the stop. He'd started the foot pursuit unarmed, and now confronted by a drug-runner determined to kill him, he jerked his gun hand across the front of his body in a pathetic gesture of protection.

The suspect's first round ripped through-and-through his right forearm and into his abdomen. The suspect fired again, but the city sergeant, running a few feet behind Tapia, cut him down with his Glock 17. The suspect was first to die, about two hours later at a local hospital. Sergeant Tapia succumbed early the next morning after being helicoptered to a trauma center in Tucson. One hundred twenty-five pounds of Mexican marijuana—forty-one bricks packaged in dark green trash bags and sealed with duct tape—were found in the killer's trunk.

Officers in foot pursuits often are strong in emotions, weak in tactics. The gall of a suspect running away makes them mad or they mistakenly conclude that a fleeing suspect must be afraid of them, and they give chase automatically, when a more prudent course of action—certainly if you have no gun—is to stay put.

A risky, reflexive pursuit can be especially foolish on a contraband stop. If the suspect flees his unlocked vehicle and no other responsible party is around, you can usually consider it abandoned[11] or a road hazard subject to being towed in most jurisdictions. Most likely you would then be permitted to inventory the contents without having either a search warrant or consent and seize anything illicit you find inside. A fleeing suspect is likely to surface eventually, or you can track him down under more controlled circumstances. So in a sense you can have your cake and eat it too.

Any pursuit of more than a few steps should be a *considered* decision, in which tactics, not emotions, are the swaying influences.

Often the best way to win a foot pursuit, as with a vehicle chase, is to prevent one from starting. Stay on guard to abort one by reminding yourself that, as a DEA bulletin states, "escape is an option that the suspect is considering at all times"—regardless of his circumstances. A drug-runner who was stopped by two municipal officers in a small town in Arizona while he was hauling $1,000,000 worth of methamphetamine in his trunk took off running even though he was handcuffed behind his back. He ran that way not once but twice within a matter of minutes. He was caught and subdued each time, but in the process both officers were injured, including one sustaining a painful kick to the groin. Reflecting on this incident later, the officers realized that just before he ran the first time the suspect took several steps backward, building a head start from the officers, who had just recovered a folding knife and a large amount of cash from his pockets. The officers missed this indicator, perhaps assuming (falsely) that a suspect in handcuffs is beyond running.

Watch for early warning signs like that or like the suspect looking around or making a target glance at a tempting escape route or engaging in exaggerated movement. Often you will see "bob-and-weave" behavior: The suspect leans away, takes a step back, then rocks back and forth nervously as he tries to decide whether to flee or fight. The more he has to hide, the more pronounced this bob-and-weave will be. Also notice how his feet are positioned. If he's in your patrol car and they're both pointed toward the door on his side or you're outside with him and they're pointed off in a direction away from you, consider that to be a potential flight position.

If he's moving around, tell him to stand still. Legitimate people will; people with something to hide often *can't* stand still because they have to relieve their stressful energy. Anticipate his moving to run, and be ready to snatch him the instant he starts.

The most successful foot pursuit is the one you prevent. If you're alert for early warning signs, things may not reach this point.

Watch for the "bob-and-weave" and other indicators that the suspect is anticipating escape. Grab the offender the moment he or she turns to flee.

Meantime, if you have backup present, bracket the suspect between the two of you to limit his avenues of escape. Consider planting verbal images in his mind that will dampen his flight fantasies. A California traffic officer stopped a driver one night who turned out to be transporting LSD tabs in packs of cigarettes. As they talked, the suspect kept looking toward a stand of timber that lined the road. Reading his thoughts, the officer said solemnly, "Don't run into those woods. The bears will get you." The suspect settled right down.

Before racing after a suspect who does "book," evaluate these variables in deciding if that's really your best option:

Who is the suspect? Is he someone you've already patted down, or is the weaponry he might be packing unknown? Does he have a known violent background that suggests he could attack, given the opportunity? Is he the driver of the vehicle, probably the person you're most interested in on a contraband stop, or a passenger who does not have authority over the car? Do you know who he is, where he lives, and where you can likely find him again even if he gets away now?

Your physical condition vs. the suspect's is one factor to consider in deciding if a foot pursuit is safe for you. This 16-year-old has just been nabbed after a long-distance chase that started when he fled from questioning. How much of an impact do you think the exertion had on him? Now check out the condition of the officer who was chasing him (below). Who would you bet on had there been a fight at the point of capture?

Who are you? Are you wearing your vest? Are you overweight, out of shape, near retirement and susceptible to a heart attack from a chase and possible scuffle afterwards? If you catch the suspect, can you handle him physically, when you're likely to be out of breath and fatigued? Can you use your firearm after sustained exertion? If you don't know, try this on the range: Sprint for just thirty seconds, then shoot; notice the effect on your accuracy.

What help is available? If you don't have backup, can you radio for other officers in the vicinity to intercept the pursuit or block off the

287

area so the suspect is contained? Do you have at least verbal communication with other officers joining the chase? *Taking on a sustained foot pursuit all by yourself is extremely dangerous.* This is not an athletic contest but an effort to seize an actively resisting subject who apparently is involved in something serious enough to convince him to refuse to submit to your authority and your commands to stop. This resistance frequently escalates to a violent physical confrontation at the end of the pursuit, when you may need the help of other officers. Also consider what help might be available to the suspect, especially if he leads you unto his home turf.

When is the pursuit taking place? Is it at night when your visibility is limited, or near the end of shift when you're already dead tired? Is it in cold weather when ice may create a running hazard, or in summer when blazing heat may cause sudden exertion problems?

Where is it taking place? Some officers feel the most important element of a successful pursuit is knowing the territory. Do you know the area as well as the suspect is likely to, or are you running "blind," essentially ignorant about possible hazards, where he might end up, shortcuts, opportunities he might have to circle back to your patrol car, et cetera? Does the path of flight allow you to maintain visual contact with the suspect, if not continually at least sufficiently to prevent ambush? (If you lose him, you're really no longer in a pursuit; you're into a search.) Is the location inherently dangerous—like thick woods or a housing project—with numerous hiding places and vantage points for surprise attack? Is traffic a threat to you? One detective in Massachusetts chased a suspect down into a ravine that held railroad tracks. He was so intent on the pursuit that he didn't hear a train coming around a bend behind him until it was too late to get out of the way. In Texas, a patrol officer drowned when she slipped into a creek while chasing a suspect through woods.

Are the risks worth it? If the bottom line is "No," don't pursue. This should definitely be your conclusion if you know in advance that the fleeing suspect is armed with a gun. If that becomes known during the pursuit, call it off, unless you can proceed with adequate cover.

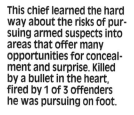

This chief learned the hard way about the risks of pursuing armed suspects into areas that offer many opportunities for concealment and surprise. Killed by a bullet in the heart, fired by 1 of 3 offenders he was pursuing on foot.

If you do decide to chase, here are some tips for improving your C.Q. (Chase Quotient)—ways to smarten your running technique to give you the best chance of catching the offender:

- Off-duty, develop your pursuit style, learning to run with your body relaxed and efficient;

- Run with the ground surface, not against it. That is, try to minimize your vertical bobbing up and down to reduce muscular/skeletal shock and energy drain;

- Run with your head over your "center" to best maintain your balance and confrontational stance;

- If you have a choice on your department, wear duty shoes that will facilitate speed, traction, and endurance; avoid footgear like cowboy boots. (Can you comfortably and safely run 100 yards in your current footwear?)

- When chasing an offender, run at a pace that will leave you a reserve of energy should you need to confront him;

- If a suspect stops running, maintain a control distance that will allow you to disengage from a physical encounter or escalate to a higher level of force if he aggressively resists you.[12]

Keep these survival principles in mind during the pursuit:

Don't automatically start running. Sometimes you can go just about anyplace the suspect can in your patrol car. Chase him with it as far as you can to conserve your energy. When you reach a place you can't go, then evaluate whether bailing out and running after him makes sense. Remember, you will have to secure your squad if you go, so no one (including the fleeing suspect) can access your equipment or steal your car.

Don't abandon unsecured subjects or run past an uncleared suspect vehicle from which an armed occupant could ambush you. Remember, the person you're chasing may not be your greatest threat. An Oregon officer stopped a car with four occupants after they left a drug-sale location. The driver ran, the officer chased him. They scuffled briefly, but the officer subdued and cuffed him. This suspect was unarmed. But among the three passengers left behind (two of whom were females) were a revolver and a Marine Corps Ka-Bar combat knife. The male passenger ran after the officer, intending to help the driver. He showed up—with the Ka-Bar knife in hand—just as the officer completed cuffing. The officer drew down on him and controlled him. But if he'd arrived seconds sooner while the officer was still struggling with the driver, the story could have had a different ending.

Sprint briefly, then follow, don't chase. If you can't catch the suspect with a quick dash that lasts no more than about twenty seconds, ease off and pace yourself. Try to keep him in sight and track where he's going, but don't exhaust yourself so that you're physically vulnerable if you do catch him. Adjust your speed to your advantage. One option is the "pace-and-charge" technique. While the suspect is running as fast as he can, you run at more of a jogging pace, about 60 to 80% of your maximum effort. Try to stay close enough to keep him in sight but with enough separation (about fifteen yards or so) to create a protective buffer. As he begins to tire and slow down, you accelerate and overtake him. When he sees you gaining on him, this will often produce surrender.

Note: Some officers as personal policy abandon pursuits if they don't catch the suspect within the first 100 yards. They figure that they're carrying about twenty pounds of equipment that the suspect doesn't have and are likely to tire faster and be in poorer shape to defend themselves if they do catch him after a long chase. In effect, they're practicing damage control by bailing early.

Also understand that launching a dead-out sprint from standing still may expose you to the risk of muscle injury. You'll be safer to start slow—and more likely to *think* rather than react emotionally—but the suspect may readily outdistance you.

As you run, scan. Look up and back from where you are to where the suspect is (and beyond), as well as scanning from side to side, just as you do in a vehicle pursuit. You're breaking your tunnel vision on him to watch for "road" hazards, possible ambush spots, or other threats that may blindside you otherwise. In a vehicle pursuit, it's important not to drive so fast that you "outrun your headlights" and are on a hazard before you can do anything to avoid it. The same holds true in controlling yourself during a footchase.

Keep your sidearm controlled. Don't run with it in your hand; the risk of unintentional discharge or disarming is too high. Don't try to shoot while you're running; the risk of wild shots and unintentional hits is too high. Especially avoid firing "warning" shots; they usually are worthless and dangerous and create a severe legal-liability risk for you. Keep in mind that you cannot shoot a fleeing suspect just because he is fleeing. In the context of a civil rights lawsuit, the U.S. Supreme Court has ruled[13] that you are justified in using deadly force only when you have

Not recommended.

290

eliminated other options for preventing the suspect's escape and have probable cause to believe that he has committed a violent crime or poses an immediate threat of serious physical harm to you or someone else or a substantial danger to the community if not immediately stopped or captured; some state laws and department policies are even more restrictive. Be sure when your gun is in your holster that it is secure. Unbelievable as it seems, guns have bounced out of holsters during foot pursuits and officers haven't realized it until they've tried to draw—and grabbed empty air. (In practice sessions, try running with all your normal duty gear and see what happens to your equipment. Do you lose anything? This may affect your future decisions about chasing.)

Don't split your forces. If a partner is with you and there are multiple runners, both of you stay together even if the suspects split in different directions. Pick your best target and stick with him. It's worth others getting away if you can safely capture one.

Use caution rounding corners and try to move from cover to cover as you run. Take time not to rush past or around corners and solid objects where the suspect may be hiding or run out in the open where he can spin and pop you. Scan ahead so you anticipate corners. Approaching them, either quick-peek around them..."slice the pie" as you would on a building search to gradually expose what's on the other side...or at the very least swing wide to "round the corner off" so you create distance from an area of unknown hazard. This will no doubt slow you down some, but a less cautious approach can slow you down all the way...permanently.

Rounding corners at full speed, you may play right into a suspect's game plan. Slow down... "slice the pie"...watch for shadows and other giveaway cues. The extra effort may be well worth it!

Watching a suspect's hands is important even during pursuit. A reach to the waist may be to toss contraband or access a weapon—in this case, a .38 with a 4-in. barrel.

Watch for movement toward common weapon areas. A suspect's hands are just as dangerous when he's in flight as any other time. As you run, keep asking yourself: Where is my nearest cover *right now*? How am I going to respond if he moves toward a weapon area *right now*?

Don't hypnotically follow the suspect's exact path of flight. This behavioral form of tunnel vision makes you dangerously predictable. Plus, you may not want to go where he goes. If you're chasing him across rooftops in a city and he jumps from one building to another across a chasm eight stories deep, or he darts across six lanes of high-speed traffic on an Interstate, do you really want to try that?

Be alert for discarded contraband. Suspects often throw away baggies and vials of dope, drug paraphernalia, and other evidence as they run. The Supreme Court has ruled that this is fair game for you to seize;[14] by discarding the item, the suspect has surrendered any reasonable expectation of privacy in it. If you see the discard take place, it can be probable cause for arrest. During a foot pursuit in Georgia, a fleeing probationer dropped a mere roach. Yet the officer's alertness to this scant evidence, which could have sent the suspect back to jail, allowed authorities to persuade him to give up the heavy-hitting leader of a Crips set on cocaine trafficking charges and to learn the location of two fugitive murder suspects.

Hey, Guys! Here I Am!

Sometimes you don't have to be a mantracking genius to stay on a fleeing suspect's trail.

In Virginia a dope dealer ran from a nighttime stop and headed toward thick woods. Pursuing cops would have lost him for sure among the trees—except he was wearing battery-operated sneakers.

Lights in the heels flashed on each time the shoes hit the ground. The officers running behind just followed them like beacons and finally grabbed the culprit, along with twelve bags of cocaine.

Anticipate the suspect's flight pattern. To some extent, you can predict where he'll run, and this can be an important survival and tracking consideration if you lose sight of him. One Canadian study[15] concludes that:

1. Suspects fleeing from a scene may first turn left but after that will tend to turn right whenever they have to turn, avoiding left turns if at all possible. Apparently this relates to the part of the human brain that becomes dominant under stress.
2. If they are forced to turn left by natural barriers or police containment, they become frustrated or confused. They generally will make no more than two left turns before they panic and hide.
3. Running down a street or alley, the vast majority will run along the right side.
4. Evidence will usually be tossed away to the right.
5. If they have a choice of where to hide they favor the right side.
6. If two suspects are running and one hides, the second will usually hide within 200 feet of the first; both will hide sooner than a subject fleeing alone.
7. If one of two fleeing suspects is captured, the other will tend to circle to the right within a 200-foot radius and come back to the scene to scope things out, so long as the prisoner is kept in the vicinity. The sergeant who documented these patterns sometimes uses this last tendency as a means of bagging the companion who remains at large. At night, he places the handcuffed first suspect on the hood of his patrol car, plays a spotlight on him, and uses him as a visible magnet to draw the second offender into the area, where he then can be taken by surprise.

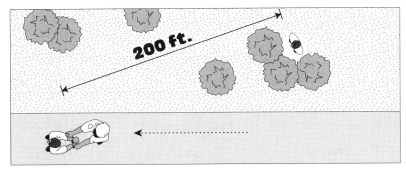

If one of two fleeing suspects is captured, the other will tend to circle to the right within a 200-ft. radius and come back to the scene to scope things out, so long as the prisoner is kept in the vicinity.

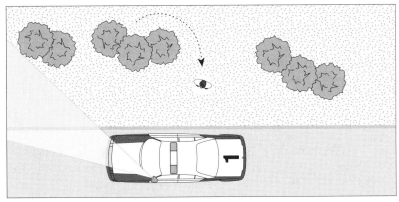

After the first suspect is arrested, handcuffed and searched, remove him from the scene. But consider the value of leaving a patrol car with high beams and spotlight activated in the immediate area for a while. Officers who use this technique claim that it works wonders, making the second suspect think his buddy is still there and drawing him out of hiding so he can be apprehended.

Use extreme caution in your final approach. If you're running full speed and closing in on the suspect, he can suddenly stop and attack before you can slow down. Your forward momentum may propel you right into him and his weapon. Trying to tackle him may end up in a wrestling match—and result in your disarming. If you use the pace-and-charge technique, slow down before you actually reach the suspect and approach in a balanced and controlled manner, ready to apply any necessary defensive and/or arrest control techniques. You're safest to draw your firearm and just stabilize the scene at a comfortable distance, avoiding a final approach until: backup is present...the suspect is physically unable to resist...or you are convinced he is fully submissive. Remember, with many foot pursuits, when the chase ends a fight begins.

Be psychologically prepared for a deadly force encounter. Unpredictability is often a core ingredient of foot pursuits. Changes in the status can take place at head-spinning speed. Consider: A sheriff's deputy discovered an ounce of crack hidden in the spare-tire compartment of a car he'd stopped for a traffic violation in Alabama. The driver seemed compliant, but the passenger rabbited. In a matter of minutes, the fleeing suspect: tried unsuccessfully to get into several unoccupied cars he approached in traffic...dived through the window of a Monte Carlo...jumped out when police made contact with that car...ran into a busy grocery store...grabbed a large knife off a butcher's table...ran through swinging doors into the back of the store and into a refrigerated storage area...confronted the original deputy who'd come after him...threatened to kill himself while the deputy tried to persuade him to drop the knife and surrender peacefully...sprayed stainless-steel cleaner into his mouth...suddenly lunged toward the deputy in a threatening manner…was shot and mortally wounded. Through all this, the deputy not only pursued the fleeing suspect successfully but maintained the necessary mental acuity and physical firearms control to protect himself and others in a fast-changing scenario.

Even when a foot-pursuit suspect is seized, don't assume your danger is over. A rookie trooper in Connecticut pursued a Chevrolet Camaro that he was trying to stop one afternoon for passing illegally. The driver screeched to a halt near a wooded area and ran from the car, leaving behind a briefcase with thousands of dollars in cash, a quantity of cocaine, and a handgun. The rookie ran after him, caught him, and had one handcuff applied when the suspect whipped out a hidden .25-cal. pistol and shot the trooper in the forehead. At this writing, more than four years later, the trooper remains paralyzed.

Ideally, you are able to conclude your concealed interrogation and obtain consent to search without the suspect fleeing or posing a threat that requires your response with firearms or defensive tactics. Even so, be cognizant that your stop is now entering a dicey period of new challenges: the Great Treasure Hunt for contraband.

By now at least one additional officer should be present for protection. Bear in mind that this is probably the most stressful phase for the suspect. Your skill at searching very likely will decide his future. Much is at stake. It is not yet safe to relax.

III
TACTICS OF SEARCH & SURVIVAL

TACTICAL SETUP

What does this number represent?

According to the Georgia State Patrol, this is the number of different places its troopers found drugs hidden in vehicles in one twelve-month period. And these are just the places they found! How many they missed is anybody's guess.

More than 90% of drug dealers surveyed by the Patrol say cops conduct lousy searches. Nearly 80% say drug traffickers can easily bluff the police, because most officers only search in the most obvious places—places where shrewd drug haulers don't hide contraband anymore.

Unfortunately, they're probably right. Unless something's so blatant it can't possibly be missed, a lot of officers never tumble to it. Or they don't even try to thoroughly search a vehicle they've stopped, even if they're suspicious about what might be hidden in it, because they think the job will take too long...or they lack confidence that they can do it right...or they're uncertain just how far they can go legally. So they settle for a "normal" toss of the vehicle: glancing under seats, peering into the glove box, or checking behind the sun visors, if they do anything at all.

The truth is if you learn how to read certain search cues, you can complete a competent and safe search of a passenger vehicle in about *fifteen minutes or less.* Even on a hectic urban beat where you don't have time to "tap every spot," the right shortcuts can still take you to treasure.

Efficiency is important. You don't want to search cars longer than about twenty-five to thirty minutes. Beyond that, on a consent search, you may encounter problems about the length of detention. Plus, if you haven't found contraband by then, you probably won't.[1] (Larger vehicles, of course, may require more time.)

The secret is:

1. Knowing certain strategies that allow you to keep your time under control, without sacrificing quality;

2. Observing tactics that safeguard your survival as your investigation becomes increasingly threatening to the suspect.

In line with what your priorities should be, we'll first explore the proper tactical foundation that will set you up for searching a vehicle safely. Then in the next chapter we'll share the distilled wisdom of scores of successful Criminal Patrol officers on precisely where and how to search probably the most common object of investigation: the passenger car.

Search Commandments

For survival, keep in mind five key principles: Survival Commandments, appropriate to any type of conveyance.

Commandment 1: Have backup present before starting your search. Call the moment you become suspicious and decide you're going to ask for consent. If you're working in teams, as is common on Criminal Patrol, there will likely be a quick response. (On some teams the back-up officer likes to park in a concealed position nearby and watch the early phase of the stop through binoculars until summoned.)

Don't go any further than getting the consent form signed, until your backup is actually there. Even if you have only one suspect to manage and even if you intend to have him or her sit in the back of your caged patrol car, ideally you're going to want another officer watching the suspect while you concentrate fully on searching the vehicle. With more than one suspect, this becomes an absolute necessity.

Don't make the mistake of a Florida trooper. When a car he'd stopped for speeding turned out not to be registered to any of its four occupants, he began to suspect it was hauling drugs. Without calling backup, he let two of the suspects out of the vehicle, apparently thinking he could watch and control them and thoroughly search the car at the same time. In the trunk, he discovered a suitcase sealed with black tape, and inside that, a garbage bag bulging with marijuana. At that instant, a third suspect started to get out on the passenger side—and the trooper's sweet triumph turned sour in an eye blink. While he was distracted with the third man, one of the others darted his hand into the open trunk, grabbed a small semiautomatic pistol hidden underneath the suitcase, and snuffed the trooper with a shot to the head. The officer was still clutching the driver's license when he hit the ground.

Another Florida trooper on a different stop waited until after he'd found a small quantity of rock cocaine while searching a trunk before calling for backup. He waited too long. Before an additional officer arrived, the desperate driver initiated a struggle. The trooper and the suspect both rolled down an embankment into a watery ditch, and the officer lost control of his sidearm. The suspect grabbed it and fatally fired point-blank into the trooper's face.

If you can't get backup when you need it and you can't reasonably and safely detain the suspect(s) until it's available, your wisest option is to terminate the stop.

Much better to accept the fact that you're not going to win the war on drugs single-handed than to take on the extreme risk of conducting a search alone when it's difficult or impossible to maintain a Position of Advantage.

Commandment 2: Conduct the search in a safe location. Be sure the vehicle is positioned so you will be safe from the suspects...safe from other civilians who may be around...and safe from passing traffic. If you're in a dangerous spot, ask the driver to move his vehicle to a nearby service station, a highway maintenance depot, a parking lot, or other location where you can search without anxiety. Your backup needs to be conscious of safe positioning, too. He or she should pull up behind or to the side of your unit, not park in front of the suspect vehicle in the immediate kill zone.

Commandment 3: With backup tactically deployed, order all occupants out before you put any part of your body into the vehicle. You need freedom of mind to concentrate fully on searching and not be distracted by subjects seated inside who may be waiting for an opportunity to attack.

To search thoroughly, you'll need to stoop, squat, twist, and stretch in awkward positions. Your sidearm will often be exposed. Your vision may be blocked. You'll be in tight quarters that restrict defensive movement. In short, you'll be *extremely vulnerable* to anyone close by with violent intent. A sheriff's deputy in a Western state barely escaped serious injury when he stuck his body halfway into a Plymouth Duster that had been detained at a truck stop. The driver, hopped up on cocaine, methamphetamine, and heroin and still behind the wheel, suddenly threw the Plymouth into reverse. The deputy was pinned against a tractor-trailer rig parked nearby. Backup officers were forced to shoot the driver multiple times, fatally wounding him, before the injured deputy could be freed.

Another deputy got the single occupant out of a car on a different stop all right. But then he let the suspect hover next to him while he searched the trunk. "What's that?" the deputy asked, pointing to a sealed garbage bag. "Dirty laundry," the suspect said. But when the deputy poked his finger through the bag, he found marijuana. In a flash, the suspect slammed the trunk lid down on the officer's arm. Only the intervention of a civilian ride-along saved him from further assault.

You're safest getting the occupants away from the vehicle and you, where your backup can monitor them.

Commandment 4: Frisk occupants first, then search their vehicle. Officers often become so intent on searching vehicles that they neglect at least to pat down the people associated with them. Weapons and contraband alike are missed.

Some offender types—street-gang members in or near their turf, for example—tend to keep all the drugs they have along in the car on their person. Even long-distance couriers hauling significant quantities are increasingly secreting drugs or money taped to their inner thighs, legs, or arms, in money belts around their waists, or in rigs that make them look pregnant.

A deputy who stopped a car on a scorching day in the South thought it strange that a middle-aged female passenger was wearing a heavy sweater and quilted winter jacket when the temperature was boiling toward 92 degrees. Patting down her waist, he felt what the bulky clothes were hiding: a special girdle with pouches that allowed her to carry a kilo of coke in front and another in back.

In one case, an observant Customs inspector noticed that a young Colombian man had an unusually stiff-legged way of walking. When the subject was patted down, the inspector first thought there was something taped to his thighs. Further examination revealed badly infected incisions, patched over with strips of adhesive tape. Incredibly, this mule had permitted a doctor to surgically implant four packets of cocaine—each about six inches long, three inches wide, and an inch thick—into his thighs, then stitch the entry slits back together. Numerous obese suspects have concealed drugs or cash in folds of fat. One 475-pound man tucked crack cocaine worth $30,000 up under his enormous gut. When they first searched him, officers in Florida couldn't find anything. Finally when a K-9 kept alerting on his abundant abdomen, they lifted it up—and eleven pounds of drugs fell out.

Caution: Before you move in for a pat-down, be sure you see the suspect's fingers spread apart. An offender may conceal razor blades between his fingers and use these to slash your face as he goes for your gun. Also check the mouth. A common gangbanger tactic is to conceal a razor blade between the gum and cheek. It can be quickly manipulated out by the tongue and then clenched by the front teeth for a slashing attack.

Commandment 5: Before reaching into any area, look! At this writing, relatively few courier cars have actually been found to be booby trapped with explosives or other dangerous surprises. But we know that marijuana fields are, to discourage rip-offs as well as foil law enforcement. It's only a matter of time before the same deadly tricks are used extensively to protect vehicles.

With the right tools and tactics, you can get a preview of even the darkest, hardest-to-reach spots that you need to search in a vehicle. It's safer to let your eyes make an initial assessment of any location than to grope up or in blindly with your hands or fingers. One officer reached into a duffel bag and grabbed a boa constrictor that was guarding a supply of marijuana! (A wide variety of dangerous reptiles are commonly used in transporting drugs, a university study has confirmed.[2] Sometimes contraband is concealed in cages of poisonous snakes to discourage searching; other times snakes are force-fed drug packets and are tormented or mutilated to make them superaggressive when approached.)

Commandment 6: Beware of possible setups by "cooperative" suspects. Some subjects readily consent to a search, then try to guide your attention. At the very least, this is probably an attempt at "verbal masking," an effort to direct you away from stash sites.

A fifty-seven-year-old Cuban male who was ticketed by a Mississippi deputy for following too closely eagerly offered the officer his keys immediately upon giving consent. "You want to search my trunk?" he kept asking. Apparently he was hoping the deputy would assume that the trunk must be "clean" and skip it. The deputy didn't bite, fortunately. Hidden among children's clothes in a suitcase in the trunk, he found 121 pounds of compressed marijuana; it was the rest of the car that was clean. A Colorado driver stopped in South Dakota hurriedly cleared out several moveable items from his camper so a trooper could have a "better look." One thing he removed was a fish-and-beer cooler, which he stood beside throughout the search. That's where the trooper eventually found over seven pounds of marijuana. On a stop in the East, a passenger who said he was a cop from

Florida flashing a badge and volunteered to search the car himself.! The sergeant who'd made the stop politely declined—and under the backseat found two kilos of coke.

Sometimes a diversion is a prelude to attack. A suspect in Georgia volunteered to cut open a taped container, ostensibly to prove to an officer that there was nothing suspicious inside. Actually the suspect was hauling 300 grams of cocaine. As the officer moved closer to look in the box, the suspect spun toward him with the knife and threatened to slash him. The officer reacted fast enough to shoot the assailant in the abdomen, but the man kept fighting as if he hadn't even been hit. At one point he had the officer on the ground, trying to disarm him. He was not controlled until a passing citizen stepped in and helped subdue him.

Step-by-Step up the Criminal Patrol Pyramid

John LeBlanc, trooper first class with the Louisiana State Police, was about to give up on a consent search as unproductive when an attempted diversion by the suspect—a la Commandment 6—convinced him to look a little longer. The result was the bust of his career.

The case began about noon on a hot July day when an eleven-year-old Ford station wagon blew past LeBlanc at 75 mph in a 65-mph zone. LeBlanc was driving to the state crime lab to deliver B.A.C. kits. He decided to ticket the driver for speeding.

As soon as the cars came to a stop, contraband cues began piling up in textbook fashion.

Immediately the Hispanic driver exited his vehicle and hurried toward LeBlanc's unit. At the same time, the trooper noticed a man's head pop up in the front seat and look back at him. He assumed the passenger had been slumped down, sleeping. LeBlanc asked the driver if he spoke English. "Poquito," the driver replied—a little. LeBlanc said he spoke a bit of Spanish, and with a little English from the driver and a little Spanish and sign language from LeBlanc, they communicated.

The driver presented a New York driver's license, but the station wagon carried New Jersey plates. Registration papers showed a third-party owner: "a friend," the driver said. The driver himself claimed to be an unemployed mechanic and said that he and the passenger were "on vacation." How can a man without a job afford a pleasure trip? LeBlanc wondered, but he said nothing. What he was most conscious of at the moment was a peculiar, powerful aroma of spicy food that hung about the driver; the guy smelled like a pizzeria!

As dialogue continued, LeBlanc noticed that the driver and the passenger frequently established eye contact with each other. The driver's hands were shaking, which LeBlanc pointed out. "Are you nervous?" he asked. The driver said he was just tired; he'd been driving long hours without sleep.

The passenger, monitored in LeBlanc's peripheral vision, seemed even more nervous and agitated than the driver, a contrast with ordinary vehicle stops where the driver is most stressed because he's about to receive a ticket. LeBlanc decided to approach the vehicle.

As he got close, he sniffed the same odor he'd noticed on the driver wafting from the open windows, but stronger. On past stops, LeBlanc had discovered such things as Mexican laundry detergent and ripe bananas used to mask the scent of drugs. He knew smugglers often overdo it.

With the driver's consent to search documented on a Spanish-language consent form, LeBlanc patted down both occupants. No weapons. Then he had them stand fifteen feet in front of their vehicle to create a barrier between them and him. Glancing up frequently to confirm that they were still in position, he then searched the station wagon, following a pattern he has found works well for him: doors first, seats second, glove box third, then the rear of the vehicle.

By the time he reached the back, LeBlanc had found nothing illegal. A colorful piñata was lying on the back floor, but it seemed too lightweight to have anything hidden inside. LeBlanc tossed it aside. He called the driver back and asked him if the bottom compartment of the station wagon opened. The driver, who now seemed extremely nervous, ignored the question and grabbed the discarded piñata. He tore one of the legs off and handed the animal to LeBlanc, telling him he could look inside and see that there was nothing there.

Now, LeBlanc figured, I must be close to something. He commanded the driver back in front of the vehicle and tried to remove the side panels in the rear of the wagon. He couldn't get them off readily, so he took his screwdriver and removed a stereo speaker that was mounted in one of the panels. He shined his flashlight into the hole and spotted what looked like a package.

Coated with what appeared to be a pungent, greasy mixture of black pepper and garlic, it was too slippery to tug out. LeBlanc thrust his screwdriver into the package and pulled out a tiny mound of white powder on the blade which tested positive for cocaine.

In all, he recovered 172 packages of coke weighing 378 pounds, with a value later estimated at $17,000,000—the second largest haul of contraband drugs in the history of Louisiana.

Searching Occupants

If you have not yet established PC for an arrest and are going to be searching the vehicle under voluntary consent, you will be limited legally in the extent to which you can check the occupant(s) themselves. Just because you suspect someone is transporting contraband in a vehicle does not automatically give you the right even to frisk that individual, just as having legal grounds to stop a subject does not automatically give you the right to frisk him or her[3] (although this is one of the most common misconceptions among officers).

Understanding what you can do regarding a frisk will not only keep your actions legal at the scene, but will help you articulate them properly in your report so they'll be seen as legal later if they're challenged in court.

You have two possible justifications for frisking:

1. You or your backup reasonably conclude that the subject may be armed and dangerous to your safety. If you can specifically articulate reasons why you reached that conclusion, you can pat down or crimp his or her outer clothing to locate and then seize weapons that might be used to assault you.[4] You must actually feel apprehensive about your safety and you should say so in your report. What you can seize includes not just obvious weapons, like guns or knives, but any object that reasonably could be used to assault and injure you. The subject's permission, of course, is not necessary for this pat-down, but normally you cannot initially go into pockets, hat bands, or inner clothing, as you can on a custodial, full-body, exploratory search. The only exceptions would be when:

- Outer clothing is too bulky to let you determine whether a weapon is concealed, in which case outer clothing such as coats may be opened to permit a direct frisk of the inner clothing, such as shirts, trousers, et cetera;

- You have a reasonable belief, based on reliable information or your own observation, that a weapon is concealed in a particular location on the person, such as a pocket, waistband, or sleeve. Then you may reach directly into the suspected area. This is an unusual procedure, though, and you must be prepared to cite the precise factors that led you to act in this manner.[5]

To justify a normal frisk, a reasonable suspicion that a person is armed might be based, among other things, on seeing the suspect make furtive or threatening movements into or toward his clothing during the stop or extraction from the vehicle...the sound or sight of a weapon...the discovery of a weapon or weapon indicator nearby... the suspect's appearance, such as wearing clothing or carrying items that are capable of concealing a weapon...bulges in the suspect's clothes suggestive of weapons or body armor...records information regarding past involvement in weapons-related offenses...a reliable informant's tip or your personal knowledge that the suspect is armed or is known or reputed to carry weapons or act violently...the fact that you are in a high-crime neighborhood where guns are common or are alone in an isolated or hostile spot where you are unlikely to receive help if attacked...darkness or poor lighting conditions that may improve a subject's ability to assault you...the need for you as a single officer to handle multiple suspects...statements by the suspect, other occupants, or other witnesses…in some cases, even the suspect's extreme nervousness, refusal to follow orders, or untruthful answers to questions. If you are alone and intend to violate Commandment 1 by searching a vehicle without backup, you may be able to justify a pat-down by explaining that the subject had to be outside your immediate control during the search and if armed, could easily kill you.

Note: Just knowing or suspecting that a subject is in the narcotics trade is not necessarily enough by itself to legally justify a pat-down. We know traffickers are a threat to officer survival, but courts do not universally accept as a general premise that a drug-dealing affiliation in and of itself is reasonable cause for frisking.[6] Check with your prosecutor for the opinion and precedent in your jurisdiction, as well as for other unique limitations your state may impose on frisks.

2. There is no reason to believe the occupants are armed and dangerous, but you ask their consent to frisk. This can be done lightly, just like you may have asked permission to search the vehicle: "You don't have any guns, knives, bazookas, or other weapons on you personally, do you?" When the suspect says "No," ask if it's okay to pat him down "just for my reassurance and safety, so nobody gets hurt." Obviously, a refusal to let you frisk is a significant danger cue.

With his consent, you have better grounds for asking him to open his jacket and pull up his pants legs so you can check in boots, et cetera. In fact, in consensual circumstances, you can explain that you'd like to check him, as well as his vehicle, for drugs, in addition to weapons. If he agrees, you can then go into pockets and other places where people typically carry narcotics. Some courts have ruled that unless the suspect objects, this includes feeling the crotch area through clothing, since both guns and drugs are often concealed there.[7] (Officers in some urban areas have testified that 75% of their drug recoveries come from this area. In hopes of avoiding inspection there, some subjects may deliberately wet their pants.)

Always ask the suspect if he or she has any weapons or "anything else that can hurt me." If he says he does, then you can frisk and retrieve it regardless of consent. It doesn't matter that the weapon may be legal for him to possess; you're still entitled to conduct your investigation of the vehicle without fear of unexpected violence from the subject. If the instrument is legal and no arrest results, you can return it when you release him. Be sure to ask specifically if he or she

Creative but Not Correct

When the passenger exited a car that had been pulled over in Florida, the officer noticed a large bulge in the subject's genital area. Rather than touch the bulge on a protective frisk, the officer decided to play on male pride.

He remarked with amazement on the size of the bulge. "I've never seen anything like that," he told the passenger. "I'm curious. Would you show 'it' to me?" The passenger responded by unsnapping and unzipping his pants and pulling his underwear away from his stomach.

Using a flashlight, the officer peered in. In addition to whatever else he saw, he spotted a brown, opaque plastic bag marked Toys "Я" Us. The suspect wouldn't say what was in the bag. So the officer retrieved it and looked inside. There he found a second bag containing cocaine.

Not good, an appellate court decided. The officer lacked PC for opening and seizing the bag. Said the court: "Seeing a bag stuffed into the genital area of someone's underwear is highly suspicious even to the average citizen. But

without testimony that the location, type of packaging, or other articulable facts led [the officer] to reasonably believe that the bag contained contraband, his suspicion never rose to the level of probable cause."[8]

Under the circumstances, the officer should have obtained the suspect's consent to search the bag. Since the subject was cooperative enough to show off "Big Ed," he might have been persuaded to go along with the officer peeking into the bag, too.

is carrying a pocket knife or any other knives; many people do not automatically think of a knife as a weapon. Also ask if they're carrying any needles. Some courts have held that hypodermic needles are dangerous weapons, subject to removal during a pat-down.[9] If a suspect denies having a weapon, you can advise him: "If I find anything, I'm really going to be mad, and it may qualify as carrying a concealed weapon." This may prompt a preemptive response.

Watch for revealing body language. A suspect who's carrying something often will tend to turn that side away from you, hoping if you pat him down that you'll only check his "safe" side.

Assuming your pat-down falls within Category 1 (an involuntary frisk), can you recover drugs, drug packages, or drug paraphernalia during it? Under some circumstances, yes.[10] But there may be some hair-splitting involved from a legal standpoint.

Legally, the purpose of a frisk is not to discover evidence of crime but only to locate weapons. However, the Supreme Court has confirmed a "plain feel" doctrine[11] analogous to the plain view doctrine discussed in Chapter 4. That is: If during a lawful frisk you feel something through the suspect's clothing that you immediately identify by your tactile sensation as contraband—recognizing by feel a small lump as a crack rock, say—you then have PC to extract and seize it. The questionable item need not feel like a possible weapon or present any threat to you. But its incriminating nature must be "readily apparent" because of its contour or mass, without further examination.

You might assume that this means you must recognize the item as contraband the instant you touch it. But some prosecutors have interpreted the Court's decision more liberally. They say you can manipulate an item in the suspect's clothing as long as it takes for you to be convinced it is not a weapon. But then at the moment you reach that conclusion, you must recognize it as contraband, based on your training and experience, to meet the Court's "immediately apparent" standard.[12] If the subject is not yet in circumstances that constitute Miranda custody, you may ask him what the item is without issuing a Miranda warning, and he may tell you.[13] Otherwise, you are expected to pass on. If you must continue to manipulate and squeeze or withdraw and visually examine it to tell that it is contraband, then you are not constitutionally entitled to seize it.

On the other hand, if you feel something you think is a weapon, you may seize it, even if the object turns out to be contraband or other evidence and not a weapon. The seizure is lawful so long as your initial belief that it was a weapon was "objectively reasonable." Courts have said that officers should be allowed "wide latitude" in examining hard objects that may be weapons.[14] You may even open closed containers (like a flip-top cigarette box) that you discover during your pat-down, if you can articulate some basis for believing they may contain a weapon (like a razor blade in the cigarette box, for instance). However, if you think the container probably holds contraband and not a weapon, you'll need the suspect's consent or a warrant to open it legally, unless the contents are clearly obvious by plain view, plain touch, or smell.[15]

If the item you find actually is a weapon, you may have grounds for arrest for carrying a concealed weapon. Then you could escalate your search. In other words, you would then be entitled to search the suspect thoroughly for contraband as well as other weapons, as a search incident to his or her arrest.

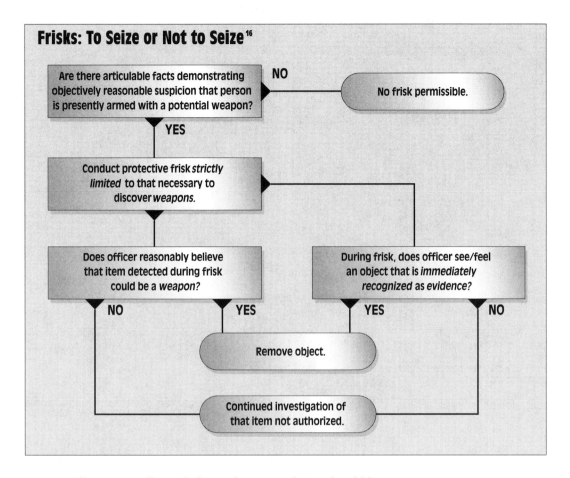

Frisks: To Seize or Not to Seize [16]

Are there articulable facts demonstrating objectively reasonable suspicion that person is presently armed with a potential weapon?

NO → No frisk permissible.

YES

Conduct protective frisk *strictly limited* to that necessary to discover *weapons.*

Does officer reasonably believe that item detected during frisk could be a *weapon?*

During frisk, does officer see/feel an object that is *immediately recognized* as evidence?

NO **YES** **YES** **NO**

Remove object.

Continued investigation of that item not authorized.

Tactically, many officers believe that a pat-down should begin at the top, with the suspect's head or hat, and work down, systematically covering each side of the body. This thorough approach works well for a search incident to arrest, where the suspect is restrained and you are entitled to be complete. But when you approach the head first on a mere frisk, many people become defensive, as this is a particularly sensitive violation of personal space.

For a seemingly cooperative and nonthreatening subject, consider starting your frisk on the right side, checking front and back along the waistband, and including pockets. Most people are right-handed and you will most often recover weapons on the right side. When that is completed, check the left side and other areas the subject can reach without bending or contorting. Then frisk down his legs and feet and leave his head for last. Even though he may seem low-risk, stand so you are not in front of him, in his area of control (i.e., not in his "inside" position). And pay attention. "Too often, officers do pat-downs like they're not expecting to find anything," observes one trainer.

With subjects you believe are dangerous, you can escalate your control measures, including having them prone out, if justified. Do not, however, resort to the outmoded but enduring prop-search or wall-search positioning. This is as hazardous for pat-downs as it is for full-fledged searches, because of the suspect's ability to use the prop surface as a platform for attacking you. Assess the frisks pictured here:

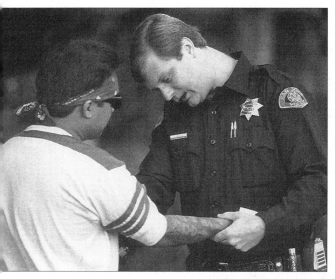

(above)
Officer stands in the "inside position" examining a suspected drug user. A safer position is to stand at an angle to the rear, which makes it harder for a suspect to assault you.

(top right)
Danger in numbers. If you were the suspect in the middle, would you be able to take this agent right now? Suspects are too close to each other. Consider a kneeling position for frisking, or peeling one off at a time to frisk, while keeping a visual on the others.

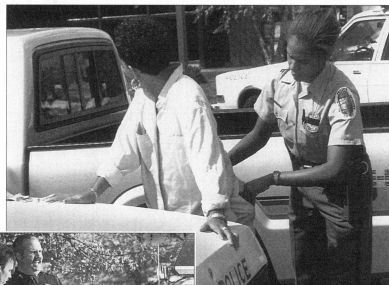

(above)
Both of this subject's hands are free, while the officer's hands are occupied. "Propping" a suspect offers no real restraint or control.

(left)
These officers probably think they've put the suspect at great disadvantage. But is he really off-balance? Is either of his hands controlled? If he were to drop and roll, the officers are at risk. Only one is even watching the suspect.

Option to counter resistance during a frisk. The subject spreads his legs and arms. You control the arm nearest you with a wrist grip. If you sense resistive tension, you can use an arm bar to bring him to the ground.

307

A variation that allows you to escalate rapidly into a takedown. If he tries to pull away or disobey, leverage him back by buckling his leg with your knee. Using your hip as a fulcrum, you'll knock the suspect off-balance and he'll slide down your leg to the ground.

For higher-risk subjects, the Faulkner frisk greatly reduces the ability to turn and attack you during contact. Suspect interlaces fingers behind his back, while you maintain distance to assess cooperation. Slip your hand behind his and grip his interlocked fingers firmly with your palm, fingers, and thumb. Quickly rotate your hand up and back toward you. This tilts him backward and off-balance. Frisk one side, change hands, frisk the other.

You may be able to handcuff a suspect during frisking, even though you have not yet arrested him—if you can articulate why you believe your safety or that of your backup would be in jeopardy otherwise. Generally, cuffing during an investigative stop can be justified when a serious offense is involved or when there is reasonable risk of flight, resistance, or violent behavior by the suspect.[17] Once you have confirmed that a suspect is not armed, however, the cuffs normally should be removed, unless you have reason to believe that he continues to pose a threat while you search the vehicle.

Although normally associated with arrest, handcuffing does not per se mean you have arrested him. Nor does placing him in a patrol car or even holding the subject at gun point. For example, when a Southern deputy stopped a car with three occupants speeding near a marijuana field, one of the suspects became belligerent and verbally abusive. All were then held at shotgun point until two eventually were taken into custody. A federal appeals court found that covering the suspects with the gun—including the suspect who was eventually freed—was reasonable, nonexcessive force and did not itself constitute arrest.[18] When you feel it is necessary to restrain a suspect without arresting him, it is best to inform him directly that he is not under arrest and is being cuffed, confined, or drawn down on only for safety reasons during your investigation.

As you're evaluating what you're feeling during a frisk, stay alert for clothing that seems unusually stiff or neatly pressed. Some traffickers starch their clothes with a cocaine-laden mixture that can be ironed into the fabric and then liquefied and extracted at the end of the run. Also keep money in mind. One smuggler brags that he can pack $100,000 worth of twenties in $5,000 packages into a built-in zipper compartment in the back of a lightweight nylon ski coat. Others remove down filling to create space or use money belts or overcoats with special compartmentalized linings that let them covertly carry fifty to eighty pounds of cash—some or all of which might be felt on a pat-down.

Be sure to pat down each person associated with the vehicle, including infants. With babies as with adults, suspicious bulges in clothing can be reasonable grounds for a pat-down. Or ask a parent's consent. A North Carolina deputy had stopped a car with a couple and their baby and was just about to start searching the vehicle when the woman asked if she could change the baby's diaper first. The request seemed so conveniently timed that the deputy decided to inspect the bag she shoved the dirty diaper into. It was like sticking his hand down a privy, but buried among a tangle of fouled cloths, he found a cache of drugs. "Check babies, baby bags, baby seats, baby diapers, baby clothing, boxes of baby wipe cloths, anything associated with a baby in any suspicious car you stop," the deputy advises. "Cops see a kid in half-shitty diapers, crying, and they think, 'Oh God, let me get outa here.' That's precisely why couriers use them."

Don't feel hesitant about frisking suspects of the opposite sex, if it's not feasible to use an officer who's the same gender as the suspect. Male officers, especially, are often reluctant even to touch a woman's coat or ask her to remove it, despite the fact that female associates of criminals are notorious as weapons carriers. But if you frisk professionally, court precedent will likely back you up. A female drug suspect in Michigan sued a male officer for patting her down, claiming he touched her breast inside her jacket, rubbed his hands on the inside of her thighs, and grazed her genital area. However, a federal court stated that the practice of male officers frisking female suspects—even in misdemeanor circumstances—is not unconstitutional.[19] Use better judgment, though, than officers with a drug task force in Tennessee. They strip-searched two sisters in the back seat of a patrol car during a vehicle stop. The dome light and a flashlight were on, the door was open, and city traffic was passing by about six feet away. No weapons or drugs were found. Not surprisingly, a court declared this to be an "unreasonable and out-rageous" violation of the women's constitutional rights.[20]

Include in your pat-down any articles the suspect is carrying, such as a purse or briefcase, if at all possible. Again you'll need consent or reasonable suspicion that they contain a dangerous instrument. Otherwise they should be placed in a secure location (such as your patrol car) for the duration of your stop. Inspecting such objects is often worth the effort. Two officers stopped a rental car speeding down a state highway in California, carrying three men and a female juvenile. The occupants smelled of alcohol, there were open beer cans in the car, and the girl held a pizza carton—intimations at first flush of a common mobile party. But the girl seemed unusually pos-sessive of the carton. When the officers peered inside, they under-stood why—the pizza's unusual topping: a clear plastic bag filled with $50,000 worth of cocaine. In Indiana, a driver about to be frisked said he first wanted to "get my money." He then pulled a wad of bills and a film canister from his sock, tossing the canister aside. An officer retrieved it, and inside found felony-size chunks of crack cocaine.

Remember to secure any weapons, as well as contraband, that you recover. A Mississippi Highway Patrolman discovered a boot knife and a vial of pills on a suspicious driver he patted down after a speed-ing stop. The trooper shoved the pills into his pocket, but he laid the knife on the roof of his patrol car, apparently thinking that was far enough removed to be out of reach. Without calling backup or restraining the driver and three passengers, the trooper then began to search the car. While he was bending in to feel under seats, a female passenger who'd gotten out to talk to the driver grabbed the knife unobserved and passed it to the driver. He rushed up behind the troop-er and stabbed him in the back. In the struggle that followed, the offi-cer was disarmed, shot in the face with his own .357 Magnum, and left in a ditch to die.

Contact/Cover

With backup at hand, you can employ the tactic of Contact/Cover to enhance your Position of Advantage during the suspect pat-down and the subsequent vehicle search. This involves a critical division of labor: Whoever the two of you designate as Contact Officer conducts the "business" of the encounter—frisking the subject(s) and carefully exploring the vehicle for hidden contraband. The Cover Officer con-centrates on watching and controlling the occupants for the protection of himself and the Contact Officer.

Because of his positioning and undistracted attention to the sus-pects, the Cover Officer conveys a silent but powerful warning that he is ready to respond effectively should they present any threat to you or him. It is this unspoken, intimidating "force presence" by your Cover that lets you concentrate on the pat-down(s) and search, with confi-dence in your security. It eliminates both of you trying to do a little of everything and ending up missing something important, like a danger cue signaling an imminent attack.

Using a Cover Officer can safeguard you legally, too. With a consent search, the driver needs to be where he can order the search halted at anytime, but tactically you probably won't want him close to you while you're searching. If the Cover Officer is with him, that still allows an avenue of communication, even though he is isolated from you and the vehicle.

Also the Cover Officer can continue dialogue with the suspect(s) while you search. If the encounter is being recorded by in-car video, this is an opportunity to see more of the suspect lying and contradicting himself or a passenger on camera. Where there's no camera, the Cover Officer being able to elicit the same kinds of statements from the suspect that you did will support your word in court.

Ideally, the Cover Officer stands where he or she has a visual of the occupants, of you, and of the vehicle you're searching. This holds even if one or more of the suspects is handcuffed and is in the back seat of a caged patrol car. The Cover wants the occupants in his line of fire, without you being in crossfire. He should be close enough that he can move in quickly to physically control them if necessary. Yet he should maintain a sufficient reactionary gap so he does not invite sudden attack.

Without an effective Cover Officer, you have the potential for disaster, as in this armed confrontation captured on in-car video. (1) Contact Officer (arrow) is caught in a standoff with passenger, who produces a gun during questioning, while unsecured driver (foreground) looks on. (2) Rather than promptly securing and monitoring driver, Cover Officer divides his focus and deploys sidearm indecisively. (3) At one point, he even turns his back on driver, leaving himself and Contact Officer vulnerable. Before this incident was resolved, passenger was shot. Contact Officer, fortunately, was not injured.

(top left/right)
Effective Contact/Cover. Cover Officer monitors suspect during frisk and placement in patrol car.

(above)
During search, Cover Officer stands where he can watch and hear suspect, while keeping a visual on Contact Officer and suspect vehicle.

(left)
Where suspect remains outside during search, he should ideally be positioned between Cover Officer and suspect vehicle, not watching the search. This Cover Officer would be safer to keep both the suspect's hands in sight.

313

Responsibilities on an Investigative Vehicle Stop

CONTACT OFFICER

1. Obtains consent to search after issuing traffic citation or warning.
2. Quickly briefs backup on the circumstances, out of earshot of the suspect(s).
3. Performs pat-down(s) of suspect(s).
4. Searches vehicle.
5. Recovers evidence or contraband.
6. Handles routine radio communications.
7. Handcuffs and searches all arrestees.

COVER OFFICER

1. Closely observes suspect(s) to discourage hostile acts.
2. Watches for escort vehicles.
3. Discourages escape.
4. Converses with suspects during search for statements useful to search or in court.
5. Listens and watches for dialogue and stress cues from suspect(s) during vehicle search.
6. Alerts Contact Officer to any attempt to hide, discard, or destroy evidence.
7. Resists distraction.
8. Intervenes with force if necessary to protect self or Contact Officer.

"Cover Officer" patiently sits among 4 unsecured suspects while their car is searched for cocaine.

Do you see him performing any of the 8 responsibilities of a good Cover Officer?

In this situation, the Cover Officer (arrow) is actively engaged in maintaining control. He monitors these suspected street-gang members who have been adequately spaced on the curb with their legs crossed to reduce mobility. Contact Officer is in foreground out of view.

One option for discouraging assault by multiple suspects who are not cuffed or caged is to seat them on a curb or on the roadside shoulder.

Command them to cross their ankles to inhibit sudden mobility, and to sit far enough apart that they can't touch, to prevent weapons or contraband from being passed. Position them where they can't quickly reach cover, like rolling under or behind your patrol car.

Seated or standing, the suspects, if possible, should be facing away

314

from their vehicle. This prevents them from having a steady, precise fix on your location as Contact Officer. In case you missed a gun during your pat-down, better to have them at a visual disadvantage should they decide to attack. If from their position they are able to watch you closely, that may mean that your Cover Officer is not in a position where he can see them and you well. And if they're watching your every move, that may also spur them to withdraw consent to search before you find the goods.

Seasoned Criminal Patrol officers say that subjects who are guilty of transporting contraband will often sneak peeks at areas where the contraband is hidden. They want to reassure themselves that it's still concealed. Otherwise, they are usually eager to distance themselves from the search; they don't want to be associated with what may be found. When they're asked, "Whose suitcase is this?" they may just shrug or claim they never saw it before. In contrast, innocent parties generally want to get close to the searching officer; they're intrigued about where he's looking and what he's finding. Of course from a tactical standpoint, you probably won't want them close, but their apparent desire can be noted by your Cover Officer.

Besides keeping subjects diverted from thinking about withdrawing consent, the "idle" conversation your Cover has with them may engender other cues. During the search of a camper beside a lake in Arkansas, the Contact Officer slipped into the water. A suspect heard the splash and exclaimed to the Cover Officer: "What happened? Did he drop some of our marijuana in the lake and go after it?" By watching and listening, a savvy Cover Officer "can read a suspect like a drug dog's tail wagging," says one Criminal Patrol specialist.

The speech pattern of guilty persons may change as the search progresses. So long as you are checking out "cold" parts of the vehicle, a suspect who manages to sneak a glance at your location from time to time may be relatively willing to engage in casual comments with your Cover. When you start getting closer to where the payload is stashed, the suspect may become more nervous and start asking your Cover questions, like: "How much longer is this going to take?" or "Doesn't he need a warrant to do that?" The closer you get to the stash, the more silent the suspect then tends to become. "When he clams up completely," says one officer, "you're there."

A trooper in Iowa confirmed this when he stopped two males for speeding. They said they'd already been stopped and searched unsuccessfully in Utah. When the Iowa officer started his search, the two were joking and laughing. But when he got to the trunk, they turned stone serious...silent. As soon as he moved on to another part of the car, they resumed their banter. This sent him back to the trunk for a second look. And this time *he* was laughing. Down around the wheel well, he found thirty pounds of high-grade marijuana, tightly wrapped in cylindrical form.

Should the suspect happen to be looking in your direction at the moment you "hit," chances are he'll automatically turn away—"doing the twist," one Criminal Patrol officer calls it—as if he can't bear to watch you find his load. During a search in Illinois, a suspected courier focused intently on the K-9 sniffing through his camper. Initially he remarked on how beautiful the dog was and made other fawning comments about it. Then as soon as the dog started clawing at the roof where drugs were concealed, the driver suddenly discovered a "prob lem" with the trailer he was towing that required him to get down and look under it—a version of the twist. Other times, the subject may shrug and throw up his hands in a give-up gesture.

If a suspect knows you've detected something incriminating, the crisis of that moment may trigger an assault. A verbal code worked out with your backup in advance can buy time to tighten controls and lessen the danger. Codes that mean "I've found something" or "Something's about to happen" can keep each of you apprised of important developments and give you both a chance to get prepared for potentially violent moments, without telegraphing an alert to the suspect. (Don't use 10-codes, though; street-smart suspects will understand them.) Regardless of what may be discovered as the search progresses, neither of you should betray enthusiasm or excitement to suspects at that point. You're usually safest with the suspects in the dark about the specifics of how successful you're being until later.

You and your partner can switch roles during the stop. The Cover Officer may note an area that you have missed, or he or she may pick up something in conversation with the suspects that arouses curiosity about a fresh area. You may find something in the car that you think will promote revealing dialogue with the suspects, or you may just want a fresh set of eyes and hands to range over the vehicle. Just remember: *At all times, one of you must be actively monitoring all suspects, without distraction.*

Where more than two officers are at the scene, it's better to deploy additional Cover Officers rather than have extra Contact Officers involved in the search, unless you are dealing with a large vehicle like a semitrailer where an area of responsibility for each officer can be clearly designated. Otherwise, multiple officers may only create confusion, getting in each other's way, increasing the risk that some potential hiding spots will be missed, and possibly compromising the chain of evidence if anything is found.

Covert Tape Recording

If the suspects are confined to your patrol car during your search, in addition to having your Cover Officer watch them consider the tactical edge you can get by surreptitiously turning on a tape recorder and leaving it on your front seat. (This is in addition to any recording you may make of the suspects' comments during your concealed interrogation.) Even if the audio you capture turns out not to be used in court, it could still make your day.

One city-county drug task force in eastern Arkansas has recorders mounted in the front seat console of its patrol cars, with a high-powered microphone discreetly attached to the prisoner screen. Here's how that worked the day a van with a father and his eleven-year-old son was pulled over for speeding:

As soon as the van came to a stop, the boy jumped out and ran toward the patrol car, crying. He was afraid for his father, he sobbed, but the officers calmed him down and assured him everything would be okay. After issuing a citation and gaining consent to search, they asked the father and son to wait in the back of the cruiser.

The officers found a Rottweiler loose in the van, so the search was at best cursory. They discovered nothing illegal and let the two go. Then they played back the audio tape. They heard the kid, now completely composed, telling the father he was afraid the cops were going to find their drugs! The father agreed that if the officers looked very hard, they were going to jail.

Immediately, the officers kicked into pursuit and pulled the van over for an instant replay. This time, they ignored the kid when he turned on the tears again...an animal control officer was called to handle the dog...and in the back of the van, sitting in the open, the officers found eighty pounds of marijuana.

An officer in New York State captured something even more startling on his tape recorder. Working alone, he left it on his front seat when he started searching, thinking the three suspects in the back of his unit might reveal where they'd hidden their contraband. Instead, when he retrieved the recorder and played the tape back out of their earshot, he heard them plotting how to overpower and kill him.

He then did what he should have done in the first place—got some backup there and used the proven survival principles of Contact/Cover.

Defense attorneys will usually vigorously attack recordings surreptitiously made in patrol cars, claiming they violate a suspect's constitutional rights. They'll argue that the taping is a form of self-incrimination, is invalid because no Miranda warnings were given, intrudes on the suspect's privacy, and so on. A good prosecutor should be able to defeat these arguments in court.

State laws vary regarding eavesdropping, but the U. S. Supreme Court has ruled that simply placing suspects in situations where they are likely to incriminate themselves does not, in and of itself, amount to a constitutional violation.[21] Secret recordings of conversations between suspects are *not* the same as unlawful custodial interrogation, the Court has said. Comments among suspects in the back seat of a patrol car are spontaneously made to another civilian, not responses to questioning by an officer. Miranda warnings are not necessary if the suspect is conversing with another nonofficial individual. Moreover, other courts have ruled that a suspect does not have a reasonable expectation of privacy in a police vehicle or other "government space." Make sure that you don't say or suggest that conversations in your car will be private, as that may muddy the situation.[22]

Single-Officer Search Tactics

Many officers ignore the Survival Commandment about having backup present, and not only frisk suspects but also search vehicles all alone. They perceive backup to be too far away, too busy, too inexperienced, too inept—or simply nonexistent. And in their imperfect world—whether real or imagined—they are willing to accept the significantly higher risks of working investigative stops by themselves, from start to finish.

Incarcerated drug couriers interviewed for this book were asked when they most likely would choose to attack an officer working alone, given the opportunity. The most common answer: when the officer is searching their vehicle.

To search intently and still watch the suspect closely may be impossible for an officer working alone. Divided focus leaves you vulnerable to sneak attack.

If it is your choice (or your necessity) to conduct a search without a Cover Officer, understand that in its larger context your approach is undeniably defective from a tactical standpoint, somewhat like choosing to interview suspects in your front seat. And yet in limited but important ways within that faulty big picture, you can still maintain a level of survival consciousness that could save your life.

First, let your dispatcher know that you are embarking on a single-officer vehicle search. Be sure she or he knows your location and all other relevant information about the suspect vehicle and driver. Also be certain you pat down the suspect as thoroughly as possible before you begin the search.

If you don't feel there are grounds enough for you to order the suspect to sit in your caged patrol car while you search, you still may be able to get him there voluntarily. You will then be safer than if he is free to stand or move wherever he chooses (including directly behind you) while you are absorbed in searching. After the pat-down, ask: "Would you like to have a seat in my car while I'm doing this? You'll be more comfortable." With the right tone, you can make this come across as a directive, although technically you're "inviting" him into your squad for his "benefit."[23]

Of course, if you have no cage, that exposes him to your equipment, including, probably, your shotgun. Also, confining him to your car makes it difficult for him to effectively withdraw his consent during your search, potentially a legal drawback. Officers on one Florida department handle this by not closing the back door completely. The suspect usually either does not notice this or hesitates to leave, even though he's told before the search that he's free to do so. With the door unlatched, he is able to get out and withdraw his consent at any time.

An alternative is to ask the suspect to stand about three or more feet in *front* of his vehicle and stay there. By day, have him face away from the car. At night, you want him facing toward it, so he's looking square into the headlights. Even if he closes his eyes, he will still have temporary blindness if he moves and opens them. As you search inside, pop up frequently to check that he's still there. If he moves, the pattern of light reflected back into the car should change, and the shifting shadows can tip you off.

To eliminate the danger of the suspect wandering into traffic (or traffic "wandering" into him), some officers prefer to have him stand on the passenger side of his vehicle. But there you lose the blinding effect of the lights. If there's a guardrail, you could tell him to step onto the other side of that, so at least there's a barrier working in your favor. If you have a K-9 with you, consider letting the dog watch the suspect as your Cover Officer while you do the searching.

Other possibilities include having the suspect perch on the hood of his car, facing away with his feet resting on the bumper, while you search. You'll feel his movement even if he just shifts his weight. Or tell him to wait about 100 feet up the road till you're done. This buys distance but may invite escape.

Even though they have frisked the suspect, some officers searching alone are too uncomfortable ducking below dashboard or window level, regardless of lights, barricades, or distance. They compromise by conducting their search strictly by "blind feel," keeping their heads up and the suspect always in at least their peripheral vision. However, this violates the Commandment about looking before you touch or reach, and also prevents you from detecting subtle visual cues that may indicate the presence of contraband.

Some officers avoid at least having to crawl beneath a vehicle to search the undercarriage by affixing a broad-surfaced mirror onto a cane-length pole. Then they can glance under the car while they walk slowly around it, without making themselves susceptible to attack by proning out. What they lose in search quality, they gain in Position of Advantage. Likewise, some avoid entering the vehicle all the way, so they can't get trapped inside by a suspect who rushes the car. They lean in through open doorways and search as best they can.

Do not attempt searching alone even with precautions if you are dealing with more than one suspect. Too many things can go wrong for one officer to handle. An escort vehicle may cruise by and launch an ambush. You may have to announce and effect arrests at some point. Can you be aggressive enough, commanding enough, or surprising enough to control all suspects at once, especially when they may know before you do that you're getting close to their stash and they've had time to psyche up for a fight? The difficulty of controlling multiple aggressors is easy to underestimate, until the moment of no return when you're fighting for your life against a barrage of hands and feet—or guns. "I've made the decision more than once to release what I strongly feel were drug couriers because I didn't have backup available," says a municipal officer from Minnesota. "I've never regretted it. No amount of dope is worth dying for."

Two final words about searching alone: Sherman Toler.

In the Tucumcari District of the New Mexico State Police, Officer Sherman Toler Jr. was pepper hot. In scarcely six months, in addition to handling his normal patrol duties, he'd discovered and seized more than $1,000,000 worth of marijuana, cocaine, and PCP, and had been responsible for the forfeiture of nearly a dozen vehicles used in drug smuggling. His efforts produced a laundry list of criminal arrests apart from narcotics, and many of the offenders he'd taken off the highways and byways were armed and dangerous.

His performance was so exceptional that his captain wrote a formal commendation of his work, and one Wednesday in March he called Toler on the phone and read him the handwritten draft before giving it to the typist.

A few hours later, as evening was settling over the desert Interstate, Toler stopped a speeding eastbound Cadillac, carrying a male driver and a female passenger. It looked like a cinch for another score. The driver's inside door panel was missing, and he grudgingly admitted that he'd been stopped and searched twice earlier in the day by other officers looking for drugs. Toler figured he'd take a crack at finding what they must have missed, and got the driver's consent for a third toss.

Whether Toler sensed it or not, the driver was seething. Passing truckers later recalled seeing him making "threatening gestures" at the officer. But Toler persisted with the search alone.

While he was concentrating on a black garment bag in the trunk, with no other cop around to warn him or intervene, the driver attacked. He was physically stronger, a karate instructor and ex-con with an "overwhelming rage" at police officers.[24] He grabbed Toler's .357 Magnum, and Toler, startled, fought to get it back. Toler had a survival hunting knife down in his boot, but he grappled desperately for the gun. "The gun was between us," the driver later testified. "He kept trying to point it toward me. I kept trying to push it away, and it would point toward him."

When he finally wrenched the gun loose, the driver smashed Toler so hard on the back of his head with the barrel that it fractured his skull. Then, "I fired. I kept firing. I fired until it clicked."

Five shots hit the pride of Tucumcari. He was already unconscious from the whipping and probably never knew it. The fatal round tore into his chest at the edge of his vest. He lived, gasping on the concrete, for maybe ten minutes more.

Twenty-seven years old...a wife...twin boys, age three...a baby daughter...a commendation in the typewriter.

If you could ask him, what do you think Sherman Toler would say now about searching without backup?

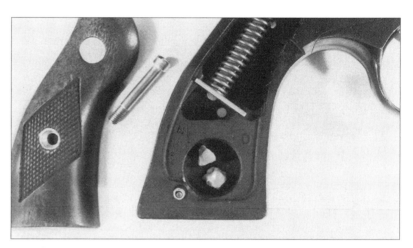

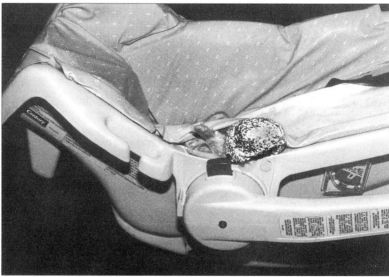

Drugs can be hidden anywhere, anytime, and without any limits on creativity.
(top)
Cocaine rocks were found once a grip was removed from this Ruger revolver in Alabama.
(bottom)
Wrapped inside foil, drugs were hidden under the liner of a car baby seat in North Carolina.

STRATEGIES FOR DISCOVERY

Cars and trucks are like the Trojan horse. They're riddled with natural cavities, and perfect for adding "unnatural" ones. Their design works to the smugglers' advantage, not yours. Thus, discovering efficiently what does not immediately meet your eye about a vehicle becomes perhaps the most difficult part of a successful investigative stop. "It's a game of wits," says an Iowa trooper. "It's the criminals' creativity in hiding stuff against our creativity in finding it."

For some officers, this pressure-cooker phase of Criminal Patrol makes careers. For unfortunate others, it makes widows or widowers. It's these high stakes that bring the rush when you win.

Some officers approach this challenge with just the standard equipment already carried on patrol. Others who've refined vehicle searches into a fine art have compiled tool kits that rival a shade tree mechanic's.

At both ends of the spectrum and in between, the most important "tools" of all, though, are a tactical strategy for searching, a familiarity with how traffickers work, a vivid imagination, patience, and commitment. Whatever you bring to the job beyond that is all gravy.

Searching is like the sensory pat-down of the vehicle and the concealed interrogation you did earlier: You're looking for things—often subtle things—that just don't seem quite right. And you're seeking more than just cocaine and marijuana and their paraphernalia. You may find evidence of other illegal drugs, as well as clues to other crimes. An officer who specializes in Criminal Patrol in the Chicago area says that what you can expect to find, in decreasing order of frequency, are: 1) guns ("You'll be amazed at how many concealed weapons you'll run across"; one study of traffic stops in a violent urban neighborhood in the Midwest showed that officers found an average of one gun in every twenty-eight stops[1]) , 2) drugs, 3) alcohol, 4) drug paraphernalia (needles, razor blades, mirrors, drug packaging), and 5) illicit money. Besides outright contraband, be observant as you search for materials used to process and package drugs. These can be important in building probable cause for continuing the search in case the suspect withdraws consent.

"You can't stop and search cars on a regular basis and not find *anything*," says a North Carolina officer. An Illinois trooper estimates that in 40% to 50% of his searches, somebody goes to jail for *something*.

The first few times you start going through people's vehicles and belongings on a consent search, you're likely to feel uncomfortable doing it. It may seem embarrassingly intrusive. But keep in mind: You're doing it because there's reason to believe that these people are involved in criminal activities. Seeing the process work a time or two will build your confidence and comfort.

Part of the adventure of searching vehicles is knowing that almost anything can be hidden inside. This cache of military firepower, including plastic explosives, was discovered on a vehicle stop in Kansas.

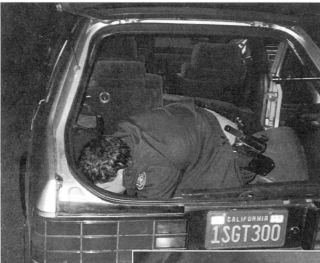

The secret to successful searching is to actively, not passively, get involved. It took this officer (left) searching intently to discover 2 kilos of coke (below) in the rear of this hatchback in Oregon. Imagine the moment of discovery if this had been you.

Tools for Detection

A Southern sheriff's deputy who has recovered millions of dollars in drugs, guns, and "dirty" money on investigative stops estimates that from 60% to 70% of his discoveries are "difficult" finds. In other words, the contraband is hidden in secret compartments, in vehicle body cavities, or in other inconvenient, hard-to-reach spots. Your accessing these places (so long as you don't inflict permanent damage to the vehicle without PC to do so) is not a problem with most courts. As one stated in approving the removal of a door vent: "Any reasonable person would know that the [consent] search of a car's interior for drugs would go beyond a mere 'visual sweep' of the inside of the car."[2]

To be truly thorough and look in the kinds of spots you need to look ideally requires some skill in taking things apart and a few simple hand tools, in addition to what you normally bring on patrol. These can easily be carried in a small canvas bag in your patrol car. Trying to search effectively without them, in the opinion of one trainer, "would be like trying to build a house without a hammer."

Thoughtfully assembling a tool kit for searches will save you time and add to your success. The 2 officers who carry these tool sets on every shift have been responsible for uncovering some of the largest drug seizures in their respective states.

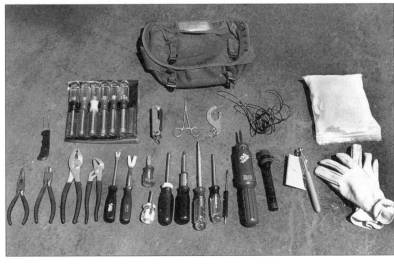

A basic "starter" kit includes:

- A high-intensity miniflashlight, essential even in daytime (the slim barrel lets you hold the light between your teeth when both hands are occupied);

- A small automotive mirror, for peering into hard-to-see-spots (its square or rectangular shape will reveal more of a search area than a round mirror and will also give you a better perception of what you're seeing; a mirror, says one deputy, is "worth its weight in gold ten times");

- A screwdriver set or a battery-operated or ratchet screwdriver with interchangeable tips (besides the conventional Phillips-head and flat tips, you should have a torx-head for removing window cranks and some other parts on some cars);

- A length of firm but flexible wire (like a coat hanger), as a probe;

- Regular and needle-nose pliers;

- A steel tape measure, for checking dimensions on semitrailers, pickup trucks, campers, and other special vehicles;

- Ziploc and large paper bags, for collecting evidence;

- Camera and color film, for documenting your finds.

In time, consider adding:

- A cordless drill (or at least a $1/32$-inch drill bit that can fit into your power screwdriver);

- Socket wrench, crescent wrench, and Allen wrench sets;

- Small crowbar;

- Valve-stem remover;

- A jump wire with alligator clips, for completing electrical circuits to activate lock releases on hidden compartments;

- A flexible, fiber-optic wand attachment for your flashlight (used with your mirror, it will let you see around corners and illuminate other tight places your flashlight alone can't reach);

- A hemostat (from a medical supply house), for picking up things you don't want to touch;

- Field scales (like a digital fish scale), for determining felony amounts of narcotics;

- Cotton-tipped swabs, for collecting drug residue from inside "empty" vials or tubes (any amount of residue may be enough for an arrest or conviction for possession in some jurisdictions[3]).

The more tools you have, of course, the more thorough and efficient you can be. To be absolutely thorough, you can easily double the time you spend searching, to thirty or forty minutes, when you have the volume of calls that permits that. But in reality *even in the absence of any tools, much can still be done and with much less time.* In fact, some officers feel that whipping out tools and starting to unscrew things is a good way to prompt a suspect to change his mind and revoke consent. It's amazing how much of a car you can get apart with just your *hands*—and how much you can find quickly just by using your *eyes.* If 60% to 70% of contraband is difficult to find, that means that 30% to 40% is easy, if a 5%er attitude of curiosity, observation, and determination is in gear.

As you search, be on the lookout for tools you may encounter inside the suspect vehicle that might lead you to a hiding place. Usually couriers carry with them somewhere in the car any tool(s) necessary to open hidden compartments. These will generally be in the glove box or lying in the car; if you find a toolbox, the special tool(s) will usually be marked. One North Carolina officer came across a brand new socket wrench set in a car he was searching, with one of the sockets attached to the ratchet handle. He kept it with him as he moved through the vehicle, trying it against every bolt head he came across to see if it fit. High up under the dash, he finally discovered two bolts that the socket slid onto perfectly. Loosened, they yielded access to a specially constructed compartment containing thousands of dollars in drug-transaction money. In Mississippi, a deputy found a torx-head screwdriver lying on the floor of a car—an unusual tool for the average motorist. He used it like the suspects had used it: to remove a window crank so the inside door panel could be popped off to access the cavity behind it. Sure enough, five kilos of coke were tucked inside. Ask the driver about any extra keys you may notice on his key ring, apart from ignition and trunk keys. Smaller keys, especially, may fit locks to hiding places.

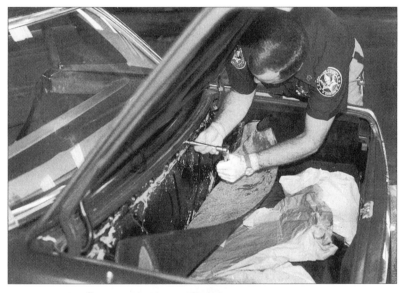

Sometimes tools can be found inside the vehicle, like this socket wrench, which was found to fit bolts on the panel of a special compartment in the trunk.

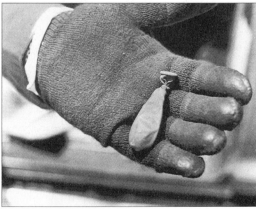

Protective gloves not only may save you from injury from sharp objects while searching but can also serve as a barrier against narcotics absorption when you handle evidence.

Use care in handling tools you find in a vehicle. If they do open up a contraband compartment, your evidence technician may want to try to pull prints off them.

With any tools you use, be careful not to permanently damage the car. If you fail to find contraband, you'll need to release the vehicle in the same condition you started searching it. If you do find something and you can persuade the driver to continue on his run for a controlled delivery, you want the car to appear undamaged so as not to alert the other suspects you hope to net.

Anytime you search, you want to wear gloves. Latex or leather will help keep your skin from becoming contaminated by narcotics; woven-Kevlar gloves with specially treated fingertips worn over a latex pair may provide some additional protection in case you inadvertently jab into needles or other sharp objects. Some of the drugs you may encounter can be easily absorbed through the skin. One officer reportedly used his bare hands to handle LSD blotters that he found in a glove box. Later he turned toward his partner and hallucinated that the other officer was a threatening snake—and shot him. Protective gloves can prevent this kind of tragedy.

Search Patterns

Resist the temptation to "explode" into the car and start tearing everything apart or to jump immediately to some favorite spot where you may have found contraband before. "This is not like going fishing in your favorite part of the lake," explains a California Highway Patrol officer. "Each car is a new lake. Hiding spots vary, just as the people involved vary." Be orderly. Using a consistent, systematic pattern for searching will help assure that you don't overlook any area or forget where you've been or where you're going because of distractions, and it will also help you build speed. Think of the acronym TOM. You want to be:

Thorough

Observant

Methodical.

With passenger cars, the most frequently encountered vehicle for transporting drugs,[4] you want to cover nine search zones or potential zones of concealment:

- The exterior of the vehicle;
- A quadrant inside the vehicle, including all doors;
- The trunk (and its lid);
- The engine compartment (and underside of the hood);
- The roof;
- The underside.

Note: With some obvious modifications, these same search zones pertain as well when you're investigating semitrailers, vans, campers, motor homes, and other types of vehicle.

The sequence you select will depend on the environment around your stop, your time constraints, and your personal preferences, based on what tends to work best, safest, and most comfortably for you.

Some officers like to give the whole car a fast once-over, looking for anything that catches their eye as a place to start, regardless of what zone it happens to be in; or if they've seen something suspicious during their initial approach and dialogue with the driver, they begin there. Some favor a progressive pattern that commences with the driver area and proceeds counterclockwise around—and through—the vehicle. Others like to start on the passenger side and move clockwise, arguing that this better shields them from traffic hazards in both urban and rural settings during the early phases of the search. Still others claim that these approaches are too slow when you're pressed for time and give the suspect too much opportunity to change his or her mind about consent. These officers zero in first on the glove box or the trunk, figuring that the popularity of these spots for concealing contraband offers the best odds of quickly discovering probable cause for arresting the suspect(s) or holding the vehicle for a less pressured search. "Seventy-five per cent of the time you can find something in the passenger compartment that will give you PC for searching the rest of the car, regardless of whether you have consent to do so," claims an Ohio trooper.

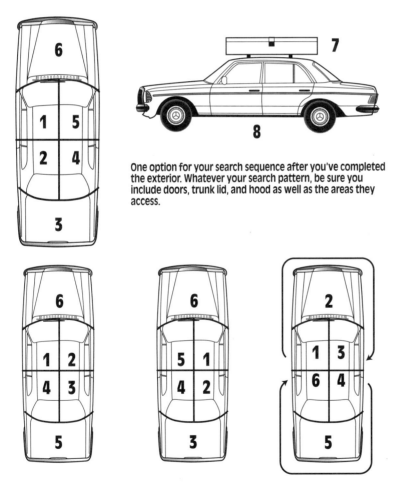

One option for your search sequence after you've completed the exterior. Whatever your search pattern, be sure you include doors, trunk lid, and hood as well as the areas they access.

Alternative patterns for the 6 contiguous search zones. Pattern on right incorporates checking exterior as you move from zone to zone. Try different patterns in the field to determine which one(s) you favor.

More important than any particular order is making certain that before you are finished you search all zones of possible concealment.

Officers who work in protected environments (like secondary inspection areas at border stations) like to get all doors open...the hood up...the trunk lid up before beginning to search, to allow easy access to each section. On the street, however, this is rarely practical or even desirable. Wind whipping through an open car can easily disperse incriminating odors or blow away other evidence. You're better keeping as much of the vehicle closed for as long as possible, opening a door or lid only to gain access to the portion you're actively searching.

Consider having the driver open at least the trunk to reinforce that the consent is voluntary,[5] while you stand off to one side. This also allows you to watch the suspect's reaction. That may buy you some protection against booby traps. An officer working alone in Arkansas, for example, had just taken the keys for a suspected courier car from the driver and was turning to open the trunk when the driver took off running. The officer ran after him—fortunately. When the suspect was caught, he explained that his boss had rigged the trunk lock with blasting caps and several sticks of dynamite. When the key was inserted, the trunk would explode. There were drugs inside...but the officer let the bomb squad find them.

Once the trunk is open, move the suspect to a location where he can be watched by your Cover Officer before you start searching it. Don't permit him to stand there holding the trunk lid, which he could slam down on you, and don't let him rummage in the trunk's contents, where he might retrieve a weapon.

This is not what is meant by the suspect being watched by the Cover Officer after the trunk is opened. These officers watch the search, watch the ground, watch the residence but don't watch the suspect who is standing close to the search, improperly handcuffed. This search, incidentally, resulted in the seizure of cocaine, LSD, Quaaludes, amphetamines, and weapons.

Earlier when asking for consent to search you presumably have gotten him to deny that there are any large sums of money in the vehicle. Give him one more chance to admit it. Tell him: "If you have any large amounts of cash in there, tell me now so you don't have to worry about it blowing down the street or about me stealing it." By denying the presence of money again, he reinforces your right to seize any significant sums you find.

Caution: Some drug suspects train pit bulls and other aggressive-breed dogs to protect their vehicles. The dogs lie quietly within enclosed areas (like trunks or van compartments) and attack anyone other than the owner who opens up the hiding place. Before opening any large, closed compartments, bang on the vehicle and listen for noise from within. Be ready for a nasty surprise. When an officer in Canada opened the trunk of a car driven by a known gang member, he found a man curled up inside with a gun in his hand. This individual was part of an armed robbery team. On holdups, the getaway driver (usually the girlfriend of the gang) would leave the trunk open, the stick-up man would jump in after the heist, and the car would speed away. The officer in this case was quick-witted enough to drop to the pavement before the gunman could pull the trigger.

Zones of Concealment

Each search zone has its unique opportunities for concealment. With at least 975 possibilities known to exist, we can't explore them all, and without infinite time you won't be able to either on any given stop. What follows is not meant to be a comprehensive list of every conceivable place you can or should search in a vehicle. It is merely a sampling that demonstrates the ingenuity of contraband smugglers and some tactics for focusing your search to help you expose them.

Note: In some cases, your search will lead you directly to contraband. In other instances, you may follow cues to a highly suspect area, but to access it and see what's inside will demand significant disassembly and possibly permanent damage to the vehicle. Under those circumstances, unless you are thoroughly experienced and comfortable with Criminal Patrol procedures, you will probably want to hold the vehicle and occupants and seek a search warrant so that you have official judicial sanction before going further. If possible, get a drug-trained K-9 to the scene. If the dog alerts, you'll then have probable cause to justify the necessary probing search.

Keep your in-car video camera running throughout your search. The tape will document matters of time and your behavior and will help refute any accusations that you planted contraband in the vehicle.

Exterior. During a slow, careful outside inspection of the vehicle's four sides, ask yourself:

Is the vehicle tilting to one side or riding unusually low? One old Ford stopped for a traffic violation in Georgia was almost scraping the highway. Officers began checking cavities in the body and around the chassis, and ultimately extracted twenty-eight packages of pot, each about the size of a laundry bundle.

Tap your knuckle on the door panels and quarter panels as you circle the car. Do you hear a uniformly hollow sound, indicating lots of empty air...or a heavy, dull thump, like something solid might be inside? Detecting such a clunk when he rapped the front fenders of one car, an officer found seventy-five pounds of cocaine secreted behind each headlight, in "dope-on-a-rope" packages strung together like sausages. (In most cases, access to quarter panels, one of the most frequent hiding spots for drugs, will be from inside the vehicle.)

Do you see evidence of body work, like welding seams, disturbed metal, fresh paint, silicone caulking, fiberglassing, or Bondo patching?

When you inspect wheel wells, watch for welded seams (arrow) and other metal alterations. When peeled back, this weld accessed a hiding place for 39 kilos of cocaine.

During exterior inspection of this vehicle, stopped for speeding in Kentucky, officer noticed smell of marijuana at the rear of the car. With this as PC, bumper was taken apart, revealing secret metal compartment with 43 lbs. of pot inside.

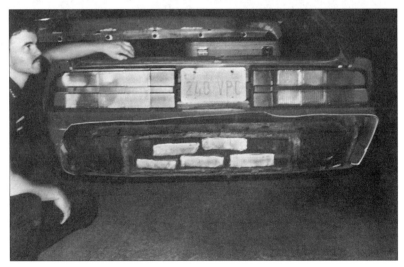

It's unusual for a new car, especially, to have had any legitimate repairs. Examining the exterior of a Volkswagen, a Border Patrol agent noticed a rectangle of steel that appeared to have been cut out, then welded back in place high up in a rear wheel well. When this "trapdoor" was popped open, a cavity loaded with drugs was revealed behind it. On another vehicle, paint on the exterior near the windshield looked fresher than the rest. That area had been cut out to gain access to the ventilation system, then covered with Bondo and sprayed.

Look and feel up inside fenders for contraband or compartments that may be attached there. Is any headlamp obviously out of adjustment, like it has been removed and put back carelessly?

Is there any element of the car that is cleaner or dirtier, newer or older than the rest? If so, you need to wonder why that part is different. Are there fingerprints or smudges on the hubcaps or in unusual places, like on the headlights, taillamp covers, bumpers, or the grille? Closely inspecting a taillight on a station wagon he'd stopped, one officer noticed that the screws holding the cover in place were burred. He backed them out, expecting to find dope hidden behind the light. Instead, he discovered a small plastic panel with a toggle switch. The suspect explained that when the car's brakes were put on, the gears were shifted to reverse, and the switch was then flipped, it electronically released two doors to a secret compartment built under the wagon's cargo area.

On old vehicles, traffickers can easily build hiding places into the oversized bumpers; on newer cars with shock-absorbent bumper systems, they may remove front or back bumpers (or both), take out the Styrofoam or plastic filler that's part of the bumper assembly, and replace it with contraband. Or they use the bumper to cover over trap doors cut into the body of the car. On some models, you can pry the plastic around the bumper apart enough with a screwdriver to look down in with a flashlight and hunt for alterations.

Examine closely as you explore the exterior. Sometimes you'll see two license plates held together by a frame, with thin packages or vials of drugs sandwiched between them. Thousands of dollars worth of contraband can be carried in this way.

What do you see when you open the gas-tank flap? If it's the kind that has the rear license plate framed on it and is hinged to pull down, look first for weapons. Drug transporters, especially street-gang members, sometimes mount a gun or a knife there, so they can quickly flip the flap down and grab the weapon while they are lounging against the back of the car. This is one strong argument for keeping suspects away from you and any part of the vehicle while you're searching.

Stick your flexible probe down the gas tank's filler pipe. On short runs where refueling isn't necessary, couriers may hide contraband in there, inside plastic plumbing pipe that's slightly smaller than the filler pipe's diameter. With most gas flaps open, you'll generally see three bolts or screws holding the filler neck assembly in place. Are these missing, scratched, or burred? If so, they may have been taken out to allow the gas tank to be removed and chocked with drugs. One trooper, sharp-eyed enough to spot peculiar scratches made on one vehicle when the spout was taken in and out, eventually found $140,000 in drug money—plus cocaine residue—in the gas tank and another $25,000 in the glove box. Another officer, after unscrewing a gas cap, found a string with a sealed package tied to the end that had been dropped down into the tank.

Check the windshield wiper trough. This is a common hiding spot
for small quantities of drugs. Some mules add a metal cover over the
trough and paint it to look like part of the car.

Consider bleeding off and sniffing (or having a K-9 sniff) some of the
air in the tires. A developing trend among traffickers is to compress
drugs in metal containers or PVC pipe fitted around the tire rims, or in
loose packages inside the tire with just enough air for driving. Border
agents in Texas, who decided to search one vehicle because the driver
nervously avoided eye contact during questioning, recovered nearly
ninety pounds of marijuana from boxes spot-welded to the inside of all
four wheel rims like this:

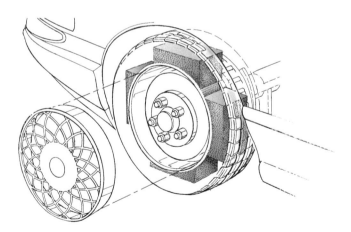

Caution: Do not stick your nose directly against the air valve and
inhale deeply while bleeding a tire. If drug packages have broken and
are leaking, you may suck in some of the product. You're safer to keep
your face back a bit and use your hand to lightly waft a little of the
expelled air toward your nose. You'll catch enough of the scent if
something's inside without making yourself vulnerable. This same
tactic can be used for "sampling" odors from bottles, jars, and cans
you find in the vehicle.

During your circuit of the exterior, inspect the ground around the vehicle, too. You may find contraband discarded by occupants earlier in the stop.

Driver Zone. In this zone and others in the interior quadrant, take a moment just to sit in the seat and look around. What do you see, just from alert observation?

This zone, within arm's reach of the driver, is where personal weapons are most likely to be hidden. During the search of the Driver Zone in one vehicle, a California officer found two fixed-blade knives strapped to the roll-bar, a billy club under the seat, a gun magazine in a small bag in a seat pocket, a loaded .380 Beretta in another bag, and a machete secured to the backrest!

If the driver's a drug user, he or she may also keep small amounts of drugs in this zone for easy access during the transport. All you have to find in most jurisdictions is a coke packet inside a cassette case or a roach in the ashtray or seeds on the carpet to have PC for searching, even if the subject withdraws consent. More than one big score has blossomed from an officer initially spotting just such a minor clue.

Do your feet seem to be unusually high as you sit behind the steering wheel? The floor should dip down below the door sill, but couriers sometimes level it off to create a cavity for contraband.

If nothing seems immediately suspicious, turn the ignition on and quickly check the instrument panel. Does the gas gauge work? If not, it may have been disconnected when a smuggler removed the gas tank to conceal contraband inside. Try the windshield washers. If fluid won't squirt out, maybe the reservoir is jammed with drugs. Do the radio, the CB, the radar detector, the horn, and other accessories work? If not, they may be hollowed out and packed with drugs. Do the air conditioner vents expel air uniformly? If some aren't blowing right, packages hidden in the air ducts could be blocking the flow. Feed your flexible probe through a vent louver and wiggle it along the air duct toward the center of the car to see if it bumps anything. Or remove the louver (most pop out easily if you push hard against one side, pressing toward the center), stick your mechanic's mirror into the duct and bounce your flashlight off its surface for illumination so you can eyeball the interior. Probing or looking, you'll confirm whether there even is a duct connected to the vent. Sometimes smugglers remove ductwork to make more space for drug packages, then cover the backs of the vents with black electrical tape. If you just glance at the vent grille without a light or probe, you'll think you're seeing innocent darkness.

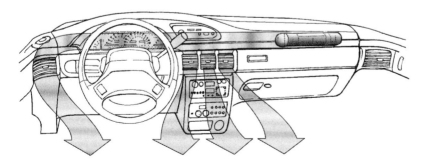

If air ducts are not obstructed, air flow should be evenly dispersed. Here that is not possible because a drug pack in the ductwork is blocking air flow to the passenger side.

In other cases, air conditioners have failed to function because the compressor motor has been removed and replaced with drugs.

Check under and behind any center armrest and inside any console. Take ashtrays out and look in the cavity behind them. Also check their bottoms and backs; keys to hidden compartments or the trunk may be taped there. Empty the contents of ashtrays onto a piece of paper and see what else may be hidden in their midst. Use the same procedure with trash containers in the car. Officers in Texas discovered eighty grams of crack worth $8,000 in a crumpled-up McDonald's bag. Others have found crack concealed in wads of snotty tissues.

Move the seat as far back as you can and look under it. Check the steering column for welds or fingerprints, especially around the base. Check on the backs of brake pedals and the accelerator and also inside their rubber covers. Look and feel under the dash. In many cars, the lower edge of the dashboard curves up into a lip or trough where packages can be stuffed. Some street-gang traffickers attach custom-made sleeves for guns or drugs under the steering column, behind the stereo, or up in the heater vent.

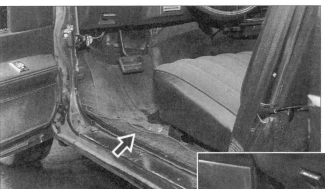

Loose wiring on the floorboard is a cue worth noting. Arrow at left indicates a wire running from a button on the inside wall at the left of the emergency brake (arrow below).

Following the wire, a searching officer found a hidden compartment with drugs in the left-rear wall. When the button (arrow) was pushed, the compartment opened.

Inspect the dash area for nonfactory equipment, like strange dangling wires, switches, latches, extra fuse panels, or remote-control buttons that may connect to electronically controlled hidden compartments elsewhere in the vehicle. *Close scrutiny may be necessary to detect these.* Carefully scanning surfaces in the Driver Zone with his flashlight, one trooper noticed a tiny hole that appeared to have been drilled in a dash panel just under the steering column. That didn't make sense to him, so he pried the panel off. In the cavity behind, mounted in a metal bracket and aligned with the hole, he found a yellow plastic push button. The driver could stick an ice pick through the hole, shove it against the button, and thereby activate an electrical circuit that caused the back seat to fall forward. Behind the seatback was a secret metal container mounted on the trunk wall to carry drugs and drug money. A trooper searching an old Lincoln in New Jersey found a similar compartment crammed with a kilo of coke and $100,000. All that tipped him off were two small screws which didn't seem to have a purpose under the dash. Shorted out with a jump wire, they activated a latch to release the compartment. In Illinois, suburban officers discovered hidden compartments in rear armrests that were opened by sticking toothpicks from a box carried on the front seat into small holes drilled in the back of the glove box.

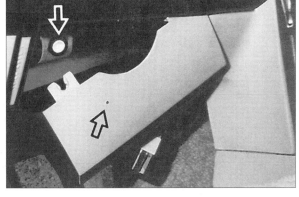

Pinhole (lower arrow) through which an ice pick could press an electric button (upper arrow) to access secret compartment behind rear seat.

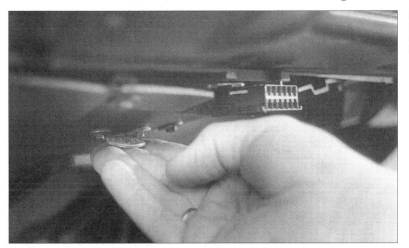

Sometimes hidden compartments are opened by placing a coin across a solenoid under the dash.

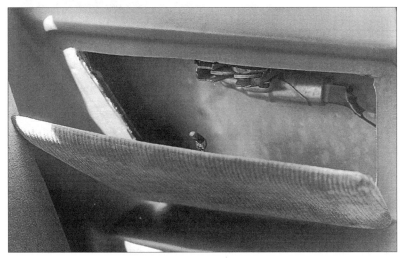

Compartment opens above armrest when the solenoid (above) is activated. Lots of room inside for hiding contraband.

Watch for coins that may show burn marks from electrical arcing. Or you may find a bobby pin spread apart with no tips on the ends. This may need to be stuck into small holes in the dash to complete an electrical circuit and open a compartment. When you make the proper electrical connection, you should be able to hear the compartment's locking mechanism click open and thus be able to trace its location. Sometimes locks are activated by small magnets, which are kept behind the rearview mirror or behind the ashtray. (Activating hidden caches can sometimes be astoundingly complex. One of the most sophisticated systems cropped up in California, when a female driver and her brother admitted to carrying fifty to 100 pounds of pot in their T-bird. To reach the dope, officers first had to open both doors, then turn on the headlights, then turn the air fan to full, then turn the air conditioning on maximum, then turn on the defroster, and finally push a hidden button beneath the glove box while simultaneously pressing the release buttons for the gasoline access door and trunk lid. In another vehicle searched in Ohio, traffickers had drilled two small holes in the bottom of a coin holder in a center console. When coins were removed, two pieces of hanger wire could be poked through the holes to depress two trunk release buttons underneath. If the rear window defogger was on at the same time, an electrical impulse would cause rear side panels to open.)

(left)
If you discover components of an improvised electrical system, beware of booby trapping. A California officer leaning into a car during a search hit one of these toggle switches (arrow). Car instantly collapsed on his foot and the roof conked his head. He was off work for 3 months and feels he was spared a violent attack only because his partner was watching the 4 suspects from the vehicle when the "accident" occurred.

(right)
Batteries filling the trunk powered the hydraulics responsible for the sudden collapse that injured the officer.

Your chance of figuring out a complicated compartment release by experimentation is slim. But confronted with unexplained buttons and toggle switches, the suspect may explain how they work. Some are quite proud of their craftiness. An Illinois trooper overcame one courier's reluctance to talk by grabbing a crowbar and acting as if he was going to wreck the vehicle. The suspect broke down and babbled directions for nondestructively unlocking a compartment in which he was toting forty pounds of marijuana.

Rather than immediately pushing buttons or flipping switches, you're safest to try to trace the wiring to pinpoint just where—and to what—it leads. Try to bluff the suspect by saying you want him to activate the system ("Show me how it works") or at least to stand close beside you while you do it. If he knows it's rigged, his reaction will betray the danger. If you have grounds for a search warrant or an arrest, get the car towed and let EOD personnel deal with the problem.

In the Driver Zone, as well as elsewhere in the interior, lift headrests and look for altered or repaired areas. Test the door locks and roll down all windows. If a lock won't activate or a window won't lower completely, packages may be stuffed inside the door panel, blocking the mechanisms. Remember, though, if a lock or window does go down, that does not necessarily mean that the door cavities are free of drugs. With the door open, shake it; feel the weight and listen for contraband inside. Check the door panel to see if it feels loose. With a flat-tip screwdriver, pry the rubber away from the inside of the window glass and put your eye right down against the slot. With your flashlight, you will then be able to peek down into the window well, usually clear to the bottom of the door. Doing this several places along the window, you'll confirm whether the door is really empty. If you're not convinced, pull out a corner or the bottom of the door's upholstered panel, which normally pops out or unscrews. You can also pop out the plastic plugs you'll find in most doors and shine your flashlight inside to look for packages. (Generally speaking, you won't take the door panel completely off unless you actually see contraband inside. Use your flashlight in searching these and other areas even in daylight. Officers have overlooked drugs when searching without their flashlights, then have discovered what they missed by searching a second time with their lights.)

In the Driver Zone and others, look for telltale marks: slits in upholstery where something may have been shoved in…white crease marks on panels or flooring, indicating that it has previously been bent back…handprints and finger smudges on removable parts like speaker grilles and seatbelt assemblies…scratches on plastic or paint surfaces around screws that might have been made by a slipping screwdriver. It's unusual for screws ever to be removed or replaced in a legitimate car, but drug couriers often take them out to access hiding places. It's almost impossible to remove screws from a rocker panel sill strip, for example, and get them back in without burring them because they are of such soft metal.

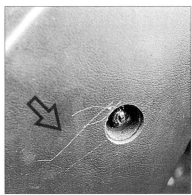

Scratches made by screwdrivers or other tools may signal the gateway to a hidden stash.

Really *look* for evidence of tampering, including screws that seem suspiciously new or free of dirt in their slots. A Southern deputy discovered rocker panel compartments filled with broken-down machine guns and cash—booty from a marijuana deal in Texas—because he first noticed traces of new spray paint on a sill strip. Ironically, the driver had two recent traffic citations in his possession. He'd gotten stopped and ticketed twice on his delivery run, without the dope being detected or probably even searched for. Also unsuspected was a potentially fatal reality: The courier traveled with a fully operative machine gun wired under the gas tank, where he could roll beneath the car and grab it in a crisis if he was not carefully controlled.

Inside rocker panels is another place you may find cables running to electric or mechanically operated hidden compartments. One cable in Arizona was traced on up through the firewall and into the engine compartment. It terminated inside the air cleaner, where a bolt was welded to the end to make a handle. When this was pulled, a secret, hinged compartment behind the rear seat fell forward.

(above)
Does this screw look suspicious to you? It should.

(above right)
Rocker panel on driver side crudely altered to conceal guns underneath.

Most rocker panels have Phillips-head screws when they come from the factory. If you see a rivet or a flathead screw in place or a screw missing, the vehicle has almost certainly been tampered with. One deputy noticed a screw lying on the carpet by the driver seat. He couldn't find anyplace it fit up front, but then he noticed an empty hole in a rear armrest. He suspected the armrest had been removed and stuffed with dope—and he was right. (Missing screws can be a tip-off in other vehicles besides cars. Florida agents searching a small charter plane noticed an inspection plate in the floor, with ten of its fifteen screws missing. In the well underneath, they found nine packages of cocaine, worth $1,000,000.)

Left-rear Passenger Zone. First, slide the front seat forward so you have maximum room to work. Check the back of this seat for bulges that could suggest bundles stuffed inside, and also look under the seat from the rear to be sure you didn't miss anything there during your search of the Driver Zone.

Examine the center doorposts in four-door vehicles for signs or sounds of tampering. Usually there are natural compartments in these posts.

Remove the vent plate, as you should in any zone that has one. Legitimate people have no logical reason for removing these, but drug dealers often take these plates off to pack contraband in the quarter-

340

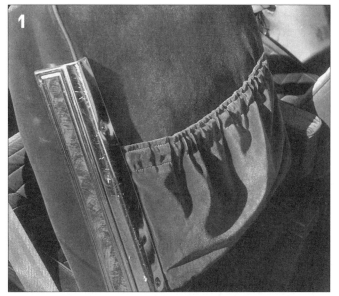

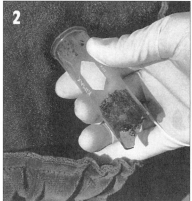

(left/above)
Drug users often hide paraphernalia behind the driver's seat for easy access. Look before reaching into such places to avoid injury—and remember that glassware like above can be important evidence.

A Phillips screwdriver, some curiosity, and a little time may lead to an important discovery inside the driver's seatback.

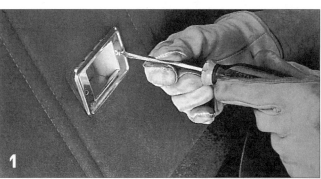

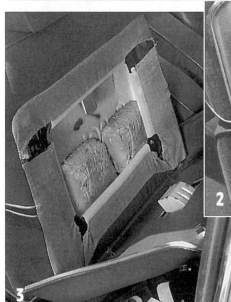

Not until the ashtray was removed could the officer see the cavity in the seat, which held drug packs.

341

panel cavities. Shine your flashlight and poke your probe inside. Sometimes transporters create a baffle of tin or stuff a towel sprayed with undercoating between the vent opening and the hidden drugs. They're hoping that without good illumination you'll think you're seeing the back of the empty cavity and not realize there's still hidden space behind their rigged-up barrier.

Caution: Before reaching into any vent, always check first with your flashlight. Couriers sometimes booby trap these spaces with mousetraps.

Anywhere there are hollow spaces, in the rear passenger zones or elsewhere in the car, check them. With the side ashtrays removed, for example, you'll usually be able to view large hollow spaces in the rear doors and behind interior panels.

Also check inside any containers you find loose in the vehicle, such as cans of what appear to be commercial products. Some metal "stash

With station wagons, especially, tap the rear side panels from inside the vehicle. These contain natural compartments and should give a heavy, solid sound if loaded. Also check for screws along the rear windows that are burred, unusually clean, new, or otherwise look suspicious or like they've been tampered with. 40 lbs. of marijuana was discovered inside the rear compartment of this station wagon.

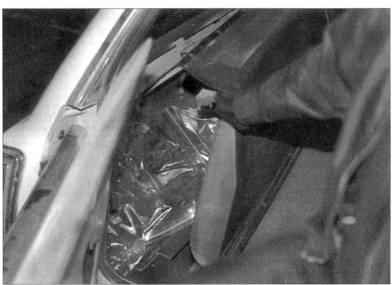

342

cans," sold as disguised "safes" for storing valuables, are designed to look exactly like popular brands of oil, hair spray, soft drinks, carpet cleaner, beer, and so on—even fire extinguishers. Some may even be partly filled with the actual product. *Don't take things at face value.* Unlike legitimate packaging, the top or bottom of a fake will screw off (often when you turn it opposite to what's normal) to access a hidden compartment. One California officer who found a six-pack of Coca-Cola cans on the rear floor set it on the roof to get it out of his way while he searched. When he didn't find anything in the car, he

(left)
Commercially available "security containers" may really be hiding spots for drugs and dirty money.

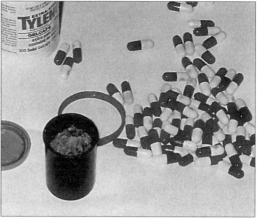

(above)
35mm film canister filled with pot was hidden inside Tylenol bottle and covered with capsules.

replaced the cans and moved on to the next zone—never realizing that they were phonies and that the contraband was inside them. Although these "safes" may look like some 140 different legitimate products, you may get a cue that they're fake by checking for a date/shift code on the bottom of the can. Real ones have these codes stamped or printed on by manufacturers to identify when and where they were filled; phonies usually won't. Also fake aerosol-product cans generally won't spray.

Caution: Gang members are said to rig these containers as bombs. The hollowed-out interior is filled with C-4, two AAA batteries, and a wiring/detonator ensemble. When the bottom or top is unscrewed a quarter-turn, the bomb is activated. When you find a container you think is a safe, consider having the suspect stand beside you while you twist it open. He'll likely stop you if he knows it is rigged.

Scrutinize *every* article you encounter, from every angle. One smuggler trick is to ball cocaine inside aluminum foil and stuff it into the cores of toilet paper rolls, expecting unobservant officers to toss these aside without inspection. Another is to shove drugs into tennis balls through a one-inch slit cut with a razor. The slice is invisible unless the ball is squeezed just right. In Georgia an officer found a package of cocaine hidden in a coffee can under an inch of

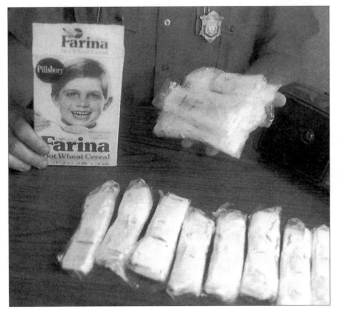

Creative packaging: 300 lbs. of pot concealed inside baby-food cans, pot transported inside trashbags, cocaine found inside cereal boxes, and cocaine "cookies" (worth $45 each) hidden inside potato chip cans—all discovered by careful officers during vehicle searches.

ground coffee; he struck the package when he probed the contents by sticking his screwdriver down into it. Another smuggler, who claimed to be a traveling salesman, showed an officer boxes of his product, a cologne. He even gave the officer a free sample. But during a consent search, the officer noticed that on some boxes, a certain stripe was diagonal, while on others it was straight. Closer inspection revealed that all the boxes with diagonal stripes contained money, not product.

Contraband has been found, *ad infinitum*, inside cereal boxes, boom boxes, portable cellular phones, film canisters, wheelchairs, bags of charcoal, fire extinguishers, flashlights, TV sets, garbage, sanitary napkin bags, pet cages, jacket sleeves, the false bottoms of chests and chewing tobacco spit cups, in briefcases under fouled handkerchiefs, even inside a watermelon (an end was cut off, the melon hollowed out for the stash, then the end taped back on and placed down in a shopping bag).

An officer searching a car in southern Illinois found cans of peach es and sauerkraut, still factory sealed. But they had Mexican brand names he'd never heard of, so he shook them. They "shook funny"—because cocaine, not food, had been sealed inside by a conspiring factory worker. Cartons of baby-food cans seized in New Jersey proved to contain 300 pounds of marijuana. Here officers alerted to a coupon on the label that supposedly could be redeemed for infant underwear—but there was no address given for where the coupon could be sent.

Bounce with your hands or punch or knee against the seat cushions to see if they feel uneven or exceptionally hard and rigid instead of flexible. Some smugglers replace seats with hollow fiberglass compartments, which are then upholstered to simulate normal cushions. Others pack the seat springs or foam padding with hard, packaged contraband. One Louisiana trooper who thought the backrest of one rear seat felt too solid tucked his hand between the seat and the side of the car. There he could feel a seam in the foam-rubber padding, like it had been split and glued back together. It had. The foam rubber had been hollowed out and packed with ten large bricks of cocaine, bundled in duct tape and plastic wrap.

Probing seat cracks can produce rewarding results, but use your miniflashlight or expandable baton to spare your fingers from unseen hazards.

Behind the back seat, incidentally, is where street-gang members often hide weapons when they go mobile. Grasp the seat top and try to shake it. From the factory, it should be so tight you can't move it and probably can't remove it without special tools. If you feel play in it, suspect tampering and probably an improvised electrical release. Run your expandable baton in along the crack at the top of the seat and you may hit the locking mechanism. Pull the top of the rear seat forward, if you can. With your flashlight you may then be able to see down into a large natural cavity. Also look for fingerprints and smudges along the top of the seat, which may have been left by others removing it. Don't feel you can ignore areas like this because you are searching a rental vehicle. Officers in Arizona stopped a rented California Oldsmobile headed toward St. Louis, in which the occupants had torn out half the rear seatback padding to accommodate nearly 1,200 grams of crack. On other rental cars, gas tanks, bumpers, and wheel wells have been modified.

To remove seat cushions quickly and painlessly, place your knee against the cushion, push back, and raise up to dislodge the seat.

In, around, and under rear seats are common hiding places you can't examine until the seat is out. An empty cushion is normally light and easy to move. If it's loaded with drugs, you should sense the added weight almost immediately.

Officer noticed a back seat that felt hard and had a bumpy contour. The reason was simple: Drug packages were crammed inside so tightly they protruded up against the seat surface.

Always take out the seat bottom when you search (is it already loose before you touch it?), and look on the underside of the cushion. This is a common hiding place not only for drugs but for cash, which can be stacked in bundles two to three inches high under most seats without being obvious. (In most cars, you will also find a confidential VIN number clipped to the framework of the back-seat cushion.)

Caution: In searching the crack between seat cushions, first run your miniflashlight barrel or expandable baton along the crevice. Some suspects insert hypodermic needles between the seats, pointed so they will prick you if you reach your fingers in without checking. Some reportedly have been recovered with HIV+ tainted blood.

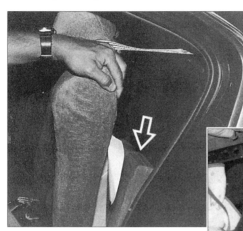

Cocaine packages were detected behind this left-rear seatback in North Carolina by simply pulling it forward.

(right)
False floor (arrow) discovered after rear seat cushion was removed. Don't forget to examine the underside of the cushion itself, as well as what might be below it.

Factory wiring is easy to identify, because it is secured and conforms with the contour of the metal stamping. When the back seat was removed from this vehicle, loose wiring (arrow) was discovered leading to an electrically controlled hidden compartment in the trunk.

Trunk Zone. Ideally, before you start searching the trunk, one of the most commonly used hiding places, take out all the contents and place them at roadside or on the curb so you won't be encumbered or distracted in assessing this highly suspect area. If that's not practical because of time or place, pile the contents from one side of the trunk onto the other side so you clear an initial search area, then later switch sides. Of course you'll want to search whatever you move or remove, one item at a time.

The majority of narcotics found in trunks have been either unconcealed or hidden in luggage or other containers. What looks like ordinary "trunk junk" may be the object of your treasure hunt—like the battered old ice chest an Arkansas drug team found in a Chrysler's cluttered trunk, which yielded over $90,000 in "cold" cash; nearby was a man's shirt with $4,000 in the pocket, a "gift" package with $4,500 inside, and a plastic "baby wipes" bottle containing $23,000. Remember that deceptive "stage props" may be part of a courier's camouflage. One deputy stopped a couple with two young children who said they were driving from Texas to Florida for a wedding,

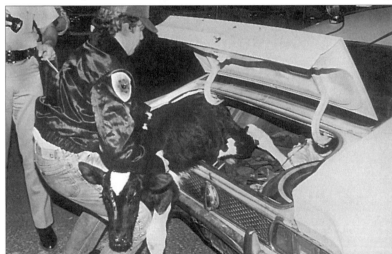

Searching the trunk can lead to discovering almost anything! This vehicle was pulled over for speeding and weaving. 6 occupants were inside with DUI driver. Calf was detected when the officer's interview with the driver was interrupted by loud thumps from rear of the car.

Among other citations, driver was charged with cruelty to animals.

Have a system for removing the trunk's contents so you can return items to their original location.

348

(left/below)
Drugs often are easy to find. Large, black garbage bags were first thing officer saw when he opened the trunk. Inside: 110 smaller white bags, each holding 1 lb. of pot.

(below/bottom)
One birthday present that never got delivered.... Don't be fooled by creative camouflage.

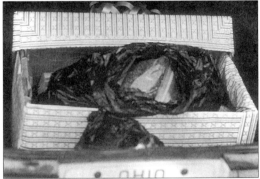

(above)
Florida plates on the outside, Arizona plates inside, along with a duffel bag loaded with drugs.

although they had no luggage. In the trunk, the deputy found two gift-wrapped packages, marked: "May God Bless Your Marriage." The driver said they had cookware inside, his wife said dishes. Neither box rattled when the deputy shook them. He stuck his pocketknife through the sides and discovered...no pots and pans—just pot. A couple stopped in Florida by a sheriff's patrolman said they'd been on vacation, and in their trunk he found a big pile of dirty laundry, plus a bottle of bleach and a box of soap that appeared unopened. Strange, he thought, that the couple had all the ingredients for washing clothes, but hadn't. Not so strange when inside the soap box he found 126 grams of crack. The box had been opened, then resealed after the dope was concealed inside.

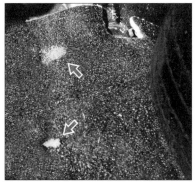

Burn marks on trunk carpet made by sparks from a welding torch. This became an early clue to discovering a secret compartment in the trunk roof.

With the area as empty as is practical to get it, take a moment to just look at the trunk. Let your sixth sense surface. What impressions do you get from this area? Do you see weld splatter, burn marks, or smoke trails that might have come from metal being altered or added?

Do the trunk's dimensions seem right—front to back, side to side, up and down? Squatting close to the rear bumper, reach one arm up into the trunk and the other under the car and see how close your fingers come to touching. The trunk floor should be so thin that your fingers come within about an inch of meeting, so you can "feel" them tapping. If they're four or five inches apart, what accounts for the void? Start looking for a built-in compartment. (You can perform this same test on the roof, with the door open. It also works on luggage and other containers that may have false bottoms.)

Does the trunk mat look like it's been pulled up or damaged? Once carpeting has been tampered with, it's often hard to get it to lie down flat again without bumps or ridges. If sections have been cut out and patched, the colors may not match. Is any Bondo, welding, spray paint, fresh tar, fresh adhesive, or their associated odors evident, or newer carpeting in an older trunk? Is carpeting glued down? In most vehicles, carpeting is rarely glued in the trunk or in the interior. An officer checking out one car trunk noticed not only that the mat was wavy but that it was littered with little chips of plywood, which

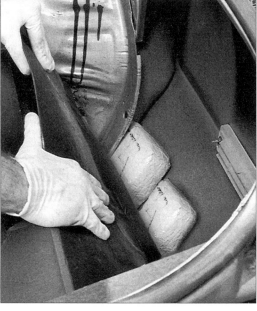

With trunk contents removed, you have plenty of room to climb inside and search thoroughly and closely for hidden drugs.

350

seemed out of place. That, combined with the fact that the trunk looked unusually shallow, front to back, kept him searching until he finally found a plywood compartment between the trunk and back seat—loaded with dope. (The condition of carpeting in station wagons and vans and the rubberized mat in many pickup trucks is important to observe, too, because the equivalent of the Trunk Zone in those vehicles is abundant with potential hiding places.)

Study any luggage that's visible. *More contraband is found in luggage than any other single place.*[6] Is the luggage in a logical spot? A Mississippi deputy found a suitcase being carried inside a toolbox. That didn't make sense until he opened it—and found it packed full of pot. Is the luggage brand new? Pot is often transported in luggage because its bulk is hard to conceal other places in the vehicle, and this luggage is generally bought new for each trip, then discarded after delivery. Does the luggage smell perfumey? Hoping to throw off drug dogs, couriers sometimes wrap the contraband contents of suitcases in blankets soaked with cologne. Other masking agents may be evident in luggage or elsewhere—layers of carpet freshener or coffee grounds, carpet soaked with antifreeze…even the rotting heads of dead birds turned up on one Florida stop (so did $108,000 cash, hidden in a false compartment built into the trunk floor). Closely examine clothing or other "innocent" articles you find in luggage. When three Jamaican males driving from New York to Virginia were stopped in New Jersey, three guns were found in obvious hiding places in their rented Pontiac. But the dope they had—more than 2,800 grams of heroin—was in clear plastic bags that had been sewn inside the lining of a coat, including the sleeves. Checking the luggage of a California woman stopped in Florida, agents found soda cans amidst her clothing. This seemed strange, considering the easy availability everywhere of soft drinks. After determining that the cans didn't slosh when shaken, the agents discovered they were filled to their brims with Colombian heroin.

First cue on this search was brand new luggage. Inside, clothing had been tugged around a large bundle—a shipment of marijuana.

If luggage is locked, does the suspect have a key? Few legitimate travelers go on vacation or business with luggage they can't open. Also, check whether the zipper is Super-Glued shut. This may be done to discourage the courier—or you—from tampering with the load. (Remember: Without specific consent to do so, you usually should not break open locked containers, including luggage—unless you have PC, such as a K-9 alert, as a foundation.)

Are there boom-box speakers mounted in the trunk? They're a favorite of gangbangers for concealing guns and drugs. Here, 7 lbs. of marijuana were found inside huge stereo speakers.

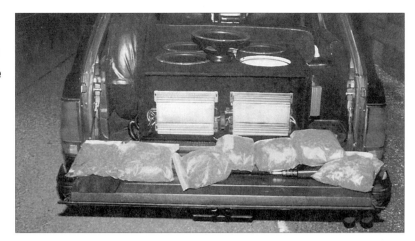

Is there a repair kit for dealing with highway breakdowns that seems overequipped compared to what the average motorist carries? Do you notice spare gas cans, or gasoline in antifreeze jugs or other "disguised" containers? A suspect may say his gas gauge is broken and this is protection against running out, but in fact the normal capacity of the gas tank may have been reduced to just one to three gallons by loading it with dope, making it necessary to haul extra gas for frequent refueling. (As you patrol, watch service stations for motorists filling up multiple gas cans, a potential courier indicator.) The vehicle may not be powered by gasoline at all. If the courier is smuggling goods in the gas tank, you may see a propane tank mounted in the trunk that's actually fueling the car.

When the officer at the scene removed the gas cap on this vehicle, he could not detect the normal odor of gasoline. In the trunk, he found a propane tank that actually fueled the car. The gas tank was carrying drugs.

You may notice more than one spare tire, certainly an unusual circumstance with legitimate motorists. One Kentucky officer who found two spares in the back of a Mercury Capri soon found forty-nine packages of marijuana inside them. In fact, one how-to book for smugglers claims that "more cocaine, cash, and jewels have successfully [been hauled] inside tires than in any other car location."[7] An Arkansas trooper thought the spare of a car he was searching looked flat when he first saw it anchored in place. But when he took it out and bounced it, it seemed unusually heavy. No wonder. Thirty-six packages

352

(left)
Trooper who found these drug packages inside a spare tire thought the tire looked flat when he first saw it anchored in place. When he removed and bounced it, the tire seemed unusually heavy.

(right)
Once the trash bag was pulled back, officer examining this spare noticed marijuana gleanings plainly evident around the wheel rim.

Trooper holds a new scheme for hiding drugs inside a tire—metal cylinders, wrapped around the rim to conceal drugs. Vehicle was stopped for tinted windows. After the occupants gave conflicting stories about how long they had known each other, consent to search was granted. After vehicle was towed to a service station for further inspection, a suspicious, strong smell of ether was detected from a valve stem. Inside the tire were 91 lbs. of marijuana.

of drugs hidden inside the inner tube weighed a lot more than air!

Before you move a spare, notice if it's in the factory position; it may have been relocated to camouflage a hidden compartment. A New Jersey officer searching a Ford LTD noticed that the spare was standing almost vertically at the back of the trunk. Checking his own trunk (same model car) he verified that his spare was mounted differently. Behind the suspect's tire, the officer then found a retrofitted compartment and eight kilos of coke. Are you searching a late-model car that has a full-size spare? Newer cars should have a minispare. Take any cover off the spare to be sure that only a tire is under it. A California officer found 1,362 grams of methamphetamine in a whisky decanter box under a spare-tire cover (as well as a 9mm semi-automatic hidden behind the liner in the glove box). See that the spare's lug holes align with the wheels on the car. Is the spare the same brand as the mounted tires? Traffickers may grab a spare randomly for hiding drugs or buy one already loaded. Are there fingerprints or smudges on the inner side of the spare or shiny marks on the rim, as if the tire has been taken off and put back?

You can check for a concealed load by sharply striking an inflated tire with your expandable baton in various places. Hold the tire vertically and rest your off hand on the sidewall opposite each spot you hit. You should feel and hear a distinct vibration if it contains only air; a dull "thud" is incriminating. If you shake the spare or roll it, you may hear something rattle or slide around inside. A Georgia officer cut into the spare of a car he'd stopped for weaving after hearing a "flopping sound" when he rolled the tire. Moreover, the spare was from a different manufacturer than the other tires, the rim was rusted, the factory wheel cover did not fit, and the tire seemed unusually heavy. The officer found not only ten kilos of cocaine inside, but also a machine gun, a silencer, and multiple rounds of ammunition. (Although consent to search is not consent to destroy property, a federal court ruled that the noise he'd heard, plus the other circumstances, constituted probable cause for slashing the tire, given the officer's articulable interpretation of these cues.[8])

You can also bleed air from spares, as you do other tires. But again, be cautious about inhaling deeply from close up. In one Southern incident, an offender allegedly filled a spare tire with acetone, which nearly killed a sniffing trooper.

In the trunks of some cars you can pull up the carpet edges and get access to the areas around wheel wells, often rewarding places to investigate. Also under the carpet, you can inspect electrical wiring coming from the interior of the vehicle. Factory-installed wiring generally follows the molded contours of the trunk, usually lies in special grooves, and is held in place with clips or bands. If you see wiring that's loose or separate or looks different from the rest, it may have been retrofitted to connect with a booby trap or hidden compartment.

Also check the space between the back trunk wall and the rear seat, especially if the trunk seems shallow, front to back. With most cars, if you climb into the trunk and pull down the wall lining a bit you'll expose the holes that will let you look or reach into this area; with most cars, you should be able to see the springs on the back side of the rear seat. Or test the seatback by poking your expandable baton through the wall's portholes. It should be soft; if it feels hard or "clinks," you've probably found a compartment. If for some reason this is not possible

These wires which connected to 2 exterior bolts seemed suspicious during a trunk search.

When electrically activated, the wires opened the metal box (arrow) revealed between the trunk wall and the rear seat.

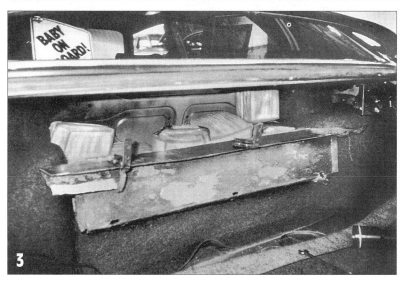

Cocaine ultimately discovered inside the secret compartment. Note "good guy" camouflage in rear window.

Texas Border Patrol agent checking this Chevy sedan noticed its floor was bare metal, with a drainage hole (in the position of the dotted line). When he removed the drainage cap, he should have been able to see the ground or the gas tank. Instead he saw a secret compartment with 80 lbs. of marijuana. Floor has been peeled back here to remove drugs.

While searching from inside the trunk, deputy peels back wall lining and discovers drugs in frequent concealment area for contraband—in the space between trunk and rear seat.

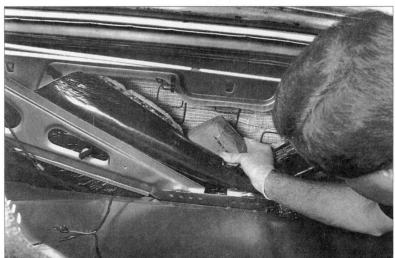

When searching the trunk, remove carpeting and other materials down to bare metal. Then you have the greatest opportunity to detect secret compartments and their contents.

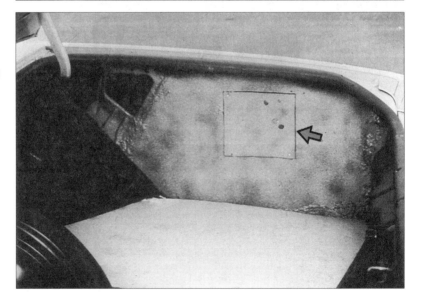

to do, stand to the side of the trunk with the lid up and eyeball the space where the back of the trunk and the back of the rear seat meet. There should appear to be virtually no gap between them. If there is, something's probably wrong and you need to "account for the void."

Before you leave the Trunk Zone, look up at the inside of the trunk lid. Do you see evidence of spray paint, welding, or anything that appears to have been added or altered there? Are fingerprints or smudges evident in unlikely spots? Are any access pulls visible, like ropes or wires? Can you see the metal braces on the lid, or have they been covered over to create cavities? Does the lid seem exceptionally heavy when you lift it? On station wagons, of course, the rear door, which offers large interior cavities, deserves the same thorough inspection. Tap it along the bottom for the dull sound of being loaded.

Caution: If in the trunk or elsewhere you find one or more aluminum foil balls being transported inside jars of alcohol or wrapped in heavy padding, such as cotton or foam rubber, do not shake these or attempt to open the foil. These may look like narcotics packages, but they may actually hold a volatile chemical cocktail of red phosphorus and potassium chloride, called an Armstrong mixture, which is extremely sensitive to shock or friction. Ranging from the size of marbles to the size of baseballs, they are designed to explode when jarred. Their deadly force is said to exceed that of military dynamite. Bikers and other traffickers of methamphetamine and cocaine use them to booby-trap drug houses, but you may encounter them when they are being transported from place to place. Some officers have lost fingers and hands and suffered other physical injuries by unwittingly handling or trying to unwrap them. Similar devices have been recovered in southern California, but folded like a foil bindle. Watch for blood-red residue from the phosphorus on the outside of packets you may encounter.

Crumpled foil, loaded with volatile chemicals and projectiles, can be homemade bombs, capable of mangling fingers and hands.

Right-Rear Passenger Zone. This represents the area inside the car that is farthest from the driver door, and because most officers on most vehicle stops spend most of their contact time at or near the driver's window, couriers of contraband often feel this zone is least vulnerable to inspection and detection. Some get downright sloppy. One stopped for speeding in Florida had made virtually no effort to disguise the contents of a shopping bag he'd set on the floor in this section. A searching trooper quickly spotted its ten kilos of cocaine—which led to seizing over thirty times that much from the suspect's residence.

In the Right-Rear Passenger Zone, you search the same kinds of locations you searched in the Driver Zone and the Left-Rear Passenger Zone, continuing to look not only for the obvious but for things that don't quite fit with what's normal. If for some reason you passed over certain interior components in the first two zones—like armrests, rocker panels, ashtrays, seat cushions—seeing these same potential hiding places again in this zone can be a reminder to check them out.

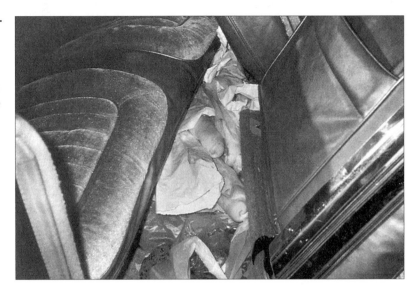

Search beyond your assumptions. To an unaware officer, this might look like just groceries. But the Mississippi deputy searching the Right-rear Zone of this vehicle, driven by a Cuban male, dug further. Hidden under bread, spices, and meat: a kilo of cocaine.

An Arkansas trooper who stopped two Jamaican males for speeding noticed a strong smell of deodorizer in their hatchback coupe. During his concealed interrogation, he managed to establish that they had conflicting stories about their trip. But the only thing he noticed unusual about their vehicle was that directly behind the front seats, in space that's normally open in that model car, they had installed two large, custom-made speakers, which occupied the entire area. By the time he got around to the Right-Rear Passenger Zone, the trooper decided to do a little disassembly. The speakers themselves checked out. But the carpeted wall they were mounted on sounded odd when he rapped on it. Behind the carpet, he found a panel of plywood. Behind that, he found a layer of insulation. Behind that, he found a sheet of metal. And behind that, along with strips of Bounce, he found sixty pounds of marijuana.

A Louisiana officer stopped a white limousine because its directional signals weren't working right. He became suspicious that something more might be involved when he discovered that the driver was carrying half-a-dozen operator's licenses from different states. With permission to search, he found plastic garbage bags in the rear passenger compartment, containing an unusual collection of police paraphernalia—portable radios, scanners, gunbelts, uniform shirts, a PBA baseball cap. But what really caught his eye was a vent plate in the Right-Rear Passenger Zone held in place with a rivet instead of a Phillips-head screw. When he snapped the plate off and shined his flashlight inside, the first thing the beam hit was the butt of a gun. The driver was hauling a load of MAC-11s and other firearms hidden in the cavities of the limo.

(above)
Anywhere you find vents, search them. They access large natural cavities in most vehicles.

(left)
This right-rear sidewall bore smudges and subtle signs of tampering. Behind a removable panel, officers found the drug cache.

Same search location, different automobile, similar results. An amazing quantity of drugs can be hidden in this zone.

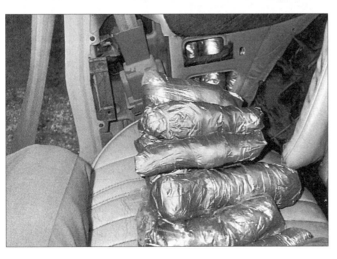

Conflicts between 2 Jamaican male occupants and a strong smell of deodorizer led to consent search that eventually brought an Arkansas trooper to this search area. Behind the speakers, bolted in very tightly, were successive layers of carpet, plywood, insulation, and sheet metal. Finally, wrapped with strips of laundry deodorizing sheets, were 60 lbs. of dope.

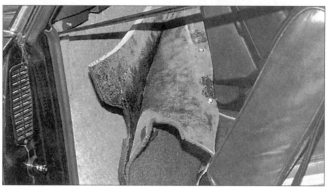

Front Passenger Zone. This is another high-risk area for personal weapons—hidden under the seat, up under the dash, inside air vents, inside the glove box.

On some vehicles right above the glove compartment there's a decorative panel on the dashboard, and behind that is a natural cavity. As illustrated in Chapter 3, some offenders pry this panel off and paste Velcro strips on the back of it and on the framework it's mounted on to allow it to be ripped off quickly for fast access to guns or drugs stashed behind it. When you're searching, you can wedge this panel open enough with a screwdriver, a pocket knife, even your finger to see what contraband might be in there.

With the glove box open and emptied out, give it the same visual assessment you gave the trunk. Do the dimensions look right? If it seems abnormally narrow or shallow, a hidden compartment may have been added behind its walls. In most cars, the glove box liner pulls or snaps out easily. With your flashlight and mirror, you then can look into the cavity behind the dash, all the way to the left to the instrument panel. If the liner does not come out easily, there may be a factory-made hole in its left side that will permit you the same inspection. Also reach up under the dash and feel on top of the glove box as well as the radio and ashtray.

In addition to checking for drugs in the same kinds of hiding places you checked in the Driver Zone, be alert in the Front Passenger Zone for floor carpet that has been slashed or removed and replaced with a loose pad or cardboard square. This may have been done to give ready access to a "dump hole" cut in the floorboard, which lets offenders jettison contraband when they notice you following or approaching their vehicle. This technique is frequently used by inner-city gangs and bikers, among other drug traffickers.

Also check the front footrest. Does it appear built up? Look at the bolts holding the seat to the floor. Are they shiny or burred?

Besides weapons and contraband, this zone (and others) may yield documents that suggest drug connections and that can be extreme

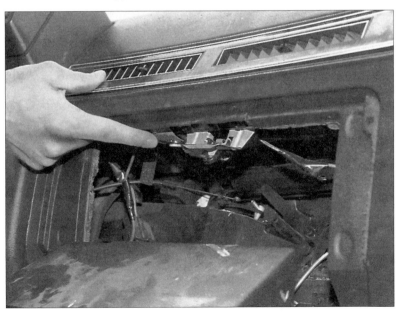

Remote-control buttons for releasing electrically activated, hidden compartments are often located in the glove box. This one, on a vehicle stopped in Oregon, was detected by an officer using a mirror after the liner was removed. Would you have been curious enough to give this area a special look?

Bouncing your flashlight off your inspection mirror, you can check down the air conditioning duct for obstructions.

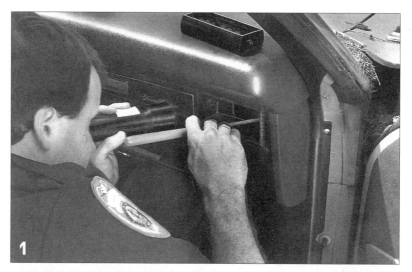

If you spot something, unscrew and remove the dashboard trim bezel on the dash to better access the ductwork.

Separating the ductwork at a joint, you are now able to remove a section through the glove box and retrieve the contraband causing the blockage. This procedure may vary slightly, depending on the model vehicle involved.

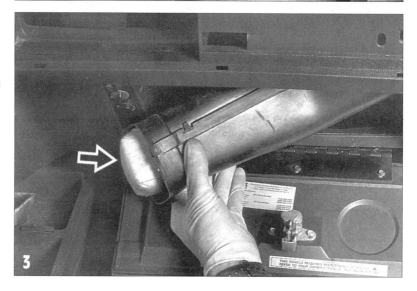

Inspecting the front passenger door involves the same techniques described earlier for searching the driver door. If the window will not roll down or you see an obstruction when you peer inside the window opening, search further.

With reason to suspect that the door cavity has been compromised, you can remove the protective panel to check inside. If you're wrong—which this officer wasn't—the panel can easily be replaced without damage.

363

ly valuable in building a bigger case: hand-jotted tallies of names and numbers, including boat names, flight times, beeper numbers, phone numbers, and locker numbers; address books; diaries; business cards (especially for attorneys); and cashier's checks, money orders, and Western Union receipts, which may represent payment for drugs or hauling or money-laundering instruments.

Airline tickets or receipts may reveal the origin or destination of travel or names of additional players; names on tickets can be compared to names on luggage tags and other identification you discover. Be alert for gasoline receipts. If you find that the suspects have been buying just eight to ten gallons of gas at a time, that could be a clue that the gas tank has been altered to hold less than its normal capacity in order to accommodate drugs hidden in it. By contrast, a trooper in Louisiana who found receipts in a passenger car for hundreds of gallons of diesel fuel deduced that he had stopped the escort car for an eighteen-wheeler that was hauling dope. His suspicion was confirmed when good interrogation at the next weigh station exposed the courier trucker.

Watch also for incriminating photographs. Many drug traffickers enjoy taking snapshots and videos of themselves and their cohorts using drugs, packaging drugs, or posing with drugs or money. When such photos turn up in a vehicle you're searching, they can be powerful leverage for prying information out of the people you've stopped. Photos of another sort turned up in Iowa. A trooper opened a jewelry box he found on the floor of one car and found snapshots of several elderly white people having a picnic. The driver he'd stopped was black. That doesn't seem to fit, he thought. Also inside was an envelope with an address on it. He called local police and discovered that the home at that address had been burglarized. That explained the VCR the trooper then found on the backseat, covered with an Army jacket.

Beware of pillows or cushions you may find during your search. They may be booby traps. Some Asian gangs drive nails through boards, then cover them with thin cloth to resemble cushions. These are then laid on car seats. If you lean on the cushion with your hand or arm during a search, the nails will puncture the cloth—and then puncture you.

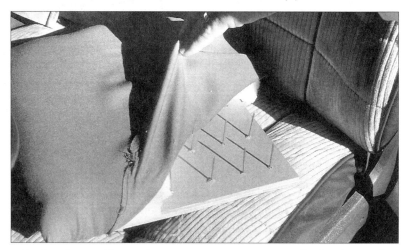

Engine Zone. The engine compartment statistically has been a little-used place for hiding drugs, but it's a popular hiding spot for weapons. Besides the fact that officers rarely look there during a car toss, offenders, especially street-gang members, like to hide guns in this zone because that allows them to be doing something that seems innocent and ordinary (checking for problems under the hood), while in reality arming themselves for a surprise assault—putting a new twist to the term "Boyz 'n the Hood." During the search of a Chevrolet carrying two Chicago gangbangers, Illinois troopers first found fifty rounds of .25-cal. ammunition behind the temperature-control panel inside the vehicle. Then wedged inside the windshield-wiper motor compartment under the hood, they discovered three semiautomatic handguns. In other vehicles, rifles have been located resting across radiators and engine blocks, and handguns have been recovered from behind the grille and inside the air cleaner. On occasion, switches to electronic compartments may be hidden in the Engine Zone, also.

To search this zone: After an initial over-all assessment, move systematically from one side of the engine compartment to the other, making active use of your inspection mirror and flashlight as your only hope of searching the many spots that will otherwise be impossible or too messy to reach.

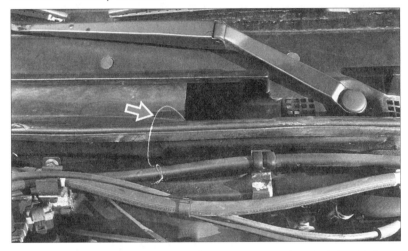

During the Engine Zone search of this vehicle, deputy noticed a rectangular hole cut in the cowling between the windshield and the firewall, with a piece of fishline sticking out. Slowly withdrawn, the line was attached to a sock containing heroin.

Even in daylight, use of a mirror and flashlight will make your search of the engine compartment easier. These tools greatly shorten search time and allow your detection of contraband in dark, tough-to-reach areas.

Cocaine hidden inside paper bag stuffed down behind the ignition coil. Just like any other zone, some discoveries under the hood are easy and others require help from a flashlight and inspection mirror.

Look for bags, boxes, tape, and other materials that noticeably don't belong. One none-too-bright courier in California crammed a duffel bag full of marijuana down against the radiator where, of course, the heat only accentuated the pot's give-away smell. A Louisiana trooper spotted a binoculars case shoved down behind a headlight. Lifting the flap, he found $30,000 in drug cash in one fat roll. Another officer who stopped a suspect in Missouri found 681 grams of crack in a shaving kit under the hood. More subtly, what caught the eye of a Mississippi deputy searching a car that had a PBA sticker prominently displayed on one window was a nearly invisible fragment of monofilament fishline, peeking out from under the horn. The deputy had been about to give up, because he'd found nothing in the trunk, in the interior quadrant, or behind the door vents. But at least this was something that didn't fit. And it was enough. He traced it and found tied at the other end an athletic sock, tucked far out of sight down behind a wheel well and filled with more than a pound of cocaine.

As you check the firewall, do you notice any painted area, new welds, or shiny new bolts coming from inside the vehicle? Some biker groups transport kilos of coke duct-taped to the firewall, and sometimes you may find drug packages disguised with black electrician's tape, to look like part of the vehicle's electrical system. In Idaho, officers peeled back insulation in the engine compartment of one Ford and found a natural cavity packed with 37 grams of Mexican tar heroin.

On and around the engine, look for hoses, air filter, or other components that are clean, like they've been wiped off, and, conversely, that are smudged with dirty fingerprints. Anything that isn't uniform in terms of dirtiness suggests movement that requires further investigation. Does the oil filter look new but oil on the dip stick looks dirty? Is the filter cool even though the engine still seems hot? It may be a fake, hiding drugs. Does the radiator show any freshly welded or painted areas? Follow all hoses to their destinations to be sure they're hooked up to something. Hoses can be disconnected and the probe run through those openings, too. Or squeeze hoses by hand to see if you feel obstructions.

366

Note: In respect for the vehicle's future safety, do not remove any bolts or engine parts without consulting your supervisor.

Does the battery fit down snug against its pan, or does it seem loose and riding high? Are there fingerprints or smudges on its top or sides? Are the hold-down bolts shiny? Is there a second battery, which could be a phony filled with drugs? Does there seem to be the normal oxidation you'd expect on cable connections?

Pop open all fluid containers and, if the contents are too dark or too deep for a satisfactory visual inspection, swish your probe down in to see if you hit any packages or other solid matter. Rock cocaine, for example, is heat-soluble but not water-soluble, so it is sometimes transported in the water-return container of a car's coolant system. Powdered cocaine is sometimes dissolved and transported in the windshield washer tank. Here you can take strips of paper towel from your pocket, dip them in the liquid, and continue to search while they dry. Then use your drug field-test kit to check the paper.

Take the caps off all tubes and run your probe down; small quantities of drugs often are wadded up and jammed down there, especially in urban areas. Check inside the air filter. Also visually inspect and probe through all open grille work; contraband may be taped behind it.

Before you leave this zone, grasp the hood and shake it. Do you hear anything rattling inside? Does the hood seem too heavy? Feel the insulation for lumps or bulges. Also check the underside for fingerprints. You'll rarely find any there unless the hood has been tampered with, possibly to create hiding places.

Roof Zone. On passenger cars, you're probably least likely to find contraband hidden in this zone; it will generally yield more when you're searching campers, vans, and other special vehicles, as described in the next chapter. Still, there have been some spectacular car-roof hits.

A Midwestern trooper stopped a family in a station wagon, with enough luggage to support their story of being on vacation. But when he checked them through EPIC, they came back with a history of drug smuggling. In his consent search, he couldn't find anything. Then inspecting the roof, he tried the trick of seeing how close his fingers would come when reaching from underneath and on top simultaneously. His fingertips ended up about five inches apart—way too much. Inside the wagon, the trooper noticed the dome light was loose. He started to check it, and it literally fell off in his hands. He looked up into the hole—and saw the first of seventy-two kilos of cocaine that eventually were removed from a false compartment built into the roof.

Besides the fingertip test, check for roof packing by rapping your knuckle against the headliner at various places inside the car, looking for lumps and for spots that sound different than the rest. Money is sometimes concealed there, especially right above where the roof meets the rear windshield. Check the screws on the molding strip around the edge of the roof for signs of recent removal. A California officer who noticed that screws on a molding were only half-way in and were of mismatched shapes and sizes found 160 pounds of marijuana hidden in the headliner of a Jeep Cherokee.

Also thoroughly rap and press against vinyl roofs from the outside, and look for signs the covering has been tampered with. One smuggler scheme is to carefully remove the vinyl, then beat broad depressions

Obvious signs of a tampered roof include surface wrinkles, multiple indentations, and inexplicable hard spots—all potential indicators of hidden drugs.

in the roof with a hammer, stopping just short of protruding into the headliner on the inside. Contraband is then cradled in these big dents, the vinyl is coated with a thin layer of fiberglass or resin to stiffen it, then is tightly stretched back over the doctored areas, and reglued. One Texas courier created a cavity across the entire roof of his Olds. It was only an inch deep, but it held 100 pounds of marijuana.

When the vehicle has a roof-top luggage carrier, this should be unloaded, with both the apparatus and its contents searched, similar to what you do for the trunk. Drugs have been recovered from inside the tubing of roof racks, as well as from the folds of convertible tops when they are retracted.

Underside Zone. Under the vehicle is saved for last. After all, why get your uniform dirty if you can find what you're looking for someplace else, right? Actually, even if you do find drugs or guns in another zone, you should still search underneath. But you may not want to do it on the spot, under "combat" conditions. The car can be towed and the underside checked more comfortably on a hoist.

In fact, some stashes are likely to be discovered only under garage conditions. Crip gang members in Los Angeles have frequently escaped police detection by transporting cocaine in the oil pans of rented cars, which were driven by young women with kids. For that area to be searched, you're going to have to develop at least strong dialogue cues and other suspicion that justifies the car being impounded.

To check the underside short of that, prepare at your stop site to get down and maybe a little dirty, with a mechanic's mirror and your flashlight. You can protect your uniform somewhat by using floor mats from the vehicle to kneel or lie on. Some avid Criminal Patrol officers buy a mechanic's wheeled creeper that they carry in their trunk.

Chop shops and some auto repair places these days have an active sideline installing electronically operated secret compartments and creating other underside concealments for short- and long-haul trips. Many of these modifications are fairly obvious if you take the effort to look.

You're checking for materials that aren't functional as part of the undercarriage...for evidence of welding, including on the bottom of

Checking under the car, see if metal straps supporting the gas tank have been tampered with. Are they smudged with fingerprints or unusually clean? Do they appear to have been moved? Do you see fresh undercoating on the tank that could be hiding welding seams?

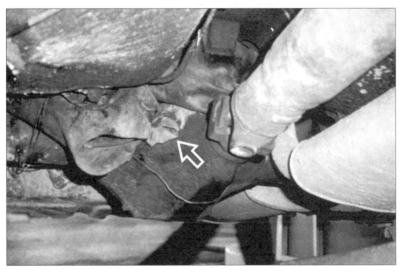

Rags (arrow) stuffed underneath don't belong there for any legitimate purpose. In this case, when an officer pulled them down, he discovered drug packages hidden inside.

the radiator...for shiny new metal...for unusual bolt placement...for packing material shoved up into the chassis or around the drive shaft...for fingerprints on underside elements—again, things that don't belong. The size of the vehicle is immaterial. Texas investigators found three underside compartments on one VW Beetle: one accessed by a plate on top of the rear axle, another under the trunk, and a third in a natural cavity housing the brake, clutch, and gearshift cables—holding in all fifty-two packages of cocaine. A Colombian couple made it all the way from New York to the outskirts of Los Angeles before a CHP officer finally stopped them for a traffic violation and looked under their Toyota on a consent search. Right away he spotted new bolts, new paint, and new silicone sealer on a false compartment that had been welded to the underside. Beyond a trap door were nearly sixty kilos of coke. In New Jersey, the cue officers spotted on another car was a hood-release lever installed near a muffler. They pulled it and the gas tank fell down. On top of that was a hinged door to a secret compartment.

Some vehicles have rubber drain plugs in the undersides of the rocker panels. Pop these out and check up into the cavity with your flashlight. One such panel in Texas had eleven pounds of marijuana packed inside.

Is there a dual exhaust system? Be sure both tailpipes heat up when the motor's running. A city officer in Florida found that one pipe on a vehicle he'd stopped stayed cold. The muffler it was attached to was fake, loaded with drugs. Even with legitimate mufflers, contraband may be wrapped in aluminum foil and secured to the tops. A book written for traffickers advises smugly: "This method will survive quite thorough examination."

Tap the drive shaft. It should sound hollow. If there's a dull thud instead, there may be drugs concealed. Also knock mud off any bolt heads that are covered with it. Some traffickers deliberately paste mud or clay on to hide shiny wrench marks made when the bolts were removed or newly installed. If there's mud anywhere, is it everywhere? Customs inspectors in California checking under a Ford LTD noticed mud on the gas tank, while the rest of the undercarriage was relatively clean. Inside the tank were three pounds of black-tar heroin and nearly twenty-seven pounds of marijuana. Sometimes the clue is just the opposite: the tank is shiny and new while the rest underneath is old and dirty.

When you tap the tank with your expandable baton or flashlight, you should get a ring as the vibration carries through the liquid if it has only fuel in it; a heavy, dull sound probably denotes something else. Border Patrol agents who seized forty-one pounds of cocaine from the gas tank of an old Chevrolet at a checkpoint in California found the drugs after noting five strong indicators related to the tank alone: the fuel gauge didn't work, there was no cap on the filler spout, fresh mud and sand appeared to have been applied by hand to areas surrounding the fuel tank, fresh sand was packed on the bolts that held the support straps, and scratch marks on the tank and frame nearby indicated recent removal.

As always, be alert for weapons, as well as drugs. Some street gangs bind small handguns to heavy-duty magnets with duct tape, then attach these units to the frame or body underneath their vehicles.

The keys for successfully searching each concealment zone are to:

1. Expand your imagination so you can start to think like smugglers think when they're selecting hiding places;
2. Understand enough about vehicle construction that you know what concealment possibilities exist and how to reach them.

You'll benefit greatly in both regards by spending a few hours periodically at an auto salvage yard. Here, with the owner's permission and perhaps with pointers from a helpful mechanic, you can leisurely practice "searching" the same wide variety of vehicles that you encounter on the street. Bring a partner along and take turns hiding simulated drug packs. You'll discover design features unique to each make and model that aid concealment; you'll become more familiar with what should and shouldn't be in a vehicle; you'll practice how to remove and replace door panels, air conditioning vents, seat cushions, and so on, and, with the ability to make and correct mistakes in a nonthreatening environment, you'll build your knowledge, speed, and confidence for real-life investigative stops.

Confidential from EPIC

Every week the federally funded El Paso Intelligence Center sends confidential teletypes on highway drug interdictions of significance.

The purpose is to acquaint law enforcement with the latest information on contraband movements and hiding places. If you have access to these bulletins, read them religiously. They'll remind you of productive places to search, as these typical samples suggest:

MARYLAND STATE POLICE SEIZED 536 GRAMS OF HEROIN AT 0203 HOURS ON SOUTHBOUND I-95 IN CECIL COUNTY FROM A BLACK FEMALE RESIDENT OF HIGH POINT, NORTH CAROLINA. THE VEHICLE WAS A DODGE WITH NORTH CAROLINA TAGS. THE SUBJECT WAS STOPPED FOR A TRAFFIC VIOLATION AND THE TYPE OF SEARCH WAS CONSENT. THE HEROIN WAS CONCEALED IN A SHOEBOX WRAPPED IN BLACK ELECTRIC TAPE.

NEW JERSEY STATE POLICE SEIZED 20 KILOGRAMS OF COCAINE AT 1635 HOURS ON WESTBOUND I-80 IN WARREN COUNTY. THE COCAINE WAS SEIZED FROM THREE BLACK MALES; ONE AKRON, OHIO, RESIDENT AND TWO HOLLYWOOD, FLORIDA, RESIDENTS. THE VEHICLE WAS A RENTED 1992 PONTIAC GRAND AM WITH OHIO TAGS AND THE SUBJECTS WERE EN ROUTE TO AKRON, OHIO, FROM NEW YORK. THE SUBJECTS WERE STOPPED FOR A TRAFFIC VIOLATION AND THE SEARCH TYPE WAS SIGNED CONSENT. THE COCAINE WAS CONCEALED IN A DUFFEL BAG LOCATED IN THE TRUNK OF THE VEHICLE.

OREGON STATE POLICE SEIZED $160,000 IN U.S. CURRENCY ON I-5 SB IN LANE COUNTY FROM A MEXICAN MALE RESIDENT OF CALIFORNIA. CURRENCY WAS DISCOVERED INSIDE A DEFLATED SPARE TIRE IN THE TRUNK OF A 1983 BUICK LESABRE WITH WASHINGTON TAGS. CURRENCY WAS IN ONE THOUSAND DOLLAR INCREMENTS, BANDED IN BUNDLES OF TEN THOUSAND DOLLARS, AND PLACED IN A PLASTIC BAGGIE.

LOUISIANA STATE POLICE SEIZED 510 GRAMS OF CRACK COCAINE ON I-12 EB IN ST. TAMMANY PARISH FROM A BLACK MALE RESIDENT OF LOUISIANA. THE CRACK LOOKED LIKE WHITE PRALINE "CANDY." THERE WERE 18 INDIVIDUALLY WRAPPED PACKAGES OR "CANDIES" CONCEALED WITHIN A PAPER BAG UNDER THE FRONT SEAT OF A RENTED 1991 CHEVROLET BERETTA FOUR DOOR WITH LOUISIANA TAGS. ARRESTEE CLAIMED HE WAS EN ROUTE TO PICAYUNE, MISSISSIPPI, FROM THE HOUSTON AREA TO DELIVER THE COCAINE FOR A PRICE OF $14,000. HE CLAIMED TO HAVE DELIVERED THE SAME TYPE OF CRACK TO SAME CUSTOMER TWO DAYS EARLIER FOR $14,500.

CALIFORNIA HIGHWAY PATROL SEIZED 59.9 KILOGRAMS OF COCAINE AT 2021 HOURS ON EASTBOUND I-40 IN SAN BERNARDINO COUNTY. THE COCAINE WAS SEIZED FROM A COLOMBIAN MALE AND FEMALE; BOTH JACKSON HEIGHTS, NEW YORK, RESIDENTS. THE VEHICLE WAS A 1987 TOYOTA PICKUP WITH NEW YORK TAGS AND THE SUBJECTS WERE NOT THE REGISTERED OWNERS. THE SUBJECTS WERE EN ROUTE TO NEW YORK FROM LOS ANGELES AND WERE STOPPED FOR A TRAFFIC VIOLATION. THE TYPE OF SEARCH WAS SIGNED CONSENT DURING WHICH A FALSE COMPARTMENT WAS IDENTIFIED, THUS LEADING TO A CANINE SEARCH AND SUBSEQUENT ALERT. THE COCAINE WAS CONCEALED IN A FALSE COMPARTMENT WELDED ONTO THE UNDERSIDE OF THE TRUCK BED. THIS COMPARTMENT WAS VISIBLE FROM UNDERNEATH THE TRUCK AND EXTENDED THE LENGTH OF THE BED AS WELL AS FROM WHEEL WELL TO WHEEL WELL. THE BED ITSELF WAS RAISED APPROXIMATELY TWO INCHES FROM THE FRAME WITH OBVIOUS RED SPACERS WHICH HAD BEEN COVERED WITH PLASTIC. NEW BOLTS WERE NOTICEABLE SECURING THE BED, AS WAS NEW PAINT ON THE COMPARTMENT AND NEW SILICONE SEALER ON SCREWS SECURING A TRAP DOOR. ALTHOUGH THE COMPARTMENT AND SPACERS WERE VISIBLE TO THE OFFICER WHEN LOOKING UNDER THE VEHICLE FROM THE BACK, THE TRAP DOOR WOULD ONLY HAVE BEEN VISIBLE FROM UNDERNEATH.

ARIZONA DPS SEIZED 1,589 GRAMS OF CRACK COCAINE ON I-40 EASTBOUND IN NAVAJO COUNTY FROM TWO BLACK MALES, BOTH RESIDENTS OF TEXAS. THE CRACK WAS CONCEALED WITHIN A MODIFIED COMPARTMENT BEHIND THE CENTER DASH WITH ENTRANCE TO THE COMPARTMENT BEING THROUGH THE CHEVROLET EMBLEM COVER IN FRONT OF THE DASH. ARRESTEES, TRAVELING IN A CHEVROLET CAPRICE WITH TEXAS TAGS, EN ROUTE TO LUBBOCK FROM COMPTON, CALIFORNIA.

MISSOURI STATE HIGHWAY PATROL SEIZED 269 KILOGRAMS OF COCAINE AT 1347 HOURS ON EASTBOUND I-44 IN ST. LOUIS COUNTY. THE COCAINE WAS SEIZED FROM TWO WHITE MALES, BOTH ARIZONA RESIDENTS. THE VEHICLE WAS A 1985 CHEVROLET PICKUP WITH ARIZONA TAGS AND THE SUBJECTS WERE EN ROUTE TO HARRISBURG, PENNSYLVANIA, FROM TUCSON, ARIZONA. THE SUBJECTS WERE STOPPED FOR A TRAFFIC VIOLATION AND THE TYPE OF SEARCH WAS CONSENT, DURING WHICH A SUSPECTED FALSE COMPARTMENT AND ADDITIONAL GAS TANKS WERE IDENTIFIED. THIS LED TO A CANINE SEARCH AND SUBSEQUENT ALERT. THE COCAINE

Eureka!...Now What?

Roadside dramas with happy endings go like this:

Act I: You make the stop and get consent to search.

Act II: You find something illegal.

Act III: The suspect submits safely to arrest.

For Act III to play right, your tactical and psychological performance can't end with Act II.

Rather than declare an arrest the instant contraband is found and thereby fuel the suspect's sense of desperation, a Milwaukee-area detective says he feels safer trying to play the good ol' boy one step further.

With a tone of puzzlement and concern, he tells the suspect, "Something's not right here. I don't want anything to go wrong, so for your safety and my safety, I'm just going to put cuffs on you until we get this cleared up. Okay?"

The suspect may feel that by going along, there's still a chance things will work out in his favor. If he submits, the detective handcuffs him—and then says, "You're under arrest." If he's uncooperative, he can still be stabilized with the help of backup, but at least the effort has been made to lure him into restraints in a less confrontational and potentially dangerous manner. Of course, once the arrestee is handcuffed, search him thoroughly. (Occupants of a courier vehicle are usually subject to arrest for "constructive possession," if nothing else, even though illegal substances are not actually found on their person. Constructive possession means that they had "intent and capacity to maintain dominion and control over the contraband."[9])

Once you've discovered contraband, do not permit the suspect(s) to reenter the vehicle. Also do not remove any contraband from its hiding place immediately. When you discover what appear to be packages of an illegal substance, you can reasonably articulate your impressions to the point of probable cause to permit an arrest before you move them.

What is in front of you now is a bona fide crime scene. Protect it. The greatest threat to its integrity may come from overeager police. Before touching anything, *think!* Once you or other officers disturb the scene, you lose an authenticity that may never be reproduced. Photograph your find in place, from various angles. Include closeups of any unusual markings, plus photos of the vehicle (with license plate), of any physical indicators you may have detected, of hidden compartments and switches, and of the suspect(s) at the scene, with drugs, guns, and other contraband and packaging in the pictures, if possible. (Al-

Can you tell what this shows? A jury can't either. Evidence photos that look like this are useless.

though the U. S. Supreme Court has ruled that the mere proximity of a gun to drugs can no longer be used to automatically enhance an arrestee's sentence,[10] defense lawyers still hate guns in pictures because that makes their clients appear more sinister. Getting the

372

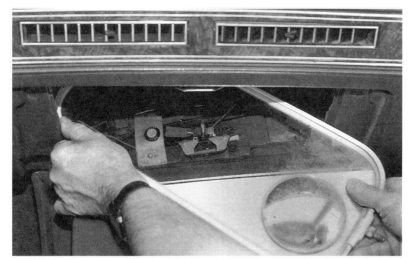

Creative solution to photographing hidden evidence at the scene. A truck mirror is used to reveal the remote-control button, anchored to the roof of the glove box, which opens hidden compartment.

Photos of seizures that show guns and drugs together can have special impact because of the implied violence they convey. Defense attorneys hate them.

suspects to smile adds a nice touch, too.) Photographs will help later in mentally putting you "back in the scene" and remembering important details. They will also save time and confusion in court when you try to describe what you were dealing with. Take "too many" pictures rather than too few; fifteen or twenty shots to document a sizable bust is not overdoing it. This is a one-time opportunity.

Handle the evidence as little as possible, dealing with any cash you find before you touch any narcotics, if that's feasible, to minimize the risk of contaminating the currency. Lift packages at the corners, where latent fingerprints are least likely to be. Prints may be recoverable from some packaging (including the sticky side of tape) and from the area around the spot where the contraband was found. These could be crucial in refuting a suspect's claim of being an innocent dupe, as well as in tying other parties to the case.

While processing the scene, keep the suspect separated from the evidence. Officers in Colorado put a suitcase containing cocaine in the back seat of a patrol car with the subject who had been carrying it. While the officers weren't looking, the subject ingested much of the coke and later died of an overdose.[11]

Multiple Stashes

An officer monitoring traffic on a California freeway one afternoon clocked an old Nova beater exceeding the speed limit. When he approached the car, he saw cans of beer inside and thought he smelled marijuana. The driver, as it turned out, was free on bail in a murder case. He granted permission to search. The officer found one small bag of cocaine hidden inside the body of the car, and arrested the driver and two passengers. Then the car was towed and the search resumed. By the time it was finally over, 400 grams of powder and rock cocaine packaged in small plastic bags were found concealed throughout the auto.

Searching for drugs or other contraband in a vehicle is like searching for weapons on an individual. Just because you find one stash, don't stop. Couriers commonly hide contraband in several places to increase the load and spread their risk, especially when they're hauling a relatively concealable drug like cocaine. Follow the "1 + 1 Rule": If you find drugs look further, not only for more drugs but for one or more guns, their frequent traveling companions. Conversely, if you find guns, look for drugs.

You may be able to use your first discovery to pry more information out of the suspect. He's especially likely to be cooperative if you appear knowledgeable about the type and quantity of drugs you've seized. If he thinks you know what you're doing, he'll likely feel that he'll get in even more trouble if he screws with you.

One psychological trick is to play on his ego. Referring to your initial find, tell him: "This is nothing. Tell me where the rest of it is, and show me how shrewd you really are." (Depending on circumstances, of course, the subject may be entitled to a Miranda warning before you play this card.) If he won't cooperate, you may just want to arrest him at that point and get him off the scene so you can continue the search under less pressure.

Don't take a suspect's apparent cooperation at face value. He may try to bluff you into leniency or disinterest with a small quantity of "give away" dope. One deputy, motivated to search a car after spotting four cans of deodorizing spray and a nearly depleted roll of duct tape in it, readily found several roaches in the front ashtray. A criminal-history check revealed that the driver had numerous priors for transporting marijuana. Confronted, he offered to "give up" his load in hopes the deputy would "go easy" on him. He indicated a bag in the back seat with two smaller bags of marijuana inside, about two pounds. The deputy, however, persisted with his search— and found the *real* load when he peeled down the panels above the rear armrests: twenty packages of compressed weed. Missouri officers found a bag of cocaine in a driver's shirt pocket and a gun under a rear seat of his van. Six hours later, an inventory of the car disclosed $125,000 worth of heroin in the engine compartment that earlier had been missed.[12]

Even if you hit *big* in one hiding spot, don't stop. Two officers searching a suspect's car in Oregon found fourteen packages of money, total-

Search of a suspected courier car uncovered large amounts of cash in multiple locations. In hopes of discovering more cash or drugs, an officer took the time to also examine this shirt, found in the car. $4,000 cash was inside a pocket.

Drugs were found in the door panels of this van being driven from San Antonio to Memphis. This discovery justified further searching, including the inside of this spare tire, with additional positive results (arrow).

ing nearly $80,000. They arrested him and had his car towed to temporary storage. The next day, another officer, transporting the car to a different location, flipped the visor down to shield his eyes from the sun—and a package of cocaine fell into his lap. Now officers excitedly searched the suspect's house, and found more money, coke, and drug paraphernalia. They were congratulating themselves when the suspect told them they'd better go back to the car. They'd still missed drugs there, hidden in a secret compartment. In Arizona, after developing good visual and dialogue cues during the stop of a pickup truck, exuberant officers found 186 pounds of cocaine in false gasoline tanks—a sizable haul in anyone's book. They arrested the driver and confiscated the truck. Later it was sold at a police auction. The new civilian owner was preparing to drive it off the city lot when he noticed that one of the windows wouldn't work. He took off the door panel—and discovered twenty packages of cocaine still inside. Hidden in the other door, he found twenty more packages. In all, officers in their original search had missed $880,000 worth of drugs because they stopped too soon.

Searching thoroughly means searching to the very end—through every potential concealment zone. If you bail out along the way, you may end up with just peanuts when you could have had the peanut farm.

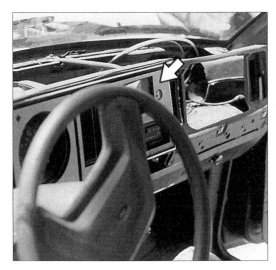

This vehicle was first searched after the arrest of its 2 female occupants for transporting cocaine. Eventually, police sold it to an innocent party. To his shock, he discovered behind the radio (removed in these photos) a number of packages filled with white powder. When officers searched this time, an additional 21 lbs. of cocaine were recovered.

375

Having to Say You're Sorry

Instead of hitting the jackpot, suppose you come up with zip.

First, take one last glance inside the vehicle. When one officer looked back after an unsuccessful search, he saw a .357 Magnum lying on the front seat. How'd I miss that? he wondered. Then he realized it was *his* gun, which had fallen out during his search contortions earlier.

Barring anything new, replace all the subject's personal possessions in the vehicle as close as possible to the way you found them...apologize for his or her inconvenience...and express your thanks for the cooperation.

Be guarded about revealing the indicators that led you to ask for consent to search. On the chance that you've actually missed a load, you don't want to give away information that will make that person—and everyone he tells—even more careful the next time. If some explanation seems necessary to soothe ruffled feathers, stay general: "You were coming from a source city for drugs, going to a high-demand city" or "You have the kind of car that lends itself to transporting drugs." Explain: "I know you're not a bad guy *now*. I didn't know *before*."

If you're convinced you simply misread a solid citizen, a little extra stroking may further diminish the risk of a beef: "The only way we're going to stop drugs from hitting the streets is to conduct searches like this. I really appreciate your help, because it's only through the cooperation of people like you that I can do my job."

Even though the subject seems clean at this point, maintain your survival awareness as he leaves the scene. Stand where you can have the benefit of some barrier—behind your open passenger door, for example—and don't get back into your car until his vehicle is back in traffic.

Before going on to your next stop, consider filling out an F.I. card on the subject and his or her vehicle. Articulate the cues behind your original suspicion and search, to protect yourself in case of a liability or privacy question later on. This card can then be routed to narcotics investigators in your department for their intelligence files and may contribute to some current or future investigation you're not even aware of.

Especially if you patrol an urban beat, accept the fact that you are bound to miss some contraband simply because of the speed with which you're often forced to search; it just may not be practical sometimes for you to do much more than a "vehicle frisk." Also accept that not every bust has to put you in headlines to make your efforts worthwhile. "A quarter gram is just as good as a kilo," says one officer. "Even a little bit is important."

Understand, too, that even the best Criminal Patrol officers hit dry spells. Sometimes these frustrating and discouraging periods last for weeks at a time. Hang in. Contraband and couriers are out there. You are out there. It's only a matter of time and numbers before you come together again.

BUSTING MOTHER-LODE VEHICLES

If a Drug Courier "Haul" of Fame is ever established, it will be dominated not by the drivers of passenger cars but by offenders who jockey oversized vehicles: preponderantly semitrailers and tanker trucks and their smaller cousins, rental trucks, vans, pickups, campers, and motor homes.

The mother lodes of contraband and cash in transit today are rolling over streets and highways in these conveyances, for reasons both physical and psychological.

Obviously, their larger size gives these rigs more square footage of hiding space, yielding profit-hungry traffickers an appealing economy of scale. It's a proven rule of thumb: As the value of the means of transporting the contraband increases, the value of the contraband itself tends to multiply. In other words, the more expensive the rig that's used, the more precious its hidden cargo is likely to be. Indeed, confiscations of 100 to 300 kilos of cocaine from large trucks are considered "average."[1]

Besides that, transporters shrewdly perceive that where commercial carriers in particular are concerned officers are much more reluctant to stop them, more baffled about how to develop suspicion of nefarious activity, and more likely to be paralyzed at the prospect of searching because it seems like such a needle-in-the-haystack crapshoot. Officers in urban areas, especially, may not know even what the inside of an eighteen-wheeler's cab and trailer is supposed to look like. The bigger and more complicated the vehicle, the more likely it is to be passed by on Criminal Patrol.

Just how intimidating commercial vehicles can be to officers is dramatically illustrated by the case of a tractor-trailer rig that loaded up 4,540 pounds of marijuana in Texas, then drove for more than 600 miles without any law enforcement interception, even though it had no license plates. The load was interdicted only because FBI agents, who had followed it from the beginning, finally notified a department of public safety to stop it.[2]

Yet officers who have cultivated the confidence and skill to stop and search big vehicles—both commercial and noncommercial—have scored some spectacular busts, by following basic investigative principles of contraband interception:

The photos you see on pages 378-379 show just a small sampling of the rewards that can result from careful investigation of oversized vehicles. Notice the variety of vehicles involved and the efforts by drug traffickers to provide realistic-looking camouflage in an effort to throw you off.

(right)
Going fishing? This van was pulled over because the boat had no license plates. After a deputy searched both the van and the boat, cocaine and marijuana were found in the van, along with incriminating photos of the occupants doing drugs. The boat was only window-dressing.

(left)
Couriers use every conceivable size and type of vehicle to transport narcotics. After stopping a motor home, officers discovered 191 lbs. of cocaine hidden in this couch.

(below)
2,500 lbs. of cocaine being unloaded from a tractor-trailer where it was hidden inside boxes of cabbage. A definite mother-lode victory!

(above/inset)
After a false wall was removed from the nose of this rental truck, this incredible stack of cocaine was uncovered.

Sheriff in New York State inspects a truckload of yucca plants that were hollowed out and filled with 142 lbs. of high-grade cocaine. Included among the shipping papers was a map which showed where the cocaine was hidden in the shipment.

Other cases underscore the opportunities for large-truck victories. A New Jersey trooper, for instance, initiated a stop when he saw something leaking out of a trailer. The driver said he was just hauling Italian olive oil, nothing hazardous. He had been ticketed twice in Maryland during his run for being overweight. Examining his papers, the officer noticed that the bills of lading bore no dates for pick up and delivery. With the cargo doors open, the officer noted that many of the cartons and skids appeared to have been severely damaged by a forklift. The driver would have had to sign for accepting the load in that condition, but he hadn't. Part way up in the trailer, the officer could see several U-Haul boxes that were different from the rest of the cartons. Bingo! He opened these and found 400 pounds of cocaine.

At 4 o'clock one January morning, another East Coast trooper stopped a pickup truck/camper for speeding and asked the driver where he was headed. The subject said he was a migrant farm laborer, looking for work picking lettuce—highly unseasonable in the dead of winter. The trooper noticed that the vehicle had three gasoline tanks and that its odometer had logged 75,000 miles, although the rig was less than a year old. In the glove box during a consent search, he found a tiny screwdriver that matched some unusual screws in the ceiling of the camper compartment. Other campers the trooper had seen had rivets holding the ceiling in place. Hidden there, he found 526 pounds of cocaine.

Two Ohio troopers stopped a motor home with a black male driver and a white female passenger for following too closely behind a semi. Questioned separately, the pair offered conflicting stories. One said they were coming from Las Vegas and headed to Buffalo. The other said they were en route to Rochester, New York, from Los Angeles. During the concealed interrogation, a K-9 officer arrived and ran his dog around the vehicle. The dog alerted and the troopers conducted a probable-cause search. The first place they looked, in the natural compartment under one of the beds, they found 65 kilos of cocaine. Searching all the beds and table benches, they accumulated a total of 491 pounds of coke, including some they discovered in a floor-to-ceiling false wall in a closet.

In a small town in Texas, the driver of an eighteen-wheeler suffered a fatal heart attack while headed north for a town in southern Indiana along a route nicknamed "the Marijuana Highway." Local officers investigating his death tried to track down the owner of the leased truck and the consignee of the $5,000 worth of fresh cabbages it was hauling. The driver, they discovered, had been fired a month earlier and wasn't supposed to be in possession of the rig. The shipping invoice was a phony. License plates on the rig were stolen. And the 771 cartons of cabbages were just window-dressing. Officers found the *real* load buried among them in burlap sacks: over 2,400 pounds of cocaine.

Another vehicle stopped for following too close—this one a rental truck pulled over in Texas—contained a man and a woman who couldn't agree on where they were coming from or where they were going. With backup on hand, the officer opened up the cargo door and saw a sorry-looking collection of beat-up appliances, an obvious junk load not worth the expense of transporting it. He opened the door of the nearest piece, a refrigerator. It was stuffed to overflowing with packages of cocaine. So were an oven, a washer, and a dryer—873 pounds in all, said to be worth nearly $35,000,000.

Although there are some important differences in where and how you search oversized vehicles, the same fundamentals that guide you in investigating passenger cars underlie the play at this championship level. If you are to depend on anything more than sheer luck, you *still* need to be alert for sensory cues...to know what's right so you can pick up on what's wrong...and to employ time-saving, systematic search strategies. You just adapt your investigative procedures to different vehicular parameters. A support strap that looks to have been removed and replaced is just as suspicious on a diesel saddle tank of a semitrailer as it is on the gasoline tank of a passenger car. You should wonder as much about a pickup truck tailgate that seems unusually heavy as you do about a trunk lid that feels overweight. Missing screws in campers and vans have the same significance as in automobiles, as do finger smudges in unusual places, windows that won't roll down, or switches and wires that don't seem to have a purpose. The structural and operational differences between passenger cars and oversized vehicles can actually work to your advantage. Once you understand them, they can provide even more clues that you can check for. Says one Criminal Patrol officer: "If you can think of a place in a truck that dope could be hidden and you think it's not going to be there, rethink."

The same cues that make you curious about cars can arouse your suspicions about oversized vehicles, too. This 26-year-old, traveling from Texas to Michigan in a 3rd party rental, was nervous, had no luggage, and showed a Mexican driver's license. Consent search yielded 272 lbs. of marijuana hidden behind junk furniture.

You, too, can bask in the glow of victory from major busts once you commit to stopping and searching large vehicles. Officers stopped this rental truck for a minor infraction. During concealed interrogation, they detected conflicts between the driver and the passenger. Checking the cargo area on a consent search, they noticed sheets of Bounce and mothballs—indicators of masking. Some cartons were filled with pottery, mostly broken. The rest held 1,600 lbs. of marijuana.

No place seems off-limits for contraband in big vehicles. This pickup was pulled over for upside-down temporary license plate on a flatbed trailer it was pulling. 625 lbs. of marijuana was found sealed inside the load of food service counters it was hauling.

It's true that even with some advanced insights into searching oversized vehicles you are still likely to find contraband more frequently in passenger cars. But the surpassing quantity that's to be found in bigger rigs is what makes them such a necessary part of your patrol.

And they're becoming more so. Confidential intelligence bulletins from EPIC repeatedly reinforce the growing importance of these carriers to the narcotics pipeline: a ton of cocaine every week is reported being shipped from Tucson to Miami, Philadelphia, and New Jersey via moving vans...a smuggler is using motor homes "tricked out" with false compartments that hold 100 kilos of coke to run drugs from Houston to New York...a "major distributor" of marijuana and cocaine employs trucks and RVs as "preferred transportation" for his deliveries to South Carolina...members of a Canadian religious group use tankers, flatbeds, and box trailers to transport multi-kilo quantities of cocaine...one smuggling organization uses frozen-food trucks designed to haul orange juice to transport marijuana north to Massachusetts from south Texas...another trafficker operating in Texas maintains a fleet of vans and RVs, bearing New Mexico plates and fitted with large false compartments...still another carries marijuana in a horse trailer towed behind a large pickup or Ryder rental truck...interstate commuter vans are transporting cocaine and heroin between New York and Rhode Island…semis with false trailer noses hidden by loads of onions are trucking pot on a "large scale" from Mexico and Texas to Chicago and at least 2,500 kilos per month from Arizona to Pennsylvania and New York…a driver from Mexico is carrying marijuana in crates on a gooseneck flatbed loaded with construction equipment and building supplies…smugglers moving across the Rio Grande at night are filling hidden compartments in big trucks and cars on lonely south Texas roads, then reloading the goods into tractor-trailers in large Texas cities for dispersion to Minnesota, Wisconsin, Illinois, and Michigan…a lone operator has carried six to ten tons of marijuana every four to six weeks from Mexico to North Carolina in a Ford Bronco…a Jamaican organization in Houston conceals marijuana in false roofs of semitrailers…and on and on.

An EPIC survey of marijuana seizures in four states—Texas, Louisiana, Missouri, and New Mexico—showed that during just one reporting period, nearly one-fourth of the total quantity of pot discovered was recovered from pickup trucks and that two-thirds was being transported by tractor-trailers. In a nine-state region, pickups were also carrying one-fourth of the currency seized. Traffickers' growing affinity for oversized vehicles has prompted the Idaho Department of Law Enforcement to advise: "Every contact you make [with these carriers] has the potential of developing into a felony arrest."

Don't forget important danger cues while you focus on searching. Cocaine transported in this landscaper's truck is hidden in storage compartments under tools that include a pitchfork (arrow) and other edged weapons. Remember that the driver may be adept at using such tools and if you permit him to stand too close during your search, they could be within his easy reach.

We won't try to cover every type of large vehicle that you may need to stop and search. Contraband has been confiscated from tow trucks, cement mixers, hot asphalt tankers, garbage trucks, boats being pulled by trucks, hayracks, dry bulk hoppers, buses, even steam-rollers. If it has wheels and a motor, chances are it has been or will be used to smuggle something somewhere. We'll concentrate on the uniques involved in discovering illicit goods in some of the more common ones you'll encounter, both private and commercial.

As you become as familiar and comfortable with investigating over-sized vehicles as you are with passenger cars, remember: *Bigger stakes mean bigger risks.* The Search Commandments and other survival principles apply here—in spades. And keep in mind, too, that just like other couriers, you will encounter "dirty" truckers in places besides the Interstates, where they perceive weigh stations and interdiction-trained troopers to be their greatest risks.

Just as with passenger vehicles, you begin the search with a high level of articulable suspicion developed earlier in the stop and usual-ly with the driver's voluntary consent to search. We'll assume you are the Contact Officer, responsible for searching. But, as with passenger cars, you should not start until all occupants are out and frisked, recovered weapons are secured, and a Cover Officer is tactically deployed to watch and control the suspects.

Private Vehicles

Dividing the vehicle into distinct zones for searching still works for oversized carriers as a way to keep organized and focused during your hunt. So does being alert for small amounts of drugs or other evidence that will quickly establish probable cause, so you can search thorough-ly under less pressure. Pictured here are some examples of key search opportunities with just one type of oversized vehicle, a cargo van.

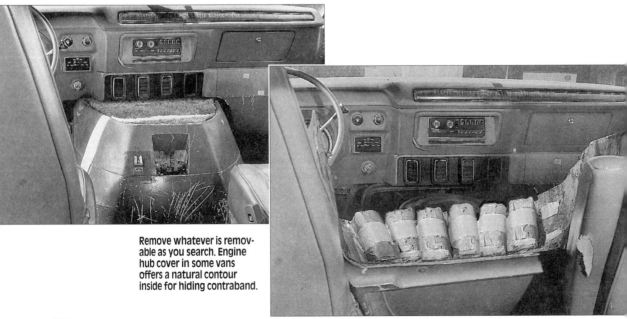

Remove whatever is remov-able as you search. Engine hub cover in some vans offers a natural contour inside for hiding contraband.

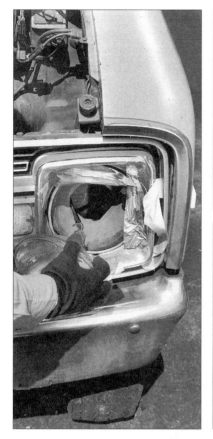

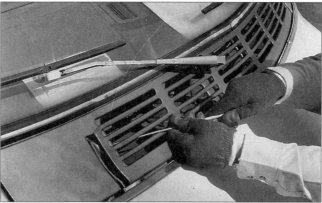

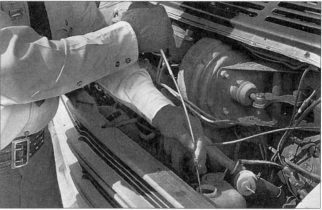

(above clockwise)
Small hiding places outside the cargo area can be fruitful to check, like behind the headlights. Use your probe to poke beyond grilles and to check liquid reservoirs.

(above/left)
Kilo of cocaine was hidden in this air filter of a van stopped for speeding. Package (arrow) was wrapped in black rubber for camouflage and concealment and for waterproofing when shipment was initially air-dropped off-shore. Drugs ultimately were traced to a major drug cartel.

(above)
Intake hose for the air cleaner is an ideal hiding place for a kilo.

(left)
Fuel filler hose can be gently squeezed to determine if something more solid than gasoline is inside.

(below)
Bumpers on a van or pickup may be even bigger concealment areas than on a passenger car. Sliding tray in customized rack carried large load of drugs behind bumper of this van.

Given that with oversized vehicles you may be in pursuit of colossal loads of drugs, currency, and other contraband, certain search zones warrant special attention, because they represent the biggest potential hiding places.With private vehicles—such as vans, pickup trucks (the second most commonly encountered contraband vehicle after autos[3]), campers, and motor homes—the possible treasure vaults include:

Roof. Smugglers using private vehicles often construct false compartments in this area. With vans, they generally build *down* to create hiding space below the top surface; you'll be able to detect this work more easily from inside the vehicle. With campers and motor homes they usually build *up*, often leaving cues that are visible from outside.

If the metal trim strip that runs around corners and along the top of campers and motor homes has been removed during the alteration, it almost never can be put back exactly right. From outside, carefully check its condition. Does it lie straight along the roof line, like it should, or is it crooked, curvy, bent, scratched, or otherwise damaged? Does all the trim match, or is some a different style or color from the rest? Also, large campers and motor homes generally have air vents or skylights. If you don't see these on the roofline or they are sealed over inside the vehicle, they may have been incorporated in hiding chambers. Officers in Texas discovered 558 kilos of marijuana concealed above sheet metal panels that had been riveted to the roof frame of a rental truck headed for New York.

Does the roof align properly with windows and doors? An officer inspecting a Dodge Caravan driven by a woman with two small children noticed that the top of the rear door didn't seem parallel to the roof. That led him to discover that the roof had been altered to conceal 195 pounds of marijuana.

When you duck inside the vehicle, does the ceiling seem lower than you expected? An Arkansas trooper searching a camper he'd stopped for speeding on a state road thought the ceiling "felt" about a foot lower than the rooftop looked from outside. After finding a .22 derringer in the vehicle and sniffing a strong odor of marijuana, he pulled down a section of the ceiling and discovered what turned out to be nearly 400 pounds of pot that had been compressed into neat bundles by a trash compactor.

Roof of a camper can provide an incredible concealment area for drugs. Do you take the time to carefully inspect the roofline for evidence of tampering when you see or stop such vehicles?

Confirm and compare inside and outside distances with your steel tape. Measure floor to ceiling inside and floor to rooftop outside. An unexplained gap of several inches or more could be improvised space that's packed with contraband. With cab-over style campers (extremely popular for smuggling) be sure to measure heights in the sleeping section that extends over the cab—a favorite concealment zone. Compare the distance from the top of the side window to the ceiling inside the vehicle and to the roof line outside. Also compare the distance from the bottom of the window to the floor of the bunk inside and to the bottom of the compartment outside, to detect hiding space that may have been created on the underside of the cab-over extension. Verify, too, that similar measurements on other windows and doors roughly match inside and outside the vehicle.

Remember: Small indicators can add up to big results. U.S. Border Patrol agents in California built suspicion one piece at a time regarding a camper shell that was mounted on an old Chevy pickup truck. Then detected that: paint on the roof looked fresher and shinier than paint on the sides...when tapped, the roof produced a solid, "loaded" thud instead of a hollow sound...bolts that anchored the shell to the pickup had fresh scratches, as if they'd been recently put in...inside-outside measurements revealed that the roof was unusually thick (about four inches), and the ceiling inside the camper sagged. Ultimately, the roof was peeled open—and yielded ninety-five pounds of marijuana.

Walls. The walls of campers, vans, and motor homes often are "insulated" with contraband. Tampering from the outside may be revealed by damage to the metal sealer strip that runs vertically up to the roof line at the corners of some vehicles. Inside, where walls may be paneled with plywood, look for new paneling in an old vehicle, loose paneling, screws missing—all can be visual cues. You may be able to pry paneling out a bit with a screwdriver to look behind it with your flashlight and also to discover what odors are released.

More controversial is drilling through wood or metal with a small bit, then checking the grooves when you pull it out to see if they're filled with cocaine or marijuana instead of just sawdust or metallic grit. You're safest legally to drill and possibly damage property only when you have probable cause to believe you're dealing with a courier vehicle. Some officers, however, routinely ask permission to make "unobtrusive" holes as part of a consent search. A California officer explains: "I tell the suspect, 'A lot of officers take a long time to search. They take out the seats...there's a lot to put back together. I like to use a real small drill and drill a few quick holes to be sure everything's okay. All right?' They usually consent, figuring I won't drill in the right spot. Sometimes they tell me where the drugs are, just because they see the drill."

Sometimes traffickers expand the walls of pickup-truck beds for smuggling. This can be done by adding a commercially available plastic bed liner, then stuffing contraband behind it. Or they may build a false compartment in from the front of the bed just behind the cab, or in from the sides, to create dead space. This is often hidden by placing a camper shell or a large fuel tank over it. Again, your steel tape can confirm discrepancies between inside and outside measurements of the bed's length. If measurements don't seem normal, you may have PC for getting a warrant and having the camouflaging shell or tank removed.

Inside/Outside Measuring Tells the Tale

The rattletrap pickup truck looked suspicious to Deputy Grant Willis the minute he saw it on the expressway in Jefferson Davis Parish, Louisiana. The GMC truck was at least a dozen hard years old, but the camper shell perched over its bed and cab looked brand new, and bigger than normal. The driver made an improper lane change, and Willis pulled him over. Walking up, he could see a collection of paint cans, a ladder, and two duffel bags in the bed under the shell. Two Hispanic males in their mid-thirties were in the cab.

The registration showed that the truck had been recently purchased. The occupants told conflicting stories. One said they were on their way to look for a painting job in Alabama. The other said they already had a painting job there. Willis obtained written consent to search.

He patted the suspects down, then put them in front of the truck. First he searched the cab for weapons. Nothing. Next he measured the height of the camper shell, outside then inside, with a twenty-five-foot tape he keeps in his trunk.

The inside distance was a glaring four inches shorter.

Willis tried to turn on the roof light inside. It didn't work. He unscrewed the screws holding it in place. When he pulled the light down, the distinct odor of marijuana flooded out.

Two hundred pounds of pot were recovered from the false ceiling. Later a secret compartment was also exposed in the bed of the pickup.

The two "painters" never made it to their "job." They currently reside in Jefferson Davis Parish Prison.

(above)
Peeling back the camper shell exposes the load, a job safer to do with heavy gloves.

(left)
200 lbs. of pot recovered from false roof.

Another roof deception exposed by comparing inside and outside heights. Agent's cap shows depth of compartment created by false ceiling.

(clockwise)
Remember to check the cargo as well as the conveyance. Driver of this rental truck said he was moving, and the boxes looked like they fit his story. But when officer lifted a couple, they felt empty. Those farther back were full—of drugs.

Check wall panels on rental trucks carefully. They usually won't exist in legitimate rigs. This plywood panel seemed hastily added and poorly secured. A gentle tug pulled it loose, exposing 9 kilos of cocaine stacked behind.

Floor. Like roofs, the floors of private vehicles, including the beds of pickup trucks, are also susceptible to being built up or down to create "load space." Some pickup floors may be rigged to tip up or completely to the side on hydraulic lifts.

Alteration of floors appears to be growing as a smuggler tactic. One of the largest seizures of cash in the history of Operation Pipeline—$1,920,540, discovered during a stop in Texas—was taken from a false compartment that ran the full length under a Voyager minivan. Other sizable recoveries from floors occur regularly: Louisiana officers, initially suspicious because the couple traveling together in a camper from Maryland lived half a continent apart, unscrewed the camper's back step and exposed an improvised compartment under the floor behind it, crammed with 159 kilos of marijuana.... An agent searching a Chevy van in the Southwest lifted up a plastic floor mat and saw a small, square plate screwed and sealed in place in the floorboard. This accessed a false compartment carrying 124 pounds of pot, en route to Michigan.... Customs inspectors in Arizona became curious about a Ford pickup when they saw that the glove box was completely empty, except for the registration. Then they noticed that the truck's bed had been freshly painted. Checking more closely, they found that it had been raised, to accommodate 285 pounds of cocaine.... In Utah, a trooper measuring the sides of a pickup because the bed looked too shallow confirmed a ten-inch vertical difference between inside and outside distances. Built under the bed he found the secret compartment he suspected, stuffed with bundles of marijuana.... Another pickup truck was seized in Louisiana after an officer noticed fresh paint behind the license plate. Bondo over the area was peeled away, revealing a compartment under the bed, loaded with cocaine. The truck was part of a fleet of cars and pickups used to ferry coke to New Orleans after it was brought across the Rio Grande from Mexico by smugglers using scuba gear.

Using one hand on top of the floor and the other below it, evaluate whether or not there is space for a false bed.

In assessing floors, especially pickup beds, your naked eye can tell a lot even without tape measuring. Drop the tailgate of the truck. The bed and gate should be level; a bed that has been built up for a false compartment will be higher. Also remember to compare the bed level to the rear tires as you may have already done before stopping the vehicle (explained in Chapter 2).

In a van, one indication of a false floor added on top of the real one may be the base of the seats. The base will often need to be cut down after the floor's rigged to keep the occupants' heads from hitting the roof, so the base will appear noticeably shorter than those you ordinarily see.

With vehicles that have carpeted or matted floors, look for signs of patching or for new coverings in an older vehicle, which can also indicate concealed compartments. Are there creases in the carpeting that could have been made by a trap door being swung open?

And don't ignore what's *on* the floor. Sometimes smugglers pack coke and heroin inside PVC pipe, cap the ends, and toss it casually into a pickup bed, figuring no cop will think to inspect anything that commonplace. Contraband is also commonly concealed inside cardboard moving boxes. Couriers heading to Ohio had 159 kilos of marijuana inside three such boxes in their van when arrested during a vehicle stop

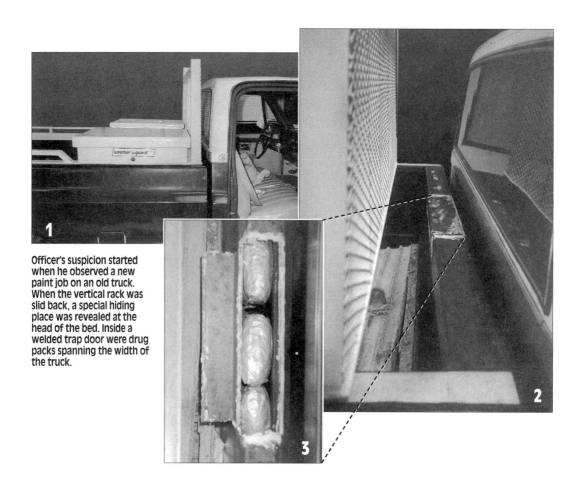

Officer's suspicion started when he observed a new paint job on an old truck. When the vertical rack was slid back, a special hiding place was revealed at the head of the bed. Inside a welded trap door were drug packs spanning the width of the truck.

Cocaine (arrow) worth $1,900,000 was packed into special compartment under this pickup. Entire bed could be raised and propped up for access.

Narcotics hidden in false pickup bed, accessed via removal of the rear bumper.

Sawdust and trash were used to "alter" this Canadian pickup bed to conceal drugs.

in Missouri. During another search in Louisiana, moving boxes discovered behind an assortment of used furniture inside a Ryder rental truck yielded 974 kilos of marijuana. You may see boxes that have been used many times, reinforced with duct tape at the corners; couriers can be cheap in small ways, and one way is to collapse U-Haul boxes after a delivery of cash or drugs and reuse them on trip after trip. (You may notice such "recycled" containers in commercial rigs, too.)

Ask yourself: Does what's on board make sense? One group of couriers hauled marijuana in pickup trucks in 1,000-pound lots from south Texas to Michigan inside hollowed-out fence posts. Detachable caps on the bottoms of the posts were smeared with tar and cement to give the impression that the posts had been previously used. If you had stopped the driver of one of these pickups and found out where he was coming from and where he was going, would you have wondered why there was such a need for used fence posts in Michigan that they had to be hauled there 1,500 miles from Texas?

Trooper examining this pickup in Utah thought bed looked shallow vertically. (Rubber mat was lying flat when he first saw it.)

Lifting rubber mat, he saw evidence of disturbed metal and welding seams (arrow). Bed had been modified to accommodate hidden compartment for drugs.

False floors in vans are common. This one, accessed by trap doors under loose carpeting, carried 383 lbs. of cocaine. Border Patrol agent in Arizona originally pulled this van over for weaving after he observed a suspension system that seemed unusually high and freshly painted fender wells that seemed to extend too low.

Fuel tanks. According to U.S. Customs, "The most favored overall hiding area in [pickup] trucks remains the gas tank[s]." Not only tanks that provide engine fuel for oversized vehicles but auxiliary tanks that presumably supply cooking gas and work-related fuels are highly prone to contraband conversion. Because propane tanks are frequently installed by legitimate workers in the beds of pickup trucks, a popular courier scheme is to cut a hole in the underside of an empty tank, insert drugs, then reseal the opening. A small decoy bottle of propane may be placed inside along with the contraband and hooked to a bleeder valve or the tank's main valve so that some pressure will register and gas will hiss out if the valves are tested.

Shiny, loose bolt and washer spotted on floor of pickup bed near large propane tank led an observant and suspicious Illinois officer to conclude that the tank had been newly and carelessly installed. Touching and tapping, he felt the seams of the trap door, which had been painted over on the tank's back side. Drugs (arrow), not propane, were inside.

Unless you know what you're doing, randomly cranking valves as you search is risky because of the hazardous qualities of propane and other fuels. The investigative technique called "touch-and-tap" is safer, plus it will often allow you to overcome a decoy bottle ruse.

With touch-and-tap, you run your hand over all surfaces of the tank you can reach. Feel for imperfections or alterations in the metal. Assess the temperature of the tank (with fuel inside, it should feel cool, but with marijuana inside, for example, it will feel warm because organic matter generates heat). Strike the tank with your knuckle, a coin, or your pen to see if it chimes as if filled with gas or thuds because something solid is packed inside. If a filler cap can be removed, dip your metal probe into the tank to see whether you hit obstructions or whether suspicious white residue might be visible on it after it's extracted.

At a Customs checkpoint in Texas, one pickup driver was almost waved through because he was "clean-cut, nicely dressed, and generally presented the appearance of a very low-risk subject." But his passport showed extensive travel to Colombia, Haiti, Santo Domingo, and the Antilles, so inspectors decided to at least give his truck the once-over. Touching-and-tapping quickly focused attention on the propane tank in the truck's bed. When an inspector rapped it, he heard "a dull, solid sound rather than a resonant echo." When the tank was unbolted and rolled over, it was then possible to feel the faint outline of a rectangular hatch that had been cut through the bottom, resealed with body putty, and repainted. Breaking through it, inspectors found 138 pounds of cocaine.

Be sure you tap and touch multiple places on any tank you're checking. The tank may be sectioned inside, with some chambers containing gas, others filled with drugs. Also tap pressure gauges. In a bona fide system, the gauge needle will normally move when tapped. (Understand, though, that the use of a decoy bottle may compromise the reliability of this test.)

Touching can also help you detect one of the most vexing concealments: a double-walled tank. This consists of an inner core where drugs are packed and a surrounding chamber where fuel is carried. Built well, such tanks will defeat tapping or bleeding. But they may not defeat your sensitive fingers. Sometimes you can feel what is difficult to see.

For example, New Mexico officers encountered an unlicensed driver at a highway checkpoint and noticed fresh paint and new bolts on the propane tank in the back of his Ford pickup—definite search cues. He had cut a door in the bottom of the tank, enabling him to insert and brace a hidden inner chamber holding bags of cocaine. He'd repaired the loading hole so deftly that it was virtually undetectable by sight. Only the slightly different feel where the tank had been puttied and sanded before painting finally gave it away. That, as it turned out, was a "touch" of double-bad luck for the driver. Tipped off by New Mexico, officers in his home state, Texas, found another propane tank with the identical modification in the bed of a Chevy pickup at his house—with another 105 kilos of coke inside ready to go.

A form of touching is to run a small magnet over the tank's surface. Plastic repair compounds won't attract it, and this may help you find patches covering trap doors. Also carefully inspect the ends of tanks. In double-walling, these may be taken off so the inner chamber can be put in place, then resealed with Bondo and repainted. A Chevy pickup being searched in Texas seemed to have a fully functioning propane tank: The fuel gauge registered full, opening a relief valve released gas, the sides rang just right when tapped. But feeling the surface of the tank's end caps with the attuned touch of a Braille reader, the searching officer detected a recessed bolt hidden with putty and painted over. In the truck's cab, he found an Allen wrench that fit it—and opened up the tank end to an inner cylinder holding 115 pounds of marijuana. Understand that Bondo or any other patching compound should never be found on any legitimate tank that is under pressure. If it's there, it's not right, no matter what excuse you're offered.

Flexible probe can help you examine inside of a fuel tank for solid objects and partitions.

Both gas tanks removed from this pickup contain false compartments for drug transport.

Besides what you can detect with tapping and touching, be alert to other indicators: brand new propane or motor fuel tanks on a worn-out vehicle...fuel lines coming out of a tank but not connecting any-where...propane tanks not bolted to the truck bed...scratches that may have occurred when tanks were set on their sides, and so on. An officer in a Western state noticed what looked like an auxiliary fuel tank in the bed of a pickup truck, a large, rectangular metal contain-er standing flush against the back of the cab. Looking closer he real-ized it had no spout for filling. When he tipped it forward, he found it did have an opening: a trap door cut into the side that was hidden next to the cab. This was used to fill the tank—with drugs.

Note: Don't let zeal overwhelm your common sense. *Think* about what you're doing. An Arizona officer decided to investigate the fuel tank of one oversized carrier by *drilling* into it. He struck gasoline, not dope—and was left with a pool of it widening on the highway, an irate driver, and a reputation he'll never live down.

Caution: If your search produces strong suspicion of tank tamper-ing and you are not fully familiar with the kind of tank you are inves-tigating, get a fuel dealer, a mechanic, or other experienced personnel to the scene. They can advise how to investigate further. You may need a search warrant to detain the driver longer, but the extra time and effort are better than impulsively overreaching. Don't turn a bust into a blowup by pushing beyond your competence.

Searching a large private vehicle can seem like searching a house because there are so many potential hiding places beyond the primary checkpoints listed above. With those carriers that actually resemble small houses—custom vans, campers, and motor homes—there should be another similarity. They should look and smell "lived in." After a long trip, they normally are not clean and neat, so be suspicious of any that seem exceptionally so.

House-type vehicles require the same dissection in searching as a room. New Mexico agents discovered 160 kilograms of marijuana in one motor home from Canada, but it was in scattered locations: under a bed, in a closet, under bench seats in the dining area, in a luggage carrier. When time and suspicion permit, be prepared to measure the depth of cabinets and closets for unaccountable space. Look behind and under drawers. Remove table posts to check for hollowed-out spaces in or under their bases. Inspect all the vehicle's outside compartments, including water filler spouts, septic tanks, electrical panels, storage areas, air conditioning units. Test all electrical outlets and investigate behind any that aren't working. Hidden in a natural cavity under a cigarette lighter in one custom van, a Southern deputy found $37,000 in cash; he was amazed at how much money could fit into so small a space. "You can search hard in an oversized vehicle for thirty minutes," says one municipal officer, "and at best you'll hit only half the places that one or two kilos of coke can be hidden."

If you strike a dry hole one place, keep searching. Officers in a small Florida town who were searching a customized van after a K-9 alert first found a piece of unexplained plywood screwed to the floor. When the board was lifted up, they saw that three compartments had been constructed under it in the floor frame. These were empty, but the

118 kilos of marijuana were found under a false floor of this motor home when the table and carpet were removed.

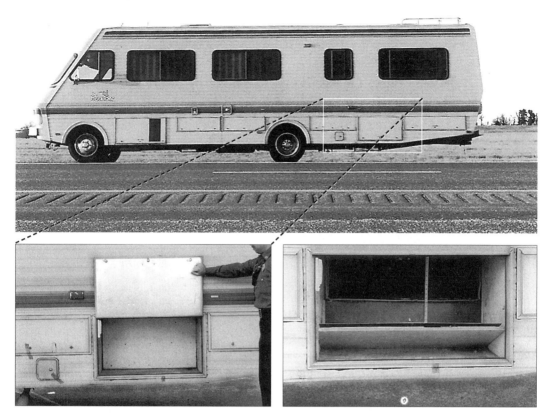

Stay alert for what "doesn't fit" when searching larger vehicles, the same as smaller ones. This motor home looked unexceptional when stopped for improper passing and weaving. Officer began a consent search when he learned owner was a 3rd party, unknown to driver. He noticed that back wall of one storage compartment was held in place by drywall screws. Walls in other storage areas were stapled. Behind the "different" wall was the drug hideaway.

More Tips for the Bad Guys

Just as drug-culture magazines and gray-market publishers regularly advise their readers on how to successfully haul contraband by automobile, they also offer tips of the trade for using trucks. This excerpt is from a book, aimed at drug smugglers and wanna-bes:

New trucks with new camper shells on them are more suspicious than older ones that look like they've been around the block a few times.

Three-quarter-ton, eight-foot-bed pickups are the most desirable. The springs and shocks are such that the vehicle won't tilt back if it has a two-thousand-pound load, and these trucks can handle the heaviest camper rigs. Half-ton pickup trucks are far more popular in the market-place, but unless you beef up the rear suspension, a half-ton pickup will show that it's carrying a heavy load by tilting slightly to the rear.

It is essential that your truck have four-wheel drive. No matter what the mission, you will need a vehicle to off-load to, so have one that is equipped to go anywhere.

Once purchased, if the truck isn't new, then give it the complete razzle-dazzle. The minimum would be four new steel-belted, all-terrain tires and a complete tune-up, including all fluids checked plus new oil and oil filter, plugs, ignition parts, ignition wires, battery, and a radar detector. Additionally, the vehicle should be equipped with a pair of jumper cables, a small tool kit, a flashlight, a road atlas, extra fuses, extra bulbs for the running lights, an extra headlight, a shovel, and a high-lift jack in case you get stuck in sand, mud, or snow.

Each state has different regulations for licensing and registration, but two general rules are to have a legitimate mailing address where you can receive the title and to use "RV" plates as opposed to "business" plates. Recreational vehicle plates on a truck generally exempt you from having to stop at weigh stations. Call the division of motor vehicles in the state in which you are thinking about registering your vehicles to find out the ins and outs of getting the job done. Then you'll know what kind of paperwork to expect when you go in to get your license plates....[4]

town's chief, who was participating in the search, then noticed an unmatching piece of carpeting stapled to the wall behind the driver seat. Pulling this off, he discovered another compartment cut into the side. Here he found a plastic bag filled with mustard, spices—and twelve kilos of coke.

Keep in mind: The probabilities are greater that big loads are carried in big vehicles, but that's not all they carry. Couriers are hauling smaller amounts in these vehicles, too, right down to personal-use quantities. Don't be looking so hard for a forest that you miss seeing a tree.

Commercial Rigs

With a courier who's driving a commercial tractor-trailer, a tanker truck, or other "working" rig ("large cars," as truckers call them), there are three possibilities:

- **His true load is the dope,** and any freight or other commodities in the cargo area are there strictly for disguise;
- **He's hauling a legitimate load,** along with drugs that are concealed amidst it, or around it in the walls, floor, or roof of the cargo carrier;
- **His load is strictly untainted** and the contraband is hidden elsewhere in the truck.

From your dialogue with the driver and any passengers, your knowledgeable examination of the documents, and your observations before obtaining consent, you may have strong suspicions about the extent to which the load is involved. But with one important exception, the cargo area is probably not the place you're going to start looking. The exception is when that area is alleged to be empty or lightly loaded and exploring it is relatively easy. Otherwise, try first to develop more evidence for reasonable suspicion or probable cause, because getting into the cargo area can complicate your stop. With a semitrailer, for example, you may have to snip a shipper's metal seal on the rear door latch, which potentially has certain ramifications. Then unless the contraband is obvious once you get the doors open, you may face a search through several tons of boxed freight, fresh produce, or other wares. In the end, probably the only practical means of completing the job will be to recruit a K-9.

Consequently, the most realistic search pattern generally will be to leave the cargo area, which you may consider the "best" spot (in terms of potential payoff) or the "worst" (in terms of difficulty), for last. Start with the cab, where you may find personal-use or modest-to-significant quantities of drugs...progress around the exterior of the rig...and finish with the interior of the trailer. Searching the cab and exterior can keep your investigation active while you're awaiting arrival of a K-9 and possibly additional officers. Of course, a Cover Officer should already be there monitoring the suspect(s) before you begin searching any area. (This search pattern, incidentally, can also apply for searching smaller trucks with enclosed cargo areas, including rental vehicles.)

Use spare moments on patrol or off-duty to look over a lot of different rigs. Legitimate drivers at truck stops will generally be willing to show you the ropes if approached in a friendly, curious manner. Get a feel for what's right and what isn't and for the way trucks come from the factory. Then you'll more quickly tap into suspicious variances you may see on a contraband stop.

Besides the basic strategies appropriate for searching any vehicle, these additional considerations can help you successfully investigate trucks:

CAB. First, be sure the engine is turned off before you enter the truck. This eliminates the risk of your inadvertently nudging the gear shift as you rummage around the cab, and it reduces noxious fumes that may hamper a K-9's search.

When you're actually up in a tractor cab, your perspective changes radically from when you're standing at ground level looking up. There's a great deal more hidden from you when you're outside a truck than outside a car. An Iowa trooper arrested a money courier who had already been stopped and cited for speeding by two different officers in Nevada. The driver rode with a big knife hanging from a strap on his steering column, he had a gun tucked beside his seat, and ammo was scattered on the console. But the Nevada officers hadn't tumbled to any of this because they couldn't see it from where they stood down on the roadway.

Sit for a moment after entering the cab and absorb what's now noticeable to you. What drug- or masking-related odors are you now conscious of? Is the windshield unusually dirty? Maybe instead of fluid in the washer reservoir there's dope. Do you see multiple toolboxes in the cab? Usually there's just one; all should be checked. Is the CB set to a channel other than 19, the communications channel legitimate truckers usually use? In the Southeast, for example, Cubans involved with drug hauling often stay in touch with each other over Channel 22, on highly accessorized, top-of-the-line CBs. Cuban couriers may also be involved in the Santeria religious culture that flourishes among some immigrant groups in south Florida. You may see shrines, icons, burnt offerings, bow-and-arrow symbolism, and other evidence of appeasement to Santeria figures in hopes of winning protection from the police.

Because the cab often doubles as a home for days at a time and gives the illusion of lofty isolation, you may see the kind of drug paraphernalia around that you'd expect to find lying out in some suspect's pad—roach clips, cigarette papers, straws cut in half, the tube casings of writing pens, razor blades, mirrors, sometimes even scales, funnels, sifters, tourniquets, heating spoons, cotton balls, mixing and cutting agents (like powdered milk and lactose, baking soda, starch) or personal-use drug packaging (toy balloons, capsules, folded paper bindles, heat-sealed plastic bag corners, vials, tinfoil).

Search for hidden contraband much as you would in the front seat of an automobile, van, or pickup truck. Divide the driver-passenger area in two to organize your hunt. Then systematically knock off the usual places: inside door panels, under and behind seats, under the dash, in vents and speakers, under mats (look for bulges and signs of disturbance in the floor covering over the angled floorboard on the passenger side; there's a natural cavity under this "kickboard" on many trucks), behind visors, overhead, et cetera. Roll windows all the way down, and look for screws that have been tampered with or removed, as you do in other vehicles. Also check under the gearshift cover; truckers often hide weapons there. Fully pull out all seat belts. One courier trick is to lay currency flat on a stretched-out seat belt, then retract it so the money rolls up inside. A portion of a $300,000 load of cash was smuggled into New York from Canada this way.

Read all papers you encounter, including phone bills (any calls to source areas?), love letters (which may include references to drugs or things deteriorating in the driver's life that could motivate a drug run), and old shipping papers (same load being carted around for months?). Also be alert for airline tickets that can provide you an additional topic for dialogue with the driver.

If there's a sleeping berth, consider that to be an additional search zone. U-Haul boxes or other containers stacked up there would be unusual on a legitimate trip. Likewise, clean and pressed clothing on

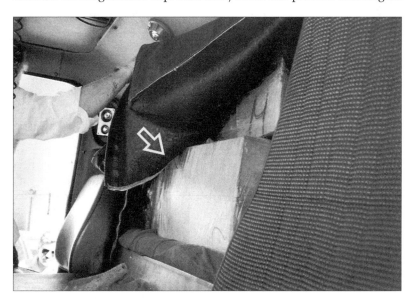

Boxes containing a total of 449 lbs. of pot found in tractor sleeping berth. Driver, 19, too young to drive a commercial truck, was stopped for reckless driving. He told officers he was headed toward a vacant lot to sell the truck.

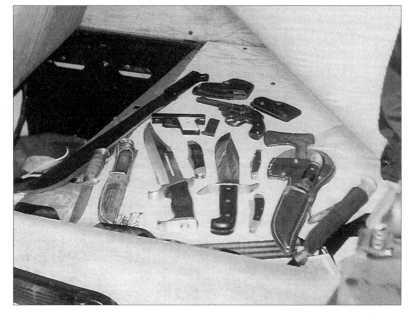

Weapons found during search underneath the bed of a semi's cab. Hideout was accessed by unscrewing bolts and removing a piece of plywood.

hangers is not typical of the average trucker but may be of some of the more fastidious drivers for the Colombian cartels. Under the mattress where the driver can easily reach back is where you'll often find guns and sometimes drugs. Below the sleeper compartment in most cabs is a tool or storage cabinet that is usually accessed through small outside doors. On many trucks you can see into this compartment from behind the seats; if you can't, it may have been partitioned and sealed off to create a hiding spot.

Note: Top-of-the-line trucks like Peterbilt, Kenworth, and Western Star are well-made vehicles. Any evidence of shoddy workmanship or modifications, like missing screws, paint drips, Bondo, and so on, should be considered suspicious. These vehicles come from the factory the way they need to be for legitimate truckers and don't require alterations.

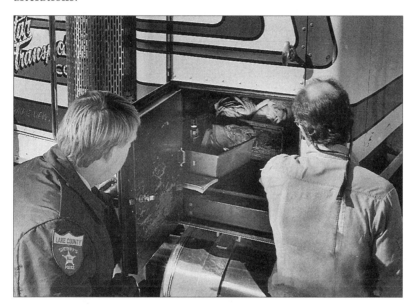

You may be able to see into some storage compartments from inside the cab. If the driver has to unlock one for closer inspection, remember the risks of letting him reach inside or remain close while you search.

Lights Out

A small infraction led Patrolman Charles Simmons of the Fairmont (Illinois) Police Department to the biggest bust of his career.

At about midnight one night in May, he spotted a Kenworth tractor rumbling through his jurisdiction with no clearance lights illuminated. The twenty-two-year-old driver said they'd burned out about an hour ago and he intended to get them fixed at the next truck stop.

As Simmons looked over the truck's documentation, the independent driver, a Cuban from Florida, seemed unusually nervous. He claimed he was traveling alone with a trailer full of broccoli and lettuce. At one point, he said his destination was New York. Another time he said Ohio, then Pennsylvania. His permit card lacked a stamp from Illinois.

With backup present, Simmons headed for the cab to begin a consent search. His first surprise was finding a passenger, who'd just awakened in the sleeping compartment. After he was rousted, Simmons noticed four taped cardboard boxes sitting on a ledge above the berth.

The passenger, a native of the Dominican Republic, said the driver had approached him in Miami and asked if he wanted to make a run for extra money. They first drove to California with a load of Spanish produce, then started on the present run to New York. The passenger didn't know anything about the boxes, he said, except that the driver had told him not to mess with them.

Simmons now questioned the driver about the boxes, which bore no address labels. He said they were his personal property and that they contained auto parts. He wasn't carrying any guns or anything illegal, he insisted, so he had no objection to the officer looking inside the cartons. In fact, he cut the first one open himself.

Inside were twenty individually wrapped packages, about the size of a kilo, each stamped with "Uno."

After a K-9 borrowed from the state police alerted to each of the boxes, the rest were opened. The contents field-tested positive for cocaine. Grand total: seventy kilos with an estimated local street value of $3,000,000.

EXTERIOR. Inspecting the exterior of a commercial rig, you have a dual mission: You're looking for contraband caches that can be directly accessed, and at the same time you're seeking clues that may indirectly suggest that the cargo area has been compromised. *Completely* circle the truck, evaluating what you see. Keep in mind that much contraband carried in trucks is hauled in hiding places that can be quickly accessed, so it can be readily off-loaded into smaller vehicles at a transfer point. Of course you'll want to check all compartments that open from the outside. In addition, pay particular attention to these other popular direct-access hiding places:

Bumpers. Be especially suspicious of trucks on which the factory bumpers have been replaced with fabricated round "cattle-guard" pipes. Two to six inches in diameter, these may run the full width of the rig. Officers in North Dakota found that such pipes on trucks hauling machinery were stuffed with cocaine packages, then a plate was welded at each end. The original bumpers were carried in with the cargo so they could be reattached when the loaded tubes were removed at the end of the run. Similarly, caps are sometimes taken off and rewelded to the hollow metal framework on automobile carrier trailers. One carrier hauled 140 bricks of marijuana, strung together with wires, inside this framework. A K-9 alert may be your best bet for detecting these hiding spots.

Oil-bath air cleaner. Couriers may replace the filter soaking in oil in this fat cylinder with contraband. You'll need a wrench to open it but you can do a rough test of it closed. If it's working properly and the engine's running, the cleaner should always feel hot when you hold your hand close. If not, it may have been compromised. There's no functional need for more than one cleaner on a truck. A second cold one should draw your immediate attention.

What's inside the oil-bath air cleaner? It may pay big to be curious enough to investigate.

404

117 lbs. of marijuana were found inside this oil-bath air cleaner. Cab is tilted to assure thorough search of other possible hiding places in the Engine Zone.

Battery boxes. Most big rigs have one box on each side; one holds the batteries (normally on the driver side), the other is for show or storage. Besides checking the spare space, inspect for fake or altered batteries. These may look brand new without the usual patina of grime and oxidation, or the layer of dirt may look disturbed.

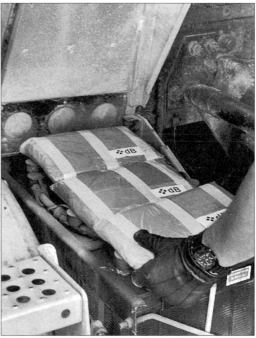

Battery box and interior drug concealment.

Fuel tanks. Diesel-fuel saddle tanks often are rebuilt with a false chamber in the center. Once packed with drugs, these tanks may then be switched from truck to truck for shipment throughout the U.S. Tap fuel tanks for suspicious dull sounds, probe for obstructions, and look for signs of tampering with the bands...for shiny or newly scratched bolts...and for a possible access panel cut into the underside. Remember,

405

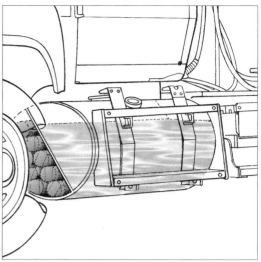

Don't touch and tap just in the easiest, most obvious places. Tanks may be partitioned with drugs hidden on the side hardest to reach, in hopes that a weakness for convenience will defeat your search.

fuel inside a tank should make it feel cool. If any part of it feels hot, be suspicious of a hidden chamber packed with heat-generating drugs. Welded seams may be concealed under the broad metal bands.

"Reefer" fuel tank. A semi with a refrigeration unit will have a separate fuel tank serving that unit, usually located under the trailer. With dope runs, the reefer unit may be shut down and this tank used to carry drugs. Check it in the same way you do the saddle tanks.

Air-brake tanks. A tractor-trailer typically has from one to four air tanks for its pneumatic brake system. These are favorite hiding places. One group of cocaine couriers modified the air tanks on a fleet of flatbeds and semitrailers to hold thirty-six kilos apiece and moved 300 to 500 kilos every week, until Texas officers intercepted them. Look for brake lines that don't connect to either a tank or a wheel...fresh weld marks where lines meet the tanks...places where a uniform coating of dirt has been disturbed. Strike each tank with a hammer or other metal tool to see if it rings like it should. It should sound hollow, since it legitimately carries only air. The driver should be knowledgeable enough about his equipment that he can readily open bleeder valves to release an air sample for K-9. Even without a dog, you can ask him to operate the valves to test his familiarity with the rig.

Caution: Do not mess with the air-brake *chambers*, which are separate from the air-brake *tanks*. These small units at each brake are pressurized and incorporate spring-loaded parts which, if released, can become deadly projectiles capable of penetrating a vest. The chambers are not large enough to contain significant quantities of dope and are not worth the risk to attempt to inspect internally.

Running boards. Look underneath for possible false compartments or taped contraband. Some traffickers weld "toolboxes" there on big rigs as well as on pickup trucks, confident that you won't risk getting your hands and pants dirty by kneeling down to check them.

Exhaust stacks. Dual exhausts are a style option on big rigs, but a truck really only needs one stack to run right. Consequently the other can make a convenient hiding place. Just by putting your hand close you can tell if both are really hooked up and working. If one's cold, it warrants further checking, preferably with K-9.

406

Engine compartment. This often-neglected area offers tremendous potential for concealment. If it's located under the cab, ask the driver to unlatch and open it. He may have to use a hydraulic pump to tilt the cab forward, but he'll know how. Look up into the underside of the tilted cab, too.

Questionable equipment. Any equipment on a truck that doesn't seem to have a normal function or that is difficult or impossible to operate—from running lights to the refrigeration unit—may indicate a repository for concealed contraband. If accessories aren't working because of neglectful maintenance, that can be a cue, too. Drug transporters often pay little attention to "nonessential" equipment. Their focus is on their illicit load and keeping it moving.

Tires. On big commercial rigs, tires inflate to about 80 psi. If you check with a gauge and find an exceptionally low reading—say, 30 psi or less—the tire may contain something other than air. Place your off hand on each tire and strike the tread with a hammer to see if you feel the vibration you should. Are there hubcaps on the tires? That's very uncommon on over-the-road rigs.

Look for fresh marks on lug nuts...fresh mud, grease or paint applied to wheel assemblies to hide evidence of tampering...new tires on a truck that's old junk. Officers in Dallas found 147 kilos of marijuana in a forward set of tires on a car-carrier trailer, after noticing that the lug nuts were scratched and wiped clean of grime as if they'd been recently removed. The tires were lifted up by adjustable air shocks so they wouldn't touch the road when the carrier was under way.

The inner tires of dual tire sets are especially favored for contraband concealment because they're harder to reach and less likely to be examined closely. Spare tires are popular, too. In contrast with a rolling tire that's carrying contraband, there's no risk with a spare of a blowout spraying the load all over the road.

Air bags. These are big black balloon-like devices near the tires of the tractor and/or trailer, designed to absorb shock. If they're functional, they'll be blown up like a ball. You can hit them and they should sound like a rubber air ball. If they appear less than taut, be suspicious that something else is inside.

Air bags and interior drug concealment.

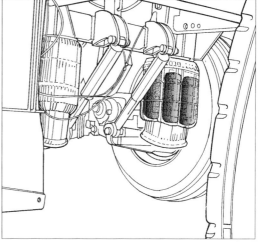

Roof. With refrigerated trailers, there normally is four to six inches of insulation in the roof, which is often removed by smugglers and replaced with narcotics. Look for evidence of a new top, new or creased trim, fresh caulking, misaligned or overlapped seams where the roof and sidewall join—similar to indicators that you check for on motor homes and campers. Some compartments added on top of trailer roofs are hinged, so that the entire second roof can be unlocked and swung up to one side. Check for hinges that may be visible along the roofline.

Reefer vent. On most refrigeration units there are small vent doors in front and rear ends of the trailer that allow a look inside. The front one is usually more easily reached, up a small ladder attached to the rig. Peering through, look for a load that doesn't match the driver's story and for containers that look different from the rest, which may signify contraband amidst a cover load. If there's a padlock on the vent, be suspicious. There's rarely a legitimate reason for it to be there.

Reefer vent provides an exterior inspection opportunity for discovering drugs inside the trailer. Note that drugs have also been hidden inside the wind deflector which normally is hollow with no rear wall.

Chassis. You should be able to see the wood or metal floor of the trailer showing through between all girders when you look up from underneath the chassis. If not, be suspicious. Smugglers sometimes create compartments under the trailer by welding metal plates across the chassis girders. Are the girders filled in? Do you see burn or buckle marks made from torches or welding? With flatbed trailers, which many officers ignore because they feel there are no concealment areas, the trailer's wood flooring is sometimes hollowed out to accommodate dope. Or contraband containers designed to look like storage compartments may be added to the undercarriage. If flooring seems unusually thick, check further. In New Jersey, troopers searching one flatbed found $3,000,000 worth of cocaine concealed in beams supporting the chassis, inside special compartments that had been added to the undercarriage, and inside foreign car engines that were being hauled as cargo. On some flatbeds, the flooring lifts on hydraulics. Have the driver tilt it enough for you to see if any compartments have been constructed in the framework underneath.

Look underneath the trailer to see if cross beams and flooring are visible.

Cocaine revealed after plywood closure was removed. Compartments under the chassis of over-the-road rigs are highly suspicious.

Fifth wheel/kingpin plate. Drugs are frequently packed into the natural cavities or easily created compartments in the "kingpin plate," the apparatus on the bottom of the trailer where it hooks onto the tractor's "fifth wheel." Factory cut-out holes in some plate assemblies are favorite stash places for the personal-use amphetamines and other uppers popped by many truckers. Larger quantities of drugs can be hidden there, too. In one bust, officers found 394 pounds of marijuana divided between the fifth wheel/kingpin plate area and space under the sleeper berth in the cab. The kingpin plate is often removed so contraband can be packed above it, too. Besides looking in natural recesses with your flashlight, check for bolts and nuts that have been recently painted or are noticeably chipped or shiny from being frequently taken off and put back.

CARGO AREA. There are different concealment opportunities in the cargo area, depending on the type of truck.

Tanker trucks. With these vehicles, the kingpin plate is one of several sites that can offer clues to suggest that the cargo area has been compromised. In southern California, a sharp-eyed officer checking a propane tanker noticed gouges and chips in the paint on the nuts and bolts holding the plate up in place. With the help of narcotics task force members, the plate was removed, revealing a hole above it that had been cut through the tank belly. Inside the "empty" tanker were two tons of marijuana, packed in cardboard egg boxes that had been loaded through this cutout. Other tankers with similar apertures concealed by the kingpin plate have been found in Texas and Arizona, including one chemical tanker nailed on a traffic stop while hauling 846 pounds of cocaine and another truck that had delivered a whopping six tons of pot in one load shortly before being discovered.

Access holes are also sometimes cut in tanker bellies above the spare-tire rack. Here the cut-out metal is usually welded back in place after the load has been inserted, then puttied over and repainted. You may need to look and feel closely for evidence of alteration. Also check the circular manhole inspection plate located at the top rear or top front of tankers. This is another popular loading hole. In their careless haste, smugglers sometimes fail to replace the gasket which normally fits between the inspection plate and the tanker wall, or they damage or leave off some of the sixteen lug nuts that ordinarily hold the plate in place. In legitimate operations, this plate is not often removed, so nuts that are shiny, stripped, or missing should be immediately suspicious.

During your outside circuit of a tanker, take note of the intake and discharge valves near the middle of the tank's belly. Are they rusty or do they look as if they would be very difficult to open? With propane tankers, that doesn't fit because propane does not rust metal, and these valves have to be in good working condition so the tank can be filled and emptied.

As you move along the side of a tanker, use the touch-and-tap technique, seeking variations in sound or temperature that may suggest a false compartment in the cargo area. (Legally you can touch and tap even without consent to search because this technique is not considered a search.[5]) A propane tanker should give a "hollow resonance" when tapped, whether empty or filled with gas; a solid sound, as

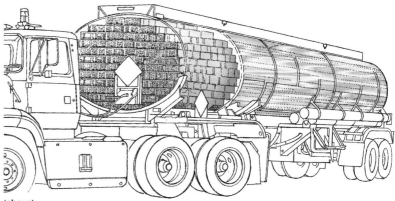

(below/below right)
Drug concealment in the hose container. Container cap may be sealed and, with adequate suspicion, should be opened to view inside tube with your flashlight.

(above)
With tankers, traffickers can make a number of internal alterations to conceal contraband. Here a vertical partition separates a compartment for marijuana from legitimate contents. You may be able to detect this deception by touching and tapping the exterior. If one section feels cold and another warm, you have reason for further investigation.

410

usual, suggests it's loaded with something else. Along the shady side of the truck, where surface temperatures will be less affected by the sun, feel the metal every foot or so. Is it cool…cool…cool—then a lot warmer in some spot? You may be touching a secret compartment that's filled with heat-generating marijuana. In summertime, condensation may form on the outside of tankers carrying cool loads. If part of the tank has condensation and the rest doesn't, wonder why. Ditto with refrigerated trailers; their cold, sweaty outside "skin" should feel consistent from nose to tail.

Caution: Trucks hauling explosives, fuels, acids, and other toxic or volatile materials can be extremely dangerous. Some tanks are even more hazardous empty than full because of the internal buildup of fumes. *Do not approach these vehicles with any open flame (such as a flare, cigarette lighter, or even burning cigarette) during your search.* A manual published by EPIC itemizes various valves on tanker trucks that can be opened and tested as part of a search. However, unless you have specific training or experience, you are safest to avoid manipulating any valves, handles, hatches, or other gear related to tankers. Use K-9 assistance instead. If the truck is hauling drugs, residue will almost certainly have been left somewhere on the exterior during the loading process. If the dog alerts on any part of the vehicle not familiar or readily accessible to you, get expert help before proceeding further.

Enclosed trailers. Learning what's inside an enclosed trailer can be complicated, too. But this investigation is usually more direct and less risky than dealing with a tanker.

On some semitrailer loads, particularly with company-owned trucks, the back latch may be sealed with a metal strip bearing a serial number. This seal is supposed to remain intact throughout the transport, to discourage theft and tampering. However, when you have dialogue cues, behavior cues, document cues, and/or other strong indicators that something is wrong, do not skip searching the trailer interior, even though it is sealed.

If the driver has given you consent to search (which should include his consent to search the cargo), he'll likely also give you permission to cut the seal. Get this in writing. He will often have a fresh seal to resecure the load and will note the change in his log book should you fail to find anything illegal inside.

If the driver won't cooperate (and a peek inside through the vent doors on a reefer unit doesn't satisfy you), call the trucking company, explain your suspicion, and get approval to break the seal. Legitimate firms are very concerned that contraband may be hauled without their knowledge and will generally cooperate.

With probable cause (like a K-9 alert) to believe that the cargo area contains contraband, you are on good legal grounds to cut the seal even without permission. Ditto for opening the rear doors of a refrigerated unit, where the infusion of outside air may adversely affect the temperature and the load. However, know your department's policy and state and federal regulations about this. Confer with your supervisor if you have doubts. Many officers and agencies in practice won't disturb seals for fear they'll be held liable if no drugs are found and the load ends up damaged. But with adequate suspicion and the proper approach, you should not be intimidated.

Oddly enough, independent owner/operator rigs (which are most

Don't try to break a metal seal (arrow) with your fingers. You'll get cut. Use a real or improvised tool.

411

Driver with suspicious shipping papers had no key for lock on his rear doors. Entry was made with bolt cutter. Over 1,300 lbs. of marijuana was discovered in 8 canvas bags inside. Sometimes easiest access to concealed drugs is a side door (arrow). Try that before forcing entry—it may be unlocked.

often involved with drug hauling) tend not to use seals as much. Their doors may be fastened with a padlock, for which the driver will normally have the key. If he doesn't, that in itself could be suspicious.

To directly access the cargo area, first have the driver open the trailer's rear doors about four to six inches. This provides you some protection from booby traps and also against poorly secured piles of boxes or other freight that may be tipped against the door ready to fall out. (If anything does fall out, the driver may be in violation of a statute regarding unsafe loading.)

As you stand about three to four feet behind the driver, sweep your flashlight around inside to check for individuals who may be hiding there. Then have the driver open the doors fully and lock them in position. The driver and any passenger[s] should then be monitored by your Cover Officer while you continue the search. You are alert, as always, for anything that seems unusual or altered. Do you smell any of the traditional masking odors—baby powder, deodorant, coffee grounds, spices, cedar shavings, air freshener, mothballs—not noticeable outside the truck? Do you see crushed boxes (maybe being recycled for another drug load) or boxes that look different from most of the load (possibly contraband added to legitimate freight)? Assess what the load looks like. Are you seeing odd or useless commodities, kind of a flea-market look?

Be suspicious when boxes are mismatched in a truck loaded with cargo.

If the cargo is *produce* (the most popular cover load), is it spoiled, frozen, or in disarray? One early indicator in a bust of 700 pounds of marijuana in a semitrailer in Missouri was the fact that the driver was hauling perishable produce in an unventilated trailer. Produce is normally kept at carefully regulated temperatures and should be delivered quickly. It should have a fresh, crisp smell when you get the doors open. Marijuana will taint this natural aroma and make it acrid or spoiled smelling. Boxed produce is usually stacked with narrow aisles on a ridged "T-floor" or on pallets, so the cooled air can flow around it.

With freight, is the top of the load level, or is some part higher than the rest? Freight pallets are normally stacked evenly for the whole length of the trailer; an uneven load may suggest a false compartment or nonmatching containers under the uneven portion. If the trailer is only partially full, be sure the log book indicates that drops have already been made along the way; it's highly unusual for over-the-road trucks to travel far while less than fully loaded.

With couriers, spoilage of produce may occur through negligence, or it may be deliberate to mask drug odor. In this case, rotten cabbage was packed floor-to-ceiling, with a mother lode of cocaine buried in the middle (arrow). The traffickers thought the stinky mess would defeat drug dogs. But the idea that a legitimate trucker would haul a load of spoiled vegetables was so nonsensical that it drew suspicion rather than diverted it.

Light Load = Heavy Suspicion

Officers watching a hotel in California saw three empty trucks parked in the hotel's lot for three days and a group of men who seemed to be holding meetings in the hotel restaurant. The subjects made frequent pay-phone calls and from time to time engaged in what the officers interpreted as "countersurveillance driving."

On the third day, the men hastily loaded the trucks with cartons without securing them, filling only a small fraction of each cargo area.

After two of the trucks left the lot, the officers stopped all of them and questioned the drivers. The drivers gave written consent to search. From the boxes, the officers recovered 2,000 kilos of cocaine.

Later, a court ruled that "legitimate truckers will not use their vehicle as inefficiently as these trucks were used, do not generally use hotel parking lots to transfer loads, and do not normally behave as the people in this case did." The officers were justified in stopping the trucks on the basis of reasonable suspicion, and the resulting arrests were upheld.[6]

Still standing at ground level at the rear of the trailer, look back and forth, inside and outside, down its full length. You can do this whether the truck is loaded or not. Does your comparative depth perception convey that the inside distance from back to front is noticeably shorter, suggesting a false compartment built back from the nose?

On some trailers you may also be able to count the vertical "ribs" along an inside wall or across the ceiling. These should match the number of corresponding riveted seams on the exterior. Fewer ribs visible inside than there are seams on the outside again suggests a false-nose compartment. The most reliable test, of course, is to actually "measure and match" inside and outside distances. Use your steel tape. Or if your radar gun has been replaced with a laser speed-measuring device that also computes distance, you can use that. Have your backup hold a clipboard at one end of the truck and bounce the laser beam off that out side, then bounce it off the nose of the trailer inside for comparison. Because of a laser's plus-or-minus allowances, a false partition that's only a few inches deep may be hard to detect except by *precisely* measuring with a tape. Also *vertical* distances in a truck can't be accurately measured by laser. But, says one city officer from Arkansas, "just whipping out your tape or laser is often intimidating" to the suspect[s].

Some officers feel that checking for nose compartments is "too much trouble." But if you slight it, you're potentially bypassing one of the most popular smuggler devices. The biggest cocaine seizure ever recorded anywhere in the world was at a warehouse under the control of a Mexican drug cartel in Sylmar, California: 21.4 tons, plus about $12,000,000 in cash. The drugs in that enormous cache (plus much more) had first been hauled, about 650 pounds at a time, from Mexico to El Paso in the large trunks of Mercury luxury cars. Over an eighteen-month period more than 900 runs bringing in some 250 tons of cocaine had been made without a single detection. From a stockpile in El Paso, the drugs were then shipped in refrigerated semitrailers along secondary roads to the warehouse in California. These undetected loads were concealed in false-nose compartments, generally hidden behind a cargo of *piñatas* and Mexican crafts. Up to five tons of cocaine a week were shipped back out from the warehouse to other destinations in California, New York, and Florida, similarly concealed in other trucks. In some of the trailers, the false compartments were two deep—another one hidden behind the first. Again, none was detected; the warehouse was fingered and raided after a citizen's tip.[7]

To the extent you can see walls and floor as you survey the trailer, do you see what looks like any excessive amount of caulking anywhere (possibly to cover seams of a false wall)? Do the upper front wall corners seem to be of the same shape as the corresponding exterior corners? (With a false nose they may have different angles.) Note whether the coverings of surfaces look consistent in size, condition, texture, material, and color from one panel to another. Are there plywood wall panels that appear newer than the rest, or that have new or damaged rivets, nails, or bolts? Do you see screws used where rivets are appropriate or rivets, bolts, or screws that are not in symmetrical order? Do you see or smell fresh paint, glue, or caulking? Be prepared to drill suspicious walls with a long, thin bit.

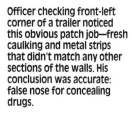
Officer checking front-left corner of a trailer noticed this obvious patch job—fresh caulking and metal strips that didn't match any other sections of the walls. His conclusion was accurate: false nose for concealing drugs.

One of a fleet of jerry-rigged semitrailers seized in the world-record Sylmar (CA) bust. After establishing suspicion of a false nose, officers remove the improvised wall. Behind it: a huge load of cocaine ready to roll.

With flooring or walls that are sheets of ribbed metal, do you detect any fresh welds along the seams or new or burred screws along the ends of the panels? Such cues to structural modifications may indicate that below or behind the suspicious panels are false compartments or contraband. Use your drill to check them out. A federal agent inspecting a commercial truck in Arizona noticed that the interior had been completely refurbished, although the exterior still looked old. Also the floor looked higher than normal and was "irregular" instead of level. Actually, the floor he saw was false. It had been jerry-rigged over the original to hide nearly 1,500 pounds of marijuana. An agent in Texas found marijuana packed in the front wall of a livestock trailer carrying sheep and goats after he noticed that a piece of the wall's sheet metal covering was loose. Curious, he lifted it and discovered a false compartment that had been sealed with silicone caulking.

If the trailer has a rear door that slides up along tracks suspended from the roof, lower it enough from inside so you can shine your flashlight into the "dead space" that is created between the door and roof when it's open. False compartments are sometimes built there on assumptions that the open door will shield them and that "cops don't look up when searching."

Usually the toughest payload to detect is one that traffickers have concealed amidst seemingly legitimate cargo. They do this about as often as they modify the structure of a vehicle. Drugs have been ferried in virtually every type of load, from dog food to crystalware. Depending on the style of truck and your own time and equipment, you may still be able to find it on your own. With open-top grain trucks, for example, you can shove a small-diameter steel probe about six feet long down into the grain at various points to seek unexplained obstructions and be sure the cargo really goes as deep as it should. With a flatbed truck that's hauling lumber or sheets of drywall, look closely for indentations in the outer edges of the boards that would suggest that the metal bands securing the load have been removed and reapplied.

Contraband is sometimes inserted in the center of lumber stacks, or the middle of a stack of drywall is cut out to create a hiding cavity. With an auto carrier, not only can the framework be used for concealment but drugs may also be hidden in one or more of the cars being transported. One m.o. is for the trafficker to buy junk cars at an auto auction as a cheap cover load and then hide contraband in the one that would be hardest for you to reach and check out, like the one on top near the front.

In some cases, contraband can be discovered only by unloading cargo piece by piece. Obviously undertaking a chore like that requires extremely solid grounds for suspicion and probably a warrant, as well as a forklift, manpower, and a secure staging area for off-loading.

On the whole, your success in detecting contraband in cargo will most likely depend on the help you can get from a good K-9. One drug ring shipped heroin by truck from California to the Atlantic Coast by cutting open and hollowing out solid rubber tires of the type used on wheelbarrows. Loaders then inserted drug packages, glued the tires back together, and mixed them inside boxes of real tires. Realistically, even if you develop rock-solid suspicions for consent to search, your chances of finding a load like that without a K-9, a suspect's cooperation, or information from a confidential informant are infinitesimal.

Mobile Clan Labs

An officer in California stopped a motor home for a traffic violation, and while standing at the driver's window he caught a whiff of something inside that smelled like cat urine. Keeping close watch on the driver and vehicle, he immediately returned to his patrol car and radioed for help from a narcotics task force.

Exactly right.

What he'd stopped was a mobile clandestine laboratory for the manufacture and transportation of crystal methamphetamine— "ice." Inside, task-force officers eventually found nearly seven grams of 53% pure meth in a plastic bag, an array of chemicals that had been used to "cook" it, and a variety of laboratory glassware encrusted with drug residue. They did it safely because they had special training and the proper protective gear for the job. But had the original officer tried to search the vehicle himself, he would have been embarking on a highly unpredictable and treacherous undertaking. He could have suffered serious physical injury from toxic chemicals, through inhalation or skin absorption, and, because of their extreme volatility, he could have touched off a deadly explosion by unintentionally mishandling them.

As it was, his sensory alertness still resulted in getting a dangerous vehicle off the streets, and his professional restraint kept him from being harmed in the process.

While clandestine laboratories are used to produce LSD, PCP and synthetic heroin, as well as other hallucinogens, stimulants, and depressants, their predominant output is methamphetamine[8] in its various forms, including ice, the smokable version.

An increasing percentage of meth production is being exported out of this country, using the same routes by which other drugs are smuggled in. Because of the distinctive odors involved in mixing and heating meth's chemical ingredients, much of it is produced in isolated houses or outbuildings in rural settings and distributed from there. To elude law enforcement scrutiny and get closer to their domestic markets or export sites, however, a growing number of outlaw laboratory operators are going mobile—either moving frequently from motel room to motel room or setting up crude distilleries inside oversized vehicles so they can change location even quicker. These developments are bringing the meth-production problem out of its traditional rural location into the suburbs and inner cities.[9]

A driver or passenger who's in possession just of the finished product—methamphetamine powder, pills, or crystals that are ready to sell or use—should be handled like any other drug offender you detect. But if you discover that you are dealing with a van, motor home, or other vehicle that is used to manufacture meth or to transport the equipment and chemicals for its production, *special caution is mandatory.* Because of the chemicals, processes, and byproducts involved, you essentially are dealing with a *hazardous-materials scene.* The sooner you can realize what you've stopped and get specialized personnel there, the safer you will be. This is one vehicle you should not attempt to search; leave that to other experts.

Sensory cues you should be on guard for include:

Vehicle appearance. Semitrailers, rental trucks, and other commer

You'll most likely encounter mobile clan labs in vans or motor homes. If one is parked, even the windshield may be covered to keep out prying eyes.

Mobile labs may park in secluded spots for hours at a time while batches of product are cooked. Park Service ranger discovered this meth lab in the California desert after following tire tracks into an unauthorized area. (Contents have been removed during the search and placed on the ground.)

Generator, hoses, and other equipment used in manufacturing methamphetamine were readily visible during a "plain view" glance into the vehicle.

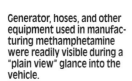

418

Would you go this far in searching a mobile methamphetamine lab? Officer on this stop, who pulled the driver over for weaving, unloaded vials, bottles, scales, a vacuum pump, and chemicals used for meth cooking, plus firearms and cocaine. Not advisable without protective gear or hazmat help.

cial vehicles are sometimes used as meth labs or to haul lab equipment. More often, though, a mobile laboratory will be set up in a van or motor home, with liquid propane or butane used as the fire source for heating the raw chemicals into the finished product. Shades, heavy curtains, or sheets of aluminum foil are likely to cover the windows for privacy, even when the vehicle is moving. When it's parked, the windshield will probably also be covered. If a batch is being produced, the cooking may take place in a parked vehicle for up to eighteen hours or more at a stretch. Watch for occupants who leave a parked vehicle to smoke, then go back in. Because of explosive fumes and vapors that build up during the distilling process, smoking inside may be too risky.

Occupant appearance. Motorcycle gangs and ex-con members of prison gangs currently dominate the meth business, with some inroads being made by Hispanics and middle-class Caucasians. Suspects who simply haul the finished product may not display distinguishing characteristics (other than the usual biker or joint "skin art"), but those who cook it—and use it—often betray tattletale signs of their activity.

On rare occasions, cookers are "normal" looking. But most who've been in the trade for very long tend to "look like walking zombies," says an Oregon investigator. Most have lost muscle mass and bone size. Their jaws especially look sunken and shrunken, and they may have difficulty breathing because of lung problems. You may notice little bumps all over their bodies, as if the meth they've taken is trying to "get out." Or they may have oozy, scabby, bleeding sores— "meth sores"—from scratching and picking at their skin. Long hair, bad teeth, dirty clothes, poor personal hygiene—absolute filth—often complete the picture. From the effects of the drug, they may seem irritable and hyper, restlessly tapping hands and feet and speaking fast. A single dose of meth (sometimes called "the poor man's cocaine") can keep a user "speeding" for six to twelve hours, compared to twenty minutes for a line of coke.

Caution: Some meth suspects may have needles in their pockets or their vehicles. These frequently are shared and are usually tainted with

419

blood residue. Meth suspects are prime candidates for AIDS. They are frequently armed with a variety of weapons, ranging from boot knives that they've compulsively honed to razor-sharpness to fully automatic assault rifles, and often travel with pit bulls or other attack dogs.

Meth can make a suspect paranoid and highly predisposed to violence. Suspects are likely to react automatically to fight their way out of stressful situations. "You're like a freight train trying to find a place to jump tracks," says an ex-cooker. "You're wound up so tight you'll pull a gun [at the slightest excuse]. It's like having your adrenal gland crack open and stay wide open. You don't think, you just do it." Besides calling immediately for specialists to handle the suspected mobile lab, get backup to the scene ASAP to help you control the occupant[s].

Visible contents. When you're able to see inside a mobile lab, you're likeliest to key on laboratory glassware and chemical containers inside the vehicle. In more sophisticated labs, the glassware will be professional chemist's equipment—flasks, test tubes, beakers, funnels, heating mantles, reflux condensers, reaction vessels. In cruder operations, you may see a jumble of jars, bottles, pots, and pans.

The cooking process often leaves a dark brown waste sediment called sludge, which may be visible in the bottoms or on the sides of some of these utensils. Raw chemicals may be in drums, five-gallon cans, or smaller containers. Particularly dangerous ones may have suppliers' labels that are coded red, red-and-white, or black-and-white to signify extra caution, or the labels may be obliterated to hide their names and colors. Be alert also for liquid filters, boxes of Red Devil lye, cheese cloth, heat lamps, vacuum pumps, plastic trash cans, buckets, and Ziploc bags, which are commonly used in the manufacturing or packaging processes.

Avoid touching any equipment or substances in the vehicle. Some cooking ingredients—mercuric chloride, for example—can be deadly to the touch. Some crystalline formations on the rims of containers

(right)
Hydrogen chloride in a cylinder removed from a clan lab—extremely hazardous under pressure. Can you believe that officers at the scene were actually kicking this container around?

(far right)
Glass containers like this, with evidence of carelessly handled chemicals, should be warning signs to you to back off.

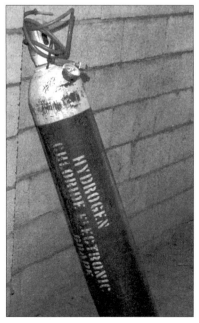

420

Walking up on the driver side of a pickup she'd stopped, an officer noticed a number of boxes and a metal drum marked "Methanol—Flammable Liquid" through a side window of the camper top. Asked about the chemicals, the driver said they were liniments for horses. Later he admitted they were being delivered to a clandestine meth lab.

may be explosive. Particles of some chemicals no bigger than a grain of salt can cause serious bodily contamination and in some cases even death. K-9s should not be exposed to environments where these risks are present, either.

Odor. New cooking methods are being used to diminish noticeable odors, but in many cases both the cooker and his vehicle still may reek of a chemical smell that has been described as resembling "very heavy cat urine," "dinosaur piss," or "wet baby diapers that have fermented in a pail for six weeks." The suspect may not be conscious of the stench, because cooking quickly destroys the olfactory sense. But you'll probably notice it even as you're approaching the vehicle.

The urine-like smell comes from mixing and cooking phenyl acetic acid, anhydrous sodium acetate, and acetic anhydride. Recipes vary (there are nearly 200 different methods of manufacturing methamphetamine), but the production process customarily involves a multitude of other chemicals with distinctive odors, among them ether (which is also highly explosive; one gallon is equal to six sticks of dynamite), chloroform, hydrochloric acid, acetone (smells like nail-polish remover), and hydriotic acid (has a sulfur smell of rotten eggs).

Caution: Vapors and fumes from clan-lab chemicals and their byproducts are highly toxic and can cause eye, skin, kidney, liver, lung, and genetic damage. In the case of one chemical used in some labs, one small dose may cause irreversible Parkinson's disease, according to the federal Environmental Protection Agency. Some can be fatal. Once you smell any pungent or unsavory chemical odor in a vehicle, *don't stay in close or breathe in deeply.* Get back to fresh air immediately.

If you suspect you are dealing with a mobile clan lab, your job is to command the driver and any other occupants out of the vehicle and get them stabilized, with the help of backup. If you do not have prompt access to law enforcement personnel who are trained to deal with the potential hazards of the vehicle, ask your dispatcher to summon the fire department and to brief them on the circumstances you're facing. They will likely have the haz-mat training that's need ed, as well as the "moon suits," breathing apparatus, and other specialty gear required to safely dismantle the lab. The nearest offices of the DEA and the EPA can also assist; DEA may even help fund some of the costly cleanup that may be involved. The same procedure is required if you encounter any questionable chemicals. Criminal Patrol officers have run into everything from solid rocket fuel to tanks of nitrous oxide (laughing gas) to drums of toxic waste on vehicle stops. These—and many more—can be life-threatening if mishandled.

Do not initiate towing a suspected clan-lab vehicle until it has been thoroughly investigated and secured by trained personnel. On the West Coast, a lab discovered in a rental truck was prematurely ordered towed to a place where a sergeant thought it could be more conveniently explored. As the wrecker yanked it away, bottles and cans shattered and spilled inside…liquid poured out the back, vaporizing. Eventually the truck exploded, and ammunition hidden inside fired out in all directions.

There are times when the best survival tactic you can use is to pull back, de-escalate your efforts, and let others with greater expertise take over. The discovery of a suspected mobile clan lab is one of those times.

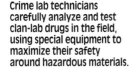

Crime lab technicians carefully analyze and test clan-lab drugs in the field, using special equipment to maximize their safety around hazardous materials.

K-9 SEARCHES

A team of undercover tactical officers approached a car that had stopped in front of a known drug offender's house on Chicago's South Side. They thought the driver was a major supplier for a drug ring operating near a school. As they moved up to identify themselves and question him, he suddenly opened fire with a fully automatic TEC-9 he had hidden in a garbage bag.

Nearly sixty rounds split the night air. An officer fell, injured. The suspect was wounded in the head and tried to drive off, then skidded to a stop and slumped over the wheel. Moments later when an officer crept up to the car, the wounded driver shot him through the door with armor-piercing rounds, without even lifting his head. Then he sped away. He was arrested later at his girlfriend's home, and his car was confiscated. When detectives searched it, they came up empty-handed. Not so much as a nanogram of drugs could be recovered from the vehicle, an ironic disappointment that salted the wounds of the two hospitalized officers.

Later another member of the police department re-searched the vehicle—a narcotics-trained German shepherd. The dog was scarcely inside when he "went berserk," a lieutenant remembers. Guided now by the dog's wet nose, detectives discovered a trap door between the rear seat and the trunk. And from the secret compartment it covered, they withdrew a pistol, $53,000 cash, and multiple kilos of rock cocaine with an estimated local street value of $1,200,000.

The would-be killer's "clean" car was, in fact, a dirty mobile vault....

When it comes to super snooping, it's sometimes tough to beat a four-legged crime fighter. Trained and handled properly, a good drug-sniffing K-9 can expose some offenders you might not suspect otherwise and keep some you do suspect from getting away.

No one knows for sure how superior a dog's sense of smell is compared to a human's, but most experts agree that overall it is perhaps a thousand times more sensitive.[1] While our visual sense usually dominates our sensory intake, a dog's sense of smell is his strongest source of information. He has exponentially more olfactory cells, and he identifies everything by scent first, before using his senses of sight and sound. Some dogs inhaling some odors have been able to detect chemical compounds at the phenomenal level of one part per quadrillion!

Nor surprisingly, K-9s sniffing odors in and around vehicles not only often find drugs faster than some officers but they frequently alert to sophisticated hiding places cops tend to miss: false compartments, bumpers, gas tanks, and unconventional containers, like the innocent-looking toy rabbit that attracted a dog inside a vehicle in Florida and was then discovered to contain crack cocaine. Sometimes a dog's alert

After a shoot-out (arrow points to bullet hole) with a dangerous drug dealer, Chicago detectives could not find drugs in his car—until a K-9 led them to a secret compartment broken open here at the back of the trunk.

Compartment was filled through a hole hidden behind the rear seat. Electrical system controlled by the driver caused seat to fall forward.

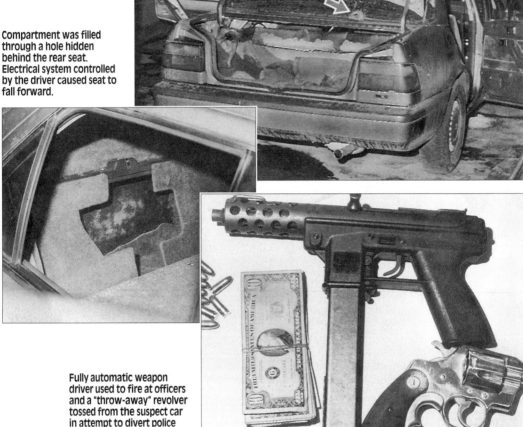

Fully automatic weapon driver used to fire at officers and a "throw-away" revolver tossed from the suspect car in attempt to divert police attention.

will be the only sure indicator. Traffickers busted in Texas, for example, carried marijuana sealed in metal containers in the natural firewall compartments of Ford LTDs. There were no external signs, and the compartment could be reached only by removing a front fender and a door. But a K-9 detected it just by walking near the car.

Even if you find a hidden compartment on your own, it's reassuring to get K-9 confirmation that drugs are inside before you begin disassembly or drilling. New Jersey officers were suspicious of a pickup truck pulling restaurant steam tables on a trailer. The metal tables looked carelessly exposed to the elements (the weather was cold and snowy), the tops had been welded shut, and the touch-and-tap technique had produced a dull thud and resistance, apparently from the bulk of something hidden inside. When the driver was told the tables would have to be torn apart, he withdrew consent. But he did agree to wait until a K-9 arrived. The dog alerted under the tables, providing PC for dismantling them—and leading to the discovery of 625 pounds of marijuana wrapped in plastic and covered with fabric-softener sheets.

The Smell of Success

A small sheriff's department with six road deputies in Missouri has confiscated more than 1,300 pounds of marijuana and 257 kilos of cocaine in just one year, working with a newly acquired K-9. Based on their success, four other departments in the area have purchased dogs and now others are considering it. One case where the dog proved its worth:

A highway patrolman stopped an RV for speeding and found the occupants to be unusually nervous and unconvincing. Both the driver and his female passenger insisted they were on their way to buy Western jewelry, but they were headed east. The driver refused consent to search, and with no PC to hold them the patrolman let them go.

Still eager to search the RV, he radioed down the road for any agency that might have a K-9 nearby. Deputies from the sheriff's department responded with their dog in about five minutes and urged the patrolman to track down the vehicle and find a reason to stop it again.

The minute the driver saw the patrol car following him, he exited the highway. At the top of the ramp he turned left without signaling, and the patrolman pulled him over.

While the patrolman discussed this infraction with the driver, the sheriff's dog arrived and walked around the car for a "free" sniff. Not surprisingly, it alerted.

From above a sleeping area inside, garbage bags filled with 280 pounds of pot were recovered, along with a sawed-off shotgun, a handgun hidden in a boot, and a quantity of methamphetamine concealed inside a phony can of lubricant.

K-9s can be valuable allies in your search for contraband. Most couriers would rather risk your searching their vehicles than a K-9 sniffing around, whether they're carrying drugs or money.

Some of the nation's biggest seizures, especially from hard-to-search oversized vehicles, have been K-9 related. Some sharp-nosed dogs have built such stellar reputations that bounties of $30,000 or more have been placed on their heads by traffickers. One Belgian malinois whose keen nose helped ferret out more than 680 pounds of marijuana and over a ton of cocaine during a twenty-four-month stint along the Texas border was found poisoned in his kennel, after smugglers issued a "contract" on him.

Despite the successes of K-9s, some cops still scorn the idea of involving dogs in their Criminal Patrol stops. They argue that K-9s "miss a lot," particularly contraband currency. They fear that dogs will "false alert" and damage credibility. They worry that handlers will be so riveted on the K-9 that they'll be vulnerable to traffic hazards and suspect threats. Some believe that dogs are futile because "smugglers now test their caches with their own drug dogs to be sure they can't be detected." A few claim to be virtual narc hounds themselves; one California deputy testified under oath that when he stooped down to retrieve a bunch of keys he'd dropped next to a suspect's suitcases, he could smell cocaine (a notoriously low-odor drug) hidden inside the luggage! "If I

425

can't find dope in a vehicle without using a dog ," brags one New Jersey officer, "it's not there."

Certainly drug dogs are not free of occasional shortcomings, and some of the claims in their support are clearly farfetched (like the handler who insists that his K-9 can unimpeachably sniff drugs in cars that are speeding along at 60 mph). Certainly, too, your personal skills can result in impressive drug busts even without K-9, as they have for countless other officers.

Yet the fact remains that where dogs are available and are put to work appropriately, they can improve Criminal Patrol results. One study showed that the seizure rate of illicit drugs by Border Patrol officers working with trained dogs is about 1,000 times greater per year on average than that of officers without dogs.[2] "There are times," says an expert from New York, "when one good nose is worth 100 pairs of eyes." Adds an officer from North Carolina, "If a dog is good, the chance of him missing drugs is a lot smaller than the chance of me missing them."

The temptation some officers succumb to is to defer too much to K-9 as a cure-all. The best approach is one of balance and teamwork. *A dog should never be relied on exclusively or regarded as replacement for diligent police work.* Instead, use him or her as a tool to supplement your own investigative talents, with each of you performing according to your unique strengths.

If you're a handler riding with a K-9 partner, the dog's presence will be automatic. Likewise, if you're part of a Criminal Patrol team working a given area, a K-9 car will probably be close by. If you patrol on your own without K-9, you'll need to weigh several factors in deciding whether to call one to the scene of a stop:

- Is a dog available, from your own agency or possibly from another department?

- Are the dog and handler currently on duty?

- How long will it take to get K-9 to your location?

- Do you feel you can sustain the driver's cooperation until K-9 arrives?

- Are you dealing with an oversized vehicle where K-9 may be crucial to a truly effective search?

- Do you have indications of a "hide" in a hard-to-find place (like a secret compartment) or one that is difficult to investigate (like inside a gasoline tank)?

- How confident are you in your searching ability without a dog's participation?

Understand that most K-9 handlers want their dogs to participate in drug searches. Most are eager to respond to vehicle stops to help other officers even if off duty; they won't consider being called an imposition. In fact, many appreciate being summoned even if you've already found drugs on your own, just so the dog gets an opportunity to sniff the contraband as part of practice and reinforcement.

What follows assumes that you are not a K-9 officer. It is intended to help you better understand how a K-9 realistically might aid you and to better appreciate dog-and-handler practices so that you will know what to expect once a dog reaches the scene. This will help you conduct yourself to enhance the dog's work rather than hamper it, to the benefit of yourself and other officers and to the detriment of guilty parties.

If you are a handler, this is the kind of information you should share with regular patrol officers you work with to eliminate mystery, misconceptions, and false expectations and enable them to make full use of the valuable skills and resources you have to offer.

Doin' It Doggie Style

Dope-sniffing K-9s are trained in "olfactory lock work"—to lock in on the scent of cocaine, heroin, marijuana, hashish, methamphetamine, their derivatives, and other illicit drugs and then to "alert" or signal when they detect the odor. They alert in one of two distinct styles:

1. Aggressively, by scratching, chewing, or biting through whatever is in their way to get to the source of the odor and actually produce the drugs they smell (one reason these K-9s should not be used to search people). This reaction is good for showing the exact location of the stash, but it increases the risk of the dog ingesting drugs and also makes him or her much more vulnerable to booby traps. It may increase your vulnerability, too, if a suspect you're monitoring while the handler and dog are searching the vehicle is able to key off the dog's excited reaction and catch you off-guard with a sudden attack. (Of additional consideration, aggressive alerts can also cause public relations problems. Say a dog rips up a car because the driver earlier gave a ride to a hitchhiker who had narcotics in his backpack that left an odor residue on the back seat. The dog will smell the lingering odor, even though the contraband is no longer present.)

Aggressively-trained K-9 digs and chews at cardboard section of appliance carton to reveal a hidden "prize."

2. Passively, by sitting down at the site where they've picked up the contraband scent.(A variation of the passive response is "casting." Here the dog, upon picking up a suspicious odor, will suddenly move his head or whole body quickly in the direction of the smell. He may not be able to track the scent to the source, but the handler, by watching the cast, will be able to tell the general direction the smell is coming from.) Passively-trained dogs are less likely to cause damage, tend to be quicker to learn booby traps, in some training programs show more stamina, and don't telegraph their finds to civilians so clearly. But they do not pinpoint the exact source of the stash as well as their aggressive counterparts.

Dogs with each style of alerting are used on vehicle stops, as they are on building searches. Each response has its strengths and weaknesses, including officer and K-9 survival considerations. Whatever the style of alert, a dog is only as good as his handler, and vice versa. Age, disease, lack of motivation, exposure to tobacco smoke in the patrol car immediately before a search, and poor direction from his human partner can all negatively impact a dog's discoveries. A handler's inability to accurately "read" the dog's reactions, of course, can result in false conclusions about the vehicle.

Also a dog is able to react only to those drugs for which he has been specifically trained. If the courier is carrying something the dog hasn't been prepared for, he'll miss it.

On hot days, dogs are not as likely to be effective. Among other things, panting interferes with smelling, and their efficiency rapidly diminishes. Even in mild weather, dogs tire easily and asked to search multiple vehicles in a row without rest or play they may lose interest or stress out and become unreliable. At a roadblock inspection site in Alabama, for example, two dogs directed to search a string of cars were both exhausted within ninety minutes and unable to continue, even though the temperature was in the 70s.

It's a myth that dogs are deliberately addicted to drugs to make them search for a fix. In fact, they're highly allergic to most drugs, and even small amounts of some can be fatal to them.

They are trained to detect drug odors by a conditioning process: They're rewarded for valid finds not only by being praised and petted but by being allowed then to play with a rubber ball, a "tug" (as in tug-of-war), or some other "gift," like morsels of food. (Even dogs that don't get food rewards should be searching on an empty stomach. Like humans, they tend to be more on edge and alert when hungry, sluggish when full.) Dogs make the association between action-reward to such an acute extent that it is difficult for the human mind to comprehend. Not giving the dog the gift he wants unless drugs are actually discovered is so instilled in training that by the time the dog hits the streets the risk of a false alert is almost nonexistent. In fact, says one nationally known K-9 expert, "A poorly trained dog is more likely to fail to indicate the presence of drugs when they're really there than to falsely indicate that they are present when they're not."[3]

Some drug traffickers try to promote false alerts in hopes of confusing the dog and handler. They may soak rags in antifreeze, which tends to attract dogs, or carry a cage of mice in the car. They hope that the dog will alert to these decoys and convince the handler that they are all the dog is reacting to in the vehicle. A good handler won't be misled by such ploys.

For training purposes, *pseudo* drugs are available that simulate the odors of real drugs, but many leading trainers consider it unwise for a K-9 to be trained on these products. When pseudo narcotics are used, it cannot truthfully be testified that the dog is conditioned to find genuine drugs. This, in turn, gives defense attorneys an opportunity to challenge the dog's credibility.

Couriers often think they can fool dogs by camouflaging the vapors of drugs with other odors, by carrying deodorizers, fabric softeners, coffee grounds, onions, baby powder, chlorine crystals, gasoline, and other aromatic masking agents with their loads. With well-trained K-9s, this usually doesn't work. Dogs have an exceptional ability to separate odors. In good training, they are exposed to a wide variety of potential masking agents and made accustomed to distinguishing drugs despite them. Indeed, some masks, like fabric-softener sheets, have a strong, unique smell that a dog won't normally encounter in such intense concentration. This may actually call his attention to the package and cause him to examine it more closely.

What's more likely to defeat a dog than distracting smells is careful, airtight packaging. If drug odor can't get out, a dog can't pick it up. One dog, for example, missed 1,400 pounds of marijuana hidden in a hermetically sealed compartment in the floor of a semitrailer. Other smugglers have created "dog proof" containers by stuffing drugs inside plastic PVC pipe, which is then tightly sealed with standard end caps, glue, and hot wax, making it virtually leak-free. Such efforts often are flawed, however, because the packagers have drug residue on their hands which then contaminates the outside of the container as they handle it. This may have helped a municipal K-9 in Louisiana that successfully detected eleven pounds of pot packed into a PVC pipe and submerged in a gas tank. Similarly five kilos of coke were detected under the hood of a rental car by a sheriff's K-9 in another Southern state, even though the coke was tightly wrapped in clear plastic, swathed with industrial tape, heat-sealed in heavy-duty aluminum foil, put in a cardboard box, and sealed with plastic again.

Despite complex training, a dog will certainly work best where there is a minimum of competing odors. For this reason, incidentally, drug dogs should not wear flea collars. The strong chemicals can affect their scenting ability. Also some odors are irritants to dogs. For example, couriers may mix Clorox bleach with powdered detergent, let the mixture dry out, then pack it into the hiding places for drugs. Although the Clorox odor will dissipate enough that you can't smell it, a dog will. He'll tend to pull back or turn his head away because the scent is repulsive to him. An alert handler who knows his animal well will mark this move as a signal. If you see a Clorox bottle, detergent, or other cleaning supplies in the vehicle with no laundry in evidence, that may be a further indicator of what's happening.

Unfortunately, some departments think that narcotics-detection dogs are like programmable computers or robots—that once they're trained, they'll stay trained. That's not so. Even the best need ongoing reinforcement to maintain their scent sensitivity. Experts recommend an hour a day—or a minimum of four hours a week—of in-service training, with the handler keeping detailed records of exercises and performance as a means of evaluating the dog's effectiveness under a variety of conditions and as future evidence for court.

Continuous training and recertification are essential in establishing the legal credibility of both the dog and the handler. Part of the handler's training should concern ways to keep the dog motivated and fine-tuned for accurate and reliable performance, day in and day out, for all his working life.

Free Sniffs

A drug-trained K-9 sniffing the open air around the outside of a vehicle or other object in a public place is not considered a search by U. S. case law.[4] Therefore, such sniffing does not require that you obtain consent or a search warrant and cannot violate anyone's Fourth Amendment privacy rights. (Most courts, including the Supreme Court, have held that the same is true of a dog putting his nose to the outside of luggage in a transportation terminal or other public location.)

The thinking is that there's no reasonable expectation of privacy in the air space surrounding a car's exterior nor in odors released to the public air. A dog's sniff is virtually nonintrusive. It detects only the presence of drug contraband and does not cause embarrassment or inconvenience by identifying or exposing noncontraband items otherwise hidden from public view. So long as the vehicle is legally stopped, the dog and related officers stay where they are legally entitled to be, and the travelers are not unreasonably detained, a dog evaluating the air space surrounding a vehicle is, in effect, a "free" sniff, unencumbered by legal restrictions. You do not need even reasonable suspicion of wrongdoing to justify it. (However, you may need reasonable suspicion or consent to detain the vehicle so the dog can perform the sniff.)

K-9 sniffing the exterior of a vehicle is not a search, courts have ruled. Such "free sniffs" are often the beginning of major drug busts.

The courts' support means that with the creative and efficient use of K-9 you can significantly expand the opportunities for legally investigating vehicles that you may encounter on patrol. Indeed, with free sniffs you can open up the secrets of vehicles you would otherwise have no legal grounds to inspect.

Consider these possibilities, based on actual Criminal Patrol practices:

- While you are talking to a driver and completing paperwork or running a license check on a stop, a handler walks a dog around the violator's vehicle to see if the dog will alert to any narcotics odors. This can be done without your having to ask for consent since it is not a "search." It takes only a minute or two and, if the dog is readily available, will not at all delay your completion of the stop;

- As cars are backed up at tollbooths, a dog is walked up and down the lines, searching for suspicious odors that may be wafting from any of the vehicles;

- Vehicles stopped at lawful roadblocks where registrations, licenses, insurance, and sobriety are being checked are monitored by K-9 in the same fashion, while other officers process the drivers;

- Similarly, a dog is encouraged to sniff around trucks that pull into roadside weighing stations, while the driver confers with attendants on his paperwork;

- A dog is directed around buses, trucks, motor homes, and passenger vehicles parked at highway rest stops. If he alerts to the luggage compartment of a bus, for instance, individual bags can be removed and sniffed. A specific alert may then lead to the identification and arrest of the owner. If no one claims the bag, it can be declared abandoned and then be confiscated or traced to the owner through investigative means;

- As a place to walk his dog during his shift, a K-9 officer chooses a motel parking lot. He "exercises" the dog in and out among the cars, with the K-9, of course, sniffing for anything hinky all the time.[5]

Note: Restrict your free sniffs only to vehicles and, when appropriate, luggage. *People usually should not be approached and sniffed by K-9,* even though they are in a public place. This is considered too physically threatening and intrusive, especially with aggressive-trained dogs, and legally too intrusive of their privacy.[6]

An alert during a free sniff at the very least is probable cause for you then to detain the vehicle or other object and try to obtain a search warrant. Indeed, substantial case law in some jurisdictions has held that an alert from outside a vehicle by a properly trained and reliable K-9, when interpreted by a knowledgeable handler, can be sufficient PC for even a warrantless search of the interior,[7] and some courts say an alert may be enough for an arrest.[8] Check with your local prosecutor to see for sure what prevails in your area. If you're anticipating turning the case over to federal authorities for forfeiture purposes (see Chapter 12), pursue a search warrant before going further, as that tends to be the fed's preference in most areas.

Free sniffs may sound like needle-in-the-haystack gambles. But the results can be astounding. An Illinois suburban officer was on patrol with his dog early one morning when he spotted an Econoline van with tinted windows and without license plates parked at a Best Western motel. He pulled into the lot and approached with the dog. They'd scarcely started to walk around the van when the passive-trained dog suddenly plopped to the ground. The officer peered through a window and saw what looked like "a lot of taped packages." After police obtained a search warrant and staked out the vehicle for several hours, two men approached the van and were taken into custody. In the vehicle, packages of greenbacks wrapped with duct tape were recovered from shopping bags, cardboard boxes, suitcases, a garbage can, and a duffel bag. It took officers more than twelve hours to count the hoard—the largest single seizure of suspected drug-related cash in the history of that county: $5,203,165.

The K-9 officer, who'd had his dog only eight months before hitting this jackpot, said: "It's like seeing your kid win the Little League World Series." The suspects denied ownership of the money and vehicle and refused any explanation. No claim was ever placed for the cash, and it was all forfeited to law enforcement. In Tennessee, an officer let his dog sniff a semi-trailer at a highway weighing station while the two drivers were inside trying to clarify a fuel-tax matter. Not surprisingly, as it turned out, the dog alerted. Inside the trailer under a cover load of peppers was 3,276 pounds of marijuana, estimated to be worth nearly $20,000,000.

Ringing up the proceeds of a free sniff. Over $5,000,000 was recovered from a van after a suburban officer exercised his K-9 in a motel parking lot.

Attractive as they can be, free sniffs probably won't become more than welcome but irregular exceptions to your patrol pattern. More commonly, the K-9 searches you employ will be like most of your human ones: They'll come after you've carefully constructed a foundation of suspicion through your sensory perceptions and dialogue and after you have obtained the driver's voluntary consent to search his vehicle.

No special permission has to be sought to use a dog on a consent search. Any time you have the right to make a manual search, as you do when you get consent, a dog can participate, too.

Reasonable Delay

Because Criminal Patrol teams often work with a K-9 car in their group, a team officer who knows he's going to ask a driver for consent to search can generally get a dog there within three to ten minutes. That usually allows time for the dog to take a quick free sniff around the exterior before the citation or warning is completed.

But say you *can't* get a dog fast and say further that you have now obtained the driver's voluntary permission to search: How long can you keep him or her waiting for K-9 to arrive if you want a dog to help you search the vehicle?

Unfortunately, a precise answer can't be given.

If you're depending on voluntary consent, the driver actually can leave anytime he gets tired of waiting. Unless your glib tongue can persuade him to stay, all he needs to do is withdraw consent and go.

To detain him involuntarily when he wants to leave, you need at least reasonable suspicion; in other words, a reasonable inference that criminal activity is afoot, based on articulable, accepted indicators, as discussed in earlier chapters.

If he withdraws consent while now being officially detained, you can still have the handler walk the dog around the exterior of the vehicle and see if he alerts. If he does, the time factor is no longer a problem; now you have at least the PC necessary for a search warrant. In the absence of an alert, you'll need other probable-cause information to get the dog or yourself inside to search without the driver's permission.

The length of time you can keep the suspect waiting for a dog without your temporary detention being considered unreasonable or turning into an arrest depends on "the totality of the circumstances" and must be judged on a case-by-case basis, according to most court rulings. In other words, the more grounds for suspicion you can articulate and the more incriminating they appear, the longer will be acceptable. Detentions of up to an hour or even ninety minutes, have been sanctioned as reasonable by some courts, where the officer had clearly established reasonable suspicion.[9] However, the longer you hold a suspect the more you cause a major intrusion in his or her life. If you can keep the time to twenty or thirty minutes maximum, even with reasonable suspicion, you'll be on more solid ground.

Search Tactics

Ideally, a consent search with K-9 involves three officers: the handler to work the dog, an officer to watch and direct traffic, and another to monitor the suspect(s) and assess their reactions during the dog's search. *A handler and dog should not attempt a search without backup any more than you patrolling without K-9 should.* The handler's inevitable distraction from the suspects because of the need to closely observe the dog (watching his head, body, and tail and listening to his nose for signs of excitement) is simply too dangerous to risk without at least a Cover Officer present.

Some Criminal Patrol officers like to search the car themselves before the dog arrives, feeling that once a guilty suspect sees a K-9 he's more likely to withdraw consent. You won't interfere much if you confine your inspection to the exterior, but if you rummage through the interior you can diminish the dog's subsequent chances. Odors you introduce will complicate the scents and by opening doors and windows you may dissipate the smell from hidden contraband.

It's best to let K-9 search first. The exceptions, of course, are when you have already fruitlessly conducted a search but still feel something's wrong and you then decide to call the dog in as a last resort to double-check or when you feel that time constraints are such that you have to get started with a search while you're waiting for K-9 to arrive.

Watch the driver when the dog shows up; his reaction may be revealing. A sergeant who'd stopped a tractor-trailer in Ohio for following too closely called for a dog after the driver was unable to produce a bill of lading, had a cockamamie story about his destination, and offered a logbook that seemed to contradict what he said about his trip. The driver vehemently denied any drug involvement. But when K-9 arrived, the sergeant observed a significant change in his behavior; his shoulders slouched down, he stopped making eye contact, and he got very quiet. After the dog alerted at the rear of the trailer, officers found eight canvas bags and seventeen cardboard boxes inside, with

(top)
Even with backup officers at hand, you want occupants far away from the K-9 and handler during a search. Too close, they may be able to distract or threaten with subtle movements. Cover Officers, incidentally, should be monitoring the suspects in a position of readiness.

(center)
An organized and controlled response to the arrival of K-9 and handler. Contact Officer debriefs handler before search begins, while Cover Officer monitors suspect seated in caged patrol car. While search is underway, Contact Officer acts as a 2nd Cover Officer.

(right)
Stay back from the dog just as you keep suspects back. When searching, a K-9 is keyed up. If you crowd him or try to pet him, you may get a reaction you won't like.

1,300 pounds of pot wrapped in sheets of Bounce and covered with coffee grounds and spices.

Before the dog begins to search, consider asking the suspect what the dog will find. A Missouri officer did this after radioing for K-9, and the driver said, "All we've got is a pipe and a little baggie." As it turned out, the K-9 unit wasn't able to respond to the scene, but the driver's admission convinced the officer to search even though the driver had declined to give consent. She found forty-five pounds of marijuana in the car.[10]

Some officers like the dog to make an initial exterior circuit while the driver and passengers remain inside the vehicle. "If they have dope in their pockets, it may generate an odor," explains one trooper. If this strategy is followed, be sure the engine is off before the dog and handler pass in front of or behind the vehicle. Even then, some handlers will not have their dogs check the forward part of an occupied vehicle because of the increased vulnerability to assault with weapons. This, of course, limits the thoroughness of the search.

Most handlers prefer that occupants be out of the vehicle before the search starts and under the surveillance of a Cover Officer at a distance where the dog cannot readily see or hear them. If other officers are present, they should stay back, too, to minimize noise and confusion. Allowed close, some suspects know how to appear to be mildly threatening the dog or handler with "innocuous" gestures and noises. Officers may ignore or not even perceive these distractions, but a dog that is cross-trained in handler protection will immediately be diverted from the search to "defend" his human partner.

Once the occupants are out, keep the doors and windows shut. This helps preserve a concentrated build-up of incriminating odor if drugs are present.

If you have seen or heard anything that may suggest a contraband location or know from experience where drugs commonly are hidden in the kind of vehicle at hand, let the handler know at the outset. He may want to start the search there so the dog is freshest for the most critical area. Otherwise, the dog will normally begin by circling the vehicle. Your having chosen a stop location where the vehicle is unobstructed on all sides (clear of a guardrail, for example) will now help the dog and handler, just as it may have helped you earlier in making a passenger-side approach.

Exterior strategy. Before the dog is brought up, the handler should check the exterior for potential hazards: broken glass, jagged pieces of metal, anything else about the car that could hurt the dog. If the radiator is leaking, for example, the sweetness of dripping antifreeze may attract the dog, and he may try to lick it.

The engine should be off to minimize the K-9's exposure to hot metal and carbon monoxide, although the catalytic converter and other exhaust system components may stay hot enough to be a continuing hazard when he sniffs the undercarriage. (The good side of this is that heat from the system may warm up any drugs stored in compartments under the car and intensify their smell.)

When the dog first arrives, the handler should walk him to clear the dog's nose before they start searching. Then just before the dog begins his outside circuit, you or the handler should quickly reach in and turn the ignition key to activate the electrical system (but not start the en gine). Now engage the car's ventilation system: Set the temperature selector on "cool"…the air selector on "vent" or "heat"…and turn the fan on "high." Within a few seconds, stale air will be forced out around windows and through door and trunk seams, vents, rocker-panel drainage slots, and other ventilation points, where the dog may then more easily pick up on drug odors. (The actual drugs, of course, may be inches or feet away from where the dog alerts under these circumstances.)

On-leash to best assure his protection from passing traffic and his direction by the handler, the dog should begin on the downwind side of the vehicle, working into the wind so that odors are blown toward him, making them easier and faster to find. If wind direction is not obvious, holding a cigarette lighter aloft or tossing a handful of grass, leaves, dog hair, or light trash into the air may help define it.

The search should be from an "anchor point," from which the handler and dog circle the car then return in the opposite direction. The handler may walk backwards, directing the dog's attention to the exterior surface and making sure he is sniffing.

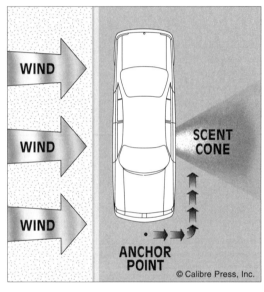

K-9 search should progress first along the downwind side of a vehicle to give the dog the maximum chance of catching a drug scent.

As odors emanate from a hiding place, they are shaped into a "scent cone" by air currents. If the wind is moving fast, the cone will be long and narrow; if the air is still or blowing slowly, the cone will be wide. When a K-9's nose intercepts the scent cone, he can then usually follow it back to the source. The handler should help the dog all he can, without influencing the dog's reactions. The handler must guide the dog to intensely snuffle along each and every crack and seam completely, assessing every possible scent secretion. Odors, like water, follow the path of least resistance and after building up inside will seep out through or around doorjambs, key locks, door handles, window tracks, and other gaps, large and small, as well as air vents. Cracks and seams around hubcaps, head- and taillights, bumpers, and the gas cap must be checked, too. The handler should release air from all tire valves so the dog can also inspect it for evidence of contamination—or release air onto a gauze pad, which he then places behind the wheel to see if the dog alerts.

Some handlers like to make successive circles of the vehicle, working the dog low the first time, which is easier because of his low build, and directing him to sniff higher cracks and seams the next, like the common pattern for a K-9 room search. Others zigzag the dog up and down as they go. Odors tend to rise, so one way or another comprehensive high-and-low coverage is necessary in an effort to get the dog above any emerging scent. A brisk pace usually keeps the dog more interested and alert than going slowly. It's better to search an area twice at a fast pace than once slowly. Thoroughness is what matters most. "Search a car like you're going to buy it, checking out the details," recommends one handler.

Just as when you search, the handler must be careful not to dismiss the obvious. Handlers sometimes naively pull dogs off the scent, ignoring what the K-9s are trying to tell them, because they think smug glers would never hide contraband in such "stupid" places. Yet they often do, of course—and the dog's objective reaction may, in fact, surpass the handler's subjective one. It's important that the handler go into every search without predisposed notions as to whether or where narcotics exist. He must trust the dog, not taint the dog's reactions.

Suspects can be obvious in their actions as well as their hiding places at times, and you must remain alert to this as you monitor them during the search. A man and a woman were stopped in Ohio in a truck that was pulling an empty horse trailer. They said they were on their way from Colorado to Pennsylvania to buy horses, although it was the dead of winter, not the usual trading season. They were carrying their cash rolled up in a Styrofoam cup, which seemed odd also. As a handler and dog searched the exterior, the couple were quiet—until the dog approached the gas tank. Then the woman suddenly yelled out to the handler, asking if she could have one of his business cards. No drugs were discovered on that stop. It was not until later when he was reviewing the in-car video of the encounter that the handler realized that the dog was just starting to alert on the gas tank when the woman distracted him. He pulled the dog off to respond to her, not realizing he'd been tricked. "When you start to work the dog and the suspects start to raise hell," says the handler today, "it's a smoke screen."

If the dog alerts during the exterior circuit, some handlers like to take him away from the vehicle for a bit, then bring him back for another tour around to see if he hits again in the same spot.

If he alerts to someplace like a gas tank, which will require moving the car and/or performing major dismantlement to properly explore, consider calling a second K-9 to the scene to confirm the "hit" before you act. The handler for the backup dog should not be told where the first alert occurred. Some departments call a second dog routinely, regardless of where the first dog alerts or of how strong other indicators seem to be. On a stop in Arkansas, an aggressive-trained K-9 alerted to the left gas tank on a pickup truck by biting and scratching it with his paws. The officer who'd made the stop for speeding had already heard the nervous driver, a welder, say he was driving alone from Texas to Canada on a week's "vacation"...had smelled a strong odor of incense coming from the cab...had observed new tires and heavy-duty shocks on the truck...and had detected evidence that both gas tanks had been lowered and remounted. Yet a second K-9 was still called to search the exterior from the beginning. When it passively alerted on the same tank by sitting down, officers felt completely confident to take the pickup to the city shop to drop the tank, even though the driver continued to insist there was nothing in it. Actually, there were two compartments in it, containing sixteen packages of marijuana. The right-hand tank proved to hold another six packages of pot, one with a .45-cal. pistol also inside, plus a gram of cocaine.

An alert may prove to be only the midpoint in a search. A municipal officer in Florida became suspicious of a woman he'd stopped in a big Oldsmobile and called K-9, which alerted to the undercarriage. But he and other officers still required "a considerable amount of serious looking" before they deciphered the hide: The gas tank had been put on hinges and wired to an electrical release cable located beside the emergency-brake lever. When the cable was pulled, the tank swung down to the ground, revealing a hidden compartment packed with seven kilos of coke.

Once the dog has alerted to the exterior, you will probably also have to continue the search inside the vehicle on your own, because the K-9 will not likely be so useful from that point on. He may want to keep going back to the spot where he got his reward rather than to search new areas diligently.

When the dog alerts, consider talking to the driver *before* you try to pinpoint or extract the contraband. Some courts would require a Miranda warning at this point, but even so you may get him to tell you what the dog is reacting to, exactly where it's hidden, how it's packaged, how much there is, whether it's booby trapped, what else he is carrying, et cetera. You may even get him to participate in a controlled delivery, in which case you may not want to disturb the cache now, so as to save time and preserve the appearance of the hiding place.

Interior strategy. Don't be misled by a driver who claims that he sometimes smokes pot and the dog may alert to the lingering odor of smoke or other residue in the vehicle. He may be trying to discourage the search or undermine the importance of an alert. Proceed according to plan.

Aside from the immediate harm, a dog who's hurt on a search may lose his enthusiasm for entering and checking interiors in the future. So before a dog searches inside, another hazards check is necessary. The handler should quickly scan for interior damage that could cause injury, like sharp or protruding metal, and for threats like needles, razor blades, open knives, or visible drugs that the dog might bite into and ingest. If test tubes, chemical containers, or other evidence is visible that suggests the vehicle carries clandestine laboratory materials (as described in the last chapter), the dog should not enter. Toxic chemicals associated with methamphetamine production can seriously injure or kill the dog.

With the driver's permission, remove any food or food containers before the K-9 enters. Also extract any dogs or other pets belonging to the suspect. Some couriers carry along personal protection dogs or bitches in heat in hopes they'll threaten or distract a K-9. Offender dogs should be kept outside on leash until the search is over. If the owner objects, he should be reminded that a dog that becomes aggressive can be considered a deadly weapon. Tell him: "I don't want to run the risk of having to shoot your dog." Also be sure the interior is clear of any bees, wasps, or other stinging insects.

After the hazards inspection, let the vehicle sit with doors and windows closed for a few moments to allow the air to settle and the odors to accumulate again. If you have already found and removed drugs from the interior before the K-9's arrival, advise the handler where you found them so he can react with the proper commendation when the dog alerts to this location because of the residual smell.

If no exterior alerts have focused attention on a particular area, the handler should guide the dog through the interior according to some search pattern that assures a thorough canvass. With the dog now off-leash for easier movement, he may start at the driver's door, sniffing the door frame and panels while still standing outside, then entering under the steering column. In a four-door car, the entire front will usually be searched first, including under the dash, or the floor, under seats, along the headlining, between windshield and dash. In a two-door, the dog may move roughly in a Figure-8 pattern, jumping from

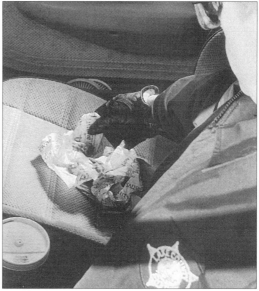

(above left/above)
Handler should inspect the interior for hazards or distractions before dog enters the vehicle. Some couriers plant chicken bones and fast-food leftovers in hopes of confounding a K-9 search.

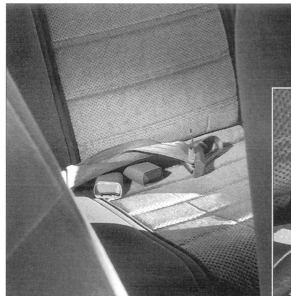

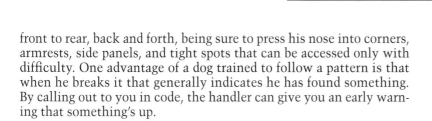

(above/right)
Hidden hazards can harm a dog, the same as a human officer. Piled on the cushion, the seat belt looks harmless, but behind it lurks a nasty knife.

front to rear, back and forth, being sure to press his nose into corners, armrests, side panels, and tight spots that can be accessed only with difficulty. One advantage of a dog trained to follow a pattern is that when he breaks it that generally indicates he has found something. By calling out to you in code, the handler can give you an early warning that something's up.

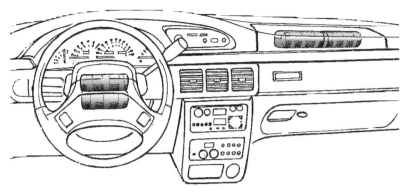

Be sure a searching K-9 checks all interior surfaces carefully. He'll be the best chance of detecting certain "difficult hides," like these cavities, filled with contraband after airbags have been removed.

Odors of cocaine and heroin are more subtle than marijuana, and the dog will need to get quite close to the source to detect them. The handler can help in some places by pressing down on seats and especially the sides of luggage to "breathe" them; i.e., to expel the air—and odors—inside through cracks and seams.

Some dogs may need to be lifted into the trunk in order to sniff all its surfaces closely. To contain odors, the lid should be raised just far enough to let the dog in. If the trunk is loaded with luggage and other possessions, they should be removed and placed in a line safely at roadside or curbside so the dog can screen them there.

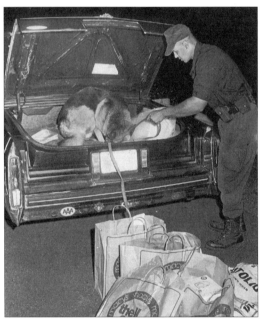

K-9 and handler search the trunk interior after the major contents are removed. Aside from being a courier suspect, the driver from Massachusetts had outstanding warrants.

The engine compartment should be checked last. Unless the engine is cool, the dog should never be lifted atop it. Even then, many handlers feel the risk of the dog getting cut or otherwise injured atop the engine is too high. They may ask you to check under the hood or rely on the exterior search to have provoked an alert if any contraband is present. Indeed, the heat from the engine may make drugs hidden there readily detectable by K-9 even at ground level.

On an ordinary passenger car, the K-9 search, inside and out, normally will take no more than three to five minutes.

After the dog is finished, whether he has alerted or not, you should thoroughly search the vehicle yourself, if you have not already done so. *A dog's negative reaction does not necessarily mean a vehicle is clean.* For one thing, the driver may be hauling contraband other than drugs. Rare, exotic birds, for example, are often smuggled in false bottoms of suitcases and in the wheel wells of cars, and their traffickers often use some of the same routes as drug smugglers. Also a dog's alerting to one spot does not necessarily mean that's the only hiding place. He may quickly find a relatively small amount of marijuana and quit, for example, while there are still several kilos of cocaine stashed elsewhere in the vehicle.

Dogs aren't machines. They can have "off" days and unexplained failures, the same as humans. On rare occasions, a dog's nose may be clogged by dirt or pollen, like a dirty vacuum-cleaner filter; until it's washed out with a spray bottle of water it won't sniff with results. Besides missing drugs, dogs frequently miss hidden currency and, of course, weapons. Occasionally there may be so much narcotic present that the dog is overwhelmed by the odor and can't pinpoint the origin. Or if a courier is carrying more than one type of drug, the dog may alert to both scents but pinpoint only one. *The dog's limitations make your searching essential.* You may pick up on visual cues, like telltale scratches, that are beyond a dog's capability. If you do find contraband the dog has missed, this can understandably damage his credibility. But better that than for a load to escape detection. (If the dog has failed to alert, your searching after he finishes will probably have to be with the driver's continuing consent to keep your actions legal.)

Occasionally, a dog will alert but you won't be able to find any narcotics. Assuming the dog is well-trained and is not being influenced by the handler's preconception about drugs being present, one of two things is probably happening:

1. Narcotics have been present in the vehicle previously and the dog is reacting to what's called "dead scent," the residual odor that is left behind after the substance has been removed (some dogs may react to residual scents that are up to four to six weeks old[11]);

2. Drugs are present but you don't recognize them. For example, some smugglers have developed a process of mixing cocaine with plastic to form figurines and other objects that in no way resemble drug packs but that can be chemically separated at the point of destination.

Under these circumstances, your only hope is more dialogue with the suspect(s). The dog's alert may give you enough leverage to pry out the truth.

Oversized Vehicles

With semitrailers, motor homes, and other large vehicles, the K-9 ideally should start searching about fifty to ninety feet away on the downwind side. Wind blowing across the top of the rig will drop at about this distance, carrying toward the ground any scents from drugs hidden high inside. "If the dog is too close," explains one handler, "the scent may blow right over him."

After initially circling at a distance, the dog should then move in close for a second circuit around the rig, starting from a different place.

To promote consistency and thoroughness when dealing with a semitrailer, for example, the handler should mentally divide the exterior into three zones:

1. **The front,** extending from the forward bumper through the last of the tractor wheels, including the fifth wheel;

2. **The center,** starting at that point and ending with the first set of tires on the trailer;

3. **The rear,** beginning with the first set of trailer tires through the back of the rig.

Working the dog one zone at a time helps focus the search and better pinpoints any alert to a more confined area.

441

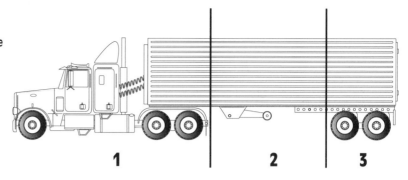

Searching semitrailers involves the K-9 working one zone at a time until all 3 zones have been searched.

1   2   3

Where a sparse "junk" load is being carried in the cargo hold, there may be little to compete with the radiating smell of contraband. But even with well-disguised loads, dogs can score some remarkable alerts. One, for example, reacted to a stack of one-kilo bricks of cocaine that were hidden behind 27,000 pounds of apples. Another found 945 pounds of coke that was surrounded by 42,000 pounds of potatoes.

The bigger drug loads typically carried in big rigs make it easier for the dog to detect contraband odors even when separated considerably from the source. In fact, some Criminal Patrol specialists won't bother checking the insides of loaded semitrailers unless a dog first alerts to the exterior, which may be placing too much confidence in K-9, especially if other indicators exist.

Selling Shares in "Bubba"

Drive-by shootings, crack houses, street-corner drug markets—Fulton, Missouri, has not escaped the scourge of the drug epidemic that has spread through even rural cities in recent years. As part of combating the problem, the Fulton Police Department wanted to buy a drug dog to make searching of vehicles and other locations more effective, but couldn't afford the cost. Then Deputy Chief Charles Latham got a novel idea: Have the department sell shares and give contributors certificates of stock in the K-9 that would be bought with the proceeds. Latham describes the results:

The first council member to speak after hearing the share-selling plan [described at a city-council meeting] asked, "Where can I purchase shares for my kids?" Suddenly, the very people whom the department had hesitated to ask for more money started to contribute to the fund and challenged others to do the same....

Shares in the dog could be purchased at three levels: individual for $10, civic for $25, and corporate for $100. Stock certificates were designed and made on a computer, and officers delivered them in person to stockholders. The day after the council meeting aired on the local cable-access channel, school children and teachers met the police department's DARE officer at the door of his first school stop to give him money to buy shares in the dog.

Two days after the original announcement, civic organizations began presenting the chief with rather large checks. The local newspaper traded several quarter-page ads for one share in the dog. The paper also ran a daily front-page progress report free of charge. The project became known as Operation Drug Dog, and when all three local television stations began to carry the story, contributions started to pour in from all over central Missouri.

Within the first week of the program, the department reached the initial goal of $5,000 to cover the cost of the dog and training for the handler. It accepted additional money only after announcing that the goal had been reached and that the remaining funds would be used for care of the dog. Ultimately, Operation Drug Dog raised approximately $8,500.

With the funds, the department purchased Bubba, a three-year-old Golden Retriever, trained his handler, and equipped a K-9 vehicle for them. The new team started conducting drug searches within approximately ten weeks of that initial council meeting.

The program also spawned a newsletter, The Bubba Times, which is produced quarterly for the supporters of Operation Drug Dog. The newsletter allows the department to maintain the close contact with the public that was established during the campaign. It also informs stockholders of how their money is being spent....

Operation Drug Dog illustrates that police officers need not and should not shoulder complete responsibility for solving a community's problems. It shows what can be accomplished when officers team up with citizens to "take stock" in the community, or in this case, a drug dog![12]

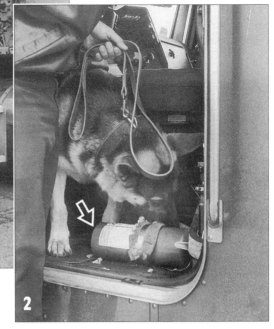

K-9's alert during the exterior circuit can signal where to check inside first. In this case, only a small quantity of drugs was found—in a phony fire extinguisher (arrow).

If K-9 had failed to alert to this sleeper berth, would you have checked it carefully anyway? You should. Dogs should be a supplement to your search, not a substitute. K-9s have been known to miss incredibly large loads of drugs.

Underneath rigs, K-9s "have proven very effective in the discovery of narcotics within drive shafts," according to an EPIC report. A dog's exterior search should also be sure to include the axles of semitrailers and air-brake tanks, where compressed air can be released for sniffs through bleeder valves. Even more carefully than with a car, a handler will have to assure that the dog is protected from the profusion of hazards associated with trucks and other large vehicles, ranging from dripping grease and antifreeze to sharp protrusions. Before the cargo area of a refrigerated truck is checked, the cooling unit should be shut down. Otherwise the smoky output of the reefer may affect the dog's nose.

Because of the steep height, the dog may need to be helped up to check inside the trailer, as well as the cab. The cab invariably should be covered inside, even in the absence of an exterior alert, because drugs at least in personal-use quantity will often be found there. If you're stopping trucks, you'll want a dog that's trained to detect methamphetamine, one of the drugs common to cabs.

Be sure the dog searches as high as he can in truck cabs and in other oversized vehicles, in pursuit of roof concealments. In cargo areas, the handler should beware of possible subtle booby traps. Couriers may spread ground-up hot peppers on the floors of trailers to make it harder for a snuffling dog to work.

K-9 First Aid

To a handler, knowing how to give first aid to an injured dog is an important part of "officer" survival. During a search, a dog can be cut, stuck, even shot. He may break a leg. He may encounter packaging that has been saturated with dangerous chemicals to burn his nose. But probably the most prevailing threat is overdosing. Particularly aggressive-trained dogs may occasionally break through to a cache they've sniffed and in their excitement ingest drugs before the handler can intervene. This can happen fast and without warning, especially in low-light situations.

If treatment is not administered promptly, the consequences from some substances—especially cocaine, heroin, and amphetamines—can be fatal from respiratory arrest, heart attack, or extreme overheating. Even swallowing marijuana, though not likely to cause death, can make a dog depressed and slow-moving, which could threaten his safety on duty.

Based on training from a veterinarian, a handler should know how to diagnose drug exposure or overdose in a dog, induce vomiting and defecation, select and administer antidotes, and provide respiratory assistance equivalent of CPR. As fast as possible, the dog should be transported to the nearest veterinary clinic. But at the scene and en route, the handler should be able to perform first aid on his stricken partner to lessen the effects of the drug and its absorption from the digestive tract. Dog handlers who work drugs extensively often outfit a briefcase as a first-aid kit to have with them on call-outs.

Caution: Proper dosage and administration of detoxifying medications are important to avoid adverse side effects. If the handler is not competent to diagnose and treat, it's probably safer to wait for the vet. Some short-term emergency help may be obtained for a modest fee by calling the National Animal Poison Control Center at the University

Saving a Dog

Getting a veterinarian's help is always essential when a K-9 is stricken. But until then, a handler's emergency first aid to the dog may prove critical to saving the dog's life and his future working career. Here are on-the-spot treatments for four circumstances that may arise during drug searches. Some may require supplies from the handler's emergency kit.

MARIJUANA INGESTION

Induce vomiting. Give the dog one teaspoon of 3% hydrogen peroxide for every five pounds of the K-9's body weight, or one tablespoon for every fifteen pounds, to a maximum of three tablespoons. The dog should vomit within ten to fifteen minutes. If not, repeat the process every ten minutes until the dog vomits. This should be done immediately in hopes of preventing seizures and other ill effects from the drugs.

NOTE: A dog will not vomit on an empty stomach. Carry a small, moist meal that the dog can be fed before the hydrogen peroxide is administered.

COCAINE INGESTION

DO NOT induce vomiting. Cocaine produces a high potential for seizures, and if a dog convulses while vomiting he may breathe the vomit into his lungs and drown. For cocaine (and also for marijuana after vomiting has occurred), administer charcoal. Give the dog oral doses of one-half to one gram of activated charcoal per pound of body weight, mixed with one-quarter teaspoon sodium or magnesium sulfate for every ten pounds body weight. Repeat two or three times. To save time at the scene, use premixed squirt bottles of charcoal in solution.

HEART FAILURE

Perform CPR. If the dog's heart stops beating, place him on his right side on the ground. Pull his tongue out to be sure the airway is open. Place one or both hands on the chest behind the dog's elbow in his brisket area and rapidly compress the chest six times, pausing one or two seconds between compressions. Give three breaths by artificial respiration. Repeat compression and respiration until you feel a heartbeat. This procedure is difficult even for experienced technicians. Do the best you can.

NO RESPIRATION

Give artificial respiration via mouth-to-nose resuscitation. First be sure the mouth is clear of all foreign materials. Then with the dog lying on his side, hold his mouth and nose closed and cup your hands around his muzzle. Blow firmly into the dog's nostrils once every six seconds. You should see his chest rise. Let it fall back naturally. Continue the procedure until breathing is sustained or coughing occurs. This procedure can also be accomplished with a full-muzzle resuscitation bag, which can be included in the handler's first-aid kit, along with emergency medications.

Remember: The key to saving K-9s exposed to illicit substances is fast action.

of Illinois College of Veterinary Medicine, which can offer guidance for aiding overdosed dogs and can answer life-saving questions by phone. Calls are handled by licensed veterinarians and board-certified veterinary toxicologists. Call: 900-680-0000 or 800-548-2423.

If the dog has ingested bags of drugs, a veterinarian may also need to perform immediate surgery to remove the plastic or other wrapping and prevent an obstruction or the rapid absorption of a lethal dose.

After any incident, a dog's heart rate and breathing should be carefully monitored, and electrocardiograms should be taken periodically to be sure that recovery has been made without lingering after-effects.

Courtroom Questions

When a contraband bust involving K-9 gets to court, the dog's training and ability may be vigorously challenged by the defense in an effort to cast doubt on the legality of the search or on the dog's credibility in detecting drugs. One court has likened the process of "certifying" the dog in the courtroom as "similar to that of qualifying an expert witness at trial."[13]

It will help if the handler has kept an accurate logbook of all the dog's training and finds, including (where finds are concerned) dates, amounts, types of narcotics, concealment locations, and so on.

Also knowing in advance the kinds of questions that may be asked will help a handler best support his dog—and, consequently, protect your arrest. Here is a small sampling of common questions by defendants' attorneys regarding dogs, compiled from actual court transcripts by the Los Angeles Police Department and the California Narcotic Canine Association. Share these with handlers you work with, so they can anticipate how they would answer them in court in order to present themselves and their dogs as the most effective witnesses possible in your cases.

TRAINING QUESTIONS

1. Have you had the opportunity to take any classes regarding scent molecules and their relationship to drugs?

2. Can you summarize your dog's training and experience with respect to detecting the scent of controlled substances?

3. Has your training utilized a manual or textbook?

4. How often do you train? Is your dog weak in some areas?

PSEUDO-NARCOTICS QUESTIONS

1. What are pseudo narcotics? Have you trained with pseudo narcotics?

2. How many times has your dog alerted to pseudo narcotics or any other substance that was not actual narcotics?

3. Would you mind if we put out some pseudo narcotics to see if your dog would alert?

4. Are you aware that non-narcotics training aids contain ingredients that are common with perfume, throat lozenges, and Ben-Gay, for example?

5. Why don't you use pseudo drugs to train your dog?

6. Would you agree that [some prestigious] dog training school is one of the foremost training schools for drug detection dogs in the United States? Are you aware that [this] dog school trains with non-narcotics or pseudo drugs?

CURRENCY QUESTIONS

1. Is it true that there is literature suggesting that a very high percentage of bills that are in circulation have odor of drug residue on them?

2. Do you have an opinion as to how recently or what period of time elapsed between the time your dog alerted to the presence of narcotics and when the currency was exposed to cocaine or other narcotics?

3. Would you agree with me that dog sniffs of money ideally should be done as contemporaneously to the seizure as possible?

4. Was the U.S. currency counted prior to your dog sniff? Did they use a money counter?

5. If you have marijuana, cocaine, or heroin on your hands, is it reasonable to say that some of those drugs could rub off on the currency?

GENERAL QUESTIONS

1. Are you aware that the police department seized my client's vehicle after your dog alerted to it? As you know, no drugs were found. Can you explain how the police can do this?

2. Would you be willing to bring your detection dog to court and demonstrate the effectiveness or lack of it to the jurors? If not, why not?

3. Did you have permission to have your dog where he was prior to using him? From whom?

4. Do you know what the scent ingredients are in marijuana, cocaine, heroin, or methamphetamine?

5. Does pure cocaine have a scent?

6. What is the smallest and largest amounts of narcotics your dog has alerted to?

7. Does your dog alert to methamphetamine? Do you know what is the chemical makeup of methamphetamine? Which of those chemicals is your dog alerting to?

8. Are there any substances that can, in your opinion, confuse the dog or that in anyway can diminish his ability to alert to narcotics? In your opinion, are there any particular scents that are effective in masking?

9. Has your dog ever falsely alerted?

10. Doesn't your dog have good days and bad days like any other living thing, like people? I notice that you have all Es for Excellent in your dog's training records over the last six years. How is that?

11. What does the term "dead scent" mean to you?

12. In how many situations has your dog given you an alert to a container and after opening said container, you observed no usable narcotics?

13. Isn't it true that on occasion your dog might alert and you don't have a clue as to why? Why does that happen?

Of course, in a closely fought case, many more questions will be asked. But if handlers you work with review this list and research answers they don't know by conferring with prosecutors and K-9 training organizations before becoming involved in a trial, they'll at least be familiar with and prepared for the type of questioning they'll likely encounter at trial. Then they'll better be able to take the stand with confidence and successfully parry cross-examination.

IV
TACTICS OF FOLLOW-THROUGH

BEYOND THE BUST

The vehicle search is over. You've found and secured the goods. You've got the suspect. And now what you've got is a *new opportunity*—a chance to catapult your stop to an even greater investigative level.

With a bit more effort and expertise, you can expand your impact significantly by one or both of the following options:

- Enlisting the suspect's cooperation to implicate his contacts or collaborators in the drug business and produce more arrests;

- Initiating an asset forfeiture, whereby ownership of money or property related to criminal activity passes to the government, to the ultimate benefit of you and your fellow officers.

These are the potential "Bonus Benefits" that can be achieved at the peak of the Criminal Patrol Pyramid, beyond your initial investigation and discovery of contraband.

Asset forfeiture has been variously described as "the dash for the cash"…"putting meat in the smokehouse"…"the H-bomb in the war on drugs." Drug-dealing is a money-motivated crime, and forfeiture procedures are part of the strategy of attacking it with unlimited tactics. When you help your agency confiscate suspicious currency you encounter on a stop, as well as other valuable property that appears to be linked with lawbreaking, drug traffickers are hit where it hurts most—in their profits and in the wealth they've accumulated. A traffic stop by a deputy in Mississippi, for example, resulted not only in the loss of sixty pounds of coke he discovered but through forfeiture proceedings led eventually to the confiscation of $6,500,000 worth of hard assets in Texas, including a ranch and several warehouses. When such seizures are liquidated and the proceeds shared with the agency whose officer(s) initiated the action, law enforcement gets what it needs most and has the hardest time getting these days: funds for training, new equipment, and more manpower. In some communities, officers have even gotten direct cash bonuses from forfeitures they were involved in.[1]

Currently there's a vocal movement underway among police critics to severely curtail the forfeiture process. They mock agencies that have benefited from forfeitures as "the new drug profiteers" and imply that taking ill-gotten gains away from criminals is somehow unfair. They've had their influence; the process that used to be relatively easy now requires more hard work.[2] But the results can still be worth it. The forfeiture honeymoon may be over, but the marriage with law enforcement is expected to endure.

Presently, over 90% of state police agencies and major municipal or sheriff's departments receive forfeiture money in a typical year.[3] Many progressive departments in smaller communities are taking a share, too. Some have reaped more than $1,000,000 a month from forfeiture, and in some communities police agencies take in more cash than the local banks.

With these funds they're able to buy state-of-the art equipment and training they could never afford solely from today's tax-supported bud-

gets. Examples: a $72,000 LaserDisc-shooting simulator for a state police agency in the East...a fleet of unmarked cars with Vascar units, shotguns, and racks for a department in Maryland...a $400,000 communications van and new 9mm pistols and leather gear for an entire sheriff's department in Colorado...a $177,000 infrared nighttime aerial reconnaissance system for a sheriff's office in Florida... raid jackets and special helmets for a Southern public safety department...new leather jackets, uniforms, and sidearms for a 1,200-officer department in Illinois. One seven-officer department in Rhode Island has gained more than ten times its annual budget from forfeitures. The chief has bought new cruisers with high-tech gear, soft body armor, semiautomatic handguns with laser sights, a $50,000 indoor-outdoor range, and has financed three officers attending college, funded a school drug awareness program, and hired an animal-control officer and a kid to wash patrol cars—and still hasn't put much of a dent in his special treasury.

(top)
In these tight-budget times, this Mercedes (seized for hauling marijuana) may be worth 2-3 patrol cars for your department.

(above)
No money for training? Maybe you can help. With good forfeiture procedures, money you confiscate can be converted into improved training and equipment for you and fellow officers.

Much of the forfeiture windfall for departments has resulted from raids, stings, and other traditional narcotics enforcement activities. But an increasing portion is coming from uniformed officers committed to aggressive Criminal Patrol, like the patrolman in New Jersey who stopped a van for speeding, discovered a sack of marijuana money inside, and earned his twenty-six-officer department $325,000 for his alertness, the single biggest revenue infusion it had ever received. On one Midwestern department, five officers were responsible for money confiscations worth $1,200,000 emanating from traffic stops in just one six-month period. Even more revenues will come from such efforts as patrol officers are better trained to recognize the necessary elements of forfeiture and forfeiture opportunities. "The assumption that only organized crime and narcotics units need training in forfeiture is incorrect," declares a Florida legal advisor. "There are opportunities for every officer."

How much you personally get involved in pushing your successful bust to the top of the Pyramid will depend largely on your department's policies, size, and structure. What happens after your street encounter may rest almost wholly in the hands of others. Even so, your role is pivotal.

Earlier, your knowing how to approach the situation turned a vehi

450

cle stop into a criminal investigation, with a successful climax. Now by understanding what's needed on your part, you can lay a foundation that will result in success on the next plane. Even if there is no "bonus" development, your proper attention to details after you leave the scene, at the very least, will help you strengthen your original case in court.

As you wrap up your duties at the scene and prepare to shift your attention to the station or some other location for the next phase, continue to keep your priorities in mind. *Stay tactical.* The activities you embark on "beyond the bust" should always begin—and continue—with your foremost concern on your personal safety.

Survival First

A tempting pitfall is to regard an arrest as the end of an encounter from a survival standpoint. You get so focused on controlling the dangers of approach and confrontation that when those periods are safely past you relax. In reality, the worst may be yet to come in the often-treacherous "follow-through" phase.

This period can be especially risky after the seizure of a significant quantity of contraband or cash. Then there's a natural excitement about the find, and the anticipation of weighing or counting what you've nailed can easily overshadow everything else unless you consciously remind yourself that so long as you have contact with a suspect, there is danger. Your vulnerability does not end until you have turned him over to someone else and you are free and clear of him.

You're well aware of the standard post-arrest precautions: Stabilize and control the suspect before attempting to handcuff...handcuff before you search...thoroughly search places that are often ignored or slighted but where weapons are frequently secreted, like the groin... be sure the arrestee is cuffed behind his or her back before transport... avoid hog-tying and placing the prisoner chest-down in your squad, because of the heightened risk of potentially fatal breathing difficulties ("positional asphyxia")...search again before turning the subject over to booking personnel, and so on.

In addition, here are six other cautions of follow-through, in the special context of contraband stops:

Be prepared for multiple handcuffings. By estimate, about half the cross-country drug couriers travel in pairs...or your arrest may include occupants of an escort car as well as a primary vehicle. In urban settings, with street gangs or other drug-related groups potentially involved, there's also a high likelihood of multiple suspects.

It's possible to hook up more than one arrestee with a single pair of cuffs, as illustrated in *The Tactical Edge.* But your preference is one set of cuffs for each prisoner. Depending on the design of your squad car, you may be able to carry backup pairs hooked over your emergency-brake pedal, your hood release, your spotlight handle, or some other protrusion under or near the dash.

If you use flexcuffs, remember that some styles of these are uniquely vulnerable to breaking or cutting. If the cuffs do not have a thin metal core, for example, they may be cut apart by rubbing dental floss or other strong, string-like material against the plastic so it "burns" through.

Also keep in mind that you may need to improvise once cuffs are

(above)
Don't shortcut your search. You're safest to inspect the suspect's belongings after you secure him in your patrol car. Then you can look down and concentrate on the contents of his pockets with less risk of a sudden assault or escape attempt.

(right)
Cover Officer monitoring the suspect promotes more thoroughness by the Contact Officer. Here the Contact has a good wide stance, which will help him maintain balance if the suspect gets frisky.

Is this how you want to search, even with the prisoner in handcuffs? In the "inside" position, with your hands in pockets, a headbutt or sudden twist can daze you or jerk you off balance. Search at an angle from the rear.

on. One Southern deputy bagged an elderly mule who was too stiff to get his hands close enough together behind his back for cuffing. The deputy cuffed him in front, but then with a second pair of cuffs hooked his hands up high to the metal screen in his patrol car, so he couldn't cause trouble. Another night, the same deputy busted a courier with sixty-five pounds of coke along an isolated stretch of road. With only a rookie as a partner, the deputy became alarmed when the offender claimed he "didn't know" whether an armed escort car was accompanying him. Taking no chances of an ambush while awaiting backup, the deputy cuffed the suspect to the grille of his patrol car. From separate hidden locations in the dark—behind

Storing multiple handcuffs for quick access: hooked on the emergency-brake pedal.

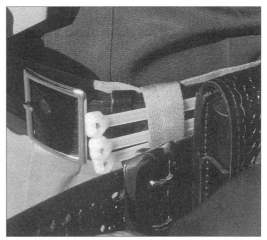

(above)
Storing multiple flex cuffs for quick access: Tucked inside your belt loops.

If your prisoner can't get his hands behind him for conventional, tactical cuffing, this may be an alternative for transport.

bushes up a hill and down in a ditch—the deputy and the rookie then kept a rifle and a handgun trained on the prisoner, ready for a gunfight while they awaited the arrival of three more squads.

Search arrestees as thoroughly as vehicles. Prior to the vehicle search, you may have just patted down a suspect for weapons. Now, with an arrest, you should completely search from head to toe, including not only the groin but other areas that sometimes are not checked at all at the scene. Once an arrest is made, time is now on your side. Slow down. Bring the same thorough scrutiny to finding weapons and possible tools of escape that you brought to finding contraband in the vehicle.

Suspects may have cuff keys hidden in their mouths, taped to their belts, or hung on necklaces. These may be disguised to look like something else, including crosses. Needles may be carried, point up, inside socks. Guns are sometimes concealed in hats or inside baby diapers. Some suspects hollow out the soles of athletic shoes to carry small handguns.

One Wisconsin deputy prided himself on the fact that a jailer had never found a weapon during booking that the deputy had missed on the road. Yet the deputy had never searched a suspect's wallet at a scene of arrest—until one night just twenty-eight hours after he'd experienced training about edged weapons at a seminar. He and two backup officers were handling three males who'd been stopped in a "seedy" car with no license plates. The suspects denied having any "guns, knives, atom bombs, drugs, or drug paraphernalia." But after learning that all had outstanding warrants and finding a roach clip on one, the deputy searched them thoroughly. In the middle compartment of one suspect's tri-fold wallet, he found a single-edge razor blade—just as he'd seen illustrated at the seminar. "With the subject's hands cuffed behind his back, he could have very easily retrieved the blade," says the deputy. "After unhandcuffing at the jail, he could have done some terrible bodily harm to myself and the jailers."

When you go inside pockets to retrieve things, use just your index and middle fingers to pinch and extract; you're less likely to get pricked or cut than if you jam your whole hand in, and you can get your fingers out faster if the suspect tries to trap your hand.

Of course, you should also be looking for contraband as you search. Include inspection of not-so-obvious concealment places, such as trouser cuffs, inside socks, inside linings and behind labels in jackets (look for evidence of re-stitching), items inside other items (like a bindle of heroin inside a matchbook). Check inside the offender's hands, since drug users are very skilled at palming contraband until it can be thrown away or eaten. In one Florida case, a suspect smuggled two kilos of cocaine—nearly five pounds worth—hidden in his sneakers. Buxom females often carry hypodermic needles, drug packets, even guns taped underneath their breasts. (Sometimes an early cue to this is an attempt by the suspect to intimidate you about her breasts. She may brazenly accuse you of wanting to look at them or touch them, in hopes of scaring you away from searching that area.)[4]

Today's offender can be well prepared for violence and worthy of a thorough search. Two bikers in Arizona had with them all of these weapons when arrested.

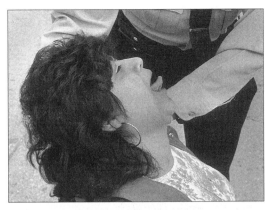

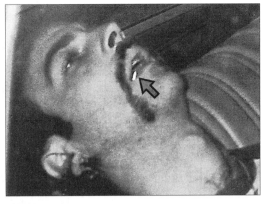

(above left)
Part of searching thoroughly is remembering to check areas often overlooked. For example, the suspect's mouth.

(above)
This suspect hid a handcuff key (arrow) inside his mouth. He never got to use it because he died first, in a confrontation with an officer. Suspects may also hide razor blades there.

(left)
Don't forget the weapon capability of "jewelry." Remove such items before transport.

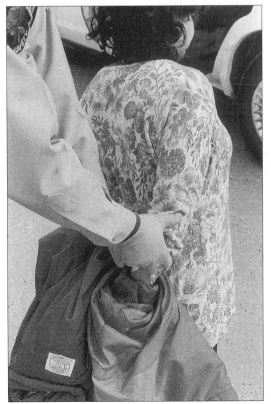

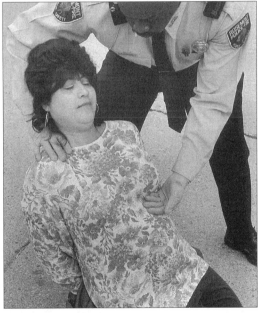

(left)
If the suspect is wearing a jacket, search it first, then pull it down low and continue a thorough check of the suspect's back and arms.

(above)
Searching the breast area of a female arrestee can and should be done, even if a female officer is not present. Checking the area with the backs of your fingers is professional and appropriate for detecting contraband and weapons.

455

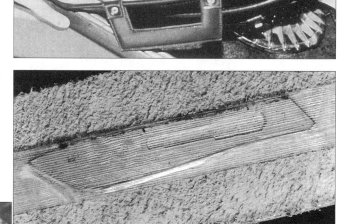

(above)
Carefully inspect all items you recover while searching. This pager has been hollowed out to conceal narcotics.

(top right)
Purses are frequent carrying places for knives, guns, and drugs. Separate purses from suspects before they enter your patrol car and search them thoroughly.

(right)
Knife blade found taped to the inside of an arrestee's pants belt.

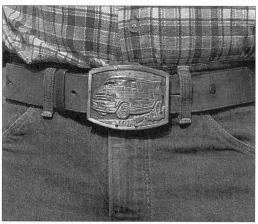

(left)
Search both sides of the suspect's belt by feel and sight, using this or comparable technique. Weapons and/or drugs may be affixed.

(below left/right)
This belt buckle was converted to a double-barrel .22, using mail-order instructions. When the trigger atop the buckle is pushed, the front flips down and the barrels snap out simultaneously, firing 2 shots at belly-button height.

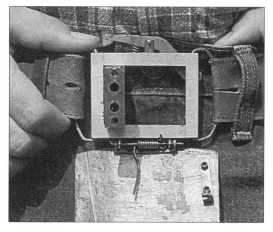

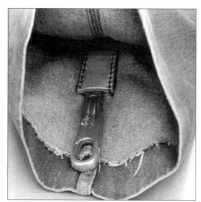

(left/below)
As your search focuses on the lower limbs, remember to check cuffs, socks, and inside the pants legs. Some offenders hide weapons, as well as contraband, for quick access.

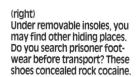

(above)
Remember this the next time you're tempted to just run your flat hand quickly down a suspect's leg.

(below)
Weapons can easily be hidden inside tennis shoe soles. Inside one pair, deputies confiscated this .22-cal. minirevolver frame, cylinder, 5 hollow-point bullets, and 2 handcuff keys.

(right)
Under removable insoles, you may find other hiding places. Do you search prisoner footwear before transport? These shoes concealed rock cocaine.

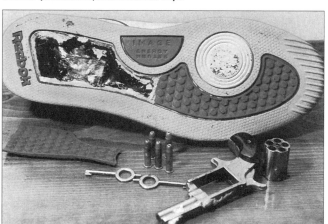

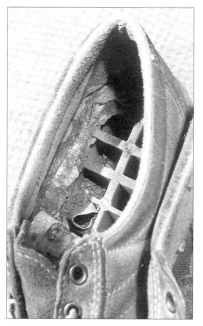

Why Searching Must Be Thorough

Drug users and transporters can show as much ingenuity in hiding contraband on their persons and in personal effects as they do in concealing it in their vehicles. Here's just a partial list of places from which drugs have been recovered during personal searches. Some of these same spots are capable of concealing weapons or escape tools.

Lipstick tube	Under false teeth	Fountain pens
Cigarette lighter/packs	Zippered belts	Inside fly trap of pants
Taped under breast	Belt buckles	Hearing-aid battery box
Processed hair/buns/wigs	Behind collars/stays	Thermos jugs
Rectum	Foreskin of penis	Luggage liners
Vagina	Under bandages	Canteens
Nose	False limbs	Inhalers
Ears	Rings	Change-purse lining
Mouth	Hearing-aid glasses	Under helmet insulation
Cheeks of buttocks	Jock straps	In love beads
Lapels	Swallowed with string to teeth	Earrings
Inside/back of watch/jewelry	Between toes/taped to feet	Knot of tie/handkerchiefs
Taped behind ears	Wallet	Military patches
Cuffs/waistband	Eye-glasses case	False caps on teeth
Socks/shoes	Behind uniform ribbons	In hair beret
Pill vials	Film cans	Hat band
Inside sanitary napkins/tampons	Money belts	Inside colostomy bag
In lockets/bracelets/charms	Cane/umbrella handles	Tobacco tins/pouches
Cigarette filters	Compact	Lining of clothing
In addressed envelopes	False buttons	In gum sticks
In swim trunks	In stem of pipe	Casts
Pinned to shorts	In artificial eyes	In hollowed-out crutches
In baby's diapers	Tie pins/clasps/cuff links	In gum stuck behind ear
In corsets/girdles	Breath freshener dispenser	Inside ID bracelets

Be aware of post-arrest booby traps. Couriers sometimes rig up decoy drug packages by combining sugar with either chlorate or sodium cyanide to form a powdered mixture that looks like narcotics, which they then plant on themselves or in their vehicles. These are designed to turn field drug-test kits into small bombs or mini gas chambers.[5]

Some commonly used kits include ampoules containing highly concentrated sulfuric acid as part of the reagent. When sulfuric acid hits chlorate, an immediate, acid-spraying violent reaction occurs that can produce chemical burns and permanent blindness. One officer lost several fingers in such a blast. When sulfuric acid contacts sodium cyanide, it releases poisonous hydrogen cyanide gas, the "death chamber" ingredient. An Arizona officer almost fell victim to this when he seized what looked like a quantity of methamphetamine. The booby trap in this case apparently was aimed not at cops but at enemies in the drug trade, for the suspect kept telling him not to test it and tried violently to get away. The officer backed off and let a lab analyze the "meth," where chemists confirmed the deadly set up. Hydrogen cyanide is colorless, but has a faint smell of almonds. If you detect that odor during a drug test, clear the area immediately. If you have any other suspicion that materials may be booby trapped, call for immediate assistance from the nearest bomb squad.

Otherwise, take care in using your field kit. Don't taste or inhale vapors. Use protective eye- and headgear and breathing apparatus, if possible. At the very least, don't stick your face right over where you're testing...wear heavy gloves...try to be in a well-ventilated

458

area…if possible, conduct tests in an open dish so gases can vent…and keep your back to the wind, so fumes will blow away from you. (Substances may also be mixed with drugs to affect test validity.)

Also be cautious in handling the drugs themselves. One officer busted a suspect with 200 sheets of LSD. Counting them, the officer wet his finger to turn the pages, and ended up with a bad reaction when the hallucinogen absorbed into his skin.

Maintain your alertness throughout the transport. Designed by the U.S. Marshals Service after two of its deputies were savagely attacked and critically injured while moving a prisoner by car, this diagram reflects the dangerous psychology of many transports:

Dynamics of Transport

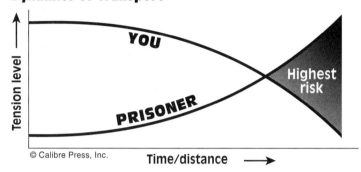

© Calibre Press, Inc.

Time/distance ⟶   Jail

As a transport nears its end, officers tend to relax, thinking they're almost at a place of safety. A prisoner's tension level increases, as he realizes his time for action (escape) is running out. Be ready for a last-ditch move for freedom by keeping your alertness level high.

Officers are most likely to be in Condition Yellow, the mental state of heightened awareness, at the beginning of a transport and to allow their alertness to flag the closer they get to the destination, which represents to them a "home base" of safety. The prisoner often experiences just the *opposite* pattern of tension, becoming more desperate as he gets closer to the point where he'll be behind bars and his opportunities for escape will be radically diminished. Consequently, the most dangerous period of a transport will often be the final stretch, when the prisoner is likeliest to make a last-ditch move and the typical officer is likeliest to have dropped his guard.

Even in a caged car, an unmonitored arrestee can do considerable damage and, at the very least, may be setting you up for an assault when you stop the vehicle and open the door to extract him. Some devious suspects know how to use seat-belt latches to break apart handcuffs. Others are able to open cuffs with the teeth of a comb. Limber ones can "step through" cuffs to bring their hands to the front, where they're capable of innumerable deadly deeds.

If you are transporting with a partner, the passenger officer should turn in his seat so he can watch the prisoner throughout the transport, a version of the Contact/Cover tactic. If you're alone, position the prisoner on the far right side of the back seat, building maximum distance between you. Turn your rearview mirror so it reflects him and use your side mirror for looking back at traffic. If you've seat-belted him in and have tied his ankles with a hobble that you've closed in his door, he'll be bound in place. In the mirror or with a slight turn of your head, you can now keep an eye on him. (This might benefit him, too. If he's a drug user and there has been a struggle, a foot pursuit, or use of chemical agents prior to the transport, he may be vul-

Dynamics of Transport—Written in Blood

Proof that the final stage of transport can be a countdown to death. NYPD Detective Richard Guerzon (below) lies murdered outside personal car used for transporting a suburban crack dealer to jail. Prisoner killed Guerzon and partner, Detective Keith Williams (below right), with a revolver he concealed before he was placed alone in the back seat for transport. Handcuffed in front, not adequately searched, and not properly controlled or monitored, he accessed the gun during the ride and fired on the officers. Both were killed instantly with point-blank shots to the head—just five blocks from the end of the transport

Detective Richard Guerzon, 8 meritorious awards, 5 citations for excellent police duty, less than 1 month from retirement.

Detective Keith Williams, 8 years on the job, 2 citations for excellent police duty.

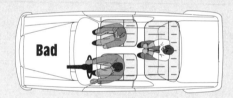

No cage. Suspect alone, handcuffed in front, not thoroughly searched. Officers' attention focused elsewhere.

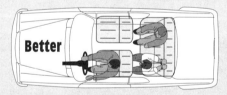

With uncaged car, prisoner searched and properly restrained, including tightly cinched in seat belt. Officer seated in rear with gun side away to monitor him.

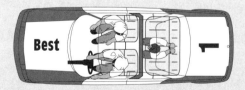

Caged patrol car, prisoner properly searched and restrained. Prisoner in rear where driver can watch in mirror and passenger officer can turn to monitor throughout transport.

(above)
Even with a screen, relaxing is risky. This heavy-duty partition installed in a Texas patrol car supposedly was prisoner-proof. Yet a suspect rammed his head against it until it broke, removing the barrier between him and officers up front.

nerable to a dangerous level of systemic excitation that can lead to a heart attack or breathing arrest. He needs to be monitored for medical as well as safety reasons. Should any symptoms of distress appear, drive directly to an emergency facility.)

Remember, before any suspect enters your patrol car, caged or not, he must be thoroughly searched. A trooper in Oregon stopped a pickup truck with three Hispanic males. He put them all in the back seat of his unit, with one handcuffed, the others not. Apparently he failed to search them carefully. When the trooper was behind the wheel, one of the suspects drew a hidden gun and shot him three times in the head through the Plexiglas shield. The killer then shot out the rear window, and all the suspects climbed through it and fled, leaving the trooper's body to be discovered by fellow officers after he didn't respond to the radio.

Don't be lulled by a "safe" environment. When you finally reach the station and your suspect seems nonthreatening and cooperative, it's easy to feel that you're on secure, solid ground when you actually may be treading on the brink of disaster.

This point is perhaps best reinforced by the fate of a young chief in a tiny Southern town. Late one spring night he stopped a pickup truck for speeding and during a search found three baggies of marijuana and about an ounce of cocaine. He brought the truck's occupants, a twenty-year-old driver and a seventeen-year-old girl, back to his office in Town Hall to interview them. They were *not* handcuffed, the girl was *not* searched.

At some point she allegedly slipped the driver a semiautomatic pistol that she'd been concealing. Firing multiple rounds that hit below the chief's vest, the driver inflicted mortal wounds. Before dying, the chief fired back with his 9mm service weapon, but couldn't stop them. He was disarmed and shot more times with his own gun before the suspects stole his unmarked car and fled.

Secure the seizure. Usually this is thought of in terms of protecting the cash or drugs you've confiscated from being contaminated as evidence. But occasionally there are survival considerations, too.

Officers in a "Mayberry" town of 2,200 in southern Illinois busted a semitrailer with seventy kilos of coke. The drugs were so valuable ($3,000,000 estimated worth) and the police force so small (fourteen) that the chief was reluctant to keep the haul at the station for fear the place would be attacked and overrun by a commando force from the traffickers. So he rented safe deposit boxes at the local bank and stashed the seizure there. No problem.

Search your patrol car before resuming patrol. You may have missed something when you searched the prisoner, and en route to the station he or she may have hidden something in your back seat which could become available to the next occupant—like drugs or, worse, a weapon.

Controlled Delivery

With survival considerations in proper perspective, you can now explore ways in which to parlay your discovery beyond a one-stop, one-subject, one-arrest bottom line.

One important option is to get the courier back on the road and headed toward his intended destination, with the plan of pulling a "sting" at the end to snare other players higher up the ladder in the trafficking network. You may be asked to escort him in an unmarked car or another disguised vehicle for surveillance purposes, or the whole operation may be taken over by investigators in your department or by federal agents.

In any case, if you keep the possibility of a "controlled delivery" of either drugs or cash in mind when you make the bust, you very likely can play a key role at the arrest scene in persuading the suspect to cooperate. He'll feel caught between his fear of you and his fear of his bosses. You want to use your unique leverage to bend him your way.

"You need to 'sell' yourself to the suspect...and 'ask for the sale' in convincing him," says one Criminal Patrol specialist. "When a K-9 has alerted or you've found contraband, explain to the suspect that this is not a mistake, it's hard evidence. Tell him that in the past you've seized X pounds of pot, X pounds of coke, X dollars in cash. Let him know that this is your business and he's been caught by someone who really knows what they're doing. Let him see that you're his worst nightmare because you're going to put him in prison for as long as you can.

"Then tell him if he helps you, you'll see what the DA will do for him. Keep it vague, like you'll talk to the prosecutor and try to help him out. Ask him to cooperate by completing his run just like it was planned. Don't expect him to volunteer. But tell him: 'If you don't help us *right now*, there will be no deals.' There's nothing untruthful in that." Drivers who have their families along on the run may become especially cooperative if they feel you'll try to help their wives and children be treated leniently.

Many couriers, hoping for a "break," will turn over anyone they can; with enough time and information, the suspect may be wired, phone calls can be tape recorded, and the delivery videotaped. Deputies in Tennessee parlayed the arrest of two Mexican brothers with more than 350 kilos of cocaine into multiple arrests in L.A. and Washington, D.C., and seizures of major drug warehouses. You never know where your "simple" vehicle stop might lead.

To facilitate the sting, to possibly develop other promising avenues of investigation, and to strengthen your case even if you're not planning a controlled delivery, you'll need to find out from your arrestee as much as possible of the following, guided by the time you have and his or her level of cooperation:

- Whether escort vehicles are accompanying and surveilling him and whether their occupants are armed;
- Under what circumstances and in what way can the escort offenders be expected to react;
- How he is supposed to arrange delivery at the other end, including phone or beeper numbers he's to call, locations he's to go to, deadlines he's expected to meet;
- Names, addresses, and hangouts of contacts at both ends of his run;
- Whether he is aware of any storage facilities;
- How and by whom was he recruited;
- Who provided the vehicle and how he got it;

- Where and by whom the contraband was packed and loaded;
- Who gave him his instructions;
- When, where, by whom, and how much he's getting paid;
- Who else knows about the smuggling;
- What travel routes have been designated, and the locations of any delivery points, pickup points, transfer points, stash points, or check-in points along the way;
- Any special devices, codes, or procedures associated with this transport;
- Are there any secret compartments, other hiding places, or booby traps you have not discovered;
- If the vehicle has been modified, where and by whom was the work done;
- Whether he's aware of other couriers working for the same bosses, and, if so, their number, frequency, and routes of travel, size of load, type of contraband, and kinds of vehicles to give an idea of the scope of the organization;
- What he knows, if anything, of the contraband's point of origin and how it entered the country, including descriptions of methods, locations, personnel, boats, and aircraft involved;
- Some idea of his own and his associates' assets, including bank accounts, real estate, businesses, cars, and so on that might later be tied to drug dealings;
- Are any law enforcement personnel illicitly involved;
- Are the contacts he'll be meeting likely to be armed; if so, with what types of weapons.

Remember: The suspect is likely to be under tight time pressure. If he misses a delivery or check-in deadline, this will be a red flag to his associates. Although there's a risk he'll shake a police tail along the way, it may be best to leave as much of the load as possible in place to minimize delays and mask your interception. Consider having him call his delivery contacts and claim that he has experienced a breakdown, to account for the lost time. If he's close to the delivery point, they may even send a rescue party to meet him, creating opportunity for additional arrests at the discovery scene if that is considered desirable. Troopers in New Jersey have used this ruse numerous times, with officers dressed in mechanics' uniforms awaiting the responding delegation. In some cases, rescuers have flown in by private plane. After pulling the sting, arresting officers have then added the aircraft to the property seized for forfeiture.

Of course, watching your legal Ps and Qs is important on a controlled delivery, as elsewhere. Care must be taken to assure that the illegal substances that get delivered are in fact what you discovered initially and not something that a lawyer could claim got "planted" along the way. Interestingly, the U.S. Supreme Court has made it easier to convict co-conspirators who may be arrested in the follow-through. In a case from the West, officers stopped a car for driving too slowly, perceived that the driver fit various drug-courier indicators, searched, and discovered 560 pounds of cocaine in the trunk. The suspect cooperated with a controlled delivery which bagged various codefendants. The sec ondary arrestees challenged the search as illegal and claimed that it violated their Fourth Amendment right to privacy that derived from their "supervisory role" in the smuggling operation. An Appeals court agreed and suppressed the coke as evidence. But the Supreme Court reversed, holding that conspirators do not have standing to challenge illegally seized evidence solely because of their supervision over the place searched.[6] In other words, even if your initial seizure proves faulty, co-conspirator arrests may still stand. Indeed, in a case from Alaska, the Supreme Court has ruled that parties accused of conspiring to sell drugs do not even have to act in some way to carry out the scheme in order to be convicted of conspiracy; the criminal agreement itself is a criminal act.[7] These cases mean fewer shields that the upper echelon in drug operations can use to hide behind.

Even if a suspect won't cooperate with a controlled delivery, there may be ways to expand beyond the initial arrest. Your search of the vehicle and his or her personal effects may yield records or phone numbers that will incriminate others. With gangbangers, especially, you may find boastful photographs of traffickers with money, weapons, and drugs that can be valuable to intelligence officers. The suspect may have a pager or cellular phone that can be used to catch calls that will lead back to other players. During a vehicle search by a small-town officer in California, for example, a pager in the car went off. The officer went to a nearby pay phone, called the number, and set up a meeting with the female who answered when he learned that she wanted to buy heroin.

Once you've discovered a substantial amount of contraband, you'll usually have grounds for getting a search warrant for the residence of each occupant of the vehicle. And that not only may yield more contraband but may open the floodgate to asset forfeiture. After a deputy in North Carolina stopped a motorist early one morning for driving erratically and then found forty-three grams of cocaine in his Lincoln Town Car, a search warrant for his home led officers to discover that he had ten different bank accounts with over $500,000. They drilled a safe in the place and found several guns, a collection of porno videos, more cocaine, and $204,000 cash. All this was seized, plus his $75,000 condo and luxury automobile—more than $800,000 worth of money and property that eventually was forfeited.

Not bad for a stop that started out with the deputy thinking he was pulling over "just another DUI."

Asset Forfeiture

The lucrative game of asset forfeiture is played a number of ways by rules that keep changing.[8]

The idea—depriving wrongdoers of the spoils of their criminal activities without compensation—dates back to Biblical times, but it has become objectionable to some legislators and judges in recent years because of the myth, fostered by radical civil libertarians, criminal-defense attorneys, and a hostile media, that forfeiture regularly and widely victimizes innocent people.

Despite their opposition, asset forfeiture remains one of law enforcement's most powerful weapons in the war on drugs, both in the U.S. and Canada. Even though a suspect may not be charged with a crime, questionable money you find in his vehicle can still be seized for forfeiture, if his explanation of its origin and purpose is not supported by evidence and the circumstances seem to fit with drug-trafficking patterns.[9] Of course, the vehicle itself is usually forfeitable, too. Officers in Michigan reduced local drug traffic in one high-volume county by seizing the vehicles of even casual drug buyers. In less than three years, they confiscated over 2,000 automobiles.[10] (With the right support from prosecutors, forfeiture can be used in other types of cases, as well. Police in Portland, Oregon, for example, have brought vehicle-forfeiture proceedings against certain drunk-driving offenders and against subjects who solicit prostitutes. Some observers have credited this strategy with a 60% decrease in fatal accidents involving alcohol.[11])

Because forfeiture rules are changing rapidly, you will need to consult your local legal advisors to confirm what's possible in your area. In fact, close coordination with a prosecutor's office (usually the U.S. Attorney) is necessary to make forfeiture work successfully. As most legislation and case law stand at this writing:

All types of property are subject to forfeiture, including money, bank accounts, securities, vehicles, boats, airplanes, jewelry, livestock, art, electronic gear, weapons, real estate, and, of course, contraband itself. Even attorneys' fees paid with illegal funds can be confiscated.[12] The property in question must have been used or intended to be used to facilitate an illegal activity, like the production, possession, transportation, or sale of drugs, or it must be traceable to the proceeds from crime.

There are four types of forfeiture:

1. Summary, the automatic surrender of contraband, without hearing or notice;

2. Administrative, where, according to guidelines, certain other property (such as hauling conveyances and some monetary instruments) can be forfeited solely upon order of the investigative agency or through a negotiated settlement with the owner or other claimant;

3. Criminal, where a bid for forfeiture is included as part of the trial of a defendant;

4. Civil, where proceedings are brought in civil court against the property itself, not against the owner or possessor.

Some state laws require hearings and even jury trials regardless of the nature of the property at issue, unless waived by the claimant in writing. Where forfeiture of real estate and other costly or contested property is involved, pre-seizure notice and an adversarial judicial hearing are universally required,[13] except in extraordinary circumstances.

So far, civil forfeiture has been most popular with law enforcement agencies because of the burden of proof required. With criminal forfeiture, the connection between property and crime must be established, like the defendant's guilt, "beyond a reasonable doubt;" if the defendant is acquitted, the property will not be forfeited.[14] With civil forfeiture, you do not need a criminal indictment or conviction or even an arrest. Depending on the jurisdiction, all that's required may be a showing of probable cause that the property in question is associated with illegality, regardless of whether the owner is ever charged separately with a crime or convicted. Circumstantial and hearsay evidence is acceptable, and the property need not be traced to specific illegal transactions. For example, an officer stopped a rental truck for speeding on an off-the-beaten-path road in Alabama, a state where major routes are closely watched by state troopers. Although the occupants, two cousins headed from Florida to Texas, were not using their air conditioning on that sweltering day, a background check turned up nothing and no drugs were found during a consent search. However, the officer and his backup did smell marijuana, and when they opened a number of sealed cardboard boxes in the cargo area, many of them were empty. One officer tried to pick up a mattress that

Plucking Victory from the Jaws of Defeat

Sometimes even when your initial search comes up dry, forfeitures can be possible with the right follow-through.

When highway patrol officers in Ohio stopped and questioned the occupants of a brand new Cadillac Fleetwood after a speeding violation, they developed plenty of drug indicators. One suspect said he embroidered jackets for a living, the other worked in a body shop. The car, which didn't seem to fit those occupations, was allegedly rented by an absent "aunt" of the passenger, but the rental agreement bore someone else's name. The suspects had flown from Dallas to Indianapolis, where they rented the car, then drove to Chicago to "visit relatives," and now were en route to Toledo, supposedly for the same purpose. They'd racked up over 600 miles in just two days. They couldn't

explain why they'd flown to Indianapolis, where they apparently had no business, instead of Chicago, supposedly their first stop. Both suspects denied previous arrests, but a criminal-history check revealed an alias for the driver and an earlier bust for possessing eighty pounds of marijuana. During a search, officers found receipts from luxury motels, including phone records showing thirty to forty brief long-distance calls a day. This seemed unusual during a vacation trip but not so unusual for setting up drug deliveries.

Yet aside from one roach in an ashtray, the officers found no drugs in the car and only about $800 cash.

Still convinced something was amiss, they contacted DEA before sending the suspects on their way. The feds tailed the Caddy to a

neighborhood in Toledo where "no one who's legit can afford to pay $79 a day for a luxury rental." Surveilling the house the two suspects entered, agents noted "a lot of traffic in and out every few minutes all night long." Periodically a woman emerged with a purse and made trips back and forth to a car parked in the back yard. The agents figured she was ferrying drugs from the car to the house.

With a search warrant, they finally recovered about thirty pounds of marijuana from the back-yard car, $15,000 cash from a closet in the residence, and a MAC-10. The owner of the place was an ex-con. Arrests were made, the gun and dope were confiscated, and forfeiture proceedings were successfully brought against the back-yard car, the house, and the cash.

A gratifying outcome for a roadside search that "didn't work out."

was propped behind the boxes and found it unusually heavy. Inside it, he discovered $511,780 in cash, which also smelled like pot. The cousins objected to a forfeiture action that was later filed, but the court ruled that the odor of marijuana on the truck, money, and mattress, plus some marijuana residue found in the cargo area and the fact that the mattress was stored behind empty boxes provided "substantial evidence to establish probable cause." The money was ordered forfeited.[15]

Claimants who want to contest a forfeiture usually must first demonstrate that they have a viable interest in the seized property, and then must prove the property's "innocence" by a "preponderance of evidence" or establish that they did not know of or consent to its illegal use or origin.[16]

Forfeiture can take place under state or federal process. All but one state have civil-forfeiture laws, and a few also provide for criminal forfeiture.[17] Federally, in addition to provisions for criminal forfeiture, there are over 100 civil-forfeiture statutes contained in the United States Code.

Even though you work for a state, county, or municipal agency and you encounter the questionable property in the process of enforcing nonfederal laws, your case can sometimes be "adopted" by a federal agency, like the FBI, DEA, or Immigration and Naturalization Service, for federal civil or administrative forfeiture. The property must be worth certain minimum values, the agency petitioned for adoption must be willing to expend the resources to pursue the forfeiture and to provide custodial care for the property involved, and your department usually must obtain a state court "turnover order" or the sanction of your state attorney that transfers the seizure under federal auspices.

Although new rules in the early '90s made federal adoption more difficult, this is still an appealing option, when possible. At this writing, federal forfeiture cases are generally more aggressively pursued by prosecutors, tend to move faster, require the least burden of proof (probable cause), and provide better paybacks to local law enforcement. With federally adopted cases, the initiating agency generally gets back up to 80% of the net proceeds, while under state process the return generally runs only about 50% to 75%, the rest being shared with the prosecutor's office and other public entities; in some states, all proceeds from seized assets go into general state or local treasuries.

Property forfeited must be in balance with the criminal activity with which it is associated. Forfeiture has been declared a "monetary punishment" by the Supreme Court and consequently it cannot be "excessive" compared to the seriousness of the crime, under the Eighth Amendment.[18] No precise "proportionality guidelines" have yet been established, but at least one lower court has said that the determination must weigh the "inherent gravity" of the offense, whether the property was an "integral part" of criminal activity, and whether such activity was "extensive."[19] This likely means that a roach you discover in a driver's ashtray cannot in and of itself be used as grounds for seizing for forfeiture the driver's $60,000 Jaguar, although this was possible—even popular—in the past under so-called Zero Tolerance drug interdiction programs.

Successful forfeiture involves a blizzard of paperwork and the right massaging of various bureaucratic backs. When you notify your supervisor about any discovery that you feel could lead to worthwhile forfeiture, he or she will decide how best to proceed. There should be a written checklist of procedures kept up to date with the latest regulations. Close conferring with your department's legal advisor, with federal agents and attorneys, or with your local prosecutor will be necessary.

As with a controlled delivery, you may have little if any direct involvement in forfeiture proceedings once your initial seizure has been processed. However, the groundwork you lay through dialogue with the suspect and the information you convey in your report can be crucial to the outcome. You set the scene for success or failure.

Shaking the Money Tree

Eighty per cent of people affected never contest forfeiture.[20] This includes situations where cash money—sometimes *big* money—is at stake, especially if they've lied and told you before you began searching that they weren't carrying any large sums.

When you discover currency (as some Criminal Patrol officers say they do in about one out of every fifteen vehicle searches), the suspects most likely will claim they didn't know it was there...don't know who it belongs to...and for sure it isn't theirs. This may occur even if you find the money in their clothing during a pat-down!

Which is fine, because with no claimants it's considered abandoned property. If no one comes forward after proper public notice, it's easy to forfeit, usually by administrative procedure. Just be sure you aid the process by documenting in your report the suspect's denials and, if possible, have him read and sign a form disclaiming ownership of the property. Every person at the scene should be interviewed about the origin of the money, as well as persons you learn about later who may be potential claimants.

If a suspect protests your seizing money at the scene, solicit whatever story he wants to offer to establish some credible legal interest in the funds. Encourage him to talk, even if he lies. *For you, lies are the next best thing to the truth.* He may claim, for example, that he's a dealer of some sort—livestock, automobiles, diamonds—and is on his way to make cash purchases. Ask him to show you a receipt for his bank withdrawal of the funds or other paperwork that would document his purpose. With most money seizures there will be no documents which could establish a legitimate source for the cash.

Simply possessing money, whatever the amount, is not a crime, nor is it by itself PC for an arrest or forfeiture.[21] With some good interviewing techniques, though, you may get the subject to admit that the money is drug proceeds. With forfeiture in mind, you want at the very least to tie him down to a story that investigation can later rebut. Explore his story with him in detail. Press him to come up with an explanation for the money early on, before he has time to invent a yarn that later is difficult or impossible to disprove. A trooper in Iowa, for example, seized $20,000 he found stuffed up behind a headlight on a car he'd stopped for an equipment violation. Although a mirror, a razor blade, and a large quantity of ammunition were found in the car, no narcotics could be located. The suspect insisted that the cash was from tips he'd received as a dealer in Las Vegas before his retirement. However, a check of the serial numbers showed that the currency, which a K-9 alerted to, hadn't even been printed until three years after his alleged retirement. When a Florida deputy found $95,000 in a trash bag in a car, the driver said his uncle had given it to him to buy a dump truck. Called, the uncle denied that the money was his.

Among logical questions that will help you test a suspect's story are:
- Who did you get the money from? When? Where? Why?
- Who else was with you when you got it?
- Do you know where it originated?
- Who packaged it?
- Did you count it or get any accompanying documents?
- Where were you taking the money?
- To whom (including full name, address, and phone number)?
- What is your relationship to these persons? To the money itself?
- Why is it being taken by you rather than being sent by some other means?
- Why is the money in cash? In small denominations?
- Are you dealing drugs in this city? County? State? Elsewhere?

"Please Take Me to Jail!"

Everyone's heard of situations where drug dealers offer cops huge sums to escape arrest. But when officers in Jacksonville, Florida, stopped a mule and found $365,000 in two duffel bags in the back seat of his Blazer, he sang a different tune.

He'd been sent to Miami from South Carolina with the money to buy dope but had missed his contact. He was headed home without any goods, so he was already in trouble with his bosses.

Now the officers told him they intended to seize his vehicle and the dough for forfeiture. The suspect dissolved in a fit of nerves. "Please take me to jail!" he pleaded. He figured being locked up a far better fate than having to face his irate employers. The officers declined; since he had no drugs, they had no grounds for arrest.

"If I attack you, will you put me in jail then?" he asked. Forget it, the officers said, and cut him loose.

No one ever came back for the money. The suspect has not been heard of in Jacksonville again.

Carrying thousands of dollars in a vehicle, in common drug-dealing denominations, is not in itself illegal. But the driver needs to have a credible explanation, or you may have grounds for a successful seizure and forfeiture.

If the suspect is under arrest or otherwise not free to leave, of course Miranda must be observed if you are interrogating him. Otherwise, the questioning will be limited only by your curiosity and his willingness to respond.

If he sticks to his story but you still feel that you have articulable reasons to believe the money may be connected with or intended for a drug transaction or other criminal activity, tell him:

"This money will be taken to headquarters for safekeeping until we get this all investigated and straightened out. Let's set up a time right now when you can come in and talk about it...and I'll have an agent from the IRS there."

This ploy was tried in Ohio with typical results after a highway patrolman stopped two rental cars for speeding in tandem. The lead driver was an eighteen-year-old, with two women passengers. The tail car carried two muscular males, who appeared to be bodyguards. Both cars had been rented by a party who was not present, and the occupants gave conflicting stories about why they were on the road. They strenuously denied having any drugs, guns, or large sums of money, but during a consent search the officer found $42,500 in cash in the first car's trunk. The driver said his father had given it to him to buy a new Corvette and that he'd "forgotten" it was there. He insisted it was his and that they'd be back to check on it the next day. But after the IRS was mentioned, they never appeared. Says a Wisconsin officer who paints this "word picture" with fair regularity: "I've never had anyone show up."

Whether the suspect seems inclined to fight for the cash or not, ask him to accompany you to the station (assuming he is not under arrest because of other evidence and is already headed there involuntarily), watch while you count it, and get a receipt. If the suspect agrees, do not leave him or yourself alone with the money at any point. If he declines to go with you, that should go into your report also, further indicating his dissociation from the funds.

Of course, if you've found drugs, drug records, or drug paraphernalia in the vehicle in addition to the cash, that supports forfeiture. Courts have ruled that "money found near forfeitable controlled substances is presumed to be forfeitable."[22] The funds do not have to be traced to a particular illegal transaction.

The next best evidence will probably be a history of drug offenses by the supposed owner of the money, so run a criminal-records check on everyone in the vehicle and on all the names you can get from them as supposedly being associated with the trip. Explore possible gang involvement. Gang connections combined with drug running may increase the punishment if an arrest is involved. (If you are not anticipating an arrest, you should run an NCIC check before the subjects leave; you may learn about warrants or other information that will change your mind.)

If a K-9 is available, consider a sniff test on the money. This is not required in order for cash to be eligible for forfeiture, but some departments feel that when money is found in the absence of drugs a positive alert to it by a trained dog can help clinch the case; certainly if you don't do a sniff test, the defense attorney will try to make a big deal out of that. However, understand the limitations of this. Some extreme estimates claim that traces of cocaine can be found on a staggering 97% of circulating currency; one federal test of one-dollar bills from fourteen locations (including Yellowstone, Wyoming and Whitefish, Montana) showed that 79% bore traces of the drug. If the forfeiture is contested, the suspect's attorney will use this to cast doubt on the dog's alert, arguing that the money wasn't contaminated by his client but by someone before him on the circulation chain. Some K-9 experts insist that properly trained dogs "[do] not false alert on general circulation money." However, some courts have ruled otherwise. Because of the controversy, a dog alert on money should only be regarded as one element of your case.[23]

Currency does pick up scents easily, so to keep the K-9 sniff as credible as possible, the suspect bills should be carefully protected from inadvertent officer contamination during seizure, transportation, counting, and other handling or storage. After you've photographed it undisturbed in the spot where you discovered it, the cash should be removed by an officer who has not been in contact with any narcotics, placed in paper bags, and *then* transported in a drug-sterile patrol vehicle where it is further protected from contamination. Cash discovered in separate locations or on suspects should *not* be commingled, nor should the money be put close to any drugs you've recovered. In an uncontaminated location, with each batch of questionable money isolated and processed one at a time, the suspect currency can then be positioned, in effect, in a "line up" and a K-9 brought in to pick it out.

Ideally, this K-9 "search" is conducted *before* the money is counted, to keep handling to a minimum. If it must be counted first, it's best to do so by hand, with officers wearing clean latex gloves, rather than by a counting machine, which may be contaminated from previous use.

(Also to help blunt possible accusations of impropriety, it's best to have a minimum of three officers present for the tally.)

One K-9 testing option is to put the suspect money into a new paper bag (or envelope), fold the top over, and staple it shut. Another officer who has not been in contact with narcotics nor with the confiscated cash then prepares three to five other bags in the same fashion. At least two of these bags should contain currency as a control, bundled in the same way as the money you found. These funds may be pocket money, borrowed from other "uncontaminated" officers. The remaining bag(s) may contain plain paper or newspaper cut to resemble the bulk and dimensions of the questionable bills. Holes should be punched in all bags to let air escape, and they should be lined up or grouped about twelve inches apart. Then the handler brings the dog in and directs him to sniff each of them.

Any K-9 search of confiscated cash ideally should be done before the money is counted and processed as evidence. Otherwise, defense attorneys may claim that the currency was contaminated by officers handling it.

Some officers like to do sniff testing at the scene, before the questionable money is moved to another location. In that case, the line-up of paper bags is usually positioned along the side of the street or road.

Also have the dog separately check each container in which money was found, the areas where the containers were discovered, and the exact spots they sat on. The more places the dog alerts, the more ammunition you'll have in countering the argument that drug residue on the money is "normal" by modern standards; now the argument can be made that the container has been used to carry drugs and/or a suspect's personal items, like clothing, that were in close contact with drugs.

Besides the sniff, also consider a laboratory analysis of currency and/or containers. One Criminal Patrol task force in Arkansas always counts suspicious money on brown wrapping paper to catch any drug residue that may fall off. In one case this was done after an officer found $287,455 in a suitcase in a third-party rental vehicle he stopped for speeding. The driver said he was headed home to Texas from a fishing trip in Indiana, although the closest thing to angling equipment in the car was a magazine with a trout on the cover. He claimed he'd earned the cash playing drums for Willie Nelson and was hiding it from his wife during divorce proceedings. After the count, the wrapping paper was brought to the crime lab—where it tested positive for marijuana. The driver denied any drug involvement and was not arrested. But he never came back for the bucks.

Be aware that a K-9 alert or lab test without a trained detective conducting a thorough interview of the subject is worthless. Also results of K-9 and lab tests are most effective when presented in context with other evidence. Be sure to note for your report, for example, the appearance and packaging of the money: whether it is in stacks secured with rubber bands...the denominations and amount in each stack (thousand-dollar bundles of twenty- and hundred-dollar bills are common in drug transactions)...the containers that are

471

holding it (Ziploc or garbage bags?)...any markings that appear on its wrappings...coded slips of paper or ledgers that may have been found among or near it. This can help distinguish the cash you've seized from the way legitimate people normally carry funds.

Just as you took photos of the money and/or drugs at the scene before extracting them from the vehicle, the money should be photographed again at the station, with pictures of each stack or bundle before counting.

The larger the quantity of cash you've discovered, the greater the probability that it represents drug-trafficking proceeds, according to the DEA.[24] Smaller quantities require more evidence of a drug relationship, because they are more common and more likely to be "innocent." What constitutes a large or a small amount will depend partly upon the circumstances of your seizure; that is, a suspect plausibly claiming to be a dealer in precious gems is more likely to be in possession of a larger amount of cash than one claiming to be unemployed or on welfare.

As part of your evidence processing, photograph the suspect with the money you are confiscating, just as you photograph it in its original hiding place.

The small versus large issue can also pertain to contraband and its relationship to money. A small quantity of drugs in a vehicle may mean you're dealing with just a personal-use offender—but if the small amount is sweepings, it could indicate the recent presence of much larger amounts, which would suggest trafficking and that the money is trafficking proceeds.

Checklist in Drug Money Cases

This form is carried by all officers on one suburban Illinois agency as a reminder of the kind of forfeiture evidence they need when they encounter unexplained sums of money in vehicles. This checklist can also help you in questioning suspects and writing reports about money finds.

DIRECT EVIDENCE

☐ Evidence that money was furnished or intended to be furnished in exchange for a controlled substance.

☐ Evidence that money is proceeds from drug transactions, such as the presence of drug records or drug paraphernalia.

☐ Statements made by the possessor concerning the sources of, or intended use of, the money.

CIRCUMSTANTIAL EVIDENCE

☐ Prior drug record by the owner of the money.

☐ Positive alert by a drug-detector dog.

☐ Positive laboratory analysis of currency and/or containers for drug traces.

☐ Use of false or multiple identities by the owner of the money.

☐ Lack of employment by the owner of the money.

☐ Large amount of money.

☐ Lack of other legitimate source of income.

☐ Connections with others involved in narcotics trafficking.

☐ Evasive behavior exhibited or evasive or incomplete answers supplied concerning ownership of the money.

☐ The particular location of the money—hidden where the amount of money involved would not normally be found.

☐ Nationality (illegal aliens from Colombia, for example) of those connected with, if not in the possession of, the money.

☐ Presence of weapons.

☐ Presence of surveillance equipment.

Documenting Criminality

Your written report regarding your suspicions of the suspect is probably the single most important element in any criminal case or forfeiture proceeding that results from your stop. On your report may hinge the admissibility of other evidence when a criminal case goes to trial. Where no arrest has been made, the evidence for forfeiture will likely be wholly circumstantial, which means that the impression of criminality you build with the facts you have must be especially incriminating. Information you capture during and after a stop may also prove invaluable if the case requires some sophisticated financial investigation, like a "net worth analysis" to show that a claimant's income or business could not support the possession of large amounts of cash.

To be effective, your report must be a clear, detailed, accurate, sequential narrative that blends what you said and did with what the subject said and did, both at the scene and afterwards, and the conclusions you drew from your various sensory perceptions, based on your training and experience. Take care with what you write; *you don't want your report to become the defense attorney's best evidence!* Other important documentation or investigation that you initiated or contributed to—like a criminal-records check—may supplement and support what you personally experienced.

Beginning with your assignment and your actions immediately prior to observing the vehicle on through to the arrest and/or seizure of contraband, money, or other property and beyond, lay out the accumulation of events and your perceptions as they developed. One government attorney advises: *"Give details, details, details, and more details,"* reconstructing the event one fact at a time as it occurred. Give specifics, not generalities. For example, refer to "2 or 3 minutes" rather than a "short period of time" and describe the suspect as "fidgety, perspiring, established no eye contact," not as "appeared nervous."

In addition to specifics about any contraband recovered, be sure to include the elements that allowed you to move up the Criminal Patrol Pyramid, such as:

The circumstances justifying your initial stop. You must show that you had the legal right to pull the suspect over. Without that, your subsequent efforts will likely have been fruitless.

Indicators that aroused and built your suspicion. Judges and juries like to hear in detail about the cues you detected—things that seemed out of place, that made bells go off in your head. These should add up to more than a traditional "profile"; with money seizures, as with initial stops, courts have held that drug-courier profile characteristics alone are not enough.[25] *The more things you can add to the list, the better off you'll be.* Include the suspect's evasive behavior or incomplete answers regarding ownership of any money that you found.

Preposterous elements of the suspect's story, including a lack of employment or other legitimate resources if you've found money. The owner of $34,000 found in a car trunk by an Ohio officer claimed he was using it to bankroll a business in Indiana. He couldn't offer a name for the business and said it didn't have an address. Another suspect caught in Florida with $50,000 said he made it plucking chickens in Maryland for $3.60 an hour. Such details will help reduce a suspect's credibility and provide fodder for questioning later during a deposition, hearing, or trial. Naturally, any admissions by the suspect should be included also, as should any lies he or others told you and any inconsistencies you were able to develop between the stories told by various occupants of the vehicle. Use verbatim quotes where possible, including curses, threats, et cetera.

The use of multiple or false identities. This can add to a suspect's circumstantial appearance of criminality. (Of course, where potentially forfeitable property is involved, you also want the full true name, DOB, address, phone number, Social Security number, driver's license number, and vehicle identification information for each potential claimant.)

The suspect's consent or other grounds you had for searching the vehicle. If the search was not permissible, evidence may be tainted and thrown out. Be sure to reference your return of the suspect's papers before asking for consent to establish the de-escalation of the stop into a consensual encounter. Report the exact words you used to get consent and the suspect's exact answer, including his demeanor at the time.

Description of any money found. Include the total amount, the amount and denominations in each stack or bundle, and exactly where it was found, particularly if you discovered it in a place where cash normally would not be carried. Also describe how it was bundled or packaged and any markings on it. Give the precise location of money or weapons in relation to any drugs in the vehicle. If guns are found on a drug bust, notify the U.S. Bureau of Alcohol, Tobacco, and Firearms; federal charges may be possible.

This is not where most legitimate people carry cash when they're traveling by car. In your report, describe exactly where money was found. The more unlikely the place, the better.

The absence of receipts or other documentation that would attest to the legitimacy of money found. You must establish that such documents were requested or searched for and that none existed at the time of seizure.

Description of the packaging of any drugs found. This will help distinguish between the packaging reasonably associated with personal-use quantities, as opposed to trafficking quantities. Include any apparent codes or other markings on the packaging. With packages of cocaine, names and logos are typically affixed by the chemist who processed the drug, to indicate his brand.

474

Include photos and descriptions of special markings that appear on confiscated drugs. These typically are "brands," affixed by processors early in the distribution chain.

Unqualified identifications. If you smelled marijuana, say so. If you smelled meth, say so. If you found a crack vial, say so. Don't say that you smelled an odor "like cut grass or leaves" or "like cat urine" or that you found a glass container "like perfume could be put in." This applies when you are testifying later in court, as well. If you offer "legitimate" comparisons, a defense attorney will seize on them to cast doubt on what you actually did smell or see. Nothing else resembles precisely the contraband or paraphernalia you encountered. Have the confidence in your training and experience to say so. If you are not currently familiar with drug odors and appearances, get familiar with them in safe laboratory settings so you can write and speak from first-hand experience.

With currency seizures, be sure to include the suspect's statements about the source and possession of the money; the signing of the disclaimer form, if this was done; all phone calls you made trying to verify the subject's story, including numbers, date, time, names, and statements given by those you contacted.

Avoid police jargon and legalese. Don't write like you talk to your fellow officers in the squad room; write with dignity and precision, as you would speak in court. And as part of your report package, include whatever you can that will help avoid disputes later on, like photos, diagrams, video and audio tapes, radio logs (which can establish your continuous investigative efforts at the scene and refute claims of unreasonable and unlawful detention), K-9 alerts, field tests, consent forms, et cetera. In event of any questions, confer promptly with your legal advisor.

If you must deal with the media as a result of an arrest or seizure you've made, keep courier cues and other investigative details confidential. Stick essentially to name, date, charges filed, if any. Nothing more is public record. In deciding to release more, you must balance the favorable publicity that a good bust can garner for you and your agency with the intelligence information that may be conveyed to the offender community. Sharp, aggressive drug traffickers do try to learn from the mistakes of others. They may even visit courtrooms during drug trials to pick up information on law enforcement techniques.[26]

Winning Form

A good report should recreate the sequence of your contact with the offender and pinpoint in detail the elements that moved you step-by-step up the Criminal Patrol Pyramid.

To show the general structure your document may take, here's the outline of one successful report from Oregon,[27] regarding the arrests of a drug courier and his passenger:

CHRONOLOGY OF EVENTS

1. Purpose of Stop:
- Failing to maintain single lane of travel.

2. Early Indicators of Suspicion:
- Two occupants
- California plates in Oregon
- Vehicle registered to third party
- Driver says vehicle belongs to uncle, can't remember name
- Officer "reads" fictitious name off registration, which suspect wrongly identifies as uncle
- Odor of air freshener from vehicle
- Suspects extremely nervous, unable to maintain eye contact
- Destination is major metropolitan area (Portland)

3. Continuing the Contact:
- Request backup
- Obtain tape recorder
- Decide to de-escalate into a consensual encounter

4. De-escalate Stop to a Mere Encounter:
- Overhead lights on all vehicles turned off
- All patrol cars behind suspect vehicle, not blocking path
- Return documents and warn driver for violation
- Told driver that overhead lights were off
- Asked suspects if they understood they were free to go
- Both suspects indicated they understood
- Driver said, "Thank you"
- Driver restarted vehicle (actually leaving!)

5. Obtaining Voluntary Consent:
- Suspect reinitiates contact, asking how far to gas station
- Officer then asks about drugs
- Driver responded "no" in laughing tone
- Officer asked to search vehicle in English and Spanish
- Driver responded, "Oh sure!"
- Driver exited vehicle without being asked
- Driver reaffirmed that officer could look anywhere in vehicle
- Driver declined backup officer's offer to sit in patrol vehicle

6. Outcome of Search:
- Search of vehicle led to discovery of large quantity of cocaine and meth
- Specifics of contraband, its location, and recovery

The passenger in this case was not prosecuted. In court, the driver's attorney attempted to suppress the evidence, alleging that:

1. The traffic stop was illegal because "defendant committed no traffic infraction and was stopped only because he was Hispanic."

2. The defendant did not feel free to leave because "patrol cars were blocking his path and two officers were standing in his way."

3. The defendant's consent was not voluntary because "he felt he could not leave unless he allowed the search."

The state's response, in the vernacular of the arresting officer:

1. Bullshit.
2. Bullshit.
3. Life is tough.

Motion to suppress was denied. Under a plea bargain, driver pleaded guilty to charges of delivery of cocaine and methamphetamine and was sentenced to the Oregon State Penitentiary.

HELPFUL HINTS

Write your report in chronological order and keep it unbiased. Unless your superiors or your prosecutors object, consider using descriptive informational headings within the report as a means of organizing your material and making the sequence clearer to civilian readers. For instance:

- Assignment/Arrival
- Observation of Vehicle/Driver
- Conversation with Driver
- Summary of Suspicious Indicators
- Consent to Search
- Evidence Located
- Statements by Driver
- Developments away from Scene
- Disposition
- Additional Information

Although it can be tedious, writing thorough reports and compiling other comprehensive documentation on even small cases is important. They help build up your background, your credibility. When you get to court, chances are you'll be asked how many drug cases or other contraband stops you've worked. Numbers count.

Winner's Circle

If aggressive Criminal Patrol sounds like a lot of hard work, it is. It's not, as one officer so vividly puts it, "all bouquets and blow jobs."

Some of your peers may resent your successes. Some will gripe that you must be doing something wrong—illegal—to snag the busts you do. Some may mock you: "I get my paycheck the same as you, and I don't have to do all that crazy shit." Especially at first, your supervisors may be suspicious, even fearful that your proactive patrolling will "stir up trouble." One supervisor told a highway patrolman in the Midwest that he should operate in the Criminal Patrol mode only two hours a shift.

"You want me to work felonies only two hours a day?" the officer asked.

"Yep, I want you out there just giving tickets," the supervisor declared.

The officer was silent for a moment, then: "Can I use your phone?"

"Who you gonna call?"

"Mike Wallace and *60 Minutes.*"

No more talk about just two hours.

To overcome such conflict, you may need to educate your supervisors about the philosophy, techniques, and successes of Criminal Patrol. You may need to educate your administrators to pursue forfeitures and then to actually spend the proceeds, not just horde them. You may need to educate some inexperienced prosecutors about the case law of search and seizure. You will need, continually, to educate yourself, talking to suspects and more experienced officers about what's new with the bad guys and what are the best ways to defeat them. You'll need a positive expectation to stay motivated through dry spells, and to remind yourself that one person can get out there and make a difference. And you'll need repeatedly to reinforce your ability to stay focused on survival tactics in the face of both deadening routine and blasts of adrenaline.

It's far from the easiest way to spend your tours of duty. In fact, it's one of the most demanding.

But then Criminal Patrol is not for wimps. It's for 5%ers, and 5%ers are accustomed to demands...because they demand the best of themselves, always, whatever it takes.

What will keep you going is that rush of triumph when you uncover what someone thought no cop could ever find...that look on the suspect's face...that *moment* that is out there waiting for you.

**The Pride
of Success...**

The last photo in this series has not
yet been placed. This spot is reserved for a
picture of you and your score on Criminal
Patrol, as a committed member of the
5%er elite.

The Andy Lopez Stop

Nine months after the murder of Constable Darrell Lunsford (Chapter 1), Trooper Andy Lopez stopped three men on a lonely country road. Indicators surfaced quickly: unusual nervousness, excessive eye contact between driver and front passenger, a tendency by that passenger to answer every question Lopez asked the driver. When Lopez inquired about drugs, one of the men popped the trunk open even before Lopez could request consent to search.

In the trunk, Lopez saw just a backpack. From its squared-off shape, he figured, correctly, they were hauling marijuana.

The suspects were out of the car now. One attempted a distraction. Another pulled a gun....

1 Already in Condition Red, Lopez shoves the gunman to create time and distance.

2 Zigzagging to make a harder target, he runs into the dark—and concealment.

3 Even mobile, he fires one shot—and drops the suspect. He reapproaches, ready to respond.

4 When the fight resumes, he uses cover. He scores eight hits...fatally wounding his assailant.

Andy Lopez admits that under stress his tactics weren't all perfect. But he understood his priorities: Survival first.

481

Would you believe that ducks in selected cages on this truck were force—fed packets of cocaine as the means of concealing the load?

Don't underestimate your adversaries! Some work extremely hard at creatively staying one step ahead of you.

482

CHAPTER NOTES

INTRODUCTION:
MAKE-A-DIFFERENCE PATROL

1. *Criminal Interdiction through Traffic Enforcement* (Salt Lake City: Utah Highway Patrol, n.d.), 1.
2. "Drugs, Crime and the Justice System," special report (Washington, D.C.: U.S. Bureau of Justice Statistics, December 1992), 152.
3. "FBI, DEA Leaders Cry Foul over Staffing Cuts," *Narcotics Control Digest*, 11 May 1994, 5.
4. "More than 18,000 Officers Are on Full-time Drug Enforcement Duty," *Criminal Justice Newsletter*, 15 April 1992, 7.
5. Rogers Worthington, "Trial Program Gets Aggressive about Guns," *Chicago Tribune*, 11 December 1994. Also see: Lawrence W. Sherman, et al., "The Kansas City Gun Experiment," research brief, National Institute of Justice, January 1995.
6. Gordon P. Whitaker, et al., "Aggressive Policing and the Deterrence of Crime," *Law and Policy* 7 (1985), 401.
7. Gerald Godshaw, et al., "Anti-Drug Law Enforcement Efforts and Their Impact," report for U.S. Customs Service, August 1987, 2.
8. Bill Clede, "Spotting Subtle Signs," *Law and Order*, March 1989, 52; Col. Wiley McCormick, "Criminal Patrol Techniques," *FBI Law Enforcement Bulletin*, January 1988, 19-22.
9. William Harris, "Buzzword of the 90s: Drug Interdiction," *Law Enforcement Technology*, July/August 1990, 38.
10. U.S. Attorney's Forfeiture Training Seminar, Rocky Mount, North Carolina, 19 October l989.
11. "Drug Enforcement by Police and Sheriff's Departments," special report (Washington, D.C.: U.S. Bureau of Justice Statistics, 1990), 3.
12. Tom Jarriel, "Your Tax Dollars at Work," *20/20*, ABC News, 8 January 1993.
13. "Crack Said to Be Spreading to Small Towns and Rural Areas," *Drug Enforcement Report*, 8 July 1994; Michael McCabe, "Crime Surge Worries Yosemite Rangers," *San Francisco Chronicle*, 2 June 1994, 1+.
14. "Drug Courier Interdiction," training course, Wisconsin State Patrol, 25-29 March 1991.
15. Sam Vincent Meddis, "Nation's Drug Scene Again Deteriorating," *USA Today*, 12 May 1994; "U.S. Facing a Resurgence of Heroin Abuse, Trafficking, DEA Administrator Warns," *Narcotics Control Digest*, 17 August 1994, 1+; "Household Survey Finds Growth in Numbers of U.S. Drug Users," *Drug Enforcement Report*, 25 July 1994, 7; "Marijuana Use Is 'Exploding'; Cocaine Use Is Reported Stable," *Drug Detection Report*, 20 September 1994, 7; Theo Francis, "Officials View Rise in Teens' Drug Use as 'A Call to Action,'" *Chicago Tribune*, 13 December 1994; "Drug Use Rising among Teens, Annual Survey Finds," *Narcotics Control Digest*, 21 December 1994, 1-5; "Hospital Survey Indicates Increase in Heroin Cases," *Drug Enforcement Report*, 23 December 1994; "Drug Use by Arrestees Was up in 1993, Study Finds," *Drug Enforcement Report*, 9 January 1995; "Methamphetamines Making Comeback," *Narcotics Enforcement & Prevention Digest*, 26 January 1995, 6; Robert H. Feldkamp, "Heroin Use Expanding to Teens, Females and Middle-Income Americans, Says New U.S. Study," *Narcotics Enforcement & Prevention Digest*, 16 March 1995, 1.
16. Lawrence Sherman, et al., "Police Murdered in Drug-Related Situations," report (Washington, D.C.: Crime Control Institute, 1989).
17. *Commonly Encountered Concealment Methods in Selected Land Vehicles* (El Paso, Texas: El Paso Intelligence Center, 1990), 2.

CHAPTER 1: 5%ER MIND-SET

1. *Killed in the Line of Duty: A Study of Selected Felonious Killings of Law Enforcement Officers* (Washington, D.C.: Federal Bureau of Investigation, September 1992); author interview with Training Instructor Edward F. Davis and Forensic Psychologist Anthony J. Pinizzotto, PhD, members of the study team, 18 September 1990.
2. Summary based on information supplied by the Institute of Police Technology and Management; the Internal Revenue Service; "Follow the Money Trail to Follow the Drug Traffic," *Narcotics Control Digest*, 27 April 1994, 10; "Trafficking Narcotics Via Tractor Trailer," report, FBI Drug Intelligence Unit, 11 May 1992; Bill Knight, "Recent Seizure Illustrates Role in War on Drugs," *The Minnesota Police Journal*, June 1994; "Drug Runners Switch to Land, Sea as U.S. Chokes Air Deliveries," *International Drug Report*, July/August 1994; "Heroin Is Cheaper, Purer, More Available than Ever," *Narcotics Control Digest*, 12 October 1994, 1-2; "RCMP Says Drug Trade Money Laundering in Canada Involves Billions of Dollars," *Narcotics Control Digest*, 20 July 1994, 3-4; "ONDCP Designates Puerto Rico and Virgin Islands as a HIDTA," *Drug Enforcement Report*, 8 November 1994, 1-2; "House Considers Creating Three New HIDTA Regions," *Drug Enforcement Report*, 8 July 1996, 3.
3. "Trafficking Trends," *Narcotics Control Digest*, 27 April 1994, 10.
4. Paul Weingarten and James Coates, "Menace on Main Street," *Chicago Tribune*, 12 September 1989, 6.
5. Brian A. Reaves, "Drug Enforcement by Police and Sheriff's Departments," *Texas Deputy*, Fall 1992, 51.
6. Jerry Seper, "Awash in Drugs on the Rio Grande," *Insight*, 11 June 1990, 26-27.
7. "Coast Guard Drug Seizures Found to Be Decreasing" and "Central American Interdiction is Ineffective, GAO Report Says," *Drug Enforcement Report*, 23 August 1994, 4-5; "Inspections Eased, Seizures Plunge," *Narcotics Enforcement & Prevention Digest*, 2 March 1995.
8. Daniel Heinz, instructor-coordinator, North Carolina Justice Academy.
9. "Drug Use Soaring Among Criminals," *Chicago Tribune*, 13 April 1992; "Drug Use Forecasting," *Law Enforcement Technology*, May 1993, 10+; "Half of All Homicides Tied to Drug Use, Report Says," *Narcotics Control Digest*, 2 March 1994, 1.

CHAPTER 2: LOOKING FOR MR. WRONG

1. James Bovard, "Drug-Courier Profiles," *Playboy*, November 1994, 47.
2. "Observable Factors & Manifestations of Nervousness," internal document, U.S. Border Patrol, n.d.
3. M.C. Finn, *The Complete Book of International Smuggling* (Boulder, Colorado: Paladin Press, 1983).
4. *Identification & Information Manual* (Irvine, California: National Consumer Publications, Inc., 1994), A2-A5.
5. Alan Harman, "State Police Drug Team," *Law and Order*, March 1993, 81.
6. Donovan Jacobs, "In Harm's Way," *The Informant*, September 1992, 14-15+.
7. Doug Levy, "Reckless Drivers May Be High—on Drugs," *USA Today*, 25 August 1994, 1.
8. Cases and interpretation related to elements needed for reasonable suspicion include: *Terry v. Ohio*, 392 U.S. 1 (1968); *Delaware v. Prouse*, 440 U.S. 648 (1979); *U.S. v. Place*, 462 U.S. 696 (1983); *Florida v. Royer*, 460 U.S. 491 (1983); *U.S. v. Williams*, 876 F.2d 1521 (1989); *U.S. v. Salinas*, 940 F.2d 392 (1991); *U.S. v. Cervantes*, 19 F.3d 1151 (1994). Also see: Devallis Rutledge, "Frisky Business," *Police*, November 1994, 14; Paul R. Joseph, *Warrantless Search Law Deskbook* (Deerfield, Illinois: Clark Boardman Callaghan, 1991-92), 11-34; Jerome O. Campane Jr., "Investigative Detention and the Drug Courier: Recent Supreme Court Decisions," *FBI Law Enforcement Bulletin*, November 1983, 27.
9. *U.S. v. Sokolow*, 490 U.S. 1, 109 S.Ct. 1581 (1989).
10. Cases where reasonable suspicion has been accepted as justification for a stop include: *U.S. v. Sharpe*, 470 U.S. 675 (1985), cert. denied, 485 U.S. 965 (1988); *Bethea v. Commonwealth*, 429 S.E.2d 211 (1993). Also see: "Suspicion of 'Scout Car' Activity Found to Justify Border Stop," *Drug Enforcement Report*, 8 February 1995, 8, reporting on *U.S. v. Carter* (1994). Cases sustaining infor-

mants' tips include: *Alabama v. White,* 496 U.S. 325 (1990); *U.S. v. Watts,* 7 F.3d 122 (1993); *People v. Faucett,* 499 N.W.2d 764 (1993); *Johnson v. State,* 862 S.W.2d 290 (1993); *People v. Brown,* 627 N.E.2d 340 (1993); *State v. Warrington,* 884 S.W.2d 711 (1994). For cases rejecting informants' tips as grounds for a stop, see: *Sapp v. State,* 592 So.2d 786 (1992) and *Commonwealth v. Avalo,* 636 N.E.2d 1362 (1994).

11. *U.S. v. Salinas* (see 8 above).

12. *U.S. v. Robert L.,* 874 F.2d 701 (1989). For another case in which an officer was rebuked for stopping a vehicle for insufficient cause, see: *State v. Carter,* 630 N.E.2d 355 (1994).

13. *Reid v. Georgia,* 448 U.S. 438 (1980). Also see: *Street Level Narcotics Enforcement* (Boulder, Colorado: Paladin Press, 1992), 9-10; Charlotte Sellers, "'Drug Mule Profile' Works for Indiana Trooper," *Wisconsin Trooper,* Summer 1988, 53.

14. *U.S. v. Armijo,* 781 F.Supp. 1551 (1991); *State v. Letts,* 603 A.2d 562 (1992).

15. *Whitfield v. Board of County Commissioners of Eagle County,* 837 F.Supp. 338 (1993). For the outcome of another case challenging profiling as allegedly race-based, see: "Pennsylvania Municipality Settles to End Minority Driver Lawsuit," *Drug Enforcement Report,* 25 October 1994, 3-4. Also see: "Maryland State Police Settle Suit over Drug Profile Search," *Narcotics Enforcement & Prevention Digest,* 19 January 1995, 8, and "Maryland Police and ACLU Settle Drug Courier Profile Case," *Drug Enforcement Report,* 23 January 1995, 1+.

16. *U.S. v. Laymon,* 730 F.Supp. 332 (1990).

17. *U.S. v. Mendenhall,* 446 U.S. 544 (1980); *U.S. v. Sokolow* (see 9 above); *U.S. v. Crichlow,* 812 F.Supp. 379 (1993); *U.S. v. Ramos,* 55 CrL 1036 (1994); *State v. Patterson,* 55 CrL 1006 (1994). Also: Campane (see 8 above).

18. Cases that deal with probable cause for initiating a stop include: *U.S. v. Castenada,* 951 F.2d 44 (1992); *U.S. v. Barahona,* 990 F.2d 412 (1993); *State v. Hunt,* 514 P.2d 1363 (1973); *Nodd v. State,* 549 So.2d 139 (1989); *Vela v. State,* 871 S.W.2d 815 (1994).

19. *Whren v. U.S.,* 116 S.Ct. 1769 (1996); "Court Approves 'Pretext' Traffic Stops," *Legal Defense Manual,* No. 4 1996, 20.

20. *State v. Lopez,* 873 P.2d 1127 (1994). Other cases and interpretation regarding "pretextual" stops include: *Scott v. U.S.,* 436 U.S. 128 (1978); *U.S. v. Villamonte-Marquez,* 462 U.S. 579 (1983); *Maryland v. Macon,* 472 U.S. 463 (1985); *U.S. v. Causey,* 834 F.2d 1179 (1987); *U.S. v. Pino,* 855 F.2d 357 (1988); *U.S. v. Cummins,* 920 F.2d 498 (1990); *U.S. v. Hernandez,* 901 F.2d 1217 (1990); *U.S. v. Colin,* 928 F.2d 676 (1991); *U.S. v. Pasciuti,* 793 F.Supp. 373 (1992); *U.S. v. Ferguson,* 989 F.2d 202 (1993); *U.S. v. Scopo,* 19 F.3d 777 (1994); *U.S. v. Miller,* 20 F.3d 926 (1994); *U.S. v. Parke,* 842 F.Supp. 281 (1994); *State v. Vasquez,* 842 S.W.2d 841 (1992); *People v. Miranda,* 17 Cal.App.4th 917 (1993); *People v. Uribe,* 12 Cal.App.4th 1432 (1993); *Vercher v. State,* 861 S.W.2d 68 (1993); *Ex Parte Scarbrough,* 621 So.2d 1006 (1993); *People v. Todd,* 30 Cal.App.4th 617 (1994). Also see: "Traffic Arrest was 'Pretextual,' Results Are Inadmissible," *The Law Officer's Bulletin,* 23 July 1987, 152; "Arrest: Pretext; Objective Standard," *Law Enforcement Legal Review,* May-June 1993, 5.

21. *U.S. v. Smith,* 799 F.2d 704 (1986); *U.S. v. Miller,* 821 F.2d 546 (1987); *U.S. v. Guzman,* 864 F.2d 1512 (1988); *U.S. v. Cardona-Rivera,* 904 F.2d 1149 (1990); *U.S. v. Harris,* 928 F.2d 1113 (1991); *U.S. v. Valdez,* 931 F.2d 1448 (1991); *U.S. v. Mans,* 999 F.2d 966 (1993); *U.S. v. Millan,* 36 F.3d 886 (1994); *U.S. v. Fernandez,* 18 F.3d 874 (1994); *U.S. v. Castillo,* 864 F.Supp. 1090 (1994); *People v. Smith,* 581 N.Y.S.2d 240 (1992). Also see: "Objective Test Set for Evaluating Legality of 'Pretextual' Stops," *The Law Officer's Bulletin,* 28 April 1988, 115; "Black Motorists Being Targeted, Critics Say," *The Macon (GA) Telegraph,* 10 May 1992, 2B.

22. Mark T. Baganz, "Pretext Training?" *The ASLET Journal,* July/August 1994, 43.

23. *U.S. v. Lyons,* 7 F.3d 973 (1993).

24. *U.S. v. Rodriguez,* 737 F.Supp 85 (1990).

25. *U.S. v. Gant,* 858 F.Supp. 74 (1994).

26. *People v. Guerrieri,* 551 N.E.2d 767 (1990).

27. *U.S. v. Werking,* 919 F.2d 1404 (1990).

28. *U.S. v. Miller* (see 20 above).

29. Cases pertaining to roadblocks and checkpoints include: *U.S. v. Martinez-Fuerte,* 428 U.S. 543 (1976); *Delaware v. Prouse* (see 8 above); *Michigan Dept. of State Police v. Sitz,* 110 S.Ct. 2481 (1990); *U.S. v. Morales-Zamora,* 974 F.2d 149 (1992); *U.S. v. Duncan,* 52 CrL 1443 (1993); *U.S. v. Seslar,* 996

F.2d 1058 (1993); *U.S. v. Rascon-Ortiz*, 994 F.2d 749 (1993); *U.S. v. Santiago*, 846 F.Supp. 1486 (1994); *State v. Bolton*, 801 P.2d 98 (1990); *Cains v. State*, 555 So.2d 290 (1990); *Galberth v. U.S.*, 590 A.2d 990 (1991); *State v. Thill*, 474 N.W.2d 86 (1991); *People v. Chaffee*, 590 N.Y.S.2d 625 (1992); *People v. Wells*, 608 N.E.2d 578 (1993); *State v. Claussen*, 522 N.W.2d 196 (1994). (In an exception to the prohibition of random stops on patrol, some federal courts have ruled that police can make random, warrantless stops of vehicles used in a closely regulated commercial activity, such as trucks traveling in interstate commerce.)

30. *U.S. v. Magee*, 816 F.Supp. 1511 (1993).
31. "Missouri Supreme Court Limits Privacy Rights at Checkpoints," *Drug Enforcement Report*, 8 July 1994.
32. *U.S. v. Jefferson*, 906 F.2d 346 (1990); *U. S. v. Soto-Lopez*, 995 F.2d 694 (1993); *Ozhuwan v. State*, 786 P.2d 918 (1990); *Commonwealth v. Tindell*, 629 A.2d 161 (1993); *People v. Bouser*, 32 Cal.Rptr.2d 163 (1994).
33. M/Officer M.L. Martin, *Asian Gang Activity* (Garden Grove, California: Garden Grove Police Department, 1992), 153-154; Officer Robbie Levensbaum, "Gang Weapons," warning bulletin, Chicago Police Department Gang Crimes Unit, n.d.
34. *U.S. v. Mason*, 982 F.2d 325 (1993).

CHAPTER 3: POSITION OF ADVANTAGE

1. Harvey Hadden, "Vehicle Stop Survival," in *Total Survival*, ed. Ed Nowicki (Powers Lake, Wisconsin: Performance Dimensions Publishing, 1993), 193.
2. "Motor Vehicle Stops," concepts and issues paper, International Association of Chiefs of Police National Law Enforcement Policy Center, April 1992, 3.
3. NRA Firearms Fact Card, 1994.
4. George I. Miller, "The 'Right' Vehicle Approach," *The Police Marksman*, September/October 1994, 30.
5. For a fuller account of this confrontation, see: "'Collinsville, 115, I'm Shot!'" *10-43 Magazine*, vol. 4 no. 2, 6-12.
6. *Pennsylvania v. Mimms*, 434 U.S. 106 (1977).
7. *Criminal Interdiction through Traffic Enforcement* (see 1, Introduction), 63.
8. *Kaisner v. Kolb*, 543 So.2d 732 (1989). Also

see: *Belding v. Town of New Whiteland*, 622 N.E.2d 1291 (1993).
9. *Pennsylvania v. Mimms* (see 6 above). Also see: Devallis Rutledge (see 8, Chapter 2).
10. "California Cop Says 'Sixth Sense' Saved Him with Hall in '78," *Albuquerque Journal*, 12 June 1994, A14.
11. *Maryland v. Wilson*, 117 S.Ct. 882 (1997).
12. *State v. Wight*, 790 P.2d 385 (1990).
13. *People v. Maxwell*, 206 Cal.App.3d 1004 (1988).
14. "Search Limited to Weapons," *Front Line Report* (Newsletter of the Missouri Attorney General's office), May 1994, 1.

CHAPTER 4: SENSORY PAT-DOWN

1. *State v. Aubin*, 622 A.2d 444 (1993).
2. *U.S. v. Ryles*, 988 F.2d 13 (1993). Also see: *U.S. v. Pierre*, 958 F.2d 1304 (1992).
3. *New York v. Class*, 475 U.S. 106 (1986).
4. *Horton v. California*, 496 U.S. 128 (1990); *U.S. v. Jimenez*, 864 F.2d 686 (1988); *U.S. v. Diotte*, 846 F.Supp. 236 (1993).
5. *People v. Mason*, 574 N.Y.S.2d 589 (1991); *Toth v. State of Georgia*, 444 S.E.2d 159 (1994).
6. *Texas v. Brown*, 460 U.S. 730 (1983); *U.S. v. Landry*, 903 F.2d 334 (1990); *People v. Rogers*, 21 Cal.3d 542 (1978).
7. *U.S. v. McGuire*, 957 F.2d 310 (1992).
8. *Chicago Tribune*, 11 February 1994, reporting on study by Columbia University's Center of Addiction and Substance Abuse, based on figures from the National Institute of Drug Abuse's National Household Survey of Drug Abuse.
9. *Texas v. Brown* (see 6 above). Also see: M/Sgt. Steve Emberton, "Plain Feel: Implications for the Tactical Officer," *ITOA News*, Winter 1993, 8. For a case in which a conviction was reversed because cocaine came into plain view during an "illegal" pat-down, see: *Rouse v. State*, 643 So.2d 696 (1994).
10. *Horton v. California* (see 4 above); Kevin B. Zeese and Eve E. Zeese, *Drug Law: Strategies and Tactics* (Deerfield, Illinois: Clark Boardman Callaghan, Supplement, August 1994), 1-72.
11. Zeese, ibid., 1-71.
12. *New York v. Belton*, 453 U.S. 454 (1981). Also see: *U.S. v. Holifield*, 956 F.2d 665 (1992); *U.S. v. Richards*, 967 F.2d 1189

(1992).

13. *Texas v. Brown* (see 6 above).

14. "Drug Agents Crack Down on Possession of Toad Venom," news report from the Associated Press, *International Drug Report*, March/April 1994, 4.

15. *People v. Cabot*, 450 N.Y.S.2d 489 (1982).

16. *U.S. v. Russell*, 665 F.2d 1261 (1981).

17. Cases and interpretation relating to "plain smell" include: *U.S. v. Dallas*, 672 F.Supp. 362 (1987); *U.S. v. Reed*, 882 F.2d 147 (1989); *U.S. v. Caves*, 890 F.2d 87 (1989); *Minnick v. U.S.*, 607 A.2d 519 (1992); *Utah v. Naisbitt*, 827 P.2d 969 (1992); *State v. Fuente*, 871 S.W.2d 438 (1994). Also: Andrew L. Zwerling, "Establishing Probable Cause in Drug Searches and Seizures," *Search and Seizure Law Report*, May 1984, 29-30.

18. *People v. Walker*, 273 Cal2d 720 (1969); *People v. Martin*, 23 Cal3d 444 (1972); *People v. Faddler*, 132 Cal3d 607 (1982).

19. "Use of LSD Highest in Seven Years," *Hoosier Policeman*, Summer 1993, 20; "Adolescent Drug Use Said to Be on the Rise," *Drug Enforcement Report*, 8 February 1994, 5; "Teen Drug Use Increasing," *Narcotics Control Digest*, 2 February 1994, 1; "Hallucinogen PCP Reported to Be Regaining Popularity," *Drug Enforcement Report*, 25 October 1994, 6-7.

20. "Researchers Warn of Connection between 'Blunts' and Violence," *Drug Enforcement Report*, 23 March 1994, 8. Also see: "Marijuana Is Drug of Choice among Washington, D.C. Youth," *Drug Enforcement Report*, 8 November 1994, 4-5.

21. Gary J. Miller, *Drugs and the Law: Detection, Recognition and Investigation* (Altamonte Springs, Florida: Gould Publications, Inc., 1992), 262.

22. Mike Snyder, "Steroid Use Linked to Violence, Drugs," *USA Today*, 10 February 1993. For a report that tends to belittle the association between drug use and violence, see: Jeffrey A. Roth, "Psychoactive Substances and Violence," research paper, National Institute of Justice, February 1994.

23. Gary Wisby, "LSD Makes Return Trip," *Chicago Sun-Times*, 4 February, 1993.

CHAPTER 5: DETECTING DECEPTION

1. Paul Ekman, *Telling Lies: Clues to Deceit in the Marketplace, Politics and Marriage* (New York, New York: W.W. Norton & Company, 1992), 326.

2. *People v. McGaughran*, 25 Cal.3d 577 (1979); *People v. Lusardi*, 228 Cal.App.3d Supp.1 (1991); *People v. Samaniego*, 25 Cal.App.4th 1717 (1994); *Rouse v. State* (see 9, Chapter 4). Also see: *U.S. v. Hardy*, 855 F.2d 753 (1988); *Aureguy v. Town of Tiburon*, 825 F.Supp. 902 (1993).

3. "Vehicle Searches," *The Law Enforcement Legal Reporter*, October 1991, 118-119. Also see: *U.S. v. Ramos* (see 17, Chapter 2); *People v. Lingo*, 3 Cal.App.3d 661 (1970).

4. Miller (see 21, Chapter 4). Also see: *U.S. v. Sanchez-Valderuten*, 11 F.3d 985 (1993); *U.S. v. Gonzalez-Lerma*, 14 F.3d 1479 (1994); *U.S. v. Sharpe*, 845 F.Supp. 791 (1994); *Haddox v. State*, 636 So.2d 1229 (1994).

5. *Aureguy v. Town of Tiburon* (see 2 above).

6. *State v. Cohen*, 549 So.2d 884 (1989).

7. *U.S. v. Place* (see 8, Chapter 2); *U.S. v. Sharpe* (see 10, Chapter 2). Also see: Joseph (see 8, Chapter 2), 9-2; John C. Hall, "Investigative Detention: An Intermediate Response," *FBI Law Enforcement Bulletin*, December 1985, 19-20.

8. Example: *I.D. Checking Guide* (Redwood City, California: Drivers License Guide Company) is updated annually with color photographs of driver's licenses and other documents from each state, with advice on how to examine them for evidence of counterfeiting.

9. Based on a bulletin issued by the National Park Service, Great Smoky Mountains National Park, Gatlinburg, Tennessee, March 1991. Also see: Officer X, *10-8: A Cop's Honest Look at Life on the Street* (Northbrook, Illinois: Calibre Press, 1994), regarding attitude and staple holes.

10. Social Security Administration, April 1994.

11. *U.S. v. Wellons*, 32 F.3d 117 (1994); *Littlepage v. State*, 863 S.W.2d 276 (1993).

12. "Trafficking Narcotics via Tractor Trailer" (see 2, Chapter 1).

13. *Code of Federal Rules and Regulations for Motor Carriers*, Title 49, Statute 39260.

14. "Trafficking Narcotics via Tractor Trailer" (see 2, Chapter 1), 1.

15. *Berkemer v. McCarthy*, 468 U.S. 420 (1984); *People v. Vasquez*, 14 Cal.App.4th 1158 (1993).

16. Wendell C. Rudacille, *Evasive Speech and Deception* (Ellicott City, Maryland: Veri-

facts Systems, Inc., 1992).

17. *State v. Galloway*, 859 P.2d 476 (1993).

18. "Interviews and Interrogation," program, Law Enforcement Satellite Academy of Tennessee Teleconference, 20 May 1992.

19. "Roadside Interviewing and Interrogation: Lie Detection," handout by the Institute of Police Technology and Management, Jacksonville, Florida, distributed at the American Society of Law Enforcement Trainers Annual Seminar, 4-8 January 1994, Washington, D.C.

20. Charles C. Brougham, "Nonverbal Communication: Can What They Don't Say Give Them Away?" *FBI Law Enforcement Bulletin*, July 1992, 17.

21. *Expert Body Language: The Science of Reading People* (San Mateo, California: Intelligence, Inc., 1992). Videocassette.

22. Dave Proctor, Federal Law Enforcement Training Center instructor, "Neurolinguistic Programming," lecture, American Society of Law Enforcement Trainers Annual Seminar, 4-8 January 1994, Washington, D.C. Also see: Don Rabon, *Interviewing and Interrogation* (Durham, North Carolina: Carolina Academic Press, 1992), 25-37; Carl Stincelli, *Reading Between the Lines* (Elk Grove, California: Interviews and Interrogations Institute, n.d.), 14.

23. "Interviews and Interrogation" (see 18 above) and *Expert Body Language* (see 21 above).

24. Fred E. Inbau, John E. Reid, and Joseph B. Buckley, *Criminal Interrogation and Confessions* (Baltimore, Maryland: Williams and Wilkins, 1986), 49-51.

25. Ekman (see 1 above), 22.

26. Ibid., 283-286.

27. Daniel Goleman, "Can You Tell When Someone Is Lying to You?" *Psychology Today*, August 1982, 18.

28. Inbau, et al. (see 24 above), 53.

29. Edward F. Connors III and Hugh Nugent, *Street-Level Narcotics Enforcement*, monograph, U.S. Bureau of Justice Assistance, April 1990, 6.

30. The government refuses to reveal detailed information about the nature of the NADDIS system, even in trials. In one recent case, the court regarded NADDIS as an informant and narrowly ruled that a report from it constituted reasonable suspicion for the stopping of two suspected drug dealers.

Also see: *U.S. v. Ornelas-Ledesma*, 16 F.3d 714 (1994).

31. Anne Keegan, "The 'Yugo Gang,'" *Chicago Tribune*, 3 November 1993.

32. *U.S. v. Angell*, 11 F.3d 806 (1994).

CHAPTER 6: CONSENT TO SEARCH

1. James A. Foster, "Narcotics Interdiction at the Street Level," *Law Enforcement Technology*, May 1992, 20-21.

2. Zeese, Supplement (see 10, Chapter 4), 1-67.

3. *Commonwealth v. Parker*, 619 A.2d 735 (1993). Also see: *State v. Tijerina*, 811 P.2d 241 (1991). For a contrasting view, see: *People v. Galdino*, 229 Cal.App.3d 1259 (1991) and Patrick Mahaney, "Rulings in Two Search and Seizure Cases Made during Traffic Stops," *The Blue Light*, July 1994, 4.

4. *U. S. v. Dewitt*, 946 F.2d 1497 (1991). (When the contact is taking place in circumstances where the subject can't readily walk or drive away, like on a train or bus, the test is whether the person feels "free to end the conversation." See: *U.S. v. Kim*, 27 F.3d 947 [1994].)

5. *Ohio v. Robinette*, 117 S.Ct. 417 (1996).

6. *U.S. v. Walker*, 112 S.Ct. 1168 (1992), 751 F.Supp. 199 (1990), 941 F.2d 1086 (1991), 807 F.Supp. 115 (1992). Also see: "Supreme Court Lets Stand Limits on Questioning During Traffic Stops," *Crime Control Digest*, 2 May 1992, 1+. For a case involving a federal agent [inappropriately] retaining an alien registration card while asking permission to search a vehicle, see: *U.S. v. Chavez-Villareal*, 3 F.3d 124 (1993). For a case in which failure to inform a suspect of his rights to leave and to refuse consent was an issue, see: *U.S. v. Fernandez*, 18 F.3d 874 (1994).

7. *U. S. v. Chaidez*, 906 F.2d 377 (1990). For examples of courts that have accepted permission to "look" as permission to search, see: *Guerrero v. State*, 401 S.E.2d 749 (1991); *Popham v. State*, 449 S.E.2d 150 (1994), and "'Permission' to Search Vehicle," *Police Times*, Fall 1993, 6.

8. *State v. Swanson*, 838 P.2d 1340 (1992).

9. *Schneckloth v. Bustamonte*, 412 U.S. 218 (1973); *U.S. v. Matlock*, 415 U.S. 164 (1974); *Illinois v. Rodriguez*, 110 S.Ct. 2793 (1990); *Florida v. Jimeno*, 111 S.Ct. 1801 (1991); *U.S. v. Walker* (see 5 above). Also see: De-

vallis Rutledge, "Consensual Relations," *Police*, February 1995, 8-9.

10. Cases relating to voluntariness of consent include: *U.S. v. Tapia*, 912 F.2d 1367 (1990); *U.S. v. Chaidez* (see 7 above); *U.S. v. Turner*, 928 F.2d 956 (1991); *U.S. v. Quinones-Sandoval*, 943 F.2d 771 (1991); *U.S. v. Vizcarra*, 835 F.Supp. 1160 (1993); *U.S. v. Hernandez*, 5 F.3d 628 (1993); *U.S. v. Fernandez* (see 5 above); *U.S. v. Kozinski*, 16 F.3d 795 (1994); *U.S. v. Gleason*, 25 F.3d 605 (1994); *State v. Prahin*, 455 N.W.2d 554 (1990); *State v. Dezso*, 512 N.W.2d 877 (1993); *Rouse v. State* (see 9, Chapter 4).

11. *U.S. v. Brennen*, 251 F.Supp. 99 (1966). Also: *Criminal Interdiction through Traffic Enforcement* (see 1, Introduction), 44-45.

12. *U.S. v. Dudley*, 854 F.Supp. 570 (1994). Also see: *U.S. v. Melendez-Garcia*, 28 F.3d 1046 (1994).

13. Cases and interpretation regarding authority to give consent include: *U.S. v. Daniel*, 725 F.Supp. 532 (1989); *U.S. v. Jefferson*, 723 F.Supp. 619 (1989); *U.S. v. Jefferson*, 925 F.2d 1242 (1991); *U.S. v. Dunson*, 940 F.2d 989 (1991); *U.S. v. Eldridge*, 984 F.2d 943 (1993); *U.S. v. Henao*, 835 F.Supp. 926 (1993); *U.S. v. Stapleton*, 10 F.3d 582 (1994); *U.S. v. Lewis*, 24 F.3d 79 (1994); *U.S. v. Moore*, 849 F.Supp. 206 (1994); *U.S. v. Kimball*, 25 F.3d 1 (1994); *U.S. v. Crain*, 33 F.3d 480 (1994); *People v. Harris*, 557 N.E.2d 1277 (1990); *State v. Cantrell*, 853 P.2d 479 (1993), 875 P.2d 1208 (1994). Also see: W. Dale Talbert, "Legal Standards for Stops, Searches, Seizures, and Arrests," presentation for North Carolina State Highway Patrol In-Service Training, February 1993; "Consent by One Occupant of Vehicle Suffices for Search," *International Drug Report*, July/August 1994, 13. For a case in which a driver's consent to search was ruled not to extend to a passenger's property, see: *U.S. v. Infante-Ruiz*, 13 F.3d 498 (1994). Also see: "Search of Passenger's Purse Was Invalid," *The National Law Journal*, 20 February 1995, B13, reporting on *People v. James* (1994), and "Court Requires Actual Authority for Driver to Consent to Search," *Drug Enforcement Report*, 23 February 1995, 8.

14. *Phipps v. State*, 841 P.2d 591 (1992).

15. *Bumper v. North Carolina*, 391 U.S. 543 (1968); *Florida v. Royer* (see 8, Chapter 2).

16. *U.S. v. Archer*, 840 F.2d 567, *cert. denied*, 488 U.S. 941 (1988); *U.S. v. Phillips*, 640 F.2d 87 (1981). Also see: Joseph (see 8, Chapter 2), 16-9.

17. For a case involving a Spanish speaker and his comprehension of consent, see: *U.S. v. Sanchez*, 32 F.3d 1330 (1994).

18. *U.S. v. Tavarez*, 834 F.Supp. 55 (1993).

19. *Schneckloth v. Bustamonte* (see 9 above). Also see: *Criminal Interdiction through Traffic Enforcement* (see 1, Introduction), 46. For a contrasting view, see: *U.S. v. Daniel*, 804 F.Supp. 1330 (1992).

20. *U.S. v. Carbajal*, 956 F.2d 924 (1992).

21. Cases pertaining to scope of consent include: *California v. Acevedo*, 111 S.Ct. 1982 (1991); *Florida v. Jimeno* (see 9 above); *U.S. v. Gutierrez-Mederos*, 965 F.2d 800 (1992); *U.S. v. Martinez*, 949 F.2d 1117 (1992); *U.S. v. Rich*, 791 F.Supp. 1162 (1992) and 992 F.2d 502 (1993); *U.S. v. Nicholson*, 17 F.3d 1294 (1994).

22. *State v. Huether*, 453 N.W.2d 778 (1990).

23. Cases and interpretation regarding locked containers on consent searches include: *Florida v. Jimeno* (see 9 above); *U.S. v. Martinez* (see 21 above); *U.S. v. Martel-Martines*, 988 F.2d 855 (1993). Also see: Joseph (see 8, Chapter 2) 16-21; "Searches and Seizures," *The Law Enforcement Legal Reporter*, May 1992, 49-50.

24. *State v. McDaniels*, 405 S.E.2d 358 (1991); *State v. Paredes*, 810 P.2d 607 (1991).

25. Greg Connor, *Vehicle Stops: Tactical Procedures and Safety Strategies* (Champaign, Illinois: Stipes Publishing Company, 1993), 147-148.

26. *U.S. v. Ibarra*, 725 F.2d 1195 (1989). This finding was later vacated by the U.S. Supreme Court: 112 S.Ct. 4 (1991).

27. *State v. Zelinske*, 779 P.2d 971 (1989).

28. *U.S. v. Crabb*, 952 F.2d 1245 (1991). Also see: *State v. Newberry*, 560 So.2d 121 (1990).

29. If you apply for a warrant when you reasonably should have known that you lack probable cause, you risk losing your normal qualified immunity from civil damages. See: "Immunity Denied for Deputy with No Probable Cause for Warrant," *Drug Enforcement Report*, 23 January 1995, 8, reporting on the 1994 federal case, *Greenstreet v. County of San Bernardino*.

30. *Criminal Interdiction through Traffic Enforcement* (see 1, Introduction), 50-51. For a

court decision favorable to warrants by phone, see: *U.S. v. Clutchette*, 24 F.3d 577 (1994). For a discussion of civil liability risks an officer may incur by applying for a warrant with obvioujsly inadequate PC, see: James Peva, et al., "Searches & Seizures," *Hoosier Policeman*, Summer 1994, 16+, reprinted from the book, *Essential Case Law for Policing America*, 2nd edition.

31. *U.S. v. Stone*, 866 F.2d 359 (1989).

32. *U.S. v. Garcia* and *U.S. v. Miranda-Garcia*, 1994 U.S.App.Lexis 9567 (consolidated) (1994) and 23 F.3d 1331 (1994).

33. Richard V. Graylow, "Autos May Be Searched without a Warrant," *Wisconsin Trooper*, Winter 1989, 69+. Also see: *Rakas v. Illinois*, 439 U.S. 128 (1978); *California v. Carney*, 471 U.S. 386 (1985); *Pennsylvania v. LaBron*; *Pennsylvania v. Kilgore*, 116 S.Ct. 2485 (1996).

34. Cases and interpretation regarding the searching of vehicles for weapons include: *Michigan v. Long*, 463 U.S. 1032 (1983); *U.S. v. Lott*, 870 F.2d 778 (1989); *U.S. v. Peoples*, 925 F.2d 1082 (1991); *People v. Weston*, 869 P.2d 1293 (1994); *People v. Molina*, 25 Cal.App.4th 1038 (1994). Also see: John C. Hall, "Investigative Detention," *FBI Law Enforcement Bulletin*, January 1986, 27.

35. *People v. Weston* (see 34 above).

36. *People v. Lafitte*, 211 Cal.App.3d 1429 (1989).

37. Cases and interpretation regarding the searching of vehicles with probable cause include: *Carroll v. United States*, 267 U.S. 132 (1925); *U.S. v. Ross*, 456 U.S. 798 (1982); *California v. Carney* (see 33 above); *U.S. v. Chadwick*, 433 U.S. 1 (1987); *California v. Acevedo* (see 21 above); *U.S. v. Strickland*, 902 F.2d 937 (1990); *State v. Poole*, 871 P.2d 531 (1994). Also see: "People v. Boissard," *The Law Enforcement Legal Reporter*, November 1992, 124; *Criminal Interdiction through Traffic Enforcement* (see 1, Introduction). For a case in which multiple indicators were ruled not to constitute probable cause for an involuntary search, see: *State v. Perrone*, 872 S.W.2d 519 (1994).

38. *U.S. v. Adams*, 845 F.Supp. 1531 (1994).

39. *State v. Cohen* (see 6, Chapter 5). Also see: *State v. Alonzo*, 587 So.2d 136 (1991); *State v. Fuente* (see 18, Chapter 4).

40. *State v. Burkhardt*, 795 S.W.2d 399 (1990).

41. Cases and interpretation regarding search-ing a vehicle incident to an arrest include: *Chimel v. California*, 395 U.S. 752 (1969); *U.S. v. Robinson*, 414 U.S. 218 (1973); *Gustafson v. Florida*, 414 U.S. 260 (1974); *New York v. Belton* (see 12, Chapter 4); *People v. Boissard*, 5 Cal.App.4th 972 (1992); *People v. Prance*, 277 Cal.Rptr. 567 (1991); *People v. Bosnak*, 633 N.E.2d 1322 (1994).

42. *Connor* (see 25 above), 135; *Commonwealth v. Shiflet*, 670 A.2d 128 (1995); *Perry v. State of Wyoming*, 927 P.2d 1158 (1996).

43. *People v. Hunt*, 225 Cal.App.3d 498 (1990). Also see: *People v. Stoffle*, 1 Cal.App.4th, 1671 (1991).

44. Cases regarding an inventory "search" after impoundment include: *Michigan v. Thomas*, 458 U.S. 259 (1982); *Colorado v. Bertine*, 479 U.S. 367 (1987); *Florida v. Wells*, 110 S.Ct. 1632 (1990); *U.S. v. Harvey*, 16 F.3d 109 (1994); *U.S. v. Decker*, 19 F.3d 287 (1994); *U.S. v. Agofsky*, 20 F.3d 866 (1994); *People v. Lloyd*, 562 N.Y.S.2d 257 (1990); *People v. Aguilar*, 228 Cal.App.3d 1049 (1991).

45. *Autran v. State*, 887 S.W.2d 31 (1994).

46. *U.S. v. Andrews*, 22 F.3d 1328 (1994).

47. *Sammons v. Taylor*, 967 F.2d 1533 (1992); *People v. Aguilar* (see 44 above).

48. *U.S. v. Taddeo*, 724 F.Supp. 81 (1989); *U.S. v. Gilmer*, 793 F.Supp. 1545 (1992).

CHAPTER 7:
SINGLE-OFFICER SELF-DEFENSE

1. *Law Enforcement Officers Killed and Assaulted* (Washington, D.C.: Federal Bureau of Investigation, 1991).

2. Robert Dent, "¡Habla Ingles!" *Law and Order*, September 1993, 70.

3. Brougham (see 20, Chapter 5), 16.

4. Handout, prepared by San Bernardino County (California) Sheriff's Regional Training Center in cooperation with the Verbal Judo Institute.

5. *Mathis v. Parks*, 741 F.Supp. 567 (1990).

6. Christopher A. Hertig, *Protection Officer Survival* (Bellingham, Washington: International Foundation for Protection Officers, 1991).

7. For a strong statement against interviewing subjects inside patrol cars, see: "Motor Vehicle Stops" (see 2, Chapter 3), 4.

8. George Demetriou, "To Punch or Not to Punch," *Law and Order*, September 1994,

179.

9. *Mastering Floor Fighting Techniques: Vol. 1*, Arthur Cohen, instructor (San Clemente, California: Panther Productions, 1986). Videocassette.

10. Tracy Robinson and Douglas Chu, "Tactical Groundfighting," in *Total Survival* (see 1, Chapter 3), 301-2.

11. *U.S. v. Tate*, 821 F.2d 1328 (1987).

12. Tim Powers, Fitness Institute for Police, Fire & Rescue, Appleton, Wisconsin.

13. *Tennessee v. Garner*, 105 S.Ct. 1694 (1985).

14. *California v. Hodari*, 111 S.Ct. 1547 (1991). Also see: *U.S. v. Levasseur*, 816 F.2d 37 (1987); *In Re Baraka H.*, 6 Cal.App.4th 1039 (1992); *People v. Green*, 25 Cal.App.4th 1107 (1994).

15. Unpublished study conducted throughout the 1980s by S/Sgt. Ross MacInnes, Calgary Police Department Organized Crime Division. Also see: Bob Eden, "On Automatic Pilot: Subconscious Flight Patterns," *Police*, March 1994, 21.

CHAPTER 8: TACTICAL SETUP

1. Isaac T. Avery III, "Legal Standards for Stops, Searches, Seizures, and Arrests," Operation Pipeline training, March 1987.

2. David Chiszar, et al., "Reptiles in Association with Illicit Drugs," *Bulletin of the Chicago Herpetological Society*, 27(1):1-4, 1992.

3. Jeremy M. Miller, "The Exceptions to the Warrant Requirement of the Fourth Amendment," *Daily Journal Report*, n.d., 19. Also see: *U.S. v. Thomas*, 844 F.2d 678 (1988); *Chauncey v. State*, 382 So.2d 782 (1981); "Search Limited to Weapons," *Front Line Report*, May 1994, 1.

4. *Terry v. Ohio* (see 8, Chapter 2); *U.S. v. Knox*, 950 F.2d 516 (1991); *U.S. v. Roach*, 958 F.2d 679 (1992); *Sapp v. State* (see 10, Chapter 2); *People v. Wilson*, 582 N.Y.S.2d 106 (1992); *In re D.E.W.*, 612 A.2d 194 (1992); *People v. Dickey*, 21 Cal.App.4th 952 (1994). Also see: "Field Interviews and Pat-Down Searches," concepts and issues paper, International Association of Chiefs of Police National Law Enforcement Policy Center, May 1993, 3. For a case in which a court held that shoes cannot be included in an involuntary frisk because the subject would not have easy access to any weapon that might be concealed there, see: *U.S. v. Douglas*, 854 F.Supp. 383 (1994).

5. Douglas R. Mitchell, "Legal and Physical Safety Considerations in Investigative Stops: Part 2," *The Police Marksman* (May/June 1994), 15-16.

6. *U. S. v. Oates*, 560 F.2d 45 (1977); *U. S. v. Ceballos*, 654 F.2d 177 (1981). Also see: *U.S. v. Stewart*, 867 F.2d 581 (1989). For contrary opinions, see: *U.S. v. Alexander*, 907 F.2d 269 (1990) and *U.S. v. Clark*, 24 F.3d 299 (1994). In the latter case, the court observed: "Twenty-five years ago...it might have been unreasonable to assume that a suspected drug dealer in a car would be armed; today, it could well be foolhardy for an officer to assume otherwise."

7. *U.S. v. Rodney*, 956 F.2d 295 (1992); *U.S. v. Ashley*, 37 F.3d 678 (1994); *State v. Valrie*, 597 So.2d 1218 (1992).

8. *Gray v. State*, 550 So.2d 540 (1989).

9. *People v. Autry*, 232 Cal.App.3d 365 (1991).

10. Emberton (see 9, Chapter 4); William U. McCormack, J.D., "Supreme Court Cases: 1992-1993 Term," *FBI Law Enforcement Bulletin*, October 1993, 27-28; Hall (see 34, Chapter 6); A. Louis DiPietro, J.D., "The 'Plain Feel' Doctrine," *FBI Law Enforcement Bulletin*, February 1994, 27-32; J. Shane Creamer, "Understanding the 'Plain Touch' Doctrine," *The Police Chief*, August 1994, 42+.

11. *Minnesota v. Dickerson*, 113 S.Ct. 2130 (1993). Also see: *U.S. v. Craft*, 30 F.3d 1044 (1994); *People v. Mitchell*, 630 N.E.2d 451 (1993); *State v. Hudson*, 874 P.2d 160 (1994); *Huffman v. State*, 56 CrL 1166 (1994). For an analysis of why the Supreme Court's explanation of the Plain Feel Doctrine is "absurd," see: "Minnesota v. Dickerson," *The Law Enforcement Legal Reporter*, October 1993, 117-120. For a decision that refuses to accept the plain-feel concept, see: *People v. Champion*, 518 N.W.2d 518 (1994).

12. Joe Weeg, Polk County (Iowa) prosecutor, "Terry Analysis of Search and Seizure," presentation at the Iowa State County Attorneys' Conference, 11 November 1993, Des Moines.

13. *State v. Scott*, 518 N.W.2d 347 (1994).

14. *People v. Salvator*, 602 N.E.2d 953 (1992).

15. Miller (see 21, Chapter 4), 503.

16. Louis DiPietro, "The 'Plain Feel' Doctrine," *FBI Law Enforcement Bulletin*, February 1994, 30.

17. Cases regarding restraint of a nonarrested subject include: *U.S. v. Parr*, 843 F.2d 1228 (1988); *U.S. v. Glenna*, 878 F. 2d 967 (1989); *U.S. v. Crittendon*, 883 F.2d 326 (1989); *U.S. v. Hastamorir*, 881 F.2d 1551 (1989); *U.S. v. Merkley*, 988 F.2d 1062 (1993); *U.S. v. Sanders*, 994 F.2d 200 (1993); *U.S. v. Ortiz*, 15 F.3d 1093 (1993); *U.S. v. Tilmon*, 19 F.3d 1221 (1994); *Reynolds v. State*, 592 So.2d 1082 (1992); *State v. Reid*, 605 A.2d 1050 (1992).

18. *Courson v. McMillian*, 939 F.2d 1479 (1991).

19. *Martin v. Swift*, 781 F.Supp. 1250 (1992).

20. *Timberlake by Timberlake v. Benton*, 786 F.Supp. 676 (1992).

21. *Kuhlmann v. Wilson*, 106 S.Ct. 2616 (1986).

22. Kimberly A. Crawford, J.D., "Surreptitious Recording of Suspects' Conversations," *FBI Law Enforcement Bulletin*, September 1993, 26-32. Also see: *U.S. v. McKinnon*, 985 F.2d 525 (1993); *State v. Fedorchenko*, 630 So.2d 213 (1993); *U.S. v. Clark*, 22 F.3d 799 (1994).

23. For a case in which a trooper's request for a violator to sit in his patrol car was ruled not to be a coercive or objectionable action, see: *State v. LaMasters*, 878 S.W.2d 485 (1994).

24. Colleen Heild, "Why a Cop Killer Goes Free," *Albuquerque Journal*, 12 June 1994, 1+.

CHAPTER 9: STRATEGIES FOR DISCOVERY

1. "Program Reduces Crimes with Guns," *Chicago Tribune*, 24 November 1994, 28.

2. *People v. Crenshaw*, 12 Cal.Rptr.2d 172 (1992). Also see: *PORAC News*, March 1993, 10.

3. *State v. Hill*, 823 P.2d 201 (1991). For a contrasting view, see: *Taylor v. State*, 805 S.W.2d 609 (1991).

4. *Commonly Encountered Concealment Methods in Selected Land Vehicles* (see 17, Introduction).

5. One federal case that supports this position is *U. S. v. Dallas* (see 17, Chapter 4).

6. Avery (see 1, Chapter 8).

7. Finn (see 3, Chapter 2), 150.

8. *U.S. v. Strickland* (see 37, Chapter 6).

9. *Jackson v. State*, 588 N.E.2d 588 (1992). Also see: *People v. 1984 BMW 528E Auto*, 567 N.E.2d 654 (1991).

10. *Bailey v. U.S.*, 116 S.Ct. 501 (1995).

11. *Weimer v. Schraeder*, 952 F.2d 336 (1991).

12. *U.S. v. Lewis*, 3 F.3d 252 (1993).

CHAPTER 10:
BUSTING MOTHER-LODE VEHICLES

1. "Commercial Motor Vehicle Drug Enforcement," course, Institute of Police Technology and Management, 2-4 May 1994, Jacksonville, Florida.

2. *U.S. v. Hernandez* (see 20, Chapter 2).

3. *Commonly Encountered Concealment Methods in Selected Land Vehicles* (see 17, Introduction), 86.

4. K. Hawkeye Gross, *Drug Smuggling: The Forbidden Book* (Boulder, Colorado: Paladin Press, 1992), 38-39.

5. *U.S. v. Muniz-Melchor*, 894 F.2d 1430; cert. denied, 110 S.Ct. 1957 (1990). Also see: Joseph (see 8, Chapter 2), 7-18.

6. *U.S. v. Mejia*, 953 F.2d 461 (1991).

7. "What Happened to the Drug War?" PBS *Frontline*, television documentary, 2 February 1993. Also see: Douglas Jehl, "Route to Cocaine Outlined in Report," *Los Angeles Times*, n.d. For data on how relaxed border interdictions are creating more opportunities than ever for drug-laden trucks to enter the U.S., see: "Inspections Eased, Seizures Plunge," *Narcotics Enforcement & Prevention Digest*, 2 March 1995.

8. *Drugs and Crime Facts, 1992* (Rockville, Maryland: Drugs and Crime Data Center and Clearinghouse, 1993), 9. Also see: Sherman L. Hermann, "Clandestine Drug Laboratory Hazards," *Law and Order*, May 1994, 93.

9. "Methamphetamine Makers Seen Avoiding Controls on Precursors," *Drug Enforcement Report*, 8 August 1994, 5.

CHAPTER 11: K-9 SEARCHES

1. William Kane, "Olfaction," *McGraw-Hill Encyclopedia of Science and Technology*, vol. 12 (New York, New York: McGraw-Hill, Inc., 1992), 342.

2. Lawrence J. Myers, "The Dog-Handler Team: An Old Technology on the Leading Edge," article distributed by the California Narcotics Canine Association, n.d. (circa 1993).

3. Charles Kirchner, *Training Narcotic Detection Dogs for Law Enforcement: Tape 2* (Littleton, Colorado: Canine Training Systems,

1991). Videocassette.

4. Cases in which the use of K-9 to sniff the exterior of luggage or a vehicle is declared not to be a search include: *U.S. v. Place* (see 8, Chapter 2); *U.S. v. Lovell*, 849 F.2d 910 (1988); *U.S. v. Morales-Zamora*, 914 F.2d 200 (1990); *U.S. v. Rodriguez-Morales*, 929 F.2d 780 (1991); *U.S. v. Harvey*, 961 F.2d 1361 (1992); *U.S. v. Ludwig*, 10 F.3d 1523 (1993); *U.S. v. Chavis*, 841 F.Supp. 780 (1993); *U. S. v. Rascon-Ortiz* (see 29, Chapter 2); *U.S. v. Jeffers*, 22 F.3d 554 (1994); *U.S. v. Brown*, 24 F.3d 1223 (1994); *State v. Williams*, 565 So.2d 714 (1990); *Joseph v. State*, 588 So.2d 1014 (1991); *Brown v. Commissioner*, 421 S.E.2d 877 (1992). For a case that does not conform to customary case law regarding "free sniffs," see: *Commonwealth v. Martin*, 626 A.2d 556 (1993), involving a satchel containing marijuana and a large amount of cash that was sniffed by a K-9 in a restaurant. The Pennsylvania Supreme Court held that police must have probable cause before initiating such a sniff; see: *Police Times*, Fall 1993, for a report on this case. Also see: Djuna E. Perkins, "The Nose Knows: Using Trained Dogs to Detect Drugs," special report, Quinlan Publishing Company, 1995.

5. For a case supporting the walking of K-9s in motel parking lots, see: *U.S. v. Ludwig* (see 4 above).

6. *Horton v. Goose Creek Independent School District*, 690 F.2d 470 (1982). Also see: Perkins (see 4 above).

7. Cases and interpretation regarding K-9 alert being probable cause for a warrantless search include: *U.S. v. Dovali-Avila*, 895 F.2d 206 (1990); *U.S. v. Hernandez*, 976 F.2d 929 (1992); *U.S. v. Barbee*, 968 F.2d 1026 (1992); *U.S. v. Ludwig* (see 4 above); *Cardwell v. State*, 482 So.2d 512 (1986); *Brown v. Commissioner* (see 4 above); *State of Kansas v. Barker*, 850 P.2d 885 (1993). Also see: Kevin B. Zeese and Eve E. Zeese, *Drug Law: Strategies and Tactics* (Deerfield, Illinois: Clark Boardman Callaghan, 1993), 1-83 to 1-94.

8. *U.S. v. Williams*, 726 F.2d 661 (1984); *U.S. v. Massac*, 867 F.2d 174 (1989).

9. *U.S. v. Hardy*, 855 F.2d 753 (1988). Also see: Perkins (see 4 above). For a case in which insufficient suspicious facts were said to make detention unreasonable, see: *U.S. v. Tapia* (see 10, Chapter 6).

10. *State v. Fuente* (see 17, Chapter 4).

11. Zeese (see 7 above), 1-86.

12. Charles M. Latham, "Operation Drug Dog," *FBI Law Enforcement Bulletin,* October 1994, 16-17.

13. *U.S. v. Diaz*, 25 F.3d 392 (1994).

CHAPTER 12: BEYOND THE BUST

1. "Utah Cops Get Share of Seized Goods," *Chicago Tribune,* 1 February 1995.

2. For reports on proposals to make forfeiture proceedings even more stringent, see: "Uniform Laws Conference Approves Model State Asset Forfeiture Law," *Drug Enforcement Report,* 8 August 1994, 1+, and "Asset Forfeiture Legislation to Get High Priority in House," *Drug Enforcement Report,* 23 January 1995, 4. For details on how "emergency" legislation drastically tightened forfeiture regulations in one state, see: "New Asset Forfeiture Statute Is Enacted into Law in California," *Drug Enforcement Report,* 12 August 1994, 1+. For a Justice Department "reform" proposal that the National Association of Criminal Defense Lawyers considers "too friendly to prosecutors and police," see: "Justice Department Circulates Asset Forfeiture Reform Proposal," *Drug Enforcement Report,* 25 July 1994, 1+.

3. Reaves (see 5, Chapter 1). Also see: *Criminal Justice Newsletter* (see 4, Introduction).

4. Connie Fletcher, "On the Line: Women Cops Speak Out," *Chicago Tribune Magazine,* 19 February 1995.

5. "Dangers Involved in Field Drug Testing," *Law and Order,* February 1990, 5. For information on newer field tests that involve no strong liquid acids, see: "Company Produces Innovative Field Drug ID System," *Narcotics Control Digest,* 12 October 1994, 9-10. Also see: "New Battery-Powered Device Detects Illicit Drugs on Surfaces," *Drug Detection Report,* 20 December 1994.

6. *U.S. v. Padilla*, 113 S.Ct. 1936 (1993).

7. *U.S. v. Shabani*, 993 F.2d 1419 (1993).

8. Zeese (see 7, Chapter 11), 5-1 through 5-33; "Justice Dept. Amends Forfeiture Rules for 'Innocent' Victims," *West's Legal News,* 9 January 1997, 1; *A Guide to Equitable Sharing of Federally Forfeited Property for State and Local Law Enforcement Agencies* (Washington, D.C.: U.S. Department of Justice, March 1994); "New Asset Forfeiture

Guidelines Require Financial Accountability," *Drug Enforcement Report,* 8 June 1994, 1-3. (The U.S. Bureau of Justice Assistance has published a set of sixteen manuals covering different aspects of asset forfeiture. For more information, call the BJA Clearinghouse at (800) 688-4252.) Also see: *U.S. v. Ursery* and *U.S. v. $405,089.23,* 116 S.Ct. 2135 (1996).

9. *Idaho Department of Law Enforcement by and through Richardson v. $34,000 U.S. Currency,* 824 P.2d 142 (1991).

10. "Campaign PUSH-OFF Targets Vehicles of Drug Buyers," *Drug Enforcement Report,* 23 February 1994, 8.

11. "Automobile Seizures and Forfeitures," International Association of Chiefs of Police *Policy Review,* vol. 4, no. 4, 1993. Also see: "Detroit Police Seize Vehicles of Routine Drug Offenders," *Drug Enforcement Report,* 11 October 1994, 4-5.

12. *U.S. v. Monsanto,* 491 U.S. 600 (1989); *Caplin & Drysdale, Chartered v. U.S.,* 491 U.S. 617 (1989).

13. *U.S. v. James Daniel Good Real Property,* 114 S.Ct. 492 (1993). For reports on this case, see: Irving B. Zeichner, "Inside Justice," *Law and Order,* February 1994, 9; William U. McCormack, "Supreme Court Cases—1993-94 Term," *FBI Law Enforcement Bulletin,* October 1994, 32. Also see: *A Guide to Equitable Sharing of Federally Forfeited Property for State and Local Law Enforcement Agencies* (see 8 above).

14. For a case in which pursuit of civil forfeiture after criminal convictions were obtained was ruled to be double jeopardy, see: *U.S. v. $405,089.23 U.S. Currency,* 33 F.3d 1210 (1994); "Separate Forfeiture Case Held to Constitute Double Jeopardy," *Drug Enforcement Report,* 11 October 1994, 1+; "Administration Seeks Rehearing on Asset Forfeiture Restriction," *Narcotics Control Digest,* 16 October 1994, 1-2. Also see: "Forfeiture Ruling Heartens Lawyers," *The National Law Journal,* 22 August 1994, A10, and "Supreme Court Refuses Review of Major Asset Forfeiture Case," *Drug Enforcement Report,* 23 December 1994, 1+. At this writing, conflict exists among federal judicial circuits on the double-jeopardy issue. For a case in which a state supreme court held that a suspect does not have to choose between his Fifth Amendment

rights and his right to contest a forfeiture, see: *Wohlstrom v. Buchanan* (1994), described in *Drug Enforcement Report,* 9 January 1995, 8.

15. *U.S. v. $511,780.00 in U.S. Currency,* 847 F.Supp. 908 (1994). For a case in which a state supreme court ruled that the mere possession of a large sum of curency, without any proof of a link to criminal activity, is not sufficient for forfeiture, see: "Court Rejects Forfeiture Where Money Wasn't Linked to Drugs," *Drug Enforcement Report,* 8 February 1995, 8, reporting on *$107,000 U.S. Currency v. State* (1994). For a case in which the U.S. Supreme Court ruled that an "innocent" owner's property may be forfeited, even though she did not realize it was being used for criminal purposes, see: *Bennis v. Michigan,* 116 S.Ct. 994 (1996).

16. Cases regarding the ground rules of civil forfeiture include: *Calero-Toledo v. Pearson Yacht Leasing Co.,* 416 U.S. 663 (1974); *U.S. v. $321,470.00 U. S. Currency,* 874 F.2d 298 (1989); *U.S. v. 7715 Betsy Bruce Lane Summerfield, N.C.,* 906 F.2d 110 (1990); *U.S. v. Certain Real Property,* 922 F.2d 130 (1990); *U.S. v. One 1987 Mercedes 560SEL,* 919 F.2d 327 (1990); *U.S. v. Parcels of Land,* 903 F.2d 36 (1990); *U.S. v. Certain Real Property,* 943 F.2d 721 (1991); *U. S. v. Elgersma,* 929 F.2d 1538 (1991); *U.S. v. Four Parcels of Real Property,* 941 F.2d 1428 (1991); *Cade v. One 1987 Dodge Lancer,* 874 P.2d 542 (1994).

17. "Drugs, Crime and the Justice System" (see 2, Introduction), 156.

18. *Austin v. U., S.* 113 S.Ct. 2801 (1993). Also see: *State v. Hill,* 635 N.E.2d 1248 (1994). For an earlier contrasting view, see: *U.S. v. Premises Known As 3639-2nd St., N.E.,* 869 F.2d 1093 (1989).

19. *U.S. v. Real Property at 6625 Zumirez Dr.,* 845 F.Supp. 725 (1994).

20. David A. Kaplan, et al., "Where the Innocent Lose," *Newsweek,* 4 January 1993, 43; Erwin Chemerinsky, "Civil Forfeiture: A Diminishing Power," *Trial,* April 1994, 66+.

21. *U.S. v. $121,100.00 in U.S. Currency,* 999 F.2d 1503 (1993).

22. *Davidson v. State of Arkansas,* 831 S.W.2d 160 (1992). Also see: *U.S. v. $91,960.00,* 897 F.2d 1457 (1990).

23. For the strengths and weaknesses of K-9s

alerting on currency, see: *Jones v. U.S. Drug Enforcement Administration*, 819 F.Supp. 698 (1993); *U.S. v. U.S. Currency, $30,060.00*, 39 F.3d 1039 (1994); *People v. Sommer*, 12 Cal.App.4th 1642 (1993); "Crime and Chemical Analysis," *Science*, 24 March 1989; "Dirty Money," *United States Banker*, October 1989, 10; "Evidence of Narcotics Detections Dog's Alert to Cash Deposits Is Admissible in Money Laundering Case," *Daily Appellate Report*, 5 February 1993, 1637; Arthur S. Hayes, "Cocaine-Tainted Cash Faulted as Evidence," *Wall Street Journal*, 2 June 1993; Stephen H. Green, "Changing Trends in Asset Forfeiture," *The Police Chief*, January 1994, 16; "Currency Contamination Cited as Bar to Forfeiture Action," *Drug Enforcement Report*, 23 November 1994, 3; Perkins (see 4, Chapter 11); "Federal Study Confirms Extensive Cocaine Contamination of Cash," *Drug Enforcement Report*, 8 October 1996.

24. Green, ibid.

25. *U. S. v. $53,082.00 in U. S. Currency*, 985 F.2d 245 (1993).

26. "Old Methods Seem to Fail Against Drug Groups in Capital Area," *Drug Enforcement Report*, 9 January 1995, 3.

27. Handout distributed at the Western States Information Network Training Conference, 8-10 June 1994, Sacramento, California.

End of a thorough search. (Just kidding!)

ADDITIONAL RESOURCES

Additional information on the legal aspects of Criminal Patrol is both plentiful and easily accessible. A number of excellent newsletters are published monthly with explanatory updates on the latest court decisions regarding investigative stops, detention, search, seizure, and arrest. Additional sources regarding the tactics and techniques of contraband discovery are harder to come by. The confidential bulletins and manuals published by the federally funded El Paso Intelligence Center, which offer invaluable insights into current trafficker methods, are often difficult for most patrol personnel to acquire. Apart from personal contact with Criminal Patrol specialists, the best supplementary instructional information at this time appears to be available from videocassettes, seminars, training sessions, and lesson plans developed by instructors and agencies that are involved first hand in this style of patrol. Resources that were particularly helpful in the research of **Tactics for Criminal Patrol** include the following:

Books and Manuals

Amaral, Michel. *Officer Safety: Police Tactics for Survival.* San Jose, California: Calprinting, 1991.

Billington, Mike, et al. *Profit in the Name of the Law.* Ft. Lauderdale, Florida: *Sun-Sentinel* newspaper, 1991.

Commercial Motor Vehicle Drug/Currency Seizure Data. Oklahoma City: Drug Interdiction Assistance Program, April 1994.

Commercial Vehicle Enforcement: A Guide for Police Traffic Personnel. Washington, D.C.: National Highway Traffic Safety Administration, U.S. Department of Transportation, n.d.

Commonly Encountered Concealment Methods in Selected Land Vehicles. El Paso, Texas: El Paso Intelligence Center, 15 November 1990.

Connor, Greg. *Vehicle Stops: Tactical Procedures and Safety Strategies.* Champaign, Illinois: Stipes Publishing Company, 1993.

Connor, Michael. *Duty Free: Smuggling Made Easy.* Boulder, Colorado: Paladin Press, 1993.

Criminal Interdiction through Traffic Enforcement. Salt Lake City: Utah Highway Patrol, n.d.

Criminal Patrol Drug Enforcement Manual. Jacksonville, Florida: Institute of Police Technology and Management, n.d.

Cunningham, Cindy. *Drug Detector Dog Training.* Oklahoma City: Oklahoma State Bureau of Narcotics and Dangerous Drugs Control, n.d.

Dent, Robert L. *The Complete Spanish Field Reference Manual for Public Safety Professionals.* Bend, Oregon: The Constable Group, Inc., 1991.

Drug Identification & Symptom Manual. Irvine, California: National Consumer Publications, Inc., 1992-93 ed.

Drug Movement Indicator Profile. El Paso, Texas: El Paso Intelligence Center, 22 April 1991.

Drugs and Crime Facts, 1992. Rockville, Maryland: Drugs & Crime Data Center & Clearinghouse, 1993.

_____, *1993.* Rockville, Maryland: Drugs & Crime Data Center & Clearinghouse, 1994.

Drugs, Crime, and the Justice System. Washington, D.C.: U.S. Bureau of Justice Statistics, December 1992.

Drug Use Forecasting: 1993 Annual Report on Juvenile Arrestees/Detainees. Washington, D.C.: National Institute of Justice, 1994.

Duncan, Martin V. *Drug Interdiction.* Florida Highway Patrol, n.d. [circa 1993].

Ekman, Paul. *Telling Lies: Clues to Deceit in the Marketplace, Politics and Marriage.* New York, New York: W. W. Norton & Company, 1992.

Finn, M.C. *The Complete Book of International Smuggling.* Boulder, Colorado: Paladin Press, 1983.

Fisanick, Christian A. *Vehicle Search Law Deskbook.* Deerfield, Illinois: Clark Boardman Callaghan, 1996.

Gang Manual. Santa Rosa, California: National Law Enforcement Institute, Inc., 1992.

Gross, K. Hawkeye. *Drug Smuggling: The Forbidden Book.* Boulder, Colorado: Paladin Press, 1992.

Guide to Equitable Sharing of Federally Forfeited Property for State and Local Law Enforcement Agencies, A. Washington, D.C.: U.S. Department of Justice, March 1994.

Guide to Semitrailers as Concealment Vehicles. El Paso, Texas: El Paso Intelligence Center. 3 December 1984.

Hermann, Michele G. *Search and Seizure Checklists.* Deerfield, Illinois: Clark Boardman Callaghan, 1993.

Hertig, Christopher A. *Protection Officer Survival.* Bellingham, Washington: International Foundation for Protection Officers, 1991.

Highway Interdiction. El Paso, Texas: El Paso Intelligence Center, 15 January 1992.

Inbau, Fred E.; John E. Reid; Joseph P. Buckley. *Criminal Interrogation and Confessions.* 3d ed. Baltimore, Maryland: Williams & Wilkins, 1986.

Ingraham, Barton L. and Thomas P. Mauriello. *Police Investigation Handbook.* Albany, New York: Matthew Bender & Co., 1990.

Joseph, Paul R. *Warrantless Search Law Deskbook.* Deerfield, Illinois: Clark Boardman Callaghan, 1991-92.

Kappeler, Victor E. *Critical Issues in Police Civil Liability.* Prospect Heights, Illinois: Waveland Press, 1993.

Kessler, Stephen L. *Civil and Criminal Forfeiture.* Deerfield, Illinois: Clark Boardman Callaghan, 1993.

Killed in the Line of Duty. Washington, D.C.: FBI Uniform Crime Reports Section, 1992.

Knapp, Mark L. and Judith A. Hall. *Nonverbal Communication in Human Interaction.* 3rd ed. Orlando, FL: Harcourt Brace Jovanovich College Publishers, 1972.

Lodovico, Thomas P., ed. *An Introduction to Seaside Street Gangs.* Seaside, California: Seaside Police Department, n.d.

Marnell, Tim, ed. *Drug Identification Bible.*™ Denver, Colorado: Drug Identification Bible, 1993.

Martin, M/Officer M.L. *Asian Gang Activity.* Garden Grove, California: Garden Grove Police Department, 1992.

Miller, Gary J. *Drugs and the Law: Detection, Recognition & Investigation.* Altamonte Springs, Florida: Gould Publications, Inc., 1992.

NNICC Report, The: The Supply of Illicit Drugs to the United States. Washington, D.C.: National Narcotics Intelligence Consumers Committee, July 1992.

Nowicki, Ed, ed. *Total Survival.* Powers Lake, Wisconsin: Performance Dimensions Publishing, 1993.

Nowicki, Edward J. and Dennis A. Ramsey. *Street Weapons,* Powers Lake, Wisconsin: Performance Dimensions Publishing, 1991.

Ouellette, Roland. *Management of Aggressive Behavior.* Powers Lake, Wisconsin: Performance Dimensions Publishing, 1993.

Pickel, Sergeant Duane, with Mary R. Burch and Lieutenant David Frisby. *The Administration of Police K-9 Units: Standard Operating Procedures.* No publisher, n.d.

Rabon, Don. *Interviewing and Interrogation.* Durham, North Carolina: Carolina Academic Press, 1992.

_____. *Investigative Discourse Analysis.* Durham, North Carolina: Carolina Academic Press, 1994.

Remsberg, Charles. *Street Survival: Tactics for Armed Encounters.* Northbrook, Illinois: Calibre Press, Inc., 1980.

_____. *The Tactical Edge: Surviving High-Risk Patrol.* Northbrook, Illinois: Calibre Press, Inc., 1986.

Rudacille, Wendell C. *Evasive Speech and Deception.* Ellicott City, Maryland: Verifacts Systems, Inc., 1992.

Semitrailers and Large Trucks as Concealment Vehicles. El Paso, Texas: El Paso Intelligence Center, 4 March 1994.

Shearer, Robert A. *Interviewing in Criminal Justice.* Acton, Massachusetts: Copley Publishing Group, 1993.

Sourcebook of Criminal Justice Statistics. Washington, D.C.: U.S. Bureau of Justice Statistics, November 1996.

Stincelli, Carl. *Reading Between the Lines: The Investigator's Guide to Successful Interviews and Interrogations.* Elk Grove, California: Interviews and Interrogations Institute, n.d.

Street Level Narcotics Enforcement: Successful Elements of Stings, Raids, and Other Tactical Operations. Boulder, Colorado: Paladin Press, 1992.

Vehicle Concealment Handbook. Baton Rouge, Louisiana: Louisiana Department of Public Safety and Corrections, n.d.

Zeese, Kevin B. and Eve E. Zeese. *Drug Law: Strategies and Tactics.* Deerfield, Illinois: Clark Boardman Callaghan, 1993; *Supplement,* August 1994. [Kevin Zeese is former chief counsel for the National Organization for the Reform of Marijuana Laws. This reference work appears to favor abandonment of the drug war and liberalization of drug laws. Includes advice to defense attorneys.]

Zulawski, David E. and Douglas E. Wicklander. *Practical Aspects of Interview and Interrogation.* Baton Rouge, Louisiana: CRC Press, 1993.

Videotapes

Aspects of Interrogation. Dr. Tom Streed, instructor. Inform Video Lecture Series, n.d.

Asset Forfeiture. International Narcotic Enforcement Officers Association in cooperation with Instructional Video Productions, Inc., n.d.

Clandestine Drug Labs: Kitchens of Death. California Attorney General's Office, 1989.

Drug Courier, The: Criminal Patrol Techniques. Louisiana State Police, 1984.

Drug Interdiction. Chesterfield, Missouri: L.E. Net, n.d..

Drug Interdiction: Narcotics Arrests and Seizures Stemming from Motor Vehicle Stops. Connecticut State Police Video Unit, n.d.

Drug Smuggler Interdiction. Trooper Marvin Johnson, instructor. Inform Video Lecture Series, n.d.

Drug User Recognition. Santa Barbara County (California) Training Task Force, consultants. Distributed by Aims Media, Van Nuys, California, n.d.

Drugs on the Street. Instructional Video Productions, Inc., in cooperation with the National Sheriffs Association, 1986. Includes study guide and instructor's manual.

Drugs on the Street: Drugs in Motor Vehicles. Instructional Video Productions, Inc., in cooperation with the National Sheriffs Association, 1989.

El Paso Intelligence Center. Oklahoma Department of Public Safety Video Section, n.d.

Expert Body Language: The Science of Reading People. San Mateo, California: Intelligence Incorporated, 1992.

Hidden Compartments of Drug Traffickers. Sheriff Don Blankenship, instructor. Springfield, Missouri: Hornbeck Productions, 1994.

Land Concealment Techniques. Federal Law Enforcement Training Center Media Production

Branch, n.d.

Mastering Floor Fighting Techniques, vols. I and II. Arthur Cohen, instructor. San Clemente, California: Panther Productions, 1986.

One on One: Handling a Prisoner under the Influence of PCP. Frank Swaringen, producer. Santa Clara County (California) Sheriff's Department, 1988.

Operation Pipeline Training Video. New Mexico State Police and U.S. Drug Enforcement Administration, 1986.

Overview of the Georgia State Patrol's Aggressive Criminal Enforcement Program, An. Georgia State Patrol Safety Education Unit, n.d.

Rolling Stoned! Part I: Drug Identification and Detection of Drivers Under the Influence. Idaho Department. of Law Enforcement, State Police Division, 1989.

_____. *Part II: Commercial Vehicle Drug Interdiction.* Idaho Department of Law Enforcement, State Police Division, 1990.

Stopping Large Vehicles. North Carolina Justice Academy, 1991.

Trailer and Container Inspection. Office of the Comptroller in cooperation with U.S. Customs Service Office of Inspection and Control, n.d.

Training Narcotic Detection Dogs for Law Enforcement: Tape 2. Charles Kirchner, instructor. Littleton, Colorado: Canine Training Systems, 1991.

Vehicle Concealment Areas: Part I and *Part II.* Sergeant Rob Bishop, instructor. Butts County (Georgia) Sheriff's Department, n.d.

Magazine Articles, Newsletters, and Professional Papers

Albrecht, Steven. "Contact & Cover." *Police*, April 1989, 33-36+.

_____. "Streetwork: Every Day Is M-O-T-H-E-R-'S Day." *The Informant*, June 1992, 11.

_____. "Streetwork: Mastering the Double 'Huh?'" *The Informant*, November, 1993, 21.

Allard, Reginald F. Jr. "Plain Touch Doctrine." *Narcotic Enforcement Officers Association Newsletter*, n.d., 6-8.

Andersen, Austin A. "Inventory Searches: The Role of Discretion." *FBI Law Enforcement Bulletin*, May 1991, 26-31.

Arrest Law Bulletin. All issues, 1990-early 1995.

"Arrest, Search, and Seizure." *Case Commentaries and Briefs*, February, 1990, 4+.

Ayoob, Massad. "Observation—Your Key to Survival." *Combat Handguns*, n.d., 56+.

Baganz, Mark T. "Pretext Training?" *The ASLET Journal*, July/August 1994, 42-44.

Blystone, David A. and Andrew J. Bodzak. "Warrantless Searches of Vehicles in the 1990s." *Law and Order*, March 1994, 97-98.

Bovard, James. "Drug-Courier Profiles." *Playboy*, November 1994, 46-48.

Brougham, Charles G. "Nonverbal Communication: Can What They Don't Say Give Them Away?" *FBI Law Enforcement Bulletin*, July 1992,15-18.

Buckley, Joseph. "Behavioral Profile Helps in Identifying the Liar." *PORAC News*, February 1993, 26.

Burroughs, W.E. "Forced Vehicle Stops: What the Academy Didn't Tell You." *Police and Security News*, January/February 1993, 5+.

Caeti, Tory J. "My House Is Not My Car: Federal Courts Expand the Automobile Exception to the Fourth Amendment." *Police Liability Review*, Winter 1993, 1-7.

California Gang Investigators Association *Newsletter*. Miscellaneous dates.

Campane, Jerome O. Jr. "Investigative Detention and the Drug Courier: Recent Supreme Court Decisions." *FBI Law Enforcement Bulletin*, November 1983, 23-30.

Chemerinsky, Erwin. "Civil Forfeiture: A Diminishing Power." *Trial*, April 1994, 66+.

Chiszar, David, et al. "Reptiles in Association with Illicit Drugs." *Bulletin of the Chicago*

Herpetological Society, 27(1):1-4, 1992.

Clede, Bill. "Spotting Subtle Signs." *Law and Order*, March 1989, 51-52.

Collins, Sue Carter. "Legal Aspects of Search and Seizure," in *Criminal Patrol Drug Enforcement Manual* (Jacksonville, Florida: The Institute of Police Technology and Management, 1 October 1992).

"'Collinsville, 115, I'm Shot!'" *10-43 Magazine*, vol. 4, no. 2, 6-12.

Confidential teletype bulletins on Operation Pipeline seizures. El Paso Intelligence Center. Miscellaneous dates, 1990-1992.

"Congress to Cops: Watch Your Asset Seizures." *Law Enforcement Technology*, April 1994, 20.

Connor, Greg. "Transitional Traffic Stops: A New Challenge for Training." *Law and Order*, March 1992, 26-28.

Connors, Edward F. III and Hugh Nugent. "Street-Level Narcotics Enforcement." Monograph. U.S. Bureau of Justice Assistance, April 1990.

"Consent Searches of the Person: Groin Searches." *International Association of Chiefs of Police Policy Review*, August 1992, 2.

"Constructive Possession." Special supplement. *Narcotics Law Bulletin*, 1992.

Copeland, Cary H. "National Code of Professional Conduct for Asset Forfeiture." *The Police Chief*, October 1993, 86-87.

"Court Adopts 'Plain Feel' Doctrine." *Law Enforcement Legal Review*, July/August 1993, 3-4.

"Court Reacts to Criticism of 'Drug Courier Profiles.'" *The Law Officer's Bulletin*, 21 January 1988, 73-74.

Crawford, Kimberly A., J.D. "Surreptitious Recording of Suspects' Conversations." *The Training Wheel*, publication of the Las Vegas (NV) Metro Police Department, January/February 1994, 4-10. Reprinted from *FBI Law Enforcement Bulletin*, September 1993, 26-32.

_____. "The Consent to Search Doctrine: 'Apparent' Refinements." *FBI Law Enforcement Bulletin*, July 1992, 27-32.

Creamer, J. Shane. "Understanding the 'Plain Touch' Doctrine." *The Police Chief*, August 1994, 42+.

"Currency Contamination Cited as Bar to Forfeiture Action." *Drug Enforcement Report*, 23 November 1994, 3-4.

"Dangers Involved in Field Drug Testing." *Law and Order*, February 1990, 5.

Danielson, Kay. "Headway on the Highway." *Police*, June 1992, 78-79.

"Debriefing Questions in Specific Areas of Drug Trafficking." Handout. The Institute of Police Technology and Management, n.d.

Dedenhoff, Peter. "Robert L. Vogel: Developer of the 'Drug-Courier Profile.'" *Law Enforcement News*, 15 August 1989, 9+.

Demetriou, George. "To Punch or Not to Punch." *Law and Order*, September 1994, 179.

DiPietro, A. Louis, J.D. "The 'Plain Feel' Doctrine." *FBI Law Enforcement Bulletin*, February 1994, 27-32.

"Drug-busting Sheriff Says He Welcomes State's Review." *Law Enforcement News*, 15 October 1992, 7.

"Drug Courier Profile Alone Can't Support Vehicle Stop." *The Law Officer's Bulletin*, 23 June 1988, 143.

"Drug Enforcement by Police and Sheriff's Departments." Special report. U.S. Bureau of Justice Statistics, 1990.

Drug Enforcement Report. All issues, 1993-early 1995.

"Drug Smugglers Have New Trick up Their Sleeves." *International Drug Report*, March 1992, 5.

"Drug Trafficking Twists." *Texas Deputy*, Fall 1992, 71+.

"Drug Use Forecasting." *Law Enforcement Technology*, May 1993, 10+.

"Drugs Are Everywhere and So Are the Cops." *The Empire State Sheriff*, vol. 9, no. 1, 1993, 5-8.

Dula, Andy. "Troop K Patrols Florida's Main Street." *The Florida Trooper*, Spring 1988, 6+.

Dumonceaux, Genevieve A. and Richard Beasley. "Emergency Treatments for Police Dogs Used for Illicit Drug Detection." *Journal of the American Veterinary Medical Association*, 15 July 1990, 185-187.

Dunston, Mark S. "What's Available in Drug Testing Kits." *The Police Marksman*, September/October 1994, 20-21.

Eckholm, Erik. "Who's Got a Gun? Clues Are in the Body Language." *New York Times*, 26 May 1992, B3.

Evans, Daniel D. "10 Ways to Sharpen Your Interviewing Skills." *Law and Order*, August 1990, 90+.

"Evidence of Narcotics Detections Dog's Alert to Cash Deposits Is Admissible in Money Laundering Case." *Daily Appellate Report*, 5 February 1993, 1634-1640.

"Field Interviews and Pat-Down Searches." Concepts and issues paper. International Association of Chiefs of Police National Law Enforcement Policy Center, May, 1993, 1-3.
_____. Model policy. International Association of Chiefs of Police National Law Enforcement Policy Center, February 1992, 1-2.

"Florida Forfeiture Law under Scrutiny." *Law Enforcement News*, 15 October 1992, 7.

Foster, James A. "Narcotics Interdiction at the Street Level" *Law Enforcement Technology*, May 1992, 20-21.

Garner, Gerald. "The Game is Afoot." *Police*, September 1990, 34+.

Godshaw, Gerald; Ross Koppel; Russell Pancoast. "Anti-Drug Law Enforcement Efforts and Their Impact." U.S. Customs Service, August, 1987.

Goleman, Daniel. "Can You Tell When Someone Is Lying to You?" *Psychology Today*, August 1982, 14-23.

Graylow, Richard V. "Autos May Be Searched without a Warrant." *Wisconsin Trooper*, Winter 1989, 69+.

Green, Stephen H. "Changing Trends in Asset Forfeiture." *The Police Chief*, January 1994, 14+.

Hall, John C. "Investigative Detention: An Intermediate Response (Part 1)." *FBI Law Enforcement Bulletin*, November 1985, 25-31. "Part 2," December 1985, 18-23. "Conclusion," January 1986, 23-29.

Harman, Alan. "State Police Drug Team." *Law and Order*, March 1993, 80-82.

Harris, David A. "The Police May End up Frisking Everyone." *The National Law Journal*, 19 August 1994, A21.

Harris, William H. "Buzzword of the 90s: Drug Interdiction." *Law Enforcement Technology*, July/August 1990, 36-38.

Harrison, Robert. "Use of Nonverbal Cues to Detect Deception." *Law and Order*, September 1986, 57-58.

Heilbroner, David. "The Law Goes on a Treasure Hunt." *The New York Times Magazine*, 11 December 1994, 70+

Hess, John. "The Myths of Interviewing." Handout. Law Enforcement Satellite Academy of Tennessee Teleconference on Interviews and Interrogation, 20 May 1992.

Hinton, John E. Jr. "Criminal Patrol Safety Survival Tips for Felony Criminal Enforcement Officers." *The Police Marksman*, July/August 1993, 36+.

Holden, Richard N. "Police and the Profit-Motive: A New Look at Asset Forfeiture." *ACJS Today*, September/October 1993, 1+.

Humes, Charles E. Jr. "High Impact: Getting the Most from Your Knees." *The Tactical Edge* Magazine, Fall 1994, 54-58.

"Integrity Interviewing: Part I." *Military Law Enforcement Association Newsletter*, 15 May 1992, 1-2."Part II," 15 June 1992, 2-3.

"Intelligence Trends." Confidential bulletins on contraband seizures. U.S. Customs Service and Drug Enforcement Administration. Miscellaneous dates, 1990-92.

International Drug Report. All issues, 1993-94.

Jacoby, Tamar, with Lynda Wright. "When Cops Act on a Hunch." *Newsweek*, 10 October 1988, 79.

Janofsky, Michael. "In Drug Fight, Police Now Take to the Highway." *The New York Times*, 5 March 1995, 7.

Jernigan, Chet. "Drug Enforcement for Patrol Officers." North Carolina Justice Academy, July 1989.

Jones, Sheila L. "Cocaine Bust—Largest on Kansas Records." *The Kansas Trooper*, Winter 1991, 21+.

Jons, John. "Narcotics Detection Dog Competition." *Schutzhund USA*, July/August 1993, 63-65.

_____. "Training the Narcotics Detection Dog." *Schutzhund USA*, July/August 1993, 51-54.

Kingston, Kimberly A. "Forfeiture of Attorney's Fees." *FBI Law Enforcement Bulletin*, April 1990, 27-32.

_____. "Hounding Drug Traffickers: the Use of Drug Detection Dogs." *FBI Law Enforcement Bulletin*, August 1989, 26-32.

Knight, Bill. "Recent Seizure Illustrates Role in War on Drugs." *The Minnesota Police Journal*, June 1994, 32-33.

Kuboviak, James. "Reasonable Suspicion." *Law and Order*, March 1995, 81-86.

Kukura, Thomas V. "The Vehicle Exception to the Warrant Requirement: Clarification by the Supreme Court." *FBI Law Enforcement Bulletin*, August 1992, 27-32.

"Large Vehicle Stops." *FBI Law Enforcement Bulletin*, February 1990, 18-19.

Larson, Charles W.; Martin J. McLaughlin; Steven M. Badger. "Federal Asset Forfeiture: Law Enforcement's Guide to Preparing a Case for Judicial Forfeiture." Narcotic Enforcement Officers Association of Connecticut, Inc., December 1990.

Law Enforcement Legal Defense Manual. All issues, 1990-early 1995.

Law Enforcement Legal Reporter, The. All issues, 1988-early 1995.

Law Enforcement Legal Review. All issues, 1990-early 1995.

Mackenzie, Stephen A. "It Makes Sense: Narcotics Dogs Track down the Possibilities." *Police*, September 1992, 16-17.

_____. "K-9: Fulfilling the Function." *Police*, January 1993, 16-17.

Mahaney, Corporal Patrick. "Trooper Drug Interdiction and Consent Searches." *Florida Trooper*, Fall 1990, 51+. Reprinted from *The Alabama Trooper*, vol. 5, no. 1, June 1991, 30-32.

Martin, Deirdre. "Assets Seizure: Poetic Justice or Taking Justice into One's Own Hands?" *Law Enforcement Technology*, October 1993, 46+.

McCormick, Colonel Wiley D. "Criminal Patrol Techniques." *FBI Law Enforcement Bulletin*, January 1988, 19-22.

McCormack, William U. "Detaining Suspected Drug Couriers: Recent Court Decisions." *FBI Law Enforcement Bulletin*, June 1991, 27+.

_____. "Supreme Court Cases, 1992-1993 Term." *FBI Law Enforcement Bulletin*, October 1993, 27+.

McGivney, James. "Made in America: the New and Potent Methcathinone." *The Police Chief*, April 1994, 20+. Reprinted in *The Training Wheel*, July/August 1994, 44-48.

Messina, Phil. "Fighting from the Ground up." *Police*, April 1994, 18-19.

Michaels, William. "Car Nab Knowledge." *High Times*, September 1985, 57-58.

_____. "25 Hot Tips for Good Car-ma." *High Times*, September 1985, 59.

Miller, George I. "The 'Right' Vehicle Approach." *The Police Marksman*, September/October 1994, 30-31.

Miller, Verne W. "A Nose for the Job: Using Narcotics K-9s with Raid Teams." *The Tactical Edge* Magazine, Winter 1993, 58-59.

"Minnesota v. Dickerson." *The Law Enforcement Legal Reporter*, October 1993; 117-120.

Mitchell, Douglas R. "Legal and Physical Safety Considerations in Investigative Stops." *The Police Marksman*, March/April 1994, 17-21. "Part 2," May/June 1994, 15-17.

"Motor Vehicle Inventories." Model policy. International Association of Chiefs of Police National Law Enforcement Policy Center, January 1994.

"Motor Vehicle Searches." Concepts and issues paper. International Association of Chiefs of Police National Law Enforcement Policy Center, May 1993, 1-5.

"Motor Vehicle Stops." Concepts and issues paper. International Association of Chiefs of Police National Law Enforcement Policy Center, April 1992.

Narcotics Control Digest. All issues, 1994.

Narcotics Enforcement & Prevention Digest. All issues, early 1995.

Narcotics Law Bulletin. All issues, 1990-early 1995.

National Law Journal, The. All issues, 1994-early 1995.

"Negligence: Vehicle Related." *Liability Reporter*, November 1989, 169+.

Nope, Wendell M. "Police Service Dog Psychology." Report. California Narcotic Canine Association, 1993.

Norling, Dave. "Foot Pursuits: Chasing the World's Most Dangerous Game." *The Police Marksman*, November/December 1991, 50-51.

"Observable Factors & Manifestations of Nervousness." Internal document. U.S. Border Patrol, n.d.

Ouellette, Roland W. "Eye Contact." *Defensive Tactics Newsletter*, July 1994, 12-13.

Parlor, Michael B. "L-Unit Stop Procedures." Los Angeles Police Department, 1992.

"People v. Maxwell: Detentions." *The Law Enforcement Legal Reporter*, August 1989, 1+.

Perkins, Djuna E. "The Nose Knows: Using Trained Dogs to Detect Drugs." Special report. Quinlan Publishing Company, 1995.

Peva, James, et al. "Searches & Seizures: Warrantless Searches." *Hoosier Policeman*, Winter 1995, 16+.

Pollan, Michael. "How Pot Has Grown." *The New York Times Magazine*, 19 February 1995, 31+.

Ponticelli, Theodore. "Deception Detection." *Police*, October 1993, 46+.

Post, Michael S. "Colombian Organized Crime and Cocaine Trafficking." *The Narc Officer*, December 1989, 11-33.

Powers, Tim. "Controlled Foot Pursuit." *The ASLET Journal*, September/October 1988, 13-14.

Quick, Sergeant Burt. "Canine First Aid." *Police*, April 1994, 20+.

Reaves, Brian A. "Drug Enforcement by Police and Sheriffs' Departments." *Texas Deputy*, Fall 1992, 43-57.

Reidinger, Phillip A. and Major Mark D. Cashio. "Multi-Agency Cooperation Leads to Drug Interdiction along the Southwest Border." *The Police Chief*, October 1992, 68+.

"Roadside Interview and Interrogation: Lie Detection." Handout. American Society of Law Enforcement Trainers Annual Training Seminar, 8 January 1994.

Robin, Gerald D. "Hounding Drug Couriers." *Law and Order*, November 1993, 88-89.

Roman, Mark. "The Cop Who Caught His Killers." *Reader's Digest*, November 1993, 67-72.

Roth, Jeffrey A. "Psychoactive Substances and Violence." Research brief. National Institute of Justice, February 1994.

Rudacille, Wendell C. "Lies in Disguise." *Training Aids Digest*, October 1992, 1+.

_____. "Lies in Disguise: How to Detect Verbal Deception." *PORAC News*, August 1993, 30. " Part 2," October 1993, 32.

Rutledge, Devallis. "Consensual Relations." *Police*, February 1995, 8-9.

_____."Frisky Business." *Police*, November 1994, 14-15.

_____. "Stopping with Precision." *Police*, December 1994, 14-15.

Ryan, Kevin. "Technicians and Interpreters in Moral Crusades: The Case of the Drug Courier Profile." *Deviant Behavior*, July/September 1994, 217-240.

Sanow, Corporal Ed. "Head out on the Highway." *Police*, December 1993, 59-63.

Sauls, John Gales. "Traffic Stops: Police Powers under the Fourth Amendment." *FBI Law Enforcement Bulletin*, October 1989, 27-32.

Scuro, Joseph E. Jr. "Significant Supreme Court Decisions." *Law and Order*, May 1992, 94-96.

Search and Seizure Bulletin. All issues, 1990-early 1995.

Secher, Judith E. "Asset Seizure: Building Better Cases." *The Police Chief*, July 1992, 12.

Sellers, Charlotte. "'Drug Mule Profile' Works for Indiana Trooper." *Wisconsin Trooper*,

Summer 1988, 53+. Reprinted from *Indiana's Finest*, December 1987.

Seper, Jerry. "Awash in Drugs on the Rio Grande." *Insight*, 11 June 1990, 26-27.

Sherman, Lawrence W., et al. "Police Murdered in Drug-Related Situations." Crime Control Institute, 1989.

_____. "The Kansas City Gun Experiment." Research brief. National Institute of Justice, January 1995.

"Signs of the Times? Drug Dealers Targeting the Deaf." *Law Enforcement News*, 15 June 1993, 3.

Stoddard, Brooke C. "Asset Forfeitures: A Training and Technical Assistance Project." *The National Sheriff*, February/March 1990, 38+.

"Stop for Traffic Violation on Pretext to Search Ruled Permissible." *Law Enforcement Legal Reporter*, August 1993, 94-96.

Sullivan, Craig A. "In the Trenches of the Drug War." *Police*, September 1992, 42-46.

"Supreme Court Lets Stand Limits on Questioning during Traffic Stops." *Crime Control Digest*, 2 March 1992, 1-2.

Talbert, W. Dale. "A Guide to Seizure and Forfeiture of Property Used or Acquired in Violation of State and Federal Controlled Substances Laws and Assessments Under the State Excise Tax Law." Office of Special Deputy Attorney General, Raleigh, North Carolina, 1991.

"36 Illegal Pat-Downs...Frisks...Warrantless Searches." Special supplement. *Search and Seizure Bulletin*, 1991.

Thomas, Ron. "Pipeline Interdiction." *The ASLET Journal*, September/October 1991, 22+.

Tousignant, David D. "Why Suspects Confess." *FBI Law Enforcement Bulletin,* March 1991, 14-18.

"Trafficking Narcotics via Tractor Trailer." Report. Federal Bureau of Investigation Drug Intelligence Unit, 11 May 1992.

Truncale, Joseph J. "Reading Body Language for Survival on the Street. *Law Enforcement Technology*, July 1994, 82-85.

"Use of K-9s in Narcotics." Handout. California Narcotic Canine Association, 1993.

"Vehicle Stop Procedures Handout." Tactical paper. Los Angeles Police Department, May 1990.

Weingarten, Paul. "Profits, Perils Higher for Today's Bootleggers." *Chicago Tribune*, 14 September 1989, 1+.

Weisheit, Ralph A., et al. "Rural Crime and Rural Policing." Report. National Institute of Justice, October 1994.

Whitaker, Gordon, et al. "Aggressive Policing and the Deterrence of Crime." *Law and Policy*, vol. 7, 1985.

Wilson, Captain Dave. "Practical Drug Recognition Expert Training." *Sheriff*, January-February 1995, 18.

Zwerling, Andrew L. "Establishing Probable Cause in Drug Searches and Arrests." *Search and Seizure Law Report*, May 1984, 29-36.

Seminars, Training Sessions, and Lesson Plans

Anderson, John and Walt Markee, Oregon State Police; Douglas W. Fong, deputy district attorney, Josephine County, Oregon. Lesson plan. "Interstate-5 Drug Trafficker Profiles and Interdictions." Western States Information Network Training Conference, 8-10 June 1994, Sacramento, California.

"Asset Forfeiture: Partnership for Law Enforcement." Workshop. International Association of Chiefs of Police Convention, 18 October 1993, St. Louis.

Avery, Isaac T. III, et al. "Legal Standards for Stops, Searches, Seizures and Arrests." Operation Pipeline Training, March 1987, North Carolina.

Cabral, Senior Agent J.D. and Agent Jeffrey Richards, U.S. Border Patrol. "Drug Interdiction."

Missouri Sheriff's Training Institute, 5 April 1994, Rolla, Missouri.

"Commercial Vehicle Interdiction." Course plan. Operation Desert Snow, January 1994.

David, Joe, California Highway Patrol. "Operation Desert Snow: Advanced Highway Drug Interdiction." Training program and course plan, 28 February-3 March 1994, Laughlin, NV.

"Drug Courier Interdiction." Lesson plan. Wisconsin State Patrol, March 1991.

"Drug Enforcement for Patrol Officers." Lesson plan. North Carolina Justice Academy, 1989.

"Drug Interdiction Training." Instructor and student outlines. Lakeshore Technical College, 11-13 November 1992, Cleveland, Wisconsin.

Duncan, Agent John and Detective Roy Wunderlich. "Clandestine Laboratory Training: Enforcement and Safety Overview." Institute for Law and Justice, 17-18 October 1990, Hammond, Indiana.

"Gang Seminar." National Law Enforcement Institute, Inc., 23-24 July 1992, Phoenix, Arizona.

Gravel, W.J. "False Compartments." Training package. Royal Canadian Mounted Police/Canada Customs Joint Forces Operation, 3 March 1992.

Hauk, Blake and Frankie Floied. "Interviews and Interrogation." Teleconference. Law Enforcement Satellite Academy of Tennessee, 20 May 1992.

Hinton, John. "Roadside Interview Technique—Lie Detection." Lecture. American Society of Law Enforcement Trainers Annual Training Seminar, 8 January 1994.

"Forfeiture Training Seminar." U.S. Attorney's Office, Eastern District of North Carolina, n.d.

Klugiewicz, Lieutenant Gary, Milwaukee County (Wisconsin) Sheriff's Department. "Close-quarters Defensive Tactics." Law Enforcement Television Network, *Drug Crackdown* program, 1992.

Maurer, Kevin M. "Officer Survival." Lesson Plan. Rocky Mount (North Carolina) Police Department, 1992.

"Observational Techniques/Behavioral Symptoms Analysis Training Course for Land Border Inspectors." Lesson plan and handout materials. United States Customs Service Academy, Federal Law Enforcement Training Center, n.d.

Parent, Bruce, law enforcement officer and drug recognition technician with Florida Department of Transportation, and Narcotics Investigator Don Klein, with the Anaheim (California) Police Department. "Commercial Motor Vehicle Drug Enforcement." Training program. The Institute of Police Technology and Management, 2-4 May 1994, Jacksonville, Florida.

"Passenger Vehicle Interdiction." Course plan. Operation Desert Snow, January, 1994.

Rosell, Trooper Rich. "Operation Pipeline Lecture Program." New Jersey State Police, 1992.

Stevens, Trooper Robert and Trooper Dick Unger, with the Ohio State Highway Patrol. "Drug Interdiction Techniques." Owens Technical College, 29 July 1993, Toledo, Ohio.

Street Survival® Seminar, Calibre Press, Inc.

Talbert, W. Dale. "Legal Standards for Stops, Searches, Seizures, and Arrests." Lecture. North Carolina State Highway Patrol In-service Training, February 1993.

Training Seminar. California Narcotic Canine Association, 9-11 September 1993, Van Nuys, California.

Twenty-fifth Annual Regional Criminal Investigation School. Narcotic Enforcement Officers Association, 2-5 November 1992, Worcester, Massachusetts.

Walters, Training Specialist Harry, with the Florida Marine Patrol (Reserve), and Patrol Officer and FTO Greg DiFranza, with the Jacksonville (Florida) Sheriff's Office. "Criminal Patrol Drug Enforcement." Training program. The Institute of Police Technology and Management, 21-25 February 1994, Jacksonville, Florida.

Weeg, Joe, Polk County (Iowa) prosecutor. "Terry Analysis of Search and Seizure." Lecture. Iowa State County Attorneys Conference, 11 November 1993, Des Moines.

ABOUT THE AUTHOR AND THE PHOTOGRAPHER

The creative team of **Charles Remsberg** and **Dennis Anderson** has been a major force in law enforcement training for nearly two decades, beginning in the 1970s with their collaboration on an award-winning film-and-print training program on hostage negotiation for police.

As writer and photographer, respectively, they have created the best-selling books, *Street Survival: Tactics for Armed Encounters* and *The Tactical Edge: Surviving High-Risk Patrol*...conceived, developed, and instructed the widely acclaimed Street Survival® Seminar...and produced an on-going series of groundbreaking instructional videos, including *Surviving Edged Weapons, Ultimate Survivors: Winning Against Incredible Odds,* and the two-part *Deadly Force Decisions.*

Calibre Press, the firm they founded in 1979, is today recognized as the world's leading private source of training materials for officer survival, and their projects have been credited with saving hundreds of officers' lives in more than fifty countries. Police academies and law enforcement agencies have modeled much of their tactical training on Remsberg-Anderson productions, and these books and films have been frequently cited in court as the standard for modern police performance.

Among many awards, Remsberg and Anderson have been honored with the O.W. Wilson Award for outstanding contribution to law enforcement from the American Criminal Justice Association and the Honor Award for distinguished achievement in public service from the American Police Hall of Fame. They have also served as members of the FBI's Critical Incident Management Advisory Council.

Photo Sources

During three years of research, writing, and production, more than 1,500 photographs were acquired from the field for consideration in this book. Our deepest appreciation goes to the photographers and sources listed below for the photos finally selected. Any photographs not credited were provided by sources who wish to remain anonymous.

Dennis Anderson—front cover, 14, 17, 39, 51, 54-56, 59, 69, 76, 79, 83, 86, 89, 90-96, 99-100, 103, 105-108, 110, 113-116, 120, 122, 122-128, 130, 137-138, 143, 145, 147, 201, 203-205, 214, 219, 226, 245-255, 257-266, 268-271, 274-279, 281-283, 286, 291, 307-309, 313-314, 318, 325, 327, 339-341, 346, 348, 350, 356-357, 362-365, 368, 383-386, 390-392, 403-411, 427, 434, 439, 443, 453, 455-457, 481, 496, 507; Jandy Viloria—ii-iii; Honolulu Police Department—iv; Sheila Smith—vii; Don Klein—11, 379, 412; Don Lamont, Matrix—12; Bill Lovejoy, *Santa Cruz (CA) Sentinel*—12; Agence France-Presse—12; Neil Schneider, *New York Post*—12; Eugene Richards, Magnum Photos—13; *Chicago Tribune*—13, 432; Art Vivaros—14; Bill Collins—14, 17, 36, 46, 53-55, 57, 59, 135, 137, 141-142, 144, 150-151, 188, 191, 194, 207-208, 299, 327, 340, 343-345, 349-351, 355, 358-359, 366, 369, 373, 378, 392, 450, 453, 469, 471, 478; Wayne Corcoran—15, 87, 418, 420, 454; David Rentas, *New York Post*—15; W. J. Gravel—15, 135, 235, 343, 352, 393, 398, 402, 414; Sarah Hardaway—21; John Looper—21; Mike Haustad, Scientific Services Bureau—22; Bob Stevens—26, 27, 62, 140, 146, 212; *California Highway Patrolman*—29, 344; Charles Arrigo—30; Glenn Scroggy, *The Daily and Sunday Courier-Post*—30; Mark Poulsen, *Albuquerque Journal*—30; Craig Herndon, *The Washington Post*—30; Nacogdoches County (TX) Sheriff's Department—32, 33; Mark Parks—35, 479; Rich Wemmer—38; Francis M. Roberts—39; Wide World Photos—40, 452; Marc Pesetsky—43; Walt Markee—46, 324, 336, 346, 361, 373, 422, 475; Richard Jimerson—46, 133, 192, 202, 381, 399, back cover; Kirk Simone—46, 324, 385, 393, 474; Tony Miller—48, 332, 374, 375; Chris Parkerson—55; Dennis Doherty—57, 387; Robert Cole—58, 394; Volusia County (FL) Sheriff's Department—72; Auto Safe Manufacturing—76; M. L. Traina—77; Boris Yaro, *Los Angeles Times*—78; John Witoshynsky—88; Francis E. Morgan—88; Paul Adae, *New York Post*—89; Louis Kleeman—89; Westchester (NY) Rockland Newspapers—92; Robert Magaletti,—104; Jeff Green—104, 412, 425; Dave Audsley—105; Vern Walker, *Boulder (CO) Daily Camera*—107; Lloyd DeGrane—112; Peoria (IL) Police Department—112; Don Blankenship—139, 352; Gerry Gropp, Sipa Press—145; Jim Jenkner—146, 356, 359, 395, 456; DEA (Chicago)—146; Chicago Lincoln Park Zoo —153; Larry Cuslidge—155, 213; Denis Blake—156; West Covina (CA) Police Department—161; Jim Mallory,—161; *San Gabriel (CA) Valley Tribune*—161; U. S. Marshals Service—161; Jim Gensheimer—162, 306, 454; Robin Holmes—162; Cloe Poisson, *The Hartford (CT) Courant*—164; Kirby Kennedy, *New Haven (CT) Register*—164; Milford (CT) Police Department—164; Sandy Pritchett—177, 421; Frank Hanes, *Chicago Tribune*—186; Dan Dyer—187; Keith Buckley—192; Tony Carannante, *Staten Island (NY) Advance*—220; *Journal of American Insurance*—226; South Carolina State Highway Patrol—238, 239; South Carolina Department of Highways and Public Transportation—238; William Meed, Times Publishing Company—273; Arizona Department of Public Safety—284; Jim Romano—287; Mark C. Ide—288, 337, 334, 440; Michael Heller—290; *The Arizona Republic*—291; John Bell—306; Tom Carter—306; Jim Baird, *The San Diego Union*—306; Georgia State Patrol—312; Michael Fryer, *Chicago Tribune*—314; *The Police Marksman*—322; Dan Heinz—322, 347; Naval Investigative Service—330; Bill Healy—332, 378; Barry Dunn—334, 347, 356, 359, 389, 397, 405, 430, 434, 472, 478, 479; John LeBlanc—337, 349, 381; Greg Kilpatrick—338; Grant Willis—389; John Scarberough—342, 353, 360; Bob Bolling—348; Jeff Cook, *Quad-Cities (IA) Times*—353; Bill Artiaga—375; Jack Compton—378; Chris O'Brien—379; Dan Chidester—394; Gary Leyba—402; U.S. Border Patrol—413; Paul Hagerty—415; Dale Antonich—418; Bob Melton—419; Frank Goff—424; *National Centurion*—456; Davidson County (TN) Sheriff's Department—457; Mark Kantralis—460; David Handschuh, *New York Daily News*—460; Jerry Engel, *New York Post*— 460; Kleberg County (TX) Sheriff's Department—478; John Kringas, *Chicago Tribune*—480; Texas Department of Public Safety—481; and Charles Remsberg—507.

Photographer's Acknowledgments

A number of law enforcement agencies cooperated and provided personnel during original photography for this book. Their department liaisons include:

Lieutenant **Rick Drehobl,** Rosemont (IL) Department of Public Safety; Sergeant **Lou Tessman,** Waukegan (IL) Police Department; Sergeant **Joe Truncale,** Glenview (IL) Police Department (retired), and Corporal **Michael Blazincic** and Deputy **Dave Drushinin,** Lake County (IL) Sheriff's Department. I also wish to thank the many officers and deputies who assisted from these agencies as talent.

Executive Director **Jane Homeyer, PhD,** and Forensic Scientist **Chris E. Hedges,** Northern Illinois Police Crime Laboratory provided assistance with weaponry nomenclature and drug paraphernalia identification.

I wish to thank two on-site technical advisors who worked with me during photography: Sergeant **Robert Stasch,** Chicago Police Department, and Sergeant **Michael Irwin,** Illinois State Police.

The following individuals assisted generously in the creation of the cover photograph: Chief **William Gallagher** and Officer **Patrick Kreis,** Winnetka (IL) Police Department, and **Marc Miller,** lighting director.

Additional assistance was provided during photography by: Sergeant **Mary Conner,** Northbrook (IL) Police Department; **Al Visovatti,** VIZ Charger Service Center, Highland Park, IL; Frank's West Side Auto Parts, Chicago; CP Motor Freight, Park City, IL; Systems Transport, Inc., Wood Dale, IL; Chalet Landscaping Company, Wilmette, IL; **Dave Bagby** and **Bryan Levernier,** professional truck drivers; **Richard Davis,** Founder, Second Chance Body Armor, and **Perry Franks.**

Original illustrations were created by **John Riska** on pages 90, 105, 334, 335, 404, 406-408, 410, and 440 and by **George Strehlow** on pages 9, 11, 19-20, 41, 49, 65, 79, 80, 91, 97, 106, 108-109, 113, 118-119, 121, 124, 126, 128, 136, 173, 176, 180, 293, 305, 329, 436, 442, 459, and 460.

The production of this book involved the combined dedication, talent, and efforts of three individuals with whom I am proud to be associated:

Scott Buhrmaster, research coordinator, was involved in amassing the large number of crime-scene photographs and assisting with logistics for shooting original photography.

For assistance in layout and design and in helping to make the identity for this book a reality, I thank **George Strehlow.** His countless hours of dedicated work and concern have helped to make the pages of this book distinguished.

Creatively, it would be impossible for me to express my awe at the talents of this book's author, **Charles Remsberg.** Chuck's unlimited enthusiasm and commitment toward the goals of this book, its quality, accuracy, and its insightful expression of information could only have been captured by him. I am honored to be his partner and friend.

I want to also thank my wife, **Chana,** and my son, **Aaron,** for their patience and understanding during these many months of production. Their sensitivity, love, and belief in me provide a continual source of energy and purpose to my life.

Dennis Anderson
Northbrook, Illinois